**Vedanta**

**[An Invaluable Guide to Happy and Successful Life)**

# VEDANTA

**[AN INVALUABLE GUIDE TO HAPPY AND SUCCESSFUL LIFE]**

***THE "KNOWLEDGE SUPREME"***

**Edited By**
**Dr. T. N. Achyuta Rao**

KALPAZ

*Published by*

Kalpaz Publications
C-30, Satyawati Nagar,
Delhi – 110052
Ph.: 011-47034999, 9811692060
www.kalpazpublications.com
E-mail: kalpaz@hotmail.com

*Distribution Network*
gyanbooks.com
India, USA, Canada, UK, Australia, France



ISBN: 978-93-5722-873-2 (PB)

First Published, 2024

*Printed at:* Gyan Press, Delhi.



**Vedanta: the Knowledge Supreme**
Author: Dr. T.N. Achyuta Rao

***Dedicated***
***to***
***My Parents***
***and My Brothers***
***Girish & Krishna***

# CONTENTS


| | | |
|---|---|---|
| | *Prayer* | 9 |
| | *Preface* | 11 |
| | *Introduction* | 18 |
| 1. | The Veda | 28 |
| 2. | Vedanta | 44 |
| 3. | Upanishads | 75 |
| 4. | Brahma Sutras | 154 |
| 5. | The Puranas and Epics | 165 |
| 6. | The Bhagavad -Gita | 177 |
| 7. | Mahaveera and Buddha | |
| | The Great Acharyas | 187 |
| 8. | Vedantic Way of Life | 207 |
| 9. | The Art of Creative Living | 218 |
| 10. | Yoga for Health, Peace, and Happiness | 267 |
| 11. | Sansar – Ripples and Waves | 283 |
| | Conclusion | 334 |
| | Think it Over | 343 |
| | Acknowledgments | 347 |
| | Further Reading | 348 |
| | Glossory of Samskrut Terms | 351 |
| | *Index* | 359 |

# Prayer

***"Om! Mahat Pradhana Kala Purusha Hiranyagarbha Roopine! Sat-Chit-Ananda Svaroopine Name Sree Narayane Harih!***

This in brief is the 'Truth' (Satyam) and 'Order (Ritam), the foundation of this universe, – all about the Creator, the creation, the created, and the seeker. The Supreme devotee Bhakta Dhruva uttered the above words describing the Lord when he was enlightened by the touch of the Lord Shree Vishnu's Conch. These wonderful, mystic yana is the Supreme Consciousness, Space, Time, Energy, Nature, all living and non-living beings as the manifest and the supreme Truth. Knowledge and, Bliss that is unmanifest in all.

**II**

*Om! Sham no mitrah sham Varunah*
*Sham no bhavatvaryammah*
*Sham no Indro Brihaspatih.*
*Sham no Vishnururukramah*
*Namo Brahmane. Namaste Vayo.*
*Tvameva Pratyaksham Brahmaavadisham.*
*Ritamavadsham. Satyamvadisham.*
*Tanmamaaveet Tadvaktaaramaaveet.*
*Aveenmaam, Avidvaktaaram.*
*"Om, Sahanaavavatu. Sahanau bhunaktu.*
*Sahe Veeryam Karavaavahai.*
*Tejasvi naavadheetamastu. Maa vidvishaavahai."*
*"Om! Shantih! Shantih! Shantih!"*

*Meaning,* *May the Sun (Mitra) be good to us!*
*May Varuna be good to us!*
*May the Sun (Aryama) be good to us!*
*May Indra and Brihaspati be good to us!*
*May Vishnu of great strides be good to us!*
*Prostrations to thee Brahman!*
*Prostrations to thee, O Vayu!*
*Thou indeed art the visible Brahman.*
*I shall proclaim thee the visible Brahman.*
*I shall call thee just!*
*Om! Peace, Peace, Peace!*

Agni and Vayu are the only two of the Devas that ever went very close to Brahman but could not recognise Him. Indra could know about Brahman only through the effulgennt Knowledge Uma, the daughter of Himavat! When Indra asked Uma who the Yaksha was, Uma told Indra that it is Brahman Who governs this Universe; all that exists here and elsewhere derive their energy from him. Nothing will move without His 'Will' and support.

[KENOPANISHAD].

*"Advaitam Achyutam anaadim Anantarropam*
*aadyam puraanapurusham navayouvanam cha;*
*Vedeshu durlabham durlabham aatmabhaktau*
*Govindam Aadipurusham tam aham bhajjami.*
*[Brahma Samhite 533. Bhagavad Gita 5.5]*
*Krishnah svayam samabhavatparamapumaan yo*
*Govindam Aadipurusham tamaham bhajaami.*
*[Brahma Samhite 5.39]*

*Meaning*
*I bow to Govinda, who is the One and only Supreme Brahman, The changeless, deathless, beginningless, endless; and He who Appears in innumerable forms, the One who is praised in all The scriptures as the ever youthful, radiant, resplendent, the First-ever born and unassailable, the One who is not easily Reachable through Vedas, knowledege of scriptures, but can be accessible to the devotees through the knowledge of their Self.*

*I bow down to Sri Krishna who is the Parama Purusha, the First ever-born, protector of the cows-Govinda.*

*Mantra*
*"Arvaaj trichakro madhuvaahano ratho jeeraasho*
*ashvinoryaatu sushvutah,*
*Tribanduro Maghavaa vishvasoubhagah sham na*
*Aavaksha dvipade Chatushpaaade!"*
'RK Veda' [1.157.3]

*"O Lord Indra, Maghavan, the God of the Gods, make our family life blissful and giv us success, wealth, happiness, and make our life praise-worthy, fit for others to emulate; help us to develop an integrated personality, body, mind, and soul integrated and harmonious, to bring all happiness. Let all creatures - biped as well as quadrupeds, be happy and peaceful!"*

*Om Shantih, Shantih, Shantih!*

# Preface

*"We are all drops of water in the ocean; we know it and we know not it"*

India* has made a distinct and impressive contribution to human development thought and has got a significant place in the history of Civilizations. The significance is not just limited to one or two fields like fine arts- dance, drama, music, and painting, nor is it limited to mathematics and science. It is beyond all these. It extends to the field of supernatural and ecstatic, mystic trance experiences. The ancient sages of India discovered the 'magic' of the Lord's creation by tapas, contemplation, meditation; what the modern science and technology fails to explain even today, the ancient sages could easily grasp in their deepest contemplation, state of transcendental meditation. According to these Sages, there is nothing that we can search for outside of us; we do not know that all the secrets lie buried within us. They, the Seers and the Sages, say that 'man is like a drop of the ocean and; as such, he is the ocean by himself! Since he is a part of the ocean he can never come to know the ocean since the part cannot see the whole; nor he can deny the knowledge of the ocean since he himself is a part of it and has all the qualities of the ocean since the part cannot be different from the whole. The difficulty with man is that he wants to know the ocean that is so vast and beyond his ability to grasp. He can never know the vastness of its expanse or its depth and, still he says he knows it! He knows it is vast and deep, so vast and deep that it is beyond his ability to grasp and he also knows that it has been in existence, almost beyond time. This is the vision or ' darshana' that the ancient sages had had in their deep contemplation, state of transcendental meditation, supreme conciousness.

'*Vedanta*', the Indian i.e., the Hindu Philosophy holds the key. The history of Indian philosophy, known as 'Darshanas', is as old as human evolutionary history and many a distinguished scholars have tried in vain to give a precise date to it. It is said to be as old as the first human ever born on this planet and, at least half a million years have lapsed since the first word uttered by the archaic Man. The earliest known human beings- anatomically and physiologically different from all other living creatures, belonging to the species technically known as the '*Homo Sapiens sapiens*', may have appeared simultaneously or at different times in different places in China, Germany, Africa and Java in Indonesia, may be a hundred thousand years ago. The earlist known fossil of humans has been dated a few tens of thousands of years ago in Israel. The artifacts of man stand testimony to his creativity and the earliest known cave paintings are dated

---

*The Japanese called India, 'Indie' (Paradise) and, the map of India, i.e., BHARAT- '*Vedic India*' extended from Iran (Persia) in the West to Indonesia and Malaysia in the East. The Sindhu Valley, the Indus considered the cradle of Indian Civilization, the '*Vedic Civilization*'. May be, advanced civilization flourished around Thirty thousand years. [See 'Dawn of Humans', National Geographic, February 1997].

What makes man so different from other living creatures is his ability to think, discern, discriminate, and express his feelings, emotions, and thoughts. But it remains to discover the source of the ingenuity of his thoughts, and expressions. It is still a mystery how man attained this power of discerning, discrimination, and ability to reach higher levels of consciousness. It is beyond all science, or technological means to explain the mystic experiences that some of the outstanding spiritual leaders have attained. Certain things still remain beyond thoughts and words! It is said,"*Yatra vaacho nivartante...*" meaning, 'where the thoughts and words return without reaching it'.

India has the most valuable treasure of Knowledge in the form of Veda and Vedic Literature that are as old as man himself. The Veda, meaning 'KNOWLEDGE', emphatically proclaims that the first spoken alphabet of the word (Akshara) 'A' came out of deep Silence, cosmic silence (supreme consciousness) known as *'Atyanta- Abhava' in Samskrut language.* The first sound *'Om'* came out with a 'Big Bang' (the 'Sphota') out of this silence in that deep and dark expanse of space, where lie all the primordial dark matter and the elements like hydrogen, oxygen, nitrogen, ozone, argon, methane, carbon, aluminum, magnesium, iron, gold, silver, uranium, &c. that are responsible for the material objects of this world. In a sense, the secret of evolution of this universe, the cause of the causes, lies in that deep cosmic Silence, *'Atyanta-Abhava'* also called the *'Purusha'*, or the golden Silence (Hiranyagarbha or the golden egg that holds the universe). This *'Abstract Silence'* is eternal, full, knows all, i.e., omniscient. It is called the *'Self-Referral'*- the all-knowing, dynamic flow (of impulses), and when merged in the *'Anyonya-Abhava'*, a lower level of Consciousness (called 'Prakriti') has created this material world; it is the quality of Consciousness, the impulses, the vibrations, that create the thoughts and sounds.

*"God willed"; 'so the universe came into existence'* say the Great Seers! The material objects of the world, the thoughts, the sounds, the elements, the living and the non-living creatures have all emanated from this one single source, the thought force. The source of 'thought force is 'Absolute Silence'. The secret of the origin of the universe is thus explained in the thought force, the impulses, the vibrations, the archaic sound that emanated from this deep Silence. The first impulses and vibrations producing sound lapsed into deep Silence again and again producing a series of letters and words. For instance, the sound "Om" reverberated in the universe and merged into silence; the first letter 'A' collapsed into Silence only to re-emerge as a new sound 'k'; and, thus, the first word "Ak' was formed. This 'Ak' collapsed into silence and re-emerged as ' n', to foform 'Agni' meaning fire, the Sun. The word 'Ak-shara' of Rk Veda stands for the process that explains the creaion of the Universe. The 'Ak' is the Universe and 'Agni, the Sun sustains it. The "Ak" consist of the Macrocosm and the microcosm in the letters 'A' and 'k' respectively. This self-emanating dynamism of the Silence (between GAPS of Sounds of letters and words) containes full KNOWLEDGE and all creative ability and, has

made the Veda 'Apaurusheya'. The first letter word' Ak' holds the key! It is the Universe, its own cause and effect. 'A' holds the Universe and 'k' is a part of it. 'A' is the ocean and the 'k' is the bubble! We are all part of this Infinite Ocean of Consciousness; the immutable lies dormant in all of us. It is silent, eternal, self-effulgent, omniscient, omnipresent, and omnipotent. It is called the 'Brahm'.

Modern science reaffirms these facts. It is affirmed in the 'Rk Veda' that the entire universe emanated from the Silence and reverts back to Silence. It emanated from the 'Sphota', explosion of primordial matter from the depth of Silence (the Big Bang) and its reverberating sound "Om"merged into it (the Silence). In the first word of Rk Veda Mantra 1.1, '*Agnimeele purohitam*', the first Akshara (letter) 'Ak', the syllable 'A' stands for the Akhilanda Koti Brahmanda, the Universe, the Hiranyagarbha, the macrocosm; and, the syllable 'k' is the 'kana', the sub-atomic microscopic particle, the stellar dust particle, the micrososm, that carries all the qualitiesof the macrocosm. This is expressed as *'Anoraneenyan mahato mahateeyaan'* (*Poornamadah poornamidham...*'), or the 'world in a grain of sand'. The atom, or the molecule, or the cell is complete by itself in all respects. All the material objects of this world are thus formed in the dynamic flow of the Silence, supreme Consciousness. This is the *Natural Law* of the 'Unified Field' where WHOLENESS or, 'Totality', or Full 'KNOWLEDGE' exists. This is the 'Brahm', the 'Atma'. Out of this supreme 'Brahm', the Self-existent, omniscient, omnipotent and all-pervasive 'Avyakta' (Unmanifest), all other Principles such as space, time, causality manifested, thus creating many out of the 'One', the 'Uni-verse'. The Ancient Sages or Rishis visualized this Totality of supreme knowledge, the *'Samhita', the' WHOLENESS'.*

The entire human history is conceived in a spatio-temporal (space-time) framework while the scope of spiritual antiquity of India transcends time and space. In fact, Indian philosophy starts with the words 'Ananta' and 'Achyuta' that stand for the 'eternal', 'endless', or' the 'beginning-less' and 'end-less'. It is significant to note here that the 'Geo-centric theory' of Ptolemy swayed the world till Copernicus dared to put his 'Helios-centric theory' in 1530. People believed that the earth goes round the sun, and the days and nights are caused due to this movement of the Sun round the earth. Copernicus, Tycho Brahe, Kepler and Issac Newton perfected the Helios- centric thery and stated that all the planets go round the sun and the sun moves between two centers (Foci) at the center causing the days and nights as well as seasons. But, the Indian astronomers and mathematicians like Varahamihira, Bhaskara, Brahmagupta, and Bhattacharya who calculated the position of the planets and forecast eclipses accurately.

The Veda proclaims that 'Man' is the 'center of the universe'. *"Purusham eva idham sarvam..."* [Purusha Sukta, 'Rk Veda' Mandala X. 90], meaning, "Purusha alone is everything (this whole universe)". In other words, '*Brahm*', or '*Brahman*', derived from 'Brihat' (meaning, 'to grow without limit'), resides within the Spiritual heart- Adhidaivika, the subtle heart of every creature; but only man can realize the Lord by contemplation in deep meditation. It is reiterated in Ishavasya Upanishad that "Ishavasyam idam sarvam" meaning, 'the Lord encompasses this whole universe and what all we see or hear resides in Him; and He resides in the thumb-sized cave of the heart as Light, the 'Atman' (Atma Jyoti).

It may be mentioned here that the earliest known cities, the artifacts of man are believed to have existed Five- to Six- thousand years ago. But, the Veda is much older. If modern science teaches the Solar System is a part of the Galaxy called 'Milky Way' that consists of millions of stars and, the Milky Way is a part of the 'Uni-verse', rather the 'Multi-verse', that consist of thousands of Galaxies like the Milky Way; the Veda says that the Universe is One and is centred around the 'Brahm', or the 'Atma', the Soul. The Vedic statement that the 'Purusha' who resides in the *Soul or Atma is the 'centre of the universe', "Purushamevam idham sarvam"* ['Rk Veda', Mandala X- Purushasuktha] should come as a surprise to scientists who hold that the Sun is the center of the solar system and man is an insignificant part of it. The Veda treats the Sun as the eye of the Brahman from whom it gets all its energy, heat and light- chetana or Shakti. The entire universe is centred on this Supreme Purusha, the Brahm or the source of energy and Man is a part of this supreme Brahman. In fact, the 'Atma', the 'Soul', and the 'Brahman' are the same. The human 'Mind' (that resides in his heart) is capable of discerning this 'Reality'. It is said that, 'God has created Man in his own image, as a replica and He resides in him'. Man constitutes the sum and substance of the evolutionary history of the earth. The cosmic body (the Universe) is held by the 'Brahman' and He is the container; He stays ten fingers above that what is called the universe that is ever expanding! His body is 'Hiranyagarbha', the ether; the sky or space, is his 'Mind'; and, all the creatures of the world are His Soul. Similarly, Man, the counter-part of the Brahman, has derived his physical body in the human form, the Mind, and his Soul. Thus, Man is partly 'matter' and partly spirit; he is matter in his body (physical), mind, and intellect, and is partly 'spirit' in his 'Atma' or Soul. This Atma or Soul is extremely subtle and almost impossible to see or touch, but can be experienced in a very deep state of 'Mauna' or 'Silence' called 'Atyanta-Abhava' felt in Nirvikalpa Samadhi, deep contemplation or Transcendental Meditation. So far, it is doubtful whether anybody has experienced this. It is impossible to know this Brahman since it is knowable, but not known. It is not even unknown since it is knowable, but not known. It is inexplicable and as such no body can ever define it by words or sound. The experience of the Brahm cannot be transferred and as such it remains a secret forever. When one realizes the Brahm or knows the Brahm, he becomes one with It and remains no more a human being for, he merges in supreme Consciousness. When a person attains to that exalted state of supreme Consciousness, he becomes completely, absolutely silent and, 'Absolute Silence' ('Atyantaabhaava') is 'Brahm'. Thus, the mystery continues and man wants to 'know'; his curiosity knows no bounds! Whoever says, 'he knows It, knows not; and, whoever says he knows not really knows It'! It is knowable but not known. It is far far away and beyond reach of thoughts, words and sound; t is also very very close, nearer than our hands and feet. It is in our heart of hearts! There are three hearts- one physical that pumps the blood (Adhibhautika), the other- 'anthahkarana' (Adhyatmika), and the third, the cavity where the subtlest invisible Brahm resides as the source of all KNOWLEDGE, light, or Prana, the Consciousness (the Adhidaivika).

The evolutionary history of the earth is the history of Mankind according to 'Rk Veda', and the Veda do not make any difference between the animate and the inanimate objects of this world. This concept is beautifully explained in the Text here. Every sub-atomic particle, cell, algae, phyto-plankton, or zoo- plankton, or the unicellular amoeba, or the multifaceted intellectual known as the modern Man is but a 'part of the whole and the whole of the part' as explained in the first mantra, 'Poornamadah Poornamidam"- the Peace Invocation of 'Ishavasya Upanishad'.

What constitutes the spiritual heritage of India holds good to the entire world since the Veda proclaim that the 'World, indeed, is one family' in the concept of "Vasudhaiva Kutumbakam". Indian philosophy made no mistake in asserting "Universal Brotherhood" and stood for world peace ever since the dawn of human civilization. The Peace chanting called the "Shanti Mantra"– "Om, Shantih, Shantih, Shantih", covers the entire humanity; there is the mantra, "Sarve Janah sukhino bahavantu", meaning, "Let all people be happy" and 'Let there be 'Peace, Peace, Peace' everywhere in the World'. It is significant that these concepts emanated from the Creator Himself for He is the Protector, too. The Creator (Brahma), the Protector (Vishnu), and the Destroyer (Mahesvara) are one and the same (Brahman), who holds and controls this Universe!

*Thus, Man is the 'Be-all' and 'End-all' of Vedanata, the sum and susbstance of the Veda. Whichever religion, philosophy, or culture upholds universal peace and brotherhood, love and compassion, upholds dignity of Man and proclaims and practices universal peace, and desist from maiming, hurting others- body and mind, is the greatest religion and philosophy. In this sense, Hinduism called 'Sanatana Dharma' is considered to be the most idealistic as also practical leading man with animal propensities to more human state of love and compassion, and onward to the divine state of existence.*

Indian philosophy is based on a number of Ancient Indian Scriptures. These Scriptures consist of the Veda and the Upanishads, Shrutis, Smritis, the Brahma Sutra, the Puranas, the Bhagavad-Gita, Paatanjali's Yoga Sutra, Ayur-Veda, Dhanur-Veda, and the like. Since these scriptures constitute an invaluable guide to sensible living, they constitute 'Applied Philosophy' than merely the theoretical renderings or teachings of Veda and Vedic Literature, or Religion of the Hindus. The ancient Indians lived the philosophical way, the 'Hindu Way', an austere way, of life with the spiritual goal of "Self Realization" and enriched human life. Thus, India came to be known as the "Yoga Bhoomi", 'Karma Bhoomi', or the 'Punya Bhoomi', a place of 'fulfillment', - 'spiritual' attainment on earth. The Veda are an invaluable storehouse of the secrets of Lord's creation and an invaluable Guide to Life.

We must have a clear understanding of the Ancient Indian Scriptures and the Indian Philosophy. The Veda and the Vedanga, the Upanishads, the Brahma Sutra, and the Bhagavad Gita form the basis of Indian Philosophy. The 'Rk', or Mantras (Samhita) constitute the main body of the Text of Veda and these are called 'Shrutis'. These Mantras are meant for 'intent listening', hearing with rapt attention involving body, mind and soul, and not just 'hearing', for the latter gives the feeling of 'sound' without its direction and meaning. 'Shrava' (from which the word 'shravan' is derived), means 'line' or 'direction'. Philosophy is 'darshana' which means seeing or looking and denotes 'visibility'; it is the way we look at the created world. In a sense, the 'Suktas' of the Veda are actually what the Sages (Seers) visualized in their Meditation. Darshana (Philosophy) gives a general view of life, of the world; and, particularly the Indian Philosophy, six in number (Shat-darshan), helps to understand the spiritual way of life, the 'Hindu' way of life, the Vedic Way of life. Of these, the Samkhya forms the foundation and the *Vedanta forms the crown of Knowledge.*

Max Mueller has put it in a very striking way, He says, *"In the history of the world, the Veda fills a gap which no literary work in any other language could fill. I maintain that to every body who cares for himself, for his ancestor, for his history, for his intellectual development, a study of Vedic literature is indispensable".*

The beauty of Indian philosophy is that it makes no difference between man and man, and treats the entire world as one place transcending national boundaries or political frontiers. What holds good to Indian saints and sages also holds good to all people of the world. All the religions and philosophies of the world have their roots in the Veda, i.e.,'Knowledge', i.e., the 'Sat' (Truth), established in the Veda.'Ritam' (Right or Dharma) and 'Satyam' (Truth) constitute the foundation of the universe and all the celestial bodies obey these laws. The Vedic Verses that establish these principles are explained in the Text here. The Epics, the Puranas, the Brahma Sutras, the Bhagavad Gita, the Teachings of Mahaveera and the Buddha as well as the Great Acharyas uphold these spiritual laws. But unfortunately, these values are not much appreciated in these days of 'get rich quick', or become rich and famous by any means-"enakena prakaarena prasiddho bhava" This book comes as a reminder to the modern day youth and warns not to take recourse to unrighteous or foul means whatever may be the reason and implores to adhere to 'Satyam' and 'Ritam' at any cost.

An effort has been made in this book to bring as much of the available important ancient scriptures as possible in a nutshell and provide an insight into the Vedantic doctrines, the spiritual heritage of India. This book serves as a source of inspiration to youngsters and serves as a guide to sane and sensible living. It is our great luck and fortune that we have a source of 'Knowledge' in the Veda, the Upanishads, the Brahma Sutras, the Bhagavad-Gita, and the Puranas and the Epics; and, our ancient Sages have shown us a path to realize our potential to the full and attain all success and happiness in life here, as well as liberation hereafter. A few aphorisms of the Vedic Hymns and Upanishads are given here. However, this is not an exhaustive Text or description of all the ancient scriptures. It is only a brief summary of a few selected ones and serves as a pointer.

Those who want more detailed versions may as well go to the original works, or Commentaries that are easily available. Some eminent authors have been elaborately quoted here in order to impress on the readers the need to go to their works. Select References are provded for this purpose.

I am indebted to all the great thinkers, writers, and the publishers from whom I have quoted texts at length. The ultimate objective of the study is to bring the hitherto inaccessible sources of supreme Knowledge to the doors of the readers. The author feels obliged for any valuable suggestions to improve upon this work from the readers as well as the learned scholars in the field.

**T.N.A.R.**

# Introduction

The search for 'That' ultimate thing which makes man so special is still on despite the fact that some knowledgeable persons declare that they have known 'It'! Everytime a person declares that he had the vision, he knows it like Reni Descartes, the 17th century French philosopher, scientist and mathematician, who declared –*"cogito, ergo sum" ('knew he was because he thought').* Being a scientist, he went to the extent of looking for the source and ultimately located in the pineal gland in the brain supposed to be the part of the body most immediately associated with the Soul. The Soul is the inner, vital and ineffable principle people have always believed is uniquely human and makes humans so special, different from all other animals except the apes. Apes also have this unique capacity to think. But, of course, it is only the humans who have ingeneously built up institutions of religion and culture with temples, mosques and churches and what not, to practise the thinking of 'That' special thing in the form of prayer, worship, etc. The search goes on; the search for that exclusive factor that can validate the doctrine, that 'God has created man in his own image'. There are innumerable expressions such as spirit, atma, soul, jiva, psyche, anima, etc. to qualify man that makes him very special besides the qualities of God often displayed by man.

Still, the question remains. What makes man so special? What makes man so different from other animals who are quite intelligent, and the ones capable of thinking? Some scientists have come very close to the answer and have crossed the border of the physical and entered the mystical and are trying to know the quintessence that makes man more human, giving a sense of humanity leading towards divinity. Setting him apart from the other animals. The essential ingredienssts that bring out emotions, compassion, love, sympathy, reasoning, morality, self-awareness, and the knowledge of 'free-will' are all traced to this source, lying outside the biological; the pineal gland may not be the source but, it may be something else- a group of other spcialised brain cells and their enormously cpmplex system of wiring connecting to brain. Neuro-scientists are of the opinion that 'a large cigar-shaped neurons' called 'spindle cells' produce the impulses, vibrations, and signals that carry human emotions, qualities of love, compassion, morals, etc. as also the animal tendencies, from the source near the heart and broadcast all over the body. The apes too have this spindle cells that give them the animal tendencies, impulses instincts, etc.

There is another angle to the story of Man, rather, the history of man. Remember the social contract theory. It is Hobbes, Locke, and Roussou who put forth their own views of man's struggle for freedom and release from bondage; one of them said, "Man is born free and everywhere he is in chains". Now the question is what freedom and what bondage? Who said that man is born free? Eversince the conception, the bondage is real in the umbilical chord and even when it is cut off, the emotional bondage, continues. The bondage of the anthahkarana, bondage of the three internal organs- the manas, the budhdhi, and the I-sense, or the 'ego' continue to exist even after death; In fact, this bondage is so permanent that they continue even after death, cling to the soul as karmic particles and desires and transmigrate to other bodies carrying all the impressions, memories and images as 'samskaar'. So where is freedom? But, it is paradoxical to say that there is no freedom and still ask the question where is bondage. What is bondage? There is no bondage unless you think it is bondage, a binding of the soul. The embodied soul itself is bondage. The Soul that is eternal, free, immortal, becomes embodied due to its blemishes such as desires and karmic particles and make it undergo all the troubles and travails of life on this earth since the desire to enjoy the pleasures of the senses is very strong; and, 'desire is 'Brahman'. The moment It (the Soul) realizes its true nature, it is released and becomes free. This is the 'realization of self', or enlightenment, or liberation.

In Kena Upanishad, there is the question: "What is that from which everything else becomes known'? If the secret of the source of this KNOWLEDGE is known everything becomes known. But, as already said, It is knowable but, not known. This supreme knowledge, the 'Truth', God or 'Brahm' is always eluding us.

Thus, the field of Knowledge is so vast and complicated that it is not easy to answer everything and some of these things remain mystery even after somebody knows and tries to explain what he knows. In fact, it is simply in explicable and it remains a mystery forever. The urge and the search go on.

An attempt is made here to bring out all these known and knowable things and what all has been thought and said, in a nutshell. It is an exploration into the unknown.

There are two types of Knowledge. One, the Lower Knowledge (Apara Vidya), the knowledge of the mundane objective world; and the Second, is the Higher Knowledge (Para Vidya). The latter is the Supreme Knowledge, Knowledge of the Self, Knowledge of the Atman. Vedanta is Supreme Knowledge. Vedanta, the sum and substance of the principle doctrines of the Veda, is summed up in the Upanishads. The Veda, the Vedangas and the Upanishads, the Brahma Sutra and the Bhagavad Gita are considered to be very sacred ancient scriptures. The Veda is 'Knowledge Supreme'. Although Veda is one, there are four divisions viz, the 'Rk' Veda, the Yajur Veda, the Sama Veda and the Atharva Veda, and the essence of these Veda is found in the Upanishads that number about 250 of which more than 110 are vailable in print. These Upanishads are of mystc nature and highly potent. These Upanishads were kept beyond the reach of the skeptics, non-believers, and persons of impure mind, and unscrupulous persons for fear of being misused and abused. Only a Guru, an enlightened person could initate his son or trusted pupil and impart the Vedas and Upanishads. Normally, the recipients of the instruction of the Upanishadic lessons were expected to be highly obedient, devoted, earnest and humble. The Guru used to test the pupil very rigorously before accepting him for imparting instructions. Sometimes, the Guru would not speak for ten years and the pupil had to simply carry out the daily chores like bringing water and fuel wood ('arani' or sticks of Peepual tree), assisting the teacher in Puja and other rituals in the Guruji's ashram and wait for the teacher's grace and goodwill. Even the Gods visited the Sages well versed in Vedas and stayed for several years in the Ashram before they could get their doubts cleared! Not only the teachers tested the pupils but, the pupils, as well, tested the teachers before accepting them as 'Guru'. This system of mutual trust was one of the essential requirements of the 'Gurukula'. The teacher was held in high esteem and the pupil who did not respect his Guru would forget what all he had learnt and all his knowledge would be a waste! The Teacher–Student relationship was very sacred and the divine knowledge imparted by such revered teachers was much more sacred. One of the Vedic prayers asks for 'mutual trust and protection of the teacher and the pupil.'

Vedanta is all about the 'endless quest'. It holds the key to sane and sensible living and answers all questions about life. It is about the nature of the universe; it is about life, and problems of life and death and thereafter. It is about emancipation. It is about freedom, liberation, and eternal bliss and happiness. It is about the goal of life. It is about the meaning of life. It is about the proper understanding of the problems of life as also to equip oneself to face life as it comes. It is about experience of life in its full. It is about salvation, or 'mukti', i.e., the purification of the mind. It is about 'Moksha' that is burning of all desires of impure mind and to 'dwell in Him', attaining the Supreme Bliss. It is about the sensible way of living that the ancient Indian Sages taught us that is brought out in this small book. When we say 'Vedanta' it is generally treated as something that does not concern our day-to-day life. It is often mistaken for the 'other-worldly' pursuits. That is how Vedanta has been misrepresented in all early texts. Modern expositions differ entirely from this approach. Modern spiritual science reveals the secrets of life, secrets of happiness and success in life and shows the way. Vedantic way of life is the sensible way of living that promotes a healthy, happy and successful life. Vedanta is also the source of material wealth that many have not properly understood. There are Mantras, Yantras and Tantras in Vedantic way of life that brings immense health, wealth and wisdom to all those who have firm faith in the Lord and follow this way of life. Vedanta does not mean abandoning the great opportunity given to man to live and enjoy on this earth, of which even the Devas are jealous. In a way, it is the Vedantic way of life, not of abandonment, but of fulfillment!

Vedanta is the spiritual heritage of India. It is the Veda and Upanishads that give us simple formulae for success and happiness in life. In modern day life, the mad pursuit for material wealth and prosperity sans morals and ethics has brought misery to man. Spiritual aspects of life are as important as material wealth. Vedanta is not opposed to material progress as often made to think of in many earlier texts. There is no doubt that this life is for enjoyment. Vedanta does not advise you to abandon worldly life; in fact, it advocates enjoyment of life and there are mantras to propitiate the Lord Indra to bestow health, wealth and happiness. Vedanta by itself is an invaluable guide to life. It helps to enjoy life so well that you will not hanker after wealth and sensual pleasures any more, taking repeated births. It advocates a life of 'Sat, Chit and Anand'. Take to Vedantic way of life and live sensibly. Enjoy your life so well that you feel happy and contented. Enjoy your life so well that it leaves no desires for further fulfillment in the next birth. There are Vedic prayers for the Grace of the Lord to enjoy good health and good life. But, the most important thing is to realize one's own Self by a deeper understanding of the Self, the Soul, and the Spirit within. A number of techniques derived from our ancient scriptures are given in this book that will help to understand the meaning of life and this helps to lead a happy and successful life.

Spiritual heritage of India consists of ancient scriptures like the Veda, the Upanishads, Puranas, the Bhagavad-Gita, Bhagavata, Puranas like Brahmanda Purana, Padma Purana, the Vishnu Purana, Garuda Purana, Kurma Purana, &c. The ancient Gurukula system was just like any University with a few specialists in particular Vedas and Upanishads and had their own rules and regulations. They taught eighteen subjects starting from astronomy and astrology to politics and warfare. The syllabi as well as the methods of teaching varied from Gurukula to Gurukula. The students consisted of children of wealthy as well as poor parents and even the Kings sent their children to Gurukula for instructions. The Guru made no discrimination between rich and poor, upper caste and lower castes! The ancient scriptures were taught more by chanting in chorus with utmost care for accents and pronunciation. Intent listening and absolute adherence to phoenetics and bhavartha of mantras was strictly enforced. The medium of instruction was Samskrut. The texts were written in 'Devanagari lipi' on 'Taalegari', i.e., the palm leâves. The ink was prepared out of plants and quill (porqupine quill or the bird's quill) constituted the pen. The scriptures were taught orally and learnt by-heart; rigorous training in phoenetics, musical and rhythmic expression of the Verses and repetition constituted the regular exercises in Vedic chantings very early in the morning. Memory played very important role in the entire learning process.

Even today, there are many Scriptures in manuscript form that have not seen the light of the day. In the absence of a proper scientific method of preservation and suitable Publishers these manuscripts may be lost forever. One such ancient scripture is the Brughu Samhita and the other, the Brihad Jataka. The scripts are in the form of mantras and tantras and these cannot be deciphered without a proper knowledge of Samskrut language and the codes inserted in between words and the intricate science of interpreting goodarthas (hidden meaning) of these scriptures. There are very few copies of these texts and many are disjointed and pages are missing and, this makes it difficult to use. Some scripts appear to be incoherent and, that again makes it very difficult to use. Some scripts are deliberately made incoherent using code words or syllables for purposes of secrecy. Efforts are being made to decipher these codes in some newly found rare manuscripts. Samskruta Vidhyapeetha of Tirupati Tirumalai Devasthanam (TTD) have taken up a project to collect and publish thousands of these ancient scripts and put them on their web sites for use by scholars in India and abroad.

These invaluable spiritual writings constitute the Ancient Indian Heritage and more is yet to come. The ancient scriptures cover a wide range of subjects like: astronomy including space science, astrology, ayurveda, mathematics, vyakarana (grammar), arthashastra (economics), rajaneeti (politics), metaphysics, tarka (logic), ethics, philosophy, armoury and warfare, yantra vijnyana and tantra jnyana, fine arts, -in all 18 subjects, were taught at various stages over a period of 12 twelve years in Gurukula. A student had to learn and be proficient in eighteen subjects before graduation.

This book helps to bring an awareness of the spiritual wealth, the legacy that constitutes the Spiritual Heritage of India. The puritanical and ritualistic (Yagnya) approach to the study of Vedanta has kept the youngsters away from these important sources of scientific knowledge over the millennia and, now a new wave has been created by the recent publications of modern scientific versions of these ancient scriptures. What is called biotechnology or genetic engineering in present-day curriculum is beautifully covered in the Veda. Many scholars have taken to advanced research in computing the mantras, the formulae of Vedic literature.

The very first mantra of the 'Rk Veda "Agnimeele purohitam yajnyasya Devam Ritvijam Hotaaram Ratna daataaram" is so interesting that some scholars are looking into the various aspects of its study; the phoenetics, the vibrations, the effect of the sound, the literal and the metaphorical aspects, the meaning of the GAPS between letters, words and sounds, etc. are all under intensive study. Maharishi Mahesh Yogi says that all KNOWLEDGE (VEDA) exists in the GAPS (Silence) between the letters, words, Verses, Suktas, and Mandalas and the Thirty-nine Vedic Literature and the Rk Veda. It is so interesting that references to cloning, transplantation of organs, control of the internal organs of the human body including the heart-beats and pulses by yogic powers, surgery by Yogic methods, transmigration of souls, etc. are all beautifully described in the Veda, particularly in Atharva Veda. Even amputation was done without surgical instruments! Psychic or mystic powers are explained in Atharvana Veda. Spiritiual healing and touch therapy are practised even to-day. As already stated, someof the Upanishads are of great mystic force and any spiritual aspirant gains the mystic powers within a fortnight of sincere, steadfast, and rigorous practice. The Upanishad guarantees God -visioning within six months provided the aspirant is very strict in personal discipline, morals and ethics, and carries out the stipulated yogic exercises methodically, according to Bhagavan Paatanjali. Many people, including the author of this work, have experienced the mystic experiences at very early stages of Meditation. Many obstacles follow early successes and dishearten the aspirants; but much depends on the faith and earnestness and steadfastness.

There are many more interesting aspects of modern science in the Vedic Scriptures that enthrall the readers. This opens up a new field of research in future research. The total number of Upanishads is estimated to be around 250 and about 108 have been treated very authentic. Some of the Upanishads are not exactly Upanishads of Vedic Texts and seem to be later additions to the list so as to give some sort of authenticity and respectability to these scriptures; however, all these demand moral and ethical discipline from the spiritual aspirants. Another interesting aspect of the Upanishads is that only ten or twelve of them are from Rig Veda and Sama Veda and have been expounded and commented upon by Shankara, Madhva, Raghavendra Teertha and other Swamijis. The rest are all of mystic nature and the Revered Swamijis and Teachers did not want them to be made easily accessible to unscrupulous pupils. The most popular Upanishads widely commented upon are: the Ishavasya, Katha, Kena, Prashna, Mundaka, Mandukya, Chandogya, Brihadaranyaka, Mahanarayana, and Shvetasvatara Upanishads. Many non-traditional and more scientific versions of the commentaries on a large number of Upanishads are coming out these days.

As one pervades the depths of these different Upanishads, a very striking thing happens to the readers. These Upanishads appear to be inconsistent, incoherent and, at times, sound illogical and to be at cross-purpose! But, the readers have to keep in mind the fact that the goal of all Upanishads is to herald the Unity of existence, singularity of the 'Brahman', the 'Absolute' 'Ekameva advitiyam'. The ultimate goal of life is 'Realisation of the Self', the 'Brahman'. It is a spiritual exercise, inexplicable, purely personal and non-transferable; and, each spiritual aspirant gains higher and higher levels of Consciousness in this exercise and experiences the beauty and splendour of the inner world that is revealed to him only in the meditative state.

The Earth is supposed to be the only planet so far known to have a very highly developed life form in the species 'Homo sapiens sapiens', the Man. The entire Solar system operates under the influence of a small red young star that is a mass of Hydrogen (H) getting fused to become Helium (He4) and in the process sheds light, heat and the life-supporting actinic rays- all traveling at speed of 1,86,000 miles per hour in the form of electromagnetic waves of different wave lengths. A number of theories and hypotheses like the 'Big Bang' theory, the nebular hypothesis, the tidal theory, the planetismal hypothesis, have been put forth by modern scientists to explain the cosmic origin; there are the theories of the origin of the Universe, origin of the Solar System, origin of the Earth and evolution of landforms, etc. Physicists go to the extent of studying the behaviour of the sub-particles and divide atoms and, have successfully harnessed atomic power.

All scientists simply dismiss the source of energy in atoms as just a property of matter. They do not investigate the metaphysical or the spiritual aspects simply because it does not come within the purview of material science. Physical Science or Biological Science deals with matter; and, spirit lies outside scientific enquiry that depends on the faculty of senses. So far, no scientist has ever found out what constitutes the source of this atomic energy, other than the molecular movements, and do not know who decides to give what property to matter, or for that matter, what brings forth life from the rudiments, whereas, the Ancient Sages have visualized these by Meditation!

Very plausible explanations are given about evolution of life in the Veda; not only the theory of evolution, but the theory of involution explains the origin of the myriads of life forms! While physical science needs the senses that go out to look for the answers, the spiritual science needs no senses and mind that look outward, but needs a spiritual inquiry that looks inwards towards the 'Atman' who holds all the answers for that is the Brahman who is the source of all creations in this universe. The answers come as revelations, mystic experience, and only the aspirant gets it with intense spiritual practice.

Veda are the repository of the Knowledge concerning spiritual as well as materoal sciences. Rk Veda has 10,552 verses or mantras that carefully unravel all the mystery of this Universe. There are Ten Mandalas each one is replete with lot of potent mantras that can suffice scientists to explore this universe for a million years and still the universe remains mysterious! In fact, the Veda itself says that, 'it is ignorance, Maya, or illusion that shrouds this Universe!' Each Vedic verse is pregnant with meaning and each of the ancient Sages of India like Gautama, Aruni, Yajnavalkya, Shvetaketu, Raikva have explored the depth of the meaning of these magical or mystic words and have come out with his own experience. A mantra, for example "*Annam Brahma*" has all the secrets of the origin of life on this Planet! More than a thousand -page exposition and commentary of this mantra is available and, still, scientists do not know the secret of life. Most of the Upanishads are of mystic nature and Atharva Veda is full of Tantric expositions! Sama Veda is beautiful to sing and the vibrations create wonderful effect. Yajur Veda has a number of Upanishads that give mystic experience to spiritual aspirants. Thus, each of the four Veda has its own grandeur. A well-versed person in Veda has no dearth for any of his needs if only he practices a moral and ethical way of life and uses the knowledge and mystic power for welfare of others!

There are about 250 Upanishads (so far in print), of which only 108 are significant and these have been classified as Vedanta Upanishads, Physiological Upanishads dealing with human body, Yoga Upanishads dealing with Asanas, Pranayama and Kundalini, Sanyas Upanishads or the ascetic way, and the Mantra Upanishads or Prayers. All the Upanishads drive home the fact that the real goal of life is 'Realization of the Self', the Atman or the 'Brahman'. They proclaim 'human life form is the divine plan with a purpose. It serves the purpose of evolution as well as involution. Liberation of the soul is for involution and evolution is for fulfilment. Veadanta holds the key to sensible living and fulfillment'.

From the fossil records found in Neanderthal (Germany), and Beijing, former Peking (China), and Islands of Java, Sumatra and other places it appears that man first appeared about a 100,000 years ago. Of this, nearly half the time has gone in the development of the Brain and the establishment of 'homeostasis' to control the functions of the body. It is only during the last 10,000 years or so a highly developed human being moved about the world with his philosophy and artifacts. The region around Asia Minor and the Indus Valley where the Aryans lived is supposed to be the cradle of this ancient civilization. The Vedas are the 'Revealed Words' of God (apaurusheya) and it is said Brahma initiated his son Atharvan with the Veda ('Vedh' meaning, 'that pierces through Ignorance', i.e., 'Knowledge').

Here, it may be interesting to observe the significance of each and every word spoken by man in the form of Veda. The word 'Rk' means mantra, the sacred spoken word or the written word that has its root in Atma and the 'Saman' means the song in praise of the Lord. Since Man is the first ever animal in human form to speak words, it is no wonder that every word spoken by him has attracted the attention with awe and wonder. The first word is 'Om', supposed to be the word vibrating in the universe since the very beginning, i.e., 'Big Bang' or 'Sphota' that caused this world. Similarly all the Samskrut alphabets that form seed words (Bijaksharas) are meditated upon and worshipped for the potency and effect they produce. Man's speech got power and strength from these seed words (Veeja akshara) and every word or a half of the word (hrsva) conveys a world of meaning! For example, 'Aap' or 'Aaps' stands for water and a man dying of thirst is seen breathing heavily producing the sound 'Aaps'. Even small children say 'aapu' (even before anybody taught them) to ask for water. These are explained later in the text.

No wonder, the ancients Sages enjoyed singing the praise of the Lord for giving the power of speech- "Rk" and 'Saman', to evolve into a distinct life form on this earth. Also, the enlightened Rishis, or the Sages believed that the Lord created Man in his own minature form with all the qualities enshrined in Himself. The divine qualities like 'Anand' (Bliss), the ambition to acquire name and fame, 'to shine', to become powerful, great, etc. are all his attributes. Man has grown over the Millennia and the Vedas proclaim these in unmistakable terms. What all that has been created, or all that would be created in the future, shall come from the human Mind and the human Mind is the repository of the Divine Power! These qualities, creative intelligence, omniscience, omnipotence are the qualities imbibed from Him! Vedas teach how to harness this hidden power within us through contemplation, Meditation.

Vedanta says, life is a journey to be accomplished with single-minded devotion, dedication, steadfastness, and un-wavering mind; it is a 'yajnya', an offering to the Lord Almighty who created us with a purpose. Finally, it is a total merger with 'That'. It is all contemplation, mind tuned towards sublime bliss; the mind turned away from the gross, mundane, sensate world. There is no more hankering after the sensual desires once the 'Reality' is felt 'within'. The mind is under the supervision of the Consciousness, 'Sakshi' the inner eye that perceives the fickle and irrational behavior. 'Buddhi' keeps the mind under control; the mind that puts the senses under its command to irrational errands will thus be checked. Mind plays a very important role in life. Upanishads declare Mind is the world, Mind is Brahman, and Mind is the key to happy successful life. Hence 'Manoniyantran' or mind control is an essential part of life. Swami Shivananda of Rishikesh says that, "a knowledge of the ways and habits of the mind, and its operations, the laws of the mind and the method of mental control and mental discipline, is very necessary if you want to enjoy real happiness and peace of an unruffled and abiding nature". You cannot`expect everlasting happiness and perennial joy in the world of sense around us. The mischievous monkey- mind plays havoc in a variety of ways and causes and cares, worries and anxieties. Money, property, women and children do not give permanent satisfaction. This is the experience of all people.

The sooner one gets a glimpse of the truth behind the human mind's mischievous play offering false notions of happiness, promising escape routes to drudgery of life and thus getting trapped, better it is! The simple method of attaining supreme bliss is through 'Realization of the Self and this is possible by observing the nature of Mind; simply watch the behavior of Mind with a sense of 'choice-less awareness'. The restless Mind stops to rest for a while; continue to remain in that state as long as possible; by continuous practice one can continue to be in this state of blessedness. This is the true path ('sat- nyas') from wretchedness of the mundane sensate objective world to blessedness of the heavenly world.

These things are analyzed in great detail with reference to the 'suktas' and 'mantras' obtained from the Vedas and the Upanishads, Shrutis, the Puranas, Bhagavatam, the Bhagavad Gita, and other sacred works that constitute the Spiritual heritage of India. In fact, the Upanishads, the Brahma Sutra, and the Bhagavad Gita are the 'prasthaanathrayas' that constitute the foundation of Indian Religion and Philosophy. Our ancient Sages and Seers, Saints and Sadhus, Scholars and Pundits paid rich tribute to our ancient scriptures, which constituted a store house of knowledge and wisdom. It is our misfortune that these source materials were not available to us till recently; and, suddenly now the awareness has come and this has made everyone search for these source materials. It seems that there are 250 Upanishads in print and not all are original and authentic. Some of these are altered and new ones are added without the name of the author to give a sense of sanctity and authority; but the differences can be easily made out. All the 108 Upanishads are mentioned in Muktikopanishad and someof these are listed here in the Index.

Most of the original and authentic Upanishads are lost to us due to the fact that these Upanishads have been conveyed from the teacher to the pupil by way of 'manana', learning by-heart and 'Smriti', remembering what is heard in rapt attention. Moreover, the Upanishads are dated back to more than five thousand years. Veda and Upanishads existed since time immemorial and the Upanishads found in Kali Yuga, called the 'Iron Age', are not the same as those that were found in the earlier Dwapara Yuga, Treta Yuga, and the Satya Yuga. Many have been discarded as unsuitable or redundant, too. Many Upanishads have undergone much change over the ages due to different interpretations. At the end of each Yuga, some of these Upanishads have been rendered either useless or simply ignored by the Sages and only those that suited to the general conditions of the people, spiritual level of the people, were retained. It is stated that more than twenty Kali Yugas, or Dwapara Yuga, Treta Yuga, and Satya Yugas have lapsed till now. As a result, no wonder, the available Upanishads found today are entirely different and seem to be incomplete, incoherent, and at times incomprehensive. It is very difficult to reconstruct the Upanishads that are not available and one has to be content with what is available and make full use of them!

# 1
# The Veda

What constitute the sacred Scriptures that make the spiritual heritage of India so proud is 'Jnyaan' ('Knowledge)', called the 'Veda' ('Vid" meaning, 'Knowledge'). The essence of the 'Veda' is culled into teachings called the "Upanishads", also known as "***Vedanta***". According to the '***Purusha-suktha***', the 'Rk', 'Yajus' and the 'Saman' are the three 'Veda generated at the beginning of creation from a mental sacrifice of adoration performed by the divine Prajapatis and sages with the Supreme Being as the material of the offering'. Some believe that the fourth Veda, the '***Atharva Veda***' came later as the one elucidated by Brahma to his eldest son Atharvan. But, it seems that the Atharva Veda is the only Veda and all the other three Veda are its divisions – one dealing with the Principles 'Rk', second dealing with chandas and songs, 'the Saman', and the third, Yajus dealing with the practical aspects of Yajnya.

*"Om, Brahmaa Devaanaam prathamah sambhabhuva*
*vishvasya kartaa bhuvanasya goptaa;*
*sa Brahmavidyaam sarvavidyaaprathishtaam*
*Atharvaayajyeshtaputraaya praaha"[Mundakopanishad, 1.1].*

The Puranas and epics are considered to be the Fifth Veda. In fact, all the Veda convey one and the only 'Truth', i.e. the Brahman or "Brahm".

The Veda are, thus, "transmitted from beginningless antiquity through a continuous chain of teachers and pupils, who, relying upon the statements in the Veda themselves considered them to be eternal and '***apaurusheya***, i.e., having no human source." Maharishi Bhagavan Mahesh Yogi makes it amply clear that Veda are 'Apaurusheya'. [See his Commentary on "Rk Veda": "Apaurusheya Bhashya"]. He says, "the sounds of'Rk Veda' evolved from the self-interacting dynamics of Silence as expressed by the four qualities of Consciousness- Atyanta-Abhava, Anyonya-Abhava, Pradhwamsha Abhava and Prag-Abhava available in GAPS (Sandhi) between the sounds. Further, he says, "Looking deeper into the structuring dynamics of Consciousness- ***Pradhwamsha-Abhava, Atyanta-Abhava, Amnyonya-Abhava and Prag-Abhava***- in the GAPS between the sounds of Rk Veda, we locate all the forty qualities of the creative intelligence of Consciousness- all forty qualities of the Vedic Literature including the Rk Veda, which is involved in the structuring dynamics of its own expression."

The Brahma-Sutras declare that 'Brahman' is the source of the Veda and these are eternal. According to Puranas, 'God, the Supreme Truth, caused the Veda to appear in the mind of Brahma, the first poet. [***Srimad Bhagavata***]. The Veda is also known as 'Nigama', meaning, a settled text handed down from beginning less antiquity. Veda is considered 'Amanya' since these are learnt by repetition and reflection. The Veda are also known as 'Shrutis' since the pupils learn Veda by '***listening***' carefully ***(not hearing)*** to their Guru (teacher).

All these denote that the Veda is self-manifest, the revelations made to Atharvan, the eldest son of Brahma in the beginning, who, in turn, imparted it to Ghora-Angiras [***Mundakopanishad***]. It is Vyas, Krishna-Dvaipayana, an incarnation of Lord Narayana, who systematized the Veda (thus, came to be known as Veda Vyaasa) into the four divisions by making his four disciples Paila, Vaishampayana, Jaimini, and Sumantu as the recipients and transmitters. Each one of them came to be further divided into 'Shakas' (Branches). Thus, we have different Shakhas, schools of thought (21 Schools of 'Rk Veda', 1000 of 'Sama Veda', 109 of 'Yajur Veda', and 50 of 'Atharva Veda') and thus, 1180 Upanishads in all at the rate of one Upanishad for each School. These Schools of Veda and Upanishads are identified as Schools of 'Samhitas', (collection), 'Aranyakas' (specially for the ascetics living in forests), and 'Brahmanas' (Grihastas or householders), consisting of directives for the right use of material of hymns and texts during the sacrificial service (for the householders who take to spiritual life) and the like.

Every Veda has a Samhita containing 'Sutras' (aphorism or formula), or a manual of instructions and is similar to the 'Brahmanas'. Although numerous Upanishads have been constructed from the Veda, in reality, only a few Upanishads have been identified for each Veda. For example, the Aitareya and the Kaushitaki Upanishads in Rk Veda, the Chandogya and Kena in Samaveda, the Taittiriya, the Mahnarayana, the Kathaka, the Svetasvatara and the Maitrayana Upanishads of the Krishna Yajurveda, the Brihadaranyaka, the Ishavasya of the Shukla Yajurveda, and finally, the Mundaka, Mandukya, the Prashna Upanishads of the Atharvaveda.

'***Rk Veda***' is by far the most important and the other Veda, more or less, to some extent repeat the verses or adopt the verses from the 'Rk Veda'. In 'Sama Veda', only selected verses of 'Rk Veda' are set in 'samans', musical tone called 'matras' for singing. 'Yajur Veda' consists of both verses and prose. There are 1028 metrical hymns in 'Rk Veda' praising the aspects of the Divine arranged in ten Mandalas (Sections). Practically every possible detail about the origin of the universe, evolution of life, and the various intricate relationships of 'Man-Nature' are described in the 10,552 Verses of 'Rk Veda'. The Upanishads bearing on 'Rk Veda' are many and the most important are the Aitareya, Kaushitaki, Paingi, and Sankhyayana Brahmanas. Aranyakas of Kaushitaki and Aitareya supplement the Brahmanas. There is no count of the actual number of Upanishads and at least about 1200 Upanishads are known to have existed. There is at least one Upanishad for each Shakha (Recension or Branch) of the Veda. Only 108 of these are supposed to be of some importance and Sri Shankaracharya selected only ten Upanishads out of these and commented upon them. Five of these are the well known 'Samhita' (Collections) or 'Aranyakas' (to be recited in forests by Sanyasins). For fear of being misused by the unscrupulous, many Upanishads remained inaccessible for some of them contain most powerful mystic verses.

As already stated, the ***Atharva Veda*** is believed to be the Veda dictated by Brahma to his eldest son and pupil, Atharvan. Thus, *Veda is 'One' only* and it is '***Atharvaveda***'; the other three, i.e., Rk, Saman and theYajus are its divisions. ***Atharvaveda*** is said to be the essence of the other three Veda and the Atharva mantras are called 'Sidhdha Mantras'. ***One who performs Japa with Atharva mantras with shrudhdha and bhakti gets all desires fulfilled. [Kamalaalaya Khanda, Skanda Puarana].***

"Yasthathraatharvanaan japedchadhadhasamanvitaa;
Tejaam arthodhbhavam kruthsnamphalam praapnothi sadhruvam."

*Maharshi Mahesh Yogi believes that "every aspect of the Veda and Vedic literature is a specfic aspect of the dynamics of the 'unified field'- the dynamics of WHOLENESS- the Dynamics of Consciousness" This can be seen in the structure of the word and sound of the words of Veda and Vedic literature. In a sense, the Veda and Vedic literature are established in the supreme Consciousness and thus Veda is called 'Apaurusheya' since it has emanated from the Abstract Silence called 'Atyanta –Abhava' . It (the Veda, rather the entire Uni-verse) has emanated first as the impulses of sound gradually evolving into vibration culminating in the sound 'A'. This again relapsed into silence only to re-emerge as sound 'K'. Thus the first word of the Rk Veda, that explains the origin and evolution of this universe 'Ak-shara' by akshara by akshara and, word by word, Richa by Richa, Aphorism by Aphorism or Mantra by Mantra, Sukta by Sukta, and Mandala by Mandala- each evolving out of the previous, from silence to sound and collapsing into silence- evolving and merging, re-evolving out of silence and merging again to silence.*

*Thus, all the Veda and the entire range of Vedic literature numbering 39 other than Rk Veda are truly emanated from the vast and deep seat of Silence, the Abstract Silence or the seat of Supreme Consciousness. Hence, the Veda is truly 'Apaurusheya'. No man have ever understood the true inner meaning of the Veda, so far, and the secret remains a secret forever since it is beyond human capability to understand and explain the hidden meaning of the Veda that has come in sounds of Devavani (Geervani-Bharati), a language of the Gods. The problem here is that each Vedic letter, word, phrase, verse and chapter has six meanings and one of them is the secret that can be visualized or experienced in deep Meditation, Samaadhi State or State of Supreme Consciousness attained in Transcendental Meditation. This is not simply possible for ordinary persons without any spiritual attainment that requires thousands of years of practice! Only a few Yogins have attained this state of Consciousness and have revealed this secret. Still, it is very difficult to understand. One must study the entire Veda and Vedic Literature in order to understand the 'Secret of Life' and 'Method of Sensible Living' on this earth.*

*The first sound of letters 'Ak' of 'Rk Veda' came in vibration, rich with not only sound and meaning, but objects as well! All the materials of this objective world has emanated from this Silence between Gaps of Vedic sounds! The 'Rk' Veda starts with the words 'Ak' of "Agnimeele purohitam....", where the letters 'Ak' stands for the beginning and end of theUniverse, in the sense, 'A' stands for the beginning of the Brahmanda* *(multiverse) and the 'k' ends as the minute particle or sub-atomic particle, 'Kana'; the gap between the letter A and ' k' holds all the diverse creation! It is the GAP or the silence between 'A' and' k' that is the source of all material objects of the universe. Everything has emanated from the "Silence' (Mauna) or 'abhava'. It also creates and holds the clue to what comes next. In fact, everything that has come out and is yet to come in this universe is hidden in the Silence of supreme consciousness. This means, so far, any invention has come from deep silence,'abhava'- deep contemplation. 'Rk Veda' holds the key! 'Rk Veda' is 'Samhita'-Unified, 'Holistic' (dynamic silence) quality of Consciousness- it is characterized by its sequentially evolving sounds, and these sounds are structured by the sequentially evolving dynamism of Consciousness- the dynamism of Silence within the GAPS between the sounds. Maharishi says, "Thus the intelligence that motivates the structuring dynamics of the sounds of 'Rk Veda' are Pradhwamsha- Abhava, Atyanta-Abhava, Anyonya-Abhava, and Prag-Abhava – the four qualities of Consciousness". "The silencing dynamism of Pradhwamsha-Abhava evolves into the silent WHOLENESS of Atyanta-Abhava (Purusha) with the liveliness of Anyonya-Abhava (Pradhaana or Prakriti holding all possibilities) in its silent nature, which evolves into the specific quality of Prag-Abhava, which in turn experiences itself in sound –the sound of Rk Veda. It is enlightening to see that the sounds of Rk Veda evolve from the 'self-interacting dynamics' of the four types of Silence-i.e., 'Abhavas'- the qualities of conciousness, available in the GAPS between the sounds".*[ See Celebrating the Enlightened Consciousness of Every Professor, 'Heavemn on Earth', Maharishi Mahavidyapith of Management, Jabalpur]*

*According to Maharishi Bhagavan Mahesh Yogi, 'Rk Veda Samhita' is 'Wholeness'- 'Poornam', rather 'Paripoorna', and Sama Veda is flow of Consciousness in the nature of Pradhwamsha–Abhava flowing or evolving into Atyanta-Abhava and the Atyanta-Abhava (All-Knowing Purusha) flowing into Anyonya-Abhava (Always Active Prakriti), and again, Anyonya-Abhava flowing into Prag-Abhava and finally, Prag-Abhava presents the new value, the more evolved value of the previos sound- and with it the new sounds, and new objects! Rather, everything is a flow, Sri Hari Narayana- flowing or evolving into new things! Maharishi says, "we have located the' flowing quality' of Sama Veda within the GAPS beween the sounds of 'RkVeda'; in other words, Sama Veda is located or discovered within the structure of Rk Veda as enunciated in the first Mantra of Ishavasya Upanishad: "Poornaath Poornam udachyate".*

*The vision of total reality- the total field of knowledge and its infinite organizing power- demonstrated by the essential nature of the self-interacting possible values of its structure.*

*Similarly, YajurVeda is the' offering and creating quality' of Consciousness. The character of Yajur Veda is that it dissolves the prvious structure and evolves the new structure of Law, and this process is well displayed within the holistic structure of Law ('Dharma')- Ritam and Satyam, the basis of 'Rk Veda' and its flowing wakefulness (awareness), Sama Veda, at the basis of creation.*

***Maharishi says, "Atharva Veda is the ' reverberating** wholeness* ***quality' of 'A-Tharva" ('Tharva' meaning vibration) and it can be seen*** *wherever there is holistic dynamic silence, Rk Veda; flowing wakefulness of Sama Veda; and offering and creating Yajur Veda. All these are the dynamics of the GAPS and all the four Veda function together as the self-interacting dynamics of the GAPS, expressed through the four types of Abhavas- (Silence, Mauna) in deep contemplation of Transcendental Meditation.*

*Atharva Veda is the 'Tharva (Vibrations) of 'A' (Universe), i.e., the impulse of WHOLENESS, the impulse of 'A' which is clearly seen in the nature of Atyanta-Abhava (Purusha) where the impulse of WHOLENESS is fully awake in terms of Anyonya-Abhava (Prakriti). This Tharva of 'A' is also easy to locate in the flow of 'Rk Veda', Sama Veda, and Yajur-Veda, within the structure of the four Abhavas (Silence), within the structure of the Sandhi ie GAPS.*

*Atharva Veda is endowed with the qualities of all the four Veda in the same way as each of the four Veda is endowed with the quality of very other; and, all are fully awake in their unified state at the center of the GAP- where the Samhita (the Unified state) is eternally fully awake in the potential dynamism (Anyonya-Abhava) in the state of Silence – Atyanta –Abhava. In this sense, the Atharva Veda is located within the intelligence of 'k" in the 'Rk' of Rk Veda. 'k' is the last point in the name 'Rk'. From this point, the name 'Rk' evolves into form of 'Rk'. which starts with 'A' as in Ak-nimeele purohitam (Rk Veda 1.1.1.) The vision of total knowledge at the central point of the relationship between the two sounds of 'Rk' –'R' and' k'- is the point of the Self-Referral nature of Abhava, where all four Veda and all the structuring dynamics of the Vedic literature can be accessed by anybody within his own Consciousness, within his own Self-Referral consciousness- within his own Tanscendental Meditation. Silence is the quality of Consciousness and it is Self-Referral because it has nothing else to refer to. It is the ultimate, the Absolute and the Infinite.*

*Thus, all the four Veda are obviously, virtually, literally, and in all repect 'one and only' since each Veda evolves out of the other and has a forward-backward linkage.*

The Mantra of '***Atharva Veda***' are very potent and mystic; and, sparingly used by yogins for the welfare of society. There are many result-oriented mantras like Shanti and Mahashanti mantras with details of methods of performance (vidhi-vidhana) of Shanti extolling the respective deities, like the Raja Karma, etc. from which abundant riches are obtained. Only those well- versed in Atharva Veda are permitted to perform Homa, Havana, etc in Kings' Court. Pourohitya in Rajabhisheka is described in Atharva Veda [***Vishnu Purana***].

The ***Atharva Veda*** has many mantras for specific purposes such as ward of death, jala gandaantha, ward of burglary and theft, to find the lost things, prevent diseases and cure diseases, cure body pains and ailments, remove toxic materials and extract poison from infected parts, getting relief from 'black magic', for achieving desired ambitions, getting married, getting children (Shruti of Prajapathi Mantra), money, education, jobs or position, power, fame and other earthly possessions and 'purushaarthas'. There are Shanti such as 'Mahendri', 'Kubera', 'Achintya' Vyashnavi, Roudri with Vaasthu (for wealth), Varuna (those facing jalagandanth), Yamya (for those fearing loss of life), Varuni, Aparajitha (to obtain success), Gandharva, Kumari Maha Shanti (to overcome diseases of children), Abhaya, Vaasthu Samskara Mahashanti (to obtain wealth), and many other Shanti and Maha Shanti Mantra in Atharva Veda. It is specifically mentiomed that 'pumasarana and other Karmas are to be performed in Homes only on the Full Moon Day (Pournima), or/ and New Moon Days (Amavasya) and other auspices days. Performing 'Black Magic' is also given prominence in Kaushika Sutra.

Normally, diseases are caused due to two reasons. One reason is due to food that is contaminated and poisonous. The second reason is traced to past karma or sins. The latter can be cured by means of Mantra of Atharva Veda through Homa. Kaushitaki Sutra 4.8 has a mantra:

*"Oushadhi vanaspathinaam anukthaanyaprathii.*
*Bheshajyaanam O holidaghbhih*
*I Thathaa sano muchchthvaram haraa."*

This is a Papanivaraka mantra (Formula for eradicating sin) that is used as medicine through the Homa Karma. This mantra is also useful in begetting children and saving children that have little or short span of life. There are certain instructions regarding the methods of performing the Homa Karma and the food to be taken after the Homa Karma.

In Nakshatra Kalpa Sutra, the poojas and Homas starting from Krithika (Star) is advocated and the Mahasmruti is performed. Vyashradeva Shanti is performed for the departed souls. Mahashanti is performed for purposes of getting over fear of agni and getting all the desires fulfilled. By performing ***Bhargavi Mahashanti*** all the fear and diseases caused by stars, planets, and satellites or upagrahas are warded off. ***Kubera Mahashanti*** is performed to obtain wealth and prevent loss of money. ***Achintya Mahashanti*** is performed to get education, wealth and good health. ***Vyashnavi shanti*** is performed to get food.

In ***Angirasa Kalpa***, the method of performing Homa, for prevention of 'Black Magic", is explained with all the details of types of firewood, ghee, etc. that are to be used.

In Shanti Kalpa, ***Vinayaka Homa*** is explained. The Atharvan Mantra are Sarva siddha mantras and can be used for various purposes. The very first mantra of the Atharva Veda, Shomakeeya Shakha, the "***Ye thrishaptham***.......", is the first Anuvaka (Section) that finds place in all the actions relating to acquisition of intelligence or production or increase of budhdhi shakti. According to Kaushik this can be done in Hastha Homa. There are three types of Hastha Homa viz Darvi Homa, Hastha Homa and Purna Homa ***[Kaushika Sutra 14-3; 7-8]***. These manthras should be recited with great care.

Some of the present-day mystics have abused these powers for self-aggrandizement despite severe warnings not to use these for personal gains. The ultimate goal of all these Veda is to reveal the 'Grandiose Plan' of the Lord in creating this universe and Man. In a way, it speaks volumes and volumes of the evolutionary history of the universe.

The '***Sama Veda-samhita***', the Veda of 'Samans' (songs) is said to be taken from the Eighth and Ninth Mandalas of 'Rk Veda' and set in musical hymns, Saman chants, to be sung by the Udgatr priests. The '***Yajur Veda***' constituted the Veda of sacrificial texts (Yajus). The '***Atharva Veda-samhita***' has 760 hymns of 6000 stanzas spread over 20 Chapters; of these 1200 stanzas are repetitions from 'Rk-samhita'. These deal with occult powers. These are 'Brahmanas' (meant for householders) and the important Upanishads belonging to this Veda are Mundaka, Mandukya, and Prasna. Unlike the Mantra-upanishads (the Upanishads in Verses), these are Brahmanas that are of academic interest explaining hidden meanings and narrating the past.

*What is important in all these is that, the Veda and the Upanishads have come to us as a great spiritual heritage that guide us and protect us in our everyday life. The 'Knowledge' imparted from the Veda is far superior (para vidya) as compared to the mundane, 'apara vidya' that we boast off as the worldly knowledge including modern science and technology which take us nowhere.* For want of sanity, we have produced atomic bombs and chemicals that are ruining us and we find strife and war everywhere. The Veda chant 'Peace Mantra'. and advise us how to live wisely on the principles of "*Vasudaiva Kutumbakam*" i.e., the world is one big family, and '*Universal Brotherhood*' i.e., all are brothers and sisters. This is the greatness of Indian spiritual heritage.

The Vedic scholars interpreted the Veda and Upanishads according to their needs and times. The Veda had different connotations in different 'Yugas' viz Satya Yuga (0.432 × 4 MY), Treta Yuga (0.432 × 3 MY), Dwapara Yuga (0.432 × 2 MY) and now, the Kali Yuga that runs for 0.432 Million Years of which about 0.4 Million Years (MY) have already passed. The moral and ethical values and the spiritual standards of life were different at different times. Accordingly, the Veda and their Upanishads conveyed different doctrines suitable to the standards of people. Veda according to the ancient Indians constituted a '***intelligent way of life***'. All Brahmins were ordained to learn at least one Veda and the family of such Vedic scholars was known as Vaidiks. Some came to be known as Chaturvedis (persons specialized in four Veda), Trivedis (specialized in three Veda, Dvivedis (specialized in two Veda), &c.

In early times, the Veda served as the basis of Yajnas (Rituals offering worship through ghee and rice to Fire God-Agni), a festival of 'Soma' sacrifice. Incidentally, 'Soma Ras' is the juice prepared out of grinding the soma plant, a species belonging to cactus family. It is a succulent plant. There are catus varieties like the agericus, hayoscomus, and stramonium (Dattura) that are poisonous, but, when used in small proportions, they induce hallucination. Also, there are ashtavargas, and the juice made of eight plants is mixed with the soma juice. The soma juice is intoxicating and unlike the opium, poppy, or marijuana, hashish and ganja that produce hallucinations, the soma juice gives mental strength for long hours of meditation and physical strength to sit straight for long hours for mediation.

The rituals of Yajnya i.e., offerings is an elaborate one. Four important persons were designated for this purpose as: 1.The Hotr, 2.The Udgatr, 3.The Adhvaryu, and, 4. The Braahman or the Chief Priest. The duties of these four designated staff are well defined. Accordingly, the Hotr has to sing the "Rk Vedic hymns' inviting the gods and this served as invocation. The Soma sacrifice is accompanied by the singing of the Samans by the Udgatr. The Adhvaryus carry out the holy rites chanting the Yajus or the sacrificial texts from Yajur Veda text. The Braahman is the chief priest who leads the whole ceremony and has no role in the chantings but he must know all the three Vedic texts. He is the nominal head or designated 'Kartr' of the Soma Sacrifice, the 'Yajnya'. These three designated priests should carry a handbook, viz the Hothr should carry 'the Samhita' (collection of works), the Udgatr should carry a 'Brahmana' consisting of- the vidhi, arthavada and Upanishad (the doctrinal text book) or Vedanta, the directives for the right use of the material during the sacrificial service of the Yajnya. The Adhvaryu should carry a 'Sutra', a manual- the contents of which are parallel to those of the Brahmanas. In fact, the Upanishads finally became almost invaluable and imperative that should be taught to only a few trusted disciples at the end of the schooling. These constituted the sum and substance of the Veda and the end, or the goal of all the Vedic scholars.

Thus, the sacrificial Soma festival constituted the basis of the Vedantic way of life. The grinding of the Soma plant, a succulent plant belonging to the cactus family, and the drinking of Soma juice is a major ritual since the soma juice gives mental strength to concentrate and physical strength to sit for long hours for meditation. Many Sadhus sat for several months at astretch for deep contemplation and meditation to realize the 'Truth'. Even today, some of these rituals are practiced, but the earlier fervour is no more there. There are the day and night rituals, the month-long rituals, and the year -long rituals. Performance of rituals like Havana, Homa, and Yajnya and Maha Yajna are practiced even to day. These are performed for world peace, for prosperity, good crops, getting rains, and success in all walks of life, and other wish fulfillment. Parjanya Yajnya is performed to propitiate the Rain-God- 'Varuna' for getting rains. Although it is very essential to perform these rituals to cleanse the toxic elements in atmosphere, the ignorant people criticize it as a waste of ghee, milk and other products. In fact, it is much more important to practise these Yajnyas for they are highly beneficial to mankind. These rituals have their own significance that cannot be understood rationally since they are of spiritual nature.

Gradually, the sacrificial rituals gave place to mere study of Veda for academic interest. Scholars like Yaaskaacharya, Sayana, Aurobindo, Swami Dayananda Sarasvati, Bala Gangadhar Tilak, Sudhakar Chaturvedi, and many others have interpreted the Veda in their own sociological, philosophical, and scientific background. Today, we have almost a variety of interpretations and commentaries on Veda and Upanishads, but the old fervour of 'ritualism' is not there.

One may ask 'what is there in the Veda and Upanishads?' The answer is very simple. Practically everything is there in these Veda and Upanishads.

The Veda is synonymous with the human physiology. It is the vibrating intelligence and Prana in Man. 'Rk Veda' is the 'Totality' of existence. It is 'Holistic', 'Brahm' quality of Consciousness. Sama Veda is the flow, the cosmic flow of energy and awareness, wakefulness as the sensory systems. It represents the totality of the Rishi or Seer value as the knower, wakefulness; indeed it works as '***sahasraaksha***', giving a thousand-eye-perception, the quality of '***Brahm***'. Yajur Veda is the dynamism and creative Intellignce represented by the human processing system, metabolism. It represents the totality of the illumining principle, the 'Devata' value or dynamism as seen in processing, integrating, interpreting, and creating ability of a person. Atharva Veda is the reverberating WHOLENESS as seen in the functioning of the human motor systems. Atharva Veda represensts the unified value, 'Samhita' with a predominanece of Chhandas value- possessing the ability of covering, hiding, expanding, and moving all over the body, is a source of concentrated Creative Intelligence; it is the basis of the creative process of Natural Law, "***Anoraneeyaan mahato-maheeyan***" (***Kathopanishad*** 1.2.20] meaning, smaller than the smallest and bigger than the biggest' is revealed in the Atharva Veda! Atharva Veda is the reality within each point of the four Abhavas (Silence) in the Gaps between the sounds of the Rk Veda. Atharva Veda is located within the intelligence of 'k' in the syllable of 'Rk' (Rk Veda). Hence, one can unearth all the powers hodden in the Mantra of these Veda. There are the formulae for sane living and sensible living. Clues abound in these Veda regarding virtual reality, genetic engineering, biotechnology, or space travel. Practically everything is found in the GAPS (Sandhi) of the Mantra of the four Veda and the Vedic students with the knowledge of modern science and technology, may, one day, reveal the hidden secrets of this universe. One can find out the origin of life in a mantra- "***Annam Brahma***" which denotes that "*life is food and food is life*"; wherever food is there, lifeforms originate and the lifeform itself becomes food. Similarly, all plants are 'sap' or 'rasa'. Ultimately, everything is 'Food' and everything is 'Brahman'. Kaala (Time), the sun, eats away everything and the sun also degenerates into matter from the state of pure energy.

Similarly, the '***Big Bang***' theory of the origin of the universe is explained in the syllable 'Om'. The sound that emanated from the "***Sphota***" or the 'Big Bang' still reverberates the universe. It is this sound that is the fist Akshara, called '***Ek-Akshara Brahma***'. The vibrations of sound and light (colours) in different intensities, different frequencies and different wavelengths have created this objective world, and everything in this world. Matter collapses within itself under its own mass (weight) as enunciated in the '***Black Hole***' theory. This constant dynamic metamorphosis going on in the universe as creation and extinction is the 'Yajnya'. Thus, "Om" is the beginning and end of this cosmic existence; it has its beginning in the Absolute, the Infinite and its end in "the Black hole', i.e., within "Itself". It is the "Beginning-less and the Endless". It is the 'macrocosm', the 'Akhand' at the one end, as well as the 'Sub-atomic particle', the 'microcosm' (Kana) at the other end. Also, it is 'Shoonya' or Infinity. It is zero the highest number for the figures conveying the negative values and the smallest numer for the others of positive value. Anyway, it is the same! It is the smaller than the smallest and bigger than the biggest! It is the causeless of all the causes. It is the beginningless source of all that we see, hear or witness. It is existence itself and has always been in existence and will continue to exist. It is One and there is no other! Sincee the Rishis did not know its name, they called it simply, "That" and gradually the word God replaced it. The universe of objects emanated from this, God and will again merge within God. This is the story of the universe.

The variety of all the life forms that exist and that will ever exist in this universe is explained in the '***Rk Veda***'. Cloning has been known eversince the asuras multiplied in different forms; every droplet of blood or the severed part of the body formed into a full-grown person! The techniques of interpreting the complex life forms and the intricacies of the universe are beautifully explained in the verses of 'Atharva Veda' in which every syllable, and every word is of potent mystic power.

There are the 'Yantras', the 'Mantras', and the 'Tantras' for interpreting this Universe. The 'Mantras' generate vibrations that create mystic experiences in the yogins and the powerful thought-force could be employed to many desired ends. The chanting of '***Mantras***' cures diseases. There are powerful Mantra that ward off death or prevent untimely death of children while the parents are alive. Poison in the body, particularly by snakebite, is extricated by chanting of particular 'Mantras'. Extra-sensorial Perceptions, telepathy, faith- healing, or touch therapy and other techniques are very popular even today. The yogins employed these methods for alleviating the sufferings of mankind. Magical numbers and colours that created or absorbed the universal vibrations could be deciphered by contemplation or Meditation and /or the formulae of the powerful 'Mantras' of Atharva Veda. Thus, the entire field of Vedic learning constituted the "Vedic way of life" of the ancient Indians. In a way, it was a life of prayers, prayer for the welfare of the humanity, prayer for the wellbeing of the person, and prayer for a life of fulfillment. This holistic approach to learning as well as living is absent in modern times anywhere in the world.

The Veda mean Prayer to the Lord, singing the Glory of the Lord. It is a mystic experience one gets in the trance of singing the power and glory of the multi-faceted Lord. Why this madness to sing and praise the lord is beautifully explained in the very first mantra of the '*Rk Veda*':

*"Om, Agnim eelay purohitam yajnyasya devam*
*Rithvijam hothaaram rathnadhaathaaram."*

Meaning, ***"Om, I pray Thee, Supreme Lord, the God of Fire, who is the chief of all Gods, who is beneficient to all, who is the Subject of all Sacrifices, who constitute the Yajnas, who is the giver of fruits of Yajnas, who is the absorber of all essences of all Sacrifices, and who is the supreme wearer of all the beautiful and the precious."***

This '***Mantra***' is the conscious desire and expression of 'Self' or the soul that is an eternal part of the Supreme Brahman. The prayer Mantra are addressed to the Supreme Lord by the Rishis, who are enlightened Souls themselves, for the welfare of humanity. The Gods are none else but the

Lord Himself for, the Supreme Self, Sri Hari narayana is found as different Gods in different names and forms performing different functions, just as the same person performs different roles or avocations by different names like the District Magisttrate, the Collector, Chairman of different Committees, or different roles as father, son, brother, or mother, sister, sister-in-law, etc., in day-to-day life.

The Veda can be better understood with the knowledge of the Upanishads. One should have a clear understanding of the Upanishads in order to understand the Veda. The basic concepts enunciated in the Upanishads will facilitate the understanding of the Veda. These basic concepts concerning the univesrse are beautifully explained in different Upanishads.

The '***Mantra***' that sums up these basic concepts is:

*"Om, Mahat Pradhaana Purusha Kaalaroopine*
*Sat chit ananda svaroopaaya namo Naaraayane namah, Om."*

Sri Hari, 'Narayana' is the supreme Lord of the universe. He is the container of the multitude of universes. He has created this universe and pervaded it as '***Antharyamin***'. He is omniscient, omnipotent, and omnipresent. His qualities are 'Sat', 'Chit', and 'Anand'.

The above mantra sums up the structure and composition of the universe. It brings out the qualities of nature. It clearly states the goal of life on this planet, Earth, i.e., realizing Him in one's own Self.

Here, the First principle is '***Mahat***'. 'Mahat' is '***Hiranyagarbha***' (the Golden foetus). This Hiranyagarbha is also the electro-magnetic power behind the Sun and its sphere, the Sun shining as a golden disc controlling the nine or ten planets and their satellites, so far known to us, like the earth and moon. The Mahat is the supreme Consciousness, the background and support of all existence. It is the Natural Law, or 'Dharma', or Order and Truth.

The Second Principle of the Supreme Brahman is '***Pradhaana***', the Prakriti (Nature). This Nature consists of 'great elements' such as the Sun (Aditya), Moon (Chandra), Earth (Prithvi), 'Dyouh' (Heaven where the gods live), Air (Vayu), Water (Apah), Fire (Agni), Mind (Indra), Intellect (Dheeh), Sky (Anthariksha) or space, and Ego (Ahamkara). These form the building blocks of life and all bodies that exist in the universe.

God has created Man in Hs own image as a replica. Indra represents the power of the Mind as well as the cosmic will, by which the whole universe is kept in ever-expanding movements.

The Third Principle of the Supreme Brahman, the all-pervading supreme Spirit, Sri Hari Narayana is "***Purusha***". Though there is no name or form of any god and also of supreme Brahman, it is referred to only as 'That'. This Purusha is also referred to as 'Jiva' or Prana; it is also called as divine energy that is never created nor destroyed.

The Fourth Principle of the Supreme Brahman is '***Kala***' (Time). All beings are created by the conjunction of matter and spirit, or Pradhana and Purusha brought about by Kala. The dissolutionis also brought about by Kala. This 'Time' exists as the interval between two events. Time is also eternal, and has no beginning or end, one of the svaroopa or qualities of Brahman.

Mahat contains in itself 'Time' and 'Space'. It is eternal and limitless. Just as the supreme Consciousness is the nature of the supreme Brahman, the individual Consciousness is the nature of the 'Soul', the Atman, or individual self, seated in all bodies, which is the means of experiencing the qualities of objects and bodies in the universe. It is called 'Jeevatman', or embodied soul. 'Paramatman', or the Maha Purusha, Purushottama, God, or whatever you call it, is the manifestation of the Brahman. Purusha Sukta in the Mandala X of Rk Veda makes it very clear that *all these four Principles are within the Mind of the person and not anywhere outside of him!*

With the help of these four Principle forms of the ***Supreme Brahman***, all other forms are created. From the Infinite and the unlimited have emerged all the limited and finite. Hence, the latter are subject to change, death, and decay or disintegration.

All forms of creation take place according to qualities of Nature; manifest bodies are created according to qualities of Nature through which divine energy, Narayana, Vishnu flows. Whatever that are experienced with the help of Consciousness are the qualities of Nature. Mind is the means and medium of experience which terms as pain and pleasure, joy and sorrow, and all dualities and relative qualities that are the nature of Mind.

The Supreme Self has created the '***tan-matras***' (great elements) or the building blocks of life, also referred to as 'Deities' ('abhimani devotees gods') ruling over their respective repository organs such as the eyes (repository of the Sun), speech (repository of Fire), Ears (repository of directions); worshipping these Deities the organs get their strength.

The 'Soul' that is filled with desire (blemish) takes birth as the body for functions that lead to the satisfaction of the desires. The Soul rules the organs through the Mind. The Mind, being the chief of organs, controls the body and the senses. Indra is the deity of mind and one gets strength and power by worshipping Indra, the God of all Gods. [***See*** the Mantra invoking Indra to grant happiness on page ii]. The Soul being the Inner Ruler, the '***Antharyamin***', experiences the world of objects through the body. It prays for the welfare of the body to the gods ruling over the elements and respective organs to strengthen the body organs for better enjoyment of the qualities of nature. In fact, mind is the instrument through which we perceive this objective world. The eye is an instrument that takes the picture of objects and projects on the active mind screen. Nothing is seen if the eye is defective or the mind is not active at the moment or active elsewhere. The world exists because of the conscious mind; *'no mind, no world'*. Mind is the screen on which the world objects are projected and the picture disappears as soon as the screen is removed. Hence the picture we get on the screen are only the reflected image; hence, this objective world is called unreal, illusory, or 'maaya', or 'asat' or ***imaginary***.

***Pradhana***, or the 'great elements' i.e., 'Nature', being the creation of the Supreme Brahman, functions as per their qualities ordained by the 'Supreme Order' ('Ritam'). They being the supreme devotees of the supreme Self, fulfill the wishes of the individual Self, seated in the bodies to fulfill desires and attain freedom from the limited adjuncts of the body. To this end, the soul offers prayers to different gods such as Indra, Agni, Varuna, Mithra, &c. [See Mantra on p iii].

Veda recognize Indra, Rudra, Marut, Mitra, Varuna, Agni, Vasus, etc. as gods and declare that these deities are a part of the organic and inorganic existence of everything. These aspects are beautifully described in the Upanishads. A correct understanding of the concept of God is essential in order to realize the 'Truth' of this universe. Since the Vedic verses are quoted and references to Veda are cited wherever necessary, detailed explanation of each and every Veda has not been undertaken here. It suffices to highlight the Veda and their significance in Hindu Religion and Philosophy, that too as a 'way of life' promoting spiritual attainments. Knowledge of Veda will promote blosomming of the human personality into its full potential!

For those interested in the study of Veda, The Arya Samaj is bringing out twenty Volumes of all the four Veda; there are eleven volumes of Rk Veda Samhita, one volume for each Mandala, and two Volumes of Sama Veda Samhita, and three Volumes of Atharva Veda have already been published. Other Volumes are in Print, edited by Veda Brahma Sudhakar Chaturvedi. The Commentaries given by Sayana, Bhatta Bhaskara, Aurobindo and many others are available for interested readers. Here, only the importance of these scriptures is highlighted.

The outstanding work on Veda till date is that of Maharishi Bhagavan Mahesh Yogi and his '*Apaurusheya Bhashya*' is the *magnum opus. Bhagavan relates the Veda and all Vedic Literature to Human Physiology and brings out the principle of Unified Field of Natural Law in' Samhita'. Persons interested in Vedic Studies must visit the Maharishi Mahesh Yogi Vishva Vidyalaya (University) at Jabbalpore, INDIA*

***Vedic Literature***

Veda, Vedanga, as well as, Upanga of Veda constitute the Vedic literature. Without any of these, it is incomplete. Veda is considered to be total knowledge, **supreme Knowledge**, 'the Brahman'. This is a flow- with backward and forward linkage, and, as such, all the four Veda and the thirty-six Vedic literature cited below constitute one single forward –and-backward- linking flow, each contributing to the evolution and sustainence of this material world. Maharishi has defined the four Veda and 36 values of the Vedic literature and has given the modern scientific perspective of these 40 qualities as follows:

*Rk Veda* is the expression of holistic dynamic silence in self-referral consciousness – Transcendental Consciousness- the home of all the Laws of Nature, intimately personal to everyone. All the forty values of the Vedic literature, including Rk Veda, are the structuring dynamics of Natural Law- the structuring dynamics of consciousness expressed in the physiology.

In its scientific perspective, the Holistic (Dynamic Silence) quality of Intelligence or Rk Veda is the Lagrangian of Superstring Field Theory. It is the holistic expression of the Laws of Nature at the infinitely dynamic

(Planck scale dynamics) and yet unexpressed (vaccum dynamics) and therefore silent level of the Unified Field; it represents the most compactified form of the Constitution of the Universe from the perspective of modern science. It knows all and it is self-referral and dynamic and unamanifest supreme intelligence, the supreme Consciousness. *The Rk Veda aspect of the Vedic Literature is the expression of this level of reality available in self-referral consciousness –**Atma**.*

*Sama Veda highlights the flowing wakefulness-flowing quality of intelligence involved in structuring the Rk Veda. Sama Veda* is the flowing quality of intelligence. The infinite variety of dynamic correlations (at the Planck scale) shows that the Unified Field is fully awake within itself. Moreover, the full propagator represent not only the aspect of flowing – propagation, but also includes self-interaction, that means wakefulness. The Sama Veda aspect of the Vedic Literature is the expression of this level of reality available in Self-referral Consciousness- Atma.

*Yajur Veda* highlights the ***offering and creating quality of intelligence*** involved in structuring Rk Veda. In the process of symmetry breaking the majority of field components become unexpressed. This offering to the unmanifest makes it possible for the other components to be expressed with their characteristic properties. The sequential symmetry breaking that brings forth these specific properties of the force and matter fields, etc. simultaneously can be seen as a creative process because it is responsible for the generation of the large variety found in the universe. This quality of offering of Sama Veda is exemplified in the process of 'Yajan' (Yagya) expressed in Yajur Veda. The phenomenon of offering – offering the Self to the Self is called 'self-referral dynamics of consciousness' – conciousness offering itself to itself. This is the dynamics of Yajur Veda, a phenomenon in the nature of Samhita, which makes the consciousness value of Samhita eternally awake, eternally self-referral, eternally performing on itself. Thus Yajur Veda is the absolute quality of Samhita. Yajur is Samhita- samhita is Yajur. *The Yajur Veda aspect of Vedic Literature is the expression of this level of reality available in self-referral consciousness- **Atma**.*

*Atharva Veda highlights the reverberating WHOLENESS – reverberating quality in every point of 'Holistic Intelligence' involved in structuring Rk Veda.* The Lagrangian of the Heterotic Superstring quantifies the vibration of loop-like closed strings. The Atharva Veda aspect of Vedic Literature is the expression of this level of reality available in theself-referral consciousness –***Atma***.

As one dwells into the respective Vedic literature, unfoldment of the hidden value, take place. Each Vedic literature has a specific quality and is the expression of the level of reality available in the self-referral consciousness- ***Atma***.

The Forty Vedic Literature including Rk Veda are evident in each and every Faculty- science, arts, commerce, medicine, mathematics, physics, biology or chemistry and each specialist arrives at the same high level of Consciousness through his or her specialization. The human physiology is tuned to this effect and every cell vibrates with energy as good as the cosmic and enliven the Being through this self-referral consciousness – ***Atma***. Ultimately, it is the" union of the microcosm with the macrocosm, 'yuj' in Brahm'. Whatever the means of attainment, the ultimate goal is 'Atmasakshaatkaar', Realisation of the Self. This is *Totality,* ***Wholeness*** or *Samhita of* ***Knowledge*** *leading to* ***Enlightment***.

The *Vedic Literature* possessing different quality of intelligence such as ***Shiksha, Kalp, Jyotish***, etc. are explained further. *Shiksha* highlights the ***expression*** quality of intelligence in structuring Rk Veda. The Unified Field expresses itself through the process of sequential symmetry breaking and thereby unfolds a great variety of values. ***The Shiksha aspect of Vedic Literature is the expression of this level of self-referral consciousness-Atma***. *Kalp* highlights the transforming quality of intelligence involved in structuring Rk Veda. *Vyakaran* highlights the expanding quality, *Nirukti* highlights ***self-referral*** quality; *Chhand* highlights the *quantifying* quality; *Jyotish* highlights the ***all-knowing quality***; *Nyaya* highlights the ***distinguishing*** and deciding quality; *Vaisheshika* ***highlights*** the ***specifying*** quality; *Samkhya* highlights the enumerating quality; *Yoga* highlights the ***unifying*** quality; *Karma Mimamsa* highlights the analyzing quality; Vedant highlights the ***lively Absolute (living WHOLENESS- 'I'-ness or Being quality;*** *Gandharva Veda* highlights the ***integrating and harmonizing*** quality; *Dhanur Veda* highlights the ***invincible*** and ***progressive*** quality; *Sthaapatya Veda* highlights the ***establishing*** quality, *Harita Samhita* highlights the ***nourishing*** quality; Bhel Samhita highlights the differentiating quality; *Kashyap Samhita* highlights the equivalency quality; *Charak Samhita* highlights the balance, holding together and supporting quality; *Vag Bhatt Samhita* highlights ***communication and eloquence quality***; *Madhav Nidhaan Samhita* highlights the 'diagnosing quality; *Sharangadhar Samhita* highlights the synthesizing quality; *Bhav-Prakash Samhita* highlights the ***enlightening*** quality; *Upanishad* highlights the ***transcending*** quality; *Aranyak* highlights the ***stirring*** quality; *Brahmana* highlights the ***structuring*** quality; *Itihas* highlights the ***blossoming*** of totality; *Purana* highlights the ***ancient and eternal*** quality; *Smriti* highlights ***memory*** quality; *Rk Veda Praatishakya* highlights the ***all-pervading WHOLENESS*** quality; *Shukla-Yajur Veda Praatishakya* highlights the ***silence, sharing and spreading quality***; *Atharva Veda Praatishakya* highlights the ***unfolding*** quality; *Atharva Veda Praatishakya (Chaturaadhyaayee)* highlights the ***dissolving*** quality; *Krishna Yajurved Praatishakya (Taittirya)* highlights the ***omnipresent*** quality; *Sama Veda Praatishakya (Pushpa Sutram)* highlights the ***unmanifesting the parts but manifesting the whole*** quality of intelligence invoved in structuring Rk Veda.

*All the Four Veda and thirty-six Vedic Literature are the expression of the level of reality available in the self-referral consciousness –**Atma**. Every individual is bestowed with this faulty and every one can fully utilize the intelligence through the Transcendental Meditation-Siddhi sadhana. There are Centres imparting this technique under the Maharishi Mahesh Yogi TM Centres. Literature pertaining to this Total Knwoledge* *can be obtained from M M Vedic Vishvavidyalaya (University), Jabbalpore 482 001, No. 871, Napier Town, M.P., INDIA*

A very interesting aspect of the study of Veda or the Vedic literature is the effect of impulses, vibration and messages conveyed by these as well as of sounds of the mantras and the reaction it brings in our physico-psychological system. Vibrations generated by the sounds of the Vedic hymns have tremendous effect on the physical environment, the social environment and the individual's mind and creates suitable psyche for alround peace and progress. The Forty Vedic Literature enlivens every cell in our body and activates the process towards attaining the 'Samhita'- the Rishi, Devata, Chaandas, (three-in-one, i.e., Totality), and Wholeness, 'Knoweldge'. This is beautifully explained in the Chapter: Vedic Way of Life. India, ie Bharat is fortunate in this respect in that it had a glorious, prosperous civilization that attracted the people all over the world. The Chinese, the Persians, the Greeks, the Afghans, the Moghals, the English, and many many others took advantage of this flourishing Vedic Civilization.

Even today, the spiritual strength of India lies in the Vedic spirit that is vibrant in a section of the population. It is in the blood of the Indians. The Vedic culture imbibed, inculcated by generations after generations, still dominates the psyche and constitutes the strength of India. Even if one per cent of India's population well -versed in Vedic Knowledge and Vedic practices is taken into account it amounts to more than ten million and another 15 percent on way makes it a wobbling 25 million- almost the population of many European Countries that boast of modern scientific culture and technological tradition. India has the potential to lead the nations of the World in this respect. This is the greatness of India.

# 2
# Vedanta
# The Complete Knowledge

'***Vedanta***' is the sum and substance of all Veda. The Upanishads, that constitute Vedanta, are considered to be the gist of the Veda and, hence it is complete 'Knowledge'. The Veda and the Upanishads constitute the foundation of ancient Indian Spiritual Knowledge. The ancient Indian civilization, the relics of which are found in the coastal Gujarat and Tamil Nadu and Andhra coasts, and the river valleys of Karnataka, narrate the story of human development as revealed in the rich artifacts, art and culture. But the little known facts are that some of the original scripts of the Veda and Upanishads are found in Telugu language and have been translated into other languages only recently. Sage Mudgala is believed to be one of the earliest of the Acharyas who systematically analysed the Veda and the Upanishads. One report from the archaeological investigations of Pune University puts that the ancient site of Indian civilization is traced to the baiiks of the Ghataprabha River of the Krishna Valley in Karnataka and other parts of Maharashtra-Karnataka-Andhra Pradesh border in India and much work remains to be done in this field. However, it is very interesting to note that the knowledge of the ancient Indian scholars dealt more with the spiritual attainments, notwithstanding, material progress; and, even accumulation of wealth for human welfare was not disregarded. India came to be known as a rich country, both materialistically and spiritually, a Paradise since very early times in human history.

The spiritual heritage of India is well known all over the world. Mysticism is borne out of spiritual practices. There are thousands of mystics who exhibit yogic powers. But these are trivial when compared to the experiences gained by Yogis like Bhagavan Ramana Maharshi, Swami Rama Krishna Paramahansa, or Maha Rishi Mahesh Yogi, and Acharya Rajaneesh of the last century. Swamy Vivekananada revelled in mesmerising the western audience through his lectures on Vedanta. But, it must be admitted here that not much is known about the Veda and Upanishads inspite of the implorings and, not much research has taken place in this field so far except that of Maharishi Mahesh Yogi. Bhagavan Mahesh Yogi has unraveled the mysteries of the very first Vedic Mantra of 'Rk Veda"- "*Agnimeele purohitham*........" and the Vedic Mantra, "*Richo Akshare*..."; he has analysed the quality of Consciousness hidden in the Silence beteen the GAPS of the sounds.Maharishi Mahesh Yogis; University of Vedic Sciences has branches in Russia, United States of America, and the M M Veda Vigyan Vidyapeetha, Jabbalpore, India, is engaged in imparting Management Education as per Vedic tradtion.

There are many institutions and organizations all over the world like the Arya Samaj, the Veda Prathisthan with its branches, interested in propagating the Vedic culture. It is very interesting that young scientists, doctors and engineers are showing more interest in these ancient Scriptures these days.

The full implications of the Veda and Upanishads are thus not very clear as yet since much research has to go into it. The Tirupati Tirumalai Devasthanams (TTD) and the Samskrut Visvavidyalaya have taken up a very ambitious scheme of bringing out thousands and thousands of Vedic literary works in their possession at the Samskrut Vidyapeetha, a deemed University. The TTD will put up all these on its web site to be male known all over the world and anybody can take up further research. A number of Veda Adhyayana Centres have come up in different parts of the world and some Vedic Schools impart Vedic education. The famous "Omkara Ashram" in the Himalayas have put the Veda on their website and the Veda can be downloaded.

There are methods of study of Veda and it is necessary to go through these preliminaries (Vedangas) before taking up the study of the Veda. *Shiksha* or discretion in pronunciation of Vedic terms, *Vyakarana* (grammar), Chhandas (metre), Niruktha, Jyothisha (Astrology) and Kalpa are the six parts of the study, and hence called 'Vedanga'. The efficacy of the '***mantra***' depends on the proper pronunciation with full knowledge of meaning and context. In fact, it is not easy to understand the Vedic mantras for there are 'goodartha' (hidden meaning) and metaphorical references in the words. Often, some words convey different meanings in different contexts. There is 'vyangyaartha, satirical meaning hidden in words and can be understood only by the tone of expression. Some ti,es the same word conveys both positive and negative meaning and one has to understand it by the context in which it is used. More often a change in accent will spoil the whole meaning of the sentence; and, some times an hrsva (short) 'a' or a dheerga (long) vowel 'Aa', where mispelt, would give opposite meaning than contemplated. The Veda have 'goodartha' (concealed meaning) that convey Yogic experiences that cannot be directly translated to words and can only be experienced in 'Meditation'. This is called the 'Samadhi Bhasha'. Hence, the difficulty in understanding the Veda and the Vedic hymns.

'***Vedanga Shiksha***' or the Vedic system of education consists of: 1.Methods, 2.Grammar, 3.Chhandas or Metre, 4. Nirukta (Connotations), 5. Jyotishya (Astrology), 6. Kalpa. These six preliminary studies are essential for all those who want to take up Vedic studies. The study of Panini's Grammar is one of the pre-requisites of the study of Veda. Lomasheeya Shiksha, Naaradeeya Shiksha, Lakshmi Shiksha, Panini Shiksha and five other textbooks of Vedic education are the handbooks of learning Veda and Vedic grammar. Much stress is laid on the metres and Chandas for the sounds and vibrations hold the key in the efficacy of the mantras. So also, Patanjali's Ashtanga Yoga is also helpful in the studies. Jyotish or Astrology is the study of 'jyoti' or light and the radiated colours of light and their wavelengths. All the stars emit light and the planets and their satellites also reflect these lights. A scientific study of these lights and the colour bands, their wavelengths has been made since very early times. The ancient Indian Sages were great scholars in several subjects like Khagol (Astronomy), Jyotish (Astrology), Ganita (Mathematics), Tarka (Logic), Phoenetics (Language) &c. They could calculate the distance of the stars and planets and their movements and accurately predict solar and lunar eclipses as also transit of planets..

Maharishi Mahesh Yogi is one of the greatest Vedic scholars of our times and has devoted his whole life to research in Veda and the task of propagation of Vedic culture. He, as a scientist, has gone deep into the phoenetic or sound aspects of the Veda. He says, "*The holistic Value of the sound is found as the expressions of the 'Rk Veda', whose greatest significance lies in its phoenetic structures, and not in a translated meaning. Within the holistic structure of sound are innumerable frequencies, which are embodied in the texts of the Veda.*" Maharishi says, "*Shrutis, the dynamic structure, the vibrancy of intelligence in the form of sound generated by the self referral dynamics of Consciousness, those specific sounds construct pure Consciousness."[See Maharishi's "Wholeness on the Move"]*. It is all very mysterious! As Aurobindo has rightly said, the secret of the Vedic Mantras remain a secret forever since nobody can ever get the hidden divine intuition behind the GAPS (Silence) of letters, words, mantras, smrutis and mandalas of the Veda.

What exactly is '***Vedanta***'? Generally, Vedanta is mistaken by many for Indian philosophy 'that is of no material consequence' and, some go to the extent of criticizing it as a source of indolence, lethargy, and inaction that has made Indian people indolent, poor, and backward. Some go to the extent of calling it the 'opium of the East', as Karl Marx said. But, it is exactly the opposite of that, in that, the 'Vedanta' never allows one to sit lazily, let alone be indolent it drives him to action without self-interest ('nishkama karma'); and, it reiterates the need for working for the welfare of the larger interests and wider groups, not the self! It abhors selfishness, warns against greed and acquisitive nature, and promotes piety, compassion, and universal brother-hood. Vedanta promotes a healthy society with stress on yogic practices such as Meditation, Pranayama, and practice of an austere way of life. It lays stress on moral and ethical values and promotes universal brother-hood and peace.

No other religion in the world strives for the betterment of life based on human values irrespective of nationality and political boundaries as compared to the Hindu Religion based on the Vedantic views and ways of life; any stress on materialistic welfare or even global co-operation for eradicating poverty and hunger will go only to feed the hungry ones temporarily and will be of little consequence in so far as 'Knowledge' and 'Enlightenment' is concerned. When compared to the benefits that accrue from the Vedantic way of life, adopting the spiritual practices, views, and ways of life, the modern scientific and materialistic approach will only aggravate the prevailing thirst for materialistic progress and its accompanyimg factors like stress, tension, strife, competition, suspicion, ill-will and jealousy creating unrest in the world. In this sense, 'Globalisation' and 'Free Market Economy' are a new threat that is spreading its net of monopoly and eradication of healthy competition. Poor nations will be subservient to rich nations and lose their freedom of existence!

***Vedanta*** brings about fundamental changes in the nature of man. It brings happiness and success, both spiritual and material. It strives for world peace. It advocates prohibition of war and removes wickedness in man. It generates piety, compassion and love. It strives for eradication of profit-oriented market economy and advocates mutual help and reliance that is beyond the scope of the present economic policies the world over. The present socio-economic trend is simply dismissed as 'illusion' leading to total delusion. This is evident from the recent burst in the global economy and collapse of the giants like the Enron and the Hyundai. These are beautifully, but indirectly, conveyed in the brief exposition of the Veda and Upanishads given below. More and more people are becoming aware of this now than ever before!

What is it that gives us immense happiness? The Veda proclaim that the entire creation of this universe is based on supreme 'Bliss', Anand. This Anand or happiness is based on 'Knowledge' and 'Truth'. Anything based on falsehood, make-believe, untruth and ignorance is sure to fail. "Satyameva Jayate nanrutam", meaning, 'Truth only will survive and nothing else'. The happiness brought by illusory worldly success is short-lived. Vedanta dictates and the Vedantins implore, "Seek the Truth". Question again and again whether it is the 'Truth'. The happiness derived from this is 'mahat-anand' or 'Supreme Bliss'; it is estimated to be 20 thousand million times the happiness of the highest pleasure and happiness that is ever experienced by any happy and successful person in this world. Vedanta holds the Key to success and happiness!

*Vedic Literature*

*Besides the four Veda, the 'Rk' Veda, the Sama Veda, the Yajur Veda and the Atharva Veda there are 36 Scriptures treated as Vedic literature. These include: Vyakarana, Kalpa, Shiksha, Nirukta, Chhanda, Jyotish, Nyaya, Vaisheshika, Samkhya, Vedanta, Karma Mimamsa, Yoga, Gandharva Veda, Dhanur Veda, Sthapathya Veda, Harita Samhita, Bhel Samhita, Kashyap Samhita, Charak Samhita, Sushruta Samhita, Vagbhatt Samhita, Madhav Nidhan Samhita, Shrangadgar Samhita, Bhava Prakash Samhita, Upanishad, Aranyaka, Brahmana, Smriti, Purana, Itihas, Pratishaakyas of the Veda- Rk, Sama, Shukla and Krishna Yajurveda, Atharva, Pushpa Sutram of Sama Pratshaakya, Taittiriya of Krishna Yajurveda and the Chaturaadhyaayi of Atharvaveda Pratishaakya.*

Unless one is proficient in all the 40 Scriptures of Vedic Science, no one can ever get near the Truth-the true meaning of Veda, for the simple reason that no one scripture is independent and complete by itself. Each scripture starting from the 'Rk Veda' has evolved into the next and all the forty above- mentioned Vedic scriptures are inter-twined -- each reverting, flowing forward and backward enriching each other! Every time one reads and contemplates on a mantra, a different, more enlightening deeper meaning is revealed; and, to complete real study of these scriptures is well neigh impossible! It is certain that, till date, nobody has ever commented on all these scriptures. How can anybody explain the meaning and depth of 'Mauna', Silence? And, the wonder of the Veda is that immense possibilities emanate from Mauna, deep silence –the Atyanta- Abhava, (Abstract Silence), i.e., the Purusha. Thus, Veda is for deep contemplation and Meditation. Sing the Saman and bring out the immense possibilities hidden in the reverberating sounds and the silence between them! It may take several lives to dwell in the Pranava "OM" and the rest! Forget It? Nay, make an earnest beginning today and hold on to it steadfast, come whatever may! This is Veda, the Truth.

*The Cosmogony*

In order to understand the place of Man and role of Man in this world, it is essential to know the nature of the cosmogony and the world we live in as well as what the Veda say about it.

According to modern science, there are multiverse, just not one universe- universes in 'strings'. These universes are constantly being born and burnt-out! Stars are born, shine out and cease to exist? Rather, they collapse under their own weight into their own self, a black hole! The rays emitted by these by-gone stars are still traveling in space and some of these rays have not yet reached us! They are so far and wide apart! All these make a mind-bogging story of the universes. Here, we have to remember one thing. This objective world cannot exist outside of us. Although it appears, as if, these stars and planets are all outside of us, actually it is in our mind since it is we who experience space and time and the objects of the uiverse in ourselves (on our mental screen). Without our mind it is impossible to conceive the idea and get the picture of this multiverse. In fact, the seer or knower of this universe sits within us as the Witness or Observer and sees it or knows it. But for our mind, and our selves, nothing exists and nothing matters! Remove the mental screen the objective world disappears. Even the inferences of the distant universes, their stars are our imaginations, images on the mental screen. These images are not real; they are transcient, impermanent, subject to disspation and decay. All that is within the grip of causalty, time and space (Triputi), or 'Asat' (Unreal). Only the 'Shakti', the power or spirit behind these objects, 'the Brahm' is 'Sat', i.e., Real.

Now, it is almost certain that our Universe is 13.7 billion years old and the first star that emitted light was not strong enough like the present-day stars. Some of the black matter that exploded with Big Bang emitted not only lighter elements like Hydrogen and Helium, but also oxygen and other heavier elements. The Black Matter is now drawing more attention as the basic matter!

There are a number of theories and hypotheses explaining the origin of the universe and the creation of life. There are the planetismal hypothesis, the tidal hypothesis, the nebular hypothesis, the theories put forth by Scientists like Laplace, James Jeans, Hoyle and Littleton, Hoyle and Nerlikar, Sri Sri Kumar of Pune. Of all the theories, the 'Big Bang' theory is the most popular and has its Vedic counterpart in the 'Sphota'. In all these theories and hypotheses, it is assumed that some primordial matter, a gaseous entity existed in the beginning. This gaseous matter like hydrogen, helium, oxygen, was hot in the beginning; if not hot, became hot due to contraction or fusion. And, the hot gaseous matter gradually cooled and expanded to assume the forms of liquid, plasma, and / or solid masses of matter. The entire process of cold gaseous matter becoming hot deriving energy from within has been explained by various mathematical formulae and equations. One such equation of Einstein is - Energy (E) is equal to mass (M) multiplied by twice the Velocity (i.e., C square). Here, it is presumed that energy is created within mass by its own movement. But, why should particles of matter, the atom and its sub-atomic particles- the electrons and protons, the fermions and bosons move is not explained convincingly; it is simply stated as property of matter, one of the inherent qualities of matter. Movement of particles in atom is its inherent quality. It is the Will, the Chitta Vritti (Thought Force) of Brahman, the Lord, the supreme Consciousness, energy latent, inherent in matter or matter latent, inherent in energy. The heat generated in the process of fusion and fission is explained in Physics. Movement or motion is one of the pre-ordained tasks and all the stars and planets keep on moving under the divine Order; whatever stops will be destroyed. Nothing can stop; the earth cannot stop its rotation on its axis and revolution about the Sun. The Upanishads declare that all the objects behave as per the divine order. "*For fear of Him, they move*!"

Now, let us see what the Veda say about these modern theories. 'Ritam' (Order) and 'Satyam' (Truth) are the two basic Principles, the foundation on which the Universe rests. First, The Pranava "Om" is the energy that emanated from the 'Sphota', or explosion. Movement is inherent in matter since the matter is formed out of energy. Radiation or light is transformed into matter as the intensity and velocity of vibration decreases. Similarly, matter turns into energy with the increase in velocity and intensity of vibration. Thought waves of the Rishis, Seers, Yogins are capable of transforming matter into energy as also transform matter from one state to another by means dharana, concentration, or contemplation during meditation. The Sadhus who regularly practise different types of yoga have this mystic power. The Yogin or Siddhi Purusha can reach this level of supreme Consciousness and create objects just as the Nature, Pradhan or Prakriti produces objects with the help of Purusha.

There is an aphroism in Samkhya Karika that explains this union of Spirit, the 'Purusha'- the sentient and the non-objective, the 'Sakshin' (Witness) with the Prakriti.

*"Tasmaat tatsamyogaat chetanam chetanaavadiva lingam*
*Guna kartrutve api tathaa karteva bhavatyudaasini".*
*Purushasya darshanaartham kaivalyaartham tathaa pradhaanasya*
*Pangu-andhavaat ubhayorapi samyogastakrutah sargah.*
*Prakriter Mahaanstatho ahamkaarastasmaad ganascha shodashakah*
*Tasmaadapi shodashakaat panchabhyah pancha bhutaani.*

***[Samkhya Kaarika, 20- 22].***

Meaning, 'through the union (proximity of the Purusha with Prakriti), the insentient evolute (Prakriti) appears as if it is intelligent, also from agency belonging to the gunas, the neutral Spirit (Purusha) appears as if it were the Agent (of creation). There is conjunction between the Spirit and Nature like the lame and the blind for the exhibition (for the sake of perception of Pradhaana, the cause of all evolutes, by the Purusha) of nature to the spirit and for the emancipation of the Spirit and creation proceds from this conjenction.

There are two interesting observations here; one is the 'lame' (Purusha) and the other is the 'blind' (Nature). Purusha is lame in the sense that the Spirit is sentient, complete, full and inactive since there is no need to move. Nature is blind, insentient and an object of enjoyment but needs Purusha, the Spirit for union. Hence, Nature exhibits objects that draw Purusha near and the creation proceeds out of conjunction of the Spirit and the Pradhaana. This union is eternal due to the continuous series of connections between the Spirit and the Nature and Purusha needs Pradhaana for its own liberation. And, this liberation is possible only by the knowledge that the Purusha is distinct from Pradhana, with all its evolutes. Though the Spirit unites with nature for the purpose of enjoyment, it unites again for the purpose of achieving liberation. Thus, creation becomes endless. Here, it is observed that, union of Pradhaana and Purusha would not suffice either for enjoyment or for liberation if Mahat and the rest were not there; hence the act of union itself brings about the evolution for the sake of enjoyment and liberation.

Here again, ***Mahat*** and the rest means, from ***Mahat***, the Great Principle evolves ***Prakriti***; and from that proceeds ***ahamkara***, the I-Principle; from that proceeds a set of sixteen ganas. From the five of this set of sixteen ganas proceed the panchabhuta, the five elements. Thus, from the Primordial Matter evolves the Great Principle ***Mahat***, and the rest.

Sage Kapila has beautifully and convincingly explained the sequence of events since evolution. This explanation suits the modern scientific explanation, too. Accordingly, from the primary element of sound, 'Shabdha Tanmatra' proceeds 'Aakaasha' (Space) since sound pervades space. Sound is the characteristic property of sound itself. Remember, sound emanated from absolute silence! From the primary element of touch as combined with that of sound, proceeds 'Vayu', (Air); Sound and touch are the characteristic properties of Vayu. From the primary element of Rupa (form) as combined with those of sound proceeds Tejas or Agni (Fire); sound, touch and form are the characteristics properties of Tejas. From the primary element of Rasa (Taste) as combined with those of sound, touch, and form proceeds, the 'apah' (water); and water possesses the characteristics properties of sound, touch, form and taste. Next, from the primary element of 'gandha' (odour) as combined with those of sound, touch, form, and taste proceeds Prithvi (Earth) whose characteristic properties are sound, touch, form, taste and odour.

This explains the sequence of events that proceeded from Sound 'Om' (the 'Big Bang') that created the Earth. It is important to note that 'Sound' emanated from 'Silence', and this 'Silence' is the source of primordial matter.

Here, again, 'Conjunction' or union of Purusha and Prakrity for enjoyment should not be misconstrued in the sense of human level of union (sexual copulation) and enjoyment. Enjoyment is the bliss of union ('Yuj'). This enjoyment is possible without the physical contact as seen in the case of sight and sound. Proximity or near-ness of fire and ice or butter will cause melting of the latter. There are the metaphysical aspects connoting the everchanging or 'dynamic metamorphism' in Nature that bring happiness and joy. We feel immensely happy when we see a beautiful flower, a beach, or riverside, a mountain peak, an absolutely silent surrounding like a lakeside park. The enjoyment of beauty of nature is one such; and, the creation of innumerable objects in nature is another example of the nature's way of captivating Jeevas! These are of aesthetic perceptions that are not easily understood by persons operating at lower level of consciousness. Normally, ignorant sensuous persons immediately jump to conclusion that creation is possible only from copulation and attribute it to even the Gods and Godesses (to produce offsprings)! That is how the Brahma-Saraswati concept (Silence and Sound), or the Love of Radha and Krishna (Soul and Consciousness), or birth of Ganesha (union and control of the elements) are misinterpreted leading to confusion in simple minds. The concept of '***Ardhanaareeshvara***' has to be understood carefully. The process of creation is indeed a mystical process to be understood in proper perspective. Eggs can be obtained without hen these days!

There are plenty of Vedic aphorisms regarding the origin of the universe and the creation of this objective world. Even today, some of the traditional Vaidic families of Brahmins perform their daily chores chanting these mantras, while taking bath very early in the morning as matter of ritual but reminding us of the importance of this knowledge.

*The Vibrations*

*Silence is eternal, deep and vast. Out of this deep silence emanate impulses that cause 'kampana', vibrations. This Kampana, 'Vibrations' is the cause of evolution. Vibrations of different intensities and wavelengths possessing different qualities (Gunas) have created multifarious objects of this universe including the multitude of life forms due to the self-referral nature of consciousness and its inter-active, creative and transforming abilities. Silence, 'Mauna' is the self existent Prajnya, the vast expanse of universal Consciousness (Mahat Prajnya – Absolute Awareness) or the 'Brahman'. In this vast ocean of consciousness, the impulses, vibrations that created the waves and bubbles turned into objects of perception due to the creative ability of the Consciousness in the depth of Silence. Silence evolvd into sound and the sound merged into silence creating a GAP that holds immense possibilities. The deep ocean of Consciousness is Purusha, the all-knowing or 'Omniscient' supreme Brahman; and, the 'impulses' are what is referred to as' God Willed'. The self-interacting dynamics of the self-referral conscousness is the 'Prakriti' that is responsible for the creation of this universe. That is how this Universe is' diversity in unity' since there is immense possibilities of creation of objects in the Silence (GAPS) between sound, objects have taken form depending on the quantity and duration of silence and the intensity of the emerging sound.*

*"In a sense, we are all bubbles in the waves and ripples of ocean of consciousness. We can see the bottom of the ocean, the supreme Brahman, if the waves and ripples cease, or the vibrations stop". In other words, we can visualise the Brahman only by divine grace, or when we reach the depth of silence and contemplate on Him through Meditation. Thus, a very scientific explanation for the origin of the uni-verse (Unity in Diversity) is available in 'Rk Veda Samhita' (Total Knowledge)*

***Vedanta*** makes most of these scientific explanations very clear and easy to understand. Accordingly, there was nothing in the beginning. This is illustrated by the analogy of a sesamum seed that contains oil, or a fig seed that contains the plan of a whole fig tree within; but nothing is found when these seeds are cut down to their minute particles. But the sesamum oil and a fig tree come out of the respective seed! Also, which seed sprouts depends on the divine will. This creation is the 'Divine Will' of the Lord. The 'Divine Will' is expressed in the form of 'Tapas', contemplation, or Meditation that generated heat. 'Is it there' or 'is it not there' are the most evasive questions to answer. It depends on 'faith' and the first thing the Lord created is 'faith'. One has to have absolute faith, enormous faith, and unwavering faith in the Lord."No faith, no life and no world", is the Vedic dictum.

Thus, the 'Will' or the 'thought force' (contemplation, meditation, tapas) of the Mahat Prajnya, supreme Consciousness, or simply, 'The Lord', the self-effulgent (Light) created energy (E) and matter (M) by mere 'vibrations' of different intensities and wavelengths. Energy and matter are inter-changeable; matter becomes energy at higher intensity of vibrations and intensity of energy becomes matter at lower vibrations. The primordial matter or the gaseous matter such as Hydrogen contains enormous energy (atomic energy) and these constitute the millions and millions of Stars, and the galaxies of the universe. Thus, it is all 'vibrations' that create energy and matter. 'Space' and 'Time' are the manifestations of the same process generated from supreme Consciousness. 'Mind' is the one basic constituent of this universe according to the Veda and this emanated from supreme Consciousness very early in the process. Thus, Mind constitutes the 'world' and the world is the 'Mind' of the Brahman. A replica of the Universal Consciousness, the Brahman (Macro -cosmic), is created in the form of Man, the Individual Consciousness of the Man, the Jeeva (micro cosmic). When the vibrations of individual Consciousness establish contact with the vibrations of the univerasal Consciousness, the individual soul, 'Jeevatman' merges with the universal soul, 'Paramatman'. This is 'Salvation' or 'Liberation' according to Vedanta.

Knowing 'Brahman' or visualizing Brahman, the 'Absolute' is thus possible from Dhyana Yoga (Jnyana Yoga). The technique of establishing this 'unity'; or 'yuj' is explained in Jnyana Yoga. Hence, 'Meditation' on Brahman is a beautiful technique of establishing the unity of Atman (A) with Brahman (B), the soul purpose of human life or existence on this planet! The unifying factor is 'Om' (=). It is this 'Om' that welds the Atman with Brahman and enough heat should be produced in contemplation, or Meditation (Tapas) on 'OMmm' to achieve this 'unity'.

The Unified Field is the Samhita of the Rishi, Devata and Chhandas, i.e., the Knower, the Process of Knowing, and the Observed. In other words, the 3-in –one concept! Maharishi Bhagavan Mahesh Yogi says, "Every aspect of th Veda and Vedic Literature is a specific aspect of the dynamics of the Unified Field- the dynamics of WHOLENESS- the dynamics of consciousness." Further, Maharishi says, "The unmanifest Unified Field of Consciousness, through its self-interacting dynamics, expresses itself in specific quantities and in a perfect sequence, assuming the qualities and structure of *Natural Law*, or the *Laws of Nature*."

The discovery of the *Unified Field* of all the *Laws of Nature* as the *Self-referral Reality, "Samhita"* having a three-in-one ***-Rishi-Devata-Chhandas-*** structure, completely corresponds with the Unified Field of Vedic Science. Now it is certain, according to both the modern Physical, Chemical, Biological, Mathametical and Technological sciences and the Vedic sciences, that 'the ***Self-Referral Field of Intelligence***, or Consciousness lies at the basis of all objective material creation of this universe." This is the Vision of Total Knowledge according to Maharishi Bhagavan Mahesh Yogi. [See Bhagavan Mahesh Yogi : 'Heaven on Earth'].

The origin and development of the universe is thus explained as the self-emanating phenomenon and its source is Silence, ***Atyanta-Abhava-*** a quality of conciousness. Vibrations – the most basic impulses of self-referral conciousness, emanating from Abstract Silence or Absolute Abstract, the dynamics of Silence reach the state of ***Anyonya-Abhava*** where all the evolutionary process starts. The silencing dynamism of ***Pradhwamsha-Abhava*** evolves into the silent WHOLENESS of ***Atyanta-Abhava-*** where all possibilities exist in silent nature, which evolves into the specific quality of ***Prag-Abhava***, which in turn expresses itself as sounds (svara) of Rk Veda. One who dwells in the depths of silence of the GAPS in the sounds of Mantras of Rk Veda can experience this marvel, as well! This is the source of *creative intelligence*. All inventions and discoveries come out of this depth of silence (supreme Consciousnss). The soul or Atma is the seat of this Self-Referral Unified Field (supreme Conciousness) for there is nothing else to refer to.

Thus the entire universe is the product of 'impulses' and 'vibrations' emanating from deep seat of Silence- seat of supreme Consciousness. Impulses and Vibrations constitute the primary requisite and, the basic constituents of all the multitudes of creation on this Planet originated from these 'vibrations'. The vibrations are explained in the 'Vedas' as 'Gunas' and these are – the Tamas, the Rajas and the Sattva. These three Gunas have certain inherent qualities depending on the wavelength and intensity of the vibration. These three Gunas rule this universe-. These Gunas are also the vibrations that are related to the vibrations of the 'thought force' of the Brahman (the supreme Consciousness).

There are the Vedic 'mantras' that help to capture the 'vibrations' in colours and mathematical numbers; and, these colours and numbers can be used to tap the vibrations in 'yantras'. The 'yantras' are graphic presentation of these 'magic' colours and numbers derived from the Vedic chantings, the 'mantra'. Yantras (graphic charts) can be made on foils or metal plates (gold, silver, copper etc.), or plain paper and may be tied to arm or worn around neck for personal benefit. Metallic, or paper charts are made using the appropriate colours and numbers suited to individual's place of birth, date of birth and the position of the sun in constellations and star at the time of birth. Thus, peace, progress-material and spiritual progress; as well as universal peace, economic prosperity, and spiritual progress are assured in the Vedic mantras (Atharva Veda).

This supreme 'Consciousness' always exists everywhere and has no beginning or end; it is self-effulgent, omnipotent, and omniscient. One can perceive this supreme Consciousness by sheer contemplation or Meditation. Thus, supreme Consciousness, the 'Brahman' is 'Absolute' and 'Infinite' This Absolute and the infinite that forms the subject cannot be perceived by human sensory organs or Mind that constitute the objective world. The supreme Consciousness, the Brahman, is also known as the Atman, the Self, the Prana (the Vital Airs), or the 'Paramatman', while the individual human beings are known as 'Jeevatmans' (atman enshrined in body). This basic knowledge of the Atman or the Self is essential for a spiritual aspirant and the method or technique of understanding this is called 'Jnyana Yoga'. By Meditating on the 'Self', one can understand the 'Self'.

*Vedic Cosmology*

The Veda trace the origin and development of this universe to a very simple source that is unmanifested, self-effulgent, omniscient, and omnipotent force that emanate from the Lord Himself, who is supreme 'Consciousness', all-pervading, and self-effulgent and hence self-luminous. The Lord says,"***I am the beginning-less and end-less (Ananat)***". [***Bhagavad Gita***]. I am 'That'; and, I am omnipresent. Everything emanates from 'Me' (the 'Sat') and finally takes refuge in Me (the so called Black Hole?). I am supreme Consciousness. I (Consciousness) am everywhere and everything. I am in every body or things what you call you and I, he, she, it, and they! The Yogins try to understand this 'Mahat Tattva', '***So* 'ham**', or '***Aham asmi***' ("I am"), the first Principle, Consciousness of the Atman, through Meditation. The Veda implore the same. All the Sages and the Gurus teach this first Principle- "***Aham asmi***"."***I think, so I am***".

Try to know who you are by asking the question 'Who am I'? The realization that, 'I am That', '***So'ham***' comes with deep Meditation and the process of eliminating all untruth by "neti" ('not this'), process. 'Neti, neti, neti,' is the method of discarding one by one all that is transient, not permanent, and untruth. For instance, I am not the body since the body is subject to deterioration, death and decay. I am not the Mind since the mind is ever changing and has no basis of self-existence. Like that one can go on eliminating all untrue and finally arrive at the Real and the Truth. Finally the 'Sat' ('Truth') alone will be revealed. This is God-Realisation. The second Mahat Tattva, Vedic Principle is: "***Tat tvam asi***" ***or*** "***Thou art that***' is the first step to Self-Realisation.

In the Vedic context, the Milky Way, the galaxy in which our solar system is located, is called the 'Goloka'; it is also known as Brahmanda the deity of which is Vishnu. Beyond this is the Svayambhu (the Visible World), of which Brahma is the Deity. A number of important Stars like the Kriththika, Jyeshta, Mrugashirsha, Ashlesha, Mula, etc are found here.

The Solar System ('Sauraman') consists of the Sun (Surya) whose deity is Indra. Indra is derived from 'Indha', meaning fire. (Indhana is fuel, a source of energy)

Radiation of energy is called 'Rudra'. Close to the source of heat or light it breaks or splits the particles. Rudra also means to break. It also exists in Shoona (Shoonya or vacuum). Intense light is 'ghora' and mild light is Shiva. Shiva is Lord or Soma, dispersed energy. Condensed form of matter or energy (or both) gives rise to 'agni' (fire). In creation, 'Agni' is the first to be formed of concentration of matter.

The dispersal of energy from the Sun is taken as the beginning of the measurement of distances from the source of heat, the Sun. One unit of the diameter of the Sun is the unit of measurement here. 108 such units of energy distance (dispersed from the Sun) take us to the orbit of the earth. Solar energy cools down at this distance. This is the ideal location for the formation of life forms. Thus, earth is ideally located for the proliferation of life forms. At distance of 100 units, the 'Siva region' begins and the moon is located on the head of Siva. This is the heat zone where the sun's heat is moderately high. This heat decreases gradually uptill 1000 units, near the Planet Saturn.

On the surface of the Sun, the heat is enormous and it is called 'Hiranya' (gold). As one comes near the earth and moon, it is rajat (silver). Near the Saturn, it is copper-red or tamra-aruna.

The exclusive visibility of the Sun is 100, 000 units from the sun, 10,000,000 times the diameter of the earth. This is the limit of our solar system, also known as the third step of Vishnu. Beyond this limit of solar system lies the Samba Sadashiva. Ambhas of Siva is the sphere of galaxy and Siva means the spread matter. Mahar loka is the realm of gods where Mahadeva rules.

Soma is radiation of energy (moves outward and up). Agni is concentration of matter due to gravitation (moves inward and down). Radiation of energy or heat is 'angira' (flame) current, pulling outside material with force is 'bhrugu' current. Balance of these centripetal and centrifugal forces or currents is the place of creation of 'atra' (here). It is one only compared to the three parts each of bhrugu or angira. Hence it is called 'atri' (not here). Thus, each region is atri whose light is moon that is source of plant and life. Thus, the solar system is explained in the Vedic context.

***Kapila's Samkhya Philosophy*** comes very close to the modern scientific vrsion. It is based on '***sankhya***' or number. ***Svetasvatara Upanishad*** describes the origin of the universe. Sage Kapila is the first Great Rishi or Sage who had a rare gift of perceiving the Truth and he knew everything! He could convincingly prove that all the multitude of objects that are visible, seen in this world are actually two only- one is Purusha and the other is Prakriti. He went on to show that the union of Prakriti and Purusha has given rise to this objective sensate world. In the beginning, the Brahman, the Absolute is the 'ekamevadviteeya, 'One' only. He 'willed' and created the 'Shakti' or 'Maya' as His own manifestation. Both the ***Brahman*** and the ***Maaya*** are the uncaused cause of this universe. The two are self-existent, in the sense that the creative power or Shakti was already there within the Brahman. Purusha is the manifest form of the Brahman, the spirit. Prakriti is the matter. It is just like the radiation of energy (light) turns into matter and the two different states are the result of variation in intensity of vibration. The electrons, the protons, the photons energise the cells and these tiny bodies- the enliven cells like the protozoa are the simplest forms of life. That is the beginning of life. Every atom, every living cell or everything, living or non-living is pervaded by supreme Consciousness.

The union of Purusha, the spirit and Prakriti, the matter, has yielded Mind and 23 entities that further produced the multitude of the material objects of the universe by permutations and combinations. The Sage Kapila has given very clear and unrefutable proof to establish the validity of his doctrine (Samkhya Philosophy). Infact, the phenomenal nature of the universe has come from Kapila for the first time and he proclaimed that the phenomenon has three factors viz., the Adhyatmika (Spirit), the Adhibhoutika (Matter), and the Adhidaiva (the ***illuminating principle***). It is the 'adhidaiva' or the illumining principle, light that unifies Prakriti and Purusha, matter and spirit. It is very simple. Light is required to unravel the matter that is lying in darkness. There must be light between the object and the seer. The Knower or the Seer is Adhyatma and the object is adhibhuta and the light that shows the object is adhidaiva, the illumining principle. It is only with the help of the illumining principle that we can understand the universe.

And, Kapila says, "*I think of the objects of the universe only through my mind. The universe exists because I think. It is an in-born faculty that makes the universe as real. But actually, it is an illusion. If I keep off mind from the objects of the Universe, the Reality or true Knowledge dawns on me that this objective universe is not real.*" So, it is in this delusion that we are all born and die, repeatedly, till the realization of the Self. The moment we realize that we re not this physical body of name, form, and function, but we are something much more than that-the infinite Self the universe disappears just as the picture disappears as soon as the screen is removed. This screen is avidya, illusion, maya. It is the Light that illumining principle that enlightens us as to the Reality of things. And, that light is within us. The whole universe is on our mind (screen) and, as soon as the mind is removed, the sensate world disappears and we become the Jnaaynis.

Another beautiful presentation of Kapila is the Vedic concept of "smaller than the smallest and greater than the greatest". The Lord Naryana or Vishnu is within our heart, as a light of the size of a thumb; it is the size of a grain, or is ten fingers above the Brahmanda and holds everything within himself without being affected by it. According to Kapila, the least number is Zero but it is greater than the negative values of any number. Similarly, any number greater than the zero is not greater than the Infinity and zero is infinity! "Anoraneeyaun mahato maheeyaan".

*The Living Planet*

This earth is pulsating and living. It is full of objects created by the permutations and combinations of what is called 'tanmatras'. The elements. Basically the five elements- water, fire, ether, air, and minerals go to constituted the myriads of living and non-living things. The same elements combine and recombine in different proportions under different temperatures and pressure to form innumerable objects of solid, liquid, and gaseous states. Water is found as ice as well as water vapour. Similarly we have carbon in liquid and gaseous forms. Why not we believe that we, the human beings also can take different forms under different conditions? We can assume the gaseous state and become invisible or wander all over in this form. It is foolish to believe that whatever we see is the only real thing. We should have the grace of the divine to *'see things as they are'*. Once we see things as they are, in their true form, the illusion disappears.

The 'Planet Earth' is supposed to be the only ideal location for proliferation of life due solely to its location in the Solar system. The elements so combined and formed simple compounds like air, water, minerals and compounds in innumerable chains in permutations and combinations, and produced all sorts of forms like the neurons and the neuronic charges conveying messages, compounds having genetic codes like the Di-Ribo-Nucleic Acid (DNA), Ribo-Nucleic Acid (RNA), the hydro-carbons and the carbohydrates, the minerals, proteins, vitamins, &c. The primary compounds like water, air, minerals, as well as heat and ether provide the basic structure; and, action and reaction continue to produce all the multifarious living and non-living objects of the world. In all these elements and compounds of primordial matter, the basic elements are derived from the stellar matter, of the Sun. It is the dynamic metamorphism and a quality of nature that has produced the objects of the world. It goes one step further and states that, 'all these different forms and names we have given them is due to our ignorance'. Practically nothing of such sort of multitude of names and forms exists! It is our illusion, ignorance that we see different things in one and the same unitary existence!

What is the source of this ignorance? The source of ignorance in this world is stated in ***Bhagavad–Gita, [Verse 7-13].***

*"All this world, deluded as it is by things made of the 'gunas' (qualities), does not know 'Me' (the Lord) who is transcendental to these and undecaying."*

The Veda declare that, 'whatever that is transcient, not permanent, not 'Sat' is not the 'Truth'. "Truth only exists" and nothing else really exist. This is the reason why we try to confirm the existence of an object by repeartedly touching it, feeling it and confirming its existence. Despite our repeated exercise we fail to perceive the real objects! We do not see the objects if something intervenes between our sight and the object; so also, we do not see the objects if we close our eyes. In fact, we do not know whether the objects really exist and do not see them due to many reasons. The objects cease to exist even when we are seeing them and many times we see objects of our own imagination! There is 'virtual reality', hallucination, and 'day dreams' and ' make-believe' things that we believe as real. This makes the whole universe complex and complicated and we are perplexed. This is called, '***Maya***' in Bhagavad-Gita, or 'illusion ' in Budhdhism. For instance, the 'one' single unicellular amoeba has multiplied itself to form the 'many'; and, it is also true that the 'first ever-formed amoeba' still exists in different forms and continues to proliferate! This is the 'Truth", the Veda proclaim. That which is unmanifest ('avyakta') is the 'Sat'. In the light of this Vedic dictum, it is made clear that "Nothing is ever born, die, or decay". Similarly, nothing can be ever created or invented; it can only be discovered since every thing exists in the universe as an illusion or Maya; and, it is all a 'myth' not the 'Truth'! 'Know' this truth, the Sages implore! What is the philosophical import of these implorations? Human sanity, avoiding rash and negligent actions, sensitivity to preserve and protect lives of fellow living beings, banishing thoughts of violence, strife and war, rather, knowing our limitations and a sensible living at that!

*The Veda hold that the Sun is the source of all life on earth. Sun is the virtual God. Besides the Sun, the air we breathe, the water that sustains our lives, the fire or heat that keeps us alive are all gods. All these Gods derive their power and strength from a 'Greater Source', Parameshwara- The Paramatman. Hence, it is the Supreme Lord, Lord Narayana, who sustains this world. He is praised in the Veda as 'Vishnu' and a thousand other names as in 'Vishnu Sahasra namam' (as in Mahabharata, Shanti Parva).*

*There are billions and billions of galaxies, at least 2000 of them in the Cosmos. Veda proclaim that this 'Akhilanda koti Brahmanda' is ruled by Sri Hari Narayana. The Milky Way or the 'Ksheera Path' is our Goloka (where Lord Sri Krishna rejoices with his cows as Govinda), the Galaxy in which the solar system exists at this point if time, Vaisvanara Manvantara.*

The Solar system is governed by a "dwarf star' of recent galactic history and is not very significant in any way compared to the 'giants' that are far and wide away from us. But, the significance of the Sun is such that the Veda sing and praise this dwarf star, 'Sun' for its sustaining force as one of the eyes of 'Narayana' and the other being the moon.. It is the central theme of all the 'Vedas'; The 'Rk Veda' praises and the 'Sama Veda' sings its glory. The 'Atharva Veda' tries to explore the hidden strength and power of the Sun. While the Veda dwell at length the spirit behind the creation, they also visualize the entire cosmogony in a single conceptual framework and tries to explain the secrets behind creation.

The central theme of study of the Veda is the decoding of the formulae, exploring the broad spectrum, and defining the Absolute, the 'Infinite'. The methods adopted by the Veda are different from those adopted by the modern science; while the modern scientists come very close to the ancient Yogins in their single-minded pursuits of unraveling the mysteries of the universe, the latter differ very much from the latter in that they take to contemplation, Meditation and Tapas to unravel the mysteries. The Seers and the Sages look inward while the scientists look outward; the Seers implore 'within' while the scientists explore outward to "Know". The objective is very clear but the methods are different. With the Unified Field of Science and the Samhita- Rishi, Devata and Chhandas of the Veda, the search is complete

Spiritual Science is based on Veda and Vedic Sciences and the methodology is based on fundamental Principles like the Mahat Vakyas for contemplation and Ashtanga Yoga Sutras that include Meditation; and, unlike physical sciences or biological sciences it has its laboratory within the spiritual aspirants' body for observation. Whatever is realized as the Truth in the process of deep meditation is conveyed as the Veda.

The 'Veda" is the 'Truth'. The Truth emanates from the seat of supreme Conciousness, the Atmnan. It emanates from the depth of Abstract Silence in deep meditation on the Self. The Truth or the Mahavakyas conveyed by the 'Veda' conveys the 'Truth'. Veda is "Rk". 'R'rrrrru.....'k' is 'Ak', the 'A'-'k', i.e., the 'Ak-shara'. The Akshara is 'the Ekakshara Brahman'- the "Om". This is the 'Truth', the 'Abstract Silence', the 'Infinite', or the 'Absolute'. The 'Rk' is 'vak', the word of mouth; and it is 'Saman' when sung in musical notes. It is this 'vak' (word of mouth), that is called 'Saraswati' created by Brahma, the Creator; and, the first letter or syllable ever uttered by a human being is the 'Akshara' "Om" (AUM). Brahma is that dynamic metamorphism and Vishnu is that 'cosmic energy' or sustaining force and both these are supported and sustained by "supreme Consciousness". As it is the quality of nature to degenerate, decay, and disintegrate, the 'death came to be the logical conclusion of all living objects that are not the 'sat', the (Truth). This quality of nature-degeneration, death and decay, is attached to objects and thus makes this 'objective world' an 'illusory' one or 'Maya'.

The modern scientists struggle in vain to touch the fringe of the "Truth", since the method employed by them is not suitable for the purpose. One cannot see the 'Infinite' through the 'Finite'. The scientists employ the sense organs such as the eyes, the ears, and the tools like the telescopes, the microscopes and the spectroscopes to study the matter, while 'Truth' or 'Knowledge' is not 'matter' or object that can be perceived by sense organs and the tools to aid them. The Sages know that 'spirit' can be experienced rather than explained and the method employed is the one suitable for 'experience', i.e, contemplation, Meditation. The scientists deal with matter and try to explain everything as qualities of matter. Einstein put forth his formula-E=M.C2 and tried to explain the universe as 'energy' (E). But, he did not explain the supreme power behind this source of energy (E). This has been explained in unmistakable terms in the 'Rk Veda'. It is the 'supreme Consciousness' that gives power to all the elements.

The 'Subject', the 'supreme Consciousness', is eternal and 'Infinite'. It is not possible to view the 'Subject'. The viewer is also an Object of the universe. There is only one Subject and that has no parallel and that is '***Ekameva advitiya***' ('One without a second'). This '***Subject***' is known by different names in the Veda and Upanishads. It is simply known as "That".

It is called the "***Brahman***", the "Atman", or the "Supreme Soul". It is known as the "Sat" (Truth), the "Knowledge", the "Eternal", the "Endless" the "Beginning less". It is also known as the "Chit", the "Anand", the" eternal Bliss". It is known as the "Self". It is "It". It is "***Om***". It is everything that is 'Known' and 'Unknown' so far, 'Knowable and 'Unknowable' forever". It is very near, but so far; and. all our energies are directed towards knowing "That".

A Yogin who knows the 'Truth" has no contradictions in these statements."He who knows knows not and who knows not knows". It remains a constant exercise to "Know" Him and continues to be so. In the course of this search for 'Knowledge' all the mysteries of the universe are revealed as 'mystic experiences' to the seeker, the Seer. Thus, the main objective is to seek "Him". The method of seeking 'Him' is through "Meditation" and the objective is the search for "Truth". When the seeker, the sought and the seeing are merged in 'One", the Absolute' is established and there is neither the seeker, nor the sought and the seeing. The duality ceases to exist. It is no more 'Two" (Seer and the sought), the 'dvandva', or the 'dvaita' ends and only "Advaita" stands. The whole universe stands "revealed" in the process and, the one's self merges in the other 'universal self'. The seer and the sought, the knower and the Knowledge, the Jnyata and jnyaana or the Kshetrajnya and the kshetra – all become one.This is "Vedanta" in a nutshell; the nut stands cracked!

It seems that the Veda and Upanishads swayed the life of people of the world; but the emphasis on different aspects of the Veda and Upanishads was different in different periods. It is also possible that many Upanishads that were very prominent in one period lost their significance in another period. Some Upanishads are known only in names and many are not available. Later scholars have tampered even the original texts and misinterpreted; one of them (Kaushiki) went to the extreme of denying the Veda as of any meaningful spiritual value. It is also discernible that the objective of different Schools of Vedic Thought were different and the methods of conveying these also vary. Some Upanishads lay stress on the Brahman and others on knowing the 'Atman', the Self. Some Upanishads laid stress on the Pranava 'Om'; and, others on Yogic practices to attain the Self. Quite obviously, it is all- confusing! The Western scholars have misunderstood the Vedic Scriptures due to their lack of basic understanding of Phonetics and Chandas of Veda. Literally, the meaning of Vedic Sanskrut (Sanskrit) words have been misunderstood by many of them. Moreover, the Western scholars try to explain the mystic Vedic terms that are beyond any ordinary person's comprehension unless he is a Yogin! Only, a Yogi will be able to comprehend the true meaning of the Veda in his Samadhi or state of superconciousness. And, these are, at times, inexplicable. That is the real problem. It can be only experienced but cannot be explained. Moreover, there are no equivalent words in other languages, particularly the European Languages, to translate the Vedic terms appropriately. But, there are some original works that only the Indian scholars have properly understood and preserved since antiquity. One such rare works is ***Muktikopanishad.***

***Muktikopanishad*** of Shukla Yajurveda narrates the account of Hanuman requesting Sri Rama to explain what are the Veda and Upanishads. Hanuman after praising Sri Rama asked, "O Rama, Thou art Paramatma of the nature of Sachidananda, be Thou gracious enough to tell me that by which I shall be easily released from bondage of mundane existence and by which I shall attain salvation". To this, Sri Rama replied: "O mighty-armed one, well as led, hearken them to the truth uttered by 'Me'. I am well established in Vedanta (the end of Veda or knowledge). Have thou recourse to 'Vedanta' well."

"What is Vedantas? Where does it abide? Pray enlighten me", asked Hanuman. Sri Rama replied, "O Hanuman, listen to me. I shall truly describe to you the nature of Vedanta. Through the expiratory breath of Myself-Vishnu, the Veda were generated as many. Like the oil in the sesamum seeds, Vedanta is well established or latent in the Veda."

***"How many are the Veda and their branches? O Raghava, What are the Upanishads? Please, through Thy grace, tell me truly."***

Sri Rama said, "Through the divisions of 'Rk Veda' and others, the Veda are said to be four in number. Their branches are many; so also the Upanishads. In 'Rk Veda', there are branches, twenty-one in number. O son of Vayu, there are 109 branches in 'Yajurveda". O conquerer of enemies there are one thousand branches in 'Sama Veda'. O best of monkeys, there are fifty branches in 'Atharvaveda'. In each branch, there is one Upanishad. Whoever with devotion to 'Me' studies even one of the 'Rks" (hymns) in these attains the state of absorption, rare for the Munis to attain."

***Muktikopanishad*** reiterates that, "the goal of attaining Brahman is only through 'Jnyaan'. It declares: "the final emancipation is only through 'Jnyaan path' and not through Karma, Samkhya- yoga, and other Upanishads. Thus is the Upanishad."

Again Hanuman requested Sri Rama to enlighten him as to the emancipated person, the 'Jeevanmukta'. Sri Rama replied, " The control of Chitta is Jeevanmukti and Videhamukti follows when through the extinction of Prarabdha. The 108 Upanishads are an authority on this subject and the objective of this Jeevanmukti is the attainment of supreme Bliss. Jeevanmukti is attained through Samadhi arising through Vedantic study, and accomplished through human efforts, through extinction of Vasanas."

True Jnyana does not arise through the vasanas of the world, scripture, and body; only pure Vasana will pave the way for attaining my (Brahman) seat. But the impure Vasanas are an obstruction in this path and should be overcome by efforts; the impure ones have to be transmuted into the pure vasanas. The extinction of Vasanas, vijnana and the destruction of Manas – all these three, when practiced together for a long time, are regarded as fruitful. Destruction of Manas is not easy; thoughts should be killed as oon as they rise and it is called 'manonasha'. Only Veda adhyayana (svaadhyaaya), association with the wise (satsang), attainment of spiritual knowledge and abdication of all Vasanas and control of vital air i.e., Pranayama – all these will help in the control of Mind. This may take a hundred years or even more! Even if one of these is practiced again and again, the Seat is not attained; just as the Mantra imperfectly done is useless, it will not yield any fuits. Through practice of these for a long long time, the knots of the heart are cut. O Mahakapi, practise the state of mind devoid of Vasanas, and attain quiescence of Mind (Manas) and practise mauna (silence). One who has a supreme Chitta with a heart devoid of all desires is an emancipated person. "O son of Vayu, always worship My Reality; I am the ever-full Brahman. I am Brahman, Om tat Sat!"

*Rk Veda'*

*The term "Rk" stands for the words of eternal"Truth" and Veda stands for the unquestionable knowledge of the Supreme Brahman.* ***"Rk Veda Samhita"*** is the embodiment of Knowledge- a storehouse of the knowledge concerning the universe, now the multiverse. The First Mandala deals with the origin of the universe and evolution of life. It gives the details of the basic structure of the universe. It holds the clue for the future. The Ninth Mandala of '***Rk Veda***' gives the details of the creation of Man (***Purusha Suktha***). In Bhagavad-Gita, which quotes copiously the verses from the Veda, these are beautifully explained. Sri Krishna says, *"I am everything that you can ever perceive; I am the past, present and the future. I am the architect of this universe and it is my divine plan and everything falls within my control and direction; nothing moves without 'My' will" [See Bhagavad-Gita].*

It is very interesting to note here that everything that the '***Rk Veda***' speaks of is about the Sun, the source of all life on earth. The Veda declare, that Brahman is the spirit behind the Gods and the sun and, the sun shines because of the fear of the Lord. The planets rotate and revolve about the sun in obedience to the Lord and nothing moves without his knowledge and will. The 'Will' of the Lord is of paramaount importance in creation. Simply, "He 'willed' it". There it is. No one questions the creative ability of the Lord since it is one of the 'svaroopa' or qualities. The other quality is "Sat-Chit-Anand". Yet another quality is that He is 'Achyuta, Adi-madhya-antarahita, and Ananta' i.e., 'eternal, beginningless and endless'. The Lord is thus known as:

*"Mahat Kala Purusha, Pradhana Sat-chit-ananda svaroopa Narayana".*

***Meaning***, *'Narayana', the Lord of this universe, is everything and He is above All.*

Consciousness, Energy, Matter, Space, Time, and Prana (Life) are the manifestations of the Lord and He contains all these and thus He is the container. Container is bigger than the contents! He surrounds everything. He is the 'Self-effulgent'. He shines. He is the Mind (Space). He is the 'Hiranyagarbha'. He is the 'Mahat'. He is 'Time'. He is beyond Time. He is 'Prana'. He is inside and outside everything. He is in 'Everything' since He is the all-pervading 'Vishnu' ('Vish' meaning, pervade). He is in the microscopic sub-atomic particles; He is in the simplest cellular body, the amoeba. He is the Supreme Self.

The Scientists deal with 'physical' objects, or 'matter'. They do not comprehend the 'metaphysical' aspects since they keep 'Spirit' outside the purview of Physics. They search and research into 'matter' and get deeper and deeper into the tiniest of the sub-atomic particles. They fail to notice the shoonyata, 'nothingness' that emanates as energy, as the by-product of supreme Consciousness, latent or hidden in the microns just as 'oil is latent in the sesame seeds', or 'the banyan tree hidden in the seeds of the tiny banyan seeds'. These simple 'truths' are hidden from the normal sense organs that always look outward towards the 'objects' for the answers. The Veda and the Upanishads make these points amply clear and one should be sensible enough to know the difference between the 'spiritual' and the 'materialistic'. Any effort to discard 'spiritual' from the existential reality is foolish. Mind, Consciousness, Prana, Breathing, the 'anthahkarana', the subtle body, and the subtler aspects of the Heart, etc. are beyond the purview of physical or biological science, since the science looks only at the 'objects' that are physical and biological and that are subject to investigation by the senses and the mind. But, spiritual implorations are a science of a different kind that can be personally experienced which needs no proof, confirmation, and no experimentation. The truth holds good for eternity!

Thus, the Veda and Upanishads give the most authentic and the most beautiful account of the mysteries of the universe as also explains the techniques to unravel them.

***Sreeman Narayana, the Supreme Lord***

It may be of special significance here to reiterate that, there is no mention of names of any God except that of ***Vishnu*** and ***Narayana*** in the Veda and Upanishads; hence, the ***Mahanarayanopanishad, the Narayanopanishad, the Atmabodha Upanishad and the Narsimha tapaniya upanishads*** get special mention. All gods are derivative of the Brahman and are called '***Deities***' designated with certain functions and, He, the Lord Himself assumes these designations and performs the self-assigned (!) functions. He himself defines the Self as the 'One' and the 'Absolute'. All other names, forms and functions are illusory. The terms 'THAT' and 'IT' are often used to denote the Supreme Self.

Thus, it is the Lord Almighty to whom we use the terms 'He' and 'Him'; or, the 'Divine Force' is referred to as 'That'. 'He' who resides in every creature as 'Soul' is the real God and He, the Lord, is common to all the six-and-odd billion people as well as the plants and animals of this Planet Earth; and, 'He' has no name and form! If you so desire, you can give a name and form to 'Him' and worship 'Him'. All these years of about five or six Millennia, we have been doing only this. Jesus Christ, Shree Krishna, Shree Rama, Gautama Buddha and Mahavira are beilieved to be the avatars, or incarnations of the Lord. In a way, these are the persons who have purified their mind and soul, raised their level of Consciousness to unite with the Supreme Consciousness and thereby developed their inner strength to become so powerful that they 'swayed the world' and have ultimately become the hope and faith of millions of people.

Many spiritual leaders like Shri Ramana Maharishi, Shri Ramakrishna, developed their inner strength, attained purity of mind, heart and soul, and they too became the hope and aspirations of their followers. That way, everybody can attain this spiritual height by mere sádhana, practice of Sama, Dama, Dharana, Dhyan, Meditation and Samadhi. The Veda proclaim that, the human life is the product of divine grace and has emerged in human form after a long course of rebirths. Even after obtaining the human life, it is not assured that the same divine grace will continue, and the jeeva may revert to any form of living organism or inanimate form according to its karma, good or evil deeds. *Love and love of God, alone paves the way for liberation.*

***The Place of Vedanta in Indian Philosophy***

The six systems of Indian philosophy i.e., Hindu philosophy comprises of Vaisheshika, Nyaya, Samkhya, Yoga, Mimamsa (also called Purva Mimamsa), and the Vedanta, also known as Uttara Mimamsa. These six systems may be reduced to only three groups viz, Vaisheshika and Nyaya as one, Samkhya and Yoga as second, and Mimamsa and Vedanta as the Third. These systems of philosophy are mainly concerned with "Truth" and nothing else but "Truth". The Indian mind is always interested in hearing 'Truth', reasoning upon 'Truth', and meditating on 'Truth'. The reasoning aspect of "Truth" is the main purpose of Hindu Philosophy. In this sense of the term the Hindu philosophy is the science of Hindu Religion. At sometime or the other, an Indian is prone to think about the 'Truth' or the 'Reality' of existence. The ancient Sages had the vision and goal; they systematized the concepts so as to enable the spiritual aspirants to easily understand and practise the philosophy and attain the goal. The credit of systematizing these concepts into codes goes to many a great sages starting from Narada, Manu, Vyasa, Jaimini. Gotama, Kanaada, Kapila and Paatanjali down to Yajnyavalkya and Mudgala and Vashishta.

No body has clear idea as to when exactly these great Sages lived and worked on these systems of Hindu Philosophy. If we consider the life span of these ancient sages, each one must have lived 1200 years and most of their time lapsed in Yogic practices. Some of them went into 'Turiya' state in Meditation and realized the "Truth". Kanaada is credited with the Vaisheshika system while the Nyaya system is credited to Gotama. Kapila is known for the Samkhya system whereas Patanjali is credited to systematizing the Yoga system. Jaimini is supposed to be the founder of the Mimamsa School, while Shree Vedavyasa founded the Vedanta School of Philosophy. The exact dates of origin of these schools of thought is a matter of one's imagination and belief for the available dates are confusing and contradictory. However, it may be safely said that these are at least 3000 years to 5000 years old. These ancient scriptures have come down to us as our spiritual heritage by word of mouth, as shrutis (heard) and smritis (memorized) and every care has been taken to preserve the exact meaning and spirit of the terms and the concepts and doctrines. The very system of learning Veda was so perfected that there was no room for doubts and aberrations in conveying the concepts. But these Scriptures that are poetical in form and consist of "Sutras' or euphorisms needed commentaries and further explanations. So many additions and supplementary notes have been added to the original scriptures making it difficult to understand who added what and when.

The six systems of Hindu Philosophy are mutually complementary and not exclusive and contradictory. They take us to higher and higher plane of spiritual understanding and reveal the "Truth". Since these are based on the Veda and the Upanishads, the approach of the different schools may vary but the ultimate goal is the same. Nyaya and Vaisheshika form the groundwork to philosophical understanding, whereas, the Samkhya, the Yoga, and the Mimamsa take us to higher and higher understanding and finally land us in Vedanta. Indian Philosophy is at its best in Vedanta that reveals the entire nature of our existence and reveal the "Truth" if we just close our eyes and contemplate on it. Just as a student of Physics or Chemistry specializes in the study of the elements and their properties or characteristics, or the students of Biology specializes in the study of 'cells' for decades and decades in colleges and universities, a student of Indian Philosophy prepares himself for a long and arduous journey of investigating the "Truth" and finally 'experiences' it. There are many interesting powerful techniques and methods, called 'mantras', 'tantras', and 'yantras' to attain the spiritual goal.

In brief, the systems of Nyaya and Vaisheshika aim at concptualising our faith and belief. Kanaada maintains that our purpose is to expound Dharma, Virtues or Righteousness in order to gain abhyudaya (progress or unfoldment) and highest good, 'Nishreyasa'. Nishreyasa is the immediate perception of the ultimate realities of Self and the universe. This system of philosophy recognizes the concept of Jivatman and Paramatman and believes in a material cause and efficient cause. 'Ignorance bars our way to liberation and this ignorance sprouts from identification of the Self with the body, the senses, and the mind. This leads to bondage, i.e., makes us slaves to raga, dvesha, lobha, mada and force us to commit sin that leads to suffering and death. Only the 'Realization of the Self' will redeem us from the cycle of births and deaths. Here, ignorance that is the cause of bondage and suffering and death is not merely a lack of knowledge of the Self, but it is half-knowledge or imperfect knowledge. Hence, this imperfect knowledge, moha or illusion can be eliminated by right knowledge. This right knowledge or the realization of the Self cannot be acquired by mere study of scriptures but need moral and ethical practices; one has to follow the prescribed code of conduct and gain Consciousness (not inherent quality). However, one cannot gain 'Jivanmukti', liberation (from the clutches of this body and mind) while living. Liberation to soul (jeeva) comes only with death. Thus, both Nyaya and Vaisheshika insist of 'enlightenment' for liberation through a strict adherence to austere life and code of moral and ethical conduct.

Kapila is a Maha Rishi (God), a Sage, Seer of deeper understanding and immense knowledge. His speciality lies in that he could easily count everything including the objects of this universe. He deduced everything to Principles of Samkhya (number), and colours and says that the union of Prakriti (matter) and Purusha (energy) gave rise to this entire universe, the objective colourful world. It is the mind that perceives these objects through the senses and, as such, the world exists in the mind. '*I think, I exist*'. All objects are the compounds, factors of phenomena and, once you remove the factors the 'Reality' is seen. There is a Seer, an Object, and the Light that helps the Seer to see the object. The Seer sees only because of the illumining principle, the Light. ***In Bhagavad Gita, Sree Krishna says,*** *"I am the Seer, Iam the object seen, and the Illumining principle, Light. I am the Kshetrajnya (the Knower), the Kshetra (the Field) and the Consciousness (the Illumining principle)." This is the Samhita-Totality or Unity, of the Rishi, the Devata, and the Chhandas of the Veda.*

The Samkhya School founded by Sage Kapila is very important for it emphasizes the need for subjecting the transcendental experience of the Self to a rational analysis of the truth. It provides a rational analysis of the truth. *Samkhya Sutra says, "The supreme goal of life is to end misery, the 'tapatrayas', the three kinds of suffering*'. The three kinds of sufferings are: the adhyatmika, adhibhoutika and the adhidaivika. The pain caused by the diseases of the body, mental disturbances, and unrest are adhyatmika. Adhibhautika sufferings are due to animals and other extraneous causes. Adhidhaivika are supernatural agencies that cause human suffering by floods, earthquakes, storms, etc. A right knowledge of Purusha and Prakriti will destroy the pain caused by these agencies The cause of human misery is uncertainity, aimlessness and a sense of purposelessness, or fleeting nature of all joy. Here again, absence of right knowledge is the cause. Whenever right knowledge dawns, giving immediate experience of Purusha as separate and detached from Prakrui, and only thn, will come complete cessation of misery.

Samkhya philosophy takes into consideration both misery and joy, happiness and delusion. Accordingly, Prakriti, the world of thought and matter, is a mixture of happiness, misery and delusion. For instance, the same beautiful girl who gives happiness to her husband also creates jealousy among women, and brings delusion to mind of lustful men. Thus, the objects of this world are a mixture of happiness, misery and delusion. Our knowledge of the objective universe is one-sided; our prejudices affect our judgement and our knowledge is bound to be personal, fragmentary and imperfect. The ultimate ideal is to transcend all Gunas and reach the state of Purushottama, a 'Nirgunaatman'. Traigunyo bhava Arjuna; says Shri Krishna.

The Samkhya Philosophy holds that the entire evolution, 'Srushti' is just a continuous process of evolution of what is already involved; it is just a reproduction, a transformation, the effect of the cause. Thus, there is no new creation; it is only a question of removing the barriers for the 'flow'. Thus, evolution is the gradual unfoldment of what is already involved. The three Gunas- Tamas, Rajas, and the Sattva, play a very important role in the 'flow', removing barriers to flow, to promote evolution. And thus seem to be the potential cause of every result. These three Gunas operate as different aspects of Prakriti (Nature) and, thus, are found in the evolution of all organic as well as inorganic matter. It is the restless activity, vibration, changes in the intensity and velocity, that causes the evolution, reproduction, and transformation; and, there is nothing like creation of new matter. Matter cannot be created. Matter already exists and no body can ever say when and how matter came into being. The primordial matter, the soul is one and it has transformed or multiplied or evolved into different names and forms, but it is always one.

The Soul, or the 'Purusha' is 'Pure Consciousness'. This does not undergo any change.; it is only released in the process of evolution. In higher evolutionary scale, the release is all the more, full and it is 'transcendental consciousness' that is pure and pristine. This transcendental consciousness, that is pure and full, is the 'Purusha'. Again, it is only in its pure and pristine form, the infinite and unchangeable consciousness of Purusha, or the Self, the Purusha is free, completely free, and it is no longer a reflection; it is free from the clutches of Prakriti. It is no more identified with anthahkarana and the mind stuff, the product of Prakriti. Hence, unless, one is free from attachment, raga or moha, the shackles that binds one to anthakarana, one cannot attain liberation. One has to remove all these binding knots of the heart in order to be free, the 'Purusha'. This is the state of supreme Consciousness, the Brahman.

Prakriti operates in the proximity of the Purusha, but Purusha is always free. Purusha is changeless, eternal and Prakriti is the opposite of Purusha and as such, cannot evolve itself without the aid of Purusha. This is the secret of the entire process of creation and existence! However, Prakriti binds the Purusha, the nature or quality of Purusha is unchangeable and Purusha seeks liberation and ultimately, remains free, free from bondage, or 'attachment'!

Kapila is more rational in his treatment of evolution, 'Srushti'. He has beautifully explained the process of evolution in a very scientific way and it has great universal appeal. Kapila says:

The Prakriti is a state of equilibrium and the process of evolution starts with the disturbance of this equillibrium. The first product of the effect of disturbance in this state of equilibrium is "Mahat", that is 'cosmic intelligence'. This Mahat is not the Pure Conciousness. 'Purusha' or Mahat is only the reflection (mirror reflection) of the supreme Conscousness. This is the basis of Individual intelligence. The individul souls that appear innumerable are indeed the reflection of the one supreme Soul like the Sun reflected in numerous glass pieces are the numerous water bodies, wells, lakes, and tanks. Thus, one has to merge the individual consciousness in the supreme consciousness by practice of meditation in order to attain emancipation, to be free from bondage of cycle of birth, death and rebirth, the clutches of Prakriti, or the' Sansar'.

After 'Mahat', or cosmic Intelligence, there came 'Budhdhi' that is illumined by the intelligence of Purusha. This 'Budhdhi' (Intellect) has the discriminative power and can distinguish objects, enables Purusha to experience the objective world through the mind and the senses. Budhdhi is the storehouse of all impressions, 'Samskaras'. The Mind and all the senses work for Budhdhi that in turn works directly for the Purusha. Budhdhi is a product of Prakriti and as such contains all the Gunas as its substantive material. However; one or the other of the three Gunas is always predominating and its attributes are significant and decide the quality or nature of the individual person. These Gunas affect the intelligence or object of the individual persons since the intelligence is depending on the reflection of the supreme intelligence and the predominating Guna affects the quality and quantity of the intelligence. That is why the individuals of different nature are of different levels of intelligence; more the Sattvic, more of pure intellignce and more Tamasic less of intelligence.

Ahamkara is the product of Budhdhi, the ego-sense or the 'I'-sense. The Gunas again dictate the quality of the person according to the prepondering Guna, the nature of the person is decided and the ego-ness in him. Sattva predominating, the 'ego-less-ness' is predominating for the 'sattva' is ego-less. Out of the 'Ahamkara' are born the 'Manas' (Mind) and Indriyas (the sense organs) and sense objects. The elements or the 'Tanmatras' and the Great elemens are the off- shoots of Ahamkara only. Together, these 24 categories of constituents go to make or constitute this objective world, this universe of mind and matter..

Sage Kapila has based his treatise of "Samkhya"on the Upanishadic doctrines that are indisputable and many Schools of Thought have adopted it without any question. In Bhagavad Gita, Sri Krishna says, among the Sages, 'I am Kapila'. In fact, Kapila is believed to be incarnation of Krishna. The Bhagavata Purana describes Kapila as a partial incarnation of Vishnu, born with the knowledge of truth for the good of humanity. Kapila is the author of Tattva Samaasa and Saamkhya Pravacana Sootra, but it is not very certain whether kapila actually wrote them. Kapila's Samkhya Philosophy clearly brings out the goal and purpose of philosophy and it is rational and scientific in the strict sense of the terms of Science. One should learn to look at things ***as they are, not as they appear to be.***

The Hindu philosophy of life believes in Karma or Metempsychosis. Except for Charvaka, all other doctrines are united on this. It is only Charvaka, who is a materialist and secular, who does not offer any reason or theory to support his version of evolution of man and a reasoned theory of man and the universe. Nyaya, Vaisheshika, Samkhya and Yoga believe in the authenticity of the Veda and accept dualism or Vishishta Dvaitism. Purva Mimamsa, and Uttara Mimansa advocate 'Advaitism'.

The Samkhya philosophy considers that Prakriti and Purusha account for everything. Purusha is the individual soul, of which there is an unlimited number. Primordial Prakriti is matter consisting of the twenty-four principles ranging from the three gunas-the tamas, rajas and sattvic, down to the gross earth. By the joinder of Purusha and Prakriti, spirit and matter, samsara is the result. Their divorce is the goal to be reached! Both are real entities that get on without any controlling force.

*The Hindu Way of Life through the Ages*

*Today, the Indian population is said to be secular, and the social and political leaders do not attach much significance to the Vedic heritage of India. The present trend is not a healthy one since it is weaning away the religious-minded, god-fearing, 'sattvic' people, and putting them in a quandary. The materialistic prosperity has never been the goal of the average Indian and the spiritual goals are all very clear and well set. But, under the changing social, political and economic circumstance, the term 'secular' has come handy to the opportunistic power-mongers and this spells disaster to the Country.*

*The Veda proclaim and dictate the Principle of Dharma (Virtue and Righteousness) and enacts the code of conduct in order to ensure a disciplined austere life and to promote peace and harmony; it creates condition and enables every individual to live a life of love, sacrifice, and atonement for the misdeeds of the past and thereby pave the way for mukti. 'Universal Brotherhood' and 'one world, one family' are principles and the soul aim, meaning and purpose of Secularism; mutual tolerance and respect are the methods of practicing it. The Veda do not hold brief for any sect or god; they are secular!*

The Hindu Philosophy and Hindu Religion are the oldest in the world like the Chinese philosophy and religion. It is almost Ten Thousand years old, or may be more than that. Rk Veda and Sama Veda eulogises the Sun God and the ancient Indian Sages have visualized the Brahman in the Turiyaateet state of their tapas. They have laid down the path of Self-realisation through Yoga. The human nature, the play of human Mind was so well understood by these wise men that they advocated 'Mind control' techniques through Pranayama and Meditation.

*Manu Smriti*

Manu is believed to be the first human born and as such he is the son of Brahma according to the story of creation. Scriptures say that Brahma gave him a set of code of laws in a hundred thousand verses which he reduced to four thousand making it easy to remember and convenient to use.

The code of conduct of Manu, or the Manu Smriti, that calls for an orderly way of life has often been misunderstood. This is a very important documented code of ethics and morals for an orderly development man and his society. The laws of Manu dictate strict adherence to an austere way of life to gain control over the senses, to be free from lust and greed, svadhyaya (study of scriptures or Shastras) and detachment from worldly way of life, meaning acquisition of wealth, jealousy and hatred and cut-throat competitioin in public life. One must always speak truth, respect parents and elders, respect ladies, honour old age and never injure others in thought, words and deed. These codified laws were strictly followed and India had attained the highest status in spiritual progress. In fact, the Japanese called India as "Indie" meaning "paradise on earth".

The goal of life according to Hindu Religion is mukti, "emancipation". It is the same emancipation that Jesus Christ strived for, and the' Nirvana' that Buddha achieved! Mahaveera advocated the same non-injury (Ahimsa) advocated by Manu. ***"Ahimsa paramo dharmah" is the Principle, the path of liberation***. All the religions of the world have derived their fundamental doctrines from one single source i.e., ***Rk Veda*** since it is the oldest Scripture that is ever available in this world. It is the most sacred ancient Indian Scripture most religiously practiced for quite a long time.

Manu has codified the laws based on Veda. In recent years, the

Varnashrama Dharma of Manu Smriti is the major issue that has come as a handy tool to divide Indian society in the name of establishing equity and social justice. Manu has never said that the humans are classified as castes- Brahmana, Kshatriya, Vysya and Sudra; rather, it is the functional classification that is the 'vritti dharma'. People take to different avocations and they are identified by the function. All are equal in the eyes of God and a Brahmana who is supposed to be a jnyaani knows it very well. No one is superior or inferior. All those born on this earth, whatever avocations they practise, are very near and dear to the Lord. Lord Krishna in Bhagavad Gita says,"*whatever is your station in life, perform your duty without any desire for the fruits of your action. Your own dharma is far superior to dharma proclaimed by anybody else. Ultimately all come to Me*".

Every human being is a Brahmana (Anglicised as Brahmin) as far as he uses his mental faculties towards spiritual upliftment; he is a Kshatriya in defending himself and protecting others; a Vysya as far as he exchanges knowledge or goods for social welfare; and, a Sudra producing food and wealth using his skills. Every person is a Brahmana insofar as he uses his faculties of Spiritual Knoweldge for universal welfare. He is a Kshatriya in valour, a Vaisya in materialistic progress, and a Sudra in production of food and wealth. The four classes of people are the economic classes that use different methods to attain spiritual progress and emancipation or liberation. There is nothing like the Sudra born this way, or the Brahmana born that way. It is all a mischievous political propaganda going on for centuries and centuries fooling ignorant and innocent people for political gains, power and money for selfish ends. Economic equity and social justice are well written in the code of Manu; he warns against exploitation of one class by the other. Dharma (Righteousness) is the guiding Principle of Manu. One who upholds Dharma shall be protected by Dharma. "*Dharmo Rakshati Rakshitah*".

'Manu Smriti' is the code of Hindu religion. It is the oldest and the well-documented code of ethics for mankind. It preaches the principles of morals and ethics, Yama and Niyama, as advocated by Paatanjali in his Ashtanga Yoga Sutra. Practically the codified laws are the Vedic doctrines of sane and sensible living with spiritual attainment and self- realization as the goal of life. The Manu Smriti emphasizes the need for clean life, a life of continence (Brahmacharya) for purposes of preserving the strength and energy with a view to fully utilize the human potential. Also, the futility of human life is stressed and spiritual attainement eulogized for eternal happiness. Poverty, hunger, disease and misery that haunt the people have been carefully addressed in Hindu religion and many useful hints are given to overcome these. Veda and Upanishads reiterate the nobility of human life underlining the need for spiritual attainment. Elaborate details are given in a number of these Scriptures as to the sane and sensible way of living. Manu Smriti is one such that advocate not only spiritual, but also moral, ethical and social code of conduct.

Hinduism as a way of life has undergone a sea of change since the Vedic Ages. It is the oldest and the most powerful religion that upholds the principles of Dharma "Righteousness", Universal Brother-hood and world Peace. There is no scope for narrow-mindedness in Hindu Religion and it treats all other Religions as equally great. There is no preaching of violence as some of the later religions developed intolerance and propagated terrorism, conversion, and despotic rule and advocated oppressions on their followers. There is no room for disagreement in some of the Religions that formed later as opposed to Hindu Religion that has a broad based liberal approach. Hindu religion is the mother Religion of all other Religions since it is based on Vedic Doctrines and advocates the principles of 'Universal Brotherhood' in "Vasudhaiva Kutumbakam" meaning, the humanity is one family.

*Human Development Through the Ages*

Human beings in the present form must have existed for almost 5 million years according to Veda. One day of Brahma is about 4320 million Man-years and it includes four Yuga that make one Maha Yuga. It seems that more than 20 Maha Yugas have already lapsed! It makes a mind-bogging estimate of almost a 8640 million man- years that goes to make Brahma's one day! It seems already five Manvantaras are over and the 6th Manvantara called Vaivasvata Manvantara is now going on. According to this, one manvantara lasts for about 300,8571,428 years. We are supposed to be living in Shvetavaraha Kalpa i.e., Brahma's 26th Day of the first month of the 51st year. It is very difficult to reconcile these estimates arrived at with the help of the fossil records now available. Of course, a long gestation period must be allowed for the formation of full-fledged Homo Sapiens sapiens from the primordial matter. Evolutionary history of Man is also given in the Vishnu Purana along with the evolutionary history of the earth.

As an interlude here, by the way," Who is this Brahma, the Creator"?

Almost all the 18 Puranas have a story of creation. Vishnu Purana, Brahmanda Purana, Padma Purana have all elaborate details. It was, first, Brahman, the Absolute, the Infinite, or the thing that we cannot see as a neem tree in a neem seed, or a fig tree in a fig seed, or for that matter, the differentiated ghee and butter in the milk, or oil in the oilseeds.

Then the Lord 'willed' to manifest himself in Pradhana-Purusha and then Ardha-naareeshvara, and the Brahma-Sarasvati, Shiva-Parvati, and Maha Vishnu- Maha Lakshmi, - all meaning, energy and matter, or matter and energy changing states according to intensity and wave-lengths of vibrations. Brahman became Brahma and then Prajapati! Shakti (energy) inherent in matter supported all the creations and thus emanated as the supreme Mother Goddess, call by whatever name viz Kali, Durga, Lakshmi or Shive, Rudre, or Vaishnavi or simply 'Devi Maa'.

It is intriguing to note the tendencies of dualities in human nature and behavior. Man is noble for, the God first created the Saints. The divine qualities are thus inherent in human nature. These qualities are to be nurtured and preserved for there arise corruptive tendencies due to the influence of nature. Nature here is the sensuousness and ego that rules the lives of people.

Thus, a very interesting aspect of the study of man is that of the 'corruptive tendencies' that developed in course of time. If Satya Yuga is a period of highly sattvic and virtuous period of human existence when human values were of the highest order, Kali Yuga marks a deterioration in all walks of human life. Virtuous life leads to happiness and this mitigates the hardships of families to some extent. Wayward life leads to misery and hence the need for a code of conduct. The Lord who created also gave a code of human conduct so that he can live in peace and ultimately attain Him, the Supreme Bliss. But, it seems that, all the 'tapatrayas'(miseries of life) are created by man himself i.e.,'svayamkruta' or self made. To realize this secret is the purpose of this elaborate study.

There have been corruptive tendencies, selfishness, greed and avarice, self-aggrandizements and jealousy, illwill, and mistrust – all leading to strife and misery. There has been a thorough degeneration, deterioration in the quality of human life; values have changed; and, it is a bad sign! The quality of human life has been declining since the very early times, say Krita Yuga, called the Golden Age. Various Schools of Vedic Thought propagated different Upanishads during these periods. Some of these Upanishads are not available now.

Satya Yuga or the Krita Yuga that lasted for 1,728,000 years is a period of an ideal or utopian existence with purity in thoughts and action. The Smritis, Puranas and Tantras depict the glorious days of Krita Yuga. It seems too idealistic to emulate these values and virtues, today. Vishnu Purana gives an elaborate description of geography and spiritual life of the people of this hoary past. It seems saints and seers had the central stage during this eon of pitrus, Gods and Goddesses, Gandharvas and Kinnaras. It is a highly romantic period charged with spiritual insight and emotions of heavenly existence.

Treta Yuga must have lasted for 1,296,000 years. Sri Ram is an avatar of the Lord Narayana. He took birth as the eldest son of King Dasharath of Ayodhya. He lived and worked amidst the common people and guided them. He is known as 'Purushottam' a model for others to emulate in virtue. The Vedic doctrines such as truthfulness, abiding the laws of Manu, etc. are highlighted in the poetic description of the story of Sree Ram.

In Treta Yuga, Sree Rama says, "I am Veda" and enunciates the 108 Upanishads to his ardent disciple Hanuman. There is a beautiful dialogue between Hanuman and Sri Ram. Hanuman tells Sri Ram, "Well, Ram you are a man and I am an animal at the body level, and we are world apart in comparison; at the level of Mind or Consciousness, you are the King and I am the Subject. We are two different entities. At the level of the Atman or the Soul, we both are the same. But as a King you are bound and as a subject I am free." In this sense, Hanuman is better placed in respect of spiritual attainments than Sri Ram, an incarnation of the Lord! Yoga Vasistha also brings out this aspect clearly. One should be free and prepared for emancipation. Adhyatma Ramayan gives an insight into all these aspects.

Dvapara Yuga must have lasted for 864,000 years and we do not know much about its history. Much of politics and geography is described in poetry in Mahabharat. Just as the Lord proclaimed that He will repeatedly take birth in every eon as an avatar to live amidst the people and guide them, Sri Krishna took birth in the family of Vasudeva-Devaki as their eighth son. The story of Sri Krishna as told in Bhagavata is written in twelve volumes and the most important are the Rasa Leela and the Geetopadesha.

In Dwapara Yuga, Sri Krishna said, "I am Veda"; and, the Bhagavad Gita enunciates the Karma marg, the Bhakti marg, and the Jnyana marg in its eighteen chapters.

Kali Yuga dawned almost at the close of the life and times of Sri Krishna, may be about 6 000 years from now, or at the most 10, 000 yeras ago.

It is said that in Kali Yuga there is no incarnation or avatar of the Lord although Kalki Bhagavan is supposed to appear when the human values detriorate and righteousness is destroyed by greed and avarice and sensuous and animal propensities assume immense proportions in the humans and work against the survival of mankind. But, Madhvacharya (1036 A.D.) had the God-visioning in the form of a Horse-faced person. And has realized the Hayavadana (Horse-faced) in his dreams and has propagated the same 'Righteousness' upheld by Sri Krishna in Dvapara Yuga..

In Kali Yuga, the people have reached a stage where they are afraid of speaking Truth. Greed, avarice and false-hood and cheating have become so common that the Government has to put up boards proclaiming Vedic statements like "*Satyam eva Jayate*" in law Courts and '*Nahin Jnyanena sadrisham*' in University emblems.

In the Krita Yuga, also called the Satya Yuga- an age of illumination and harmony, it was all a transparent life of 'Ritam' (Order) and 'Satyam' (Truth). People could see through and through the minds! In Treta Yuga, called the Silver Age, it was all 'Virtues', values of life; come what may, Sri Ram stood for values in life. Values started declining. Sattva guna declined giving place to prepondering Rajas. And, in the Dwapara Yuga called Copper Age, it was all 'Dharma' and Shri Krishna stands for 'Consciousness'. Values had declined further over the ages and we see the behaviour of Duryodhana and Shakuni in Mahabharat. Sri Krishna took birth to kill Kamsa and restore Dharma. Shree Krishna has been striving for establishment of 'Dharma', righteousness, throughout Dvapara Yuga as we can see it in Mahabharat. He says, 'I will take repeated births to re-establish Dharma'.

Kali Yuga is believed to last for 432,000 years and a recorded history of 2500 years is now available and the rest all is left to one's imagination or guess. Since there was no effort to preserve the data and historical accounts in large numbers, much of it is lost in fire, floods and devastations, and frequent wars and destruction of property. Preservation of ancient scriptures was by words of mouth and students had to learn by-heart with precision and care. So whatever we have today is the result of sheer providence! Even this we are unable to preserve and protect!

In Kali Yuga, called the Iron Age, it is total devastation of values, morals, ethics, and spirituality. It is pre-ponderance of Tamas, loss of values of life- 'Ritam' and 'Satyam'. A Spiritual Renaissance only would help restore 'Dharma' in the present situation.

In the light of Vedanta, these changes in values are all meaningless. There is neither good nor anything that is bad. These 'good' and 'bad' are the qualities that our mind dictates to us as something acceptable or not acceptable and the same depends on the state of the 'Mind'. Something that makes our mind acceptable, however 'bad' it might be in others' point of view. The same thing that we like today, something that is 'good' today, may not be to our liking another day. We may feel it as 'bad'. Where is the 'Truth' in all these things! The Lord says, "I am the Good and the Bad; I am everything in this universe". The good and the bad are the 'two'; but the truth is always 'One'. A wise person always knows this and is not perturbed about all these things! Vedanta implores: " Know this 'Truth' by contemplation, meditation, by contemplating on 'Truth'."

This way of thinking also leads to complacency. The best way is to pay heed to Lord Krishna's advice. "*Do your duty, leave the rest to me"("Karmanyevadhikaaraste ma phaleshu kadachana"). "Do not worry, I shall take care of you" (Ananyaaschintanayam..... yogakshemam vahaamyaham").* Those who 'doubt' (the efficacy of this) shall perish" ("*Samshayaatma vinashyati*"). ***"Those who abide by 'Dharma' (Righteousness) shall be protected by Dharma"***(*Dharmo rakshati rakshitah*") ***[Bhagavad-Gita].***

# 3
# The Upanishads

The Upanishads are considered the essence of the Veda. Among the Hindu Scriptures, the Veda hold the pre-eminent place and the Upanishads culled from the Aranyaka-portions of the Veda are regarded as the 'Vedantas'. The Upanishads constitute the 'Vedanta' for they constitute the 'complete knowledge', the end of all knowledge. The Upanishads derived from the Aranyakas denote that these portions were intended for study in the forests by the spiritual aspirants who had given up their worldly life and taken to ascetic life in all seriousness. The knowledge of the Upanishads is essential in order to understand the Veda. Only a person well-versed in the Upanishads can understand the Veda properly. Each Veda has its own Upanishads, rather, every one of the four Veda was taught in different 'Shakas' (branches) and each of these Shakas had its own Brahmana and its Upanishad annexed to it. This Upanishad was not exactly annexed or joined to the Veda, but was intended for meditation to the supplement of the Brahmana through an Aranyaka. In fact, these Upanishads are so sacred that these were imparted to selected students only, in confidential sessions, at the end of the students, stay in the Gurukula. After a long stay of the pupils with the Teacher and his family, there developed mutual affection and this prompted the teacher to call the pupil near ('Upa') and impart the essence of the Veda before the departure of the pupils from the Ashram. This farewell address summarizing the Vedic knowledge came to be known as the 'Upanishads'. As such, these Upanishads have special significance.

The householder (Grihasta) was ordained to take up spiritual life after his grihastashram and gradually keep away from worldy life; as a preparation to this life, even as students, Brahmacharis, these students were taught the Vedic studies and 17 other subjects like Grammar, Phoenetics, logic, economics, (arthsastra), archery or dhanurvidya, astrology and astronomy, mathematics, ayurveda (medicine). The Upanishads meant for the householder was 'Brahmanas' and to those serious ascetics, the 'Aranyakas'. Hence, it was the Vedic way of life; what for the Grihasta was the 'Brahmana' was for the Vanaprastha the 'Aranyaka'. In fact, as students, everyone had learnt these Aranyakas by heart; but, in old age, it's meaning became more clear and intelligible. This helped in clear understanding of the nature of the world ('Maya', as it is) and the nature of man's owns self (Self-realization). It was also an essential part of a Brahmana's life to carry out the Vedic rites and for that purpose he should be 'well-versed' in Veda.

Although there are about 250 Upanishads, major and minor, only 108 are supposed to be more important. Among these, only about a dozen are very popular and frequently commented by Acharyas and scholars. Most of the Upanishads are believed to be latest additions and the name 'upanishad' is added to give it a status of authenticity and respect. Not all Upanishads are available. Now, almost 120 Upanishads are available in print.

The most important Upanishads are the Aitareya and the Kaushitaki of the 'Rk Veda'; the Chandogya and Kena Upanishads of Sama Veda; the Taittiriya and Kathaka Upanishads of the Krishna Yajur Veda, and Maitrayani Upanishad that has since been forgotten. The important Upanishads of Atharvan Veda are the Mundaka, the Prasna and the Mandukya. A number of small Upanishads are also attached to the Atharvan Veda and these are of mystic contemplation like the "Om" and the related to the practice of Yoga.

There is a beautiful account of Sri Rama imparting Veda and Upanishads to Hanuman in Muktikopanishad. Hanuman wants to know about the Veda and Upanishads and asks Sri Rama, O Lord, I wish to know for the purpose of emancipation, Please enlighten me, about the means of release from bondage. O Rama, how many are the Veda and their branches? O Raghava, what are the Upanishads? To this, Sri Rama replied:

"The only means by which the final emancipation is attained is through 'Mandukya Upanishad'. If 'Jnyana' is not attained thereby, study the ten Upanishads and thereby attain jnyana and attain my seat. O son of Anjana, if thy jnyana is not made firm, practice well the thirty-two Upanishads; thou shalt get release. If thou longst after 'Videhamukti' (disembodied salvation) study the one hundred-eight Upanishads. I will truly state these Upanishads in order with their Shanti (Purification) mantra. They are:

Isavasya, Kena, Katha, Prasna, Munda, Mandukya, Tittiri, Aitareya, Chandogya, Brahadaranyaka, Brahma, Kaivalya, Jabala, Sveataṣvatara, Hamsa, Aruni, Garbha, Narayana (Parama), Amrita-Bindu, Amrita-Nada, Atharva-Sira, Atharva-Sikha, Maitrayani, Kaushitaki, Brhat-Jabala, Narasimha-Tapani, Kaalaagnirudra, Maitreyi, Subala, Ksurika, Mantrika, Sarvasara, Niralamba, Suka-Rahasya, Vajrasuchika, Tejo-Bindu, Nada-Bindu, Dhyana-Bindu, Brahma-Vidya, Yoga-Tattva, Atmabhodhaka, Parivrat (Narada-Parivrajaka), Tri-Sikhi, Sita (Yoga)-Chuda-Mani Nirvana, Mandala-Brahmana, Dakshina-Murti, Sarabh-skanda, Tripadvibhuti-Maha-Narayana, Advasya-Taraka, Rama-Rahasya, Rama-Tapani, Vasudeva, Mudgala, Sandilya. Paingala, Bhiksu, Mahat-sariraka, Yoga-Sikha, Triyatita, Samnyaasa, Pramahansa-Parivrajaka, Akshamalika, Avyakta, Ekakshara, Anna-Paarna, Surya, Aksi, Adhyatma, Kundika, Savitri, Atma, Pasupata, Parabrahma, Avadhuta, Tripurtapani, Devi, Tripura, Kara, Bhavana, Rudra-Hrudaya, Yoga-Kundalini, Bhasma-Jabala, Rudraksha, Ganapati, Darshana, Tarasara, Mahavakya, Panchabrahma, Prana-Agnihotra, Gopala-Tapani, Krshna, Yajnyavalkya, Varaha, Satyayani, Hayagriva, Dattatreya, Garuda, Kali-Santarana, Jabala, Soubhagya, Sarasvati-rahasya, Bhavricha, and Muktika. These 108 Upanishads will clear all doubts, vain thoughts, and false thoughts and confer 'Jnyana' and 'Vairagya'. These will destroy all vasanas including that of booklore, world and body. Shanti is prescribed before and after each Upanishad and the assistance of a knowledgeable Acharya or Guru in these Upanshads shall be taken to become 'Jivanmukta' after studying 108 Upanishads.

Sri Rama said, "O son of Vayu, these 108 Upanishads, which are the essence of all the Upanishads, are capable of destroying all sins through their mere study" "Whoever studies or hears the 108 Upanishads attains Me. There is no doubt about this. This is stated in a verse of 'Rk Veda'.

When Hanuman asked Sri Ramachandra to relate the Shanti Mantra of each Upanishad according to the divisions of Rk Veda and others to which they belong, Sri Rama said: Aitareya, Kaushitaki, Nada-Bindu, Atmabodha, Nirvana, Mudgala, Akshamalika, Tripura, Saubhagya, and Bhavrcha are of 'Rk Veda' opening with Shanti mantra '***Om, Vanme manasi*.....'; Isavasya, Brhadaranyaka, Jabala, Hamsa, Parama-Hamsa Subala, Niralamba, Matrika, Trisikhi Brahmana, Mandala- Brahmana, Advaya- Taraka, Paingala, Bhikshu, Turiyaateeta, Aadhyatma, Tarasara, Yajnyavalkya, Satyayani, and Muktika belong to Sukla Yajurveda. " ***Om, Purnamada Poornasya*......." is the Shanti Mantra of these 19 Upanishads. Krishna Yajurveda has 32 Upanishads with the Shanti Mantra beginning with "***Sahanaavavatu, Sahnau Bhunaktu...***"

Sama Veda has Kena, Chandogya, Aruni, Maitrayani, Vajrasuchika, Yoga Chudamani, Vasudeva,- Mahat Sanyasa, Avyakta, Kundika, Savitri, Rudrakasha, Jabala, Darshana, and Jabali with the Shanti Mantra beginning with '***Apyaayantu*......"

' ***Om, Bhadram Karnebhi*.......' is the beginning of the Shanti Mantra of 31 Upanishads of Atharvaveda and some of the most important ones are: Prsna, Mundaka, Mandukya, Maha-Narayana, Rama-Rahasya, Rama Taapani, etc.

It is emphasized here that, "Jnyaana path and not through Karma, Samkhya-Yoga, and other Upanishads that one can attain final emancipation"[*Muktikopanishad*]. It is impossible to go into all these 108 Upanishads in detail in an introductory text like this. Hence, a brief summary of the more important Upanishads is given here for the benefit of getting an insight into the significance of the Upanishads. However, those interested in further detailed study may go to full texts of individual Upanishads.

*Ishavasya Upanishad*

Ishavasya Upanishad is the Mantropanishad par excellence. It is the last chapter of Shukla-Yajurveda Samhita. It is also known as Samhitopanishad since it is found as an integral part of a Samhita. It is the Mantropanishad par excellence {***Srimadbhagavata VIII, 1,9, and 17***]. Due to its nature (spiritual) and style of expositions, numerous scholars have given commentaries on this Upanishad. 'Isopanishad' gets its name from the opening word of the first mantra that reads:

*"Om, Isavasyamidam sarvam yatkincha jagatyam jagat*
*tena tyaktena bhunjita maa grudaah kasyasviddhanam."*

Meaning, "*Whatever there is changeful in this ephemeral world, - all that must be enveloped by the Lord. By this renunciation of this world, support yourself. Do not covet the wealth of anyone*". This entire world belongs to God and those born here should enjoy it in a spirit of detachment. In other words, nothing belongs to us and there is no place for greed and avarice; one should never covet others possessions or deprive them of their possessions. It follows that the people should strive for the spiritual and temporal welfare of others. Nishkama karma (elaborately dealt in the Gita) will not taint and will not become a cause for suffering or rebirth. If these fundamentals of moral and ethical rules are not followed, suffering and misery are certain. One can live a hundred years if these moral and ethical values are imbibed in life and will live happily, too. One must always live an austere life performing the rites and duties and thinking of the Lord. Total surrender to Lord will relieve us from bondage.

*The nature of 'Self' is explained in the fourth and fifth mantra:*

*"Anejadekam manso javeeyo Nainadyeva aapnuvan purvamarshat.*
*Tadvaavato anyaanatyeti tishtat,*
*tasminnapo maatarishvaa dadhyaati.*
*Tadejati tannaijaati tad doore tadvantike,*
*tadantarasya sarvasya tadu sarvasyasya baahyatah."*

Meaning, "The Self, the Atman is one. It moves faster than the Mind and thus beyond the reach of the senses. Atman being 'all-pervading', it is ever steady and outstrips all that run. There is nothing that can go beyond it. Atman being the 'Consciousness', the principle behind life, is the sustainer of life and activities. By its mere presence (awakening), it enables the cosmic energy to sustain the activities of the living beings. The Atman really does no function; it is the cosmic energy that translates itself into all activities of life, mind itself being a manifestation of it. The cosmic energy is also known as 'sutratman' and 'Prana'. In its real absolute state the Atman is immutable, but appears ever-changing. It is omnipresent. It is very difficult to attain for the ignorant; but a wise person knows that it is not far since 'It' is his own self. It is immanent and also transcendent (i.e., beyond creation and beyond limitations). Thus, these verses 3 to 5 make it imperative that one should take to spiritual practice for the Realisation of Self. It is the ordained duty of the Veda. "***What delusion, what sorrow is there for the wise man who sees the unity of existence and perceives all beings as his own self!***"

He (the Self), the Supreme Ruler is the self-effulgent, all- pervading, eternal, and absolutely pure.

For the house-holders, performance of Vedic rituals and ordained duties of life will bring purity of Mind and hence, knowledge leading to liberation. Meditation on Isha (God) practiced by such a pure mind will lead ultimately to realizing Him leading to moksha.

Here; action (Karma) and Knowledge (Jnyaan) are important for liberation. Duties and Vedic rites are important insofar as they lead to 'Knowledge'. But ultimately, it is 'knowledge' only that brings liberation. According to an interpretation (Uvatacharya of 11th Cent. A.D.), God, the absolute is "Parabrahman' is 'sambhuti'. Asambhuti is vinasa or destruction of the physical body by the hunger and thirst (for the Lord). The spiritual practices, exercises or sadhana (effort) is an invaluable instrument; and, through contemplation of Brahman one can attain immortality. Prayers addressed to the Lord are given in the Verses 15-18. It is very interesting that the Lord, Sri Hari, Narayana is the One Supreme Self behind the blinding glare of the Sun and once the orb of the Sun is removed one can visualize Him. It is, in a sense, the materialistic attractions that blind us and we do not get the hidden glorious face of the Lord. It is in this sense, that a monastic life is said to be more suitable to spiritual practices or 'Sadhana'. In the ordinary life, that too in modern day life, it is well neigh impossible to even think of the Lord let alone take up spiritual practices!

*Kena Upanishad*

This is one of the ancient and more important Upanishads of Samaveda. It has four sections, first two in poetry and last two in prose, in all containing 35 Verses. The student asks the question (Kena?) in the beginning; hence, the Upanishad has come to be known by the name Kenopanishad. It starts with the Shanti mantra:

*"Om, Sahanaavavatu. Sahanau bhunaktu. Sahaveeryam karvaavahai. Tejasvi naavadheetamastu. Maa vidvishaavahai."*

Meaning, "May He protect us both (the teacher and the student or the Preceptor and the disciple). May He nourish us, both. May we both work together with great energy. May our study be thorough, and fruitful May we never hate each other." It is very interesting to note here the stress laid on the physical well-being and the recognition of the Almighty as the protector. Hence the prayer to keep us physically fit. It calls for sincere faith in the Lord, Brahman (the Atman, the Self in us) and the invocation to Lord to protect us without denying us his divine Grace.

The Upanishad begins with the question: Who is the hearer? Who is the seer? Who is that who is behind our Mind to perceive things and who impels the mind to alight on its objects?

To these questions, the reply is: *"There is one indomitable spirit, the Brahman, the Self who is behind everything; and, it is He who is the ear of the ear, eye of the eye, and the tongue speaks, the mind understands and life functions. The wise man separates the Atman from these faculties, rises out of the sensual life and attains immortality. The eye does not go there, nor speech, nor mind. We do not therefore know it, nor do we know any process of instructing about it. These sense organs are only the tools to perceive the external objects; and, the atman is the 'animating principle' behind action. No one can go into one's own self. It is impossible to impart the knowledge concerning the Atman to others since Brahman is beyond the comprehension of the senses and the mind."*

*"Since Brahman is the real knower of all that is known through the senses and the mind and itself is not an object of knowledge, one can never say that one has known him nor not know him. Awareness of Brahman is felt every moment of our life. But, through spiritual practices one can experience him and gain the real strength and immortality."*

*"Brahman is Supreme and not even the gods in heaven, like Indra, Agni, Vayu could win the battle against the 'asuras' without His 'Grace'.*

The Goddess Uma Haimavati, the effulgence or 'Knowledge', teaches Indra, the king of the gods. One has to meditate on him as 'tadvana' (a highly desirable one)."

The scripture have ordained the householders to adhere to an austere way of life and, desist all temptations of worldly life, and practise spiritual rites and perform duties. Self-control and karma are the means of attaining Brahman. This is Veda, the 'Truth'.

*Katha Upanishad*

This Upanishad belongs to the Krishna Yajurveda. It is also known as the Kathaka Upanishad. It deals with the story of Nachiketas and Yama. It is found in 'Rk Veda' Mandala 10. The Taittiriya Brahmana [3.1.8] gives an outline of the Nachiketas story and the whole story is given here.

Once King Vajasravasa, also known as Auddaalaki Aruni, was performing the Visvajit sacrifice. As the sacrifial offerings, he had to give away all his wealth that included the cows. Nachiketas, son of Auddaalaka Aruni, was sad that his father was offering the cows that were old and useless (do not give birth to calf or yield milk). He thought, "joyless, verily are those worlds to which he goes, who gives such cows that have drunk their water, eaten their hey, given their milk for the last time and would calve no more", and asked his father 'to whom he was being gifted'. At first he did not reply. When Nachiketas persisted twice, thrice, he lost his temper. In a fit of hot temper, Aruni said, 'he would offer him to Yama, the god of death.'

With the permission of his father, Nachiketas went to meet Yama. Since Yama was not there in his abode, Nachiketas had to wait; he did not touch water and food till Yama returned. It was after three days that Yama returned and found the young boy Nachiketas waiting for him without water or food. He enquired him about the purpose of his visit. He heard the whole story of the Visvajit sacrifice and felt sad. He offered three boons to Nachiketas to make him happy.

Nachiketas wanted that his father to be happy and cheerful; so, the first boon went to pacify his angry father and receive him well when he gets back home. The second boon is the 'Fire Sacrifice' that came to be known as 'Nachiketas fire' ("***Nachiketagni***") Yajnya that would enable a person to reach heaven.

The third boon is the one that is very interesting for it is the main theme of this Upanishad. It deals with the secret of 'death' and 'thereafter'. In the beginning Yama did not want to disclose the secrets; but he had no other go. He had to keep up his words for Nachiketas was very well versed in the "knowledge" of the rituals and there was no harm in imparting him the secrets. Thus, the secrets of death and the fate of the departed souls form the central idea of the ***Kathopanishad*** as revealed to Nachiketas by Yama, the god of death.

Nachiketas asked Yama, "***What happens to a person when he is dead? Whether he continues his existence even after the death of the physical body, or not?***

Since these questions concerning the Self are extremely subtle and difficult to comprhend, Yama offered Nachiketas option to ask for any other boon except this question. But, Nachiketas was determined to know about the knowledge of the Self and the way to get out of transmigration, repeated births and deaths. Hence, Yama, the god of death had to reveal the secrets; but he did so indirectly as follows:

Human beings have two options: shreyas and preyas. Shreyas is the Supreme Truth, the knowledge of which brings salvation. Preyas is worldly pleasure, momentarily attractive but ultimately disastrous. Those who opt for 'shreyas' will realze the Atman, the true self of all.

This Atman is difficult to comprehend and a person who is already a realized Self can guide in the matter and the path is known as adhyatmayoga, or Yoga of Contemplation. "Om is the means of attaining the Brahman. Atman is the smaller than the smallest and greater than the greatest. It is also established in the hearts of all. A person of pure, calm and controlled mind may realize and go beyond the cycle of births and deaths. Not even the study of the scriptures or memory of all that will help attaining the Self, but an intense desire 'to know' will do. 'Yama' and 'Niyama' are the basic requirements for a spiritual aspirant and one should lead an austere life if one wants to realize the Self. The consciousness of the atman is a matter of intuitional perception and as such it is to be experienced.

*"Etadhyevaaksharam brahma, etaddhyevaksharam param;*
*etadhyevaksharam jnyatva yo yad ichchati tasyatat." [16]*

Meaning, "***Om is the syllable Brahman, this syllable is the highest; having known this syllable whatever one desires, he gets that.***" Yama goes on to describe the true nature of the Self in the Verses 18 -20.

"The Self, the soul is neither born nor does it die. It has not come into being fom anything, nor anything has come into being from it. This unborn, eternal, ever-lasting ancient One Atma suffers no destruction, even when the body is destroyed. If the killer thinks that he is killing, and the killed thinks that he is killed, both of them know it not. It kills not. Nor is it killed."

This is exactly the advice (Hitopadesha) given by Sri Krishna to Arjuna in the battlefield of Kurukshetra when the latter asked, "How can I kill all these kith and kin?" [Gita II-19-20]

"*The Self is realized by the self of the aspirant who does not desire anything whatsoever except the Self or Atman*". Non-Advaitins interpret this in a different way. They put it as: the Self is attained by him alone whomever God chooses." Thus, for we mortals, it appears that only a person of the stature of Nachiketas who has a thirst and hunger for the knowledge of the Self, who has all the knowledge of the rites, can attain the Self, that too with the help of the god of death, Yama.

"The individual soul is enmeshed in a body-mind complex. The body is the chariot, the senses are the horses, and the mind is the reins. The intellect is the charioteer. The Self is the master of the chariot. The objects of the senses are the paths by which the chariot moves. If an expert, disciplined charioteer controls the horses, he can reach the right destination, the abode of 'Vishnu'. If the charioteer is indisciplined and the senses are not controlled he will go astray leading to disaster. In other words, a person of, impure mind and uncontrolled senses will end up in samsara or transmigration.

The problem with the human mind and the senses is that both need some control and guidance. The Mind needs be tutored and the senses need be disciplined. The senses always tend to go outwards and consequently our interest is more in outside world. But, once in a way, the mind the senses which are out-going shall turn inward and find that the inner world is much more fascinating! Only such persons who discover their inner world realize their 'Self'.

One ought to know that, "Nothing is superior to the Purusha, the supreme goal. The Panchamahabhutas, the five rudimentary forms of matter, out of which have come all the objects perceived through the senses, are superior to the senses. The Mind is superior to the objects because it perceives the latter and is subtler than the matter. The intellect is superior to the Mind and the Great Atman is superior to the intellect because it is the 'Hiranyagarbha' the macrocosmic soul, which is considered as the aggregate of individual souls. But, of all these, 'Purusha' is the supreme." [III-10-11].

Yama, god of death declares that, "it is possible to realize the Atman through meditation; the person who seeks Atman should strive for purity of mind and control the senses and keep away from sense objects which are constantly diverting his attention. The Atman is well within the reach of everybody. It resides in the heart; it is of the size of the thumb. Once a person realizes the atman, he becomes united with him."

The 'Atman' is further described as the Sun, the Moon, and is in every object of the universe. He is omnipresent; He directs the biological functions of the body from inside. In fact, he resides there and makes the body full of life and consciousness. Those who are enmeshed in the cycles of transmigration take different forms according to their Karma, good or bad deeds. If some are reborn as humans or any other living beings of higher or lower type, others may even enter inert objects! Only those who realize this Atman, i.e., Brahman, succeed in attaining everlasting peace and not others.

The whole world is Samsara, a tree with roots far flung outward (not inward inside earth). It is an upside-down tree with branches spread below.

The Prana, i.e., Brahman, is the source of power of sustenance of the whole creation. It is a very powerful, terrific force, that make the sun, moon and planets go round. *"For fear of him, the sun shines, for fear of him do Indra, Vayu and Yama, the fifth, proceed with their respective functions* [IV-3]. *The Mrutyu, god of death runs away for fear of him! [See Mahamantra, the Mantra raja, in Narasimhopanishad]. Those who know this become immortal. 'Ritam' and Satyam' is maintained in this universe for fear of Him. He protects all those who are God-fearing and follow his 'Ritam' and 'Satyam', i.e., 'Order' and 'Truth'. This is "Dharmo rakshati rakshitah".*

It is necessary to conquer the Mind in order to achieve this single main objective of attaining the Brahman. Self-control through Yoga, dhyan, and meditation is the sure way to achieve this mind control. It is in the state of 'turiya' in samadhi that one would realize the 'supreme Bliss' when the thousand lotus petals bloom in sahasraara through the opening up of the subtle tubular structure called the 'sushumna' nadi. The realized souls leave the body through this 'Archiramarga' the bright path of 'Devayana' and goes to Brahma Lok, the abode of Brahman, never to return to this mundane world.

One must know the art of separating the Self from the body; this is self- knowledge, 'atmajnyaan'. "Brahman cannot be seen with eyes. He is revealed by the intuition of the intellect that resides in the heart and controls the mind. Those who know Him become immortal", says the Upanishad [VI-9].

One need not despair fearing that liberation is not possible and one is condemned in this mrutyu lok forever. The Upanishad gives hope and encouragement and shows the path of achieving the goal through 'adhyatma yoga' with the help of a competent teacher. Everyone need not be a Nachiketas to attain the Brahman. Practical methods of sadhana, practice of Yoga is described in this Upanishad; and, this makes the Kathopanishad very popular.

*Prashna Upanishad*

As the title indicates, this Upanishad is called Prashnopanishad due to the fact that it answers six questions (Prashnas). This belongs to Atharvaveda, Pippalada Shakhaa. Here, the sage Pippalada answers the six questions of philosophical nature. The six students ask Pippalada to tell them about the source of all beings, the number of deities, and the chief among them, the nature and function of Prana, the vital force, the nature of waking, dream and sleep states and the function of the senses in each of these states, meditation on the sacred symbol 'Om' and its efficacy, and finally, the ultimate object, "the nature of the Supreme Brahman, the conscious 'Being'in man". 'Om, Bhadram karnobhih....', is the Shanti Mantra.

"From what indeed are all these beings born?" asked Sage Kabandhi to which the Venerable Sage Pippalada answers:

"Prajapati after deep meditation (tapas) created a pair of Rayi (food) and Prana, i.e., matter and spirit, that would proliferate in multifarious ways. The moon is the food and Prana, the fire, is the eater (the Sun). Whatever is gross or subtle is but food. The gross, as distinguished from that (subtle), is certainly food (of the subtle) [I- 4&5].

Then the question arises, "how is it the formless Prana (life), the eater, is also everything that is eaten (and hence it is all)? The answer is very simple: "The sun illumines all, thereby it absorbs all living things into its rays, that is all. In a way, everything is absorbed by something else since there is no distinction of superior or inferior; everything is food. Only when the distinction is made (due to our ignorance) the gross gets absorbed in the subtle and is considered as food.

The wise know that, "the one that is possessed of all forms (the sun), full of rays, endowed with with illumination, the resort of all, the single light of all, and the radiator of heat. It is the sun that possesses a thousand rays, exist in a hundred forms and is the life of all creatures. The wise know that, 'the sun is 'visvarupam', verily their own soul, '***tat***' exist in many and varied form (sahasrasimih), the life of all creatures."[I-8].

The Sun and the Moon are verily the Time of our solar and lunar calendar based on the movements of revolution and rotation of the earth in relation to the sun and the moon, respectively. Dakshinayana and Uttarayaan, the 'Pitrayan' and the 'Devayaan' (winter and summer solstices) are the path of the earth in the orbit; and, the Upanishad says, 'those who die in Pitrayan will come back to earth; whereas, those who die in Uttarayan or Devayan will reach the solar sphere, the heaven and onward to Brahmalok according to their spiritual attainments. The Krishna Paksha and Sukla Paksha of the lunar months denote the life of plants as food of man for there is a direct relation of life to moon. Many scientists like Norman Borlagh have studied the behavior of plants on full moon nights and found that wheat yields are related to the growth of plants on moonlit nights. However not much is known about this. But there is a certain relation of nocturnal life with the moon. Hence, 'Time' is a relative concept and it is closely associated with the rotation and revolution of the earth around the Sun. Once you leave the earth or travel at the speed of light, i.e., 186000 miles per second, time ceases to exist. Even those who travel in aircrafts faster than the speed of rotation of earth (1040 miles per hour at the Equator) can see several sunrises and sunsets within 24 hours, according to their speed. Once we get out of this earth, there is neither sunrise nor sunset and no time based on the movements of the earth.

Thus, energy, matter, and time are the manifestations of the Brahman. All life on this earth is thus, created by the Lord of the universe, the supreme 'Consciousness', i.e., the Infinite or the Absolute. Prana or food that sustains Prana is also considered as the Lord of all creatures. From food indeed issues that human seed. From that are born these beings [Verse 14].

Moral and ethical values are stressed in the mantra that follow the secrets of creation. Avoidance of falsehood, crookedness and dissimulation are valued most. Uttarayan or the northern course is 'Virajah', is pure and untainted; and, not subject to waxing and waning like the lunar Brahmalok. Those who perform rites without the 'adhyatmayoga' will get fruits according to their good deeds or bad deeds and return to earth in different forms to spend the remaining part of their karma. Chanting of the Lord's name and meditation will surely reduce the prarabdha karma and relieve one from sanchita karma and thus enable one to reach the Brahmalok by Devayaan or path of Uttarayan. This in brief is the answer to the first question of Prashnopanishad.

The second question rises from the fact that, 'Prana is the eater and the Lord of all creatures' It has to be determined how He is the Lord of all creatures as well as the eater in this body. Hence, Bhargava, the son of Bhrugu asked:

Venerable Sir, How many are the deities of the body and who is the chief of them?

The answer to this question is, Sage Pippalada said: "Space in fact is this deity, as also are air, fire, water, earth, the organs of speech, mind, eye, and ear. Exhibiting their glory they say, 'Unquestionably it is we who hold together this body by not allowing it to disintegrate'. To them, the chief Prana said, 'Do not be deluded. It is I who do not allow it to disintegrate by sustaining it by dividing myself fivefold.' Still, they all remained incredulous. To prove his point, Prana appeared to be rising up from the body out of indignation. All others too began to rise up along with Prana. When Prana was quiet all others were in their position; and, all others (senses) then realized how they depended on Prana for their functioning. Delighted at this, they all began to praise Prana.

Here, not only Prana is praised as the master of the body, the Self, but is praised as the Supreme Self, Prajapati Himself. Prana is fire, sun, rain, Indra, Vayu, the earth, in fact, he is the Supreme God. He is Paramesvara or Rudra. It is He who receives all offerings in Sacrifices and it is He that functions as the sense organs. All request Him to protect them as the mother protects her children.

Kausalya asks the third question, He asks Pippalaada:

"How does Prana come into this body? How again does he dwell himself dividing himself manifold? How does he depart? How does he support the external world and that which is within the physical body?

Thus, the essential nature of Prana is discussed here. Pippalaada answers these questions one by one.

From the Self is born this Prana He is like the shadow of the Self. He comes to this body owing to the actions of the Mind.Prana engages the other organs like a King who organizes his Provinces. He places 'Apana' in the two lower apertures. Prana himself, issuing from the mouth and nostrils, resides in the eyes and ears. Saman is in the middle and, this alone distributes equally all the food that is eaten; therefore, these issues out of these seven flames (agni). The Self i.e., the subtle body is in the heart. There are a hundred and one nerves, each one of them with a hundred branches and in turn are divided into seventytwo thousand branches. Among them moves the 'Vyana'. The 'Udana', Prana in its upward trend through sushumna nadi, leads to a virtuous world as a result of virtue, or to a sinful world as the result of sins, or to the human world as a result of both.

The Sun is indeed the external Prana. It supports the Prana in the eye. The deity in the earth supports the Apana. The Space supports the Samana and the air supports the Vyana. Teja or luminosity is the Udana that favours the vital functions of the body. When this light is extinguished the person attains rebirth together with the organs that enter into his mind. Together with whatever thought he had at the time of death, he enters into Prana. Prana in association with Udana and along with the soul leads him to the world desired by him [III-8- 10].

The Fourth question asked by Sauryaayani, the grandson of Surya of the Gargya family is:

O, adorable Sir, Which are the organs that go to sleep in this person? Which keep awake in him? Who experiences the dream? And who is the real enjoyer of the sleep? And, in whom all these get merged?

Of the six, all the first three questions come in the domain of lower knowledge and are concerning the mundane existence. But, this question and the next two questions are about the higher knowledge. They are about the auspicious, calm, unchanging, immutable 'Truth', that is called 'Purusha'. Purusha is the one beyond all; He is beyond the vital force, the mind and the senses. He exists everywhere, internally and externally and is birthless and deathless. The questioner wants to know about the absolute Self and not the Prana that supports all. That supreme immutable from which all things originate is explained in Mundakopanishad.

*"All objects are born like sparks from a blazing fire, and into which they merge again"* ***[Mundakopanishad II-i-1]***

The five questions are quite interesting in that they lead to an awareness of the Self. Who is the perceiver of the waking state? Whoever is dreaming in the second state must be an actor in the first state, the waking state for cessation of activity leads to dream. Whose job is that to maintain the functions of the body in all the three states? Who is the perceiver of the dream and who is the enjoyer of sleep? And, lastly, what is the state that is free from all the three other states- wakefulness, dream and sleep and turiya, as also in cosmic dissolution.

To this, Sage Pippalaada answers:"A person is said to be sleeping when his sense-organs with their experiences become one with the mind. But, the five Pranas like the garhapathya fire are working under the general guidance of the mind. It is this mind that gets all the dream experiences."

However, when the mind with the senses withdrawn into itself is merged in Brahman (in deep sleep), there is no dream. At this time, the body and organs that depend on ignorance, desire, and the result of past actions, become inactive. When these become quiet, the nature of the self, that appears distorted due to the limited adjuncts, becomes non-dual, one, auspices, and calm. There is an experience of happiness. Thus, it is into the Brahman that all get united and dissolved. This one is the seer, ffeeler, hearer, smeller, taster, thinker, ascertainer, doer- the Purusha, pervading the body and organs, that' is the knower by nature. He becomes wholly established in the supreme, immutable Self."

The next question is asked by Satyakama, son of Sibi, 'O venerable Sir, which world does he really win thereby, who among men, intently meditates on—"Om"— in that wonderful way till death'?

To this, Sage Pippalaada say, 'O Satyakama, this very Brahman, that is both inferior and superior, is 'Om'. "Om' is the symbol for Parabrahman as well as Aparabrahman, the manifested and the unmanifested aspects. One can choose to meditate on either of the two. Therefore the illumined one attains either of the two through this one means alone. To those who meditate on 'Om', which is comparable to the images of Vishnu and others and on which is fixed the idea of Brahman with devotion, that Brahman becomes favouravle and reveals itself. Sage Pippalaada explains the significance of Pranava or Onkara, the method of meditating on it and the consequent fruits attained.

"Om" consists of three letters 'A', 'U' and 'M'. But, then there is also a half letter 'm' to end this in a long drawn vibrating sound, that is not discussed here. Should one meditate on the first letter 'A' of the 'Rk' quickly one takes birth as a human and experiences greatness through self-control, continence and faith (Yama and Niyama). Meditating on the second letter 'U' of the Yajurveda, one becomes identified with the mind. This Yajur mantra lifts one to the lunar sphere and experiences greatness in the lunar world (Pitr lok) and retuns here. One who meditates on the third letter 'M', the Supreme Purusha, will be freed from all sins, will be unified with Sun will go to Brahmalok, the abode of Brahman, never to return to mundane existence. The three letters A, U, and M, of 'Om' are within the range of death. But if they are closely joined, one to another, are not divergently applied to different objects, and are applied to three courses of action-external, intermediate and internal- that are properly resorted to, then the man of enlightenment does not shake; he remains undisturbed; rather, becomes 'the Self' (i.e., established), and one with 'Om'. It also means that such an enlightened man is beyond experiences of old age, death and fear. This is immortality!

The Sixth question comes from Sukesha, the son of Bharadwaja. He asks about the 'Purusha' with the Sixteen Aspects (limbs) to which Pippalaada answers, 'that person is one's own body.' He is the Atman. He is the Creator.The Purusha who is partless appears through ignorance, to be possessed of limbs as a consequence of his attachment to the (sixteen parts) limited adjuncts. These sixteen parts get eliminated as one gets enlightened as to the real svaroopa or nature of the Purusha, as an absolute entity. He created Prana or Hiranyagarbha, the primary person (Sutratman), the totality of subtle creation. From this Prana evolved Shrudhdha (Faith), akasha (sky or space), vayu (air), jyoti (fire), apas (water), prithvi (earth), indriya (sense organs), manas (mind), anna (food), veerya (strength of body), tapas (austerity), mantra (Veda), karma (Vedic rituals), lokas (different worlds), and names (different names of objects of creation). All these sixteen aspects depend on Purusha even as the spokes in a wheel on its hub. At the time of dissolution of the world all these get merged in Him, the Purusha, even as the rivers merge in the ocean.

Thus, the six questions being answered the Sages worshipped Sage Pippalaada and returned to their homes. These six answers enlighten as to the nature of Supreme Purusha and the state of human life in wakefulness and sleep. The method of redemption, through 'Om' is also revealed here. Om, "Tat sat."

*Mundakopanishad*

This is an important manthropanishad of Atharvaveda. It deals with the two types of knowledge, para and apara, the need for renunciation, the specific method of meditation on 'Om', and the aspects of liberation. This Upanishad is, preferably, the one for the ascetics, of shaven head (mundaka) who have renounced the world and have taken to Sannyas. Mundaka literally means shaven head, rather 'clearing' ignorance. The Eternal and the Imperishable can be attained only by means of renunciation. First, the Upanishad lays stress on the need for Vedic rites; and later, these are discarded as sheer 'ignorance'! This aspect is to be considered. Mere discharge of rites and rituals as also duties will not help in Self-realization! At best, these will ensure success and happiness in worldly life that is perishable.

Mundakopanishad is considered to be the mini Bhagavad-Gita for it consists of all the essentials of the Vidyas. Step by step, the Upanishad leads to the highest knowledge of the Brahman; it explains all the intricacies of this creation and gives the techniques of emancipation. This Upanishad of the ***Atharvaveda*** belongs to Shaunakiya Shakha since the Sage Angiras taught this to Shaunaka. Atharvan, the eldest son and the pupil of Brahma taught this to his pupil Bharadvaaja Satyavaaha, who in turn taught this to Shaunaka. Thus, this Upanishad was taught to Atharvan directly by Brahma.

*"Om, Brahmadevaanaam prathamahsambabhuva visvasyakarta bhuvanasya gopta,*
*sabrahmavidyaam sarva-vidyapratisthaam Atharvaaya jyestha-putraaya praaha.'*

***[Mundakopanishad]***

Meaning, "Brahma, the creator and protector of the universe appeared first and then all other gods. Brahma, the Creator taught this Science of the Spirit, the basis of all other sciences, to his eldest son Atharvan." In fact, Veda is one and that is Atharvaveda; from it the three divisions, viz, the Rk Veda, the Yajur Veda, and the Sama Veda have come.

First question raised in this Upanishad is about the source of Knowledge. Shaunaka asks the Sage Angiras: "*Sir, what is that, knowing which everything in the world becomes known?*"

There are two kinds of knowledge to be acquired- one a lower and the other a higher. The lower knowledge consists of the study of Rk Veda, Yajur Veda, Sama Veda and Atharva-veda, phoenetics, the code of rituals, grammar, etymology, metrics and astronomy. Now the higher knowledge is that by which the imperishable is attained. In fact everything that does not lead to attainment of Self comes under lower knowledge. That alone which brings in the knowledge of the Self is higher knowledge. The source of all creation is 'That' which is invisible, ungraspable, attributeless, that never originated and is formless; 'It' is eternal, 'Vish' (all-pervading), immeasurably subtle and limitless in manifestation. That imperishable is the source of all creation. [I-1-6].

The Upanishad starts with the description of the universe (Upanishadic Cosmology) and the means of knowing Him, the Brahman. It explains the relation of the Jeevatman and Paramatman with a beautiful imagery of 'dva suparna' two falcons sitting on a tree. Finally, the Upanishad paves the way for the realsiation of the Self with the sacred Mantra "Om".

From the 'Imperishable', the "Om", the world springs out just as the spider emits and withdraws the web, or, the herbs sprout on the earth, or, the hair grows on the body of man effortlessly. From 'tapas' (heat generated from thought force or the effect of contemplation, or concentration) of the Brahman ('Tapasaa chiyate Brahma') has this world evolved. Brahman swells with joy of creation and this joy has produced anna, prana (energy), manah (mind), 'satyam' (Truth, or, the panchabhutas- the five elements), loka (seven world-Bhu, bhuvar, svar, mahat, janah, tapah and Satya), karma (endless entanglement in work) and its fruits (amritam), i.e., immortality. Here, the apparent manifestation of the supreme is the attribute of 'Maya', since the Supreme Brahman is attributeless. Brahman's ***creative thought*** is 'Knowledge' itself, and this is the 'all-wise' and 'omniscient'. 'Knowledge' accompanying creative thought signifies unaffectedness. No one can question this creative ability or the creative intelligence of the Supreme Brahman, the 'Supreme Consciousness'. This is one of the attributes of the Brahman and is found in all his creations as is evident from the spiritual attainments of the Sadhakas who attain mystic powers as by-products of incessant sadhana, and there is no wonder in it!

The very first question is an essential question of all sciences and philosophy. All knowledge, ultimately, should lead to 'self-realisation'. This knowledge of the Brahman, the Imperishable, is the superior knowledge called 'Para-vidya', Higher Knowledge. All other knowledge including the Veda and other Scriptures belongs to the category of 'Apara-vidya', i.e., the Lower Knowledge. By knowing Him everything else is known; the knowledge of the Self will reveal the true nature of everything else!

The Second Section of the First Mundaka deals with the Mantra (hymns). Persons desirous of enjoying the fruits of their work (Karma) should strictly adhere to the ritualistic practices as enunciated in the three Veda. They should carry out the rituals such as kindling sacrificial fire, offering oblations with full faith (shrudhdha and bhakti); use of pure ghee is also stressed here. Agnihotra is the first of all sacrifices. Details of the sacrifice is given in the Verses I- ii- 2 to7. But, it is also warned here, "that fools, thinking themselves as wise and learned, wander about suffering again and again, like the blind led by the blind. By being subject to passions and attachment, they never attain Knowledge, and they sink down wretched, when the fruits of their good deeds are exhausted. These deluded men do fancy sacrifices and charitable works to be the highest, and know naught better." [1-ii-8 to 10]. Only those ascetics, sanyasins, those who live in forests (solitude), leading a life of austerity and devout worship- peaceful, wise, and un-attached to even a spare loin-cloth and drinking bowl, these stainless men only will travel by 'devayaan' to Satya Lok, rather, travel by the solar gate to the Brahmalok, i.e., Immortality. [1-ii-11].

The First section of the Second Mundaka deals with the Nature of the Self. All Beings born out of fire go back to it like "the sparks of a blazing fire burn out and return to it." "From him are born life, mind, senses, ether, air, fire, water and earth that supports all. Verily, He is the indwelling spirit within all. Fire is His head; the sun and moon are His eyes; the quarters His ears; the revelation (the Veda) His voice; the wind His breath; the universe His heart. And from His feet the earth has originated. From Him comes the 'Svar" (heaven world), which is the first Fire, having the sun for its fuel; from moon come the rain clouds (second Fire) issue forth;and from the clouds and rain issue forth the herbs, the food of man. Indeed, the food of man is the source of strength and procreation. Practically everything on this earth including the Veda has come from Him."

The Second Section of the Second Mundaka gives the technique of reaching Him, who sits and moves in the cavity of the human heart and states that, "all that move and breath and wink are established in it. It is the cause of both the gross and subtle; and, the most adorable and beyond understanding of all creatures." "Luminous, subtler than even the atoms, the imperishable Brahman is the abode of the world and all its inhabitants. It can be reached by the Pranava mantra 'Om'. Taking as bow the mighty weapon furnished by the Upanishads, fix on it the arrow rendered sharp by constsnt meditation. Having drawn the string of the arrow (withdrawing all sense organs from sense objects) mind absorbed in His thought, penetrate the Imperishable Brahman. 'Om', the mystic syllable is the bow, the Self within, the arrow; and, Brahman, the target. Undistracted, hit the target and merge in Him. Know Him alone as the one Self of all and desist from all unnecessary talk. Meditate on that Self as 'Om'. Verily it is He who shines; He is everywhere. All this world indeed, is Brahman" [II-ii-2-11].

Section One of the Third Mundaka is very interesting. It gives the imagery of two falcons bound in close friendship, sitting on the same branch of a tree. One is eating the fruits of the tree with relish, while the other looks on.

*"Dva suparna sayujaa sakhaayaa samaanam vruksham parishasvajati*
*tayoranya pippalam svaadvattyanasnan anyo abhichakshasi.*
*Samaane vrukshe purushonim agneanishaya agochati muhyamanah*
*Justam yada pashyati anyameeshamasya mahimanam iti vita-shokah.*

Here, the two birds (falcons) are the jeevatman and the paramatman. The Jivatman is the Pure Consciousness limted by ignorance that makes one feel he is bound by body, mind, karma and moha (attachment). Paramatman, on the other hand is Pure Consciousness conditioned by Maya (cosmic power), but being devoid of ignorance, is free, intelligent, eternal and omniscient. Also, the two birds are compared to mind and consciousness since it is the mind that is considered responsible for action and enjoyment. The Jeevatman is nothing but the image of the Paramatman seen through the medium of the mind. The real Self, the Atman, remains always untainted by such modifications of the mind and simply witnesses them. Seated on the self-same tree, one of them (the personal Self) is sunken in ignorance and deluded, grieves for his impotence. But when he sees the other –the Lord, as His glory, he becomes free and joyful. When the individual comes to realize the transcendental reality of his own individual self, i.e., the Lord of all beings untouched by passing phenomena of life, the feeling of joy and sorrow vanishes; rather he realizes his own Self. When the seer realizes the self-effulgent Being, the source of the Creator, in himself, he attains supreme Unity. He becomes truly wise, devoid of his ego and never delighting in the Self. Only austerity (tapas), Meditation, jnyaan, continence, withdrawing the senses from all worldly attractions will pave the way for the realization of the Self.

***"Satyameva Jayate naanrutam'***, i.e., "Only truth prevails and nothing else", are the Vedic words reiterated in the Upanishad here. Brahman is the Truth. It is subtler than the subtlest, farther than the farthest, nearer than the nearest; it is here within the body. It resides in the heart; it is the heart of the hearts. When the thought is purified, i.e., when budhdhi is withdrawn from senses, the Self shines forth. Whatever spheres the man of purified nature desires, whatever objects he fixes his heart upon, he obtains those worlds and those objects. This is a very important Vedic statement reiterated by the Upanishad here. There should not be any hankering; one should work with a pure heart and pure mind. That is all, 'Om, 'Tat sat'.

The Second Section of the Third Mundaka says, "Whoever longs for objects of desire, brooding over them, they are born here and there for the satisfaction of those desires. Desires vanish for a wise man, a man of purified soul; and, there is no wandering! Wisdom lies in understanding, realizing the Self by contemplation, meditation and tapas, not by scriptures and rituals. Those realized souls see their own selves in every other being and the world ceases to exist as 'the other' for they have merged in 'It'. Whoever knows the supreme Brahman becomes the very Brahman. This is the very Truth.

*Mandukya Upanishad*

This is a very small Upanishad of the Atharvaveda that analyses the three states of Consciousness. It is considered the basic to the principles of Advaitic Vedanta.The Upanishad simply states that 'Om', the Ekakshara Brahma, the Pranava is everything. It is the Atman, the Self, also the supreme Consciousness. It is the same Conciousness in the state of a person's jagrata (wakefulness), svapna (dream), susupti (deep sleep), and turiya (the fourth). All this, the manifested world, is the Pranava, "OM' consisting of three letters:" AUM". Whatever exists in Time, and also beyond Time, is 'Om'. There are four aspects of Brahman. The first one is Vaisvanara; the atman of the individual self in its wakeful state. He is the cogniser. He experiences the external objects, gross material objects. The second aspect is Taijasa. It is associated with the dream state. He experiences the subtle objects. The third aspect is the Prajnya. He is the same atman who experiences the state of deep sleep. This is a state of solid cognition with no desires or dreams. It is full of bliss and the person enjoys bliss. He is the Lord, knows all and controls everything. He is the origin of the world, too. The fourth aspect is Turiya, different from all the other three. Since He is beyond the ken of the senses, He is indescribable. He is 'ekamevaadvitiya', the One without a second. He is the universal Self, the Subject of contemplation, meditation, attainment and realisation.

The Vaisvanara is the first syllable 'A' of the AUM ('Om). The Taijasa is 'U' and Prajnya is 'M'. The Turiya is beyond all and it is He into whom all dissolve. It is the vibration of the 'Om', represented by a half letter (m) and it prolongs after the 'Sphota'.

The Mahavakya: "*Ayam atma brahma*' is stated in the second verse of the Upanishad. Atman is pure Consciousness, different from the body-mind complex; it is equated with the Brahman, the cause of and the spirit behind the universe. This is the sum and substance of all the Upanishads highlighted by the Mandukya Upanishad here. One who realizes this is released from all bondage.

*Taittiriyopanishad*

Although the central theme of all Vedanta is to convey the significance of 'Self-realisation', the way the different Upanishads are imparted by different teachers is quite interesting. In this Upanishad, belonging to Yajurveda has Samhita, Brahmana, and Aranyaka. This is one of the most important Upanishads commented upon by many spiritual leaders and it is very authoritative according to Brahma-sutra-bhashya. The Upanishad starts with the Invocation:

*"Harih Om! Sham no mitrah, sham varunah, sham no bhavat aryama.*

*Sham no Indrah bruhaspatih, sham no vishnururkrumah.*
*Namo brahmane. Namste vayo, tvameva pratyaksham brahmaasi.*
*Tvameva pratyaksham brahmavadishyaami. Satyam vadishyaami.*
*Tanmaavavatu tadvaktaaramavatu, avatu maam, avatu vaktaaram.*
*Om, Shantih, Shantih, Shantih.* ***[Rk Veda, I- 90-.9; I-164-46].***

The above Invocation mantra is addressed to Mitra and Varuna to ward of all possible obstacles on the path of the seekers of Brahmavidya. Importance of proper chanting of the mantra is stressed in order to make it effective and fruitful; accent, quantity, rhythm, sequence, and the form of the speech sounds are all very important if the mantra are to be very effective.

First mind should be made pure by meditation. Hence, the proper methods of meditation are explained. The benefits of meditation not only include spiritual awakening but material prosperity is also assured. Hence this Upanishad is slightly different from the others for it goes in a methodical way from the gross to subtle in a worldly way. First, the phoenetics and then the prayer for wellbeing and success followed by methods of meditation and prayer for material prosperity; these prayers formulated are quite important in the present day context. It also highlights the need for total involvement of both the teacher and the student in the learning process that is totally absent in present day education.

The ***Taittiriya Upanishad*** is important in many ways. It teaches about the mystic expressions and unfolds the subtle relations among the cosmic regions and some vital and intellectual functions. It creates a higher capacity in the student to concentrate on the Supreme Brahman. It directs all attention of the student to the heart and inspires him to seek the effulgent, immortal and the intelligent Purusha, Brahman in the 'bright', but vacant, space called the 'spiritual heart' very close to the 'physical organ that pumps the blood. The Upanishad explains how the embodied spirit passes on to the crown center through the region of the uvula near the upper palate and unites itself with the Supreme Lord at the end. These are quite revealing! It is only in later Yogic practices like the Kundalini Yoga that the Jiva merging with the Supreme Lord is explained.

"He who realizes Brahman attains the Supreme. With reference to that very fact it has been declared: 'Brahman is Existence, Intelligence, Infinitude; he who realizes Him treasured in the cave, in the highest ether, fulfils all wants together, as Brahman the Omniscient.' [II-1-1]. As reality, as knowledge as Bliss, as Infinite, "He who knows such Brahman concealed in the cavity of the heart and in the highet space, attains allwishes".

There is need for some basic understanding regarding the single point of Unity of all existence. The superficial world is so complex, full of names, forms and functions that blind us as to the Reality. Practically nothing exists that is Real and lasting; everything is 'magical', make-believe, floating and fast disappearing! Even the wisest are tempted to believe this world as real; only a jnyaani knows it all, the spiritual reality, substance of experiential reality, the Brahman! This realization of Brahman is not limited to mere intellectual apprehension; it is really a profound experience in which the ordinary consciousness, working in the realm of time and space through subject-object relation, is transcended- widened, depened into its essence, the Brahman. Only in the state of in-drawn concentration known as 'Asamprajnyata' or 'Nirvikalpa Samadhi', one can get the vision of this 'Divine Unity'. Thus, Brahman, the ultimate Reality, is in essence "Being, Intelligence, and Infinitude". Hence, it is said that, "One who knows Brahman becomes Brahman". The word Brahman comes from the root 'Brh', meaning, 'to grow without any limit'.

"From that very Atman i.e., the Brahman, the ether came to be; from ether air, from air fire, from fire water, from water, earth and herbs, from herbs food, and from food the person, came to existence. He indeed is the man consisting of the essence of food.

'***Atman***' is the First Principle from which the whole universe has emanated; and in that sense, it is equated with Brahman. Atman is conceived as the First principle because it is the background of all that we conceive and perceive; it is, rather, the Pure Consciousness which is also the Existence and Infinitude, first emanates space embodying the subtle rudiment of matter known as ether along with time; this evolute develops into more distinct forms and becomes the whole relative phenomena. The quality of sound is associated with this spatial ether as reception of sound demands ether; air is evolved from ether with an added quality of touch; still more gross is fire- that form of energy which is cognized as heat and light- with the quality of colour superadded; water spings up from fire with its specific quality of taste; and finally the last constituent of the universe, earth, is evolved with the quality of smell included. This is the analysis of the universe and its constituents that make the sensuous perception possible as a standard measure to all humans.

This theory of '***Vedic Cosmogony***' clearly brings out the ***tanmatras***, the five elements (Pancha- mahabhutas) that constitute the universe. They sum up inorganic creation, which in its turn gives rise to organic creation through vegetation and food, and on to evolution of mankind. From the point of view of Liberation of man from cycle of rebirths and sufferings, this vedantic or metaphysical theory is more important than the scientific theories that do not help self-realization in any way. None but the absolute Reaity is truly free and perfect. Man becomes liberated only when he realizes that he is that Reality, the Brahman. His descent from Brahman is linked with the evolution of the whole universe cognized as the five elements and their products.

All organisms are produced from inorganic matter, and they subsist on it; finally, they are dissolved into it after the period of life. There is thus a fundamental unity in Nature. 'Annam', the cosmic Being who is manifest in the form of food, or matter exists both as the consumer and the consumed. Here, 'Brahman' assumes the multiplicity and diversity of aspects by being immanent in all things, essentially invisible and yet manifesting. In the form of Annam, the Supreme Being outgrows His ownm nature ***[Rk Veda, Purushasukta 2].***

This '*Atman-Brahman Reality*' is the key to liberation. Just as the most sublime Atman became gross and gross in an outward evolution to the finite and limited, it is possible for the limited and the finite, Man, to get back to the Infinite and the Unlimited by an 'involution' process. This is possible for man by realizing his own subtler existence in his own Self, the Atman, i.e., the jeevatman. Jeevatman and the Parmatman are but one and the same; and, this can be experienced in Nirvikalpa Samadhi, by meditation. Atman in the Purusha (Man) is thus merged in the Parmatman of the Mahapurusha (the God). It is the Kana, the microcosmic particle or cell merging with the macrocosm, the Akhand in a process of 'involution'. The Pranava, 'Om' is the means of this 'yuj', union of the atman with the paramatman. "Om, Namah Shivaaya" or "Om, Namah Narayanaaya" is the mantra.

This Upanishad brings out the essence as the Eternal Truth, and the object of devotion is the union with Immortal Brahman whose body is Infinite Space, whose essence is 'Truth', whose delight is 'Vital force', whose mind is 'Bliss', and who is peace consummate. The Pranava, 'Om' is the symbol of meditation highlighted in this Upanishad and one should meditate on 'Om' to achieve what he wants.

The *Taittiriya Upanishad* is important in more than one way. The ethical principles and practices of the students of Brahmavidya are obligatory and the students must be dutiful, meditative, self-controlled, calm, hospitable, worshipping, humane, and ever intent on seeking and imparting sacred knowledge. Even the teachers have their own specifics such as adherence to truthfulness, devout austerity, learning and teaching of the Scriptures. The rites, duties, and obligations of the students are all clearly explained in this Upanishad and it is a text for the would-be role models, intent seekers of spiritual knowledge. It is the ideal Upanishad for the beginners!

The fundamentals of the Reality of Existence are brought out in this Upanishad. It says, "Physical man is an evolutionary product of the Atman-Brahman Reality. The panchamahabhutas are the building blocks and, water and food are the supporting aspects. Spiritually the same Reality miraculously enters into his embodiment ensouling it! From any point of view, it is Brahman who is the foundation of the human personality and it is possible to realize this 'Self' by proper inquiry into one's own self. The five 'koshas' are the coverings of ignorance and the same is discarded one by one by the sword of Sri Hari, i.e., 'Knowledge'. The elemental self (annamaya kosha) ensouls the vital self (the pranamaya kosha); the latter ensouls the thinking self (jnyanamaya kosha), which ensouls the Knowing self (vijnyanamaya kosha). And, this last one ensouls the bliss itself (anandamaya kosha); all these are founded on Brahman residing five-layer deep. Brahman is the core of human personality. Some are prone to think that it is like a seed within the shell, which is wrong; the Atman is not the seed to be found in the Koshas as the seed in a fruit. It only drives home the fact that, 'one should go from the gross and grossier to subtler and subtler; that is the path to self- knowledge'.

The ***Atmnan-Brahman Reality*** is to be realized by our own selves by introspection. There is every possibility that a doubt arises as to the existence of Brahman. But, it is warned here that, "whoever denies the existence of Brahman in oneself denies himself". "One's own existence proves the existence of Brahman. The acceptance of 'Brahman as the innermost self of all' is very important." It is further explained here that, "Before evolution of the manifested universe, a non-Being or a 'Being that cannot be described' existed. It shaped itself of its own accord. It is this Reality, that is of the nature of boundless facility or 'Rasa', that evolved itself into the omnific universe by its own will and tenanted every being as its own very essence: He took shape but remained shapeless; took limits (adjuncts of body), but remained limitless; made its home (in the body) and remained outside; became everything and everything is Reality".

The Atman- Brahman Reality is not just an inert principle; it is the fundamental or basic principle on which the universe rests. It is the intelligent, Infinite Being and from the One, the Absolute, the supreme Bliss that is present in all emanates. All joy of creatures is the reflection of this supreme Bliss. The self in Man is the same as the Self in the Sun. This Supreme Bliss can be attained by all through renunciation of desire.

*Aitareyopanishad*

This Upanishad of the 'Rk Veda' is an aranyaka dated back to 600 B.C. and there is also the Aitareya Brahmana, also attributed to Mahidasa Aitareya. [Chand.III-16-7]. The Third Aranyaka is separately known as Samhitopanishad. Although not a Brahmin by birth, Aitareya born to Aitara, one of the wives of Mahidasa, was raised to the status of a Sage by sheer divine grace and austerity.

Aitareya Aranyaka deals with different Sastras, in a pure ritualistic manner. It describes at length the austerities and the meaning of the Vedic rites and rituals. The rituals and meditations in connection with 'Pranavidya' are given in detail; also a lengthy exposition of the Atman is given in 'Atmashatka'. Prana is considered as the First cause of the universe here. Self- knowledge attained by rites and rituals without any desire for the self is the only path to supreme Bliss and Immortality according to Aitareya. The Upanishad dwells at length on the universe and man, the Matter and Spirit, ('anna and annada') and says, 'Prajapati is also Hiranyagarbha Purusha- the innermost essence of the visible universe'. Human personality is centred on action (Karma) and that personality is the sphere in which Brahman dwells ***as the witness***. Prana is that conscious or unconscious energy animating the body, equated with Brahman.

There are five books of Itareya Aranyaka. The first book deals with the rites to be performed (by the ascetics in forest), with all details of grammar and meaning of rituals. In course of time, the vanaprasthas took to meditation and the spiritual forms of worship and kept away from the rituals or religious ceremonies of the Graihastashram. The second and the third Aranyakas are considered to be of great significance; and, hence it is considered as the whole Upanishad, Maha Itareyopanishad. Prana or Hiranyagarbha is taught as the first cause of creation (of this universe), and 'Pranavidya', its ritiuals and meditations are described in the Second Aranyaka. It underlines the need for 'Self- Knowledge' and explains the way to attain it with scripture ordained duties without any desire for fruits thereof.

According to this Upanishad, Brahman entered the body from the fore parts of the feet and rised through thighs, stomach, heart, neck, and to head and finally ramified into sight, hearing, mind, speech, and vital breaths. Thus, the stomach is the seat of Brahman as 'Vaisvanara'. Some sages meditate on Brahman in the stomach or in the heart. The superiority of Prana over the Senses is also brought out here. Prana (Life Energy) is stated to be at the root of speech and designations, on which the knowledge of the whole universe rests. Thus, 'Prana' is the source of all 'Veda' or Knowledge. Prana is Spirit immanent in the universe. The whole universe is present as 'Vak' (idea) in Brahman before it was manifested. Prana encompasses all.·Thus, it is Prana that sustains all sentient and insentient beings in this universe.

Just as Prana (Brhati) is the Cosmic Life, Purusha (Isvara) is the Cosmic Personality; both are the Divine Principle embodied in the universe. One should know that just as the shining space is supported by Prana, so also, 'all beings down to an ant are supported by Prana'. The various faculties serve the Purusha or Prana and this (idea) serves well for meditation. Prana is the Cosmic Life and Purusha is the cosmic personality; both are the same Divine Principle embodied in the universe.

The significance of this Upanishad is that Aitareya considers all creation of this universe in a 'father-son/daughter relationship'. For instance water is considered the daughter of Prana. He says, the all-comprising glory of waters belongs to Prana, who is the all. He is in water; he is life; he is existence and non-existence. The immortal Prana and mortal dwell together in food; all mortal forms are indwelt by him; this deity is immortal. Prana and body, the two, go in two directions; they separate themselves; they increase one but not the other- the body is increased but not the other – this Deity is immortal Prana. Prana is the sun that has entered the world as Purusha. Prana is 'Uktham', shreshta. One should meditate on Prana.

Once, Visvamitra asked Indra, "Who are you?" To this, Indra replied, "I am Prana and so also you; all creatures are Prana and this way I pervade all quarters. He who radiates light and heat is Prana. I am he that shines".

This Prana, or 'Brhati' (i.e., Brahman) is the total Reality. 'Beyond Prana who has become a thousand Brhatis, is what is Intelligence, Divinity, Absolute Spirit; he who knows this joins ('yuj') and become one with Him.'

Thus, "*What I am That he is, what He is that I am*". The Sun is the self of all that moves and standstill. [Rk Veda 1-115-1].

Further, the Aranyaka says, 'the whole universe has sprung up and subsist in relation of anna and annada, i.e., matter and spirit'. He who realizes the Atman with greater and greater clarity obtains the fullest manifestation of his true being. The Aranyaka explains the differences between the plants and animals, the sap or juice in plants and the instincts of hunger and thirst and live according to their intelligence. Man alone is capable of higher thought and noble activity. Man is potential Infinity. Whatever he attains, he desires to be beyond it. The desire to reach farther and farther is a sign that there is the possibility for him to achieve fulfillment when he regains his perfection in the Infinite. This aspect has been highlighted in all Scriptures, the Bhagavad Gita, Maha Bharata and

Bhagavata. "***Satyasya satymanuyatra yujyate tatra deva sarva ekam bhavanti.***"

Another Aranyaka, the third one, brings out the mutual support extended by one to the other in this universe. The earth is the prior form and the heaven the posterior form, and air (ether) is the principle that unites the two. It is also held that rain is the union of earth and sky and clouds unite them.

About speech, the Upanishad says, 'Speech is the Samhita', "***Vaacha vai vedah***"[111-1-6]. By speech vedas are strung, by speech the metres are made, by speech friends are united, by speech all beings and hence all this is speech. "When one talks or speaks, breath (Prana) enters speech and speech svallows Prana. When one is in deep sleep, or in silence or mauna, speech dissolves in breath or Prana svallows speech i.e., speech dwells in Prana. Control of mind by Yoga is beautifully explained here. Prana and chitta, breath and mind, are so intimately connected that the one follows the course the other takes. Mind and speech are intimately connected through vichara and vak (Prana); Prana is conscious or unconscious forces that are working in the universe which are synthesized in a higher unity. Thus, when one is engaged in conscious activity, such as study, talk or recollection accompanied by concentration, breath becomes soft and harmonious and united with that activity. Again, when one is in deep sleep or entirely absorbed, Prana alone functions and the modifications of the mind (chitta vrittis) are stopped. This mutual absorption of one by the other signifies the higher unitary principle from which both emerge ['Rk' Veda X-119-4].

'Vak' (speech) that comprises of sukshma, para, pashyanti, and vaikhari cover the entire range of Mind. In other words, 'vak' stands for mind. One can read the mind of a person by his talk.

There is another interesting explanation about the Self. "*Sa yesha ahahsammaanah chakshurmayah kshetramayah chandomayah vangmaya atma*" [III-2-1]. Meaning, 'the Self consist of sight, hearing, metre, mind, and speech.'

During the Upanishadic period, Kala (Time) was conceived as the Cause of the universe. Prajapati is also known as Time (Kaala Purusha). Vishnupurana also says 'Kaalasvaroopi Bhagavan', the Lord manifests as Time. 'Kaali' is the feminine symbolization of the dynamic aspect of Reality. Kaala or Time is based on the Sun. The year is the measure and condition of appraising time. But, Time is external and internal, subjective and objective. It is the Principle that is undivided and uniting. It is identical with the 'Mahapurusha' and the Principle in the Sun. So one should know that, "He who is in the Sun as also, the incorporate '***Prajnyatma***' are one and the same. The Supernal Sun becomes individualized in each person [Rk Veda I-115-1] He is Brahman. He is the 'Self' consisting of sight, hearing, metre, mind and speech and compared to the year numerically.

The Aranyaka, for some strange reasons, gives some omens of death and suggests reciting the Rk Vedic Verses IX-67-21 to 27; VIII-6-30; IX-113-6 to 11; and I-50-10. A person who gets dream prognosticating death should follow the directions given in 'Rk Veda', Verse X127-16, which suggests preparing a sweet dish (payas) and partaking it with Brahmanas.

The nature of the Purusha, who is within all, is described in the Aranyaka. Accordingly, the 'Purusha' is different from body and Mind; He is not heard, not reached, not thought, not subdued, not seen, not understood, not classified, but who hears, thinks, sees, classifies, sounds, understands, and knows, is one's own Self. This is the true conception of the Self, the Atman established in Vedanta. [See Brih. :III-7-13 & 8-11; Kaus.:!-8; Pras.,:IV-6, Kena: IV-18; and Nrsm., I-11].

Also, there is a reference to the musical instrument, Veena (lute) in this Aranyaka. 'The human lute is an imitation of the divine lute". "He who knows this divine lute is listened to when he speaks, the earth I filled with his fame, and wherever the learned speak in assemblies there he will be known".

It is very interesting that one can make the audience spell-bound by his speech using the mantra:

*"Oushtaapidhaanaah Na kuli dantaih parivrutaa pavih;*
*Sarvasyei vaacha eeshaana chaarumaamiha vaadayet."*

Then there are the questions, 'Why should we study the Veda?' And, 'Why should we practice Vedic Rites?' There are beautiful answers to these questions.

The whole universe is *a Yajna where one thing is sacrificed for the other. The Lord Himself sacrifices his own self for the creation of the universe; and, everything in this universe sacrifices one thing for the other. Breath sacrifices for the 'vak' and Vak sacrifices for the' annam', food. Ultimately, everything is 'annam', i,e., food that is sacrificed ('aahuti'). This is Supreme Knowledge, Jnyaan!*

Normally, our life is a Yajna and we all sacrifice; sometimes we sacrifice one for the other. As already explained," We sacrifice Prana in Vak, and Vak in Prana; for what is the beginning that is the end." This suggests that we all perform some sort of spiritual form of worship comprising of still contemplation without any external worship and sacrifice in our daily life. Everything is Yajna! Our life is a yajna (sacrifice) and we must know this.

In conclusion, this Upanishad emphatically asserts that Prana is everything. But some learned saints observe that although the Upanishad explains the Atman, it does not give the knowledge of the Self, 'Atmanjnyaan'. Sankaracharya says that the Upanishad teaches only Brahman, the spiritual Reality and its study leads to the Deity but not to the Brahman relaisation (Atmajnyaan). However, it suffices to say that the ***Aitareyopanishad*** imparts the true Knowledge of the Brahman. It asserts, "The Atman alone is the substance of this Universe and there is nothing except the Atman. Atman is Prajnyanan, Pure Consciousness, or the essential Self of Man. It is everything from Indra (derived from '***Idandra***', meaning, 'I have seen it') down to the grossest creation. The knowledge of this 'Atman' is '***Brahmajnyaan***' or the Brahmavidya". Hence, this Upanishad is considered to be the ***Maha Upanishad***.

There is a beautiful explanation regarding the Prana and the Atman entering the human body. While the Prana entered the human body from the feet and rised to navel, stomach and the heart, the Atman or the

Brahman directly entered the body from the head, i.e., the Brahmrandhra and reached the heart. The Atman supports Prana and when the Atman leaves the body, the Prana also leaves the body. One who knows this is immortal!

"Tal Shrishtwaa tad evaancepraavishat"

[Taittiriya Upanishad 2.6.2]

meaning, "Having created the creation, the creator - Cosmic Creative Intelligence - entered into it.

*Vishnu Upanishads*

The Vishnu Upanishads include the Maha Upanishad, the Narayana, the Atmabodha, Narasimhapoorvatapaniya, Narasimhottaratapaniya, Ramapoorvtapaniya and the Ramottaratapaniya Upanishads. These Upanishads proclaim Narayana as the One and the Absolute, even prior to Brahman; and, advocate the worship of Narayana in one form or the other.

*Maha Upanishad*

According to the Maha Upanishad, Narayana, verily, was alone. There was no Brahman, no Ishana, no water, no Agni and Soma, no heaven and earth, no Sun but only He, the Nara (Purusha) alone. He utters a sacrificial hymn of praise, as he remains absorbed in meditation. Therein originated fourteen Purushas and a girl, i.e., the ten indriyas and the Manas, Tejas, Ahamkara, Prana, (the Atman), and the Budhdhi. Besides the five subtle elements, and the five gross elements. In all, twenty-fivefold Purushas have emanated from the Lord Narayana. It is important to note that the creatures are not born with out the year, but they are born from the year.

Narayana, desirous of another, once more meditated in his mind and therefrom his forehead a three-eyed Purusha holding a trident, possessing about him beauty, truth, chastity, austerity, renunciation, intelligence and mastery; but the sound 'Om' and the three Vyahritis –bhur, bhuvar, svar, the Rk, the Yajus, Samans, Atharva-Angiras and all metres, they abided in his limbs.

Then Narayana meditated once again in his mind and then came sweat from his forehead. It expanded into the primordial waters, in them was born the Tejas as a golden egg and therein was born the god Brahma with four faces. Thus, the different Metres (Chandas) of the Veda were born with meditation towards the four directions. This is the *Maha Upanishad.*

*In all these, one may ask, where is the question of 'will' and' desire' of the Lord since the Lord is above everything- Will. Desire, etc. It is metaphorical and 'He willed, 'He desired', or' He meditated' is just a phrase that speaks of the' leela', 'Maya', or' illusory' nature of this sensate objective world that is ever- changing. He, the Lord Vishnu, is the cosmic flow, the universal Consciousness, the 'Prana' or the energy that steps down its intensity and vibration to form matter and so on, in the modern scientific sense of the terms.*

*Mahanarayanopanishad*

***'Mahanarayanopanishad' is a part of Krishnayajurveda and is believed to be very sacred to the religious Hindu for it is the most powerful and mystic mantra. Many of the Mantra from this Upanishad are selected for daily chantings and some of them are repeated here. "Om Namah Narayanaya" is an eight- word mantra "Ashtakashari", that is the path to deliverance, salvation, and liberates the spiritual aspirant from the bondage of this world. Mahanarayanopanishad is as good as the Sahasranamam of Vishnu, eulogizing the Lord. Every mantra is potent, mystic and rewarding. It is the Mantropansihad par excellence. Most of the Mantra of this Upanishad are chanted everyday as a part of the daily prayer in devout families. Some of the important mantra are quoted in the Text wherever necessary.***

*Narayanopanishad*

This is a Mantropanishad from Atharvaveda. It describes the 'One' supreme Lord Narayana as the 'Reality':

*" Nishkalo Niranjano, Nirvikalpo, Nirakhyato, Shudhdho deva Eko Narayanah, Na dvitiyo Asti Kaschit, Ya evam Veda, Ityupanishat."*

'*Narayana*' is the all pervading Supreme Being or Energy that is the elevating path ('Ayana') for humans ('Nara'). The description, 'Nishkala' is whole and undivided as enunciated in the first mantra, "*Om, Poornamadah poornamidam......;" and, 'Niranjana*' is unstained and unstinged; and, 'Nirvikalpa' is unbounded and above all distinctions. 'Nirakhyata' is beyond all descriptions. There is a similar mantra in Taittiriyopanishad, "*Yatra vacho nivartante*...." which declares that the Lord Narayana is beyond description because the words or speech return unsuccessfully; and, even mind is not capable of grasping this pure and the self-effulgent (Brahman).

*"Yatcha kinchajjagatyasmin drushyate shruyatopi va*
*antarbahischa tatsarvavyaapya naaraayanah sthitah "*
*[Mahanarayana Upa., 13.5]*

Meaning, "whatever there is in this world known through perception or known through report, all that is pervaded by Naarayana within and without"

*"Narayanah param Brahma tatvamNarayanah parah I;*
*Narayanah parojyotiraatma Narayanah parah II. "'*
*Mahanarayana Upa. 13. 4*]"

Narayana is the Supreme Reality designated as Brahman. Narayana is the Highest Self, the Supreme Light, the Infinite Self. Narayana is Paramatman described as the Brahman. The place for His meditation is the ether near the heart, a narrow space called 'Sushumna', a nadi comparable to an inverted lotus bud that would blossom and turn up to Him on 'Enlightenment'.

*Atmabodha Upanishad*

This Upanishad of the Rk Veda is in praise of Lord Narayana. It starts with prostrations to Narayana, decorated with conch, discus, and mace. He is in the form of Pranava 'Om' and whosoever utters this Pranava made of A, U, and M is released from the bondage of cycle of rebirth. The reciter of "Om Namo Narayanaya" will reach Vaikunta, the abode of Vishnu. The thousand names of the Lord are not sufficient to praise Him. He is everything. He is everything that existed in the past, that is existing in the present and that will ever exist in future. "Let Pranas according to their laws be fluctuating. Let Manas be blown out by desire. No pain will affect the body that is all 'Awareness and Bliss'. Being the nature of Bliss, there is not sorrow in 'Me'. And, it is through Ajnyaana that the universe shines as truth. Whoever recites this Upanishad for 48 minutes (Muhurta) is not born again, is not born again."

*Nrsimha-purva Tapaniya Upanishad*

• ***This is a very powerful mystic Upanishad comprising of six parts. It is a mantropanishad and the Nrsimha mantra is called the Mantra-raja. The Mantra–raja or the Maha Mantra is a powerful mystic mantra***. The old Vedic Sun-god Vishnu is worshipped in various forms. Nrsimha, Rama and Krishna that are avatars of one God Vishnu; both Rama and Krishna are deemed Gods, i.e., deified though in human form (Avatar). Narasimha, on the other hand, is a man-lion (divine lion) form or half-man and half-lion. There is a reference in Rk Veda 4-25-4, which says: '***Indraya nare naryaya, nrtamaya nrnam***', probably, the only original powerful divine hero into which the solar power was personified. As in the past, even today, a small exclusive sect (Vishistadvaitins) worship Vishnu (Narayana) in this Nrsimha or half Man and half Lion form through a sacred formula called the Nrsimha formula. It is ironical that the worship is aimed more at the formula than at the god Nrsimha.

"As in the Pranava, so in the Nrsimha formula is the whole Veda. This Mantr-raja or king of formulae (mantra) deals with all the worlds and all the Veda. It is identical with the four moras of the Pranava "AUMm' ('Om') sound; like Brahman, it has the Maya as its 'shakti' or creative power, and Akasha as the seed, the starting point of creation. From this Atman akasha is born, from akasha, the wind &c." as depicted in ***Taittiriya Upanishad 2-1***. This mantra-raja or king of formulae is artistically written and worn as an amulet. It assures super-abundant reward. This ***Mantra-raja*** has three or four 'angamantra (sub-formulae). The Mantra-raja is:

*"Ugram viram Mahavishnum, jvalantam sarvatomukham;*
*Nrsimham bhishanam bhadram mrutyu-mrutyum namamy aham."*

The four angamantra:

The Pranava- "*Om*!"
The Savitri-" *Ghrnih, Suryah, Adityah*;"
The Lakshmi-yajus (Yajurlakshmi)-
*"Om! bhur Lakshmir, bhuvar Lakshmih*
*Suvah kalakarni, tan no Mahalakshmi prachodayat."*
*The Narasimha Gayatri- "Om! Narasimhaya vidmahe,*
*Vajranakhaya dheemahi*

*Tan no simhah prachodayat."*

*The Upanishad asserts Prajapati created the world by means of the Nrsimha Formula.*

The gods asked Prajapati to explain the power (shakti) and the seed (Vijaṃ) of the powerful Nrsimha mantra, the Mantra-raja to which Prajapati said:

The Vishnu (u) and Shakti ('ham) of the Nrsimha, is the Maya and the Vijam (seed) out of which the whole world has developed. It is the 'Maya' of Nrsimha that creates the universe, protects the universe and reabsorbs the universe. Therefore one should know this Maya as 'Shakti', the creative power.

One who knows Maya surmounts the sin, surmounts the death; he attains immortality and great luck. The word 'ham' in the Nrsimha mantra has different powers according to pronouncements viz,

'Ham' (hrsva or short), 'haam' (dheerga or long), 'ha-am' (very long) and 'haa-----aam'(long drawn) sound giving rise to immortality, great luck, wisdom and liberation or mukti, respectively.

*Narasimha-Uttara-Tapaniya Upanishad*

This Upanishad is based on some of the doctrines already explained in Mandukya Upanishad. It has a remarkable unfoldment of the concept of the Atman-Brahman Unity with the help of Pranava, the 'Om'. While Atman is the psychic principle Brahman is the cosmic principle and both are equated by means of 'Om'. All these three are seen symbolically in Nrsimha. Atman identified with Om, Brahman and Nrsimha are one subject of perception, avikalpa. The inner unity of the Atman in all beings is beautifully brought out in this Upanishad.

There are four states of Consciousness ***viz*** 1. Waking and the gross world of waking 2. Dream and the subtle dream world 3. Deep sleep, and the seed-world, i.e., the kaarana prapancha (causal-world), or the vijanidrayata prajnah, (here, the Consciousness or prajna is merged in Prana); and, 4. Turiya, the fourth state of spectatorship in which the union of the subject and the object takes place under the persistence of Consciousness. Each of the first three states is mixed with all the four states. Turiya, although called the highest state is the real existence, not a state! The Turiya-turiya state reached after severing all worldly tastes and it is the Atman in its purest form and one should experience it as the Self in himself. This indeed is the most beautiful contribution of the Upanishads to the Spiritual heritage of India.

This Upanishad in brief is that, "Om is everything". The past, the present, the future and all this is the Om sound; what still lies beyond is also the 'Om'sound. 'Om' is the whole world. All this is verily the Brahman and Brahman is Atman, minuter than the minute. The sound 'Om',the Brahman, and the Atman are three-some world. The wise, the Seer merges the Atman in the Brahman and experiences the Bliss through Om. Thus, both the Atman and the Brahman merge in the' Om' and one should compress the whole world in the sound 'Om'.

This Atman is four-fold. The one present in the wakeful state (Taijasa)

experiencing the gross is 'Visva' and Vaisvanara is his first quarter. The one present in the dream or svapna state perceiving the subtle is 'Taijasa' and Hiranyagarbha is his second quarter. The third state of deep sleep where he experiences no desire and sees nothing, becomes one with knowledge and bliss, is the 'Prajnya' and Ishvara is his third quarter. He is the Lord of all, the cradle of the universe verily He is the Lord of creation and disappearance of all creatures. In fact, all these three are in reality deep sleep, dream and sheer delusion; for the Atman has thinking as the only taste. The fourth state fuses each of the other three states by virtue of Affirmation and Indifference inherent in all. Ultimately, 'Ishvara' is also devoured by the Turiya in the sense that,'Turiya is the abyss that swallows even the personification of the divine as Ishvara'.

The 'Om' sound is a connecting link between the Atman and the material world, on the one side through a, u, and m, on the other as the whole 'Om". Each of the three states of the Atman, the waking, dream and deep sleep contains the gross, subtle, unity and the spectator so that 'a' corresponds to waking, 'u' to dream and 'm' to deep sleep and the Om to Turiya. Through these four determinations the world becomes a reality, ***nama-roopaatmaka***.

*How to perceive the Atman? The Upanishad says, "Not perceiving the gross and not perceiving the subtle, not both-way perceiving, neither conscious nor unconscious, also not consisting of knowledge through and through, invisible, uncharacterizable, established in the certitude of his own self, extinguishing the expanse of the universe, auspicious, calm, without the second- that is the fourth quarter, that is precisely the Atman, that precisely one should perceive."*

He is the one who sees the eye, who sees the ear, who sees the speech, who sees the Manas, who sees the Budhdhi, who sees the Prana, who sees the darkness, who sees everything! Therefore, He is another from the universe, an essentially different one. He is the spectator, the 'Sakshin'. He is the unchangeable 'great spirit'. He the Atman is Brahman.

One should be able to see all the four states of Consciousness (gross, subtle, seed and spectator) in one' Om' sound, as also, in each and every syllable of the sound, i.e., severally in a, u, and m.

The Atman is similar to "ota", i.e., 'woven into' the world; It is the affrimer, 'anujna'; It is the indifference, 'avokalpa'. And, this world has names and forms for its substance because of the 'Turiyaness' (or thought form character) included in the 'Om' sound, as also, by means of being 'inwoven' (ota), affirmer (anujna), indifference (avikalpa) for the simple reason, the whole universe is also the form of indifference. There is no difference between the Atman, the sound 'Om', and the universe. One who knows this has his individual self merged in the highest self". [*Mandukya Upanishad* 12]. Such a man will know the Turiya through the Anushtubh relating to Nrsimha, the formula-king; one who accomplishes it is a man, is Narasimha himself. Wherever he moves, he moves like a Lion! Like a Lion-king in the forest, he who knows this will command everything!

Further, the Upanishad states that, "one should, meditating by means of 'Om', absorb (the world) in the Turiya.

"The syllable 'a' is earth, Rk Veda, Brahman, the Vasus, the Gayatri, Garhapatya Fire; And, 'u' is atmosphere, Yajur Veda, Vsihnu, the Rudras, Trishtubh, Dakshina Fire; 'm' is heaven, the Sama Veda, Rudra, Adityas, Jagati, Ahavaniya Fire; and, the fourth half mora, 'mmmm'sound is the Soma world, the Atharva Veda , is the fire of universal destruction, the Maruts, the Viraj, the 'shining'."

One who knows this is "verily 'nr' (man, hero) and 'simha' for this Nrsimha; and this one is the Turiya. He is Ugra, Vira, Mahan, Vishnu, Jvalantan, Sarvatomukha, Nrsimha, Bhishana, Bhadra, Mrityu to Mrityu, I prostrate -namami, and he is Aham." One should, applying himself to Yoga, meditate upon the Anushtubh with reference to Brahman and with reference to the 'Om'sound.

Indeed, the God Narasimha is the 'Supreme Atman', the highest 'Brahman'. One who knows this is without desires, satisfied desires, free from desires, and all his animal spirits assembled, stay there itself, for he is the Brahman, and he is merged in the Brahman." [***Brihadaranyaka Upanishad,*** 4-4-6 & 3-2-11], Thus spoke Prajapati.

The gods asked Prajapati to explain "*Tat tvam asi*," ("You, yourselves are That").

Can he now be possibly seen by (himself as) the secondless? Certainly not! For he would be a second, if he were not yourself."

"You yourself are he; if he were seen by you, then you would not perceive (know) the Atman (as he is the Self and none other). Verily the Atman has no attachment to the world. Therefore you yourself are he, and the light with which you shine is your own. Indeed this world is only yourselves, for you consist wholly of being and Consciousness."

"Though not seeing him, you should see him with the word 'Om'. This is the truth; "Om' is the Atman, is the Brahman, for the Brahman is the Atman. 'Om' is the Reality."

There are a number of Yoga Upanishads belonging to Atharva Veda that help us to understand the Atman-Brahman through the Pranava, 'Om". Some of these are: Brahmavidya, Kshurika, Chulika, Nadabindu. Brahmabindu, Amrutabindu, Dhyanabindu, Tejobindu, Yogashikha, Yogatattva and the Hamsa Upanishads. These are described in brief here.

*Brahmavidya Upanishad*

This Upanishad is the esoteric teaching of the science of Brahman restricted to only the initiated disciples. The Brahman can be understood by a process of elimination, neti, neti, neti, i.e., not this, not this, thereby eliminating all known sources. Brahman can be realized by Meditation through the Pranava 'Om' sound of "A +U+ M+ m"- 3 and a half moras (matras); the half mora is the buzzing reverberation sound (nada) of 'm', denoted by a point (bindu). The Brahman consists of three- and-a half constituents of 'Om' AUMm viz the sariram (body), sthanam (location), kala (time) and, terminus or end. The fourth half mora is laya or the vanishing of the sound 'Om' from perception.

The Shariram, the body of the sound 'Om' covers the three Veda (Rk, Sama and Yajur Veda), the three Fires (Garhapathya, Dakshina and the

Ahavaniya), and the three worlds (bhu, bhuvar and svar), and the three Deities (Brahma, Vishnu, Maheswara). The Stnnam is again located in three locations viz the Sun, the moon, the fire, and the half mora is the flame, which gradually get extinguished. The Kala or time is expressed in three- pointed flame in splendour (artery of the Sushumna), breaks through in brain (sahasrara) and penetrating through the 72,000 arteries exiting through the Brahmarandhra, thereby the Brahman is actually experienced as the supreme Bliss. These are mystical as esoteric and limited to the initiated ones only.

*Kshurika Upanishad*

This Upanishad, too, is an esoteric Upanishad restricted to the initiated disciples only. Kshurika is of 'Dharana', concentration the power of which surpasses the razor that cuts. It is aYogic exercise (dharana) comprising of asana, pranayama, and dhyana. The ethical practices of yama and niyama are very important and the Yogis should practice continence (celibacy). Mind control is possible only through seclusion, 'nirodha', detachment, and with practice of Hatayoga, kundalini power is raised to sahasrara through sushumna canal. Each and every part of the body is detached by dharana and nirodha; Manas is locked up in the heart and at the same time it is used to cut off the relationships of other parts with the heart. Devoid of all desires and attachment, the heart tentacles are cut off. Such a Yogin is not born here again.

*Chulika Upanishad*

The terms tip or 'chula', 'chuda', is used to denote the end of the Samkhya philosophy through this Upanishad. Purusha and Prakriti are not very mich distinguished in the early stages of evolution and the Purusha stays in Sattvam according to this Upanishad. Together Purusha and Prakriti create this world. The mystic expressions in this Upanishad are not very easy to understand and interpret. For instance, the Lord, at His will, enjoys (pro-) creation! There is a reference to this in Verses 6-7 but at the same time He is not at all interested , 'udaasina' in this act of (pro-) creation.

*Nadabindu Upanishad*

This Upanishad, again, is a further elucidation of the Pranava 'Om' in its three-and-a half moras and lays stress on the fading point of sound of 'Om'. The Atman is described as a bird with the Rajas and Tamas as feet and the Sattva as the body. Dharma and adharma are its right and lefteyes, respectively. The seven lokas (bhu, bhuvar, svar etc.) are located in different parts of its body; and it is the bird on which the Yogin ascends to Brahmalok. The three and- a- half moras of the sound 'Om' represent Agni, Vayu, solar orb, Varuna, respectively. The first mora is rich in sound, the second is wreathed in lightning, the third follows the flight-enjoyer and the fourth is swift as wind. And, Brahma, Vishnu and Ishvara are represented by the three other moras, followed by the great, firm, silent and the last Brahmic, together making it ('Om') twelve partial moras. These are, again, mystic yogic traditions and holds good to initiated disciples only. Yogins who practise the discipline strictly according to the Vedic guidelines of rituals with the prescribed Asana, pranayama, dharana, dhyana and tapas, only could realise this Brahmic. The rewards for the meditation and Yoga are clearly described in this Upanishad. The yogin who dies meditating on the first mora is born as a king and the Yogin who dies meditating on the second mora will become Yaksha. Similarly, one who dies meditating on the third, fourth, fifth, etc, will respectively attain Vidhyadhara, Gandharva, Soma, and Indra lokas and lives with Vishnu, Rudra, Pashupati and reaches Tapoloka and then reaches Brahma lok to become the light of Brahman This is the sum and substance of the Nadabindu Upanishad.

*Brahmabindu Upanishad*

This Upanishad highlights the significance of the anusvara 'm', the half mora of the Pranava "Om" in attaining Brahman. First, the technique of Mind-control is explained and then the significance of disbanding all knowledge including the Veda and the Pranava in attaining Brahman. The Upanishad says that, "Mind is the cause of all bondage. Mind alone can liberate us. Pure Mind , an object-less Mind can lead us to liberation. So one who aspires for liberation should free his mind from objects. The Upanishad implores, "Restrain your Mind so long until it is annihilated in the heart. This is Knowledge; this is liberation! Beginning Yoga with 'Om' one should reach the stage of word-less state; Meditate wordlessly and through wordless meditation one can attain non-being".

The highest Reality is that where "there is no death, no becoming and none bound and none aspirant; no liberated existence and no desire for it." Know the Atman as one; throwing off the state of waking, dream and deep sleep, one can become immortal. Brahman is the syllable of the Om-sound; the wise meditate on that eternal one. Discard the books of knowledge 'just as one the chaff, who strives for the corn'.

*Amritanada Upanishad*

This Upanishad is also known as the Amritabindu Upanishad. It highlights the esoteric doctrine of the point (bindu) or anusvara of 'Om' which signifies the Immortal Brahman. Here again, the bookish knowledge is condemned and upholds Meditation on the Brahman through Om-sound highlighting the anusvara in it. It says, "Only the half mora 'm' (anusvara 'ma'kaara), the reverberating sound, nada of the word 'Om' signifies immortality or grants liberation."

***Asana, prathyahara, dhyana, pranayama, dharana, and tarka (reflecting) are the seven methods of Yogasutra highlighted in this Upanishad.*** This Upanishad is important in more than in one way for a serious aspirant of Yoga for it gives details of the techniques. Besides, the ramifications of the five Pranas are explained. These are explained in brief in the following:

First, the superiority of Brahman over the academic knowledge and the significance of Om as far as reaching the goal (but not beyond) are highlighted in the verses 1-4. "The wise who read the books, throw them off, as if they burnt. 'Om' is the chariot and Vishnu the charioteer. But, the car is useful only so long as one is on the high road. Just as one goes on foot when the destination is reached, so one leaves the word symbol 'Om' also, and only with the silent 'm' (asvara 'm' kaara), one comes from 'Om' to silent, invisible peace."

Prathyahara is withdrawal of the sense organs from sense objects and stilling the chanchal manas (Mind). The six limbs of yoga are helpful in controlling the mind and the senses. These are: Prathyahara, Meditation, (dhyana), Breath-control (Pranayama), Chanting (Japa), Reflecting (Tarka) and communion (Tapas). The out-going senses are controlled by breath control. The sins committed in this as well as previous lives are burnt by constant chanting of the Lord's name (Japa).

Breath control is of three types: Rechaka, Kumbhaka and Pooraka. Rechaka is breath-out, Kumbhaka is retaining the breath and Pooraka is breath-in; thinking of the Giver of Light, the Sun, one should breath-in and breath –out holding breath for some time contemplating on the Gayatri. The Gayatri with its head, along with Vyahritis and Pranava is said thrice in one breath in Pranayama. Breath-out, Rechaka is accomplished by completely emptying, thereby creating empty space inside; and, keeping this emptiness, (kumbhaka) for equal time of breath-in is the technique of Pranayama. Breath-in, Pooraka is accomplished just as one is accustomed to drink water, one should draw in wind also. Keep the body still, but not stiff.

***Taittiriya Aranyaka*** 55-9 contains the Formula Gayatri presecribed for Pranayama. The head of Gayatri is: "Om! ***Apo jyoti rasomritam brahma***, and, Vyahriti – '***bhurbhuvasvar***', and the Pranava '***Om***'!"

As regards, Rules for the Yoga, the Upanishad states:

Select a level ground in very congenial surroundings with fresh air and without any disturbances. Sit facing north in Yogic posture like the padmasan, svastikasan, bhadrasan or any other convenient position – keeping the body, neck and head straight, so as to facilitate free circulation of blood. Sit on a piece of cloth, mattress, or piece of deer- skin, if available. There is a procedure and particular mantra to make a place clean and the evil forces cleared of the place as also making oneself fit for meditation (as is done in case of Sandhyavandana). One should sit quiet without any motion and contemplate on the Self. To start with, 'Sukha Pranayama' is invariably practiced to bring breathing under control. It is clearly stated that 'Om' (– AUMm, the three and-a –half moras with the last anusvara dying down in Turiya), should be meditated upon along with Pranayama. 'Om' is ekakshara Brahma; 'Om' should not be breathed out. Mere utterance of 'Om" will cleanse one and makes mind fit for meditation. Breath in with "Om'. Meditate and chant the Gayatri Mantra repeatedly and repeatedly, and no excess here is too much. This is contrary to some statements where the counting in 10, 108, 1008 etc. are stipulated. Sit motionless casting down the eyes within self, firmly; this is the method of practicing of Yoga.

'Yoga' is also said to be Samadhi. Concentrating Mind on the Self, try to establish communion with the supreme Self, the Lord, chanting 'Om' silently, within the hollow of the heart, slowly move upwards, opening the gate of liberation, the orb of Sun. An ardent disciple, a Yogi should always be careful about excesses, be it in food or sleep, talk or waking; too little of these also do much harm than good. If one practices Yoga in this way, as per the rules, he will, no doubt attain results in three months, First, he visualizes the Lord in the form of his choice; and, in a matter of six months, he will definitely attain absoluteness at will.

In Meditation, one should try to relax the body and mind and concentrate on oneself. Gradually, he should unite (merge) manas with atma and contemplate on Atma by means of atma. The Prana, to begin with, dwells in the region of the heart, the apana in the region of bowel, Samana around the navel, Udana in the neck region and, the Vyana continuously runs through the limbs. The Prana resembles in luster a red-hued precious stone; and Apana is reddish (indragopasamaprabha). The Samana shines in belly like a milk-coloured mountain crystal. The Udana is pale yellowish and the Vyana is of the colour of flame. Thus, the five vital breath and their ramifications are described. The Upanishad concludes: One who attains the power of ascending the vital breath to Sahasrara will attain immortality, no matter where he dies; he is never born any more!

A Yogin should avoid fear, anger, laziness, excess in sleeping and eating or fasting. If the aspirant practices diligently the yama and niyama steadfastly, spiritual wisdom will dawn in three months; in four months of steadfast adherence to the principles and practice of Yoga, his 'Ishtadevatha' can be visualized; and, he becomes a 'Brahmanishta' in five months! There is no doubt that any ardent aspirant who sticks to these and diligently practices yoga will attain 'Kaivalya' at–will! That man will never be reborn whose breath goes out of the Brahmarandhra (the suture line at the parting of head).

*Dhyanabindu Upanishad*

This is yet another mystic, or esoteric Yoga Upanishad for the intiated disciples only. It seems many of the verses of this Upanishad are repetitions of Mundaka Upanishad [2-2-4; Svetasvatara Upa. 5-9 & 20; Amritabindu Up. 21; and Yogatatva 1-2]. This Upanishad is very useful to all the serious students of Yoga. It starts with the statement:

"I will proclaim the truth of the Yoga for the well-being of the Yogin. Vishnu is the Purusha who shines highest; so meditate on Him. Yogic meditation helps to cleanse all the sins".

"Silence is higher than the first syllable and the Yogi who meditates on this will have no doubts whatsoever. Brahman is so subtle that it is impossible to perceive by the senses; He, the Brahman is present as fragrance in the flower, butter in milk, oil in sesamum or gold in the gold-ore. It is difficult to know Brahman from Mind. He is present in the body of man; He is in it and outside, as well. He, the Atman, dwells everywhere."

The Yogin meditates on Vishnu in pooraka, on Brahman in Kumbhaka, and on the three-eyed in Rechaka. The Yogin meditates on Him who dwells in the navel, heart and the ajnya (forehead) and guides us through the Pitryana, Devayana and Tritiyam paths to Divinity. He is of the three and a-half moras, the Pranava 'AUMm'. He who knows Him Knows Him."

The one akshara 'Om' should be contemplated upon as Brahman by all who aspire for emancipation. ***Omkara*** has eight parts (angas), four padas, three sthaanas (seats), and five devathas (deities). The sound "Om' is the bow, the soul the arrow, the Brahman the target of the arrow and the Yogin should merge in Him like the arrow in the target through "Om". The forehead, where the root of the nose is located, is theAjnya (between the eyebrows) the resting place of all; and, it is here Ishvara dwells. Meditate on Him, is the Upanishad. *That man is the knower of the Veda who knows that ardhamatra of the Pranava 'm' should be recited uninterrupted as long as the ringing sound of a bell-gong. He is the knower of the Veda who knows the three seats, the three metres, the Brahmas, the three aksharas, (AUM), bindu, nada and kaala. One should draw up the breath from the nadis, Sushumna, Ida, Pingala and absorb it in the middle of the eyebrows in the forehead. The middle of the eyebrow (ajnya), also the root of the nose, is the seat of nectar, the great place of Brahma.*

The convenient Yogic postures are many; Padmasana, Svastika, Vajrasana, Bhadra, Sidhdha, Brahma, etc. and in fact, there are as many postures as there are living creatures, and only Mahesvara knows their distinguishing features, says this Upanishad. Muladhara is the first and the Svadhishtana is the second. Between these two is the yoni (perineum) having the form of Kama. In the adhara of the anus is the four- petaled lotus and the Yoni located in the middle of this lotus is contemplated upon in Meditation (worshipped) by the Sidhdhas. The three nadis- Ida, Pingala and the Sushumna, carry the Prana always and their deities are the Sun, the moon and the Agni. Ida on the left, and Pingala on the right side with Sushumna in the middle are the known paths of Prana, Apana, Udana, and Vyana- the five Pranas (vital breaths) and the five vayus- Naga, Kurma, Krkara, Devadatta and Dhananjaya (Sub-Pranas). Jiva is under the influence of Prana and apana vayu goes up and down. Jiva on account of its movement all over the body is not visible; it is there at the tip of every roma (hair). Jiva tossed up by prana and apana is never at rest. Both prana and apana draw from each other. Kundalini-shakti when it is up in the throat makes the yogin get sidhdhi and the benefits of this are numerous. Jalandharabandha is the destroyer of all pains of the throat; Uddiyanabandha is a lion to the elephant of death and, Muladhara-bandha keeps one away from the effects of old age.

Thus, ***Dhyanabindu Upanishad*** highlights the essence of Dhayana Yoga and ensures success or sidhdhi; it destroys all the sins of past lives. According to this doctrine, Bijakashara (seed-word) is the supreme bindu (point); the letter 'Ya' is the Vija (seed) of Prana and resembles blue cloud, The letter 'ra' is the Vija of Agni is o Apana and resembles the Sun. The lette 'la' is the Vija of Prithvi (earth), is of Vyana and resembles bandhuka flower. The letter 'va' is the Vija of (vayu), is of Udana and is the colour of the conch. The letter 'ha' is the Vija of Akasha, is of Samana, and is of the colour of crystal. Prana stays in the heart, navel, nose, ear, foot, finger and travels everywhere through the 72,000 nadis and twenty-eight crores of hair pores and is yet the same everywhere!

If Vijakashara is supreme, Nada (sound) is above it; and, when nada ceases, the sound-less state (***anahata***) is the ultimate that enables the Yogin to visualize Brahman. And, then the Upanishad describes '***the Atma as the lotus (of eight petals) and jivatma in the center of the lotus***' of the form of jyotis; and, the means of knowing it, i.e, Meditation on 'AUMmmm."

*Tejobindu Upanishad*

The same train of thoughts on Yoga is continued in this Upanishad. It brings out the intricacies of Yoga and difficulties that arise in practice of Yoga. Indeed, it is very difficult to practice Yoga 'even for the wise and the lonely'. It is possible only for those who conquer greed and anger, worldy attachment, sensuousness and lust; and, it is possible to those who have neither ego nor any expectations from wife and children. It is they who who transcend the Tamas, Rajas, and Sattva and become the Hamsa".

"He, the Brahman can be grasped only by self-absorption. This Brahman who dwells in the self is the first cause, the highest aim of all unthinking thinking; it is the soul, unempty, unthinkable, yet thinkable. It's all and yet it is nothing! There is nothing higher than It. It is not real and is not known"

Only those who renounce greed, delusion, fear, pride, anger, love, and sin, one who control his senses and conquer the ***Ari-shadvargas-raga,*** dvesha, lobha, moha, mada, matsarya, only will ever bequalified to attain Him. It is they who know not what is fear, lust, pain or pleasure, hot or cold, hunger and thirst, and what is pride, and neither respect nor disrespect any and is free from all these will ever qualify to attain Him. He alone is qualified to attain Him. Whosoever has passed this test is a liberated person. This is the Upanishad.

*Yogashikha Upanishad*

This is a beautiful Upanishad that identifies the Atman with the light, ***a pointed flame Tejobindu, in the heart. The Yogin who sees this light has seen Him, the Highest Being!***

"Sitting in the Padmasana (Lotus-posture), or whatever comfortable position one likes and feels comfortable, fixing the gaze on the tip of the nose, and hands and limbs held close, controlling the Mind with pranayama concentrating on the Pranava sound "Om", mediate on Him, the light in your heart". So says the Upanishad.

"This human body is erect with the spinal chord as its pillar and the Ida, Pingala and Sushumna nadis (channels) as the posts, with nine openings in the eyes, ears, nostrils, mouth, and the lower two, is a temple. In this temple shines the Sun, like a flame from the wick of a lamp; as large is the pointed flame (***Taijabindu***), so high is the God there and the yogin who practses repeatedly penetrates through it (the sun). Through the Sushumna, the Yogin reaches the Sahasrara, the highest one."

"If one is lazy and inattentive, does not know meditation, he too will penetrate the sun through his daily recitation of the Gayatri thrice".

*Hamsa Upanishad*

Sanatkumara imparted this Upanishad to Sage Gautama. This is a doctrine (Tattva) expounded by Parvati after ascertaining Shiva's opinion as also inquiring all dharmas concerning salvation to the mortals. It consists of Ajapa Gayatri, and Yoga, the latter, a mystical practice comprising of Mulabandha and rising of Kundalini techniques; and, it is strictly prohibited for public demonstarations and practices. Just like the Ramtapaniya Upanishad, the Hamsa Upanishad is very effective and hence, a much treasured one.

The word "***Hamsa***" is a very mysterious one with manifold meanings. The words 'Ham' (or Aham) and 'Sa' (or ha) mean '***So 'ham***" ("I am That"). Hamsa is also Prana, the vital- breath since we exhale with Ha and inhale with Sa; in between the humming 'm' sound of the Pranava 'Om' is always there! '***Hamsa***' is like the oil permeating oil seeds and fire permeating the 'arni' (fuel wood).

"The jiva comes out with the letter 'Ha' and gets in again with the letter 'Sa'. The jiva always utters the mantra 'Hamsa", say about 21,600 times a day and night. This japa is so powerful that there is no other equal to this; the very thought of this mantra redeems the person from all ills." Hamsa is the individual soul and Paramahamsa is the highest soul. One can rise from the state of Hamsa to Paramahamsa by Hatayoga, the Kundalini Yoga.

'***Ajapa Gayatri***', where Hamsa is the Rishi, Avyakta Gayatri is the metre or chandas, Paramahamsa is the devata, "Ham' is the Vija (seed) and 'Sa' is the Shakti. '***So 'ham***' is the kilaka (the wedge). "Hamsa so 'ham" is the Mantra. "May the bodiless and the subtle one guide us (prachodayat)". There is a specific method of offering Salutations to Surya (Sun), Soma, Niranjana, and Niraabhaasa (spaceless-ness) with anganyaasa (touching the heart, head, hair with the thumb and circling the head with fingers and finally circling one hand over the other) in this chanting of Ajapa Gayatri.

It is reiterated here that, "Pranayama and Meditation on the Pranava of the three and-a-half moras, particularly of its reverberation ensures immortality." As regards the anusvara 'm' of the Pranava, there are ten ways of chanting viz cihini, chinchini, sound of bell, blowing of conch, string music, clapping, flute, beating drum, kettle drum and the Thunder in which reverberation can be brought forth [as in Chand. Upa. 2-22, and Maitr. 6-22]; the tenth of these is recommended for practice. Symbolical interpretation of the individual atman conceived in the form of a bird - 'Swan' or Hamsa, or the eight-petal lotus flower located in the heart, and graphically presented as in the 'Mantra-raja'.

The significance of Mulabandha and Uddayana bandha are highlighted in this Upanishad. Mulabandha is so effective that one becomes young even with old age through performing Mulabandha always. Pressing the yoni by means of the heels and contracting the anus and drawing up the apana is called 'Mulabandha'. 'Uddayana bandha' is a lion to the elephant of death since it binds the water of the akasha, which arises in the head and flows down.

*"Gudamavashtabhyadharaadvaayumuththaya svaadhishtaanam trih pradikshinikritya manipoorakam cha gatva anahatapratikramya vishudhdhou pranathrirudhyajnyamanudhyayanbrahmrandhram*

*dhyayan thrimathro ahamithyevam sarvada dhyayan. Atho naadamaadhaara brahmrandhraparyantam shudhdhasphatikasankasham sa vai brahmaparamathmethyuchchate."* These are further elucidated in ***Dhyanabindhu Upanishad.***

Yoga Upanishads give us the essence of the Yoga and pave the way for salvation.

*Yogatattva Upanishad of Krishna Yajurveda*

This Upanishad gives the essence of the Yoga. "***I will proclaim the truth of the Yoga for the well-being of the Yogin***", says the Upanishad.

"Vishnu is the highest Purusha and He as a lamp on the way of truth shines. He has magical powers. He is the redeemer. This Samsara is a whirlpool in which the blemished soul take repeated births, now as the father, and son, and then as the mother, wife and daughter, and there is no end to it. It is sickening to take birth in this mrutyu lok and suffer within the adjuncts of the filthy body, limited by space and time.

This has been beautifully put by Adi Shankara *as "Punarapi jananam, punarapi maranam; punarapi shayane janani jathare*"; it is, thus, the cycle or rotation of samsara. The only way out of this hell is through Prathyahara, Pranayama, Dhyana and Meditation on the 'Pranava' of the three and a –half moras, "AUMmmm."

This Upanishad imparts Yoga tattva to spiritual aspirants who seek liberation from all bondage of this mundane world. Lord Vishnu is the greatest Yogin and the divine light. Pitamaha Brahma respectfully offered his salutations to the Lord of the universe Vishnu and requested Him to impart the truth of this yoga to which Hrishikesha related thus:

*"Listen, I shall explain its truth. All souls are immersed in happiness and sorrow through the snare of 'maya'. Only, 'Kaivalya', the supreme seat is the path of redemption and it cuts asunder the snare of 'maya' and relieves the yogin from birth, diseases, old age and death. There are no other paths of salvation."*

"Those who go round the net of Sastras are deluded by that knowledge. Even the Devas cannot describe that indescribable state let alone by the ones who are illumined by Sastras. That only which is without parts and stains, and which is quiescent beyond all the free from decay, becomes the jeeva, i.e., the Self on account of the results of past virtues and sins. How did Kaivalya, that is eternal and stainless, and the seat of paramatma, become jeeva? A bubble arose 'It' as in water and in this bubble arose 'ahamkara'. To this arose a body made of five elements and bound by dhatus, know that to be jeeva that is associated with happiness and misery; and, hence is the term jeeva applied to Paramatma who is pure. That pure jeeva is freed from the stains of passion, anger, fear, delusion, greed, pride, lust, birth, death, miserlyness, swoon, giddiness, hunger, thirst, ambition, shame, fright, heart burning, jealousy, grief and gladness. So I shall tell you the means of destroying the sins."

"Jnyana capable of giving moksha is possible only with Yoga; and, even Yoga becomes powerless in securing moksha when it is devoid of jnyana. So, the aspirant of emancipation should practice yoga as also pursue jnyana. He should always remember that the cycle of births and deaths are due to ajnyana only and perish with jnyana. Jnyana marg is the only path of Kaivalya and only a jnani will cognise the seat of the Lord, of the nature of Sat-cht-ananda."

"Now, I shall proceed to describe yoga to you, said the Lord to Pitamaha. Mantrayoga, Layayoga, Hatayoga, and Rajayoga are the four important yogas and the state of Arambha, Ghata, Parichaya and Nishpatti are common to all these four yogas."

'O Brahma, listen carefully', said the Lord. 'One should practise the Mantra along with its matrikas (proper intonations and sound) and others for a period of twelve years to get wisdom, jnyana and siddhi. Only persons of weak intellect and less qualified for yoga take to this Mantrayoga. Layayoga is described in numerous ways and one of these is to contemplate on the Lord without parts; this should be done always, whether sleeping, eating, sitting or walking'. Hatayoga is said to possess eight subservients, the same as ahtanga yoga viz yama, niyama, asana, pranayama, prathyahara, dharana, dhyana of Sri Hari in ajnya and Samadhi. Mahamudra, Mahabandha, and Khechari, jalandhara, uddiyana, and Mulabandha, uttering Om without interruption for long time and hearing expositions of supreme truths of the triad- vajroli, amaroli and sahajoli, all these separately. The spiritual aspirant should avoid laziness, idle talk, playing with mantra, women, and metals (alchemy), and abandon them by forces of virtue; he should practise non-injury, moderate eating. He should select a calm and serene, secluded place like a monastery and sit on a slightly elevated place and practise Pranayama. He should sit erect in Padmasana on a piece of cloth, deer- skin or any other mattress and practise pranayama. He should first offer salutations to his teacher with the shloka: '*Gururbrahma, Gururvishnu, Gururdevo Mahesvarah; Gurursakshat parabrhama tasmai guruve namah*'. Closing the right nostril with right thumb and taking breath in through the left nostril; this breath should be retained as long as possible and then breathed out through the right nostril and again, breath in through the right retain long and breath out through left. By retainiang breath for long time, kevala kumbhakam is reached and this will bring enormous mystic powers such as levitation and power to perform great feats. Pranayama should be continued uninterruptedly till breathing becomes uniform in both the nostrils. The time gap between the breath-in (Pooraka), retaining (Kumbhaka) and breath-out (Rechaka) is of the ratio of 16: 64:32; this should be done four times a day- at sunrise, noon, sunset and midnight. This will purify the body and the person who regularly practices this will reduce fat, and becomes healthy with a glow on his face; he will keep calm and cool disposition. Dietary restrictions such as avoidance of bitter, too hot and sour dish, use of asfoetida, onion, garlic and mustard are also advised."

"Meditating on the Atma with the Pranava 'Om', the yogin will burn all the sin he has committed; and, dharana on Atma will give enormous power such as clairvoyance, claiveyance, clairaudience, levitation and transportation at great speed, invisibility at will, etc. Practice of five-fold dharana for a period of two years will give mastery over the earth. Miracles like walking on water, fire, and invincibility and invisibility are possible to such yogins who practise the five dharanas. Then, there is dharana with dhyana when practiced for two hours and twenty-four minutes restraining breath in akasha will give enormous super human powers. ***Mahabandha*** is another powerful yoga that will give extra-ordinary super human powers. There are the ***mahavedha, khecharimudra, yonibandha, mulabandha*** and other techniques of yoga practised by many sidhdhas. These yogas are of immense mystic powers that the Yogins who practice them can attain the forms and states on earth and in other spheres of the universe they wish at their will and ultimately reside in Brahman."

Many of the intricate details of techniques of these yogas and the mystic powers associated with them are not given here for it should be learnt under strict guidance of an experienced Sidhdha only. Further, these mystic powers should not be used for personal benefit and should be used for the welfare of the people. Another important point to be noted here is that these yogic practices require not one life time but several to be fruitful!

*Varaha Upanishad*

This is a beautiful Upanishad that provides answer to questions that are pestering the mortals, day in and day out. Like the Kaushitaki Upanishad, the Varaha Upanishad also covers vide–ranging aspects. When the great sage Ribhu performed a penance for twelve auspicious days, the Lord Narayana appeared in the form of a boar and offered him a boon of his choice. But, Ribhu was not interested in any thing of worldly significance; he in turn asked the Lord to impart 'Brahmavidya' Thus the Lord Imparted this Upanishad.

"The Wise Seers know that there are thirty-six Principles or Tattvas coupled with Jiva while others maintain there are ninety-six. However, the jnyaanendriyas and karmendriyas together make ten; the vital airs are five (Pranas); sound and other rudimentary principleas are five; manas, budhdhi, chitta and ahamkara are four; and, together these make twenty-four tattvas. Besides, as the wise hold, there are quintuplicated elements earth, water, fire, vayu and akasha. And there are the gross, subtle and the causal or the kaarana bodies. The states of Consciousness are three and these make thirty- six principles in all. There are six changes viz existence, birth, growth, transformation, decay and destruction; and, hunger, thirst, grief, delusion, old age, and death that are natural consequences and infirmities. There are the constitituents of the physical body, namely, skin, blood, flesh, fat, marrow and bones. The ari-shadvargas are raga, dvesha, lobha, mada, moha, and matsarya that kill a person internally. Visva, Taijasa and Prajnya are the three aspects of the jeeva. The three Gunas are sattva, rajas, and tamas and Prarabhdha, Sanchita, and Agamin are the three karmas binding man to samsara. There are the functions of the Manas like the thought (Chitta), certainity, egoism, compassion, memory, complacency, sympathy, and indifference; and, actions of the body like talking, walking, lifting, exerting, enjoying. The directions and their deities like the quarters, Vayu, Surya, Varuna, Ashvini devas, Agni, Indra, Upendra, Mrityu, the moon, Brahma, Rudra, Kshetrajnya, Ishvara, and all these together make the ninety-six Principles (Tattvas). The Upanishad says, "Those who woship, with devotion, me in the form a Boar, who am other than the aggregate of these 96 Tattvas are released from ajnyana and become jivanmuktas."

The Lord imparted Brahmavidya thus: A spiritual aspirant will attain Vairagya through adherence to one' duties, religious austerities and devotion to his Guru. He will gain the power of discrimination and will be able to distinguish between the eternal and the non-eternal, indifference to enjoyments of either this world or the other world, and will acquire the virtues and longing for liberation.

The spiritual aspirants should give up sensuousness and withdraw senses from the worldly affairs and concentrate on me who is the chaitanya, the universal 'Consciousness'. He should give up the conception of 'mine'in all objects and place the consciousness of 'I' in me.

To be born as a human being is difficult; and, more so, as a male, and that too, in a Brahmin family particularly a Madhva with spiritual bent of mind. It is sanskar of the previous births and Divine Grace. Even then, if the fool does not cognise the significnce of dhyan, meditation, contemplation, and svadhyaya of Vedanta, and realize the nature of Brahman, i.e., Sat-Chit- Ananad, when will he obtain Moksha? The Lord Narayana in the form of Boar said, "I am Happiness and there is none other. If there is another, then it is not happiness. If there is anything as love, it is on my account as I am the seat of supreme love. He who is sought after by all, saying "I should become such" is 'Myself', the all-pervading. "I am the Self, the self-shining, the self-effulgent Atman."

The Lord continued, "I am the Atma which is all-witness, of the nature of Brahman. The universe, jiva, Ishvara, maya, and others do not really exist, except my full atma. Karma that has Dharana and other attributes and is the form of darkness and ajnyana is not fit to touch (affect) me who am Atma, the self-resplendent. Whoever sees, through the evidence of Vedanta, this visible universe as the supreme seat that is of the form of light attains moksha at once. When that knowledge which dispels the idea that this body (alone) is Atma, arises firmly in one's mind as was before the knowledge that this body (alone is Atma, then that person, even though he does not desire moksha, will get it. So, such a wise person who enjoys the bliss of Brahman is not bound by karma (ajnyana). Persons with spiritual eyes see Brahman, that is the witness of the three states – Be-ness (Sat), wisdom (Chit), and bliss; that is the underlying meaning of 'Tvam' (Thou) and 'Aham' (I) and that is untouched by all stains. Just as a blind person does not see the sun, the ignorant person does not see Brahman. Prajnana alone is Brahman. By cognizing Brahman, a person becomes immortal."

"One who knows his own self, Atma as Brahman, is not afraid of anything. He is a Lion-king, (Nrsimha). Just as this world appears as dark to the blind and bright to the persons with good eyes, this world is full of miseries to the ignorant and fullof happiness to the wise. The real nature of all embodied objects is ever the absolute Consciousness. One who has thus known Atma fully has neither emancipation nor bondage. Whoever meditates even for 48 minutes through the cognition of one's own real form, he is released from all bondages. He is Vasudeva who has realized thus. "Prostrations to me who am in all the elements and the ***Chidatma*** (i.e., the Atma of the nature of wisdom). Prostration to me, who is eternal and free and who am the ***Pratyagatma***".

"The ignorant dry up the body without food and water and call it 'Upavasa'; Upavasa is dwelling near Him, the Lord, or the union of the atma and paramatma. A man is said to attain Paroksha (indirect) wisdom when he knows that there is Brahman, but he is said to attain 'Sakshaatkara (direct cognition) when he knows or realizes that he is himself Brahman. When a Yogin knows his Atma to be the absolute, then he becomes a 'jivanmukta'. The two words for bondage and moksha are 'mine' and 'not mine'; man is bound by 'mine', but released by 'not-mine'. The wise should abandon all thoughts relating to externals and so also with reference to internals. He should rest content with his Atma for ever."

"This whole universe has been created by sankalpa and exists in the form of sankalpa. The wise should abandon this universe and fix his mind on nirvikalpa (change-less), meditate on my heart, sing my glory, talk only about me to one another and devote yourself entirely to Me, as the Supreme. The Consciousness (chit) in the universe is myself, '***Chinmatra***' (***Supreme Consciousness***). O, Ribhu, you are 'Chit' and I am 'chit'; the world is also 'chit'. Make your desire nil; be without any stain (blemish). Delight only in 'Chinmatra' within. That which did not exist in the beginning, before the evolution of Atma (Jiva and Ishvara) and, that which ceases to exist anymore at the end (the deluge) is called "maya". There is no Ishvara and there is no Jiva, both the Akasha and the Ishvara evolved out of 'Me'."

"The creations, 'sentient' as well as 'non-sentient', from thinking (***Ikshana***) to pravesha [***Chandogya Upa***. 6- 2 & 3] of those having the forms of jivas and Ishvara is due to the creation of Ishvara (Illusion); while the samsara from the waking state to salvation is due to the creation of jiva, so, the karmas ordained in the Nachiketagni sacrfice (***Trinachaka***) to yoga are dependent on Ishvara (illusion). Therefore, aspirants after salvation should never enter into controversies regarding jiva and Ishvara."

"O Ribhu, when budhdhi is absorbed in ajnyana, it is sleep; 'Me' to whom there is no ajnyana, there is no sleep. The moving of budhdhi in subtle nadis constitutes dreaming state. For me, there is no dreaming, as there is no moving or changes in state of consciousness. Then, at the time of sushupti when all things are absorbed or enveloped by tamas, you enjoy the highest bliss, of your own nature in invisible state, O Ribhu."

"If the spiritual aspirant sees everything as 'chit' without any difference, he is a vijnani, He alone is Shiva, He alone is Hari, He alone is Brahma; and, all this mundane existence is a long drawn dream, illusion for him. So, from morning till going to bed, the spiritual aspirants should contemplate on 'Me', the one Brahman. As salt is dissolved in water, the manas is merged in Atman, it is Samadhi. For a person of controlled mind, disciplined mind, everything is possible. He can bring dead back to life and cure all diseases. But all these sidhdhis are meaningless when the higher purpose of spiritual attainment is realized. Most of the apirants end up in the blind alley and get lost in mystic and tantric glimmicks forgetting the main purpose of their yogic practices. They get enomoured by their yogic powers and get into delusion!

***Varaha Upanishad*** deals at length with the rules to be observed with regard to the practice of Yoga. Of course, this should be read with Yogatattva Upanishad for more details. However, certain important revelations are there. "The master of Manas is Prana, and the master of Prana is 'laya'. Therefore '***Laya Yoga***' should be practiced. ***Laya*** is said to be '***without action and changes***'. The Laya (absorption of mind) that is above speech and in which one has to abandon all sankalpas should be known only by experience, not otherwise. The person who desires all the wealth of yoga should practice with single mind, subdued mind concentration of nada alone".

The Lord said to Ribhu:

"This body is made up of panchabhutas in five spheres; these five elements are: 1. The hard one, Prithvi; 2.The liquid one, 'apas'; 3. The moving one, 'Vayu'; 4.The all-pervading 'akasha'; and 5. The bright one, 'tejas'. The body is pervaded by 'prana vayu'by breathing- in and breathing out day and night. Diminution of vayu will cause incessant tremour. Diminution of Apas will cause greyness of hair and diminution of Tejas will cause loss of hunger and lustre. One dies with the diminution of the essence of Akasha in the body. The Prana (jivita) that is supported by these elements rests in the body and, when the elements diminish, having no place in the body, Prana rises up like a bird flying up in (Udana) and the 'bandha' (binding) yoga technique associated with this Udana is called 'Uddiyanabandha', by which the flight is arrested, i.e., Prana is retained in the body.

This '***Uddiyanabandha***', postures described in ***Shiva Samhita***, is quite hurtful. It is very painful if there is much agni in stomach; hence, it is adviable to be very careful not to practice it on empty stomach or with out proper ablutions, cleansing the internal lower parts of the body. Persons desirous of taking benefit of this Uddiyanabandha Yoga should be moderate in food and practice ***Mantra Yoga***, ***Laya Yoga and Hata Yoga*** also through mild, midlle, and transcendental methods, respectively. The preliminary yogic practices i.e., the ashtangas like yama, niyama, etc. should be strictly followed. Yama consists of non-injury, truthfulness, continence, compassion, straight forwardness, patience, courage, moderate eating and sleep, physical and mental hygience (cleanliness, or purity). Niyama consists of religious austerities, contentment, belief in God and the sacred scriptures like Veda and Upanishads, charity, Ishvara pranidana (worship of personal god-Ishta devata), satsang, svadhyaya, Association with spiritual-minded and study of scriptures), modesty, good intellect, and practice of japa and vrata (chanting Lord's name and strictly adhering to religious observances of restraints). These enable a spiritual aspirant to have the right mood, and the right physical and mental preparation for the rigours of Yogic practices.

There are eleven postures or 'Asanas' for Yoga. These are: Chakra, Padma, Kurma, Mayura, Kukkuta, Vira, Svastika, Bhadra, Simha, Mukta, and Gomukha, and one more is the Vajra, normally advocated for Pranayama. Pranayama (pooraka, kumbhaka and rechaka at regular intervals in a ratio) should be practiced regularly.

And, then Muladhara (sacral plexus) is described in detail. The body of every sentient is 96 digits long. In the middle of the body, two digits above the anus and two digits below the sexual organ, is the center of the body called 'Muladhara', the Central Plexus (Chakra). Nine digits above the genitals, there is kanda of nadis, which revolves oval-shaped, four digits high and four digits broad. It is surrounded by flesh, blood and bone. The Nadi chakra (wheel of nerves), having twelve spokes, is situated in it; Kundali that supports this body is here. It is covering by its face the Brahmarandhra of Sushumna. By the side of the Sushumna, runs the 'Alambusha' and the 'Kuhuh'. In the next two spokes are the 'Varuna' and 'Yashasvini'. To the south of Sushumna is the Pingala. On the next two spokes are 'Pusa' and 'Payasvini'. To the west of the Sushumna is the nerve called 'Sarasvati'. On the next two spokes are 'Shankini' and the 'Gandhari'. To the north of Suishumna lies the 'Ida'. Hastijihva and Visvodara are located next. In these spokes of the wheel, the twelve nadis carry the twelve vayus from left to right to the different parts of the body. The nadis are woven warp and woof like a cloth. They are said to have different colours. The 'Nabhi chakra' (Navel Plexus), is the central portion of this network (cloth-like nadis). "Jvalanti', 'Nadrupini','Pararandhra', and Sushumna are called the basic supports of 'nada', the spiritual sound. These four are of ruby colour. 'Kundali' repeatedly covers the central portion of Brhmarandhra. Thus, ten vayus move in these nadis.

The spiritual aspirant should sit with his back and neck straight (erect) with his mouth shut, should meditate, contemplating on Atma (turyaka), with his mind on the nose-tip, center of his heart and the middle of the 'bindu', and should see with a tranquil mind, with his mental eye, the flow of nectar from there. Having closed the anus and drawn up the apana vayu and caused it to rise through, chanting in mind thePranava "Om", he should complete with Sri bija (***Hreem***); he should all the while contemplate upon his atma as ***Sri (Parashakti)*** and as being bathed in nectar. This is called '***Kaalavanchana***' (time-illusion), the most important of all. By this, whatever thought of, is accomplished by the mind itself. Agni will flame in jala and the flame of 'agni' will arise the branches and blossoms. Then the words uttered and the actions done regarding the universe are fruitful. By checking the bindu in the path, by making fire flame up in water, and drying it up, the body is made firm. Having contracted the anus and the yoni simultaneously, and united together, should draw up apana vayu and unite it with Samana. He should contemplate upon his Atma as Shiva and bathe it in nectar and concentrate on 'bala' (will or strength). Gradually, he should go up by the union of Prana and Apana and thus, will attain sidhdhis. This bandha, like a dam, shall contain all the energy and one can see the Devatas with the grace of this 'bandha'. If with Prana is made to rise up soon, Udana, this bandha checking up all nadis goes up. This is called "Samputayoga' or 'Mulabandha'. Through this yoga, the vayu comes under the control of the yogin; with the control of Vayu, the 'agni', ***Vaisvnara*** (gastric fire) in the body will increase and food will be easily digested. Increase in rasa (essence of digested food), dhatu (spiritual substance) will increase, and thereby wisdom in the body killing ll the sins."

It is further stated that, "There is the triangular muladhara in the center of the anus and the genitals that illumines the seat of Shiva (in the form of 'bindu').'Parashakti' called 'Kundalini' is located here. From the seat, rises vayu and with that 'agni' is increased; from that seat bindu originates and 'nada' becomes loud and clear. From the seat, Hamsa is born; and, 'manas' is born from the seat. The six plexus beginning with 'Muladhara' are the seat of Goddess Shakti and from neck to the top of the head is the seat of Shiva. To the nadis, the body is the support and to Prana, the nadis are the support; and, to the 'jiva' the Prana is the dwelling place; to Hamsa, jiva is the support and to Shakti, Hamsa is the seat and the locomotive and fixed universe."

Further, it is stated that, " Pranayama should be practiced with a pure mind and pure heart and the three bandhas contemplating on the supreme power that binds this universe. Breathing should be stopped and rest in 'shoonyaka' (restraint) and rest in Brahman. Rechaka is expiration and pooraka is inspiration and kumbhaka is keeping the vayu inside. He is an emancipated person who practices such a chitta. In the mandala of Sushumna vayu should be made to rise up through 'Mudra-bandha'. Short pronunciation of Pranava frees one from sins; its long pronunciation promotes to moksha and so also its pronunciation in apyaayana or pluta svara. He is a knower of Veda who knows pronunciation of 'Om' in these three ways and also knows the end of Pranava that is beyond the power of speech. The short svara goes to bindu and the long svara goes to Brahmarandhra; the pluta goes to the dvadashanta (twelfth center). The mantra should be uttered on account of getting mantraiddhis."

"Whoever recites this Upanishad becomes immaculate like fire and becomes jeevanmukta and always sees the seat of Vishnu, so says the Lord."

*Maitreya-Upanishad of Samaveda*

King Brhadrata retired to Vanaprasthashram and performed a severe austerity (tapas) for a thousand days in order to know about the true nature of the 'Sat' and the state of the Brahman. At the end of the thosand days, Shakayanya Muni, an Atmajnya of Tejas and a sage shining like scorching fire, appeared and said, O King of the Ikshvaku lineage, ask me anything you want. The king paid his respects to the Muni and requested him to impart the 'Knowledge of the Brahman' for I know this world is truly a veritable hell. He continued, "This body is borne out of sexual intercourse and has no wisdom. It emerged from urinary orifice; it is lnked by bones and coated over with flesh, bound by skin and replete with nauseating substances like urine, serum, fat, bile, phelgm, and indeed, a foul body worthy of discard at the earliest. Hence, I want to know about the Atma. Please describe 'That'."

To this, the great sage replied, "What all we know as artha, the senses feel, hear and see are evil (anartha) to which the Bhutatma (the lower Self) clings and prevents the vision of the Lord. It is only through severe austerities, Sattva' (pure mind) is attained and through the Sattva, the 'Atman' (Paramatman or higher Self) is reached. It is Chitta alone that is Samsara. It is an archaic mystery that whatever this Chitta (Thinks) desires it becomes. One should meditate on the Lotus of the heart (Hridayakamala) to realize Him.

In the next Adhyaya, the King reaches Kailasa and asks the Lord Mahadeva to impart the knowledge of the highest Tattva. It is said that, Lord Maitreya went to Kailasa and asked Mahadeva to impart him the mysteries of the highest Tattva. In reply, Mahadeva said, "This body is the temple; the Jiva in it is Shiva. One should worship him abstracting the mind from sensual objects and purifying it through Dhyana and shoucha. Ajnana is the obstruction in the path and this can be removed by subjugation of the Indriyas. One should live an ascetic life to attain Him; and, the knowledge of the Self, "So'ham" is the 'Jnyaan'. One should worship Him in his own heart with the knowledge of the Self, "So'ham".

The Upanishad drives home the fact that the Sansar, the wife, son, mother, etc. are all binding us due to our ignorance, ajnyaan. When 'Ahamkara' (son) is given up, the other weaknesses or attachments like the house, mother, wealth (brother), desire (wife), that are delusion (mother) are all washed out and the real wisdom (son) is born. The 'Chit' (Consciousness) of the sun is ever shining in the resplendent 'Akasha' of the heart. He neither sets nor rises; there is no sandhya to perform. There is no need to retire to forests and abandoning Karma or uttering of the mantra of a sanyasi will not constitute Sannyasa. Only the union of the Jeeva (-atma), the lower self, with the Parama (-atma), the higher self, at the two Sandhis (morning and evening) is the 'Sandhya'. Whoever has nausea for all Ishana (desires) and treats the rest as the vomited food, and is devoid of affection (attachment) of the body, is qualified for Sanyasa. Otherwise he is a fallen person who takes to sanyas on account of wealth, food, clothes, and fame; he is not worthy of salvation. Further, it is said that all thoughts of Meditation (contemplation on higher Tattvas), Sastras, Mantra are of no avail; even pilgrimages with a desire to attain Brahman is the worst. These are like mirage in the desert that appear as water and mislead us. Those, whose minds are deluded by My Maya, however learned they may be, do not attain Me and roam about like hungry crows. Therefore, the ascetic should worship the Lord dwelling in his own heart, and relinquish all external worship. Relinquishing with their Vasanaas, the seer, the seen and the visual, worship Atma alone, the resplendent supreme presence. This is the state where the Sankalpas are at rest." This is the second chapter of the Upanishad

In the Third chapter, the Upanishad teaches the Brahmavidya and goes on narrating how the Lord dwells in everything, everything that exists, or ever existed in the past, or will ever exist in the future. The Lord is in the form of Jyoti (light) in Chinmatra (Absolute Consciousness). He who has realized himself thus is Myself. He has realized the Self- the Atman." The Upanishad ends with a note that whosoever hears this Upanishad once will become Brahman.

*Amritabindu Upanishad*

This Upanishad is from Krishna Yajurveda. It lays its emphasis on Mind. It starts with "Om, Manas.... and, narrates the qualities of Manas. The desire makes the mind impure and the pure Mind is blemishless and mind alone is the cause of bondage or emancipation. Manas should be controlled and that alone is true wisdom. The only way to control mind is through Dhyana (Meditation). Other ways are but long and tedious. "It i.e., Brahman is not at all one that can be contemplated upon. It is not one that cannot be contemplated upon. It is not capable of contemplation, and yet it should be contemplated upon. Then one attains Brahman.... Whoever cognizes "I" to be that Brahman attains certainly Brahman."

"The body which perishes again and again is not conscious of its own destruction. But he (the Jiva) knows (it) always. He who is enveloped by the Maya of sound, is never able to come to (or see) the sun (of Prabrahman) from the darkness (of ignorance). Should such darkness be cleared, then he alone sees the non-dual state, Prabrahman in Shabdakshara. One should contemplate on that which remains after the cessation of shabdha and Akshara (indestructible) and such a person will attain his Self. Shabdhabrahman and Parabrahman are two vidyas to be known by all wise men. One who has mastered Shabdhabrahman will attain Parabrahman. One should preserve all knowledge in Jnyana and discard the books like separating the seeds from the straw. As ghee is latent in milk, so is vijnyan latent in every being. The Vasudeva who is support of all beings, who live in all and who protects all creatures is 'Myself'. "The Vasudeva is 'Myself'." Such is the Upanishad.

*Kaivalya-Upanishad*

This Upanishad belongs to Krishna –Yajurveda. Here, Ashvalayana aks Brahma to impart him the knowledge of the Supreme and the means to reach Purusha, the Brahman. To this Prajapitha replied, "Know It through Shrudhdha (faith), Bhakti (devotion), Dhyana (Meditation), and Yoga. It is not through Karma but through renunciation, one can attain salvation. Wise men take to Vedanta-vijnyana and Sanyasa yoga to reach That which is beyond the heaven and in the cave (of the heart) and finally become liberated.

Next, the Yogasana and the method of meditation are explained thus: "Being seated in a pleasant posture in an unfrequented place with a pure mind, and with his neck, head, and body erect, having given up the duties of the four ashrams of life, having subjugated all the organs, having saluted his Guru with devotion, having looked upon the heart-lotus as being free from Rajoguna, contemplating on Uma-Maheshvara......" Further, the Upanishad reads: "He only is Brahma, Shiva, Indra; He only is the indestructible, the Supreme, Self-shining, Vishnu. He only attains Parabrahman who sees in himself all elements and himself in all elements.

There is no other means. He uses his own body as arani below and the Pranava (Om) above, to contemplate and, burn his ajnyana."

"It is only He (Paramatma) who, deluded by Maya, assumes a body and does everything. He is the enjoyer- in the waking state is gratified with the earthly desires fulfilled, in the dream state enjoys pleasures and pains of several world (created by Himself), and in the dreamless state enjoys the Bliss. Again, reminded by the karmas of previous births, wakes up to this world and goes to sleep. From Him, arise Prana, Mind, jnyanendriyas, karmendriyas, Akasha, Vayu, Agni, water and earth supporting all. Parabrahman, which is of all forms, which is the Supreme abode of this universe, which is the most subtle of the subtle and which is eternal, is only yourself. You are only 'That'. One who knows this is relieved from all bondage. Whoever recites this Upanishad becomes pure as agni and is liberated from all sins.

*Skanda-Upanishad of Krishna -Yajurveda*

This is a very small Upanishad that eulogises Brahman and makes no difference between Shiva and Vishnu. It says, "the heart of Vishnu is Shiva. The heart of Shiva is Vishnu." There is no difference. The body is said to be the temple. The Shiva (in the body) is the God Sadashiva (in the temple)

That Achyuta (the indestructible or Vishnu), who is the seer of the Conscious and the inert, is of the form of 'Jnyana'. He only is Mahadeva. He only is Maha-Hari (Maha-Vishnu). One should worship Him with the thought "I am He". To see oneself as not different from Him is Jnyana (Wisdom). O Narasimha! O Lord of Devas! Through Thy grace, persons cognise the true nature of Brahman that is unthinkable, undifferentiated, endless and immutable, through the forms of gods, Brahma, narayana and Shankara. Thus is the teaching of the Veda for salvation.

*Paingala-Upanishad of Sukla Yajurveda*

This is a beautiful Upanishad that describes the Vedic cosmology and evolution of Mankind. Paingala the student of Yajnavalkya wanted to know about the supreme mysteries of Kaivalya from his Guru. Yajnavalkya imparts this Upanishad, thus:

"At first, this universe was 'Sat' only. It is spoken of as Brahman that is ever free from trammels of matter which is changeless, which is Truth, Wisdom, and Bliss, which is full, permanent, and one only without a second. In this Be-ness, i.e., Sat, was like a mirage in a desert, silver in mother-of-pearl, a person in the pillar (Narasimha), of colour, etc., in the crystals, mulaprakriti, having in equal proportions the Gunas, red, white and black, and being beyond the power of speech. That which is reflected in it is Sakshi-Chaitanya (the Witness-Consciousness)."

The mulaprakriti, again undergoing change, becomes (with the preponderance of Sattva in it), Avarana –Shakti names avyakta. That which is reflected in it (Avyakta) is Ishvara-Chaitanya. He, i.e., Ishvara has Maya. under his control, is omniscient, the original cuase of creation, preservation, the dissolution, and the seed of this universe. He causes the universe that was latent in Him."

"He makes it (the world of creatures) appear (to manifest itself) through bonds of Karma (of all creatures) like a painted canvas unfurled; and, again through the extinction of their Karmas, He makes (likes) it disappear. In Him alone is latent all the universe, lapped up like a painted cloth. Then, from the supreme avarana-shakti, Shiva (Ishvara) arose through the preponderance of the Rajas; Vikshepa-shakti called Mahat. That which is reflected in it is Hiranyagarbha-Chaitanya. Presiding over as He does over Mahat, He, (Hiranyagarbha) has a body, both manifested and unmanifested. From Vikshepa-Shakti of Hiranyagarbha arose, through the preponderance of Tamas, the gross Shakti called Ahamkara. That which is reflected in it is Virat-Chaitanya. He (Virat) presiding over it (Ahamkara) and possessing a manifested body becomes Vishnu, the Chief Purusha and Protector of all gross bodies. From that Atma arose akasha, from akasha arose Vayu, from Vayu arose agni (fire), from agni apas, and from apas prithvi (the Earth). The five tanmatras (elements or rudimentary properties) alone are the gunas of the above five."

"That generating cause of the universe (Ishvara) wishing to create and having assumed tamoguna, wanted to convert the elements which were subtle tanmatras into gross ones. In order to create the universe, he divided into two parts each of those divisible elements, and having divided each moiety into four parts, made a five-fold mixture, each element having moiety of its own original element and one-fourth of a moiety of each of the other elements, and thus evolved out of the five-fold classified gross elements, the many myriads of Brahmandas (macrocosm) and the fourteen worlds pertaining to each sphere, and the spherical gross bodies (microcosms) fit for the respective worlds.

"Having divided the Rajas-essence of the five elements into four, He out of three parts created the five Pranas having five-fold function. Again, out of the remaining fourth part, He created Karmendriyas. Having divided their Sattva-essence into four parts, He out of three such parts created the anthahkarana having five-fold function. Out of the remaining one part He created the Jnyanendriyas. Out of the collective Sattva-essence, He created the Deities (Devatas) ruling over the organs of sense and action. They, through His orders, began to pervade the macrocosm."

Through His orders, Virat associated with ahamkara created all the gross things. Through His orders, Hiranyagarbha protected all subtle things. Without Him, located in their spheres, they were unable to move or function. Then He wished to infuse Chetana (life) into them. Having created Brahmada and Brahmarandhras in all the microcosmic heads, He entered within. Though they were at first inert, they started functioning perform karmas like beings of intelligence. The omniscient Ishvara entered the microcosmic bodies with a particle of Maya and being deluded by that 'Maya', acquired the state of Jiva. Identifying the three bodies with Himself, He acquired the state of Jagrat, Svapna, and Sushupti, Trance and Death and being immersed in sorrow, he is deluded like water-lift of potter's wheel, as if subjected to birth and death."

Next, Paingala asked Yajnyavalkya to explain how Ishvara, who is the creator, preserver, and destroyer and the Lord of all the worlds, acquired the state of Jiva. To this Sage Yajnavalkya said, "Listen to me attentively, I shall explain how the gross, subtle and the causal bodies evolved and stated thus:

Ishvara having taken a small portion of the quintuplicated mahabhutas (the great elements), made in regular order the gross bodies, both collective and segregate. The skin, the skull, intestines, bone, flesh and nails are of the essence of the earth (Prithvi). Blood, urine, saliva, sweat, and others are of the apas. Hunger, thirst, heat, delusion, and copulation are of the Agni. Walking, lifting, breathing and others are of the essence of Vayu. Passion, anger, etc are of the essence of Akasha. The collection of these having touch and the rest is this gross body that is brought about by Karma, that is the seat of egoism in youth and other states, and that is the abode of many sins."

He continued, "Then he created Pranas out of the collective three parts of the Rajas essence of the five-fold divided elements. The modifications of Prana are: Prana, apana, vyana, udana and samana; naga, kurma, karkala, devadatta and dhananjaya are the auxiliary pranas. Of the first five, the heart, anus, navel, throat and the whole body are the seats of these. Then He created the karmendriyas out of the fourth part of the Rajas-guna. Of akasha and the rest He created mouth, legs, hands and the organs of secretion and excretion as the modifications; talking, walking, lifting, excreting and enjoying are their functions."

"Likewise, out of the collective three parts of Sattva-essence, He created anthahkarana. Anthahkarana, manas, budhdhi, chitta and ahamkara are its modifications. Thought (Sankalpa), certitude, memory, egoism and anusandhana (inquiry) are their functions. Throat, face, navel, heart and the middle of the eyebrows (ajnya) are their seats. Out of the remaining fourth part of the Sattva essence, He created Jnanendriyas (sense organs). Ear, skin, eyes, tongue, and nose are the modifications; sound, touch, form, taste and odour are their functions. Dik (the quarters), Vayu, Arka, Varuna, Asvini Devas, Indra, Upendra, Mrutyu, Prajapati, moon, Vishnu, the four-faced Brahma, and Shambhu (Shiva) are the presiding deities of the organs."

"There are the five Koshas: the annamaya kosha, pranmaya kosha, manomaya kosha, vijnyanamaya kosha, and the anandamaya kosha. The Annamayakosha is created and developed out of the essence of food and is absorbed into the earth which is the form of the food. This is the gross body."

"The Pranas with the karmendriya (organs of actions) is the pranamaya kosha; manas, with the jnanendriyas (organs of the sense), is the manomaya kosha. Budhdhi with the jnanendriyas is the vijnanamaya kosha. These three sheaths constitute the lingasarira (the subtle body). That which tends to ajnana (ignorance) of the Reality (of the Atma) is the anandamaya kosha. This is the causal body or the 'karana' sharira; moreover the five organs of the sense, the five organs of action, the five pranas and others, the five akasha and other elements, the four internal organs, avidya, passion, karma, and tamas- all these constitute the body (pura)." Further. Yajnavalkya continues:

'***Virat***', under the orders of Lord Ishvara, having entered this microcosmic body, and having Budhdhi as His vehicle, reaches the state of 'Visva'. Having 'Manas' as his vehicle, reaches 'Taijasa (Svapna) state. Then, under the orders of Ishvara, He who is coupled with "Avyakta', the vehicle of Maya having entered the microcosmic karana (causal) body, reaches the state of 'Prajnya' (in susupti). The Mahat Tattvas like "Aham Brahmasmi", Tat tvam asi", So'ham", speak of the identity with Brahman of the paramarthika jeeva enveloped by ajnana, which is but the small part of the avyakta, but not vyavaharika and pratibhashika (jeevas). It is only 'Chaitanya' that is reflected in 'anthahkarana that attains the three states."

Yajnavalkya continued, "There are five avasthas viz jagrat, svapna, susupti, murcha (trance), and death, Death dissolves the gross body. The jiva surrounded by avidya and the subtle elements takes with it the organs of sense and actions, their objects, and pranas along with the kamic karmas and goes to another world, assuming another body. Through the ripening of the fruits of previous karmas, the jiva has no rest; it is only after many births that the desire of emancipation arises in man through the ripening of good karma. Then, with the help of a Guru, one out of many may attain moksha, through inquiry (into atma). Therefore there should be inquiry about the universe, the jiva and the paramatma. Only when the knowledge of the three is attained, the knowledge of Brahman is possible".

In the Third Adhyaya, Paingala asks Yajnavalkya about the Mahavakyas to which a very beautiful exposition is given, thus:

"One should scrutinize the Mahat vakyas, "***Tat tvam asi***" (That art thou), "***Tvam tad asi***" (Thou art That), "***Tvam Brahmasi***" ('Thou art Brahman'), and "***Aham Brahmasmi***" ('I am Brahman'). The word 'Tat' denotes the cause of the universe that is variegated beyond perception, has the characteristic omniscience, has Maya as His vehicle and has the attributes of Sat-chit-ananda.It is He that is the basis of the notion 'I' which has the differentiated knowledge produced by anthahkarana, and it is He who is denoted by the word 'Tvam' (Thou). That is the undifferentiated Brahman which remains as the aim of the words 'Tat' and 'Tvam' after freeing itself from Maya and Avidya which are respectively the vehicles of Paramatma and Jivatma."

"The inquiry into the real significance of the sentences '***Tat tvam asi***' ***and*** '***Aham Brahmasmi***' forms what is called 'shravana', i.e., hearing- the first stage of inquiry. To inquire in solitude into the significance of shravana is 'manana'. The concentration of the mind with one-pointedness upon that which should be sought after by manana and shravana is nidhidhyasana. Samadhi is that state in which chitta having given up the conception of the difference of the meditator and the meditation, becomes of the form of the meditated. Then arises the modification pertaining to Atma. Siuch modifications cannot be known, but they can only be inferred through memory of the samadhi state. The myriads of karmas committed in this beginningless cycle of rebirths are anhilated only through them. Through these modifications of Atma, the collection of affinities is absorbed without any reminder whatever. When the accumulated good and bad karmas are wholly destroyed, these mahat vakyas become very clear and this realization of the 'Reality' will make one a jivanmukta."

"Ishvara wished to produce non-quintuplication or involution (reverse process of evolution) in the five-fold differentiated elements; withdrawing one by one from each organs and dissolved all things composed of the elements into their cause, the five elements. He then caused prithvi to merge into water, water into agni, agni into vayu, vayu into akasha, akasha into ahamkara, ahamkara into mahat, mahat into avyakta, and avyakta into Purusha in regular order. Virat, Hiranyagarbha and Ishvara being freed from (the vehicle of) Maya are absorbed into Paramatma. This gross body composed of the five differentiated elements and obtained from accumulated karma, is merged into its subtle state of non-quintuplicated elements, through the extinction of bad karmas, and increase of good karmas, attains causal or karana state and finally, is absorbed into Paramatma. So, one should meditate upon the identity of 'Tat' and 'Tvam', i.e., Atma. Then Atma shines like the sun freed from obscurations of clouds."

In the fourth Chapter, Yajnavalkya describes the virtues, the path to moksha and states that it, a lover of moksha, enables twenty-one generations to cross to atma. One through his being a 'Brahmavit' alone enables one hundred-one generations to cross. Know Atma to be the rider and the body as the chariot. Know also Budhdhi as the charioteer and manas as the reins. The wise say the organs are the horses, the objects are the roads and the hearts are the moving balloons. Atma, when associated with the sense organs and means, is the enjoyer. Therefore, it is the actual Narayana alone that is established in the heart; therefore, till his prarabdha karma lasts He exists in his body. Atma is invisible like Vayu. Though he is within and without, he is the immovable Atma; through the torch of wisdom, the internal Atma sees or knows."

"*One desirous of knowing what jnana (wisdom) and jneya (the object to be known) are, will not be able to know, attain his desired end, even though he may study the sastras a thousand times or thousand years. That which is alone should be known as the indestructible. That which exists in this world is only impermanent; therefore, after having giving up the study of many sastras, japa, sacrifice, pilgrimage-all these should be observed or practised till the 'Tattva', "I am Brahman" is known.* "

"There are two causes that lead to bondage and emancipation. They are 'mine' and 'not mine'. Through 'mine' creatures are bound; through 'not mine' they are released from bondage. When the mind attains 'unmani', i.e., above manas, then there is never the conception of duality. When unmani status occurs, then the supreme seat is attained. The mind enjoys salvation wherever it is. That which is equal in all is Brahman alone. Without the knowledge of "I am Brahman' no one will ever attain emancipation."

Whoever recites this Upanishad becomes immaculate as Agni. He becomes pure as Brahman; he becomes pure as Vayu. He purifies his ancestors ten degrees removed and his descendents ten degrees removed. He becomes a great personage. This Upanishad is Truth."

Thus, Paingala Upanishad is one of the most beautiful Upanishads that explain everything one wants to 'Know'. There is everything in it and nothing else is necessary for salvation. There is the knowledge of the evolution and involution; there is knowledge of life and death; and there is a well-laid path (to emancipation) that can surely lead the tired souls to liberation. What else is required?

*Kaushitaki Upanishad of the 'Rk' Veda*

This Upanishad is also called the Kaushitaki-Brahmana-Upanishad of the Kaushitaki School or the Sankhyanas. Both Brahmana and Aranyaka are joined in it including the Upanishad. In all there are 45 Adhyayas (Chapters) thirty in Brahmana and 15 in Aranyaka. The Kaushitaki Brahmana, in its first four Chapters, deals with the Soma sacrifice, Paryanka vidya (Path of the Soul and its rest place), Prana Vidya, Atma Vidya. Kaushitaki- Upanishad proper (Aranyaka), Chapter 3 to 6, is very interesting. Some of the salient features are described here.

King Chitra wanted to perform a sacrifice and asked the Sage Aruni to be the Priest. But Aruni sent his son Svetaketu to take part in the sacrifice. King Chitra asked Svetaketu, "Is there an end of transmigration of the soul in the world?" "Or, is there a way which leads to it?" Svetaketu replied, "I know it not". Nevertheless, "I will ask my father with regard to it". He then went to his father and asked him the same questions. Sage Aruni also did not know the answer. Both of them decided to come back to King Chitra to know the answer. King Chitra welcomes the Sage Aruni and his son and imparts Paryanka-vidya (Transmigration of souls), Prana-vidya, and Atma-vidya, thus:

"All that departs from this world, all of them, first go to the Moon. Through their life, the waxing lunar half of the month grows and by virtue of its waning half, it conveys the souls on the path of Pitryana to repeated rebirths. But, the moon is also the door to the heavenly world- the Devayana path leads beyond the moon; whoever answers the question asked by the moon in a satisfactory way will be allowed to go further to the solar sphere, the worlds beyond. On the other hand, whoever does not answer the question correctly, he allows them to fallback to earth in rain (souls returning to earth). He is born here, below in this or that place, be he as a worm, or as a fly, or as a fish, or as a bird, or as a lion, or as a boar, or as a bull, or as a tiger, or as a man, each according to his deeds (Karama), and each according to his knowledge.

The moon asks the question, "Who are You ?" and the departed soul answers thus:

"From the light (Moon), from the season, I came as seed
From the fifteen-fold produced realm of the fathers;
You have squeezed me in man as creator sprinkles in the mother,
Born am I and again I am reborn
As twelve-fold year, as the thirteenth beyond the moon
From the twelve-fold from the thirteen-fold father,
The 'this one' and 'the other' versus 'this' to know;
Untill ye seasons, me led to death by virtue of this truth, by virtue of this mortification (tapas), I am the seasons, I am the child of the seasons!

"Who are you? I am you"

If and when he speaks thus (to the moon), then he allows him to go beyond to the Devayana, the path of Gods.

"When he sets out upon this path called Devayana, he attains to the world of fire, then to the world of wind, then to the world of Varuna, then to the world of Indra, then to the world of Prajapati, then to the world of Brahman."

"In this world, he who knows all this, attains everything"; and Brahman says:

"Run towards him; because, through my power and splendour, he has arrived at the river Viraja (age-less) and will, truly, never become old."

There is a beautiful description of the Brahmalok and the Seat of Brahma. The chair, the cot, the bed (Soma-braids with Yajus), the bedspreads (Udgita), the attendants, is all beautifully described in the next few verses. Finally, the soul comes to the bedstead of rest called Amitaujas on which Brahma sits.

Brahma asks the Soul: "Who are you?"

Then he will reply: "I am the season, I sprouted from the season. I am born out of ether as my cradle, as the seed or sperm of my wife, as the splendour of the year, as the self of every being. You are the self of every being. What you are, I am".

And he (Soul) asks Brahman: "Who am I then?"

Brahman replies: "*the Truth*".

The dialogue goes on:

" How? In what manner, the Truth?"

*" – What is different from the gods and the corresponding living beings, that is 'true'; but, what the gods and living beings are, it is true-'ness'. It is expressed in ine word "TRUTH". This comprehends the whole world, you are the whole world."*

Then, the Brahman is described as the Veda. The power of cognition derived from Brahman is further explained. The power of the Brahman, as experienced by the manas, the prajnya, are explained. Finally, it is concluded that: "Whoever has this Knowledge of the Brahman acquires this Hiranyagarbha."

There is a different way of explaining all these. The Meaning of the Upanishad is quite simple. All human beings have to die after the assigned period of life, say a hundred years, is over on this earth. Many cut short this period due to their own folly, misuse and abuse of the body in youth. Well after the person dies, it is natural to take birth again since it is the order of'metempsychosis', as per the doctrine of 'Sansar'. Here the Samskar, Vasanas, the memories, the desire and such other accumulated karmic tendencies in the sub-conscious while living come into play. Desire, the unfulfilled ones decide th future course of action. The soul reenters a body through food (from rain, of clouds), according to the dictates of the past deeds. This is Pitruyana and thereafter.

The realsied soul on the other hand has discovered the path, the Devayana. It has acquired the nature (qualification) to eneter the heavens, the abode of the supreme Brahman. The soul is blemishless; it has no desire for re-birth. It simply relinquishes the body once for all, never to return.

This in brief is the summary of the first Adhyaya of the Kaushitaki Upanishad.

In the Second Adhyaya, Prana-vidya is explained, thus:

*"The Prana is Brahman, To the Prana as Brahman, the Manas (Mind) serves as the messenger, the eye as the watchman, the ear as the announcer, the speech as the attendant or the stewardess. Indeed he who knows the manas serves as the messenger to Prana as the 'Brahman' does not fail to have a messenger. Similarly, he who knows the roll of all the sense organs will get all he wants from these organs. Just as the organs of the human body serves the Prana without it's (Prana) asking, so also the Jeeva should serve the Brahman without His asking! He who knows this knows the 'Truth'.*

According to the teaching of Paingya, the Prana is Brahman. Manas, ears, eyes, speech, which were previously servants of Pran, appear here as layers placed one after another that surround Prana protecting him, as Prana again surround Atman protecting him. [See Taitt. Upa.,2], "*the Prana is Brahman; around this Prana as Brahman, the speech is situated beyond the speech (in the inside). Beyond the eye, the ear is situated and beyond the ear, the manas. Beyond the manas is Prana, around Brhaman itself, the Atman. To this Prana, as Brahman, all those godheads, i.e., the manas, eye, ear, speech, give offerings without his asking. Thus, all beings give gift to him who has such knowledge, without his asking!*

The Upanishad asserts, "*One should not beg or ask anything*". This is the secret of thisUpanishad. "*To him who asks nothing comes everything; and he who asks anything, or begs, will not get it.*"

Interestingly, there are some mantra in this Upanishad that promise to give what one wants! These mantra are mystical and occult in a sense, that it requires to follow certain tantra. Homa is performed and offerings of ghee are poured into Fire with the obeisasnce 'svaha'. After the successful completion of the Homa, the ash of the 'agnikunda' is smeared on one's body. The, smoke is inhaled, and the ash with ghee (ointment) is besmeared on limbs. With this, whatever wish is made, is fulfilled! These Homas are performed to get the desires fulfilled or thwart the games of the enemies.

There is also an interesting account of 'Pratardana', or what is called inner agnihotram. Accordingly, "so long as one speaks, he cannot breath-in, thereby he offers or sacrifices the breath in the speech. Similarly, as one breaths in, he cannot speak and thus, he sacrifies speech in the breath (for Prana). Both these sacrifices are unending, immortal because man offers them without interruption in jagrat as well as sleep. This method is also mystical; and, it is very powerful as a tantra (to fulfil one's desire). By deep Meditation and mauna (silence) enormous energy is built-up; and, this helps to work in the desired direction.

Another method is the Prayers are offered to the rising sun. The sacred thread is dipped in water and 'arghyam' (water is poured thrice) is offered with the request to liberate the aspirant from all sins he has commited.

There are mantra and tantras to protect one's property, progeny, and prevent any untoward incidents that may cause grief. Also, at the time of death, the father calls the son and utters these mystic mantra and transfers all his energy to him. Some of these mystic mantra are in Rk Veda. [See, 1.91.16; 18; 3.36.10; & 2.21.6; and, ***Atharva Veda*** 7.1.5 and 7.81.6].

In some of the verses, the supremacy of Prana over the sense organs and the manas is brought out and the significance of this knowledge of Prana as Brahman is the central theme of this Upanishad. There are persons who are deaf, dumb, blind and even foolish; there are persons who do not have the hands and/or legs and still live. It is Prana that supports the life of all these physically handicapped persons. Prana is 'Prajnatman' which encompasses this body and makes it erect; that is why one should adore Prana as Uktham [See ***Aitareya Aran***. Upa. 2.1]. All life forces penetrate into Prana.

But, what is Prana is the ***'Prajnya', the Consciousness or the intelligence and, what is Prajnya is 'Prana'***. When a man is in deep sleep, he sees no dream-image since he has attained his prajnya merged in Prana. The speech (with all names), the eyes (with all shapes and forms), the ears (with all sounds), and the manas (with all thoughts), enter into Prana (Him). And, when one wakes up, all these spring out of Atman just as the sparks spring out of blazing fire and scatter on all sides. The chief aim of this consideration about deep sleep and swoon is to demonstrate the identity of Prana and of Prajnya (Consciousness or intelligence). In deep sleep and swoon, the Prana continues while the Prajnya appears to be extinct. In truth, however, it is not extinct but has become one with the Prana, out of which it again rises forth during the waking state. Consequently, the Prajnya has only skipped, in a wakeful state it is different from Prana and for the rest, forms a unity with it.. In deep sleep, however, the sense organs also and along with them the sense objects dive into Prana. Consequently, they also together are united with the Prana.

What is Prana is Prajnya and what is Prajnya is Prana. This is 'Prana-vidya'. It (the Upanishad) says, "he who has such knowledge, recognizes the supremacy of Prana and he becomes the participant of Prana, of the intelligence-self, pulls, with all those organs out of this body and enters into the wind, becomes ether and attains to heaven." Thus, he reaches where the gods have reached and becomes immortal.

In the Third Adhyaya, 'Atma-vidya' is explained. This philosophical doctrine of the 'Atman' is the real core of this Upanishad. There are three aspects of this doctrine. 1. The Prajnyatman and the sense organs; 2. The Prajnyatman and the sense objects; and 3. The 'Subject' of Knowledge.

1. The Prajnyatman and the sense organs: The sense organs work in unity, in totality of the organs; and, this unity is efficient in every one of the organs. Further, this unity of the organs do not lie outside Prajna or Prajnya but in one amongst them, which has precedence over all other organs, i.e., Prana or Prajnyatman. The precedence of Prana or Prajnyatm, depends on: the dispensabil ity of the other organs; indispensability of the Prana; its (Prajnyatman's) continuance in deep sleep, and in the death.

2. The Prajnyatman and the Sense-objects: The sense-objects as organs are gathered in the Prajnyatman so that he reaches the objects through the organs. The organs have arisen out of Prajnyatman and, out of them again, it projects itself outwards towards the concerned objects; therefore the Prajnya reaches the objects through the organs. Thus, it is clear that, 'it is impos sible to know the objects through the organs without the Prana'. Indra: said to Pratardana,

"I am the life-breath; adore me as the intelligence self 'Prajnyatman', as life, as the immortal one. The Prana is life and life is Prana. So long as Prana stays in the body, life also stays in the body. Through Prana one attains a living condition and through Prajnya, intelligence, one gains true knowledge. So, one should adore me as life, as the immortal one, and attain immortality, imperishability and the heavenly world." Pratardana said:

"some say that vital forces operate in unity; none could at the same time, bring into consciousness, by itself; the names through speech, forms or shapes through the eyes, by them selves, the sounds through the ears by themselves, and the thoughts through the manas (Mind) by itself, but because, on the contrary, the vital forces, they bring every one of these to con sciousness, one after another. When the speech speaks, all the life forces speak following it (i.e.,with it), and when the eyes see, all the life forces see following them, when the ears hear, all the life forces hear following them, when the Manas thinks, all the life forces think following it and when the breath breaths, all the life forces breath following it." Indra said, But still, there is an order of precedence among life forces." For instance, Indra said, the person can live without the function of sense organs like the blind and the deaf; but, it is the Prana, the Prajnyatman, which encompasses the body and makes it erect. This is the penetration of all life forces into Prana. But, Prana is Prajnya and Prajnya is Prana. So, one should adore Uktham! The speech, breath, eye, ear, tongue. The limbs, the body, etc. are all parts of the Consciousness and taken out of it; of this, the respective function is only an externally transplanted element of being. For instance, the Manas is, as a part of it, taken out of it; of this thoughts and desires are an externally transplanted element of being. It is due to mounting of speech through intelligence, one attains all names through speech; similarly, mounting the breath, eyes, tongue, ears, eyes, limbs, body, and manas through intelligence, one attains the respective functions." Without Intelligence, none of these organs can function and one would say, "*my mind was elsewhere and that is why I was not conscious of that*!" Therefore, one should not desire to know or understand the unction of the mind, senses or body. One should desire to know the Subject, the person (Purusha) that is behind the performance of the action or deeds, thoughts, i.e., not the one which thinks or does but the one who thinks or does!" "*He is the protector of the world, he is the ruler of the world; He is the lord of the world. He is the Atman.*"

3. The 'Subject' of Knowledge: The 'Subject' of Knowledge, is the Brahman, 'Atman'. This is the core of the Upanishad. It is very important for every spiritual aspirant to know the spiritual goal.

> One should try to know the Subject and not the objects. There are no objects without the subjective organs and no subjective organs without objects. Both go together in this subject (like the spokes in the rim of a wheel and the felly in the nave or hub of the wheel). The subject is the Lord, who predestines man for good and evil, for salvation and perdition. This Lord is the Atman, the Brahman.

In the fourth and the last Chapter, the same concept of the bodily organs entering 'Prajnyatman' or Prana in deep sleep, and their re-emergence again is further elucidated. "In deep sleep and swoon, the Prana continues, while the Prajnya appears to be extinct. In truth, however, it is not extinct altogether but has become one with Prana, out of which it again rises forth during the waking state. Cnsequently, the Prajyna has only skipped in wakefulness; it is different from Prana and for the rest, forms a unity with it. In deep sleep, however, the sense organs also, and along with them the sense objects, dive into Prana. Consequently, they also together are united with the Prana."

Gargya Baalaaki, the first famous teacher of Veda, once went to King Ajatashatru and said, "I will teach you Brahman". The King said, "I shall give you a thousand cows for that." Gargya Baalaaki went on and on narrating the abode of the Spirit, i.e., Brahman. Finally, he conceded his inability to satisfactorily explain the Brahman. The King said, "Well, it is contrary to usual practice that a Kshatriya teaches a Brahmin; come! I will teach you the Brahman", and narrated thus:

The King took Baalaaki to a man who was in deep sleep and tried to wake him up by words. When there was no response, he pricked him and the man woke up. The King asked Balaki, "Where was this man when he was sleeping?"

In man there are arteries which are called 'Hita' which, arising out of the heart surround the pouch of the heart or pericardium. These arteries, as fine as a hair split thousandfold, find themselves filled by a fineness of a brown, white, dark, yellow and red sap. In these one stays when one is asleep so that he has no dreams. Then he becomes one with Prana; then enters into him the speech with all names, the eye with all forms, the ear with all sounds and the Manas (Mind) with all thoughts. And when he wakes up, then it happens that all life forces, each according to its location, come forth out of the Atman like the sparks fly out of one another from the blazing fire towards all sides.. The life forces (speech, eyes, ears and Manas) come forth the divinities (Agni, Surya, Disha, and Chandramah) and out of the divinities come the worlds of names, forms, sounds and thoughts."

"It is the Prana, Prajnatman, that has entered this body as self, down to the tip of the hair and nails. ... So long as Indra had not known this Atmnan, Self, the Asuras or demons were superior to him; but, after he had known Him, he defeated them and attained supremacy over all gods and creatures. So also man who attains this Knowledge repels all evil and attains supremacy, independence, and sovereignty." This is the Kaushitaki Upanishad!

*Subala- Upanishad of Shukla Yajurveda*

Raikva, a parama jnyani went to the Lord and asked Him, "*What was at first?*"

The Lord replied: "*There was nothing, neither 'Sat' nor 'asat*, nor Sat-asat'. From this state of neither 'Sat' nor 'Sat-asat' (Nothing?) evolved 'Tamas' (darkness). From Tamas emerged 'bhutadi'and from bhutadi emerged 'akasha'. From akasha came vayu and from vayu, Agni (fire); from Agni came 'apas' (water) and from 'apas' came Prithvi (Earth). The earth became an egg and after a divine year or so, the egg split into two-forming akasha above and earth below and a Purusha of a divine form in the middle. To this divine form, Brahma spoke and He himself entered to form the myriads of creatures and man. The Moon was born from His manas (Mind), the sun from His eye, the Vayu from His ears and Prana from His heart. Thus, all thigs were born."

The process of evolution thus continued and from Him everything evolved. The Atma (the Self or the Purusha) is Hiranyajyotis (effulgent light) into which all the universe is absorbed. He divided the Atma (his Self) into two moieties and out of these created man and woman; He became the Deva, Rishi, Yaksha, Rakshasa, Gandharva, all types of beasts and their classes. He himself became the supporter, 'Vishvambhara'. He became Vaishvaanara (fire) at the end and burnt up all objects, then (in dissolution). Prithvi was absorbed in apas, apas in agni, agni in vayu, vayu in akasha, akasha in Indriyas and indriyas in to tanmatras, tanmatras into bhutadi, bhutadi into mahat, mahat into avyakta, avyakta into akshara (the indestructible), the akshara into tamas (darkness) and tamas merged into Brahman, the Lord. And, then there is neither 'Sat' nor 'Asat', nor 'Sat-asat'. This is the Veda, the Truth."

"*Some one out of many, attain to this "Atman', by the six means of satya, daana (charity), tapas, non-injury, celibacy and vairagya. There are no other means of attaining it. Whoever feels happy with the thought 'I know that', that learned person will never get out of his body at the moment of his death, but will become absorbed in Brahman, he attains the state of Brahman Itself as he who knows this.*"

Further, it is stated in this Upanishad that, all creatures are born from Divine Deva, the one Narayana. The eye and the visible, the ear and the audible, the tongue and the testable, the skin and the tangible, the manas and that which is acted upon by it are Narayana. Budhdhi, ahamkara, chitta, everything is Narayana. Brahmanas who are perpetually awake praise in diverse ways and illuminate the supreme abode of Vishnu."

Narayana exists everywhere and still is not visible and knowable. Manas, chitta, budhdhi, ahamkara, avyakta, mrutyu, akshara, nobody knows Him. Narayana to Apaantaratma, who in turn imparted it to Brahma, imparted this knowledge of the Atman, the self. Brahma imparted it to Ghora- Angiras. He imparted it to Raikva who in turn imparted it to Rama; and, Rama to Anjaneya and through him to all creatures. "The Atma of all which is immaculate is located in the cave (the heart) in the body; thus, it is filled with flesh, fat and phelgm in a seat very closely shut up with shining multi-coloured walls and goes out like a plantain flower. It has tejas as its body and is bliss itself. He who knows this, cognizes this Atma, is a wise person."

Raikva asked the Lord, "O Lord, in whom does everything disappear?"

The Lord replied, "That which disappears in the eye becomes the eye only and that which disappears in the sun becomes sun only; likewise, whatever disappears in virat, prana, vijnana, or anand, becomes 'that' respectively."

And then, Raikva aked the Lord, O Lord, where do all things rest?" The Lord replied, "In Rasatala". And, "In what are these Rasatala world woven warp and woof?" The Lord replied, "In the worlds of Bhuh." The Lord went on, "the Bhuh in Bhuvah, Bhuvah in Suvah, Suvah in Mahah, Mahah, in Janah, Janah in tapah, and Tapah in Satya Lok. The Satya lok is woven in warp and woof in the Prajapati Lok and Prajapati Lok in Brahma Lok and the Brahma Lok in Sarvaloka. The Sarvaloka is woven warp and woof in Atma that is Brahman like the beads in a rosary. And, all these rest in Atma. He who knows this becomes Atma itself."

There is a very important Vedic dictum: "One should eat whatever has fallen to his lot and without begging; one should never beg any (food)," Further, it is said, "Anna, the primordial anna (food), came from Narayana. It was first cooked in Brahmaloka in the Maha-samvartaka fire, literally meaning, the fire that burns raw flesh; again, it was cooked in Jwalakila (the flaming kila); then it became pure not stale (or fresh)."

There is an exposition of Nirvana in this Upanishad. Everything is ultimately food that is consumed by one or the other. One is either the eater or the eaten; the consumer or the consumed! Prithvi is the food and apas is the eater; apas is the ater and jyotis (fire) is the eater. Jyoti is the food and vayu is the eater; vayu is the food and the akasha is the eater; and, akasha is the food and the indriyas are the eaters; indriyas are the food and the manas is the eater; manas is the food and the budhdhi is the eater; budhdhi is the food and avyakta is the eater; avyakta is the food and the akshara is the eater; akshara is the food and the mrutyu is the eater; and, mrutyu becomes one with the Supreme. Beyond 'Him', there is neither 'Sat' nor 'Asat', nor 'Sat-asat'. When the Vijnana- ghana goes out of the body, it burns prana, apana, vyana, udana, samana, prithvi, apas, tejas, vayu, and akasha and it burns jagrat (taijas), dreams (svapna) and deep sleep (sushupti), and it burns that which is beyond, the sunless, the limitless, the wordless, the mahat, the avyakta, the akshara, mrutyu and then it becomes one with the great Lord. Beyond Him, there is no Sat or Asat, or Sat-asat. This is the exposition of Nirvana in this Upanishad." This Upanishad is a very sacred one and the doctrines stated herein should not be imparted to those who do not qualify for the sacred instructions. Only a Guru should impart it to a devoted student after carefully testing him. Only then these truths shine in his great soul!

*Chhaandogya Upanishad of the Samaveda*

This is one of the most elaborate Upanishads in Saman or 'Chandas' for singing. It is one of the eight works of Brahmana- Upanishad-literature of the Samaveda and each one eulogises the different aspects of this universe. These eight works are: 1. Panchavimsha Brahmana, 2. Sadvimsa

Brahmana, 3. Samavidhanam, 4. Arsheyam, 5. Devataadhyaaya, 6. Upanishad, 7. Samhitopanishad, and the 8. Vamsha.

Chhaandogya Brahmana as also Chandogya Upanishad forms the eight Chapters of the Panchavimsam and its supplement, the Sadvimsham.

***Chhaandogya Upanishad*** consists of eight Prapathakas or Chapters. Each Prapathaka seems to be a collection of many different unconnected themes. The first Prapathaka praises Udgitha (Ud means High, Gita is song) of ***Rk*** and has some related legends. The Second Prapathaka has allegorical considerations of the Saman and deals with the Pranava, "Om" in an elaborate manner. The Third Prapathaka solemnizes Brahman as the sun of the Universe and goes on to praise Gayatri and the doctrine of Shandilya. The Fourth Prapathaka has the story of Raikva instructing Janasruti, an account of the instructions to Satyakama, Upakosala and Uddalaka, the theory of transmigration of soul, etc. The Sixth Prapathaka has the instruction of Uddalaka to his son Shvetaketu about the origin of the elements and evolution of man. In the Seventh Chapter or Prapathaka, there is the instruction of Sanatkumara to Narada. Lastly, the Eighth Prapathaka describes the Atman in the lotus-flower of the heart, and in the Universe and how to attain it. Also, there is Instruction of Indra by Prajapati about the nature of the Atman and the way to attain Him and the means of emancipation. Thus, Chandogya Upanishad has come to be almost an encyclopaedia of the Upanishads.

A few interesting verses are highlighted in the following.

"Om", the Pranava is the Udgitha and one should adore it. Everything starts and ends with "Om" since it is the essence of all things on earth; it is the essence of water, plants, man, speech, 'Rk', the Saman and the Udgitha, the most essential of all essences. It is the highest and the transcendent one. 'Rk' is the speech and the Saman the breath (Prana), and the Udgitha, the "Om". The speech and the breath, the 'Rk' and the Saman form the pair and they are united in 'Om' that brings forth love and desire. It is also the syllable of agreement or concurrence and one who knows this and adores the Udgitha prospers in the fulfillment of his desires. All the Veda exist in "Om". This is the significance of "Om".

"Om" is the gist of the Veda; it is the Udgitha, the symbol of Prana, the vital breath, i.e., the life force in man. It is superior to all others, the senses, the Mind and the Prajnya or Consciousness. If Prana leaves the body all others follow. The much Revered Sages Angiras, Brihaspati, Ayasya, Baka, all adored the Udgitha. Those who adore the Udgitha as Prana become singers who sing to the people their wishes. Thus, it is necessary to adore Udgitha, 'Om'.

The Udgitha is the symbol of the Sun. The Sun rises and shines, scares away darkness. One should adore the Udgitha, the symbol of the Sun, as the Vyana (Shoonyaka), the gap between out-breathing (Prana) and in-breathing (Apana). Vyana is the binding factor of Prana and Apana. Vyana is the same as the 'Rk' or 'Vak' or speech as it comes about when one utters without breathing in or out.

The activities of human beings put a heavy strain (weight) on the breathing. Breathing is held within while engaged in activity such as eating, speaking, lifting, singing, etc. One sings Udgitha, i.e., Saman without breathing in or breathing out. So one should adore Udgitha. So also, one should adore the syllables of 'Ud'-, 'gi'-, and 'tha', that stand for Prana (Ud), speech (gi), and food (tha), respectively. Also, the three letters of Udgitha stand for the three Veda- the Rk, the Yajus, and the Saman. Again, 'Ud' is svar (heaven), 'gi' is bhuvar (sky), and 'tha' is bhu (the earth)'. The wish of the person who cherishes a desire and sings the stotra, the Udgitha is always fulfilled.

Then, there is the account of Devas (Gods), afraid of death took refuge in the Veda, and covered themselves in the metre, the Chhandas. But, death espied them in the same place, in the Rk, the Yajus, the Saman. The gods again fled and took refuge in the sound 'Om', the syllable that makes one immortal, fearless. Thus, the Gods finally got protection from the Pranava, the "Om". And, he who flies for refuge in 'Om' becomes fearless and immortal. Hence, the superiority of 'Om' is established over the Veda.

The Udgitha is the Pranava, "Om" and the Pranava is the Udgitha; the Pranava, "Om" is resounding, reverberating, and vibrating causing movement. "It travels and changes itself in its rays and multiplicity takes place", said Kaushitaki to his son. Sing, praise the vital breath Prana; for, it originates in Him.

The cosmic principle and the psychic principle are that the Sun in the macrocosm and man in the microcosm are the same; and the sun is in the eye of man and man is in the sun. This is elucidated further as the light of the sun (light) makes the eyes see things as they are, and, the sun supports life (man). Thus, the man and his eyes are powerless without the sun. The 'Rk' depends on the Saman and the Udgitha is the power behind the Saman. The deities of the three spheres bhu, bhuvar and svar are Agni (earth), Vayu (sky) and Aditya (Heaven), respectively. Similarly, the out-breath (Prana) depends on the speech, the physical form (atman) on the eye, the manas (mind) on the ear (the word awakens or creates thought or idea). Just as the Udgitha rules over the 'Rk' and the Saman, the moon in the sun and the man in the eyes rule over the cosmic and psychic phenomena. Both the external world (the world beyond the sun) and the internal world (within man) are governed by the same Principle of Udgitha.In other words all our perceptions are dependednt on the cosmic forces (the Udgitha, the vibrations of Pranava, 'Om') for they rule the elements. This is the special significance of the Udgitha and one should adore it! One who sings ud-githa (high song) will conquer the world beyond the sun (without), as well as his self (within); 'he conquers all'.

A very interesting dialog takes place among the three experts on Udgitha, Shilaka Shaalaavatya, Chaikitaayana Daalbhya, and Pravaahana Jaivali. Shaalaavatya asked Daalbhya, "To what does the Saman (sound) go back?" Dalbhya answered, "The Saman goes back to sound, the sound goes back to breath and the vital breath (Prana) goes back to food. Then, food goes back to water and water goes back to the yonder world, the world beyond the Sun! To this Shaalavatya said, ' Indeed, there is support to your logic. But, to what does the yonder world go back? Dalbhya replied, "The yonder world goes back to this world, this fundamental world. There is nothing beyond this and Saman is the fundation, or support to this world." Then Jaivali said, "Indeed, if one would say Saman has an end, your head would split."

Then the discussion went on. One of them said, "This Akasha, indeed, is the source from which all others emerged and to which all would disappear. It is the endless one; this is the most excellent Udgitha. It is the endless one. Formerly, Atidhanvan Shaunaka taught this to Udarashaandilya and said, "So long as those among your descendents will know the Udgitha as such a one, they will share that long the most excellent life in the world; and, also they will share in that world a homely place".

Further, here is a very interesting account of a poor man, but a wise one, called Ushasti Chakraayana and his wife Atiki who reveal some secrets. When you are hungry and beg for some food, there is no sin. It is only to survive. But, when you beg for something that gives pleasure, it is sin!

Then, Chakraayana reveals the divinity that lies in 'Prastava', the 'Udgitha' and 'Pratihara'. The divinity of Prastaava lies in breath (Prana) and the Udgitha is sung in praise of Sun high up in the sky. The divinity of Pratihara lies in food because Prana depends on food.

The five-fold Saman are: himkara (the earth), prastava (fire), udgitha (the sky), pratihara (the sun), and, nidhanam (the heavens). The same holds good in the reverse order where, himkara is the heavens, prastaava the sun, etc. Similarly, the Saman accounts for the rain, the waters, the seasons, the domestic animals, the vital breaths, speech, eyes, ears and mind. Then there is the seven –fold Saman (adi and upadrava added to the other five), one should adore. Rather, all activities in this world goes on in an orderly way of the five-fold or the seven-fold Saman

Thus, the first and the second Chapters eulogise the Udgitha and implore us to adore the Udgitha in the form of Pranava, the "Om".

In the Third Prapathaka (Chapter), the Brahman is eulogosed and the method of attaining the Brahman is explained. All the Gods of the heavenly abode satiate themselves by looking at the nectar drawn from the flowers (the Veda) through the bees (the Verses of the Veda) and sucked by the Sunrays and stored in the Sun. The Upanishads, the Puranas and Itihasas, Epics and mythological poems are the flowers. The Vasus, the Rudras, the Adityas, the Maruts and the Sadhyaas live on different types of nectar drawn from the different Veda, Upanishads and the Puranas.

As regards the Sun, Chhaandogya Upanishad [3.11.1-6] says that, "*Truly it does no more rise nor sets for him; it is all the time the day for him who knows this Upanishad of Brahman.*" The 'Brahman' has proclaimed this (intuitionally) to Prajapati Brahma, and Prajapati to Manu, &c. Brahma proclaimed this doctrine to Uddalaka Aruni, (as his eldest son by his father).

*The heart of Man is the abode of the Infinite Brahman. This infinite Brahman dwells whole and undivided in the heart of man.* Brahman appears in the symbol of Gayatri, a Vedic Metre (Chandas) and as such Gayatri is the essence of all beings. Gayatri is 'vak', speech; Gayatri sings (gayati) to all beings, and, protects (traayate) all those that constantly chant the 'Mantra'. Gayatri is identical with the earth as support and is identical with the human body, the human heart, and vital organs. This six-fold Gayatri has four feet, one inside human heart and the other three the feet of Brahman, out side, there in heaven. This, one foot that is in the human heart is full and unchangeable, and it is the same as the other three out there in the heaven. One who knows this attains prosperity and happiness.

This infinite Brahman dwells whole and undivided in the heart of man. The path to attain Brahman is clearly explained in the Thirteenth Section of the Third Chapter (Prapathaka). There are five openings for the gods in the heart called Deva sushayahs. These are identical with the heart, body, earth, as well as space in the heart, the space in the body and the outer space (sky) and these respectively consist of prana, vyana, apana, samana and udana again, identical with the sense organs- the eyes, the ears, skin, speech and mind.

The doctrine of Shandilya, i.e., the 'identity of Brahman with the Atman' is explained in this Upanishad [3.14]. "Certainly, this universe is Brahman; one should worship it in tranquility, as 'Taijalaan' (one arising in it). Indeed, the man is made up of insight or intelligence. Just as man becomes that on which he exercises his intelligence to be, he will, after he has departed from this world, accordingly become ('***Yad bhavam tad bhavati***')." That is why one should exercise care in using intelligence!

" Mind is his stuff, breathing (living) his body, light his form, resolution is truth, his self is infinity (ether). He is all-doing, all-wishing, all-tasting, encompassing-all, silent and unconcerned-that is his svaroopa. *The soul, ie 'Atman' is smaller than a grain of rice or barley or mustard or millet, innermost heart, greater than the earth, greater than the sky, greater than the worlds since all other things are the content and He is the container. This Brahman, doing all, all- wishing, smelling all, tasting all, all-encomapassing, silent and unconcerned, is the one to which all enter after departing from here". This doctrine is the most important one and one who knows this will not doubt.*

There are certain ceremonies that serve the welfare and protection of the progeny as in ***Kaushitaki Upanishad*** [2.8.10]. The doctrine of "essential unity of man and the universe' is brought out against this background. Wind as the breath of the world is like the son in the family (for whose benefit these ceremonies were performed by miserable men, men of blind hearts!).

The most beautiful part of this Upanishad is the formula that helps us to maintain good health. "Truly man is a 'yajnya-aahuti' (sacrifice). Early part of man's life, for 24 years, is the morning of life. Gayatri has 24 syllables and the morning libation is accompanied by Gayatri hymn. The 'Vasus' who are the partakers are the vital breath. In this part of life, when man is prone to sickness, should worship Vasus saying,

*"Ye Prana, Vital Breaths, Vasus, may ye continue to spin this morning libation of mine upto midday libation; may I not be a sacrifice which is broken off in the midst, in the vital breaths, the Vasus".*

Any sickness is cured and the person will regain good health by this Formula.

The second part of man's life is of 48 years, the mid-day of life. The mid-day libation is to be accompanied by Trishtub Metre (Chandas). In this part of life, Rudras are the vital breath and hence the partakers; Rudras are the gods who make us weep. If in this part of life, one falls sick, he should pray, "Ye vital breaths, Rudras, may you continue to weave or spin this my midday libation upto evening libation. May I not be a sacrifice that is broken off in the midst, in the vital breaths, I pray O, Rudras. One will regain good health with this formula, if and when fallen sick.

The next 48 years of life is the evening of life, and the evening libation is accompanied by Jagati hymn of 48 syllables. The Aditya are the partakers of this libation and it is they who pull out and take away everything with themselves. If anyone is afflicted with sickness in this period of life he should pray Adityas, "Ye Vital Breaths Adityas, may you continue to weave or spin this my evening libation upto the full length of life. May I not be a sacrifice which is broken off in the midst, in the vital breaths, the Adityas!" This will help regain sound health. Mahidasa, son of Itaraa, knew this because he said, "Why do you afflict me with sickness, because I am not going to die with it?" And, he lived for 116 years!

The Seventeenth Section of the Third Part of ***Chhaandogya Upanishad*** is another beautiful revelation about human life. Man should live contented and happy like the persons celebrating the performance of the Soma Sacrifice. Indeed, the whole life is a 'Yajnya' or sacrifice! The ethical code is the Dakshina that consists of tapas, danam, arjavam, (honesty), ahimsa, and truthfulness- the five essential codes of conduct. Everyone should emulate Ghora, the teacher of Lord Krishna, the imperishable, imperturbable at the time of death.

The Upanishad describes the activities of man like eating, drinking, enjoying as similar to the Soma sacrifice and the dakshina to be offered is the ethical code of conduct described above. There are Verses with the same theme in '***Rk***' Veda [8.6.30; 1.15.10].

Another important aspect of Brahman is brought out in the Eighteenth Section and this is again, similar to the 'Rk' Vedic Verse 10.90.3, i.e., the four feet of Brahman. Manas (Mind) is Brahman and it is Akasa (sky) from the cosmic point of view; one should adore Manas as symbol of Brahman.

Speech, breath, eyes, ears, and directions of the heavens are the four feet of Brahman. Similarly, the Deities, Agni, the Sun (fire), Varuna (wind), and the Disha or 'dik' (the directions of heaven) are the four feet of Brahman. He who knows this will shine, attain fame, gain reputation, and will be renown.

In the last Section, the 'Rk' Vedic contention of the origin of the universe from a golden egg, '***Hiranyagarbha***' is highlighted ['***Rk***' ***Veda*** 10.129.3]. It is from this egg that split in two- the golden half of the egg, sun (above) and the silver half of the egg, earth (below) sprang up. This is, also, the reason why all creatures look up to the sun for salvation [also see ***Atharvaveda*** 2.1.1].

In the Fourth Chapter of the Upanishad, there is an account of 'Raikva with the cart' who imparts the doctrine of the Self to King Janasruti. The story goes that, "Once, some flamingoes were flying over the kingdom of Janasruti who was well-known for his liberal distribution of food. He had set up hostels for students and had arranged for poor-feeding everywhere. His fame had reached the heavens.

Once, while the flamingoes were flying over the Kingdom of Janasruti, one flamingo said to the other, "You, blinking-eyed, do not see that splendour of Jansruti lest it should burn you. Then, the flamingo said, "Who is that man whom you are speaking of, as if he is that Raikva with the cart". The King Janasruti heard this comment and wanted to know who this Raikva was. He sent his Retainer to find him. Finally, when they found Raikva, the King Janasruti offered Raikva, a thousand cows and gold and a wife and asked him, "O Revered Sir, Please teach me rhe Divinity you adore"

The 'Doctrine of Raikva' is thus made known to King Janasruti as follows:

"When the Fire blows away, it enters the wind; when the sun sets, it enters the wind; when the moon sets, it enters into the wind; and when the waters dry up, it enters the wind. The Wind gathers all these and hence the divinity of the wind."

"In regard to the Self, the breath is the gatherer in itself. Because, when one sleeps, the speech enters into the breath; the sight (eyes) into the breath; the hearing (ears) into the breath, the mind (manas) into the breath and finally, the breath gathers them all in itself". Thus, the wind among the divinities and the vital breath (Prana) in the Self are the gatherers. The God Breath (Prana) is 'Great' for he being unconsumed, consumes the unconsumable. Wind, fire, sun, moon, and water and the five others, breath, speech, the eyes, the ears and manas, together make up ten. This is the Kruta –throw (of ten) in the dice, the food in all directions. This is also Viraj (of ten syllables), the representative of matter (the Chandas or metre); thus, to him who knows this and adores, the whole world becomes visible and he becomes the consumer of food". This is the doctrine.

And, then there is the story of Satyakama Jaabala and the Sage Haridrumata Gautama. Gautama accepted Jaabala as his pupil despite the fact that Jaabala knew no antecedents and was daring enough to say that he was his mother Jabala's son. Jaabala learnt a lot about the Brahman, from the bull, the fire, the goose, the diver-bird, and finally his teacher Gautama. The bull taught him that the four directions are the four-sixteenth part the foot of Brahman, the expansive one. The fire taught him, that the four-sixteenth part the foot of Brahman are the earth, the sky, the heaven and the oceans and, hence Brahman is the boundless or the Infinite. The goose imparted the lesson that, 'the fire, the sun, the moon, and the lightning are the four-sixteenth part the foot of Brahman, the luminous one. He who knows this and adores will be luminous and shine. The diver-bird said, 'the breath, the eyes, the ears, and the manas (Mind) are the four-sixteenth part, the foot of Brahman. Since these are supporting this world, the one who knows this adores Him will attain the supporting worlds. And, finally, the sage Gautama imparted the secret of the Brahman. In all these stories, the vastness of knowledge and the hidden meaning of the world are explained. Only those who can contemplate on all these aspects will gradually "Know"that Brahman manifests in various forms.

The various manifestation of the Brahman, the principle of life, bliss and infinity cannot be understood by hard and depressing penance. The earth, fire, food, sun are the manifestations of Brahman. So also, the water, disha (dik) of heavens, the stars and the moon as well as the vital breath (Prana), sky (ether), heaven and lightning are the manifestations of Brahman. These can be identified with the Purusha, the man (person, spirit) in the sun, the moon, the lightning. Only a learned teacher will impart this knowledge of attaining Brahman to a deserving pupil and none else. All others will teach the way to reach the world-space (Brahmaanda), but only a true teacher will teach what it is! He teaches the Brahman not as the man in the sun, the moon, the lightning, but as the Purusha who appears in the eye, i.e., the seer of the seeing, the subject of knowledge, the soul in us. "***For him who has found Brahman in his own self, there remains no more attaining to the Brahman***." ***[Brihadaaranyaka Upanishad 4.4.6]***

And, then, there is the story of Satyakama and Upakosala. Satyakama's wife warned that he is neglecting the sincere and devoted student Upakosala and this may lead to an unpleasant situation. The poor boy will be gaining sympathy of fire gods and the fire gods will teach him. Just as she predicted, the fires took pity on this pupil of Satyakama and imparted thus:

*"Brahman is life, Brahman is joy, Brahman is expanse; the expanse, is the joy; and joy is the expanse. And, Brahman is life and expansive space"*

*The Fires, Garhapatya, Anvaarahaaryapachana, Ahvaaniya taught Upakosala the secret of Brahman thus:*

Fire Garhapatya: "The earth, the fire, the food and the sun are my forms". He who knows this and adores Garhapatya fire will live his full life, become expansive and the fires protect him

Fire Anvaahaaryapachana: " The water, the directions, the stars and the moon are my forms. But, the man (purusha) whom one sees in the moon, I am that, I am he".

Fire Ahavaniya:"The breath, the ether, the heaven and the lightning are my forms". But, the man (purusha) whom one sees in the lightning, I am that, I am he." He who knows this and adores fires will live longer and all fires will protect him.

When Upakosala went back to Satyakama, the teacher said, well, the fires have taught you their world-spaces, the path to Brahman. I shall teach you the Brahman and said, "The man whom one sees in the eye, is the Atmnan. He is the immortal one, the fearless one. He is the Brahman, so when clarified butter or water enters the eye it flows away towards the edges. He is the stronghold of all lovable things; He is the stronghold of love. He is the prince of splendour and shines in all the worlds. He who knows this shines, he becomes immortal"

Then, there is the doctrine of five fires and the transmigration of souls. The path of salvation is made clear in this Prapathaka of ***Chhaandogya Upanishad*** [5.3-10]. There is also a detailed account of this in ***Brihadaranyaka Upanishad*** 6.2.

The five sacrificial fires are: the yonder world where the sun is its fuel, the rays its smoke, the day is flame, the moon its coals and the stars the sparks. Into this fire, the gods give an offering of faith out of which arises the Soma. Similarly, the Parjanya (rain god) is the sacrificial fire, wind its fuel, cloud its smoke, lightning its flame, thunderbolt its coals and hailstones its sparks. Into this fire, the gods sacrifice the King Soma out of which arises the rain. The third sacrificial fire is, indeed, the man. Speech is its fuel, breath its smoke, tongue its flame, the eyes its coal, the ear its sparks. Into this the gods offer food out of which arises the semen. The fourth fire is the woman. Lap is fuel, love is smoke, vulva the flame, coition the coals and the pleasure the sparks; into which the gods offer semen and the bhroona (foetus) is the result. The last fire is water out of which comes the voice of the infant that is born. Thus, the whole universe including the life of man is a Sacrifice or Yajnya. "After one is born, he lives the allotted time of his life, say a hundred years. After he is dead, they carry him to his destination in the fire. From which he had come, out of which he had arisen."

The Sixth Prapathaka or Chapter is the most important and interesting part of Chhaandogya Upanishad. Here the Sage Aruni Uddalaka imparts the knowledge about the 'Being' and 'its unfoldment into the world' to his son Svetaketu.

At the age of twelve Svetaketu was sent to a teacher with whom he stayed for twelve years and studied Veda. He returned at the age of twenty-four, arrogant and conceited. Aruni asked him a simple question whether he knows: *"yena asrutam srutam bhavati......?" (meaning, 'That' from which even the unheard becomes heard, what is not comprehended becomes comprehended, and what is not known becomes known?")* Svetaketu said, "Sir, please impart me this knowledge for my teachers have not taught me this and they would have certainly taught me this had they known this.

Uddalaka said, "Look, all modifications are clinging to name and form for the essential thing is the same in reality; may it be a lump of clay, a piece of copper or iron, they are moulded into different forms and we believe they are all different! Tejas (fire), apah (water), annam (food), and such other basic elements are all physical substances or matter ('asat') derived from that 'Being' (the 'Sat'), the existent." ***Rk Veda*** [10.129.1] asserts that, "*nasad asin no sad aaseet tadaaneem*", meaning, "*In the beginning, there was the primeaval "Being", the 'Sat', the only one and without a second" ['Rk Veda 10.72.2-3].*

*The primeaval Being brings forth the 'Ur-matter (primeaval matter) and thus originates as the first creation of itself (out of itself!). Then the 'jiva-atman' or individual souls entered and propagated in names and forms. In this process there ensued three-fold divison of matter (elements) or transplantaion of the ingredients of the two elements into every other element. For instance, Water consists of 50% water and one-eighth earth, one-eighth fire and one-eighth ether. Thus, all the manifold mundąne things are mixtures of different sorts of three primeaval 'Ur'-matter. This is the same in the case of the sun, the fire, the lightning, and the moon. They are an admixture of fire, water and food; their differences are only in appearance, apparent. He who knows that these three basic elements emanated from the one supreme 'Being' knows all. "To him, who knows this 'Being', the supreme self, the 'unknown' becomes already the' known'"*

The constituents of human body can be explained as: fire in the form of speech, bone, and marrow; similarly, water in the Prana (Breath), blood and urine; Annam (food) in Manas (Mind), flesh and faeces. So also, the subtler and finest part of milk becomes butter (when churned). Manas, Prana and speech are the product of food, water and fire. Thus, Manas (Mind) consists of food and Prana of Water. If one abstains from food for fifteen days and drinks only water, his memory fades away and only Prana subsists (on water). Food taken at the end of fast, like a spark that kindles fire, brings the body back to strength.

What are sleep, hunger, thirst and death? The sleep is 'svapiti', resting in one's own self; or, it is 'Mind' (manas) and 'awareness' or Consciousness entering into Prana (unconsciousness or simply, unawareness). Hunger is 'food along with water entering the structure of the body. Actually, food has emerged out of water! The body has its root in food. And the food has its prime cause in water, which in turn has its prime cause in fire. Ultimately, the food, the water and the fire – all have their prime cause in the Being'. So also, Thirst. Thirst is 'carrying away' to build the structure and its roots are very clear, by now.

Death is something very interesting! First, 'Vac' (speech) enters the Manas (Mind); then the mind enters into Prana. And, then Prana enters into 'Being' or the Death. This appears to be quite logical since speech stops when the consciousness is still there. So also, Prana, the breathing is still there while the Consciousness is not there. However, it is stated that the speech has its root in fire and, manas rises out of food and not Prana. Prana rises out of water and not directly out of fire. These things have to be clarified. In deep sleep, the individual beings have no awareness of entering into 'Being'. Similarly, they have no awareness when they come back to awareness from out of deep sleep. This awareness of 'Consciousness 'getting into' and 'coming out' of Prana is important. The disappearance of Consciousness in death is only the return of 'Vac' (speech) into Manas (Mind), of Manas into Prana and return of Prana into fire and of fire into the 'Supreme Being'.

The manifoldness of mundane things rises out of the undifferentiated Being just like butter out of Milk through the process of churning. This supreme 'Being' is unperceivable and still omnipresent. He who is caught up in 'Maya', the unreality of this Samsara is bound by the dualities of existence (mundane world). Deliverance lies in 'Knowledge' of this 'Oneness', the 'Truth'. He who knows this knows all and is libearated from the cycle of brirths and deaths, i.e., 'Samsara'. Just as honey is made out of a variety of flowers and no distinction is made that this part of honey is of this flower, all beings unite in Brahman and no distinction is made there of. So also, all these creatures also know not, though they have come forth from the Being and again go forth out of Being. Whatever they are, whether a lion or a tiger, an ant or a human, they come back again. This universe consists of what that finest essence is, it is the real, it is the soul, that thou art ("***tat tvam asi***"), Svetaketu", said Aruni to his son. "*This body indeed dies if Prana leaves it; but Praana does not die. This universe consists of what that finest essence is, it is real, it is the soul, 'that thou art' ('tat tvam asi'), O Svetaketu. That finest essence that one cannot see in the gene plan hidden in a Banyan seed is the same in all creatures, hidden and imperceivable and that finest essence is 'that thou art', 'tat tvam asi'," O Svetaketu, said Aruni to his son.*

This '*Unity Principle of Brahman or Atman' is further elucidated in the Seventh Prapathaka. Rk Veda, the Prajapati hymn* [1.164, 10.121 & 10.129] has clearly brought out the concept of unity of Brahman, 'that all gods, worlds, and beings depend upon a unity- the one ultimate principle'. One has to understand this principle and adore the Brahman as the 'Atman'. The '***neti, neti***' doctrine is one such that tries to unravel the truth, the Brahman. A number of teachers have tried to impart this knowledge of Brahman to their students in many different ways and still the question remains as to how to realize this Brahamn or the Atman.

Sanatkumara, son of Brahma and the War Lord, sets forth sixteen ways of adoring the Brahman when Narada asks him as to whom should we adore as Brahman. First it is ***namam (name)***, since the very uttering of name is enough toget rich rewards from Him. Greater than the name is speech (Vac); and, the Manas (Mind) is greater than speech. Greater than Mind (Manas) is sankalpa or resolution, because the will is dependent on resolution just as the speech and name are dependednton the will. Greater than the resolution is the chitta or thought. Meditation (Reflection) is greater than thought; and, knowledge is greater than thought. Strength (balam) is greater than knowledge and greater than strength is food (annam), because all physical and mental strength comes from food and nutrition. Water is greater than food and fire is greater than water, because water (rain) comes from fire (heat of the sun). Ether or akasha is greater since the sun, moon, stars are contained in it, the space (akasha). Greater still is memory (Smara) and still greater is hope (asha), because asha kindles hope that depends on memory; the will spurs the intellect. Prana is greater than hope since Prana, as the hub, holds all the constituents of the body. Prana is also Brahman as enunciated earlier. And, still it is not the highest attainable since it is as an individual soul which has juxtaposed itself as the subject against the object and, is therefore, finite and small. This distinction between the subject and object is removed, when one elevates his self to full infinitude, 'bhuman'. That is the highest and grea test of all. This 'Bhuman', Infinitude is beyond all comprehension; it does not see, hear, or know anything outside itself and being immortal, rests alone in its own supre-mundane majesty and like the 'I' the soul, that is identical with it, is directly fully present in all places at all times. He, who knows this, knows all and is immortal; he knows no sorrow, no pain and sees 'I' in all the thousand appearances of the creation.

As regards emancipation or salvation, there is the prayer "*Aham eva idam sarvam syaam bhooyaasam*" ***meaning "May I become (merged in)***

***the universe***". Only the souls that pass through the moon in Devayana, by virtue of knowledge, will merge in Him, the sun. The souls that go to moon in Pitryaana, by virtue of ignorance, will come back to earth and serve the remaining part of their life according to their karma. Here, one thing is made clear. Good dharmic or karmic deeds bring good and enable one to enjoy life better on earth. Those who are engaged in evil and sin will suffer for their bad deeds. Ironically, everybody will suffer for their sins and enjoy due to their good deeds but cannot exchange the bad for the good. The debt has to be cleared! Unless the soul is pure, blemishless, desireless, light enough to escape the gravity, shall not escape from the earth. This is one of the reasons why, many a disgruntled souls, dissatisfied souls, souls separated abruptly from body, terminated accidentally, will hover over the place of death like ghosts. Their emancipation depends on the fulfillment of their desires. They remain two-dimensional images that did not get the touch of the fire according to the doctrine of fire. The elements surround the soul in the form of flesh, bones and blood to make it a three-dimensional body. This is the reason why the dead bodies are burnt and the ashes immersed in holy waters so that the contents of the dead body get back to the elements. Even in case of burial of the dead, it is doubtful whether there is total emancipation since there is no touch of fire. The contents remain in the earth as '*bhoo*'- *tha*, stay-put! But, a jeevanmukta, an emancipated soul needs no consecretary rites- '***kriyaakarmas' (anthya karma)***' for he is already burnt, flaming with knowledge and needs no further burning.

In ***Rk Veda***, the dead are supposed to remain in Yamalok, the 'realm of death' and there is no mention of return to earth. Whereas, in ***Brihadaranyaka Upanishad***, the souls return to earth and find suitable parents according to their Karma; they live a life of penury, comfort, or luxury according to their past deeds as stated in "***vidya-karmani purva-prajnyaa cha***"[***Brihadaranyaka Upanishad*** 3.2.13; 4.4.2-6]. In ***Chhandogya Upanishad***, the doctrine of five fires, 'passing through the five yajnyas (Sacrifices)' is the basis of new life on earth. Faith is important in attaining the different worlds. In fact 'faith' is the basis of spiritual existence! There is the possibility of attaining liberation, emancipation, i.e., residing in Brahman by virtue of acquisition of 'True Knowledge' through the performance of 'Sacrifices'; there is no return to earth for a true 'Jnyani' [***Chhandogya Upanishad***, 3.14.1 & 4.15.5-6]. Rebirth as lower animals is due to leading a reckless life and failure to reach either the path of manes (Pitryaana) or path of Gods (Devayana); it is due to lack of faith in God and sheer arrogance and ignorance governing the life. Those who have led a satisfactory life in the past will gain entry into wombs of desirous parents of good families, rich and learned; others, who lived obnoxious life will enter obnoxious wombs, that of a dog or swine! There are others who are condemned to life after life, born and die like insects. He who knows these fires, are pure and emancipated at last!

The concept of Yajnya is very clear, as stated earlier, 'Yajnya' means 'Sacrifice'. The whole universe is a Yajnya; the whole journey of life is a yajnya. Indeed born on this earth is an'Yajnya'. One thing is sacrificed for another. Silence is sacrificed for sound and sound is sacrificed for silence. Breath is sacrificed for sound and sound is sacrificed for breath. It simply means when one thing is there the other is not there; when we are here, we are not there. When it is here, it is not there. When we are on this earth we are not in heaven and we long for it. There is a lingering memory of the heaven we have left and the soul desires to be there; rather, get out of this body constraints and enjoy the freedom, liberty, emancipation and that is mukti or moksha. This is the gist of the Sacrifice. A technique or 'tantra' has been devised to achieve this and that is the 'Sacrificial fires', the doctrine of five fires. One has to satisfy the sacrificial fires to attain or achieve whatever one desires.

The early Vedic Period depicts the life of Brahmanas who were directed, rather dictated by the Vedic Scriptures to perform the Yajnyas, the sacred Soma Sacrifice in view of these predicaments. Only a satisfactory completion of Soma Sacrifice would emancipate or liberate the souls. This is the purport of '***Aham eva idam sarvam syaam bhuyasaam***', may I merge in the universe. Having understood the meaning of life on this earth, full of dualities, a wise man is prone to think of emancipation at the earliest! The path of salvation is enunciated in all the Veda and the Upanishads; this is the reason why a Brahmana should take to Vedadhyayana or study of Vedic scriptures without fail. The word, 'Brahmana' is used in the context of a wise man, a man of 'Knowledge', a man of discretion and Prajnya, and not just restricted to those born to families of namesake.

And, then, there is the question of superiority of the organs of the senses (Jnyaanendriyas), the Mind and the elements clarified by a logical interpretation of their functions and interactions. First, Prana is superior for everything rests on that. It is followed by - speech or 'vac', eyes (chakshus), ears (srotram), and mind (manas). To these five are added prajati, agni, soma, bhur, bhuvah, svar, Brahman, Kshatram, bhutam, bhavishayat, visvam, sarvamand Prajapati. [***Brihadaranyaka Upanishad*** 6.3.6]

Water is the purifier and it covers Prana as could be seen in rinsing of mouth after meals. Both ***Chhaandogya Upanishad*** 5.1.6 & 5.2.2 correseponding to ***Brihadaranyaka Upanishad*** 6.17 & 6.1.14, have this statement. The significance of water, 'Ganga jal' put into the mouth of a dying person illustrates this point. Water is the greatest purifier!

The Eleventh Part (Khanda) deals with the doctrne of Agni Vaisvanara and Atma Vaisvanara. The fire sacrifice, 'Agnihotram' offered to the fire-gods and.the fire sacrifice offered to Prana, i.e., '***Pranagnihotram***' are dealt with in Verses 11-24 of this Khanda.

***What is our Self, or 'Atman'? What is' the Brahman'? This has been explained in the following episodes.***

Once five learned, rich, and famous men came to Sage Uddalaka Aruni and asked him the above question. To this question, Aruni decided to take them to Asvapati Kaikeya, engaged in the study of Vaisvanara. A long discussion took place and Asvapati asked each one of them, what would they adore most as the 'Atman'.

First, Aupamanyava said, 'the Atman was described as '***Atman***

***Vaisvanara***', one full of splendour; and, one who adores him will see what is pleasing, hear what is pleasing and his family is one of great splendour'. Asvapati said, this is all true; but still the yonder world, the heavens, is the head of the Atman.

Next, Satyayajnya Paulusi said, 'the Sun is indeed the Atman Vaisvanara as the all-formed, who is being worshiped as the Atman. That is why all forms of things are seen in the family who adore him (sun) as the Atman'. That is all right; but still the sun is one eye of the Atman, said Asvapati.

Third, Indrayumna Bhallveya said, 'the wind is the Atman Vaisvanara whom we adore. But, Asvapati said, 'the wind is still the breath of the Atman'.

Fourth, Jana said, 'the space is the venerable Atman Vaisvanara'. But, Asvapati said, the space is only 'the constituent of the body of Atman'.

And, finally, Budila Aasvataraasvi said, the waters are the venerable Atman Vaisvanara whom we adore much to which Asvapati said, the 'waters are the blaader of the Atman'.

Asvapati clarified that all these learned men have understood Atman Vaisvanara as separate from their own selves and eat food. But actually, Atman, the size of a span, eats all the food in all the beings in all the worlds and in all the selves. If one performs the 'agnihotram' with full knowledge, he will attain the full benefit of the Sacrifice.

*'Atman' is the very small being in man* [***Chhaandogya Upanishad***, *3.14*], *the size of a small grain of rice or barley [Katha Upanishad, 4-12], or, the size of the tip of the needle, or more tiny than a hundredth part of a split hair*. [***SvetasvataraUpanishad ,5.8.9***].

The Eighth Chapter of ***Chhaandogya Upanishad*** deals with the Way to Atman. The heart is a cavity where the lotus blossoms. This cavity is a small space called '***dahara akasha***' which, in reality, is as big as the infinite world-space that contains everything. The Atman residing in this 'dahara akasa' is not affected by anything- death, decay or evil. The pity is that all those who aspire for wealth, riches, position, fame and name, and even the heavenly abode, pursue the perishable and thereby remain in bondage, fetters here as well as in the other world. Only those who have realized the Atman are free.

"Truly, the atman is in the heart. Heart i.e., hridayam, (Sansk.) '***hridi***'-'***ayam***' means, 'He resides in the heart'. Atman is the indestructible one; it is the Brahman, the fearless one. It is the 'Satyam'. Inside the human body, it is as if in a state of deep sleep and will rise in its own true form and effulgence; that is the Atman! It is the 'Sat', the indestructible one. And, 'ti' is destructible one i.e., mrityu (death). Both the 'Sat' and 'ti' are 'ayam', i.e., enclosed in the body, thereby meaning Satyam. He who knows this is immortal.

The way to Atman is through Brahmacharyam. Brahmacharyam is a grest Soma festival, a festival of joy of liberation, deliverance. It is a 'Yajna', Sacrifice. Through this Yajna, one finds the Atman. Brahmacharyam is also "Mauna', Silence, the silence of meditation through which Atman is perceived. Through meditation one finds atman and contemplates on it. Brahmacharyam is also fasting. Through fasting one finds the entry into the indestructible, the atman. Brahmacharyam is also 'Aranyakam', going to the forest, the realm of the Brahman, 'Ara' and 'nya' are the two lakes in the Brahmalok. The water of the lake is virtually a refreshing and nourishing one, bringing virtual immortality. There are the fig trees with dripping soma juice and the seat of Brahman in this Yonder Third World. One who attains this world through Brahmacharyam shall partake in the life of emancipation in all the worlds.

Indra asks Prajapati, "*What is the Self*?' Prajapati offers three elucidations of Atman or the self here [***Chhaandogya Upanishad***, 8.7-12]. The physical body, the individual soul, and the highest soul, represent the three steps of knowledge through which one can understand the Brahman.

The nature of the Self is thus, imparted by Prajapati to Indra. There are two atmas- one, the true atma and the other, a false one; one is the realistic soul in the individual self and the other is the idealistic soul in the highest self. In reality, both are same! The distinction is made due to the fact that the individual soul is entrapped, embodied, constrained in the 'asat', the perishable. When the soul is released on the death of the body, the individual soul merges with the universal soul.

There is a beautiful story to illustrate the 'identification of the Self'. Once, Lord Indra and Virochana went to Prajapati and asked him to impart the knowledge of the Self. Prajapati asked them to look in a mirror or water or each other's eye and see the reflection. This reflection seen in the water or mirror or each other's eye is the Self. Both went away being satisfied with the answer. But, Indra returned with the doubt. This time, Prajapati told him, "***Look, when one is in deep sleep and has attained tranquility of mind and body, he experiences no dream and that is his self, that is indestructible Brahman***." Indra went away satisfied with this explanation. But again returned with the doubt, 'how can one know the self when he is not conscious of his self in deep sleep'.

Again, Prajapati explained the nature of the Self thus: "***O Maghavan, this body is possessed by mrityu (death) and is destructible. But, it is the dwelling place for that 'indestructible'.*** This embodied soul is subject to joy and sorrow, but remember that the soul, the incorporeal self, is never being afflicted with all these dualities. The wind, the clouds, the lightning, the thunder are incorporeal. Just as these rise from the world space in which they are bound, enter into highest light and therethrough emerge forth in their own form, the individual soul, in deep sleep too emerges from the body, enters into the highest light and shines in its own true form. He is the highest spirit and roams about (and never remembers the appendage of the body in which the Prana is yoked). When the eye directs itself on akasha, it is then the spirit in the eye; the eye itself serves only for seeing and he who wishes to see is the Atman. Similarly, the other organs are merely agents at the service of this Self. And, he who wishes to understand that he is that 'atman', the understanding is his divine eye (that sees all-past and furture, too). With this divine eye, the understanding dawns on him and he enjoys the Bliss."

*Brihadaranyaka Upanishad*

One of the important Upanishads of Shukla Yajurveda is the Brihadaranyaka Upanishad. There are six Chapters in this Upanishad and the First Chapter deals with the Asvamedha in which the sacrificial horse is the Universe itself. The whole Universe is a 'Yajnya' wherein one thing is sacrified for the other. The Lord himself sacrificed His own Self for the creation and in turn, the process of creation went on as a sacrificial function, pressingof Soma. The Universe created by Prajapati is compared to a horse and it is sacrificed to please the Lord Himself. In a sense, everything emanated from Him and again returns to Him. Then, the importance of Prana as the saviour of the vital organs is emphasized here; it is used in both both cosmic (universe) and psychic (human) sense. Next, the Mahat Vakya, ***'Aham Brahmaasmi'*** ('I am Brahman') is emphasized followed by the description of the process of creation; the Manas, Vac and Prana are the first to emerge and it is interesting to note that these served as 'food' to the Lord. The Atman appears three-fold (creation) as Nama (name), Roopa (form) and, Karma (action). These are the forms of 'Atman', and the name and form are the imperishable one concealed under reality.

The ***Rk Veda*** [10.81.1 & 6] has the reference to the world created by Prajapati who is the life and the hunger and death- all in 'himself', and he performs the Sacrifice to offer food to himself. He creates 'apah' (primeaval waters) and earth, and spreads himself out three-fold as vital breath into Agni, Vayu and Aditya, by joining manas and Vac. He devours the products of his creation as Kala or Time; and, thereafter, as Aditi, devours them all. Prajapati himself becomes an ashva (Horse) and offers himself as Sacrifice to other gods as well. Thus, he who elevates himself into a Union with the Absolute or Prajapati, with hunger and death, becomes immortal.

In the Second Chapter, there is a dialogue between Ajatasatru and Baalaaki Gaargya. It reveals the state of Consciousness in sleep. The vital organs are withdrawn by the self, the Vijnyaana Purusha (the Subject of Knowledge), and again let out during the waking state. Thus, the world temporarily ceases to exist in sleep and again rises out of the Self after the sleep is over. The Purusha, 'Brahman' has form and is formless; He is knowable and unknowable. He is knowable for He exists in the pupil of the eye (in humans) and appears as the sun in the sky. But in all reality, He is unknowable according to its nature. The doctrine of 'neti, neti' will help in discovering Him. Prana is embodied and has entered the man through head and departs through head, the Brahmarandhra. The most important secret of knowing the Brahman is revealed in the dialogue of Yajnyavalkya and Maitreyi. Yajnyavalkya tells Maitreyi that 'everything is related to Atman'; the Brahman cannot be realized through riches or mere accumulation of knowledge. He is the objectless subject of knowledge; He can be realized in a state of 'choiceless awareness'.

The Third Chapter has dialogues of Yajnyavalkya with other wise men and these dialogues reveal many interesting philosophical doctrines. These dialogue cover many interesting things like the rewards for the sacrificial cult, the soul, the sense organs and sense objects, the fate of the soul after death, the benefit of asvamedha Sacrifice to the performers of the Sacrifice, the unknowability of the Brahman, the method of comprehending the Brahman, upliftment of the soul towards the Absolute, the wind as the binding force of the world, and, the akasha (sky) pervaded by the imperishable 'aksharam', Aksharam is the force that regulates the world actually dwells in us, and the unity of Atman with the Brahman.

The Fourth Chapter deals with the definitions of the Brahman, the fate of the soul after death and the method of recognizing the Atman (***individual***) and the Brahman (the highest). The fate of the Soul after death is discussed with a reference to identity of the Self (Jeevatnman) with the supreme Self (Paramatman). Atman in the different states of sleep, fate of unemancipated souls and the state of deliverance are all discussed in Chapter Four.

The Fifth Chapter discloses the nature of the Atman, the Svayambhu Brahman, the method of realizing self, the Gayatri, Prayer, &c. And, the Last Chapter concludes with the supremacy of the Vital Breath over the sense organs and some doctrines like begetting son, transmigration of soul, churning out happiness, etc.

Thus, the entire ***Bruhadaranyaka Upanishad*** is a store- house of valuable information given out in the form of dialogue of learned Seers. Some of the important philosophical doctrines emanating from Yajnyavalkya's dialogue with other learned Brahmanas are highlighted here.

The story goes that the King of Videha, Janaka arranged for Yajnya on a grand scale and invited many Kings and learned Brahmans. He wanted to know the most scholarly person among the learned Brahmanas and offered a thousand cows each with a quarter gold coin on its horn as the reward. Sage Yajnyavalkya accepted the challenge and invited the questions.

First, the Hota Asvala asked some questions.

*Fetters of death have seized this world and we are all afraid of death. What is the means of emancipation from this strange hold, 'Yama paasha'*? Everything in this world is pervaded by day and night, i.e., Time ('Kaala'). *What is the means of emancipation from the clutches of Time*? This sky (space) is without any steps to reach and what is the means of ascending the path to the heavenly abode? How many are the verses, sacrificial offerings, deities, and hymns of this Yajna (Sacrifice), what do these mean and what do we gain from these?

Learned SageYajnyavalkya answered, "*This world is in the clutches of mrutyu (death), Kala, waxing and waning of moon and the ladder-less space that prevenmt us from ascending to heavens. The speech (fire), the eye (sun), the breath (wind), and the manas (Moon) are the means of emancipation from the clutches of mrutyu and kaala (death and Time) and one can ascend to heavens through these means. Through the verses of invocation, verses of sacrifice, and the verses of praise in this Sacrifice, one can gain everything he wants. Three sacrificial offerings are poured into the sacrificial fire and the fire that blazes forth up wards take to the world of gods, the overflowing froth that surfaces take to the world of manes, and the offerings poured into the fire take to the world of men. Manas (Mind) is boundless; the 'Visve Devah' are infinite and through this manas one can reach the Brahman. The three hymns are the invocation hymns; the accompanying hymn and the hymn of praise are corresponding to in-breath (Prana), the intermediate breath (vyana), and the out-breath (Apana) are the breath through which one will attain the heavens."*

There is a very interesting dialogue between Ajatasatru and Gargya. Ajatasatru asks Gargya, "*When a man is asleep, where was that spirit consisting of knowledge and from where will it re-emerge after the sleep?*

Gargya did not know the answer to this question. Ajatasatru tells him, "*When one is asleep, then that spirit consisting of knowledge has withdrawn or taken itself through its knowledge, the knowledge of those vital organs, and lies in that space 'akasha' that is inside the heart; when that spirit seizes those senses withdrawn in itself, then people say that the man has gone into svapiti (sleep); then all the senses and the Mind are seized and withdrawn. Then the man enters the dream world where he wanders, carrying with him all the vital spirits, and carries them around in his body (according to his pleasure). However, when the man is in deep sleep and is not conscious of anything, then the twenty-seven thousand arteries called the benevolent, or hitah, circulate from the heart in the pericardium, enjoys abundant bliss and reposes (rests). When the man gets out of deep sleep, all the spirits spring out of the Atman, just as the tiny sparks spring forth out of blazing fire. This is the secret, the reality of Reality ('satyasya Satyam'); the living spirits are the reality and he is their reality."[2.1.20]*

Then, there is an account of the Brahman. Brahman is 'sthita' (immobile) or 'yat' (mobile) i.e., one is mortal and the other immortal, the one existing here ('sat') and the other transcending ('tyam'). Brahman having form is mortal, the immobile, the one that exists here; it is that which is different from the wind, the akasha consisting of earth, water and fire. The essence of this (having form) is that (which is formless) one which shines there, i.e., the sun; the sun is the essence of all that exists here. The formless one is the wind and the akasha, the immortal one. These are mobile, yonder or transcendental or 'tyat' ones. The essence of this mobile, transcendental, formless, immortal one is the 'Purusha' (the spirit) who is there in the orb of the sun. He is the essence of the yonder, transcendental one.

Now, the Brahman that has form is different from the breath, the inner space within the body (atman), the elemental body (of the pancha bhutas); this is the mortal one, the immobile one and the one that exists here (on earth). The essence of this mortal, immobile Brahman is the eyes; because, the eyes are the essence of mortals. On the other hand, the essence of the formless one, the immortal one, is the breath and the space within the body. Thes essence of this mobile, immortal one, the yonder transcendental Brahman, is that Purusha in the eye; because the eye is the essence of the yonder, transcendental one. Thus, the sun is the eye of Brahman in the yonder world and the eye is the essence of the atman (of mortals) here. The vital spirits are the reality and the Purusha or ***Brahman is its Reality***.

The Atman is the subject of knowledge in us. It is the sustainer of this whole world that has its reality only through it; without it, there is nothing.

All earthly goods are perishable and thus, worthless. Knowledge is more precious than these mundane things and hence it is more desirable. Everything that exists like, wealth, family, lower knowledge like the Veda and Upanishads, the gods and the beings of this world, including this universe is worthless when compared to that supreme knowledge that gives us supreme Bliss. *It must be understood here that all these perceptions of the universe, the world we live in are just an idea in our consciousness; they are true only as far as we entertain them as an idea in our mind. Atman is the knowing subject in us, so that we can know. And, nothing beyond that! The Reality is 'That' and 'That', 'satyasya satyam' only. He who has knowledge of the Atman knows everything. [Also see Chhaandogya Upanishad 6.1 & Mundaka Upanishad 1.1.3]*

The Veda are breathed out of Atman just as the smoke comes out of fire; that is why the Veda are supposed to be the direct revelation of the Brahman.

The dialogue between Yajnyavalkya and his wife Maitreyi is very interesting. When Yajnyavalkya wants to take leave of his wives to go to Vanprasthashram, Maitreyi requests him to impart the means of emancipation. Yajnyavalkya says, "*My dear, indeed, not for the sake of the husband, is the husband dear, but for the sake of the Self, is the husband dear; indeed, not for the sake of the wife, is the wife dear but for the sake of the Self, is the wife dear; So also, the children, wealth, and everything else including the universe and the gods are dear for the sake of the Self, but for the sake of the self everything is dear in the universe is dear. One should indeed, see, hear, understand and reflect over the Self. O, Maitreyi, indeed who has seen, heard, understood and reflected over the Self- by him alone, the whole world comes to be known. Whoever thinks that things like the universe, the gods, beings, are all outside his Self will be deserted by the universe, the gods, beings, etc.; the whole world will desert him who considers everything as being outside the Self.*" This universe, the gods, the beings etc. are what this Self is. One cannot see the god, the universe or the beings because 'He' is in it. How can one see oneself? Only when he goes beyond this universe, or the gods, that he can see the universe and the gods. Only when he transcends the self can one see his Self. Meditation is the only way to transcend this universe, transcend the gods, transcend the self and visualize all these.

Then, Maitreyi asked Yajnyavalkya, "*With what you say that there is no consciousness left after death*?" The latter replied, "*Because where there is quality as it were, there one sees, smells, hears, knows, addresses, etc. (different from oneself), another; but, where everything has become one's own Self, how should one see, hear, smell, address, or know, etc. or regard anybody as different from oneself; how should one know him through whom one knows everything, how should one know the knower?*"

Vedanta makes it amply clear that all plants, animals, human beings, gods, are wandering souls and as such they are all Brahman. Even the earth, fire, water, and such other inorganic substances are born out of Brahman [***Taittiriya Upanishad*** 2.1] All are mutually dependent. One powerful immortal spirit, 'Purusha' renders it (mutual dependence) possible and He is the Atman, the Brahman in all. The doctrine of '***madhuparkam***', or 'each is the honey, and thus attractive, to the other', is explained further in the Fifth Brahmana of the Second Chapter. It is the same 'honey' that is there in every organic or inorganic substance in this universe that makes each mutually attractive and binding, and that Principle is the 'Atman', the Brahman. It is the soul in man, the Brahman in the universe. Dadhyaanch, the son of Atharvan disclosed this Principle (of Madhuparkam) to the Ashvins and the Rishi saw this ['***Rk Veda***', 6. 47.18].

# 4
# Brahma Sutras

The Upanishads, numbering about two hundred and fifty, or so, deal with the various aspects of the Universe- its creation, its constitution, its purpose, etc. Each Upanishad has a theme like the Brahman, the Praana, the Atma, the Mantra, the Yoga, etc. and end up in contradictions and confusion in the minds of students. The students fail to comprehend the central theme of the Upanishads since they take them piecemeal and try to correlate and coordinate and systematise the different doctrines; confusion arises since the ancient Sages taught their students what they visualized as Brahman, Atma, Praana, etc. in their State of transcendental Meditation and Samaadhi. This led to different recensions, or shaakhaś or schools of thought teaching different things that are sometime contradictory and confusing. Since, the 'Vedanta' is the complete Knowledge, all Upanishadic doctrines contained in it should have a moderate, sensible, and universally acceptable explanation, with a note on points of difference and clarification of doubts in the form of a guidebook. All the students of Veda and Upanishads should have a compendium of 'Sutras' (formulae) or Vedanta Sutra, aphorisms that are brief but self-explanatory. In order to fulfil this need for a Guide, the Acharyas prepared their own Bhashyas, or Commentaries on Upanishadic Doctrines. Thus, we have a number of Bhashyas by Acharyas of different schools of philosophical thoughts.

'Brahma Sutras' or 'Vedanta Sutras' is the basis of Indian Philosophy; it is the foundation on which the Vedanta school of philosophy flourished and the Upanishadic teachings became popular. It is, but quite natural that contradictions and wrong interpretations were made due to wrong renderings of the aphorisms. The Devanagari and the Samskrut languages give ample scope for mis-interpretation of the words due to wrong emphasis on sounds and wrong divions of phrases in verses. One vowel misspelt would give a completely different meaning. There are Niruktas, Vyaakaranas, and standard reference works that guide the readers of Veda and Upanishads. Whenever a doubt occurred regarding the contentions of a particular aphorism or verse, the students referred to the Brahma Sutras and got the doubts clarified. Inspite of all possible efforts to make the study of Veda and Upanishads easy, many' Sutras' or 'Bhashyas' are still very difficult to understand, contradictory and confusing as could be seen from the Shankara's Bhashya and Madhva's Bhashya, or Bhaskara's Bhashya and the Ramanuja's Bhashya.

The central theme of '*Brahma Sutra*', as the name itself indicates, is the Knowledge of Brahman. Knowledge of Brahman is the ***'Knowledge Supreme'***. This supreme Knowledge is the key to all other knowledge, say, Knowledge of the Atman, Knowledge of God, Knowledge of Praana, etc. One who knows Brahman knows everything; it is the one Knowledge that leads to the Knowledge of all other. "***By knowing this all other things are known***".

Baadaraayana is supposed to be the author of the 'Brahma Sutras', the best possible explanation ever rendered to the aphorisms of Vedaantic Texts. This has been the basis on which all other Great Acharyas have worked and produced their own Bhashyas. This author, Baadaraayana is supposed to be the same author who wrote the Mahabharata and the Bhagavad-Gita, i.e., Veda Vyasa. However, there are differences of opinion with regard to the date and time of this Great Sage. The name suggests that Badarayana lived in the Himalayas, had his Ashram in Badarinath. It is said that Shri Madhvacharya used to visit this Great sage, an Avataar of Shri Hari Narayana in the Badarinath cave quite often, although the two belong to different dates! These Great Sages like Baadarayana lived for thousands of years and could appear to their disciples whenever they wanted, by sheer Transcendental Meditation!

Brahma Sutras or 'Vedanta Sutras' of Badarayana is the best among the numerous Bhashyas that are now available. Among the other important ones are 1. Shankara Bhashya that propagated 'Advait', or Monism (Atman and Brahman are same), 2. Madhvacharya's Bhashya that upholds 'Dvait' or Dualism, that treats Atman and Brahman as two different entities; 3.the exponent of 'Bhedabedhabhaava' (Theory of difference and non-difference) Nimbaraka's Bhashya; and 4. of Vllabha, the exponent of 'Shudhdhaadvaitavaada'. All these systems are based on the views of the ancient Vedanta schools. Here, the problem becomes more confusing since these five different schools of philosophical thought up hold contradictory doctrines and the same contradictory doctrines are also discussed by Badarayana, long long before these Acharyas. However, it is the contents of the Sutras that are more important than the dates and time of the authors. Who else can give a more appropriate answer to doubts than the incarnations like Baadrayana or Madhwacharya?

***Brahma Sutras*** are very brief and to the extent of being misinterpreted and give opposite meanings than the purported one. These Sutras are so confusing that they do not clearly state the exact section, text, or context in which the interpretations and statements are being made. Even Badarayana will not conclusively say anything and he merely gives the views of other sages orVedantins on the subject. Ultimately, the reader must take to meditation and contemplate; that is the only way of realization of the Truth.

The subject matter discussed under the Brahma Sutras concerns '***Brahman***'. Is Brahman the material or efficient cause of this ephemeral phenomenal world? Who is this *Brahman*? Is he/she/it/That (?) the Spirit behind all creations and perceivable or non-perceivable? Is Brahman Absolute, Abstract, and Infinite? Is Brahman with attributes (qualities, Gunas), 'Saguna'; or, is He 'Nirguna', without any attributes (Gunas)? Is Brahman inside the body or outside the body and what is the meaning 'His being all- pervasive, omnipresent'? Is ***Brahman really 'Antaryamin'*** like the differentiated Ghee derived from milk, and the oil in the sesame seed, or the detailed plan of the huge Banyan tree hidden in its seed? Is Brahman responsible for creating evil for the Jeeva? [Sutras, 2- 1- 21-23].

Brahman, though destitute of materials and instruments, yet is the cause of the world just as the milk turns into curds without extraneous help. [Sutras, 1-2-24-25]. All these and many more intriguing questions are answered in the Brahma Sutras quoting from the various Upanishads. For instance, Shruti says "*All this is but the Self*", *and "There is nothing whatsoever here*" [***Brihadaranyaka Upanishad*** 1-4-1 & 1-4-17 & 4-4-19] which mean the world is non-different from Brahman. Here, non-difference does not mean identity. The world and Brahman being mutually different, it is imposiible to identify one with the other. It only means, 'the world has no existence apart from Brahman and hence it is non-different from Brahman. It establishes the apparent identity or the illusory nature of the objective world, like the illusory snake imposed over the rope. [See ***Chhandogya Upanishad*** 6-1-4]. The Brahman cannot be immutable as well as transformed into the world, at the same time. The Shruti says, this has to be accepted; even as in the individual soul diverse creation exists in the dream state without marring its indivisibility, so also this world springs from Brahman. Badarayana considered this world unreal in a higher sense even as the dream world is Maya [Sutra 3-2-3; 2-3-50; &3-2-18]. ***Brahman through 'Maaya' possesses all powers necessary for creation.***

In ***Chhandogya Upanishad***, the aphorisms 6-1-3 & 4 state, "By which that which is not heard bcomes heard..."; and, "as one lump of clay all that is made of clay is known", meaning, the effects are not different from the cause. These texts clearly show that Brahman is the material cause of the world. The aphorism- "Brahman alone was at the beginning one without a second"shows that it is also the efficient cause; it is Brahman who was there in the beginning alone that could create this World! The material and efficient cause of creation is thus clarified in the above Sutras. Brahman or pure Intelligence is the efficient as well as the material cause of the world. [Sutra,1-4-23]. Brihadaranyaka Upanishad [4- 4-2] states, "He is indeed the great unborn Self". "Everything in this world exists and this quality is obtained from Brahman who is existence; everything is illumined by Intelligence i.e., Brahman. He is all pervading like the ether and is eternal. He is greater than the sky, greater than heaven. But then the Shruti texts also describe the Soul as all- pervasive. So, neither the Shruiti texts nor by reasoning can there be any differentiation between the Brahman and the Soul as 'all-pervading' and 'atomic' entities. According to Advaita, there is no disparity between the two. Brahman due to Upaadhi (adjunct) appears atomic but in reality, it is all- pervasive. So also is the Jeeva in its real nature all- pervading and therefore identical with Brahman.

Brahman and Maya are the cause of the world. Brahman through Vivarta (Sutra 2-1-14) and Maaya through Parinaama have caused this world and the qualities of both are found in the effect. Everything in this world has five elements in its make up- Asti, Bhaati, Priya, Naama and Roopa. The first three have Brahman for their material cause corresponding to the three factors- Existence, Intelligence, and Bliss; the last two consist of Maaya and henece they are unreal. Sutra 28 establishes the unreality of this material objective world, it being illusory like the dream world. It is just naama and roopa that gives an impression of reality. It is possible for Brahman to create this diverse world of name and form and yet remain immutable. Brahman alone is real and the world is unreal. Chhandogya Upanishad 6-16 calls one who sees variety as ignorant and the one who sees unity as a Jnyaani. For the ignorant person, the variety appears to be real through direct perception since he can touch and feel the existence (of body) without questioning as to its permanency and reality. On the other hand, a Jnyaani knows the reality of the things behind the naama and roopa, i.e., name and form.

The nature of the Soul and its relation to Brahman is discussed in Sutras 2- 3- 16 to 53. Shankara says that the Soul is all- pervasive and transmigratory in nature and it is identical with the Brahman; all others treat the Jeeva as atomic, serves as an agent, and a part of the Lord. Mundaka Upanishad [3-1-9], as well as, Chhandogya Upanishad [3-14-3] state that, "the soul is atomic"; and, "It is smaller than a grain of rice, smaller than a grain of barley". Taittiriya Upanishad [3 - 1] states, "That out of which all these creations are born ". It is clear that the world of sentient and insentient things has emanated from Brahman and therefore, Brahman is the cause [Sutra 2]. Hence, the Jeeva also emanated from Brahman, the Lord of the Universe. The Jeeva, although limited and possessive of Mind, is eternal and identical with Brahman, although it (Soul) appears as transmigrating entity. The Jeeva as we experience it is unreal [Sutra 16].

***Brahman is Existence, Knowledge and Infinitude, i.e., Pure Intelligence.*** [Sutra, 2.1]. It is reflected in Anthahkarana of the Jeeva. The Anthahkarana or internal organs, viz 'I'-ness, Mind, and Intelligence accompany the Jeeva at the time of death. Only when the upaadhi (Ignorance like 'I am the Body') is rent apart that the Jeeva attains its real nature, Brahman.

The Sutras in Chapter III and Section 2 deal with the nature of *Brahman.* The Scriptures teach us the Brahman is attributeless (Guna-less). Brihadaranyaka Upanishad makes it amply clear that "***the form is not true and that behind all Upaadhis there is one formless principle***" ***[2-5-1]. "Verily Brahman is formless"[Katha Upnishad 4-11].*** As formless light takes form, so does Brahman take form in connection with Upaadhis that serve the purpose of upasana (in Meditation); Brahman is pure Intelligence; Intlligence is the essential nature of Brahman. Brahman is attributeless and like the sun reflected in water bodies, they (the forms) are not real. Brahman is immortal and free from imperfections.

While defining the Brahman, the doctrine of "neti, neti"("not this, not this") as stated in Brihadaranyaka Upanishad, is used to eliminate all that is not Brahman and ultimately it reaches a point of 'nothing-ness', ***ad infinitum***. Here Brahman is not denied; only the forms of Brahman are denied. Brahman exists, though it is not manifest on account of ignorance; moreover, it is realized in meditation. Therefore Jeeva becomes one with the Infinite when Knowledge dawns. Brahman, although being of the nature of Intelligence, is realized by repeated meditation. Brahman is regarded as Infinite and possesses infinite attributes. Neti, neti only means that Brahman is not this form or that form, but is something different what all is seen in this manifested world.

Prajapati's instructions to Indra and Varuna's teachings to Bhrugu as in ***Chhandogya Upanishad and Taittiriya Upanishads***, respectively take us step by step from duality to Unity of existence. Although duality is asserted in the beginning, it is only to enlighten the reader as to the Unity aspect as the goal; and, duality is discarded soon and even censured as could be seen in ***Katha Upanishad [2-4-10-11]; Brihadaranyaka Upanishad [4- 4-9]; Maitrayani Upanishad [4-2 & 6-3].*** Non-duality is praised and immortality could be achieved by the knowledge of Unity. Again, we have the "*Anoraniyan mahato mahiyaan*" [***Katha Upanishad, 1-2-20***] attribute of Brahman that states, "***Brahman is smaller than the smallest and bigger than the biggest***" that negates all duality and establish Unity in Infinity. It is that 'Zero' (Shoonya or Infinity) which is the smallest of all positive and the highest of all negative values; and, Zero is not shoonya or devoid of value. It is full- "Poornam" and from Zero all other numbers get their value! This is Vedic mathematics, the greatest contribution of Veda to mankind.

In the exercise of this 'neti, neti' i.e.,'not this, not this' negating exercise where everything is negated, or discarded, the ultimate reality, the non-entity, the ***Brahman*** is established. This 'Non-entity' which cannot be negated, and which is the witness (Saakshin) of everything is established. *"We cannot say that by negation we come to nonentity, for the very fact that we comprehend this nonentity shows that it is being illumined by the witnessing consciousness, the basic reality even behind this idea of nonentity" (Brahma Sutras).*

*The real nature of the individual soul is described in the Sutras 2. 11-25. The individual soul is real, all-pervading, changeless, immutable, indestructible and illimitable. [Verses,16-18]. In the Verse 6-31, the identity of the self with Brahman is established as in doctrine "Thou art That".*

*Brahma Sutras Verses 29-30 describe the real nature of the 'thou' (the 'Self') and 'That' (the 'Brahman')-"You are Brahman", in the doctrine of "Thou art That". The verses 13-29-34 describe the real nature of the Soul as identical with Brahman. But the soul in its bondage being deluded considers itself an agent and experiencer, atomic and a part of the Whole, the Lord. The Gunas of Prakriti (Naure) perform all action and due to ignorance, hnman thinks he is the doer [3-27; 14-23 & 15-7].*

*"Brahman is not apprehended by our eyes, nor by our senses",[Mundaka Upanishad, 3-1-8]- "Pratyaksha anumaanabhyaam", ie shruti and smriti. Shruti says," Brahman is not known to those whose heart is not purified, but those who are purified realize It in the state of samaadhi, when ignorance is destroyed". Some wise men, however, with his eyes turned inside and wishing for immortality saw the Self within". Katha Upanishad 2-4-1; Mundaka Upanishad, 3-1-8]. Shruti also says, "He who is seen as light in the yogins meditating on Him sleeplessly, with suspended breath, contented minds, and subdued senses" have realized Him.*

*Brahma Sutra declares: "Brahman is that omniscient, omnipotent cause from which proceed the universe, its sustenance, and dissolution". It is the 'tatastha lakshana'. "Brahman is one without a second". There is only one Brahman without any difference [Sutra 3-2-31]. Brihadaranyaka Upanishad declares, "There is no other witness, but He"[3-7-23]. "There is nothing but Brahman. The Self is all this", says Chhandogya Upanishad [7-25-2]."That great, birthless Self is the eater of food (worship) and the giver of wealth, the fruit of one's work" declares Brihadaranyaka Upanishad [4-4-24]."Brahman is pure and unconditional; unconditioned Brahman is Truth, Knowledge, and Infinity". Brahman is to be realized for emancipation.*

*"That from which these things are born, by which they live after birth, and into which they enter at death- try to know "That". That is" Brahman"[Taittiriya Upanishad, 2-1 & 3-1].*

Vedanta holds that the Self, the Atman is identified with Brahman."Self is free from all limiting adjuncts of body and, is 'Infinitude', say the Scriptures, Shruti.The spiritual requirements to gain knowledge of the Self, or Brahman are:

1. Discrimination between things permanent and transient.
3. Not allowing Mind to externalize; keep the sense organs under check- sama and dama.
4. Uparati- not thinking of sense objects.
5. Renunciation of fruits of action, here and in the other world.
6. Fixity of Mind on God- Shrudhdhaa or Faith and Mumukshutvam (desire for emancipation).

These are the six treasures or virtues of a true spiritual aspirant.

But, the task of realizing Brahman is made very difficult by 'Pradhaana', ie Prakriti, Maaya. "*Knowledge is enveloped in ignorance, hence do beings get deluded" [Sutra, 5-15]. "This world knows Me not, being deluded by the modifications of the Gunas. Verily this divine Maaya of Mine is difficult to cross over... deprived of discrimination by Maya they follow the Asuric (demonic) ways [Bhagavad Gita, 7-13-16]."I am not manifest to all, being veiled by My Yogamaaya". The lord dwells in the heart of all beings causing them to revolve by his Maaya" [Bhagavad Gita 7-25; 18 – 61].*

Although stress is laid on Bhakti maarg, no where does it say that Bhakti is superior to Knowledge. "The fire of Knowledge burns all Karma to ashes. There exists nothing so purifying like Knowledge"[Gita, 4- 37-38 & 7-17-18]."Supremely dear is the wise man to Me. I regard him as My very Self" [Gita 7. 17-18]

It should be realized that the Upanishads do not preach a particular doctrine and stick to it. Every Upanishad is like step in the ladder taking higher and higher towards Self-realisation. The Upansihads start with dualistic approach, teach us about God out side of us, only to discard it and find it within ourselves. First, it tells us God is the creator, sustainer and destroyer and we need worship God. Then, it teaches us that God is not outside of nature, but immanent in nature. And, in the end, the Upanishads emphatically declare that "*Whatever is real is He; there is no difference*", as said to Svetaketu. *Thou art That*", '*The immanent One' is at last declared to be the same as that is in the human Soul*", as Badarayana has rightly observed.

*What after Death?*

Chapter III of the Brahma Sutras clarify some important doubts regarding what happens after death. It is said that the Soul, when passing out of the body at death is enveloped with fine particles of the gross elements. The Sutras explain whether the soul takes with it subtle parts of the gross elements as its seed (for the future body) in its transmigration. The Sutra 3-1-1 says that the soul does take with it subtle parts of the elements. The three internal organs, 'anthahkarana' viz, ego or 'I'-ness, manas and budhdhi accompany the soul and this establishes the fact that the soul transmigrates in order to help the Jeeva to attain its cherished desires. Children exhibit enormous intelligence in early child-hood and their mind is capable of extra-ordinary ways of thinking and imagination. The ego exhibited by a child even before it is one year old is astounding!

And, then, why is the transmigration of Souls? This question has already been answered. The soul takes to another body after the degeneration and death of the previous one due to the unfulfilled desires and the Karma particles, budhdhi, manas and ego drives it to achieve whatever possible in the next birth. Budhdhi enters at the time of the conception of the child as 'kalala'. Now, it must be remembered here that all souls will not enter the womans body and there are a thousand ways to take to rebirth in the form of plants, insects, animals and birds. The life form depends on the past karma and the good deeds bring good birth and evil ones bring lower forms. Some souls enter heaven for their good deeds and enjoy the proximity of gods only to return after their punya is exhausted.

It is clearly stated that Chitraguptas under the orders of Yama, the God of Death, maintains the account of good deeds and bad deeds or virtues and vices and sends the soul to the higher worlds or lower worlds for enjoyment or atonement depending on the Karma. The gods treat all these souls as their source of enjoyment or food. It is the residual karma that decides the birth of the souls descending from heaven. Smrui says, "With the remainder of their Karma they are born in a noteworthy place, caste, and family with becoming appearance, longevity, knowledge, wealth, happiness and intellect". So, the soul is born with residual karma. The path to heaven is also explained. "Knowledge and work are the means to go along the Devayana (God's path) and Pitryaana (Father's path)". Souls with good actions and spiritual attainment Jnyaan or Knowledge of the realityof this world who die in Uttaraayan (while the sun shines over Tropic of Cancer), will take to Devayaan and others with heavy souls (blemished with desire and karma) take to Lunar sphere and return to earth immediately to take birth as lower forms. The Souls of persons who constantly desire God and chanted His name burns the seed of rebirth (Karma) and gets out of the mesh of the 'golden threads of desire' and thus gets itself released from metempsychosis, cycle of rebirth.

Some souls take to forms of birth as rice or wheat and barley that are only 'connected'; but the actual birth of the soul as a child is connected to persons (father/mother) performing the act of generation. Now it is through connection to parents, the soul enters the woman and there gets a new body fit for experiencing the fruits of Karma.

*Realization of the Self, 'the Atman'*

*The Reality or Knowledge dawns on a person who turns all the senses inward, stills the mind, and contemplates on the Self. He alone who has desisted from desires and call of flesh, who dwells in the constant memory of the Lord and ardent desire of reaching Him will attain Him. By meditation on Him, the Supreme Lord, that which is covered by ignorance viz the similarity of the Lord and the Soul, becomes manifest; for from the Lord are its bondage and freedom." [Sutra 3-2-5]. The dream world is said to be false. But individual soul is a part of the Supreme Soul and therefore shares the power of the Lord-knowledge and rulership, even as a spark and fire have alike the power of burning. But, it is not so. The Sutra says, "the rulership is covered by ignorance in theJeeva state and gets manifested only when in the state of meditation on the Lord, this ignorance is destroyed by the knowledge, 'I am Brahman'."*

*The Shruti says, "In the intermediate stage (between waking and deep sleep, there is a real) creation". The question is whether the creation which one experiences in the dream state is as real as this world of ours, merely as Maya, illusory or false, as compared with this waking world. There are some who belive that 'it is just as real'. A meal taken in dream is as real as in the waking sate since it gives the same satisfaction. The Shruti also says that this real state of the dream springs from the Lord Himself. "There are no chariots, nor horses to be yoked to them, nor roads there, but He himself creates the chariots, the horses, and the roads; for He is the agent" [Brihadaranyaka Upanishad, 4-3-10]. "He who is awake in us shaping objects of desire while we are asleep... that is Brahman". [Katha Upanishad, 2-5-8].* ***But the dream world is not real and it is only an illusion on account of its nature not being manifest with the reality of attributes of the waking state".*** *[Brahma Sutra 3-2-3]. The nature of the dream world does not agree in toto with that of the waking world with respect to time, place, cause, and non-contradiction, and as such, that world is not real like the waking world. The objects that have no reality appear to exist in dreams just as silver does in a mother of pearl. Hence, the Sutra says that' the objects of the dream world are not real and not created by the Lord, but they are crfeated by the individual Soul'.* ***It is the Jeeva that creates the dreams and not the Lord.*** *Sutra 3-2-4 says, "soochakascha hi shruteh, aachakshate cha tadvudah", meaning, "Though the dream world is an illusion, yet it serves as an omen for, so we find in the Shruti, and the expert dream readers also say thus". The dreams are capable of forecasting events or good and bad fortune. The things indicated by dream are reai although the dream itself is unreal. "If in this dream he sees a woman, let him know this to be a sign that his sacrifice has succeeded." [Chhandogya Upanishad 5-2-8].*

*In the Aphorisms 3-2-7 & 8, the Brahma Sutras describes the soul in dreamsless sleep and coming out of Sushupti. "When a man is (deep) asleep, he sees no dreams, then he has entered into the nerves, the Naadis (Pulses)". [Chhandogya Upanishad, 8-6-3]. "Through them he moves forth and rests in the pericardium, i.e., in the region of the heart"; When this being full of consciousness is asleep.....lies in the ether, i.e., the real Self, the Atman, which is in the heart". [Brihadaaranyaka Upanishad, 2-1-19 & 17]. In other words, in deep sleep the soul goes through the nerves to the region of the heart and there rests in Praana, the Brahman. The individual soul covered with ignorance is lost in the Brahman. Hence Brahman is the resting place of the soul in deep sleep.*

*Again Chhandogya Upanishad says, "My son, all these creatures, when they have come back from the True, know not they have come back from the 'True', i.e., the Brahman" [Aphorism 6-10-2].*

*The doctrine of Maya is referred to in the Bhagavad-Gita. "Knowledge is enveloped in ignorance, hence do beings get deluded [5-15]. This world knows Me not, being deluded by the modifications of the Gunas. Verily this divine Maayaa of mine is difficult to cross over.... ..deprived of discrimination by Maayaa they follow the Asuric (demonic) ways. "I am not manifest to all, being veiled by My 'Yogamaayaa'. The Lord dwells in the heart of all beings causing them to revolve by His Maayaa." [Bhagavad –Gita 7- 13-16 & 25l 18-61]*

*Hence, the first and the foremost thing, is to realize that this world is not real. A person who is aware of the dream knows that the dreams are unreal. This objective materialistic world is illusory. Since the ignorant person believes it to be real, he is deluded. He cannot understand the simple fact that this' so-called real world' also disappears in deep sleep. There is a 'Purusha', the Witnessing Self, within all of us observing the dream world, the 'so- called real world', as well as, the deep sleep. In deep sleep, nothing exists except the Self, the Atman. An ordinary person who goes to deep sleep enjoys the bliss of peace and tranquility only to get back to the illusory world due to his ignorance. On the other hand, a Jnyaani will go to the state of nirvikalpa samaadhi, a state of supreme happiness, bliss, and peace and comes out 'enlightened' as to the nature of this transcient world. It is the' awareness' or 'wakefulness' to the nature of this world that brings enlightenment. The Atman is fully awake. It is not bound by the ' triputi' of causality, time, and space. There is no day or night and all dualities cease with' enlightenment'.*

*Sveatasvatara Upanishad [Aphorism 1—11] says, "When that God is known all fetters fall off... From meditating on Him there arises, on the dissolution of the body, the third state, that of universal Lordship." Till then the Jeeva cannot create at will anything real. Since the bondage and freedom of the Jeeva, individual soul, comes from the Lord, the power of creation does not come spontaneously. Ignorance of His true nature causes bondage and knowledge of his true Self results in liberation.*

*"The fire of Knowledge burns all Karma to ashes. There exists nothing so purifying like Knowledge. [Bhagavad-Gita , 4- 37-38] Though Bhakti is favoured for the mortals, 'Jnyaan' is supreme leading to immortality.*

*Even with regard to Pradhaana, ie Prakriti as an independent entity creating this diverse world, as the Saamkhya followers believe, it is not true; Prakriti is dependent of Brahman for creation and the story of blind and the lame coming together to travel put forth by Saamkhyans is utterly untenable. Neither the Purusha is lame nor Prakriti is blind; Purusha being always near Pradhaana, there would be permanency of creation. It is all wrong interpretations of the Shruti by the Saamkhyans. Brahma Sutra emphatically upholds the Shruti and says that, Maaya, although the cause of the world, is a dependent entity, being the power of the Brahman. "The Great Lord is the Maayin, the ruler of Maaya" [Svetasvatara Upanishad 4-10; Chhandogya Upanishad 3-14-4 & 3-8-7] Sutras 1 to 10 refute the Saamkhyans; "the inert Pradhhan has no intelligence to create a diverse well-designed world" God is the efficient cause in bringing out the latent tendencies of each individual to fruition. God is neither partial to some putting them in rich families and others in poor families, nor is he cruel punishing and making them suffer. God does not interfere in the affairs of people and people enjoy or suffer according to their virtuous acts and vices and bad deeds, Karma. Further, this world has not come from nowhere; it is a well- devised grandiose divine plan and has evolved through eons based on Ritam and Satyam. "The Lord devised the Sun and the Moon as before" [Rk Veda 10-190-3]. "Brahman alone is Truth, Existence, and Bliss".*

*The individual soul in its real nature is "real, all-pervading, changeless, deathless, immutable, indestructible, and illimitable" [Bhagavad-Gita 2-11, 16-18]. The Vedic doctrine of 'That thou art' is also explained in Verse 6-31 to establish the identity of the self and Brahman. The real nature of the soul as identical with Brahman is also explained. [Bhagavad-Gita, 13- 29.34]. But the embodied soul, in its state of bondage, being deluded considers itself an agent and experiencer, atomic and a part of the Lord. "The Gunas of Prakriti perform all action with the understanding; deluded by egoism, man thinks, 'I am the doer'. {Bhagavad Gita 3.27; 14.25 and 15.7]. The atomicity of the Soul is refuted in the Brahma Sutras on the ground that the atom is not a part of the whole but the whole by itself. "The soul is without parts like the atoms, and so there is no possibility of connection between the soul and the atoms". At best, the Brahman (the supreme soul) and the Atma (the individual soul) are like the fire and its sparks.*

*The Brahman, the Shruti says, is unmanifest (avyakta) on account of our being covered with ignorance. "He is neither apprehended by the eye, nor by the other senses, nor by penance". [Mundaka Upanishad, 3-1-8]. Brahman is experienced in perfect meditation. Brahma Sutra says, "that Brahman is not known only to those whose heart is not purified, but those who are purified realize it in the state of Samaadhi when ignorance is destroyed" [Sutra 23-24]. "Some wise man with his eyes turned inside and wishing for immortality saw the Self within". [Katha Upanishad 2-4-; Mundaka Upanishad 3-1-8]. The Smriti also confirms this: "He who is seen as Light by the Yogins meditating on Him sleeplessly, with suspended breath, contented minds, and subdued senses".*

*The Jeeva attains identity with the Brahman on the dawning of Knowledge, when ignorance with all its limiting adjuncts disappears. Mundaka Upanishad asserts, "He who knows that Supreme Brahman becomes Brahman itself." [Mundka Upanishad, 3-2-9]. Actually, the Jeevaatman and the Paramaatman, the Brahman, are not two different entities; it is" like the Light and its substratum, the orb. Both being luminous are non-different" [Sutra 28]. Light and its orb differ in their extensity. Jeva is limited and Brahman is all- pervading and, as such non-different.*

*Supreme Knowledge, i.e.,'Knowledge of the Brahman', is the only means to liberation from this world of illusion. This phenomenal world is illusory according to Shankara's Mayavada or 'Anirvachaniya Khyaativaada', or the doctrine of the apparent modification of Brahman into this phenomenal world called 'Vivartavada' (as opposed to Parinaamavaada- the doctrine of actual modification of Brahman into phenomenal world as held by Ramanuja's Vishishtaadviata). Knowledge of Brahman being thus the only way to Liberation, an inquiry into Brahman through the study of the 'Brahma Sutras' is absolutely necessary.*

The Brahma Sutras quote extensively from Shruti, the Upanishads and put at rest all objections raised by the Naiyaayikas, Vaisheshikaas, Mimaamsa and the Samkhya followers with regard to the Reality, the Truth, the Brahman, and the Atman, the Pradhhaan, the Vital Breaths, the Praana, and the like. No study is complete without the study of Brahma Sutras. It is the ultimate in Indian Philosophy, Bhaarateeya Darshana Shaastra. The Upanishads, the Brahma Sutras, and the Bhagavad Gita (Triputi), constitute the foundation of Indian Philosohy- Darshana Shastra.

# 5
# The Puranas And The Great Epics

What are the implications of ***Vedanta***, especially when we go deep into the Epics and Puranas? These epics and puranas appear very simplistic stories for a layman, but for a person seeking the inner meaning, the very essence of Vedanta is beautifully inscribed in these texts. It is highly educative, refreshing to go through the epics and puranas and even the history (itihasa) of Vedic Age.

The 'Veda' being 'hard nut to crack' to the common people, an easier means of conveying the Vedic knowledge became necessary and thus came a number of Puranas and the epics. Here, the essence of the Veda is conveyed in parables and stories, in simple language that could be understood by one and all. The people in general had a spiritual mind-set or a spiritual background due to the influence of the prevailing spiritual environment. This had a tremendous effect on the social milieu since the atmosphere was charged with spirituality as a result of the performance of Yajnyas, Homas, Havanas and Shanti for various purposes. The people were basically influenced by moral and ethical values imparted by the spiritual texts in their everyday life. Inspite of this, there might be aberrations and to correct these diversions, regular pravachans or lectures on the Puranas and epics were arranged and the people were constantly educated on these spiritual lines.

Thus, these Puranas and the epics became the part of everyday life of the people in India and even today, this method of reading holy scriptures, enacting drama based on the epics, and regular lectures (pravachan) are practised. In fact, the modern trend is astonishing and there is a greater awakening to spiritual learning in the young as well as the old. The Adhyatmic Study Centres are proliferating!

*The Puranas*

The Puranas constitute one of the important sources of Vedic knowledge and these are in simple language that can be easily understood by common people. These Puranas teach 'Righteousness', piety, spirituality, and morals and ethics for a sound harmonious social life. They convey the history of the universe and evolution of life; and, through the story of the life of great sages convey the essence, purpose, and goal of life. These Puranas lay stress on the need for effort on the part of human beings to realize the 'Self' and attain liberation. In a sense, these Puranas are the repository of the ancient knowledge and wisdom of the Sages and a part of our ancient Indian history and a spiritual heritage of India.

There are 18 Puranas, six each devoted to Brahma, Vishnu and

Mahesvara. The author of these Puranas is believed to be Vedavyasa of the Mahabharata fame and has rendered these Puranas in Verses. Vyasa imparted Bhagavatam to his son Shuka, a great Yogi of absolute purity of mind and consciousness and had attained unity amidst diversity. He, indeed, is the knower of Brahman. It is here that the Vedic gods like Indra, Skanda, Varuna, Mitra give place to the Trinity of Brahma, Vishnu and Maheswara as the manifest forms of the Brahman. Nonetheless there is no distinction between these three since each is a part of the other. For instance, Padma Purana treats the Trinity as one entity although their attributes vary. Vaishnavaites attach great importance to Bhagavatam and they sing and dance Bhagavatam and have come to be known a Bhgavatars. Bhagavata teaches the concept of Bhakti and no one knows better what Bhakti is than Narada. Absolute purity of mind and heart, devoid of all sensuousness and dwelling in the Lord are the devotees of Krishna; to name a few of them are the Gopalaks, the cowherds, the Gopalikas, the cowherdesses, Sudhama, and the whole lot of boys and girls who roamed about Brindavan, and ultimately Radha, the inexplicable one. Krishna, the Yogi had the power to appear in multifarious forms wherever his devotes called him and could assume 16000 forms to be with the 16000 damsels whom he promised redemption! What Pure love is beyond the capacity to understand and experience in the human form in Kali Yug for the mind and heart are wholly sensuous. One has to go back to Dvapara Yug to understand and appreciate the lore of Bhagavatam.

All Puranas deal at length on the story of origin of the universe, the story of evolution and narrate the whole history of gods and describe the features of the earth. There are the Pitru Loka, Deva Loka, Gandharva Loka, Kinnara Loka, the Naga Lok and the Brahma Loka, Kailasa and the Vaikunta according to Bhagavatam. The Four faced Brahma and the story of creation is very interesting. Puranas also reiterate the beginningless and endless chain of evolution or creation.

The term 'Purana' is found in ***Atharva Veda*** [11-7-24] and *Shatapatha Brahmana* [13-4-3-13]. It also appears in *Brihadaaranyaka Upanishad:*

*"Ithihaasam Puranam vidya upanishadah"*

*Purana or Itihasa is considered as the 'Fifth Veda' as per the reference in Chandogya Upanishad that reads: "Ithihaasa puranam panchamam Vedaanaam Vedhah."* Thus, the Puranas are as old as the Veda. The author of these Puranas is believed to be Dvaipaayana Veda Vyasa. But most of the Puranas now found in print may not be of this antiquity according to some scholars. Some of them are dated 300-550 A.D. of the Gupta period or may be still more recent. Vishnu Purana is believed to be the oldest dated 400 A.D. and is followed by Vaayu Purana 500 A.D., Bhagavatam 500-700 A.D. and Koorma Purana 700 A.D. Some repeat the story of Sri Krishna or the "***Sri Krishna Charita***". Vishnu Purana and Bhagavatha appear to be almost same.

***Brahma Purana*** repeats some parts of Vishnu Purana and Srimad Bhagavata. It is stated that Sage Shuka son of Sage Vyasa narrated the story of Sri Krishna as in Bhagavata to King Parikshit. It is quite possible that the same story has been narrated to different students who in turn narrated it in different forms in different Puranas keeping the central idea intact. Sage Vyasa's Vishnu Purana is the one narrated by his father Sage Paraashara; and, he in turn, narrated it to his son Maitreya.

The same story repeats in the case of Mahabharat. Although Sage Vyasa wrote the great epic, it was told to his student Romaharshan and he in turn to his son Ugrashrava and, then to Shaunaka, &c. Similarly, the epic Ramayana too has been rendered by different authors in different ways keeping the central idea in tact. As the story goes, Valmiki, a bandit was advised by the Sage Narada to perform japa on Sri Rama; but the bandit did not know how to chant the name 'Rama'. He was asked to chant as he could as 'Ma ra', 'Mara', and in course of repeated chantings he went on chanting the name of 'Rama' and attained enlightenment. This effort, 'tapas' enabled him to write the story of Sri Rama as the well-known epic 'Ramayana'. Sage Narada guided Valmiki in writing the great epic 'Ramayana'

Only a sinner can become a saint. It is this basic concept of converting the sinners into saints that forms the central theme of all the epics and puranas. It is with a single purpose of guiding the common people, rather educating the people how to live wise that these epics and puranas were narrated at regular sessions. This is the spiritual heritage of our country. All over India, these epis and Puranas became so popular that the people even today sing, dance, and playes the epics on occasions of festivals and auspicious days, or whenever they were free from their avocations such as agriculture, handicrafts, village Industries and other fine arts.

The Puranas are eighteen in number and these are: the Matsya, Markandeya,·Bhavishya, Bhagavatha, Brahma, Brahma Vaivartha, Brahmaanda, Vamana, Varaha, Vayu, Vishnu, Agni, Narada, Padma, Linga, Garuda, Koorma and Skaanda. Some verses are found common in all the Puranas. There are some Upa-Puranas like Sanathkumara, Naarasimha, Kaapila, Maanava and some of these are not available. Of all the Puranas the Skaanda Purana is the largest with 81,100 verses. Markandeya Purana is the smallest with 9000 verses.

*Vishnu Puranam*

Sage Parashara is believed to be the author of Vishnu Purana. Vishnu Purana is one of the most important Scriptures that have gained prominence among all the Puranas. It gives a detailed account of the origin of the universe and evolution of life and the history of the gods, semi-gods, sages and seers. Puranas include many other subjects other than the history of the universe and evolution of life forms. Puranas deal with Dharma Shastra (Principles of Righteousness), Vedanta (Philosophy), Yoga, Samkhya, Jyotisha- a study of colours emanated from Stars and the the intensity of vibrations (Astrology), Vaidya (Ayurveda and Medicine), Vyaakarana (Grammar), Dhanurveda (Archery), Samgeeta (Music), Shilpa (Architecture and Sculpture), Alamkaar (Fine Arts), etc.

*Who is this 'Vishnu'? Is it the one of the Trinity, or the one beyond these, who is formless, nameless, and the supporter of this universe? Vishnu is that One without a second, who is the 'Sat', 'Chit', and 'Anand'*

*and is called the 'Brahman'. This 'Knowledge of Brahman' is the central theme of Vishnu Purana. Vishnu is the Knowledge 'Sat' and the Knowledge "Sat' is Brahman.*

*"Vishnorjnyanamayamsyoktham, Tajnyanam Brahma sanjnitham."*
*[1-22-51]*

*It is beyond all description, unknown but knowable, and one becomes 'That' by experiencing Him. That is Brahman. He is the source of all power and strength behind the Trinity that rule this world: "VishnurBrahma svaroopena svayameva vyavasthithah.[1-2-56]. It is this Parabrahman who becomes Vishnu by his sattva, Brahma by his Rajas and Rudra by his Tamas qualities, vibrations. But in all essence, It is one and the same and "that is' That' or " Om tat sat". Vishnu purana clearly brings out this 'Sat' or 'Knowledge' of 'Ekameva adviteeyam' or advaith.*

*While Vishnu is the saguna and saroopa, Brahman is Nirguna and aroopa and all the three- Brahma, Vishnu and Mahesvara are the different forms of the supreme Brahman, "Vishnurbrahma svaroopena svayameva vyavasthithah. [1-2-56].*

*All the manifested, unmanifested, Time and Jeevatman are the different forms of the Parabrahman.*

*"Parasya Brahmano roopam purushah prathamam dvija,*
*Vykatavyakte tathaivaanye roope kaalastatha param.* ***[1-2-15]***

' Ignorance' appeared at the very beginning of the creation of this world and we all see this world as real due to our ignorance; there is no world without this ignorance. When 'Knowledge' dawns, this world disappears! "*Avidyaa pancha parvaishaa praadurbhootaa mahatmanah. [1-5-5]. "The illusion of the universe disappears through meditation on union of Sattva-bhava of Paramesvara. Through knowing the Lord, avidya and the rest are destroyed." [Naradaparivrajakta Upnishahd].*

***Vishnu Purana*** is a very sacred popular Scripture. There are six Sections and 126 Chapters with 23000 verses covering various aspects of the universe highlighting the prominence of the Lord Sri Hari, Narayana, "Vishnu". It is very significant to note that Vishnu Purana gives a detailed account of the Vedic cosmology that as well fits into modern theories. It gives the position of Stars and gives vivid description of the different spheres or realms of geographic regions, planets, the realms of lunar and solar spheres and the deities of the universe in the first two chapters. The third chapter deals with Vedic life and literature. Interestingly, the fourth chapter deals with the story of Sri Rama and hints at the nature of life in general and about the rulers of Kali Yuga. The dynasties of Vaivasvata, Manu, Soma, Ikshvaaku, Yadu and others are also given here. The story of the Yadava dynasty and Sri Krishna's life is given elaborately in Chapter Five. The sixth chapter deals with 'Kalidharma'. Here, the distortions that render whole life topsy-turvy by 'yuga-dharma' are beautifully explained. The relationship between wife and husband, parents and children, teachers and students, and amongst the brothers themselves get so strained that it leads to a state of 'demonaic' behaviour. Fearing the onset of such a state of affairs, the Lord himself assumes full control and directs the human life on earth. 'It is His divine will'! When things become worse, the Lord will take birth as an incarnation to uphold 'dharma (righetousness) as said in Gita. Sri Krishna says, "***Dushta shiksha shishta samrakshanaarthaaya sambhavaami yuge yuge***". Incidentally, it is very interesting to note that the history of Sri Krishna is elaborately dealt with while that of Sri Rama is brief. Vishnu Purana also covers the other incarnations, such as Koormaavatar, Varaahaavatar, and Nrsimhaavatar. Srimad Bhagavata deals with the history of Nrsimhaavatara with emphasis on Bhakthi as illustrated by Bhakta Prahlada's devotion and steadfastness (faith) in the Lord much against Hiranyakashipu's anger and hatred for Vishnu.

*According to Vishnu Purana, it is very significant that Sri Vishnu takes the form of 'Nrsimha' (An 'avatar') to kill Hiranyakashipu, father of Bhakta Prahlada. Hiranyakashipu hated the very name of Vishnu for the latter had killed his brother, an asura troubling the gods. Every time Prahlada took the name of 'Narayana' or "Sri Hari' Hiranyakashipu used to be wild and did not hesitate even to kill his son. Further, Hiranyakashipu had become invincible with the boon obtained from Brahma. Vishnu did not want to rescind the boon given by the Creator. As per the boon, Hiranyakashipu was invincible and could not be killed by any man or animal, by any instrument, fire, or water. So, the Lord took the form of a Lion with the man's head, ' Nrsimha' (Nara- Simha'), the half Man and half Lion, and used his teeth to pull out the intestines of the Asura and killed him. The teeth are of the strength of diamond and the story goes that Bhakta Prahlada was saved from the atrocities of the Asura-father for there was no other way of vanquishing him since he was invincible. In the Nrsimha Tapaneeya Upanishad, the Mahamantra or the 'mantrraja' describes the Lord as:*

*"Om! Ugram Viram Mahavishnum Jvalantam Sarvatomukham;*
*Nrsimham Bhishnam Bhdram Mrutyu-mrutym Namaamyaham."*

***Another Mantra set in Anushtubh Chandas of the Gayatri fame is:***

*"Om! Sri Nrsimhaya vidmahe, vajradantaaya dheemahi, tan no simha prachodayaat!"*

*Whoever chants the 'mantraraja' with devotion and invokes the Lord, the Lord will appear to protect the bhakta. The Nrsimha Gayatri is very useful for japam. Omnipresence of the Lord is evident from the fact that Nrsimha appears out of a pillar when Hiranyakashipu challenges Bhakta Prahlada to show him in the pillar. The Lord is everywhere to protect his devotees; but, only faith, devotion and total surrender are needed.*

*Thus, the Bhakta Prahlada episode has a special place in Vishnu Purana and is one of the most important episodes explaining the Narasimhavatar.* ***Vishnu Purana*** advocates both '***Bhakti***' and '***Jnyaana***' along with rites and duties for liberation. Lord's divine grace comes to those with pure heart and mind. Purity of mind and heart comes with '***karma anushtana***', nishkama karma. The Lord resides in anthahkarana of persons of pure mind and pure heart. 'Jnyaan' is the end product of all these three: rites and duties, pure mind, and pure heart derived from Meditation. Those who are following the '***Karma Marg***' will attain heaven and enjoy all that is best in this world. Those who take to 'sanyas' and '***Jnyaan Marg***' will become yogis and will enjoy the access to Brahma Lok. "***Om Namo Bhagavate Vaasudevaaya***" is the twelve- letter sacred mantra that will open the door to liberation only through 'Jnyaan'.

*"Jnyaanagnih sarva karmaani bhasmasath kurute Arjuna"* ***[Gita]***

'***Jnyaan***' is essential for liberation and this Jnyan comes from Meditation on the Lord. This is the core of ***Vishnu Purana***. Those who start with Dhyan of the Lord, '***Ashtabhuja Vishnu***', gradually drop his external appearance and reach the inner Self of the Lord in a state of '***nirvikalpa samadhi***', in which the Lord is seen as '*EKAMEVAADVITEEYA*', the '***One***' '***without any other***', will attain the Lord, becomes (in bhava) one with Him. In this state of '***Nirvikalpa Samadhi***', there is neither the *'dhyaata', nor the 'dhyeya', nor the 'dhyaan'. All the three become One, the Absolute.*

*Besides Puranas, there are the' Smritis' that are codified laws of moral, ethical, and social life as formulated by Sages like Narada, Yajnyavalkya and Manu. Due to misunderstanding the real meaning of the caste and class system, Manu Smriti has come into much debate as has been discussed here. The other Scriptures that are much misunderstood, as also practised in a corrupt form, are the 'Tantras'.*

*' Tantras' are the revelations of Veda called Agamas. Tantras literally mean, "that (Scriptures) by means of which knowledge is spread to save mankind from ignorance (delusion)". Tantras are grouped under different class, each according to the deity worshipped by the adherents of the particuar group.*

*The 'Vaishnava Agama' or Vaisnvite Tantras have Vishnu as the God for worship while Shiva Agama and Shakti Agama have Shiva and Shakti as the Deity of their worship, respectively.*

*The Shakta Group has 'Shakti' or' Kaali maa' or God Mother for their worship. The Buddhists too recognize the Tantra system and have developed their own 'Buddhistic Tantra' as in Tibetan School of Buddhism.*

*Of the three parts, the Sadhana part, the Siddhi part and the Philosophy part of the Tantras, the last one is very important, although the Sadhana part of the Tantras gain much importance in Shaakta Group. The Shaakta Group have abused the system and have brought much discredit to it, to some extent.*

According to tradition, Shiva uttered these doctrines to Shive, the Divine Consort. It is also 'Shakti', popularly known as 'Kaali Maa' or 'Maa Durga', the God Mother that is worshipped by the adherents of this system. But, in course of time the adherents of this system developed rituals using wine and women, and made it a night- long affair of worship called 'Vaamacara'. Any deviation from the Vedic doctrines and Upanishadic implorations that hold 'Self Realisation' as the only spiritual goal, is bound to have adverse effects. Mantra, Yantras and Tantras should not be used for personal gains.

The Philosophy of Tantras eulogises the Upanishadic doctrines of the unity of individual soul with Shiva-Shakti, the identity of individual self with Brahman, the Universal Self. The creative power of the Universe is "Maya", according to Shankaracharya. It is 'illusion', possessing in itself no absolute reality. Tantras call this creative power "Shakti". The universe is her play when she has become mind and matter. Ramanujacharya has adopted this Tantras in his philosophy of Vishishta advaitha and looks upon this universe of mind and matter as transformation of Brahma. In effect it is the body of the Brahman, the God.

" ***Shakti***" is the power of Shiva or Brahman, the Absolute according to the Upanishads. The one individual absolute existence and when there is no universe, the "Truth", is known as Shiva, or "Satchitananada', the "Absolute Existence- Knowledge-Bliss"; but, in the active, immanent plane (the Universe, a Yogi experiences the play of Shakti. Just as fire and the burning power are inseparable, the Shiva and the source of his power, the Shakti are inseparable. Brahman and Shakti are the manifest and the unmanfest forms of the Absolute One, the Relative and the Absolute Existence. This philosophical aspect of the Tantras is of great significance in Spiritual attainment.

*Ramayan*

*Ramayan* is one of the most popular epics. Ramayan is the story of Lord Shree Ram, an incarnation of Maha Vishnu or Sriman Naryana in the Treta Yuga (432000 × 3 MY). Shree Ram stands for 'Satyam' and Ritam' the two essential requirements that sustain this Universe. If Shree Krishna is Supreme Consciousness in Devapara yuga, the same holds good of Shree Ram in Treta Yuga. Shree Ram is '***Supreme Consciousness***'. Just as the Lord said that, "I shall take birth as human on this earth again and again, in every eon or '***Yug***' [***Bhagavad Gita***], he has taken birth as 'Ram' in Treta Yug, as the son of King Dasharatha of Ayodhya. The story of Rama is very simple and even the illiterate rural folk know it by-heart. It is common practice to stage a drama based on Ramayana at every 'Dasara' (during the month of October according to calendar) or other festivities.

In brief, the central theme of the epic is the destruction of evil in Ravana, the King of Lanka. Rama is the son of Dasharatha, King of Ayodhya, an ardent devotee of Lord Shiva, and 'Shiva incarnate is Rama'. There is an interesting story of 'King Dasharatha performing the pooja of the Idol of Shree Rama' that indicates that several (atleast, twenty-one) Tretayugas have lapsed! This reinforces the statement of Shree Krishna in Bhagavad Gita, that the Lord takes the human form and undergoes all the troubles and travails as a human being in order to live with them and guide them. May be a few miracles are displayed now and then to make us feel the incarnate person is different. But, the human memory is so short, that the divine existence amidst us is also of no impact on us. Rather, our Karma is so strong that even God cannot help us and we have to 'realise' this. Righteousness, and self- realization are the only solution to human problems.

It may be quite surprising that the King Ravana was also an ardent devotee of Lord Shiva, and a very learned person. He abducted Sita, wife of Rama, during the days of 'vanavasa'. The Queen Sita, a pregnant woman, is forced to spend her crucial days in the ashram of the Sages and the throne is denied to Rama due to his aunt's selfish desires to make her son Bharata the immediate heir to the throne. The weakness of King Dasharatha and selfishness of Kaikeyi become significant as example of human weakness. Two other persons, one Hanuman and the other Lakshmana, brother of Rama, stand out as a superb character depicting total devotion to the Lord. It is this 'devotion' and the noble qualities, adherance to Dharma under all trying circumstances that are highlighted in this great epic. Shree Ram stands unique as great 'Maryada Purusha' who abides by moral and ethical order and never crosses the limits of decency and dharma. The sufferings of Shree Rama as a person are just the reflection of mundane life that is common to all; and, it comes in different forms to different people at different times. But, the ultimate victory is to "Truth", "Satyam eva jayate". But, one must always adhere to 'Truth'.

There are many accounts of the story of Shree Ram written by different authors like Sant Tulsi Das (Shree Rama Charita Manasa), Gayatri Ramayana, besides Valmiki Ramayana. In all these, the central theme is that of 'Truthfulness'. Shree Ram stands for 'Truth" just as Shree Krishna stands for "Righteousness'. "***Dharmo rakshati rakshitah***" is the mantra. Whatever difficulties one has to undergo in order to live a life of truthfulness, it is worth undergoing since that is the only path of salvation!

Unlike the characters in ***Mahabharat***, the characters that appear in ***Ramayan*** are worth emulation. Faithful to his father, Shree Ram decides to go to forests thereby enables Dasharatha to fufil his words to Kaikeyi. Shree Ram willingly offers the throne to Bharat and goes to forests. Lakshmana follows Shree Ram and Sita. The devotion of Shree Hanuman, the friendhip of Sugreeva, the love of Laksmana and Bharata, the small service of the squirrel, the long wait of Shabari, are all striking! The strong determination and adherence to the path of 'Truthfulness' is the central theme of Ramayana.

There are many instances in the story of Shree Ram that an ordinary person jumps to point out as the pitfalls in Ramayana; a layman cannot understand Shree Ram when he is called the 'Maryada Purushottam', '***persona par excellence***'. Shree Ram deserts his pregnant wife for the sake of his father's commitment to his aunt Kaikeyi; he deserts his pregnant wife in the ashram of Sages when she ought to be rejoicing in her mother's home. Another glaring example of injustice done to wife Sita is that Shree Ram asks Sita to prove her fidelity on the heresay of a washerman! Sita jumping into fire and the real Sita emerging from underground (the world underneath) is a different story! Similarly, the omnipotence of the Lord is not seen in taking the help of Hanuman, Vibhishana and Sugreeva to rescue Sita from Ravana. These are of deeper significance for ordinary laymen to understand. The so-called rationalists take up these instances as their strong points in their arguments against the noble qualities of Shree Ram. Where to mark the line of separation for a divine avatar or incarnataion and a normal human with all his weaknesses is a matter of inference from spiritual knowledge and experience. Superficial knowledge has no place here. Spiritual experience takes over when the Mind and intellect stop their interference.

In the light of Veda and Upanishadic knowledge, what strikes most in ***Ramayana*** is the subordination of Mind to the Buddhi, and Buddhi under the control of the Intellect guided by the llight of the Atman. Hanuman is the Mind and Shree Ram is the Atman, the guiding light. Hanuman folds his hands and sits quiet at the feet of Lord Shree Ram, the eternal, effulgent, omnipotent supreme Consciousness. Hanuman who cannot represent mind cannot wag his tail in front of Shree Ram. One has to understand this relationship. Mind should be kept under the control of buddhi and buddhi under the Lord's direction. Always look up to the Lord for His guidance and surrender to His wishes. This is the supreme doctrine, the path of salvation, mukti or emancipation.

It is not the intent here to go into the details of the great epics. Only the hidden meaning conveyed by these epics are highlighted in this study. The adhyatmic interpretation is important. Those interested in the details of the story can always read the original scripts or commentaries given by scholars of repute.

*Mahabharat*

*In the light of the knowledge of Veda and Upanishads, the great epics depict a different picture than what appear at the surface. The characters appearing in the story are simply examples of people whom we find in our day-to- day life and they are in no way different. Their ambition, dreams and struggle are the same as that of the people whom we see everyday. These people are the bundle of desire, selfishness, ego, arrogant, sensuous, and do not have any control over their senses. They behave as dictated by their past Karma, "Karmaanusaarena buddhih" and experience the fruits they deserve. Even God who takes the human form, as incarnation, is not outside this natural law, law of Karma. We find, all living creatures are here on this earth according to the divine plan.*

In *Mahabharat*, Lord Krishna Himself plays a pivotal role. He takes the side of Righteousness (Dharma) and joins the Pandavas. He chooses to be a Charioteer to Arjuna, one of the Pandavas who were forced to wage the war that later came to be known as the Great Epic War of ***Mahabharat***. It is a war against injustice. The Kauravas, a hundred cousins led by Duryodhana usurp the kingdom of the Pandavas led by Dharmaraja. Duryodhana invites Dharmaraja to a game of dice and cheats him with the help of Shakuni, his maternal uncle. The Pandavas lose everything in the game and were forced to leave for the forests. The condition to regain the kingdom was to spend 14 years in forests and one more year ***in cognito***; in case they were found out, the same term is to be repeated. The Pandavas with their mother Kunti wander in the forests for fourteen years and remain ***incognito*** for one year. When they return to claim their kingdom, Duryodhana refuses to part with even five villages, let alone the vast kingdom!

Here, again, it is '***dharma yuddha***', the war of righteousness that the

Pandavas fight against the Kauravas with the Lord Krishna on their side! It is ironical that even the Lord has to blindly tolerate the injustice done to the Pandavas, despite the mystic powers vested in Him. He could have used the mystic powers to destroy the Kauravas and establish 'dharma' as proclaimed in the Gita. But, the Lord allows the 'natural law', the course of 'Karma' and the fruits of bad deeds and good deeds to run their full course. ***God will not interfere in the affairs of men***. At best, He will give the necessary strength of mind, courage, intelligence, and tactfulness to deal with the situation; but he will not take everything upon Himself and redeem us from our problems. If anybody wants such redemption he has to take to ***Ashtaanga Yoga*** and surrender to Him. As long as men live on this earth they have to enjoy or suffer for all their good deeds or bad deeds, according to their 'Karma'. Each one has to go the full circle of life and death, the 'Samsara'.

The various characters that we find in ***Mahabharat*** like Shakuni, Duryodhana, Dhrutarashtra, Bhishma, Dronacharya, Karna, or Kaikeyi are the eye openers. They warn us repeatedly not to take to the path of blind adherence to the dictates of the Mind. All these characters are the slaves of passion, senses, raga, dvesha, mada, matsarya, moha and lobha. These are the inherent characteristics of all humans. They never think of the spiritual aspects of life and let others live peacefully. In a way, they are all 'dead' creatures as the Lord Krishna Himself puts it and there is nothing to 'kill' them. They are 'already dead' due to their 'ajnyana', ignorance; they are 'asat'. They are full of ego, body-consciousness and mind-consciousness. "Ignorance is death".

But, it is surprising that even the Lord in human form and function behaves like a human being with all weaknesses (and wickedness?) in the company of the humans; for instance, he uses unfair means to defeat the Kauravas like lowering the chariot while shooting the arrows, giving hints to hit below the belt (on the thigh) in Gadayuddha, or blowing the conch declaring the death of kunjara (the elephant) named Ashvathama, etc. Is it the '***Gunaanu gunavartante***', or the company of men makes even gods or avatars as the men of blemished characters? A tiger cub in the company of sheep behaves like a sheep. Some of these riddles have to be explained as human weakness only to highlight the fact that any means is right when it comes to re-establishment of 'Dharma', righteousness. The story of Mahabharat is the eternal story of Indian psyche, Indian mind, that is representative of human mind. It is the quality (Gunas) of the elements, the earth, the food and water that shapes the quality of the Mind.

The story of Pandavas and the Kauravas with the epic war as the central idea is the story of Mahabharat. The central figure in the epic is, however, the Lord Krishna. Krishna is "Consciousness', the natural self, unblemished character of the soul, the Atman. The dictates of pure intellect guided by the light of the soul stands out as 'Krishna Consciousness'. It is the attainment of this 'Krishna Consciousness', the supreme goal of all life on earth. One should live a life of pure mind and pure heart to enjoy the bliss of Krishna Consciousness. None of the characters in Maha Bharat could come upto this ideal state and that is the sad story of humans on this earth. The story of Mahabharat is thus a reminder to us. These characters have always been like this ever since the Dwaparayuga. The same characters are seen everywhere. There is a Keechaka, a Shakuni, a Duryodhana and Dhrtarashtra, and a Karna here and there even today.

One of the outstanding characters in Mahabharat is 'the Grandsire' Bhishma. He is the celebrated Celibate, the Brahmacharin (bachelor) of the Mahabharat known for his knowledge, experience and valour. He fought the war and retired wounded. He had the rare gift of 'ichcha marana' or death at his will. He is the most respected Grand Old Man and the Pandavas along with Krishna come to his bedside to hear his words of advice. As narrated in the Shanti Parva, "*Man should always worship God with devotion. This is the greatest 'Truth'. Those who love God and are devoted are free from malice, avarice, anger and evil thoughts. Meditating on the Lord, one gains immortality and wisdom. The best thing one can gain in this world is health and the best happiness lies in contentment. He who is vain is the enemy of all and he who is kind to all is holy. They who have their mind under control never come to grief.*"

"Purity of thought and conduct, constant remembrance of God and chanting of His name, total devotion to Him, are the best way of attaining both shreyas and preyas, the eternal good. Mahabharata, according to Vyasa, is the 'Narayana Katha', the story of the Lord that reveals the greatness of the Lord.

These teachings are the constant reminders to the common people to live a life of austerity, give up vanity, greed and avarice and surrender to Him in total devotion.

*Sreemad Bhagavatham*

Sreemad Bhagavatam is the sacred Scripture of the Vaishnavaites. It has the story of creation, evolution, the story of gods, and gandharvas and kinnaras, pitrus and the nagas, as well as, the demons and angels and spirits. There are twelve volumes of Bhagavatam and the most important is the Tenth Volume that describes the story of Krishna, The Rasa Leela depicts 'Bhakti' or devotion at its best. Krishna's philosophy as revealed to Uddhava is found in the Eleventh Volume. The entire story of Bhagavatam is set in Verse and describes the lfe and times of Sri Krishna almost 432000 × 2 Z Y years ago.

When Krishna's flute lured the Gopis who neglected their household and rushed to him, the Lord tells them that 'one need not neglect the ordained duties in order to worship the Lord'. Mere adoration of the Lord and meditation contemplating on the lord is enough to reach him. Love, knowledge, service, sacrifice, devotion, and meditation are all beautifully explained in Bhagavatam. These are culled out of the Veda and the Upanishads, and the Bhagavad Gita. Every Vaishnavaite keeps a Volume of 'Srimad Bhagavatam' as a sacred Scripture and it is a ritual to read a few passages everyday. Scenes from Bhagavata are enacted with music and dance in Dusherra, Deepavali, and other festival days.

*The Story of Shree Krishna*

The story of Krishna is elaborately dealt with in Srimad Bhagavata.

Lord Krishna takes birth in human form as the eighth son of Vasudeva and Devaki. Krishna's maternal uncle, Kamsa had usurped the throne of Vasudeva and kept Vasudeva and Devaki in prison. He was killing every child born to Devaki for fear of being dethroned. The child Krishna was shifted from the prison and thus, Krishna escapes from the clutches of Kamsa. Finally, Krishna kills his maternal uncle King Kamsa and releases his parents from prison.

As a child, Krishna grew up as a cowherd boy along with other children. His antics as a child are beautifully narrated in Bhagavata. The avowed emancipation of 16,000 damsels in distress, his advice to Arjuna in the battlefield, his revelations in the mystic form of '***Vishva Roopa***' are all very important. These details are repeatedly explained in praise of the Lord. ***Sree Krishna Leelamruta*** is another interesting work based on the Bhagavata, the story of Sri Krishna. Krishna marries Rukmini and Satyabhama and the episode of Radha Krishna is highlighted as an example of true Love that depicts total devotion. In all these, the central idea is Love. Protecting the righteous and punishing the errant and the arrogant unrighteous people is highlighted in Mahabharat. 'Dharma' or righteousness is re-established when 'adharma' reaches its height making the pious people suffer at the hands of bad people.

Shree Krishna gave protection to the Pandavas. The Lord's protection is assured to one and all, to all those who surrender to Him. Those who tread the path of righteousness get the protection of the Lord. The path of righteousness is the only way to salvation. A common man who goes through this Epic Mahabharat will find many interesting details that apply as well to the present day life and the predicaments one faces in life. The answer to all these problems of life is total surrender to the Lord. Trust in Him, trust the Lord is the mantra; and, absolute faith in the Lord is the only solution to life's problems. But, due to 'ignorance this faith and trust in Lord is not forthcoming. Karma as well dictates the course of life and the sensuousness plays a major role in life. Finally it is 'Jnyan' only that liberates a person from this samsar. '***Nahin jnyaanena sadrisham***', meaning, 'there is nothing excelling Knowledge'. Lord shows the path of 'mukti' through Karma and Bhakti, and ultimately it is 'Jnyaan' that helps in emancipation. Yoga with, Pranaayaama, Dhyaan, and Japa, is the boat that helps to cross even the rough sea of Samsara and the Lord Shree Krishna himself becomes the Yogacharya, the spiritual guide. This is the significance of ***Mahabharat***. All other details become irrelevant in the light of 'path to salvation'. All the different episodes of the epic associated with Lord Shree Krishna end with the supreme doctrine of 'Love' and '***Sharanagatim***' (total surrender).

# 6

# The Bhagavad-Gita [The Song Divine]

***"Karmanyevadhikaaraste ma phaleshu kadachana"***

The ***Bhagavad-Gita***, also known as the '***Divine Song***', is the 'Vedanta', sum and substance of all the Veda and Upanishads. It is a 'Gospel' or a hand- book for ready reference, or the 'Bible' of sane and sensible living based on the principle of '***Dharma***'. It is one of the sacred scriptures like the Veda and the Upanishads. It is written by Krishna Dvaipayana, Narayana, believed to be an incarnation of Vishnu. The language of the Gita is similar to the one used in the Upanishads, particularly Mundaka and the Svetasvatara Upanishads. The entire Bhagavad-Gita is set in the background of the Mahabharata war that was fought between the Pandava and the Kauravas at the end of Dwapara Yuga and dawn of ***Kali Yuga*** say around 3100 B.C. The war is described in the great epic Mahabharata and the Bhishmaparva contains the Gita. Some scholars think that the great epic Mahabharata was written about 11th or 12th century B.C. According to S. Radhakrishnan, the epic has undergone much change and the present form took shape around 5th century B.C. Anyway, the antiquities of the great epics, puranas, and the other ancient scriptures are open to further research.

The ***Bhagavad-Gita*** is one of the most widely read and commented scriptures and has been translated into Persian, English, German, Chinese, Japanese and many other languages within and outside India. A number of Englishmen like Barnet, Warren Hastings, Charles Wilkins, Carlyle, and Aldous Huxley have taken deep interest in the study of the Gita besides the early Indian religious leaders like Shankaracharya, Madhvacharya, Ramanujacharya, Vallabhacharya, Sant Jnyanesvar, and Tukaram. Many of them have written elaborate commentaries based on their own interpretations. There are seven hundred Verses spread over Eighteen chapters of the Bhagavad-Gita and these cover a wide range of Vedanta, the Hindu philosophy, weighing the pros and cons of action and inaction, leading the path to salvation. It is in the Kurukshetra battlefield that Arjuna was hesitant to use force against his own teachers, kith and kin, and was in a dilemma due to the confused state of mind whether it was worth fighting the war and was almost determined to leave the battlefield.

Arjuna says, '*Oh Krishna, seeing these relatives and friends who have assembled here with the intention of fighting, my limbs become languid and my mouth completely dry. And, there is trembling in my body, and there is horripilation; the bow (Gandiva) slips from the hand and even the skin burns intently. Moreover, O Keshava, I am not able to stand firmly, and my mind seems to be whirling. And I notice the omens to be adverse*' [***Bhagavad-Gita, Verses 28-30***].

In reply, Sri Krishna says, "*O Arjuna, in this perilous place, whence has come to you this impurity entertained by unenlightened persons, which does not lead to heaven and which brings infamy?*"

The entire Second Chapter of ***Bhagavad-Gita*** is devoted to the '*Path of Knowledge*' where Sri Krishna tells Arjuna that he is mistaking this world, the kith and kin, the war, the fighting, the killing, and so forth as real. It is sheer ignorance to think that, "*one is killing the other, for there is 'neither a killer nor a killed one' since no one is born here nor dies here". "The soul is eternal, stationary, unchangeable, knows no degeneration, death, or decay. None can bring about the destruction of this 'Immutable Atman'. This One (the Soul or 'Atman') does not kill, nor is it killed. Weapons do not cut it, fire does not burn it, water does not moisten it and air does not dry it*" [*Gita*, Verse 2- 17- 24]. The 'Atman' is simply embodied, that is all!

"O Arjuna, the Veda have the three qualities as their object. These are: Vichara, Viveka, and Vairagya. You become free from worldliness (liberated), free from the pairs of duality (dwandva), ever poised in the quality of sattva (equanimity), without desire (vairagya) for acquisition (yoga) and protection (kshema), and self-collected (sthithaprajnya). You will be 'atmavan', self-controlled, self-collected and vigilant. You have to do your duty and there is no escape from the duty, whether it is self-ordained, divine will or any other, for that matter. '*Your right is for action alone, never for the results or fruits of action. Do not become the agent of the results of action. May you not have the inclination for 'inaction' (abstaining from the ordained duties). "Karmanyevaadhikaarasthe maa phaleshu kadachanaa" [Bhagavad-Gita, 2-47]. Your right is only to do your duty and not to look for the fruits of action. Desire for the fruits of action must never be your motive in doing action. So also, indolence, laziness and abstaining from one's duty are forbidden.'It also reiterates that 'svadharmo parama dharmah'. One can reach the goal through action or duties proceeding from the law of our individual nature (svadharma).*

One has to perform his duty in whatever station of life he is placed and under any circumstances and there is no exemption unless he is completely a '***jeevanmukta***', ***a realized soul***. This aspect has been ignored by most of the Western commentators who interpret Indian philosophy as 'the one encouraging indolence and inaction'. In Karma Yoga, Bhagavad-Gita clarifies that no duty is much sacred than one's own! Each one attains a certain status, position, here termed as station in life, depending on one's previous actions (Sanskar or karma), and one has to stick to it. Here, the concept of 'dignity of labour' is upheld. No body is big or small, important or unimportant, however rich, powerful and famous one might be. This, again, is a very beautiful doctrine that cuts at the root of 'ego' and makes one understand that all beings are equal. Surrender to the Lord and rise above both duty and virtues and the three Gunas- tamas rajas, and the sattva. Transcending the Gunas is the ultimate goal, says

Bhagavad-Gita. Transcending Gunas, i.e., 'nistraigunya' is as good as merging in God or identifying oneself with God.

What prevents us from reaching nearer to God is our 'ego', our 'I'-consciousness, our too much of self- importance, glorifying our body, our achievements in mundane existence and station in life. But, one must realize that nothing is important when it comes to spiritual attainment, except the realization of the Self through self-abnegation. Here, one should note that 'Maya' (that Karma), ignorance or 'avidya' prevents us from realizing our Self. "It is by working out one's Karma alone, according to law of one's being, can this veil be rent and the end accomplished". Bhagavad-Gita explains how 'total surrender to Lord', offering all deeds and virtues as worship, renders a person pure and helps him attain self-control, and realize his Self. Then only that person is totally free and unites with the Lord. This is liberation according to Bhagavad-Gita. [Ch. XVIII.53]. Indeed, this is the supreme goal of all Veda and Upanshads. It releases us from repeated births, sufferings, death and rebirth. It is complete cessation of pain and sorrow and attainment of immortality. It is called '*Brahma-nirvana*' i.e., union with the Lord. This nirvana comes now and here, not sometime after death.

A person.who attains '***Brahma-nirvana***' is ego-less, has transcended the three Gunas and has attained tranquility of mind and has attained supreme knowledge of equanimity, seeing the Lord in all 'Beings'. He is a Yogi living and working with the people around him. not just sitting in a cave in the mountains or living in forest. Here, it is very important to note that a Yogi who has attained 'nirvana', who has transcended the Gunas and has attained the Lord, has not deserted the social life; rather, his commitments to society increases as he has to guide the ignorant people. He has to reach the state of Samadhi now and then and come back to serve the people. That is the lessons of Gita. No one is completely relieved from his duty and obligation as long as he breathes. It is true that nobody can always be in Samadhi and in union with the Lord. Now and then, there may be a glimpse of the supreme Brahman and that only reminds the Yogi of his duties and obligations as a realized soul.

Now, there arises another question. What, if one fails to attain the supreme Brahman? What, if the spiritual exercises or attempts go awry and disrupted due to one's own indolence, lethargy, disinterestedness,or incapacities? Bhagavad-Gita clarifies that, "*One need not worry if the effort to attain self-realisation fails due to whatever reasons. Whatever efforts already made in this direction will certainly yield good results in the next life, put him in better position to achieve the goal. May be such a person is born in a rich family with spiritual background and, all conditions will help in the realisation of the goal*". Thus the spiritual exercises are of great importance. The general law is that "a person's next life is guided by his present one. What all one has achieved or attained, good or bad deeds, accomplishments, desires unfulfilled will be etched in as the blemishes of the soul and carried forward to the next birth as sanskar (Karma). A person will enjoy the fruits of his action, sooner or later, number of births no bar!

Sri Krishna says, "*Whoever looks to me for solace, guidance, emancipation, mukti, moksha, shall be rewarded without fail.*" He goes to the extent of advising one to throw away everything, including dharma, individual qualities-gunas and reach Him. "*No matter if you fail in your efforts, continue to do your duty and look to me for the guidance. Reward is sure to come.*" That way, total emancipation is possible according to Bhagavad-Gita, by mere steadfastness, adherence to one's duty, and total surrender to the Lord. The efforts will never go waste.

When Arjuna complained of his inability to fight the war against his own 'Gurujis', uncles, cousins, kith and kin, Sri Krishna dispels Arjuna's ignorance,'ajnyana' and enlightens him as to 'who he is?'

The principle, the Mahat Tattva- "*Tat tvam asi' is explained in the Bhagavad-Gita. The first six chapters explain the Principle 'Tat' (Brahman- the Supreme Soul) and the next six chapters explain the principle 'tvam' (Atman- individual soul; their relationship and the method of unifying the two ('Yuj') through Yoga is explained in the last six chapters. The Principle of 'Tat tvam asi' is* explained to Arjuna by Sri Krishna, who says that, 'He is the Veda'. The ***'Atman'*** is inscrutable and you are ***'That'.*** He says, 'O Arjuna, it is the ignorance of this knowledge of the Self that makes you feel that you are the killer in this war and, the kith and kin of yours on the other side are being killed by you. In fact, there is neither a killer nor are the beings killed since the killer and the killed are neither born nor ever going to die. They are the souls that are eternal, transmigrating from bodies to bodies without end. Only those who seek my help to get liberated and whom I liberate will stop taking rebirth. This is the Truth'.

'***Performing action without the least desire for the fruits of action***', i.e., '***nishkaama karma***' is the central theme of the Gita and Sri Krishna advises Arjuna to be a 'dhira' and face the problem of fighting the war boldly. Running away from the problems is not a solution and the advice comes in the form of 'Hitopadesha'. Sri Krishna opted to be the charioteer to Arjuna since he did not want to take active part in the war. He has always been the wise counsellor of the Pandavas, meaning the protector of 'Dharma' or 'Righteousness'. Sri Krishna took birth in human form as the redeemer of the pious and the saviour of the righteous people for the sake of establishing 'Dharma'. He reaffirmed that he will take birth whenever 'untruth' and 'wrong' tried to establish in the place of 'Truth' and 'Righteousness'.

Sri Krishna says, *"Yadhaa yadhaa hi Dharmasya glaanir bhavati Bharata,*
*Abhyuththaanam adharmasya thadhaatmaanam srujaamyaham*
*Parithraanaya saadhunaam vinaashaaycha dhushkrutham*
*Dharmasamsthapanaarthaaya sambhavaami yuge yuge."*

***[Gita Ch.4, verses 7-8]***

When the Kurukshetra war was declared, Krishna gave choice to both the Pandavas and the Kauravas to select either his army or him; and, the Kauravas took the army and Krishna remained with the Pandavas. He chose to be Arjuna's Charioteer and guide him. Krishna had special affection to Arjuna and was a constant companion to him.

The Charioteer, Lord Sri Krishna, gave divine 'chakshus' (inner eye) to enable Arjuna to withstand the blaze, power, splendour and glory of the Lord and unraveled his 'Virat-svaroopa' as 'Visva Darshan'. He sets at rest all his doubts. Finally, the 'illusion' was dispelled and the battle was won. All these are to be taken in a metaphorical sense for there is deeper spiritual meaning. The greatness of the Gita is that it lays down the principles of Dharma, Righteousness, and assures all the troubled souls that there is the 'Protector', who has taken the responsibility of safeguarding the safety and security of all the creatures in this world. He says,

*"Ananyaaschintayanto mam ye janah paryupasathe,*
*Tesham nithyabhiyukthanam yogakshemam vahamyaham"*

***[Gita, 9.22]***

The Lord says, *"Whoever has faith and trust in Me and totally surrenders to Me will always be taken care of and protected by Me."* Here, *"total surrender and absolute faith are a must; and, whosoever seeks His help will not be denied of His divine grace and protection"*. Thus, 'Faith' is the basis or foundation on which this whole universe rests.

The 'Gita' deals with Arjuna, personification of the confused Mind, and Sri Krishna who reveals the techniques of 'Mind-control', is personification of 'Consciousness'. Gita is a much-revered book of the Hindus for the simple reason that it shows the way out problems of life. Sri Krishna of the Bhagavad-Gita stands for the Lord, the supreme 'Consciousness' and Arjuna stands for the confused and perplexed common man. Kurukshetra stands for our selves, our life 'Sansar'. Arjuna looks to Sri Krishna for guidance in the midst of confusion. It is the same problem of Shakespeare's Hamlet, "***To do, or not to do, that is the question***". The answer is clear and loud. "***Do your duty and leave the rest to Me***", says the Lord. Anybody can find this ***Bhagavad-Gita*** a source of great solace in distress. It is not just a lamp or torch; it is a floodlight in darkness!

The ***Bhagavad-Gita*** has eighteen chapters. The common problems of all human beings are summarized in the first Chapter and the 'Path of Knowledge' and 'Karma Yoga' is discussed in the second and third chapters. The concept of 'Renunciation' is elaborately discussed in the Fourth and Fifth Chapters. The 'Yoga' of Meditation, Jnyana and Vijnyana are explained in the sixth and seventh chapters. Knowledge of Brahman and Divine Glory, Revelations of the 'Cosmic Form', '***Virat Svaroop***', are all disclosed in the eighth, ninth and tenth Chapters. Bhakti Yoga is explained in the Twelfth Chapter. The nature and soul, the Gunas, the supreme Person and attributes of the Divine are all discussed in the thirteenth to sixteenth chapters. The seventeenth chapter deals with Faith and the last chapter deals with Liberation. Thus, the entire scheme of life or the Divine Plan is revealed in the Bhagavad-Gita. A person who understands the Bhagavad-Giata crosses the ocean of sansar and will never take birth on this earth again. But is that so very easy to understand the Lord?

The 'Bhagavad-Gita' is commented up on by almost every scholar of repute, and who ever came in touch with it has rendered a translation and commentary in his own way. Every commentary differs! The beauty of the

Gita is that everytime one reads it will get a new insight into the meaning of life. The same words convey deeper and deeper meaning as one goes on contemplating them! Many saints and spiritual leaders have taken some particular Chapters of the Gita for a deeper study and have given their own versions according to their understanding, experience, and depth of knowledge. Some Yogins who have gained insight into the teachings of the Gita take it as a textbook of Karma, Bhakti and Jnyana Yoga. It is an invaluable spiritual text and a guide that lasts forever.

Sri Shankaracharya has given his commentaries on the Gita and a brief account of the same is given here. Aurobindo, Chakravarty Rajagopalachari and Dr.Sarvepalli Radhakrishnan, Swami Prabhupada, Swamy Shivananda, Swami Chinmayananda, and many others have given commentaries on Gita. There are innumerable works based on Gita and one will find all of them interesting since they are addressed to everybody as an individiual seeking salvation.

***Bhagavad-Gita*** is a source of solace to the troubled mind. It offers solutions to any problem since it aims at the root of the problems that originate in the mischievous Mind. It offers solution by way of providing techniques of mind control. Mind control is a very difficult exercise. ***Muktikopanishad*** says the only way to control mind is through 'manonasha', i.e., destroy it as soon as it arises. This, too, is a very difficult exercise. But both mind control i.e., mano niyantran and manonasha are possible by the technique of contemplation or Meditation and carefully understandng the nature and behaviour of the Mind. Mind can be tutored by the mind. Mind can be controlled by the mind by way of 'dhyaan', silence (mauna) and 'japa', and Meditation on "Om".

The entire Bhagavad Gita is a treatise on Mind and has the subject of Mind Control through 'Yoga' in Chapter Six -The Yoga of Meditation. Bhagavad Gita declares, "An uncontrolled Mind cannot meditate for it knows not its ' Self' or 'Atman'; Where is peace without meditation and whence comes happiness without peace? Only a still mind is capable of realizing the self and a man of calm and serene mind can perceive his self and become illumined.

***The Theory of Non-Action, 'Akarma'***

There is a beautiful concept that helps us to understand the intricacies of mind and its way of functioning called 'Akarma', or non-effort, that has its parallel in Taoism and Zen also. Both speak of perfection in terms of a life of spontaneity and naturalness; it involves no struggle or special effort and it is beyond all intellectuality. In other words, it is sheer Divine Grace by which action is performed effortlessly. All creativity and spontaneity are the fruits of the unfolding dimension of the Self or the Atman. These result in best of the life and work, morally and spiritually, and the achievement is effortless.

This non-effort is different from inaction or non-action as also different from nishkama karma, 'desire-less action'. In his 'Tao of Science', R.G.H.Siu clearly brings out the distinction of rational and extra-rational knowledge. 'Rational knowledge is rational only because it is obtainable through reason. The others obtainable through means other than reason are not irrational; they are extra-rational. Broadly speaking, intellectual progress is an advancement in concepts which man had formulated and handed down.' In rational knowledge and intuitive knowledge, there is a contrast.

Discoveries play a minor role in intuitive knowledge; science has not accelerated human development in the field of inventions and discoveries to any great extent. People have recognized all that is known intuitively, generations before and the silent and formless depth of life had passed many times before the mind of man in its full sweep. These are beyond mathematical formulae or scientific theories. There is no logic in intuition since it is fuzzy and do not follow the strictures. In fact, discursive reasoning is not possible without intuition.

At one stage, the concept of the 'sage-knowledge' or the 'no-knowledge' state is introduced to overcome the inability of the rational and intuitive knowledge to solve the problems. 'Sage-knowledge' concerns an understanding of 'non-being'. It transcends events and gunas, qualities; it has no shape, no time. It is undifferentiated whole. This concept is to be clearly understood. Having no 'knowledge' is different from having 'no-knowledge'; the former is mere ignorance, where as the latter-transcending all Knowledge is one of ultimate enlightenment and universal sensibilities. 'The mysteries of nature appear to be mysteries only to those who refuse to participate in them...'. Remember, Knowledge is also a barrier, an obstacle to self-realization!

'With rational knowledge, the scientist is a spectator of nature. With 'no-knowledge', he becomes a participant in nature. There is communion of knowledge and understanding here. One must rely on one's own ineffable awareness of the ineffable to probe or plumb the depths of no-knowledge. This is expounded as 'wu' in the East in China and Japan, and the principle of 'akarma' in Vedanta in India. This is yet another great contribution of the East to the body of knowledge.

The Philosophy of 'Non-action' and the state of 'No-knowledge' is beautifully explained in *Ashtavakra Samhita, Verses: 1.8; 4.4; 18.20, 39, 60-61, 95 and 98. [Published by Advaita Ashrama 1975 & 1998].*

"*He who is beyond existence and non-existence, who is wise, satisfied, and free from desire, does nothing even if he may be acting in the eyes of the world*". Here, actions are no longer actions when they are not accompanied by the feeling of egoism. The man of knowledge is absolutely free from it. He does not identify himself with his actions. He is, therefore, really inactive, even though he may seem to be acting.

"Knowledge of one's true nature as the Infinite and non-dual Pure Consciousness will give freedom and spontaineity in all actions. The wise one who lives on happily, doing what comes to him to be done, does not feel anxiety either in activity or in inactivity. The fool desires peace through the control of the mind, and so does not attain it. The wise one, knowing the truth, is ever of a tranquil mind". Further,"*with the fool, even inaction becomes action; but with the wise, even action results in the fruit of inaction*". Spontaineity through non-effort appears where the self is surrendered to something higher than itself, where the self has emancipated itself from stagnation of its sensate tether. Most of the discoveries and inventions have thus come from such total surrender and total involvement without any greed for fruits of action.

What the ***Bhagavad-Gita*** calls "akarma', is a very simple method of accomplishing great things by offering the work to Him; it is invoked first as 'by the Grace of the Lord', and then the entire performance is done in 'His name', and the fruits are finally 'offered to Him'. By this way, there is nothing that is done by this mortal man and everything is 'His Divine Grace'.

*The Chinese Philosopher Chuang-tze puts it this way:*
*"By doing nothing everything is done.*
*He who conquers the world often does so*
*by doing nothing.*
*When one is compelled to do something,*
*The world is already beyond his conquering".*

This is put in a different way in ***Bhagavad-Gita*** (Ch. IV. 18):

"*He who sees inaction in action and action in inaction, he is the wisest among men, he is the perfect yogi and the doer of all action.*"

Action is a basic instinct of human nature. It is the root of human progress and prosperity and is implicit in the law of life. No body can really remain inactive even for a moment. Inaction leads to decay and putrefaction. Some form of action is involved in the survival and maintenance of our body. But it is strange that action always leads to misery and sorrow. It is the attachment and indulgence that sows the seed of sorrow and misery in our actions. It is the sensual pleasure and material happiness that we anticipate as the fruit of our action that brings us the sorrow and misery. Anything done with the spirit of attachment, craving for fruits and under the impulses of ego necessarily brings frustration, mental depression, and moral degradation. This does not mean inaction is a better alternative. Rather, inaction would be disastrous and catastrophic! This prompted Sri Krishna to define the art of performing action in Bhagavad-Gita.

Perform action as a sacred call of duty and be instrumental in doing it; leave the rest to Almighty. All our actions must be devoid of selfish motives and attachment. Sri Krishna says, "*Your right is to work only but never to the fruit thereof. Be not instrumental in making your actions bear fruit, nor let your attachment be to inaction*".

Vedanta presupposes performance of action incessantly and sincerely intensely. It guides the performer in all his actions laying down the golden rules. Renunciation is one such golden rule. Renunciation is a spirit of self-abnegation, 'na mamah' in everything. It drives away the last tinge of selfishness in oneself. Human beings are essentially divine. Vedanta deals with this aspect of divinity and helps us in unveiling and unfolding this divinity. By recognizing the self as the part of the supreme Self, i.e., 'Self Realization', a divine experience, dawn of a true inner awakening, one realizes that one is not this body, mind or intellect. These three are inert without the Atman that energizes them to perform their functions. This Brahma Jnyana helps one to inculcate the spirit of renunciation. Renunciation does not mean giving up worldly pleasures or rejecting the fruits of one's action, or giving up desires and abstinence from consumption, but an attitude that reflects the level of renunciation one has attained. Spirituality does not forbid enjoyment. The ego and selfish motive attached to the action hampers progress and retards success and prevents serious practice of renunciation.

The principles of renunciation clearly lay down that one need not retire to the mountains and forests to practice it although, practically all early sages and seers retired to seek this Jnyan. Even the householders can practice renunciation, and in fact the householder's duty should revolve round this principle. Dhyana and Jnyana govern this principle and as such the householder should perform all actions in utter humility and submission to the Almighty. All actions are sanctified when performed selflessly with dedication to the Lord. Such a person understands what is called 'akarma' in Bhagavad Gita. He sees inaction in action and action in inaction. All his actions are neutralised in fire of knowledge and no longer bear any fruit to torment him either in this life or in the next. Of course, this Brahma Vidya needs initiation. In the absence of an initiator, the Guru, the pure mind of one's self is the initiator and it only needs firm determination. Ultimately, renunciation brings peace, happiness and Supreme Bliss.

In ***Ashtavakra Samhita***, freedom of spontaneity and naturalness arising from knowledge of one's true nature as the infinite and non-dual Pure Consciousness is beautifully explained as follows:

'The wise one who lives on happily, doing what comes to him to be done, does not feel anxiety either in activity or in inactivity'. Further, 'the fool desires peace through the control of the mind and so does not attain it. The wise one, knowing the truth, is ever of a tranquil mind'.

'Whoever, by virtue of the realization of his true nature, does not feel distressed even in practical life as people attached to the world do, and remains un-agitated like a vast lake, with all his sorrows gone- he shines'. 'The wise one is devoid of thought, even when he is engaged in thought; he is devoid of the sense organs, even though he has them; he is devoid of intelligence, even though he is endowed with it; and he is devoid of his ego even though possessed of it'.

'The liberated one, who abides in the Self under all conditions, who is free from the idea of action and of duty, who is always even-minded everywhere, owing to his desire-less state, remember what he has done and what he has not done'. Bertrand Russel suggested that there is a great need for modern man to surrender his inflated ego to something higher within himself'. When the self is surrendered to something higher than its own self (the sensate one), spontaneity through non-effort appears. This is evident in many discoveries and aesthetic as well as intellectual achievements.

The conscious self and the rational consciousness surrender themselves to something higher or deeper within in cases of ***intuition***. Spontaneity manifests itself giving rise to creativity and thus, discoveries and innovative techniques are achieved. ***Imagination*** is the word used in such circumstances. This is also true in evolving rich and happy, inter-human relationships. Deep thinking and intuition, daring imagination are hallmarks of great thinkers and achievers. Science of human creativity and philosophy of 'non-effort' and Divine Grace are spiritually related. Super-conscious dimension of the human mind is involved in all imagination, intuition and flash of brilliance.

The super-conscious, conscious, the pre-conscious, the sub-conscious and the unconscious, are the different states of mind recognized in Vedanta. In fact, all rational knowledge is referred to Consciousness. But one should not forget that there is a great part of existence of which one is not conscious. The function goes on irrespective of our conscious application in the case of the inner functions of the body. Thus, man functions at two different planes of consciousness - one is the conscious state with the feeling of egoism; the other, is the unconscious plane devoid of feeling of egoism. There is still higher plane that goes beyond consciousness not accompanied by egoism.

The conscious working of the mind is called ***reasoning***. This works with in small radius and it cannot go beyond that. But, everything that is dearest to heart lies outside this circle of human reasoning. Reason cannot answer questions about supreme consciousness, God, Self, etc. Similarly, there are the questions why one should be good to others, or always respect others, show mercy, pity, console, etc.; it is difficult whether science can answer these questions. One has to transcend reason to answer these questions. Super consciousness holds the answer to all these questions. When reason fails, reason itself will show the way to higher plane.

There are different planes at which mind functions, each developing into another- instincts develop into reason, reason into the transcendental consciousness. Real inspiration does not contradict reason; it fulfills it. It is not the purpose here to go into the psychological aspects of the mind, but it suffices to state that where reasoning stops, spirituality pays; ***where science fails, Vedanta shows the way***. It is important to note that the physical environment does play a very significant role in spiritual development as could be noted from the experience of our ancient Sages. The Banyan tree, also known as the Pipal tree, is the most sacred tree under which Bodhisatva gained enlightenment. The Riverside or lakeside or the hilltop environs suit the purpose of meditation. Some prefer caves for meditation.

# 7

# Vardhamana (Mahaveera) and Gautama Buddha And The Great Acharyas

*Two great Vedantins of the First Millennium B.C., the Mahaveera and the Budhdha, stand out as the crusaders against the ritualistic Hindu Religion since they represent separate Religions based on Upanishadic Doctrines. They deserted the then prevailing great Hindu religion for their leaders had discarded the 'Truth' behind the Vedic tradition, and had corrupted the practice to senseless ritualism with selfish motive. Both these persons had one thing in common, and that is, 'emancipation from bondage of human misery'. Freedom from from bondage, 'nirvana' was their 'mantra'.*

***Vardhamana, The Mahaveera***

Mahaveera is the 24th Teerthankara and as such he was associated with Jainism that was in practice for centuries before he became a Teerthankara. Jainism is an offshoot of Sanathana Dharma, the Vedic Religion or the Hindu Religion. Rushabha is the founder of Jainism and the first Teerthankara, a 'Realised Soul'. Jainism became very popular after Mahaveera became a Teerthankara and, even today Mahaveera is worshipped as the last of the twenty- four Teerthankaras. The name of Rushabha, as a great Saint, is mentioned in Rk Veda and the story of his life and work are narrated in Vishnu Purana and Bhagavata.

Vardhamana, born in Basrah, near Vaishali, Patna was married and had a daughter when he relinquished the householder's life and took to spiritual life. He became an enlightened or illumined person at 28, after a twelve-year- long meditation. Mahaveera, as he is known, is the twenty-fourth illumined person (Kevala) of the Status of Teerthankara of the present cycle of the waxing and waning universe. Incidentally, the name of Parshvanatha is also mentioned in the propagation of Jainism. Parshvanatha Teerthankara lived around 8th century B.C. There are many detailed accounts of these two great Jain Sages, but only a brief account of Jainism is given here for comparative study of Spiritual History of India.

Mahaveera propagated the doctrine of 'Ahimsa' that is expounded in Patanajali's Ashtaanga Yoga Sutra. The ritualistic practices of the Purohits and Brahmins are the root cause of rise of Jainism. Mahaveera invited all, irrespective caste and creed, to join Jainism and implored them to follow the principles of Ahimsa. There came about a class of Digambaras who are not conscious of their bodies and go naked, and a class of monks wearing white robes, called Shvetambaras. The householders could practice Jainism as a Religion without any restriction, but certain code of conduct was drafted for their use.

The most striking aspect of Jainism is that the Jains do not believe in God, so also the Veda consider Indra, varuna, Mitra, Skanda as gods and Upanishads proclaim,"*that which is worshipped here is not That*". Virtually, there is no mention of any God except as "That", the Absolute or the Supreme Brahman. Jainism denies the concept of God as the creator and sustainer, for they argue that there must be another creator to create this creator who created this universe. Any definite beginning of this universe in terms of a definite origin in time is illogical and unthinkable as the Veda proclaim that the universe is in existence since time immemorial not beginningless. The Jains question, "How can there be a God who was not creative and became suddenly creative?" Veda proclaim that"*He willed*" and produced this paraphernalia of the universe.

Jainism offers an alternative theory. Based on the concept of 'divinity in every soul', the Jains put forth the theory that the Universe consists of Jeevas (Living Beings) and Ajeevas (Non-living Beings). If it is possible for one being to exist, self-subsistent and eternal, why is it not possible for many to exist likewise self-subsistent and eternal? Thus, there is no problem in believeing that all Beings and Non-beings existed eversince. And, there is divinity inherent in every soul. Every person can work towards perfecting this and attain the Supreme called "Paramatman", a Kevala or a Teerthankara, at that. He becomes an object of worship and adoration. Thus every human being is a potential Paramatman!

When a person overcomes the bondage of Samskaras or Karma by subduing his desires of flesh, passions and realizes the supreme purity of his soul, he experiences a light within and becomes an enlightened person, a 'Teerthankara'. The revelation of infinite knowledge, bliss and power make him a Paramatman. Some have already attained perfection and divinity and many more are on their way to attain it. Thus, Jains believe in Parmatman, a human-God. The best way to worship God is to become, themselves, sons of gods, the supreme perfected spirits. A Siddha Paramaeshtin state is the unconditional state, a stae of passionless peace, in which he is released from action and is without desire. These are all the Upanishadic precepts of attaining the Brahman. Thus, there is not much difference between the Vedic or the Hindu Religion of the Sanatanis and the Jains.

A Jain devotee prays thus:

"*Him who is the revealer of the path to salvation, who is the remover of mountains of karmas, and who is the knower of all reality, him I worship, in order that I may realize his qualities within myself*".

According to Jainism, there are five stages to become a Paramatman or 'Siddha Parameshtin'. The first theree stages are that of a teacher who lives a austere life and strives for spiritual attainments. The fourth is the "Arhat" a person who has realized but is not yet perfect and illumined. The last stage is the perfect, illumined soul, a Siddha Parameshti. One has to serve humanity in order to attain the highest state. One is not touched by good and evil and has overcome the world in the final stage of Siddha Parameshtin.

Jainism accepts Karma and Reincarnation. Karma binds soul of person to material world and its attractions. Karma is a mterial substance. But, it is so subtle that it is unperceivable by senses. It is in this karma that the soul is found enmeshed in the substance (cell) of a being, and that it is embodied from the beginningless past. Though beginningless, it definitely has an end, for the soul is essentially free and divine, and just as soon as its true nature is revealed or realized karma disappears.

The bondage of the soul to Karma is caused by karma itself and no other extraneous things with contact with the outside world. Certain psychic conditions, like the desire for enjoyment arise that lead to ignorance of the soul's true nature; and cause the karmic molecules (cells) to' flow in' towards it and in the process surround it. This is '*asrava*', first stage in karmic bondage. The next stage is 'bandha'. In this stage, the Karmic molecules become settled and build up a subtle body (sookshma shareera), karmana shareera, and the soul is weighed down by its own karmas. The physical body dies with death, but the karmana shareera lingers on until the final liberation.

Moksha is attaind by three methods, triratnas- right faith, right knowledge, and right conduct. With right faith arises right knowledge and with right knowledge comes enlightened understanding of the truth. These must be united in right conduct. Janism strictly censures blind faith and senseless rituals. *Right faith includes action-oriented programme of adherence to ahimsa, satya (truthfulness), continence and asteya (non-stealing and aspiring for other's property), and aparigraha (non-attachment to world). Attainment of divine perfection is the goal and every person should strive for it. Blessed is the human form in body and soul, and even the gods and angels who reside in heaven must appear here on earth to achieve perfection, to attain the Brahman.*

***Gautam Buddha***

The 'Brahman', the 'Truth' is to be realized not by scriptures but by purity of heart derived from right conduct and austere life. The truth, that is '*realizing spiritual goal in one's own soul*' is far more important than learning all the Veda by heart. By following the Vedic doctrines, by living righteously, becoming aware of the light within one' own heart, one can attain the supreme bliss. Just as Mahaveera was disgusted with the ritualistic practices of the Purohits and Brahmins, Gautama Buddha also realized that there was something wrong with the people who professed the Vedic Religion. Their precepts were different from what they practised. Gautama realized the need for 'salvation', emancipation, liberation and, freedom from bondage. He decided to find out the cause of misery and unhappiness, old age and death.

Gautama Buddha is the founder of Buddhism. Mahaveera and Gautama Buddha are contemporaries in the sense that both lived almost around 650 B.C.; but no definite date can be assigned to them. Both these disgruntled souls had quite a comfortable life with family; in fact Gautama was born to princely family. Vardhamana also known as Mahaveera had a daughter and Siddharta also known as Gautama had a son and both left the family life and took to long period of meditation. Finally both achieved spiritual goal and realized the '*light within*', got illumined by divine grace.

Gautama was born around 560 B.C. at Kapilavastu and was married to Yashodhara and had a son by name Rahula. Gautama's father, King Shuddhodhana took all precaustion to keep Gautama away from any ugly sight and saw that he did not come in contact with the outside world for some astrologers had predicted that Gautama would take to ascetic life and would rule the Kingdom of humanity rather than the Princely State. By the age of Thirty, as they had predicted, the ugly sight of a sick person suffering from leprosy and the procession of a dead body stirred the heart of Gautama and he decided to find out the cause of the misery and sufferings. He left the Palace and wandered everywhere before reaching Gaya near Patna in Bihar. He meditated for a long time and attained the spiritual 'enlightenment' under a peepul tree. He realized that human sufferings sprout from the 'desire' and desire is the cause of repeated births, deaths and rebirths. After he attained 'enlightenment', the Buddha, the Enlightened One, went to Varanasi and delivered his sermon at Sarnath. Although Buddha never wrote any books, his thoughts have been noted down and have been preserved as the Dhammapada. The early Buddhists followed the sermons or preachings of Buddha so strictly that a section of the Buddhists came to be known as the '*Hinayana*' (Narrow Path) Buddhists. Later on, some of the Elders decided to do away with rigidity and set up the '*Mahayana*' (Great path) School where worship of Buddha became more conspicuous. Attaching divinity to the person of the Buddha, erecting huge statues in all postures, wherever possible, these Mahayana Buddhists propagated Buddhism all the world over. The Chinese who follow Tao-Buddhism adopted meditation as an essential part of their religion. Japan made Buddhism its national religion and many countries like Sri Lanka, Thailand, Myanmar (Burma), Malaya, Singapore all have Buddhists as a major chunk of their population. However, it is in Tibet that Buddhists established Monasteries to train Monks and, here they follow the scriptures and carry on Meditation in a strict disciplined way.

Buddhism got a staunch proponent in Emperor Ashoka (274-232 B.C.) who, after the famous Kalinga War, got disillusioned and took to Buddhism on the advice of of a Buddhist Monk, Upa Gupta. It is Emperor Ashoka who erected rock edicts and spread the sermons of Buddha and the first one at Sanchi near Bhubaneswar (Orissa) is very famous. During this period, Buddhism spread far and wide. It reached Syria, Egypt, Macedonia, Epirus, and became a world religion.

It is very interesting that Buddhism, a religion based on Vedic doctrines, that preach Upanishadic Sutras (Formulae) or aphorisms for a sane and sensible living, became popular, better established and practised outside India, than within India, the birth place of its founder.

***Teachings of The Buddha***

Buddhism is an offshoot of theVedic or Hindu Religion and, as such, the doctrines preached and practiced by Buddhists are the doctrines of the Veda and the Upanishads. The only difference between the Hindu Religion and Buddhism is that the Hindus have given up the practice of the virtues and principles implored by the Veda and Upanishads and have taken to lighter side of sensuous worldly life neglecting the spiritual goal while the Buddhists practice it as a divine order. One can ignore spiritual goal at one's own peril!

Buddhism preaches '*the Way of Peace*'. Peace is of utmost importance. One can attain supreme peace from meditation. The Taittiriya Upanishad declares that, *"Silence speaks 'Truth' much better than words". It implores, "to give up vain talk, for it brings weariness to the tongue"; and, they further speak of the truth 'which words cannot express' i.e., 'the mind comes away baffled, unable to reach it. "Yatra Vaacho nivartante...",* they say. Buddha insisted that one should experience the truth for oneself. There is no other path.

Buddha's concept of "***Nirvana***" is the same as the' Realization of the Self' or 'Brahman' of the Upanishads. The ultimate goal of all human beings is the attainment of the supreme 'Bliss'. Realization of 'Truth', 'Knowledge', and 'Bliss', or "Sat-chit-anand" is the ultimate goal. But, What is this Truth? Truth is existence; Truth is God. Truth is the unchangeable, permanent and eternal. All that is fleeting, changing, transforming, are unreal and thus, "Untruth". This world is not real; it is untruth; the life on this earth is unreal. It is Buddhism that used 'Illusion' for the first time to define the cause of human misery; it is the same as 'ignorance' or '***Maya***' as in Bhagavad Gita or the Upanishads. It takes decades and decades to realize the true meaning of "Truth". So, if one asks, "What is Truth?" the answer is very simple; it is the "Self". It is the 'Brahman'. It is the' Universal Consciousness'. It is the supreme 'Bliss'. It is the Absolute and the Infinite. There is no 'other' and it is 'one'. It is this 'Realization' that brings emancipation, moksha, 'Mukti'. Release from bondage i.e., the binding of the body, the desires of flesh, the attachment, or moha (Raaga) is not that easy.

This 'Nirvana' of Buddha or the Upanishadic 'Jeevanmukti' is not easily attaiable. Only a few persons like the Pure Shuka, son of Vedavyasa, or Kapila, or Raikva have attained '*Jeevanmukti*', liberation in this life, not after death. In fact, Kapila is known to have attained liberation even before his birth, right in his mother's womb. Sri Krishna says in Bhagavad Gita, that among the sages, he is the Great Sage Kapila. It requires the courage of conviction and strength of mind of Gautama who relinquished the pleasures of the Palace and left his young loving wife and son to attain the supreme spiritual goal. *Unless 'sankalpa' or desire, even the desire to attain Mukti, liberation, God, or any such thing, is given up there is no salvation. Once Gautama was undergoing a month-long fast as vrata to attain his spiritual goal. On the last day of his fast, he was suffering from fever and was very weak. While he waded into the river to take his bath he fell down and was unable to get up. Suddenly he thought, 'how foolish of me to think of crossing the' ocean of Sansar' when I am unable to lift this one foot in this small River'! Lo, then and there was the great illumination and realization that 'nothing can be achieved as long as' 'desire' occupies the mind'. 'Desire' is the cause of all misery and unhappiness of life.*

Buddha is known for his 'all-knowing smile'. It is the supreme knowledge that bestows supreme happiness and the all- knowing smile on the face. There are numerous stories to convey the Principles of Buddhism and the finest one is that of a rich merchant who wanted instant spiritual results. Shree Ramana Maharshi had the rare gift of conveying everything to everybody by his magnetic all-knowing smile and silence. Buddha conveyed more through 'silence' than through words. Great were the days when the aged people used to sit in silence under a big Banyan tree in front of a young Yogi; nothing was discussed. But everything was learnt! All knowing smile and silence were the means of conveying the 'Truth' to Budhdha. And, some of his disciples followed the same technique.

The primary truth is that "everyone must realize God in one's own soul". Nirvana, '***Sandhittakam Nibbanam***' or '***Jeevanmukti***', or release from bondage, is here and now; there is no procrastination or postponement of salvation to yet another life. And, in this sense, Gautama Buddha had enetered into the' Brahman'. The Budhdha says,

*"Be ye lamps unto yourselves. Be ye a refuge to yourselves. Betake yourselves to no external refuge. Hold fast to the truth as a lamp. Hold fast as a refuge to the Truth..."[Maha-Parinibbana Sutta II-33]*

Buddha's philosophy is different from Mahaveera's. Buddha considers the world of mind and matter as both positive and negative. "***It is, and it is not***". Because of the transitory and changing nature of this world, '*neither it is real nor unreal; it is somewhere between the two*'. A jnyaani always knows that 'it is' and 'it is not'. "Whoever perceives in truth and wisdom how things originate in this world, in his eyes there is no 'it is not'. Whoever perceives in truth and wisdom how things pass away in this world, in his eyes there is no 'it is' in this world...." *Everything Is*" is one extreme and "*Everything is not*" is another extreme. The truth lies in the middle". Just a lighted torch whirling round produces an illusion of a circle of fire; this fleeting, ever-changing world has created an illusion of 'reality'. Ignorant persons believe this world as 'real'; but this world is due to '*transitive causation*' where the past has created the present, like the seed creates a tree. Ultimately, "all are impermanent, body, sensation, perception, Shankhaaras (samskaras) and consciousness- all these are sorrow. They are not the self".

It is very important to note that Buddha never tried to explain all these complexities of the nature of this world. He knew that, "What Brahman is, none can define in words". The nature of this world is clearly explained. "There is an unborn, an unoriginated, an unmade, an uncompounded; were there not, there would be no escape from the world of the born, the originated, the made and the compounded. "It is beyond the experience of our senses and our minds". The Upanishads, too, explain the Brahman or Atman as that "which is beyond speech, and the mind comes away baffled, and unable to reach him". [Taittiriya Upanishad II-4]. When one attains samadhi, then alone comes the knowledge of Brahman, one realizes him. In that realization, all thoughts cease; one becomes perfectly silent. There is no power of speech left by which to express Brahman. 'So far Brahman is undefiled; no one has ever defined him by words to defile him by mouth', is the saying. Thus, it is very clear that Buddha had the knowledge of Brahman when he said that,"it is beyond all explanation". 'One has to realize Brahman by one's own self'. And, that is attaining the Self.

***The Great Acharyas***

The Hindu tradition has great reverence for the Acharyas who impart the "knowledge"of the Brahman'. Mother and father occupy the first two places followed by the Acharya (the Guru) next only to God; and, in fact, all these three are the living gods. Since God may come in any form, and at any time thithi without any notice, the fourth one, i.e., the 'Guest' athithi, is also added to this. The Subhashita implores:

***"Matru devo bhava, Pitru devo bhava, Acharya devo bhava, and, Athithi devo bhava".***

After the two great Vedantins, Mahaveera and the Buddha came Gaudapada, Chaitanya, Shankara, Madhva, and Ramanuja, and others who are the great, realised souls. Gautama Buddha is believed to be an incarnation, and so also Madhva, a reincarnation of Hanuma of the Treta Yuga and Bhima of the Dvapara Yuga. All these great souls have one thing in common as their goal and that is the emancipation of the distressed souls. They have large followings; people believe in their mystic and supernatural powers and hold them in high esteem and give a position next only to God. They are indeed, the living Gods. They are hope and aspiration of the troubled souls. They are the guides showing 'Path' to salvation; they show the path to Realisation of the Self. Veda and Upanishads are the Scriptures that have shown the path to salvation to the ancient sages as well as the modern. A brief account of the life and works of these Great Acharyas is given here for reference.

***GAUDAPADA***: The first Acharya to uphold the Vedic Doctrine of "*Eko Devah*", "God is One" and propagate the Advaith Philosphy is Gaudapada. It is very difficult to give an exact date and time to the life and works of this Great Acharya since he is believed to be an incarnation of Lord Narayana, and also a disciple of the Great Sage Shuka Muni, son of the Sage Veda Vyasa who wrote Mahabharat. In the absence of any written or recorded proof, all these are left to one's faith. But, it is highlighted in many early writings that Shankaracharya, who lived around 6th Century A.D., sought the blessings of Gaudapada. Shankaracharya treated Gaudapada as the teacher of his teacher, although separated by a thousand years; may be, this student-teacher relationship is on a yogic plane since it is natural to invoke the blessings of teachers before any great work is undertaken. When Shankara wanted to write commentary on Mandukya Upanishad he invoked the blessings of Gaudapada.

It is important to note here that Gaudapada's *Mandukya Karika*, a commentary on *Mandukya Upanishad*, is the most important work for which Gaudapada is famous. It embodies in itself the quintessence of all the Upanishads. Gaudapada points out the way to illumination within one's own soul. He says, "we should control our mind with patience and perseverance, than through the practice of discrimination. We must renounce the pleasures of the senses. By the practice of dharana (concentration) and meditation, we attain samadhi and experience bliss. We must give up this 'bliss' also so that we go deeper and deeper and experience "Supreme Bliss", the'Turiyateeta avastha', a state of super Consciousness". Mind must be free from all sorts of attachment including bliss that arises in meditation. Brahman is the goal. Brahman can be experienced as supreme Bliss.

*According to Gaudapada, "Anything that is non- existent in the beginning, and also at the end, necessarily does not exist in the middle. Reality is that, ' it is never contradicted at any time but persists forever'." Consistent with this, Gaudapada did not believe in the Absolute Reality of creation.*

*"The one non-dual, or absolute self, or God neither created this universe, nor did he become this universe. In reality, there is no creation, for the one infinite Existence appears to be manifold universe. The universe is not a reality but something super-imposed up on Atman". According to Gaudapada, there is no birth, no death. There is no one in bondage; no one aspiring for knowledge; there is no seeker, no one liberated. This is the absolute 'Truth'. Supreme Bliss, freedom, is the very nature of the Atman, an Absolute Reality that persists.*

*"Thinking that we are bound, we seek liberation, though liberation we seek is already within us. We must realize the Mahat Vakya "Aham Brahmasmi". 'Either that we are bound or that we seek liberation' is false.*

It is an ignorant person that clings to attachment, the enjoyments of life and finds to his despair that they elude his grasp at every moment. He does not realize the truth, that 'there is no world when life ends in death'. A Jnyaani plays the game, enjoys the life better than the Ajnyaani for he knows that this life is a game of play and it is possible to play with satisfaction, without attachment to it.

***SHANKARACHARYA***: Like that of Gaudapada, Shankaracharya's date is not very clear since many authors have given dates varying from 6th Century A.D. to 8th Century A D. And some have gone to the extent of placing his date to Pre-buddhistic Era, believed to be in 6th Century B.C. He is the leading light and has shown the spiritual path to millions through the Millenia. Shankara born in Keladi in Malabar in Kerala was a child prodigy, a scholar of repute and had studied the ancient Scriptures before he was 10 years of age. He had courage of conviction and dared to question the senior scholars and Pundits. He traveled far and wide through out India and established Maths to propagate the great Vedic Upanishadic doctrines of '***Aham Brahmasmi***' and '***Tat tvam asi***', and the principles of Advaitha Philosophy. Shankara is known as a great intellectual and his teachings have been accepted by a large number of followers even today. He had royal patronage and Shankar Maths with Sharda Devi on his Deity he established at Sringeri near Agumbe in Karnataka. The Karaveera Peetha at Nasik in Maharashtra, Kedarnath in Himachal Pradesh, Kanchi in Tamil nadu and Dwarka in Gujarat are very famous.

Shankaracharya, like Buddha, contemplated on the riddles of life and death and rebirth and decided to solve them, once and for all. He wanted to find out the cause of human misery and redeem the people from misery of life. He would renounce everything for the sake of this self-ordained task and as a boy of tender age, he was already disillusioned about the worldly life. He took the permission of his mother to renounce worldy life and took to ascetic life. He died very young; Pundits belive he never died.

He was hardly 32 when he simply disappeared in the Himalaya Mountains!

Shankaracharya wrote commentary on many Upanishads, Bhagavad Gita, Brahma Sutra, and wrote Maha Bhashya; and, many other works like Moha Mrudangam, Viveka Chudamani and Narada Bhakti Sutra are all very important. It is while writing the Commentary on Mandukya Upanishad, he sought the blessigs of the well-known Teacher Gaudapada, may be in his Yogic stance (Meditation). His 'Moha Mrudangam' is a beautiful poem that sings the tragic story of this creation and tells all about the illusory Existence. It is lke the' Bhaja Govindam' of 'Gita Govinda'.

Shankara's philosophy is called 'advaita'. According to him, the world of phenomena or the universe is beyond any description in clear terms since it is ever changing. It may be called existent or non-existent. If the universe has any real existence, it can never become non-existent; in that case, something will have to be nothing and that is absurd. But, as a matter of fact, the universe is something that is dying every moment and giving birth to new phenomenal objects. So it cannt be said to be existent or non-existent. Even our body cells die out every second only to be born anew with all the memories of the dead cells transferred immediately, well before their death. Thus, we are dying every moment and once in seven years we are completely changed persons! What more proof is required to show that this phenomenal world is unreal? But the question remains. How can a thing be permanent and impermanent at the same time? Shree Shankaracharya uses the term 'Maya' from Bhagavat Gita to explain the ever-changing nature of the universe.

***Shankaracharya's 'Mithyavaada' or 'Maya'***

Shankara, like Gaudapada thought of Philosophy as a 'interpretation of the totality of human experience, or the whole of life from the stand point of "Truth". Happiness and welfare of all human beings is the central theme of Indian Philosophy according to Shankaracharya. Shankara contended that the world of thought and matter is not real; he did not mean that it (the world) is non-existent but felt it is illusory (Maya). In the state of ignorance or 'Ajnyaan', it appears as real. "It is experienced, and it exists" as experienced, in the state of ignorance; in the state of illumination, "it is not experienced, and it ceases to exist". He compares the world to dream (illusion) as in sleep (ajnyaan); it is pratibhashika, when it is the dream of an individual in sleep (private illusions), and calls it vyavaharika or phenomenal when it is the dream of all the people all the time, a universal illusion or world illusion, due to ajnyaan or ignorance of the real nature of the world. A man realizes the truth about his dream as soon as he wakes up. But, the universal illusion, the dream world continues through out a man's waking life unless he becomes aware of the 'Truth' through knowledge of Brahman. This leads us to a paradox, 'it exists, it exists not'. It is neither real nor unreal. Yet, this paradox recognizes the existence and Shankara calls it "Maya", the apparent world. This is like virtual reality. It has its base in Brahman, the eternal and consists of names and forms and thus, depends on Brahman for its existence. It is not real, for it ceases to exist or just disappears as soon as light (knowledge) is shed on it (darkness or ignorance). The apparent world is illusion, 'Maya'; and, the Self or Atman alone is real.

It is this remarkable clarity, supreme wisdom, and profound spirituality of Shankaracharya that makes him a paragon of Indian philosophy; it is this doctrine that helps clear the smoke, clear the clouds of delusion, ignorance and brings eternal bliss to the suffering hearts. A person who knows and understands the fleeting nature of this make-belive world will not hanker after desires of the flesh, fulfilling momentary happiness, but seeks that supreme Bliss that one can attain from the Knowledge of Brahman. Who wants a brokenpiece of coloured glass that reflects the sunlight while the real diamond of the effulgent Brahman is available! Only the spark should be kindled in the heart and it comes with the sincere and devoted search for 'Truth'. Brahman alone is Truth.

According to Shankaracharya, the world of thought and matter has a phenomenal or relative existence, and is super-imposed on Brahman, the unique, absolute reality. As long as we remain in ignorance, rather until we experience transcendental conscience, we shall continue to experience this apparent world, which is the effect of super-imposition. When transcendental consciousness is achieved, superimposition ends. This 'transcendental consciousness, is defined by Shankaracharya in his commentary on Brahma Sutra as 'the apparent presentation, to the consciousness, by the memory of something previously observed elsewhere'. We tend to super-impose one thing over the other, say for instance, a snake over a piece of rope, and misunderstand its nature.

> But there arises a question, "*How can we super-impose a snake upon a rope we do not perceive?*
> *How can we super-impose a world phenomenon upon a reality that is not apparent to our senses?*
> *Who has seen the Brahman, for Brahman is not an object for Perception?*

Shankaracharya has beautifully explained that, "*Brahman is not non-objective in the absolute sense*". Brahman is the object of the ego-idea. By intuition, we know our inner self must exist since the ego-idea is a presentation of the self. Ignorant people super-impose a dark blue colour upon the sky, which is not an object of perception. In fact, ignorant people as we are, we go on super-imposing one thing over the other that we do not perceive at all. We go on to super-impose anything on evey thing else, whether perceived earlier or not. There is a manner in which we are aware of the reality, the inner self, Brahman, absolute existence, knowledge and Bliss. Only in transcendental consciousness we perceive or know this fully.

*"Brahman is Existence" and, we all know we exist. "One who denies Brahman denies his own existence". "Ignorance is the cause and the apparent world its effect like the seed and its tree".*

When did this ignorance come to us? Has it been there since the very beginning or has it been acquired recently? Upanishads say that ignorance has come with us from the very beginning. However, it is futile to ask this question. Shankara says," It is this ignorance what is called Maya" What is this apparent-apeearance? It is Maya. What is this ignorance? It is Maya. Maya like the 'Brahman' is without a beginning. Ignorance as the cause and the apparent world as the effect have always existed, and will always co- exist. Because of wrong ideas, it is natural to man to not to be able to distinguish between the distinct entities and between their respective attributes. He super-imposes up on each the nature and attributes of the other, uniting the real with the unreal. It is the ignorance that leads to identifying the self with everything.

Shankara has made certain things very clear as to who we are and what is our nature. We all believe that the body is our real existence and that is not correct. Our body is 'asat', untrue that changes often; change is death of the one and the birth of the other, exit of one and the beginning of another. Changeless, deathless, means eternal. There is the real 'I' behind the body that is 'asat' and that 'I' the knower, the enjoyer, the feeler, the seer is the real and the eternal, 'Sat', the Self', the Atman'. This Self is existence, eternal and unchanging. The Mind is everchanging and as such unreal and 'asat'. Shankara draws the conclusion that whatever is eternal must also be finite and thus proves that our soul is eternal and infinite. Shankara also proves the unity of the soul. Since there cannot be two infinities, my self, i.e., the real self behind the body and the mind, is one and this is true of all the creatures with body and mind and the self. The Self of all is one and it is called the Shankara's *Advaita Vada* or the monistic system. These innumerable souls are but the shadow of one universal eternal Soul. The eternal and the Blissful, seated in the cave of the heart, It is beyond the reach of the mind. The realization of this Self is the goal of life.

Thus, it is very clear that our ignorance is the cause of our misery for we mis-construe this apparent world as real and identify ourselves with everything in it. Unless we realize our Self, we will not be able to see the reality of this existence. 'Maya' is not only universal, but it is beginningless and endless. There is a difference between 'Maya', as a universal principle, and' ignorance' that is individual. 'Ajnyaan' or 'avidya' is individual or personal. This individual ignorance is beginningless, but it can end at any moment. Spiritual illumination or enligtenment will put an end to all this ignorance and the world may vanish from the consciousness of a person who has attained supreme spiritual height in Turiyaateeta Samadhi. Yet, the apparent world exists for others who are ignorant of the reality of existence.

### *The Concept of 'Ishvara'*

Shankaracharya has described the concept of God. He has brough in the concept of a personal god ***'Ishvara'*** to make the common people understand the intricacies of Nature, the Prakriti, and the Purusha. Brahman is the ultimate cause of the universe. The world-apparent or this 'make-believe' world is super-imposed upon Brahman. Brahman is the cause and Maya is effect. It is very important to understand that Brahman has not transformed himself into this world, nor has he created this world.

Brahman as absolute Reality is incapable of temporal action or change. Real cannot create the unreal. So, Shankaracharya brings in a creative principle here, a 'God' called "*Ishvara*", and makes him the Creator. Thus, Ishvara created this world. The Brahman united with Maya becomes Ishvara. It is the creative principle; it creates, preserves and ultimately destroys or dissolves the universe in an endless and beginningless process. Ishvara is God personified and has his own attributes. Ishvara is the ruler and controller of Maya. Here it is very interesting to note the similarities and difference beteen Samkhya Philosophy and Shankara's concepts. The Sankhya Philosophy holds that the universe is an evolution of Prakriti (Nature), the undifferentiated matter composed of the Gunas- tamas, rajas and the sattva. It is the disturbance, the vibrations, the inequillibrium that has caused this world of atoms and molecules that ended up as man uptill now. Prakruti is thus different from and independent of Purusha, the absolute Reality. Maya is dependent on Brahman and is thus not independent and has no absolute reality in itself. Therefore, Shankaracharya puts it in a better way. It is Ishvara, created by the Brahman, rather than Prakriti who is the ultimate cause, that is the Creator, the Preserver, and the Dissolver.

One should not think that Brahman and Ishvara are two different entities; they are the one and the same. Brahman becomes Ishvara like the water that turns into ice under freezing temperatures.. According to Sri Rama Krishna, Brahman appears as Ishvara under intense love of his devotees. Just as the ice melts away with the rising Sun, the apparent world vanishes with the Knowledge of the Brahman. There remains the Brahman and nothing else. Brahman is the Infinite, the Absolute Reality. Devotio is a very effective and very powerful tool to visualize the Brahman, to go beyond Ishvara, the impersonal Reality behind the personal divine appearance. One can become Brahman since Brahman is already there within. But one cannot become Ishvara because Ishvara is different from our personality; Ishvara is above and distant from our Self, that is Brahman. Since Ishvara is the ruler of the universe and we cannot become Ishvara, we cannot be the rulers of the universe. It is sheer ego to think that we can become the rulers of the universe. Veda Vyasa also states the same truth in his Brahma Sutra. Because of the fact that the liberated persons still retain their individual consciousness they cannot become one with Him and become the Ruler themselves. They still remain separate as long as they retain their Consciousness. Total abnegation of the Self, total surrender, solves all this problem of '*the other*'. As long as a person is within the control of maya, grip of illusion, the 'One' Absolute appears as 'Many'. Ignorance can do nothing but to worship Ishvara, the ruler of all appearances, the illusory world. The human mind can never grasp the absolute Reality. Of course, in the process of this worship, mind becomes purified and the ego disappears making way for the realization of the Self, the Brahman, the Absolute, the"Truth".

Shankara is an intellectual giant. His method of attaining the Brahman is through Jnyaan Yoga. Self-control, austerity, discrimination and renunciation, non-attachment are the techniques adopted to attain the Brahman. Allthe Ashtaanga Sutras of Patanjali come handy in attaining the Brahman. This world is indeed a paradise to one who sees the 'things as they are'; all things are seen as relative and in relation to the Brahman. Attaining supreme Consciousness and realizing the Brahman is the supreme goal. Union with the supreme soul is the goal.

Among the Great Acharyas, Shankaracharya stands apart propagating "***Aham Brahmasmi***" and implores the Upanishadic doctrine of "*Tat tvam asi*". Look within yourself; Brahman resides in you; you are"That" Light. Remove your ignorance (ajnyaan) by Meditation, says Shankaracharya.

***BHASKARACHARYA***: There is an interesting account of a system of 'Bhedaabhedavaada' system of Philosophy that owes its origin to one Oudulumini whose antecedents and works are not available. But, this philosphy of differentiation is clearly brought out by Bhaskaracharya, who lived after Shankara. Bhaskaracharya has criticized the doctrine of Maya (Mithyaavaada) as enunciated by Shankaracharya.

According to Bhaskaracharya, Brahman as the cause contains the whole universe (potentially within himself), and the universe is the cause actualized, though in part only, since the cause has not exhausted itself the effect. There is no doubt about the creative abilities of the Brahman. He is all- powerful, ekamevaadviteeya, and an unchangeable reality. "In effect, the Brahman is both Jeeva (individual soul) and the world. Brahman is the Bhoktr (the enjoyer) and the Bhogya, (the objective world, that evolves from Him). This power of Brahman is not Maya, but real in absolute sense. This objective world is not an illusory, or make-believe one, since the God himself has evolved in it! It is real and exists (existential realism) and it is empirical existence.

According to Bhaskaracharya, this empirical world has the experiencer- a subject, i.e., the jeeva and a world of senses, -the object of experience. These subject and objects are not different from Brahman, for Brahman himself has evolved in these forms; not only Brahman is not just the names and forms, but the transcendental Self as well ["*Na prapanchamaatram Brahma*"].

The jeeva-kotis, the myriads of jeevas, are like the sunrays. They are neither the sun by themselves nor different from the sun. Similarly, the individual souls are neither different from Brahman nor they themselves are God. When the individual souls are purified by spiritual attainments, they attain Him. In the state of Knowledge, the individual souls are liberated and become one with Brahman. But, the union with Brahman, the God is possible only after death, never at any time during the life. All consciousness of separation is dissolved in Knowledge and the person is liberated when he dies. This doctrine of liberation (Mukti) after death is different from the doctrine of emancipation, 'here and now', of others.

***RAMANUJACHARYA***: Among the Acharya-thrayas of Indian Philosophy, Ramanujacharya stands for 'Vishishta-advaitha'. It is Advaitha of a 'vishesha'. It admits dualism or pluirality both of matter and of souls. Apart from Brahman all else is non-entities. Ramanujacharya was born in Sriperumbudur near Chennai (Madras) in 1017 A.D. and studied Vedanta under Yadava Prakash at Kaanjeevaram. Ramanujacharya's Grand-Grand-father was a reknown Philosopher King Yaamunacharya. The story goes that Yamunacharya defeated a pundit in the court of King Pandu and gained half the Kingdom in bet. He ruled it for quite a long time before going back to Sri Ranganatha Temple to become an asctic and a teacher. After Shankaracharya, Bhaskaracharya and Ramanujacharya are the most important interpreters of the Veda as also the staunch critiques of Shankaracharya, followed by Madhvacharya.

Shree Ramanujacharya holds the view that matter, souls and God are inseparably connected. All the innumerable souls make up the mind of God. God is the central point and He is the 'Antaryamin', dwells in our heart. He is in the cosmos, but not the cosmos; He is behind as well as inside the atom. If anybody wants to go to God and get anything he wants, he has to go away from the world. You can come in contact with the God only when you get the contact of the world cut-off, i.e., the material world cut -off from the mind and the material world cut- off from the senses. God is Supreme and He only can give what you want. Since all that you want can be had from the God, seek Him; go beyond your mind and seek Him.

Ramanujacharya's philosophy is known as 'Vishishta Advaitha'. Ramanaujacharya declares that, "Brahman is determinate and can therefore be defined by statement of his essential attributes ".

"*Brahman is Satyam (Real), Jnyaanam (Consciousness), and Aanantam ((infinite) [Taittiriya Upanishad* II-1-3]. Shankaracharya does not accept these as attributes of Brahman. But, Ramanujacharya accepts these as the essential attributes of the Brahman. "Brahman is the basis of all existence, and since he is also the supreme good, also supreme goal. The universe is composed of 'chit' (the sentient) and 'achit' (the non-sentient). Both 'chit' and' achit' have their source in Brahman. He is the in-dwelling self in all and the ruler of all".

"Brahman 'Wills' to be many. He divides himself into the manifold universe of the living and the non-living, but there is no absolute beginning in time. In the phase of involution, the universe remains latent in Brahman and in creation of evolution is the actualization of the latent. Brahman is the material as well as the efficient cause of the Universe. From him, the universe has emerged, in him it exists, and unto him it returns."[*Taittiriya Upanishad* III-1]. Ramanaujacharya has no doubt regarding the cause of the Universe and he upholds the beginningless and countless cycles of evolution and involution. He upholds the Principles of the Upanishads and says,"God is the source of the universe, has transformed himself into the cosmic manifold, and he is the in-dwelling self in his creation and the ruler and the director of the cosmic process.

According to Ramanujacharya, Karma, the fruits of past deeds, binds the souls. The evil that the universe consists is the result of karma of individuals for whom the God is the dispenser of the law. God remains distinct and separate although he has transformed himself into the sentient and the non-sentient. Matter is the object of experience, individual souls are the experiencing subjects, and God is the ruler of all. He is defined in the Upanishads as the 'Satyam, 'Jnyaanam', and 'Anantam'. Because of these attributes, God is above all and beyond all matter, a changing phenomenon, and is distinct from individual souls caught in mesh of

Karma. This is the quality attributed to Ramanujacharya's 'Dvaitha' Philosophy and, hence, called 'Vishishta-Advaita'. Brahman, by his nature, is beyond change, and though immanent, he is transcendent.

Ramanujacharya differs from Shankaracharya on the subject of definition of knowledge. Knowledge according to Shankaracharya is self-luminous, i.e., light by itself. Thus, it is apart from and beyond the relation of subject and object. According to Shankaracharya, relative knowledge is not real knowledge. Relative Knowledge is not pure consciousness. True Knowledge is Atman, the Brahman and Infinite. Relative knowledge is finite and limited, and, hence not Absolute.

Ramanujacharya does not consider Knowledge as self-luminous and absolute. For him, knowledge is always relative and there is always a difference and distinction between the subject and the object. *The Absolute, i.e., the Brahman, or the 'Knowledge' (of Brahman) can be attained by Nirvikalpa Samadhi, according to Shankaracharya. But, Ramanujacharya does not believe in Nirvikalpa Samadhi, the unitary consciousness, i.e., the experience of the Self as one with Brahman. As a Bhakta, the devotee remains a jeeva and enjoys the Bliss of Brahman, but never merges or becomes one with Him. This is just similar to the Bhakti Vedanta as propagated by Shree Madhwacharya in the later years.*

What Shankaracharya calls '*Maya*' is in reality the '*Shakti*', the power of Brahman and it is not an illusion to be discarded to obtain the Brahman. Ramanujacharya does not believe in an impersonal attributeless Brahman as proposed by Shankara in his commentaries, but considers it an essential personal Brahman in whom all attributes are found.

Ramanujacharya does not believe in complete identity of man with God. One must live at the service of God and enjoy the supreme bliss, love of God. A devotee must be ardent in his love for God and must practise austerity, compassion, non-attachment, religious disciplines, sacrifice and possess purity of mind. Purity of food is important for it dictates the mind and purity of thought comes from purity of food. Ramanujacharya upholds the Vedic doctrines of sacrifices. One must avoid all excesses including enjoyment and excessive joy. Vain thoughts are dangerous and one should devote all his time in the thoughts of God. The devotion of Radha to Krishna is the purest form of love one can express towards God and every devotee (Bhakta) should cultivate pure love. One should surrender to god; surrendering our will to' God's will' is literally service to God; it is a union of souls like that of the father and son. It knows no distinction or separation. Rather, Ramanujacharya is a staunch proponent of Bhakti Yoga, a practical way to Brahman. This is in contrast to Shankaracharya's idealistic philosophy of attaining Brahman through Jnyaan Yoga.

Free will is given to man to enable him to eventually detach himself from the mesh of ignorance and Karma and grow into the personality of God.

Ramanujacharya admits Maya as Shakti, the power of the Brahman; but, refutes Shankaracharya in this respect, for man has forgotten that the Self is of divine origin and has divine destiny. Sansar is evil. The true self has degenerated into ego by becoming a mode of matter. Our free will, a gift of God, finds fulfillment of its purpose when we live in conformity with the will of God.

***NIMBAARAKA***: Nimbaaraka of the Bengal School of Philosophy is well known for its Bhedaabheda doctrine or dualism in non-dualism. It is a very simple philosophy based on Jnyaan and Bhakti. With Jnyaan one can realize Brahman and with Bhakti one can worship him with total devotion and surrender. The absolute and the relative, or the impersonal and the individual (personal) are, respectively, the Brahman or the Paramatman and the Jeevatman. Brahman, with all his attributes, is the creator and this universe of name and form is issued forth from him. Brahman is also transcendental and impersonal, without attributes, and as such he is greater than the universe. However, the universe is one with, as well as, different from Brahman just as the wave is one with but different from the lake. Paramatman and jeevatman are like the sun and its rays, one with, but different from the sun.

Nimbaaraka advocates the philosophy of 'Bhedaabheda",' dualism in non-dualism', and this school of philosophy has come to be known as the 'Sanaka School' that has got a large following in Bengal. It flourished in the 11th Century A.D. before Madhvacharya. Bhaskara held that the individual soul is a part of Brahman only so long it is in ignorance; in knowledge and liberation it becomes one with Brahman. Nimbaaraka, on the other hand, believes in the unity of the individual soul with the Brahman both "in the state of ignorance, and knowledge and emancipation. Nimbaaraka says, in the state of ignorance, the individual soul experiences the empirical world or the objective world; and in knowledge and emancipation, when it attains super conscious or transcendental state, it visualizes the Brahman". Thus, the individual soul is capable of realising the union with Brahman (in knowledge), as well as, remaining separate (in ignorance) from him. Knowledge reveals the true nature of Brahman and devotion is important to merge in him with love, devotion and total surrender. Here, the true love of Radha and Krishna is the divine model, of prema and bhakti (love and devotion); with all knowledge and emancipation, the individual soul, the Self, remains.

***MADHVACHARYA (1199- 1278 A.D.)***: A staunch critique of Shankaracharya, Madvacharya is the proponent of 'Dvaita Siddhanta', i.e., 'Dualism'. He was born near Udupi, near Mangalore on the West Coast of Karnataka in 1199 A.D. Like many other Seekers, Madhvacharya took to spiritual teachings and has to his credit a number of scholarly works. He has written the 'Bhashya', a commentary on Brahma Sutra; also he has written commentary on Bhagavad Gita, a number of Upanishads, and many treatises in which he has elaborately dealt with his philosophy of 'Dualism'.

Madhvacharya is believed to be an incarnation of the Lord Narayana and he had taken birth as Hanuma in Treta Yuga and Bhima in Dvapara Yuga. He, indeed, demonstrated his capabilities in physical strength, as well as, intellectual power. He traveled widely and entered into dialogues and set at right the confusion among scholars. He always kept the human weaknesses in his mind when he denied the possibility of attaining supreme Brahman. He clarified that, "*At best one can reach the abode of the*

*Brahman and go near him and he called it 'Sameepya' and 'Saannidhya'*. To achieve or attain His form, 'Saroopya', or to merge in Him, 'Saayujya' is impossible. So he declined to accept the doctrines of "*Tat tvam asi*" *and* "*Aham Brahmasmi*". Madhvacharya based his philosohy of Realism on the fact that the Knower and the object must be real in order to experience or realize the knowledge. Knowledge necessarily implies these; 'No knowledge can be known without the knower and the known'. The 'absolute knowledge' as defined in Yoga, and Shankaracharya's contention cannot be accepted. All knowledge is relative. Absolute Knowledge, or the transcendental Consciousness, in which all distinction between knowledge (Jnyaan), knower (Jnyaata), and the Known (Jnyeya) disappeared is a state impossible to attain. Ultimately, the difference between the Jeevatman and the Paramatman remains and the two can never be united in Yoga.

Shree Madhvacharya considers matter, soul and God – all the three as uncreated, eternal and self-existent. The soul is placed between matter and God and these souls are infinitesimally small, i.e., 'Anu', size of an atom. These small souls are of three types: good, bad, or mixed. These small souls are weak and obviously look to some powerful force called God for help and support and happiness. Since the souls are between God and matter, and they have a tendency to look outward by their senses for happiness and the senses really please persons. But, working through the senses and identifying oneself with the body, the persons feel misery alongside the flashes of happiness and joy experienced for these are finite bound by time and space. Real happiness can come only from a source that is infinite and the foolishness of the person makes forget that source of eternal happiness is within him as the Soul or, the Atman. Shree Madhvacharya is of the opinion that these ignorant foolish persons need some help and guidance in order to know their own eternal nature and he proclaimed himself as that infallible soul, the spiritual preceptor, or the Guru.

Further, Shree Madhvacharya says that, "it is quite natural to be attracted towards matter that is external since the body is made of matter and matter has a propensity to attract. Not only the bodies attract each other, but the bodies have created other bodies also. The Jeevas, or persons are so weak that they are easily attracted by all sorts of things and objects; hence, the objective world, the material objects of the world attract and hold these persons captive and the weak jeevas fall prey to these attractions. It is very difficult to give up the attachment, moha and weak persons cling to their family, property and do not come out of it, i.e., the raaga, moha, and other vargas'. It is quite natural that the Jeevas worship the idols for fulfillment of their hopes, aspirations and ambitions. "Since every formal entity is material, matter (idol)–worship of objects is quite natural to man."

God is distinct from the jeevas or individual souls. Living and the non-living matter also differ and the two are distinct. Each individual is distinct and differ from every other individual; and even in case of matter, there are differences and they are distinct from each other. This sort of difference and distinctness causes the duality of existence and this can never be erased by Yoga or meditation. Unlike Shankaracharya, Madhvacharya never accepted the principle of unity and maintained that each soul is independent and distinct. Only the moral souls attain some spiritual progress and gain the favour of the gods. The sensuous and worldly souls will never attain spiritual development and remain in the Samsar of birth and death and rebirths. There are a class of souls who do not believe in the god are the damned ones and never attain salvation. This opinion of Madhvacharya is based on Realism with which we see the world. In the present day world, spirituality is at a discount. People abhor Divinity and doubt the existence of their own self. They are immersed in pleasures of the flesh and their greed knows no bounds. The life is miserable and yet, they do not sek liberation for they are immersed in the ocean of ignorance. 'Pardon them, for they know not what they are; and what they are doing' is the compassionate words of Madhvacharya to these souls.

Madhvacharya has made certain things very clear. In fact, Madhvacharya is known for his extraordinary intellectual ability to 'see things as they are'. This ability comes as a rare gift of the Lord or Divine Grace. According to Madhvacharya, 'Sri Hari' is supreme. This world is real not a 'make-believe' one, or "Maya', or illusion. Everything in this world is seprate; you are separate and I am separate. We all can never be one. The individual souls are graded according to their prepondering Guna as superior or inferior. All souls depend on God for redemption or salvation. Realization of the self is the enjoyment of the Bliss that is latent in the soul. Pure and unstinted Bhakti is essential for the attainment of supreme goal and it is the means to the end and not an end by itself as many others think. The Subject (Sri Hari) and the Object (the objective world) are two different entities and this duality implied in thought as subject and object, endures forever. The two will not merge and the merger is inconceivable. The only union that is possible is in the subordination of the human will in the Divine Will. This subordination of the Jeevatma in the form of total devotion to Paramatma is in the acknowledgement of the eternal dependence of the Jeevas on the supreme Lord. Devotion, i.e., ananya Bhakti is the only way. Madhvacharya considers the Lord as the Bimba (Image) and we are all his Pratibimba (reflection). Madhvacharya believes in humility, faith, submission, gratitude, and self-sacrifice as the key to God-visioning; however small and insignificant we are, it is possible to know God by our total subordination. There are no hindrances to catching a glimpse of Him!

*"Speak to Him though, for He hears,*
*And, spirit with spirit can meet;*
*Closer is He than breathing*
*And, nearer than hands and feet".*

According to Madhvacaharya, 'Sri Hari' is the Paramatman and one can know him from the Scriptures, Veda and Veda alone. This Hari Bhakta, Madhvacharya had the God-visioning of Sri Krishna and actually found it in the form of an idol that came in a ship from Dwarka to Mangalore. Madhvacharya had dreamt that Sri Krishna would come to him! The interesting story is that Madhvacharya used to go to sea for his morning prayers and bath. One day he saw a ship that was in danger of grounding and the Captain of the Ship was giving distress call. Madhvacharya saw this and waved his angavastra (apparel) and the ship began to sail. Later on, the Captain of the Ship begged to offer some gift and Madhvacharya asked for the lump of mud kept in the ship to keep the balance and the Captain gladly gave it. And lo! That lump contained the idol of Lord Krishna. This idol is still worshipped in Udupi Krishna Math and the right of worship is given to Pontifs (Peethaadhipati) in turn-by-turn called 'Paryaaya'. It is in this context that the 'Bhakti', or 'devotion and total surrender' of Madhvacharya towards Sri Krishna became legendary. He strictly enforced cleanliness and certain rituals to go near this idol. In fact, the Madhva sect is known for its exclusiveness in Bhakti and Sanctity in the worship of the Lord. No other religion attaches so much of sanctity in the worship of the Lord. Thus, Krishna came into life of Madhvacharya, although it is believed, Madhvacharya himself is the incarnation of the Lord!

Shri Madhvacharya is a Vaishnava, an ardent devotee of Vishnu and all his followers are known as Vaishnavaites. Vaishnavaites are found throughout the length and breadth of India, but in a small proportion.

After studying Shankaracharya, and Bhaskaracharya and Ramanujacharya's philosophy, in depth, it is very difficult to agree with Madhvacharya on the principle of 'attainment of supreme goal, the Brahman'. It is impossible to attain 'Sayujya', ('to merge in Him'), says Madhvacharya. It is too much to aspire for this state of union with the Lord! May be, it is true. But, having born in human form, bestowed with the ability to perceive the Lord within one'sown Self, it is essential to strive for attainment of the supreme Brahman. The human Mind has the rare ability to perceive not only its own self but also the cosmic Self or the Brahman, as supreme Consciousness. This aspect of the power of the Mind cannot be ignored. Success or failure in attaining Him is left to the Lord's sweet will and Divine Grace! Many ardent devotees have attained sayujya with the Lord; they have simply disappeared into Him! There is a rare incident of a small girl Andal who simply walked into the *sanctum sanctorum of the temple* and disappeared!

***SRI CHAITANYA MAHAPRABHU***: Sri Chaitanya (b. 1485) is a well-known proponent of Vaishnavism that stands for Bhakti cult. True love for God, as evinced by Chaitanya in his ecstatic songs and dance, has given a place to him in every heart of the people of Bengal. At a very young age, Chaitanya came to Gaya and worshiped Vishnu in a temple and got illumination just as Buddha got illumination under the peepul tree in Bodh-Gaya. Chaitanya, earlier known as Nimali Pundit, a scholar in Grammer, spent his time in Navadveep in Bengal chanting the name of Krishna. His famous song is devoted to the praise of Sri Hari:

***"Hari Haraye Namah; Krishna Yaadavaaya Namah; Gopala, Govinda, Rama Sri Madhusudhana".***

Chaitanya, known as Gauranga by his disciples, had a very rare type of personality. He used to get into Samadhi and experience a sense of universal conciosness and, at the same time, used to sing and dance in a state of semi-concious and conscious states, respectively. Gauranga selected Puri for his residence after he was initiated into ascetic life. He took to worship of Sri Krishna as ordained by his Guruji, Shri Ishvara Puri.

Chaitanya's love for God has no parallel and his Bhakti with Jnyaan makes him a very popular Acharya of the Bengal Province of the pre-British days. A person undergoes five stages according to Chaitanya. First it is Shanta (a peaceful state), when a person finds joy in the thoughts of God; it is followed by 'dasya' (a servant of God) where God is the Master. The next stage is 'Sakhya', friendhip with God and then Vatsalya, like the parents' love for their child. God Krishna is the child. And, the devotee must take care of him. In the fifth stage, the sweet relation of the lover and the beloved is 'mathura'. Here, God is the beloved. The best form of love is the one described in Bhagavata – love of the Gopis or the cowherdesses and Krishna. None can excel this!

Thus, one can find a number of saints and Acharyas who have given a sense of direction to the ignorant people and implored them to take to spiritual way of life. The approach of different Acharyas may be different but the goal is the same. To attain the 'Absolute', the 'Infinite', there are infinite ways. It is ultimately, one's perception by one's own efforts that gives the illumination or knowledge. This experience of the Brahman, the Truth, the Absolute is inexplicable and not transferable. Total 'Shraddha' (faith) or 'devotion with knowledge' and sincere practice will definitely produce the result! Each one should experience this totality of existence, this Bliss by one's devotion, perseverence and dedication. Austerity is the Rule.

# 8
# Vedantic Way of Life

Vedanta means 'Wisdom"; it is the culled knowledge of the Veda. The Veda enunciate the doctrines of sensible life and sane living. Not only Brahma created Man but has also given a code of conduct in order to achieve the supreme goal of life. It is repeatedly reiterated here that there is a 'divine plan' and a supreme goal that promote the evolution of life on earth. For a rational and scientific investigator, it may appear a simple chain of physico-chemical-biological process, one leading to the other. In the divine order, the inherent qualities of human beings denote a different thing; it denotes the very nature, the quality, or the 'svabhaava' or the 'svaroopa' of the 'divine'. Man has been bestowed not only with the 'panchendriyas', the five sense organs to perceive sense objects through Mind but has also been gifted with an innate capacity to look inward and perceive the reality of the objective world. It is this innate capacity, or the ability to look outward through the Mind as well as look inward with the inner eye (antar chakshus), the spiritual eye, that makes Man different from other animals. Body constitutes the physical or material aspects of man that constitute the carriage bound by time and space and identified by name (nama), form (roopa), and function (karma). There is an invisible Soul (Atma) in every man that supports the body and mind; and, it constitutes the spiritual aspect that transcends time and space and perceives the Creator Himself. It is this innate capacity of the humans that calls for adopting a different type of life than the one that we have adopted, today.

Our way of life is, all, wrong. We have gone in a wrong path. There is a super- express Highway, but we have taken a very narrow by-lane. We have traveled very fast in this narrow lane, a long long distance, and it now seems wellneigh impossible to stop. and return or get back. The super express Highway that makes the journey easy, comfortable, and enables us to reach the destination early has been well described in the Veda and the Upanishads, the Bhagavad Geeta, and the Brahma Sutra. It shows the sane and sensible way of life as explained in the Vedic doctrines. The Vedic doctrines are the formulae that give details of 'dos' and don'ts' that ensure a happy, successful, and fruitful life, a life of fulfilment. It is called 'magic formulae' for this objective world is a magical, or 'make believe' world, a world of illusion or 'Maya'; and, one must know how to live here. *Bhagavad Gita* describes the nature of this objective world and how only a '*dheera*' (*a man of knowledge*) can live successfully here. In the famous epic Mahabaharat, Shree Krishna goes to the extent of calling all these human beings like Bhishma, Drona, Dhrutaraashtra, Duryodhana as ignorant lot; He says that they are not living beings in the 'Real' sense of the term and they are 'already dead' ('asat'); they are only name and form;

these human beings should not be taken for 'Real' or 'sat'. Only a 'Jnyaani' knows how unreal is this objective sensate material world and knows how to live here without involving deeply with it. It is the 'Jyaan' (Knowledge) called viveka in Samskrut and sense of detachment (vairagya) that brings liberation, emancipation, according to Bhagavad Gita. Shree Krishna, an avatar or incarnation of Shree Vishnu, Shreeman Narayana, is appearing again and again in each eon of time as Rama, Krishna, to guide the ignorant people and show them the path of salvation. He clearly defines the goal and the path to attain the goal. The goal of life is 'Realization of the Self', "Atmasaakshaatkaara". It is emancipation, liberation from the cycle of repeated births and deaths; release from the bondage, or 'mukti'. The path of salvation is through the practice of "*Ashtaanga Yoga Sutra*".

The three ancient Indian Scriptures viz, the Brahma Sūtra, the Bhagavad Gita, and the Upanishads give elaborate instructions to Vedic scholars to teach their disciples the principles of '*Tat tvam asi*' and "*Aham Brahmasmi*" and thereby reiterate the divinity inherent in every jeeva, as also implore the need for an austere way of life. See Ishavasya Upanshad. One hast to remember the purpose of life. One has to adhere to the doctrines of Manu Smriti that dictates the code of conduct for every person and live a sattvic way of life; persons who sverve from the path of 'Dharma' have to suffer repeated births and death on this earth.

The most striking aspect of the Vedantic Way of life is the doctrines that almost all the religions of the world emphasise and no one bothers to adopt them. Whether it is the Catholics or the Protestants, the Jains or the Buddhists or the Hindus, they are bound by certains ethics, morals, and they should strictly abide by them. The true religion is one that declares the whole world as one family and all humans as brothers and strives for universal peace and brotherhood. The Principles of "Vasudhaiva Kutumbakam' and universal peace are the Vedic doctrines.

The Upanishadic doctrines call for a high order of discipline in both private and public life. It is beautifully enunciated in the Ashtaanga Yoga Sutra of Patanjali, or the 'Viveka Chudamani' of Shankaracharya, or Vyasa's Bhagavata and explained in the Bhagavad Gita. These scripture are easily available. Well, it should be remembered here that, the Lord who created us, the Humans, has also given a guide or handbook in unwritten form of the Veda. First, it is Brahman who gave a lakh verses to Narada and that has been further reduced to the bare minimum in the Ashtaanga Yoga Sutra of Patanjali, or the Brahma Sutra, or the Manu Smruti, or the Bhagavad Gita and the Viveka Chudamani. A number of works based on these ancient Scriptures have been published in recent times as Commentaries and Translations. These works of sanatana dharma by learned scholars give us an opportunity to have divergent views and leaves us most confusing, too! However, the originals are also available in some form or the other for thosewho are interested. Almost 250 Upanishads have been published and how far some of these are authentic is doubtful! Anyway, some basic understanding of the doctrines of 'Dharma' as the basis of life is important here.

No nation can prosper without "Dharma" or "Righteousness". The fundamentals of 'Dharma' are very very clear. These are "Ritam" and "Satyam", "Order" and "Truth". The Principles of Dharma are enunciated in each and every ancient Vedic Scripture. 'Satyameva Jayate' is one such Principle. "*Ishavasyam idham Sarvam.....*" is another Principle. 'One should not covet the property of the other'. No one has exclusive right over the natural resources. One should protect the purity of air and water and should not pollute water and air. Ahimsa or Non-killing is yet another Principle. Many such Principles are enunciated in Chanakya's works. The dignity of human beings should be respected and no nation should harm the sentiments, faith and belief of people of other nations. The War-mongering Nations should take heed to the advice given in these Texts. In the present-day context, these are more relevant than ever. Every individual has to strive for the highest goal in life as enunciated in the Upanishads and the whole world should be a place of peace and prosperity, both materialistic and spiritual.

The Day-to day ritualistic practices eulogized in *Rk Veda* have undergone vast changes. In fact, the Veda clearly state that. "*Ultimately, all these scriptural practices have to be abandoned when the Jnyaani comes to know of his Self.*" Even in Bhagavad Gita, Shree Krishna implores. "*Abandon your dharma and take refuge in Me*". One should not cling to the steps of the ladder if one wants to climb up and up. One should know the purpose for which a partcular path is chosen. Many a spiritual aspirants fall victim to the siddhi of inferior type such as clairvoyance and thought reading. Many spiritual leaders have failed to make to the top due to inherent human weaknesses such as attachment, 'Raaga' and 'Moha' of the worldly life. A nation whose leaders are highly spiritual can make all other nations to fall in line and adhere to spritual as well as materialistic progress. The quality of the citizens is more important!

Vedic way of life is one of total knowledge. It is not simply a dogmatic religious and ritualistic way of life. Every thought and action of every person is filled with love and the joy and happiness derived from such action is self evident in every family, every village, and the whole State. During Vedic period, people lived a Vedic way of life-- a life of total Knowledge, Prajnya, and people were conscious of their actions and knew the repercussions of their action; they believed in Karma (a physical law) and never deviated from the path of dharma. The Vedic knowledge was restricted to the Brahmanas but the resounding Vibrations of vedic chantings pervaded the life and environment. There was Vedic agriculture, Vedic health care, Vedic administration, Vedic economy, Vedic industry, Vedic education and everything was Vedic in the sense it was total knowledge, knowledge leading to action of people in total awareness, Prajnya. This is something unimaginable in the present day context where intolerance, jealousy, cut-throat competition and mutual ill-will, greed and avarice, selfishness to the core are evident in all walks of life.

Vedic agriculture means a totality of existence where the farmer tended the plants with love and care and the plants smile with flowers and fruits touching the heart of the people. The gardens and agricultural fields were vibrating with energy and provided food full of strength (Sattva). The farmer need not read Rk Veda for this. The vibration of the sounds coming from a temple or a Brahmana's house was just sufficient.

Vedic health care was much more widely practiced during Vedic times. Atharva Veda was the *materia medica* of the pharmacopea of the Ayurvedic Pundit and small ailments were cured by mantra and touch therapy since the persons administering holistic medicine were highly spiritually attained persons. Dhanurveda Sushruta, Charaka , Vagbhatta, and Madhav Nidaam other Samhita formed the basis of Vedic medical knowledge.

Vedic economy is much more interesting. The State collected sufficient tax to maintain the functions of the State without burdening the people. Only a small proportion was collected in cash and kind and the people never felt the pinch; moreover, it was dharma and self- help that prompted people to do social service and not selfish service as found today. The rich were benevolent and never hesitated to give away their wealth for a social cause, may it be construction of a temple, or repair of the tanks. People had clear knowledge of effect of bad deeds, sin commited and good deeds (papa and punya) accumulating over several births and delivering the fruits of action over an uncertain period of time. When the time is ripe the fruits of good action would certainly reach the recipient and there was state honour for good deeds and benevolent action. It is ultimately dharma, human kindness and sacrifice and love that determined the course of every action. This is Vedic practice. Volumes and volumes of literature and history speak of the glorious days of Vedic life. Now it is globalisation and world trade where rich states are fleecing the poor nations and robbing off all their limited resources and enriching themselves for sheer materialistic glory and sadistic enjoyments in warfare and dirty politics.

The worst form of exploitation can be seen in modern medical and health care. Huge hospital complexes are constructed with a view to fill the ICCU with rich patients who can fuel the greed of the medical personnel. There is no kindness or sympathy in all these medical and health care since money is the criteria. Western Pharmaceutical companies prepare the drugs and dump them in thickly populated poor countries where the Governments tacitly encourage these pharmacy business allowing the drugs untested and unchecked. Most of the time spurious drugs make way into the system and none can detect or deter this under the system. Greed rules the roost!

During Vedic period, it appears as though there was total segregation in family and social life. Elderly persons in the family, particularly the men folk were more respected. It was joint family and the paternal or maternal uncles influenced the impressive youngsters more than the parents to a great extent. The head of the family was almost a demi-god and his utterances were treated almost the 'law of the family'. Women fold dominated the inner circles and elderly women had high Regards and were highly respected. It was all love and affection and the granny's love overflowed the family life.

Perverted, and, the so-called, intelligent learned persons, have misinterpreted the Vedic family system in their own perverted way. They say the women folk never enjoyed freedom since the rule was *"na stree swaatantram arhati", meaning women do not deserve freedom. The exact meaning of the word 'freedom' is not clear even today. Freedom, whether of man or woman, is the very goal of life we are desperately looking for today. Everybody, man or woman, wants freedom. 'Man is born free and everywhere he is chain's, said the great social thinker Hobbes. Then where is the question of only women's freedom during Vedic time? The freedom enjoyed by girls or women today all over the world, particularly in advanced countries, is an eye opener. The way women are treated in highly advanced countries is a shame on modern education and civilization. They have Reformatory Homes, Shelter and Homes for the Distressed women, Social Welfare Associations and special laws for protection of women. But, it is the proud privilege of Indian women that they are protected and respected in social life. Women are treated not only equal, but, more than equal, in family and social circles. She is the power behind men folk, and all decisions in family matters are taken by women folk. In Kerala, it is the women who have all the sayand control family property.*

As regards segregation in family and social life, it was felt absolutely essential to prevent moral abuse and prevent harm to women and children by perverted and unscrupulous persons. It was aimed at prevention of corruption in social life. The mingling of unscrupulous persons was treated as a danger to children's health and strict watch was kept on their movements. Though girls did not to school, they were given all the knowledge and training in running the household. In fact, the illiterate women were far wiser than the men folk who had schooling those days. Women used to the learn the Bhagavad Gita and Puranas by-heart and could render epics like Ramayana and Mahabharat extempore.

The four 'Purusharthas' viz, dharma (austerity), artha (economy), kaama (desire) and moksha (lberation) constituted the goal of life and the duties of a person in his four stages of life, viz, baalya (childhood), yauvana (youth), grihasta (householder), and vriddhaapya (old age) were well defined. Everyone was bound by dharma and karma. Marriage was a means to liberation and sex life was very much under control; partly there was not much of privacy and partly, the austere way of life relegated sex to background and deemed it a limited exercise to beget the progeny, preferably a son to perform family rites and look after family ancestral property. Of course, there may be deviations and perversions that did not get the wide publicity that one gets in the media these days. There was absolutely no contact between man and his wife during the menses period. This in stark contrast to the Doctors' advise to go in for oral sex, masturbation, mutual adjustments disregarding cleanliness and inevitable health problems of the women. It is surprising that the Viagara is widely publicized for correcting the erectile problems of the old persons! It is the time for total renunciation and contemplation on spiritual aspects in the Vedic way of life. Such are the glaring contrasts one can see today when compared to the Vedic way of life. It is no wonder that we suffer for what we do in the name of advancement in science and technology.

What a comparison to Vedic tradition of holistic knowledge and life of peace and plenty when we see the rottening social and political developments today. The very fact that there is Commission for Human Rights shows that there is no human dignity and respect for rights like right to knowledge, right to protected water supply and sanitation, let alone right to food, freedom from hunger.

The Westerners who came to India thought that the Indian villagers were poor just because they were not fully clothed and ate in temple functions that were numerous and bountiful. They never knew that the Indian hot climate does not permit full cover of the body. There was equity and justice in real practice and there was no need to inscribe these into the Constitution! It is the foreign domination that looted the wealth of India, destroyed social and economic life. Now, corruption and greed has eaten into the fabric of Indian society and morals and ethics have become history of the Vedic times. Human life and values are at a discount everywhere; one day, the slogan would be –'buy one dead body and get two free' (dead bodies are bought for dissection purposes in Medical Colleges). Indirectly, the Government and the Social Institutions play with the life of the poor and the gullible people due to their wrong policies and their implementation. Self-rule and self-help based on dharma constituted the Vedic tradition and that was true democracy aided and supported by aristocracy and oligarchy.

There are many intricate details of ritualistic practices in Vedic way of life. The human body is treated as a temple where the Lord resides and, as such, morning ablusions and prayers assumed significance; elaborate chantings of mantra accompanied these activities. Even while taking food, it is considered an offering to the Lord, Agni Vaishvanara and certain mantra are used to propitiate the five vital breaths, deities residing in the mouth and the five sacred fires residing in the body. Ultimately, health and wellbeing is considered to be the Lord's will! From morning till night, from the time of dawn to dusk, the rituals go on and on. There are a number of ritiuals that are to be practiced and mantra to be chanted. These mantra (for egxample the mantra of *Mahanarayana Upanishad or Atharva Veda*] are for purposes of purifying oneself and the environment; further, the body is treated as the temple in which Sri Hari Narayana dwells and appropriate sanctity is maintained by keeping it clean. There are mantra invoking the sacred Rivers while taking bath and mantra are chanted to ward of any unseen dangers while taking bath in Rivers. Tilak or mark on the forehead is one of the conspicuous signs that can be seen on the forehead of a spiritual person. It is the mark of his spiritual attainment. One who has attained a higher level of Consciousness upto the 'Ajnya' level puts a line or a round tilak with sandal paste. Higher level, upto 'Sahasraara' level is marked by a long vertical sandal paste mark on the forehead. In fact, one should constantly chant the name of Sri hari Narayana, day in and day out. Even while taking food, there are elaborate practices. Food is first offered to guests and then taken as if it is offered to the Fire God "Viasvanara" under the implorations of the Lord, Sri Hari Narayana, in order to satisfy Sri Krishna who dwells in all. It is stated that 36,000 deities in the nadis and plexus of the human nervous system take care of the functioning of the body. Veda Samhita is the guide for all these and the vibrations of sounds of 'Rk Veda' and 'Sama Veda' create a very smooth flow of cosmic energy in the body. It is stated that a person can live a healthy life upto 160 years.

Now, it appears as though it is difficult to practise all these things and live as per Vedic tradition; but a devout Brahmana should invariably practise it without fail wherever he is even today, there are a large number of families who practise these Vedic Rite and rituals all over India, in spite of modern life style and time and space constraints. In fact, it is the only hope of our survival; unless we revive our sanatana dharma and take to Vedic traditions, we Indians will be ruined by Western life style and crooked economic and political policies.

First, every Brahmana worth the name should read Rk Veda whether he understands it or not and sing the Sama Veda to create the Vibrations of the sound. Maha Yagnya, Yagnya, Homa and Havanas should be performed in every town so that there will be beneficial effect of the smoke and fire on the micro-level environment. Further, Vedic education, Vedic health care, and Vedic economy and administration followed by Vedic agriculture and Vedic Industry should be adopted on war-footing to stop the adverse effects of globalisation and avert the disaster due to collapse of the sustaining power of the environment and destabilization of the ecological balance as could be seen in changes in the behaviour of the monsoons, drying up of rivers and tanks and lowering of water table and total deforestation in Western Ghats and other key areas. Sustainable development is possible only with Vedic Knowledge. Here Veda should not be interpreted as a religious and ritualistic pursuit only. It is a methodology based on puire spiritual science that can bring 'heaven on earth',

Vedic way of life is not for a particular community. It is for all. Only participation is enough. All need not perform the rituals like the Homa, Yagnya. Just a few persons will do it and others can devotedly participate in it. All need not perform the daily rituals as advised in the Scriptures. Even if a few families rigidly follow it, it is enough. Others become the partners in Vedic tradition by virtue of their Vedic character of personal discipline, morals and ethics and strict adherence to truth and dharma (Righteousness). At the family level, to mention a few rituals that a Brahmana (Brahmin) has to perform in his household, morning ablustions, mantra to be chanted, dhyaan to be performed, strict adherence to sattvic diet and preparation of food, method of consuming the food, offering a part to the deities first and then to the honoured guests, mantra to be chanted to ward off evil eyes and contamination of food, strict aherence to discipline in private life such as contenance or celibacy (Brahmacharya) and preservation of energy for higher spiritual advancement, treatment of guests, neighbours and elders and women and children, adherence to dharma in daily life, particularly in earnings and spendings of money and goods, etc. Guidelines are given in many scriptures like the epics and Puranas and Teachings of Spiritual Leaders and Gurus, and handbooks issued out by the religious heads.

Morning ablution is of much importance for a Brahmin whose duty is to worship the Deities- Indra, Rudra, Varuna, Maruta, Vasus, and all other wish-fulfilling Devatas (numbering 33,000), for human welfare. He chants mantra in praise of these Deities and propitiates them, offering arghya (water). He starts from Surya namaskar (Yogic prayer to Sun God) and goes on chanting mantra from morning till he goes to bed. The most beautiful aspect of this Vedic ritual is that these prayers are for the happiness and welfare of humanity, not for the happiness and welfare of himself or his own family members! He says, "*Sarve janaah sukhino bhavantu*", meaning, '*Let all people be happy*'.

*There are some very interesting Mantra that are taken from the Rk Veda X. 190.1-3. These mantra are the mantra that describe the creation of the universe and the supreme power behind it. These mantra, although chanted at the time of taking bath for self-purification, expiation of the sins committed (prayaschitta) form the prayer for the welfare of mankind.*

*These mantra as quoted in Mahanarayana Upanishad:*

*"Ritam cha satyam chaabhiddhaattapaso adhyajaayata,*
*Tatto raatrirajaayata tatah samudro arnavah;*
*Samudraadarnavaadadhi samvatsaro ajaayata,*
*Ahoraatraani vidadhadvishvasya mishato vashee;*
*Sooryachandramasau dhaataa yathaapoorvamakalpayat*
*Divam cha prithveem cha antarikshamatho suvah."*

*[Mahanaraya Upanishad 1-63-65].*

*Ritam and Styam, i.e., 'Order and Truth are the foundation of the universe. Ritam also stands for the totality of the sentient beings and satyam for the individual souls'. The Divine Being is the source. Ratri stands for the Prakriti, nature that is non-sentient (avidya) and, samudra stands for the 'mahat' and arnava stands for the indistinguishable source of all creatures. There are mantra chanted for purification of the environment, the surroundings, and the body treated as the temple where the Lord resides! Water is sipped chanting mantra to purify the mouth and water is sprinkled around to purify the air. Water is poured down making a complete cycle of symbolic completion of hydrologic cycle. Sun is the center of all these prayers.*

*Hence, It is laudable that here are the people in India, even today, who devote their whole life to pray for the welfare of mankind irrespective of caste, creed, colour, as well as all organic beings all over the earth.* The Varnashrama dharma does not exist anymore and, anybody can practise any avocation these days and this has left little time to practise 'svadharma', one's own dharma. An individual's 'Dharma' dictates that he should attain spiritual excellnce that leads ultimately to 'Self Realisation'. Here, it should be noted *that there is no one superior or inferior and there is nothing more important than spiritual attainment, for it is this spiritual attainment that improves the quality of the individual person.*

There is no clear-cut division of caste, creed, and sex in spiritual life of a person. Spirituality cuts across all differences. All knowledgeable persons are considered 'Brahmanas' if they are engaged in the pursuit of "Knowledge" or search of 'Truth'. Einstein, Stephen Hawkings and any scientist for that matter is considered a Brahmana. Mere chance of birth in a Brahmana's family will not automatically entitle a person to call himself a Brahmana. There are certain ritualistic practices practiced in a Brahmana's houselhold and these are relevant as far as they promote spiritual attainments. They are irreleveant if they are practiced without any knowledge of their meaning and purpose. For instance, morning ablutions and offerings to Sun God are very relevant and even Brahamanas do not pracise these rituals these days. As already stated the way of life and the life style of these Brahmanas have changed. However, if one follows any one of the methods of Yoga, either the Bhakti Yoga or the Karma Yoga, it is enough; But, with these Bhakti and Karma Yoga, one tries the Jnyaana Yoga, it is the best path to spiritaul attainment. Always remember the word "spiritual attainment"; So far very few have actually attained it; all should strive to attain it. That is all. Here, the means is more important; the end is not easy to achieve in one or two, or even more than several lives, in some cases.

Individual progress is of two types. One, materialistic progress that is horizontal; a person may become very rich, famous, and powerful in his worldy life, in social or political life. But all these achievements do not ensure liberation or release from bondage, 'Mukti'. At best, it may give a satisfaction and fulfil his carnal desires and boost his ego. But it takes him nowhere. After death, persons who have rendered yeomen service to mankind may enjoy a bit of heavenly happiness in the nether world; but they are sure to return here to complete their journey. The ultimate goal is the same to all and there is only one path to attain it.

Second type of progress is the spiritual progress. It is of utmost importance in human life. It is with great trial and error, natural selection, and influence of environment, and genetic transformations that a living creature attains human life form. This great opportunity to be a 'human being' is not easily attained and, hence should not be wasted in pursuit of carnal cravings and fulfillment of desires of the flesh. Every minute of our life, we must be aware of the grandiose plan of the Supreme Lord who created us and try to find out the "Truth" of our existence. An inner search for 'truth' should constantly drive us to Self Realizion and the ultimate reality of our existence. Ultimately, we must merge in Him; rather go back to Him from whom we came here!

In a sense, everything that we practise today in modern life is wrong as compared to the Vedic tradition. Our food habits and dress are wrong; we donot have appropriate techniques for the Tropical life and we suffer in a number of ways for that incompatible way of life. We have left squatting on floor. Our sitting postures and the furnitures are all wrong and we suffer back pain, neck pain and headache as a result of the wrong style of living. As regards food, it is interesting to note that a dangerous trend of over-eating habit has been developing in a certain group or section of people of the upper middle class and the rich class in recent years. As far as one remembers, till recently, there was no system of breakfast, lunch, and dinner in Indian society. Imbibed from the west as a 'class', some people have taken to feeding the body with rich fatty diet three to four times a day. The Vedic tradition was such that the whole morning was spent in morning ablutions, prayer and rituals and one lunch was eaten by mid-day, that too after the guests were fed! There was no question of a dinner since the after-noon lunch was late and heavy; and, the evening was spent in bhajan, satsang, discourses on Epics and Puranas ended with light refreshment. Freezing, de-freezing and re-heating of food was prohibited for the food loses its nutritional value once it is cooked. There was no question of evening parties! Guests were invited on occasions of family events like birth of child, upanayanam, marriages, etc. and festivals and other religious and social functions. Birth Day parties and Marriage Anniversries were rare. Children had special treat during the Dassera and Ugadi and Deepavali festivals had these had great significance.

The dress code prohibited any use of trousers and pyjamas and the dress consisted of dhotis and upper-wears! As a child, the author remembers how the whole day went with out any dress for it would come in the way of rituals of pooja. Incidentally, the weather also favoured such a system; one cannot wear even a banian due to sweltering heat of the day. New clothes were bought on festival occasions. Dhoties, Shirts, and close-collared Coat constituted the official business dress and were sparingly used! The food and dress habits complied well with the seasons and climate of the regions and thus, a variety of dress in varied hues and colours are seen in India. Even the structure and design of our dwelling houses were in close conformity with nature and the 'vaastu' shastra defined the inter-action of the elements and flow in the dwelling houses. Mud walls, sloping roofs or flat roofs conformed to the conditions of excessive rain or heat of the region. All these are fast changing.

The traditional Indian habits and tastes varied from region to region and, from season to season, in all walks of life. This variety added jest to life and created great fun and frolic, especially amongst women and children. This variety is fast disappearing. Modern youth have no taste for tradition and treat anything Indian as ethnic! Incomaptibility with climate and seasonal changes often leads to sickness, illhealth, and untold misery and the modern life style has to revert to traditional ways, sometime or later. But, all these are treated with contempt by the modern youth. The result is quite obvious! It is a life of waywardness and misery. It is extremely important that the modern youth should be given proper guidance and advised to strictly adhere to spiritual way of life as enunciated in the Vedic tradition, of course with some modifications suitable to our modern times. But, there is no way but to strictly adhere to "Righteousness" and" Order" or discipline in life. Dharma or Righteousness should be clearly understood. Every individual, society or community, and nation and the world at large has well defined 'dharma' and each has to strictly adhere to it failing which the foundation of its existence is at stake.

Earlier School Text Books used to have some spiritual lessons and the children used to get some knowledge about 'dharma' at a very early stage in life. But, these things have become a thing of the past and educationists and the Governments are not interested in these for they consider these as anti-secular. Any use of the word 'dharma' is misconstrued as puritanical,

Brahmanic and against the so- called 'secular' Policy od the Government. People who do not know what is secular consider dharma as non-secular and partisan and treat it as anti-national. This is the sad part of the story of decline of a civilization! It is interesting to know that the Chinese and the Japanese have preserved their ancient culture despite the onslaught of the wave of modernism. They have preserved their educational system and blended it with the modern as well; so also, they have preserved their medical and health system. It is in India that the influence of the British Rule for over three Centuries erased much of our original system of education, health and medicine and left us high and dry. Even now, some vested interests are not willing to change! In fact, much of the knowledge gained by the Western countries is from the East and mostly India. It is high time that we have to revive our system of education, ayurveda, mathematics, astronomy and health sciences based on Yoga. It is reiterated here that the human potential can be harnessed much more easily by our ancient wisdom than by western methods. It is with this view that Vedanta should be carefully studied, not as a philosophy, religious faith, or a dogma but as a spiritual science.

# 9

# Yoga for Health, Peace, and Happiness

Health is very important. Without good health, it is not possible to attain anything! Healthy body and healthy Mind go together. Even if one is afflicted, it is difficult and life becomes miserable not only to the afflicted person but also to others who are near him/her. So, the first priority should go to maintenance of good physical and mental health. Brahma the Creator taught the secret of good physical and mental health to his first son Atharvan and this is elaborately dealt with in Atharvan Veda. Later on, Patanjali codified this in his "Ashtaanga Yoga Sutra". However, there is a difference between Yoga practiced for spiritual attainment of Self–Realization and the Yoga for simple health, peace, and happiness. The first one is the long -term goal and its practice is very rigid. The second one is simple and easy to practice and maintain good health. Both these are addressed in this chapter without making much distinction.

***WHAT IS YOGA?***

*Yoga means concentration. Concentration on anything is in fact yoga. If one concentrates on a flower it is pushpa yoga; and, if one concentrates on the fragrance of the flower, it is sugandha yoga. If one concentrates on dhyan, it is called dhyana yoga. "The state in which the Mind succeeds in stilling the clamour of the sense organs and itself becomes pure, steady and still, is called Yoga". This is the inner condition that all the spiritual aspirants seek; and, some are successful to the extent of perceiving God as affirmed by Sari Krishna in Gita. "Freed from attachment, fear and anger, absorbed in Me –the One Self in all, and taking refuge in me, very many people, purified by the tapas of jnyana, or discipline of spiritual knowledge, have attained to oneness with Me". [Bhagavad Gita IV.10]*

*'Man is divine'. If divinity is inherent, the innermost core of man, the path to it lies through the withdrawal of the senses and the mind from the world of sensate experience and diverting their energies inward by a supreme effort of concentration. By such inward penetration, man achieves realization of his true nature, the non-dual, immortal, changeless and pure Atman, behind his apparent self of changeful individuality. This is the well- known Yoga technique. In Mandukya Upanishad Karika, Shri Goudapada, the Revered Guruji of Shri Shankara, has affirmed this truth. "The transcendental non-dual state, in which relative existence is overcome has been attained by sages who were free from attachment, fear and anger, and who had gone beyond the Veda".*

Hinduism has four well-defined paths to mukti, spiritual perfection.

The four paths lead to direct higher intuitive experience. These are called 'Yoga'. 'Yoga' is derived from 'Yuj', meaning join, 'to unite'; Adhyatma yoga helps to unite the microcosmic individual Consciousness with the macrocosmic or universal Consciousness. By practicing the principles of Yoga as per Bhagavan Paatanjali's 'Yoga Sutra', one can attain the highest state of Supreme Consciousness and enjoy Supreme Bliss. *Kurma Purana* gives details of Yoga. It is said that the Maha Yogi Bhagavan Paatanjali Rishi learnt Yoga at the feet of Lord Brahma and handed over these 'Yoga Sutras' to future generations with his lucid commenataries. Paatanjali's Yoga Sutra is an important source on methods of practising Yoga not only for spiritual attainment but to maintain physical and mental wellbeing, as well.

***Types of Yoga***

*There are a dozen Yoga Upanishads that explain the different types of Yoga and their benefits Some of the important ones are: Nadabindu Upanishad of Rk Veda, Shandilya Upanishad of Atharva Veda, Yogatattva, Hamsa, Yogakundali and Varaha and Amritanada Upanishads of Krishna Yajurveda, Mandala Brahma Upanishad of Shukla Yajurveda, Dhyanabindu Upanishads of Sama Veda. Each one of these is a rich storehouse of knowledge of Yoga and describe elaborately the methods and their benefits. Also strict warning is there not to practise these techniques without the guidance of a siddhi purusha, enlightened person. It is dangerous to practice Yoga without a trained teacher. Many Sadhus and Saints have take to severe yogic exervises like the Hatha Yoga, the Surya Yoga, the Sankalpa Yoga and many other 'Siddhi Yogas'. They have attained fairly good results and much occult power. Many Sadhus are using these occult powers for selfless service and have devoted their lives after spiritual attainment true to Upanishadic implorations, However, there are many unscrupulous persons in the garb of Sadhus who misuse mystic powers and cheat the ignorant people.*

*Yoga is generally beneficial from the standpoint of maintaining good health and build a strong physique at early age. It is beneficial only when it is taken to its logical end, in Meditation and Samadhi, in spiritual attainment; otherwise, it is sheer pastime*

There are different types of Yogas. But, the most important of them are: 1. Karma Yoga, 2. Kriya Yoga, 3.Bhakti Yoga, 4. Jnyana Yoga and, 5. Raja Yoga.

The preliminary preparation for advanced spiritual development or Samadhi is 'Kriya Yoga'. It involves three exercises: Austerity (Samyama), Scriptural studies (Vedaadhyayana), and Devotion to ***God (Bhakti).*** Controlling the mind and the senses, and directing their energies to higher purpose comes under austerity or tapas. There should be no place for argument in any of these practices. In Yoga, the efforts are directed to rise above the sensuate level and intellect level and to reach intuition level. Repetition or chanting of the name of Ishtadevatha and absolute submission to the Lord are important. Kriya Yoga is necessary for an aspirant of spiritual attainment.

*Karma Yoga* seems to be very simple in that one has to do his duty with total humility and offer it at the feet of the Lord. Karma Yoga does not lay down numerous 'do's' and don'ts. It seeks total involvement in one's duty. Bhakti Yoga, on the other hand, has total devotion to the Lord and there are numerous instances of Bhaktas totally merging in Him. This is indeed the most simple but the most difficult method, for it involves total submission to Him. It is total merger like Radha in Krishna. Love and sacrifice are the key- notes of Bhakti Yoga.

*Jnyana Yoga* is different from the two others- Karma yoga and Bhakti Yoga, in that it requires intellect and self- realisation. In a sense, bhakti with jnyana is the surest path to Self Realization. This is a difficult path. It requires lot of discipline in daily life, study of scriptures, study of one's own self, one's own mind, and keep good company (satsang) and always think of Him. One has to realise one's own Self and the goal in life. This is a very difficult path for most of the seekers who do not have the facilities to study and get proper guidance from spiritual teachers. Jnyana Yoga along with Bhakti yoga is the best way to realise the Self.

Of all the Yogas, i.e., the Kriya Yoga, the Karma Yoga, the Bhakti Yoga, the Jnyana Yoga and the Raja Yoga (Dhyana Yoga), the last one, the Raja Yoga is called the king of Yogas. The practice of Hatha Yoga is suggested to those who opt for Raja Yoga. [Patanjali:Yoga Sutra]. It helps to control the mind since the mind is stubborn and adamant and will not take to RajaYoga so easily.

### *Bhakti Yoga*

'Bhakti' means spontaneous and continuous attraction of the mind to God under all circumstances. No motivation is involved here and a sense of total surrender to Him with Love is observed here. Supreme devotion to Lord, Para-Bhakti is the basis of Bhakti Yoga. This surrender to Lord with Love comes from the purification of soul through renunciation and knowledge. Those who think man is just a body and has got a soul think that the sole purpose of creation is to enjoy the worldy things; even their approach to God is to obtain the worldly happiness and a heavenly life after death. They live a life of sensuousness, slaves of the senses, animal life indeed! But there are those who think that 'man is a soul and has a body'; they think otherwise. They think of obtaining the supreme bliss by renunciation. They realize that 'there is an infinite, omniscient spirit behind, that can do everything, break every bond- and that spirit we are, and we get that power through love'. Narada Bhakti Sutra is a source of the 'secrets of devotion'.

Bhakti proceeds out of a real want. Ordinarily man wants only food, clothing, wealth, sex satisfaction, acquisition of power, fulfillment of ambition, etc. When all these lower desires fall off little by little, man will begin to want God in a real sense. Materilistic demands cloud the need for God. Renunciation is involved in all types of Yogas. Giving up the desires of fruits of action is the gist of Karma Yoga. In Raja Yoga, it is the eternal separation of soul from nature and in Jnyana Yoga, it is the concept of 'Maya'or illusion, that is the sum and substance.

Universal love is evident in the perspective developed by the Yogi practicing Bhakti Yoga as also in Raja Yoga. A sense of fearlessness dawns on him; he perceives all others as creationof the Lord and sees Lord in them. He experiences no pleasure or pain and feels everything including his body belongs to Him. "Knowing that Shree Hari, the Lord is in every being, the wise have thus to manifest unswerving love towards all beings". He develops a sense of total surrender, perfect surrender, and the conviction that nothing that happens is against him. Let things come as they may. "Thy will be done". He realizes that fighting, struggling, thinking always has no meaning and the awakening of attachment of love of God effectively breaks all other bondages and he is free. The best treatise on Bhakti is 'Narada Bhakti Sutra'.

Narada Bhakti Sutra is an exhaustive treatise on Bhakti. Sutra 25 states:

***"Sa tu karma-jnyana-yogebhyopyadhikataraa".***

Meaning,"*That devotion is superior to the paths of action (karma), Knowledge (Jnyana), and Yoga (mental exercises)*". Bhakti is not merely a path to salvation but it is also the goal (of Realization). It is not something that is produced but something which is the very essence of our being. It is the goal itself; hence it is not something to be achieved. It is the love of God; it is already there.

It should be noted that, *Naarada Bhakti Sutra* 28 says that, 'devotion can be generated through knowledge only'. *Sutra* 29 says that, 'knowledge and devotion depend upon one another'. This seems to be a balanced view. Mainly, however, through the grace of the great souls or through a little grace of God, can one obtain Bhakti or devotion [*Sutra 38*].

*Narada Bhakti Sutra* gives the methods of achieving pure Bhakti. Renunciation of the objects of desire and one's attachment to objects of desire is the first pre-requisite to obtaining Bhakti or devotion. The second requirement is undivided devotion to the Lord; and the third requirement is the continuous remembrance of God. Even when one is pre-occupied with various activities one should remain engaged in chanting, hearing and singing the glory of the Lord. This will keep the mind engaged in the thought of God; but mainly one attains devotion through a little Grace of The Lord Himself, or the Saints and Seers. Bhagavad Gita proclaims that the Lord takes full care of those who completely surrender and erase their ego in the sharanagati (surrender) of pure bhakti.

*"Ananyaschintayanto maam, ye janah paryupasate;*
*Tesam nityabhiyuktanam yogakshemam vahamyaham"*

Meaning, "*Persons who meditate on me in a state of oneness with me, who worship me, who are constantly in a state of yoga, I carry what they lack and preserve what they already have, and thus fulfil all their desire*" [*Bhagavad-Gita*, 9.22].

Practice of Bhakti Yoga is as difficult as Jnyana Yoga, or for that matter, even the Karma Yoga or the Kriya toga are not very easy. Of course, nothing is easy in the process of Self-realisation. Purity of thought, purity of mind and total surrender to Lord are difficult to come to mortals who are after sensuous life and who are always body-conscious. It is very interesting to quote Sri Ramakrishna here: 'the whole world is a lunatic asylum. Some are mad after worldly love, some after name, some after fame, some after money, some after salvation and going to heaven. In this big lunatic asylum, I am also mad- I am mad after God; my madness is after all the best" said Sri Ramakrishna.

"*We all begin as dualists in the religion of love. God is to us a separate 'Being'. Love comes between in the middle and man begins to approach God and God also comes nearer and nearer to man in the form of mother, father, son, friend, master and lover……, and the last point of progress is reached when the devotee feels that he has become absolutely merged in the object of his worship*". In the discipline of Bhakti, the practice of renunciation consists not in destroying any of man's affections, but in giving them a godward turn.

So, the teachers of Bhakti have taught how to channelise human affections into forms of God-love known as 'Bhavas" These Bhavas are: 1.Santa Bhava (placid or philosophical without any human element in it), 2. Dasya Bahava (attitude of a servant), 3. Apatya (attitude of a son to a father), 4. Sakhya (friendly or mitra bhava), 5.Vatsalya (parently affection towards children), 6.Madhura Bhava or sweetness that can take the form of conjugal love, or a lover's affection to one's sweet heart. In the highest state of Para-Bhakti the lover loses himself in the Beloved and attains to the state of non-duality. And, thus the highest form of knowledge and the highest from of Bhakti are one and the same in the end, though they may appear to be different at the initial disciplinary stage. Love and knowledge are thus the obverse and the reverse of the same coin even as are the personal God, Ishtadevatha and the Para Brahman.

Body consciousness is too strong in ordinary men and this constitutes a hurdle in the path of knowledge. For those who pursue the path of worship of personal God, it is easy to offer all their actions and surrender to Him and live in entire reliance on Him. Unlike in Jnyana Yoga where there is the danger of self-deception, Bhakti Yoga is natural, sweet and gentle.

Shuddha (Reverence), preeti and longing of the soul, surrender to Lord and feeling the meaningless-ness of life without Him, and a sense of belonging to Him are the essentials of Bhakti Yoga. Universal love characterizes the Bhakti Yoga.The true Bhakta does not care for the philosophical details. He goes beyond these turbulent and hazy regions of reason to the calmness and clarity of realization. He no more reasons and believes, he almost perceives. Bhaktas even maintain that serving God in truth and in spirit is higher than even moksha. This kind of whole-hearetd devotion to God is also of the highest utility.

However, there are a large number of people who do not care for Bhakti or concede that it is of the highest value. Such people have to go through many more births and re-incarnation to learn to feel even the faintest necessity for anything higher than just eating, drinking and engaging in sexual pursuits.

***Jnyana Yoga***

Jnyana Yoga is for the discriminative mind. It is impossible for an ordinary person with little learning to dwell at length the Vedanta philosophy. It is through intellectual discerning that one can realize the ultimate reality and any ne who wants to understand this mysterious world shall have to understand the basics of 'Maya'. In Svetasvatara Upanishad, the word 'Maya' appears with Nature. It says, "Know Nature to be Maya and the Ruler of Maya to be the Lord Himself". 'Maya' is not illusoriness of the world as commonly believed.

In the *Rig Veda*, it is said that, "Indra, through his Maya, assumed various forms". Here, it is the 'magical' spell that is '*Maya*'. This is the earliest one can find about Maya. In a sense, it is the 'make-believe' world that is 'Maya' and it is not 'illusory world'. The word 'illusion' came with the Buddhist interpretation; a section of the Buddhist Vijnyana-vadins maintained that 'ideas alone are there, not the external objects corresponding to them'. They considered the experience of the world outside as Maya, illusory perception, the ideas alone being real. However, for the sake of convenience, the word illusion is used in the text.

As Swami Vivekananda puts it, 'Vedanta in its fully developed form is neither idealism nor realism, nor is it a theory. It is simply a statement of fact; it is a statement of what we are and what we see around us'. External Nature that we perceive is very real to us and we try to explain it in very rational, very scientific way, as the ultimate truth. Unfortunately, it is not so. First, the Veadanta points out that, 'our investigation of Nature is limited by our mind and its associated faculties, the senses'. Second, mind is limited by space, time, and causation. Third, the world that we actually experience exists only in relation to the minds that experience as such. In a way, there are as many worlds as there are minds; and each Purusha has a mind. Another important thing is that our experience is also limited due to the limited capacity of the faculties endowed to us. If we had more sense organs, or tools as such, to perceive or experience this world, we would see the world in a different way. Thus, the world experienced externally has therefore no unchangeable and ultimate existence. But, it cannot be called non-existent, because it is experienced.

This world is full of contradictions. We feel 'it is' there and at the same time 'it is not' there. We do not know anything about this universe. Also, we cannot say we do not know. We stand between knowledge and ignorance, light and darkness (twilight), this mingling of truth and falsehood. It is as if we are walking in dream, half asleep and half awake. We do not know what is the reality. We try to explain it all in a very rational and scientific way; we are going in circle coming back to the same starting point. What we call matter, spirit, space, time, or mind, or anything for that matter, the fact remains the same that, 'they are', and 'they are not'. This external play of light and darkness, indiscriminate, indistinguishable, inseparable is always there. This is a statement of fact. This is what is called Maya. We are born in Maya, we live in Maya and we think and dream in it. This is the work of 'nama' (name) and 'roopa' (form). Everything that is bound by laws of space and time and causation is within *Maya*. The whole of human knowledge is generalization of ***Maya***, even if you call it infinite knowledge, for it comes within Maya. It is a contradictory, incomprehensible nature of the world refered to as '***Maya***'.

If one realizes this simple truth, that this world is all 'Maya', a make-believe' world and nothing is permanent in it, the whole attitude of man, his way of life, his way of thinking, his acquisitive nature, his selfish motive, his mindless actions, stress and tension, his miseries, ailments - physical and mental, all disappear in a matter of moment. Here is a warning! This does not mean that we can be indolent and need not work; this does not mean that we need not strive for the upliftment of the other less fortunate brethren. On the contrary, we have to work harder and strive much better for the welfare of others.

But, there are people who do not believe in all these; they are the agnostics. They say that, we are living in a in-comprehensible, irremediable world, let us take for what it is worth and enjoy it without any thought of the ultimate nature of things. This is the 'Theory of Nature' and accepting it we become slaves of Nature. Our intellect does not permit it; our ego prevents it. Man can rise above Nature and get out of its irremediable contradictions. He can be free.

In Jnyaana Yoga, the fundamental question is about the existence of the Absolute. The Absolute does exist for all practical purpose for without such existence the manifestations of the Absolute become unrealistic. But it is this unrealistic existence of the Absolute that we are discussing in JnyaanaYoga. That which does not exist for all practical purposes cannot give rise to that which exists for all practical purposes. This 'Jnyaana Yoga', on the other hand, is exactly trying to make us realize the Reality of the fact that nothing existed in this universe prior to origin of the first universe! If at all anything existed, it is that 'nothing' which we cannot see, hear or touch or feel, like the oil in the sesame seed and the plan of the huge Banyan tree in the tiny Banyan seed, or for that matter, the hollow part of the heart in our body where the Lord really resides!

*The Absolute and the Relative*

*Jnyaan and Bhakti are interrelated; Jnyaan brings bhakti with it only. That is perfect knowledge. Mere Bhakti willnot bring 'fulfilment'; Bhaki without Jnyaan is blind faith. It may take you nearer to God because of total devotion, but will not make you one with Him. In other words, Salokya is possible with Bhakti whereas Sayujya is possible only with Jnyaan. In order to understand these delicate, intricate, spiritual aspects, one has to have a clear understanding of the Relative and the Absolute, i.e., the material and the spiritual aspects of this whole exercise.*

*It is very essential to have a clear idea about the concept of the 'Absoluite' and the 'Relative' in Jnyaana Yoga since merging in the Absolute (Sayujya) is the aim of Jnyan Yoga. Brahman is the Absiluite and all else is Relative. Duality starts with the 'Relative' and the entire cosmos is one of duality, light and darkness; it exists now and here and it is no more; it is dynamic, ever changing, and unreal.* There is a whole lot of discussion regarding the idea of the evolution of the universe. Origin of the universe is explained away by a ***'Sphota' or 'Big Bang'*** and the consequent processes produced the space, time, etc. This leads to the idea that something existed even before the evolution of space and time and that must be something beyond what we call the universe of energy and matter. It is called simply 'That' for we do not know what it is. It is the Absolute and final, the '***Infinitude***'.

Whatever we call absolute is 'the Absolute' and cannot exist or manifest through time, space and causality. 'Absolute' stands on one side and the manifesting medium on the other. There cannot be two independednt existences, without each limiting the other, according to Advaitins. This destroys the very concept of Advaita. It can be only One without a second (Ekameva-adviteeyam!). So, time, space and causation cannot have an independent status even when these three are taken together as a unified category. In their very nature also these three are found to have no existence in them-selves, but in a relative sense only. Time is dependent on our state of mind. In sleep it vanishes; in dream its standard varies. Besides time cannot be thought of in abstraction. It can be experienced only in relation to two events. So also space can be thought of only as within limits, or coloured or occupied by something. As for causation, it is felt only in relation to two events in succession and it is therefore dependent on space and time. So, extraneously, these can be conceived only as a kind of existence dependent on the Absolute, and intrinsically, as mutually interdependent in existence. They are shadows around everything without substantiality. They have no real existence, but yet are non-existent, seeing that through them all things are manifesting as the universe.

Now the scientists have understood how the sub-microspcopic particles move in a state of inter-action creating and destroying particles. Thus, energy becomes matter and vice versa. One is driven to understand that space existed for the particles to evolve and move somewhere. All these lead to confusion. The idea put forth by the Advaitins try to solve this riddle by assuming that the Absolute is without the second (Ekameva adviteeyam); and all the duality, relative existence, interdependence, could be explained as the 'Lord's Will'. That is how the Biblical statement that, "the Lord said,'Let there be Light, and there was Light' came to be well known or assumed importance. Here, the 'Lord's Will' is also to be taken as a product of meditation, or Tapas. 'Tapa' means heat generated by concentration and one should meditate or contemplate on a mahat tattva till enough heat is generated to unite all in one, i.e., the knower, the knowledge and the seeker become one. It is like welding the seeker with the Lord to become the 'Seer' ('Rishi').

Here, again, there is some objection to the use of the concept of 'Will'. The idea of equating the 'Will' with the Absolute (Schopenhauer) and speaking of the 'Will' as this cause of the universe causes confusion. Will is something changeable. It is also the fact that, 'Will' manifests in consciousness and is thus a secondary product; it cannot come before time, space and causation. It cannot be equated with the Absolute. Hence, the question of 'how' and 'why' the Absolute has become the finite world of plurality has never been explained satisfactorily. The ancient Seers have maintained that the Absolute is unknown and is unknowable. This is explained in the Vedantic way as –"the 'Absolute' or 'God' is more intimate than objects and it is only through Him we perceive this world. He is the witness, the witness of all knowledge. Whatever we know, we have to know in and through Him". He is the essence of our own Self, of our ego, this 'I', and we cannot know anything except in and through that 'I'. He is nearer to us than our own limbs; He is infinitely nearer to us, yet He is infinitely higher. He is neither known nor unknown, but infinitely higher than either. In and through Him we breathe, in and through Him we exist. He is the essence of all this, the soul of my soul.

"*He that is the Essence of your soul, He is the self. He is the truth.* And, '***Thou art that***', O Svetaketu!"

He is the eternal Subject and it is this we often refere to as 'I', ignorantly attributing the "I" to the physical degenerating, decaying physical body, ever-changing mind, and the ever moving prana. He is our real Self.

Nothing exists, moves, inter-acts, without 'His Grace'. This is the sum and substance of Jnyana Yoga. This has to be contemplated upon. A number of manthras, statements, mahat tattvas, are given at the end of the book to think over, contemplate and chant, that help to realize the Self. This is for Dhyan, Contemplation and Meditation.

Pathanjali's *Yoga Sutra* is a treatise on 'Yogas' and his '*Eight Steps to Supreme Bliss*' is very popular. He has laid down certain ethical rules to be followed in the pursuit of spiritual life. Each system is suited to different types of persons and one can select any of these paths to attain Super Consciousness. There is nothing to prove that one system is superior to the other since all these help us to reach the same goal. Since Jnyan and Bhakti are indispensable, Raja Yoga is described in detail here.

***Raja Yoga (Dhyana Yoga)***

*Raja Yoga is called the 'Dhyana Yoga' since it involves Mind and it is the Yoga of Meditation. It involves awakened intelligence, or developing Buddhi. Dhi stands for Buddhi in Veda, and its power of truth perception. It gives us enormous power to understand the universe and the human being as integral unfoldments of cosmic intelligence. This higher intelligence arises through the energisation of speech and Prana and brings an extraordinary transformative power into the deepest level of the Mind. In Dhyana Yoga the light of truth floods the Mind and we come to know the unitary nature of all reality.*

*Dhyana Yoga as depicted in the Vedic Yoga is slightly different from Patanjali's Ashtanga Yoga Sutra. Dhyana Yoga of Vedic Yoga does include thepreliminary requirements like yama, niyama, prathyahara, but not as separate limbs of Yoga. Even Asana and Pranayama constitute an integral part of Dhyana Yoga, but not as separate limbs as in Ashtanga Yoga. Vedic Dhyana Yoga includes Dharana, Dhyana, and Samadhi, concentration, meditation and realization of Raja Yoga that are three aspects of merging the Mind into the Divine Self.*

*For Dhyana Yoga, the expanse of the Sun or 'truth- consciousness' must be created. One must contact the Divine Self or Paramatman within the heart. We should meditate on the Prana- energized Mantra and use them to move deeper into higherstates of consciousness. The space of light or light of space must be opened for the realization process to continue. Meditate on Indra, Agni, Soma and surya; Gayathri mantra is highly suited for this purpose. It will make our inner light glow and make us literally shine for shining is one of the attriburtes of the Brahman. The spark is already there within us. It has to be kindled by Tapas, concentration, meditation, dhyan with pure heart and mind.*

Paatanjali's Raja Yoga has eight steps to attain Supreme Consciousness. Hence, it is called the Ashtanga Yoga. The eight steps are: 1.Yama; 2. Niyama; 3.Asana; 4. Pranayama;5. Prathyahara; 6. Dharana; 7. Dhyana; or Meditation; and, 8. Samaadhi, or Superconsciousness.

A good book on Yoga is by Veda Brahma Shri S.Chaturvedi. Sudhakara Chaturvedi, now 111, a bachelor, an expert on Yoga, a Vedic scholar and a close Associate of Mahatma Gandhi and, incidentally, it is he who gave Gandhiji the prefix of Mahatma. Shri Chturvedi is a living legend. He has edited a number of books (20 Volumes on Veda), - 'Rk Veda' in 11 Volumes and Sama Veda in 2 Volumes. His book '***Yoga Pradeepa***' ***(in Kannada)*** is an excellent Treatise on Yoga. It is authoritative, written in a very lucid language, simple style, and easy to understand.

According to Yoga Sutra, there are eight steps to Samaadhi. The first two steps, i.e., Yama and Niyama are the ethical rules. Yama consists of five disciplines that are to be strictly practiced by all people at all times. Yama consists of: i. Ahimsa, ii. Continence (Brahmacharya), iii. Satya (truth), iv. Asteya (non-stealing), and , v. Aparigraha. In aparigraha, one should not even accept gifts; if it is inevitable, some thing in return should be given, may be it is some sort of service, if not in kind.

The terms, 'ahimsa' covers all aspects of piety, compassion and fellow-feeling for all the creatures of the world; one should not injure, or even think of hurting the feelings of the fellow-beings kaaya, vaacha, manasa and indriyas- i.e., in body, mind, words, thoughts, and deeds. Similarly, continence is such a difficult exercise. At the out set, it seems impossible for ordinary mortals to practice it. One should abstain from sex even with one's own wife after begetting one child or two children; the couple should live like brother and sister for the purpose of sex is only for procreation and not for sport and self- indulgence. Since sexual activity is dwelling at lower plane involving not much of energy, one is easily aroused in sexual thoughts and activity at the least instigation of the mind or fantasies of the mind.

Yoga demands diversion of sexual energies towards higher planes for, spiritual practices demand higher energy. Energy should not be dissipated in illusory fascinations and tantalizing dreams initiated by hidden desires. Concentration is affected by attractions of forms and figures, fascinations and wishful dreams. It is the confirmed fact according to the realized souls that continence gives enormous strength to practice japa, tapa, dharana or dhyana, and meditation. Since abstinence of sex gives a superior happiness all spiritual seekers should abstain from sexual thoughts, avoid company of opposite sex and lead a very pure life. Total purity of inner body, senses, mind and heart is the basic foundation of spiritual life.

The two other ethical rules viz, Satya and Asteya are also very difficult to practice in ordinary day- to- day life. Not only one should not indulge in untruth, one should not even abate or support others to think of, or speak 'asat' or lies. Asteya means not only coveting what rightly belongs to others, but also gaining anything by unfair means. So also, Aparigraha; here it is very difficult to practice self-less life. One should give away every thing that one does not need in spiritual way of life. Attachment is the greatest stumbling block in spiritual exercises.

The second ethical principle of Niyama consists of:

i. *Shoucka*, purity of both body and mind: Discipline in life is the first requisite for a happy and successful life. Many people do not consider the importance of physical and mental purity and, thus indulge in sensuous life without care. The spread of Aids and such other dreadful diseases is alarming. If laziness is the cause of neglect of physical cleanliness, it is also true that a sense of happiness is derived from abandoning all routine duties like taking bath, prayer and meditation; this is the result of the prepondering tamasic guna of the person. But, the end result is diseases, illness of both body and mind.

ii. *Santhosha* or contentment: Some people are in the habbit of complaining about everything. Since there is no harmony within, there is discontent everywhere for such people. They complain about their environment, about their surroundings, about their social circle. They also make it an excuse to abandon the spiritual exercises. Contentment with oneself, with what one has got, and santhosha in daily life is very important. It is the frame of the mind, the attitude and mental disposition that decides about the ultimate happiness; all mental energies should be directed towards dhyana, meditation and tapas in order get the full result.

iii. *Tapas*: 'Tapa' is heat. When the physical and mental energies are directed towards understanding the Self, the body gets heated. This heat is the 'unifying' factor. It brings harmony. It removes all dirt; virtually it burns away all mental rubbish. When the body and mind is thus cleaned, it is ready for receiving the Divine Light. It is an essential part of the yoga. It facilitates easy flow, an unobstructed flow of energies. Nerves are cleansed by tapas. All the nadis and the nerves should be cleansed by strict yogic practices. Shuddha Ahara or proper sattvic diet, and shudhdha vichara or good thoughts are important in tapas. Food here stands for food not only for the body but also for the senses. All the senses should be brought under control and should be fed only by pure thoughts, divine thoughts.

iv. *Svaadhyaya*: The Upanishads says 'Shrotvyaha manthravyaaha', meaning, 'you hear or read and then reflect on what you have heard or read'. Making our own what we have heard or read is 'Svaadhyaaya'. Study of Veda and Upanishads, as well as sacred works like Bhagavad Gita, Bible, Khoran, Bhagavata, Puranas, and even works on Budhdha, Mahavira, Confucious, Tao, are all very important. Study of one's own mind is much more Important than all these scriptures; it helps to dwell deep within oneself. Study of scriptures, sacred books and one's own mind is stressed in Svaadhyaya.

v. '*Isvara pranidhanam*' is Ishta Devata Sharanagatim and Dhyana. Self-surrender or offering all deeds to the Almighty is stressed by Sri Vyasamuni. It removes '*egotism*'. Surrender your body, mind, and soul to Him and the Lord takes care of you.

Thus, ethical culture is conditional in spiritual exercises. One should live a very pure and simple life. Purity is necessary for calming the mind. Only a pure mind can think of God in an unbroken stream. Upanishad says, "***We must meditate on Brahman with a calm mind***". [*Chhaandogya Upanishad* 3.14.1; and Katha Upanishad, 1.2.24 ]

Prayer is a very important step in spirituality. One must pray for the welfare of others for it expands one's mind and consciousness. Prayer done with concentration will do well to others; one must pray for those who are in trouble. One gets nearer to God in prayer.

Just as the physical homeostasis developed and perfected by nature through the process of evolution, there is the mental homeostasis that is the mechanism of mind control through Sama and Dama; and, that helps to still the mind and the senses at the command of the Yogi. In fact, physical homeostasis is the mechanism of a built-in-equilibrium, thermostatic to begin with and homeostatic later, within the organism itself. It enabled the person to be free from botheration of control of the internal organs and released him to use the brain to other more important spiritual tasks, particularly Meditation. It is a necessary condition to forge ahead to higher and higher evolutionary scales. Man has to achieve for himself, by himself, through the organic capacities which nature has endowed him with, says Vedanta, a mental homeostasis (Yoga). The whole purpose here is to realize the 'Atman' behind the Mind.

***Asana***

*'Asana', the sitting postures for Yoga are many and varied. Different asanas are preferred to achieve different objectives or sidhdhi. For purposes of simple meditation, a cross-legged sitting posture known as 'Padmasana (Lotus-posture) is very popular. For purposes of Praanayaama, Vajraasana is preferable. There are also the sukhasana (any comfortable posture), the Veeraasana, etc. These asanas are used for limited purpose of meditation, japam and Samaadhi. But, the more complicated ones areadvocated toachieve mystic powers like clairvoyance, omnipresence, mind or thought reading, parakaaya pravesh (entering other's body) etc. These asanas help to direct the vital breath to certain part of the body and retain there for the stipulated time so as to energise that particular portion achieving the desired results. Praanayaama is associated with the asana in all these yogicpsycho-physical exercises.*

*B.K.S. Iyengar of Bangalore is an internationally known Yoga expert who had an audience with Pope Paul at the Vatican City. He has demonstrated the various asanas and explained the utility of yogic postures in different parts of the world. He is an authority on Yoga. According to Iyengar, "There are gradations in asanas, starting from the gross, crude method and you have to refine it by regular sadhana or practice. The refined stage is the point where the various aspects of the consciousness are made to unite into a single entity. You will reach the epi-center of Consciousness, the source of Consciousness where there is no feeling of the past or future. Though time is linked with the future, the mind, the consciousness- everything remains in the state of the present. That is the highest practice of asana."*

*In a perfect yogic posture, one exists in the present, in his' Being', in his Self and that is the sole purpose of Yoga In course of time. Through regular practice of yoga, one attains siddhi, the light of 'Jnyaan' or KNOWLEDGE, the enlightenment. The entire exercise that started with the asanas, physical postures, controlling the vital breaths through different organs gradually turns to the Mind through dharana and meditation, and finally ends in a tranquil state, absolute Silence, at the epi-center of consciousness, the Atma or Soul. In a sense, there is hierarchy of yogic exercise- train the body first and concentrate on asanas, taking to dharana, meditation and samaadhi, i.e, from what one sees and feels to the sense of perception, to mind, to intelligence,to ego, and finally to the Consciousness and Atma.*

*Badarayana's Brahma Sutra* [4-1-7] lays down the rule that 'worship is possible in a sitting posture'. But, care must be taken to see that the sitting position is firm, relaxed in body and mind, and suitable for meditation. The right position, or asana for meditation is 'Padmaasana', sitting cross-legged with the body, neck and head straight allowing free circulation of blood.

Asana or body posture in sitting for prayer, upasana, dhyana or meditation is very important for it will guard against wrong postures that may hurt. Long hours of sitting may strain the back and cause back pain. Almost all the yoga experts stress 'padmasana' for a comfortable sitting posture. But, for some people even this is difficult. Ultimately, it is suggested by some yoga experts, that any convenient position that is comfortable may be adopted for the purpose of simple dhyana with 'namasmarane'.

The practice of Asanas is elaborately dealt in 'Hata Yoga'. Hata Yoga is mainly concerned with the maintenance of health and attainment of longevity of the body. But it is cautioned here that too much of attention to the body might nullify the efforts towards the ultimate goal. One may end up in perfecting 'yogasanas' for body fitness neglecting the spiritual exercises.

Shandilya Upanishad gives eight types of Asanas viz, svastika, gomukha, padma, vira, simha, bhadra, mukta, and mayura. These asanas should be practiced under the guidance of a trained Yogacharya.

*It should be warned here that the yogasanas must be learnt under a trained yoga teacher only. Yogasanas are normally taught and practised for better health and build of physique in Vyayamashalas or Yoga Schools and Yoga camps. For all spiritual practices, any simple padmasana or virasana is enough. Vajrasana is suitable for Pranayama. Always take the advice of a trained teacher before attempting the asanas. Persons with heart problems should not attempt certain asanas. There are possibilities of damage to brain, cerebral haemorrhage, nose bleeding, and split of nerves when yogasanas are attempted with out guidance. Many have lost eyesight due to wrong postures of Shirasasana. Almost all the experts agree that any comfortable asana that will enable easy blood flow and allow nerve currents to pass will do; the body, neck, and the head should be straight and sitting must be comfortable throughout the period of Meditation.*

***Pranayama***

*Pranayama, i.e., controlling the flow of vital breaths*, is the means for establishing control over the nerves and muscles involved in breathing, and through that control, over all the finer movements of the Prana in the body. The ultimate purpose of 'Pranayama' is to arouse Kundalini, the one and the only way to attain Divine wisdom, superconscious perception-realization of the spirit. This may come through the love of God, through the mercy of a spiritual leader or saint, or merely through analytical will of the thinker. When by the power of long meditation the vast mass of energy stored up travels along the Sushumna, - and strikes the centres, the reaction is tremendous, immensely superior to the reaction of dream or imagination, or even more intense than the reaction of even sense perception. It is supersensuous perception. When this energy reaches the head, the 'Sahasrara Chakra', a thousand-petalled Lotus, the whole brain reacts, and the result is full blaze of *illumination*, the perception of the Self. This is the result of rousing the Kundalini by Pranayama.

The purpose of selecting a suitable sitting posture or 'asana' is to perform dhyana (meditation) comfortably. In the course of meditation, the body, the neck and the head should be in a straight line so as to allow an easy and free flow of blood. It will be dangerous to sit in a curved position. 'Pranayama' is performed for purification of nerves.

Pranayama is the control of universal energy, the prana. Breath control is a method of achieving the optimum flow of this energy in the body. It helps in cleansing the nerves that carry energy to different parts of the body.

Pranayama should be learnt under an expert teacher. Although it seems very simple at the outset it should be started under guidance only. Stomach and the diaphram should be strong enough to hold the air that is powerfully driven in and out while inhaling and breathing out, respectively.

Shri Sudhakar Chaturvedi has described the various types of 'Yogasanas and Pranayama Techniques' in 'Yoga Pradeepa'. [Vaidika Prakashana Samithi, Udupi]

There are several exercises in Pranayama, and, at least eight are important and three are commonly practiced. ***These should be practiced under expert advice only***.

The first method is very simple and can be performed by any person without much difficulty and any danger. Sit straight in a comfortable position in a secluded place and breath in and breath out in a measured way uttering 'OM' in the process. Deep Breathing should be done with awareness, unlike it is normally done, and the breath is not held in. By doing this several times, four or five times, the mind and body becomes calm, restful and rhythmic.

The second exercise may be started after one has practiced the first exercise regularly for some days.

Press the right nostril with the thumb and breath in by the left nostril for 4 seconds retain it in lungs for sixteen seconds, and breath out through the right nostril for eight seconds. Imagine that you are drawing in energy through the Ida and sending the nerve current down the spinal column and striking forcibly on the 'Muladhara', the seat of Kundalini. Holding the current there for a while, then breath out slowly through the right nostril, the Pingala. Next, do it in the reverse manner. Again, close the left nostril (Ida) and breath in for 4 seconds retain breath for 16 seconds and breath out for 8 seconds. Repeat this procedure four times or for five minutes twice a day. This is called '***Sukha Pranayama***'. Physical and moral fitness must be ensured before embarking on Pranayama for rousing the Kundalini. It is risky for people who are not fit for it. It may cause insanity.

There is another very simple method. It is breathing in from one nostril and breathing out by the other nostril alternately. Thumb is used to press one nostril at a time while breathing in and out leaving no gap in time. These exercises should be performed early in the morning and late in the evening in a cool secluded place. It can be performed at mid-day and mid-night also for better results. 'Pranayama' helps to purify nerves in about two weeks. It is suggested that Japa, or 'Shree Hari Nama-smarane' (chanting the Lord's name) also should be simultaneously performed with pranayama for better results. But it must always be remembered here that mere Pranayama and Yogasanas are mere physical exercises; these will nothelp to make any spiritual progress unless meditation too, goes hand in hand.

Pranayama, as the name suggests, is controlling 'Prana'. Prana is the life-sustaining force. Pranayama helps in purifying the nerves, the carriers of energy in the body. Although 'Prana' exists everywhere, it cannot be perceived. It exists in the akasha. Akasha is the ultimate basic stuff out of which all the gross forms, from atoms to galaxies, from microscopic cells to the perfected human and divine bodies, take shape and in to which they resolve when they are dissolved or disintegrated to the pristine condition. Prana and Akasha are the two ultimate entities of the manifested universe. What works upon the Akasha and shapes it into all forms or manifestations is called 'Prana'.

Prana is the all- inclusive basic energy into which all forms of energy known to us as manifesting in matter and mind are reduced at the end of the cycle. It is Prana vibrating at the beginning of the cycle that shapes Akasha, the basic condition of matter, into a new universe of diverse forms of and states of subtlety. Out of 'Prana' is evolved all forms of energy, physical or mental. Thus, all physical forces like motion, electricity, magnetism, etc. are the expressions of 'Prana'. Thus, the sum total of all forces in the universe, physical or mental, when resolved back to their original state, is 'Prana' and the knowledge and control of this 'Prana' is Pranayama.

Thus, it is also clear that the quantum of Prana working our mind and body is the nearest to us of all the waves of the infinite ocean of Prana. Any person is capable of establishing control over the quantum of Prana constituting his being, will be able to establish a kind of mastery over 'Prana'. Such a Yogi will be in touch of the Whole, as the whole universe is one mass of 'Prana' and 'Akasha'.

Benefits of Pranayama are many and varied. By the control of Prana one can achieve such power that can cure dreadful diseases; faith cure or Reki is one such. Prana has the power of bringing it into a certain state of vibration that can be conveyed to others, arousing in them a similar vibration. It is also the secret of power of great men over others. The power to control the inner organs, when perfected, can heal up any diseased part of the body as also cure others. But, this requires enormous spiritual practice such as Meditation, japa, and dhyan. One must constantly keep practicing these exercises. More about this can be had from Raja Yoga.

If a country is great and can sway its power over others, it is because of the immense will-power of its leaders. The leaders of great countries have such will -power, that they can bring their Prana into a high state of vibration, and it is so great and powerful that it catches others in a moment, and thousands are drawn towards them, and half the world thinks as they do. It is also true of the Great Saints and Prophets whose teachings catch the world over; they had brought their Prana to the highest state of motion, and this is what gave them power to sway the world. All manifestations of power arise from this control.

Manipulation of the power of 'Prana' is very much evident in spirituality. The universe perceived by our senses is the manifestation of Akasha by the vibration of Prana at a certain intensity, wavelength. We are all in a state of vibration at certain wave- lengths. There are innumerable other universes like ours operating at different vibrations of Prana in Akasha; only their degree of intensity of vibration they represent is different. If a Yogi can change the vibration of his mind and attune himself to any of these vibrations representing any of the spheres, he can become aware of those spheres while simultaneously becoming shut off from his earthly contacts. All these kinds of supra-conscious experiences come under Samadhi. The highest grade of Samadhi is when we realise that substance out of which all these vibrations and beings representing them have come. The methods adopted for controlling the manifestation of 'Prana' as vital and mental force, through psychical means, is the Raja Yoga.

One of the most important prerequisites of Pranayama is contenence, or strict avoidence of sex, i.e., Brahmacharya. This is advocated for householders as well, since it is the basis of Pranayama. The semen ejected in sexual intercourse is a loss of energy, which would otherwise become 'Ojas' more useful for rousing Kundalini. It is the semen or 'veerya' that is converted into 'ojas' (psychic energy) that brings in turn 'tejas'. By channelising the creative force, the psychic energy or vital energy, through Sushumna to Sahasraara that one gains access to the hidden powers of the brain. If semen (dhatu) is wasted in masturbation by youth, they will lose concentration and, physical and mental strength; their spiritual exercises will be futile. So also, indulgence in sex, either in thought or action, by householder is detrimental to spiritual practices. Just like an escalator in a shopping Mall will take us to the various Departments located at the higher and higher levels or floors, this control over the Mind and conserved sexual energy will take us to higher and higher levels of Consciousness.

Vatsayana's Kama Sutra clearly lays down the principles of sexual practices as far as it helps Self Realisation. It is approved for procreation up to two children and none thereafter. First is the dharma putra/putri and the rest are all results of 'kama', lust. It is advocated that sexual indulgence is avoided at all cost and this can be achieved by raising oneself to higher planes of spiritual life. Reaching Kundalini to heart level and staying there will help in controlling sexual thoughts and action. The extreme step of abstaining from sex in youthful stage is neither possible nor advised. The very purpose of birth on this earth is fulfillment of desires. And, sex is one of the most powerful basic needs like thirst and hunger. After one has fully experienced this basic urge, he should develop detachment. That is real 'Prathyaahaara'.

Some uphold the view that there is a fourth aspect in the study of life of Man. Body, mind, and soul are the three aspects with which we are familiar. The fourth is the 'energy-flow' aspect. This is also the 'life-force'. This flow is in the form of sex-energy. There is a very interesting account of the Brahman appearing in the form of Yaksha to teach a lesson to the proud Devas, particularly Agni and Vayu, for the elated behaviour. The Devas were proud and boasted of their powers and took all the credit of retrieving Amrit from the churning of the ocean. When Brahman appeared as Yaksha, Indra and others could not recognize him. Indra sent Agni to find out who it was. When Agni appeared before Yaksha (Brahman) and proudly identified himself as Jataveda; Brahman placed a piece straw and asked Agni to burn it. Agni used all his powers to burn it and failed; he returned humiliated to Indra and said he could not know that adorable Spirit. Then, Indra sent Vayu. Vayu approached Brahman and faced the same problem; The Indomitable Brhaman placed a piece of grass and asked Vayu to move it. Vayu used all his force but could not move the straw a bit and returned humiliated. Indra personally came to test the Yaksha and found instead a beautiful lady, Uma, the daughter of the snow-clad Himavat.

Both Agni and Vayu are the deities of the Indriyas, eyes and ears, respectively; and Indra is the Lord of Mind under whose control the indriyas function. Indra, the mind (ignorance), cannot function in the face of Buddhi or intellect or the Light of the Self. Mind is only matter and gets burnt under the fire of the Supreme Consciousness. But, who is this beautiful Uma, daughter of Himavat? In Himavat, Hima stands for cold. Woman stands for prakriti. Beauty stands for the captivating force of the Prakruti. Woman stands for Sex. Thus, 'Indra seeing beautiful Uma' stands for 'the Mind coming under the grip of the captivating sex'. Sex is the over-powering and dominating force captivating the senses.

Sex is a powerful instinct. It exercises a captivating force and governs the life of humans throughout life. The sexual energy is the mainstay of life. If the sexual energy ceases, the life of the person ceases. A pèrson will become aware of his/her sex very early in life, say by about a year or so after birth, and continues to be aware of it till ripe old age. This sexual energy has been the central idea of the works of Sigmund Freud. He went to the extreme of identifying sex as the center of study of man. But, one cannot deny the fact that for most part of life, sex energy controls the life and activity of man. Much remains to be done in the field of sexual energy, although the ancient Seers laid much stress on strict adherence to contenance, Brahmacharya. Some of the great Sages were called 'urdhvaretasa' one who attained the power of directing the dhatu or semen higher and higher towards the Sahasraara plexus (chakra) in the head. Such was their firm determination to withdraw their mind from sex.

***Prana and Mind***

Prana is one of the ingredients of the living beings. It is accompanied by Consciousness, Intelligence, Mind and Awareness (Sakshi). Thought is the highest expression of Prana. Its expression is three-fold. First, there is instinct, which may be called conscious thought. At a higher level is reason in which thought is a conscious and well- regulated effort. But the circle within which it runs is very limited.'That', ' *that is beyond*', can be grasped by super-conscious, or Samadhi. All manifestations of the subtle forces of the body, which are different manifestations of Prana, give a push to the mind to assume vibrations that reveal facts at subtle level of existence. The whole universe is one unbroken mass of matter in flux beaten into different states of vibrations by the Prana. The Sun, the Moon, the Man, the plant, the animal, the mineral, the atom are all mere points of this one huge mass, *the Mahat.* When the action of Prana on Akasha is most subtle, it is called Mind. Mind is also one unbroken continuum. If one gets into the subtle vibration through the regulation of Prana within oneself, then that whole universe is seen as composed of subtle vibrations of thought. ***Samadhi*** brings the individual's mind to those vibrations that enable it to apprehend the facts of these subtle levels of existence.

Prana is generally, but often loosely, translated as 'vital-breath', the life force, or the vital force. The term is applied to both transcendental Principle- the subtle cause, as well as to its effects, the forces moving to activity the organs- physical and mental [*Brahmopansihad* 2].

In *Prashnopanishad*, Pippalada unfolds the whole philosophy of this Prana. Prana is espressly identified with the Atman; it is not just the manifested aspect of the Atman. The manifested aspect, Prana, is in reality is the same as the Atman; for purposes of intellectual comprehension, it is distinguished as a process of manifestation or creation. In the Upanishads, Prana is used as synonymous with the Atman or Brahman [*Brahma Sutras* I. 23 and I .28-31]. Prana is identified as the life of the Devas (Indriyas), becu use thelatter embody only its manifested functions that go to make up the macrocosm and the microcosm, the external and the internal world. It is also their death, because their dissolution meanbs nothing but resolution into it.

Prana is the Devatha of the Nadis, because they represent its functions. Prana evolves the complex of man's psychophysical activity. The Nadis form the media for evolution as well as involution. Thus, we have the conception that Prana becomes many and then functions through determinate channels built up with matter- Brahman in its self-manifesting process becoming determined as action and reaction, as Prana and Aakasha, force and matter.

***Pranayama and Kundalini***

Human body is a web of nerves, the 'nara-mandala'. Prana or vital energy working in the nervous system is called 'Psychic Prana'. There is the latent or coiled up energy at the base of the spinal column (Muladhara) technically called 'Kundalini'. Pranayama initiates the flow of this coiled up energy up-wards from the base to the brain, utilizing the power generated by the control established over the breath. The control of the breathing process works similarly on all the functioning of the Prana in the body. By rhythmic breathing all the molecules of the body gradually begin to move in the same direction and this makes a man a tremendous battery of will power. When all the electrons in a body flow in the same direction, electric power is generated. Similarly, by Pranayama, the energies of the body and mind are controlled and directed towards the base of the spinal column, called 'Muladhara', and thereby Kundalini, the coiled up power, is activated. Once Kundalini is activated, its energy begins to flow upwards towards the brain.

The vertebral column has the spinal cord running through it. It starts from the brain and ends up in the lumbar vertebrae as fine nerve fibres. Two nerve currents flow on two sides of the spinal cord, called Ida, the afferent nerve) and Pingala (the efferent nerve) carrying sensations to the brain and in turn convey the reactions of the brain to the body. Between these two nerve currents is Sushumna (canal centralis). This canal is closed at the bottom and ordinarily does not perform any function unless it is aroused to do. Yogis who practice Kundalini open this canal and let the nerve current pass through this hollow canal without the help of nerves. This is the medium that established contact consciousness with the environment during evolution but finally got entrapped. The release of the bondage of the body and to establish the contact with the universal consciousness is the purpose of practice of Kundalini. When the Sushumna canal is opened up and mental currents are passed through its empty space, the bondage of the body is released and the yogi establishes the contact with the super consciousness. This brings an extra-ordinary sense of happiness, the Supreme Bliss that cannot be expressed by words!

The Muladhara or the sacral plexus is the root receptacle, the seat of Kundalini. Enormous power of evolutionary impulses is coiled up here. It is this energy that enables the evolutionary process to continue devising the new forms and functions like the one that ended in devising man from the monkey. This is also the key that holds the future of mankind. This is attained by tremendous concentrated will power generated by Pranayama. The manifestation of a little of this is seen in the creative instincts and the sense of reality one gets in the experience of dreams and vivid imagination.

From Muladhara at the bottom, to the Sahasrara in the brain there are in all seven Plexus, the charkas or the centres of Consciousness. The body, mind, and the spirit meet at these junctions and influence each other. These centres of consciousness are: the Muladhara, Swadhishthana, Manipuraka, Anahata, visudhdha and Ajna, and the last one is the Brain, called Sahasrara, the thousand- petalled lotus. These Yogic centers are located in the regions of anus, root of genital, navel, heart, throat, in between the two eye- brows, and crown of head, respectively.

In ordinary people the first three chakras, the centers of consciousness, from the bottom upwards are active and the higher ones are dormant. The first three are connected with the animal life of man like eating, drinking, sense enjoyment or sexual pleasures. Selfish animal thoughts and emotions influence the lower centres. Tamas and Rajas gunas are dominant at lower chakras and, satva guna gains ascendency at higher centres of consciousness. Sushumna becomes active only when we become satvic. When the level of Consciousness rises or the Mind rests on the higher centers like the heart, throat, or Ajnya the spirituality is awakened in man.

Laya Yoga is Kundalini Yoga. 'Laya' is dissolution, dissolution of vrittis, thought-waves. Raja Yoga is restraint of Vrittis. Hatha Yoga helps to control Vrittis by rigorous spiritual, ethical and moral practices. The words 'Ha' and 'Tha' mean union of the Sun and moon, the Prana Vayu and the Apana Vayu (vital airs).

Rising Kundalini is not easy in the beginning and it requires enormous will- power and discipline. It is difficult to force the psychic energy along the Sushumna canal by will power alone. It is very important to note that these centres of consciousness at higher levels are extremely subtle centres which vitalize and control the gross bodily tracts indicated by the various regions of the vertebral column and the ganglia, plexus, nerves, arteries, and the organs situated in those respective regions. In a way, these are not to be disturbed unless one is physically and mentally fit to handle the enormous energy released by the control of Prana that enters this canal of Sushumna and reach the higher charkas or centers of consciousness. One must live a pure life of truth, love, sacrifice, and regulate the habits in order to operate the Kundlini, 'the Serpent Power'

He powers of the coiled up 'serpent power' in the humans, located at the base of the spinal chord is enormous. It has almost everything in its control; and, this Kundalini power or energy could be harnessed by different techniques of different types of Yoga. Some of the more important powers gained by Yogis are clairvoyance, levitation, clairaudience, parakaaya pravesha (entering other's body), thought reading, omnipresence, omniscience, etc. But one must be cautious that care must be taken to check whether the person who wants try this is physically and mentally strong enough to withstand the flow of this enormous hidden energy for it may cause immense damage to nerves and brain. Patanjali's Yoga Sutra describes all these powers of the Kundalini under the 'Powers of Samyama' [III-1-56].

The adverse effects of Kundalini are such that they may cause nervous break down in introverts, or lead to uncontrolled misadventures in extroverts. It may lead to insanity in weak persons. It may cause boosted egotism in physically strong but morally weak persons with the consequence that they become a threat to society. Some persons may gain cheap psychic powers like mind reading and gain control over other weak persons. They may, with practice of japa, meditation with namasmaranam, and with a disciplined life, austere life life, well enjoy peace and happiness.

### *Dharana, Japa, and Meditation*

*Dharana is concentration. 'Dharana is holding the mind on to some particular object' [Patanjali Yoga Sutra III.1]. Discarding the names and forms that have been superimposed on objects by ignorance, and realizing the Brahman behind every object that the mind the senses come into contact, is the culmination of Dharana.* Concentration is very important. Without concentration, it is impossible to achieve anything. Since the mind is always searching for more and more exciting things, it shifts from thought to thought and object to object. Unless a person learns to concentrate on one object or one thought at a time, it is very difficult to achieve success in anything. Regular practice is necessary to concentrate the mind on any task or thought or object. One may concentrate on any external object, or internal Chakras or Plexus. Concentrate on Trikuti or Ajnya chakra. The space between the two eyebrows is normally the one used in Dharana. The picture of Om is another good icon. Picture of Guruji is also good for those who have great faith in their master. To start with, one should hold a flower and gaze at it, or gaze at the idol or photo of one's Ishtadevatha, Ganesha, Radha Krishna, Vishnu or Ishvara, Jesus or the picture of Buddha; or simply gaze at a candle-lit light for five minutes and learn to hold the mind under control. One can concentrate on the sound of a wall-clock, or any spot on the wall in front or the tip of a pencil. All these are concrete concentration. There can be no concentration without something upon which the mind may rest. The mind can rest only on a pleasing object. It is difficult to fix the mind in the beginning and has to be practiced till the mind is well established on the object of concentration. Watch the thoughts pass by. Rhythmic breathing will also help in this process. Once concentration becomes easy, japa and meditation can be started.

The mind of worldly persons is gross. It is unfit for concentration and introspection. Sattvic mind is calm, sharp and subtle. Rajasic mind is passionate, restless and turbulent. It agitates the body and the senses and makes them subject to forein influences. The mind of a subtle seer is like a lamp that does not flicker. So one has to sharpen the mind by practice of daily meditation. There are different methods to discipline the wayward mind and try them. One should not give up even if he fails to control the mind in the initial stages. Gradually one will succeed. Control of one vasana (the subtle desire) or one vritti (thought) will give strength to control another vasana or another vritti. Patience and perseverance is all that is needed.

It is very difficult to say where dharana (concentration) ends and meditation begins. Meditation follows concentration. Patanjali says that, 12 seconds of concentration will lead to 'dharana' and twelve times this 12 seconds (12 x 12 Secs.) will take us to 'Dhyaan'. Another 12 times the time taken to Dhyan (144 Secs.X 12) will take us to lower levels of Samadhi and another twelve times the time taken to attain the state of lower Samadhi will take us to 'Nirvikalpa Samadhi' provided all the Rules and restrictions (yama, niyama and the other conditions laid down in the Sutra) are strictly followed in this exercise. But, it is very important to purify the 'nadis' (nerve centers) and the mind by proper diet and japa, tapa, vrata, nema-nishte, yama, and niyama before Dharana is attempted. Concentration of mind without purity is of no use. Some persons attempt dharana without purification of mind and get into trouble. Concentration without a goal is dangerous. Proper method is to take up ethical practices and strictly adhere to it before concentration is practiced.

'Dharana' or concentration is steadfastness of mind. Those who practise Dharana (concentration) evolve quickly and can do any work with scientific accuracy and great efficiency. Power of concentration will greatly increase when all causes of distractions are removed. Contenence, or Brahmacharya is another pre-requisite of Dharana. A true Brahmachari will have wonderful power of concentration. Attention is another important element of Dharana. One should develop the knack of visualizing things even if they are absent; one must be able to retrieve the mental picture at any moment. Only good practice of concentration will enable one to have sharp memory. Prathyahara will be of great help in sharpening Dharana. Thus, Yama, Niyama, Asana, Pranayama and Prathyahara are to be practiced before coming to Dharana, Meditation and Samadhi. Dhyana and Samadhi become easy and successful only one is properly equipped with all these ethical and spiritual practices.

The benefits of Dharana are many. One who can concentrate for half-an hour or one hour will have tremendous psychic powers; Will power will be very strong. Work efficiency will be several times better and quality will be superb. What was cloudy and hazy before becomes very clear and definite. What was difficult before becomes very easy now; what was complex, bewildering and confusing before comes easily within the mental grasp. The outcome of the effort can be easily estimated with a little concentration on the pros and cons. Nothing is impossible to a man who regularly practices Dharana (concentration). Besides, the persons who practise Dharana will have good health and very good mental vision.

Regularity in meditation is a *sine qua non.* One should select a suitable place and time, take the appropriate asana, like the Padmasana, and practice dhyana with utter sincere devotion. Concentration on a physical law like the law of gravitation, flow of light, expanse of space, or a spiritual idea like the mahat tattva with clarity and bhavartha will yield immense joy and happiness. Reading holy scriptures like the Bhagavad Gita. Through concentration, one can gain penetrative insight; subtle esoteric meanings will flash out in the field of mental consciousness. Inner depths of meaning and philosophical significance become very clear. One has to train the mind in concentration on various subjects, gross and subtle, big and small and in the end a strong mind and will power will emerge.

Meditation will become habitual and brings supreme joy after some time. Discussions result in hostility and mental disturbance. Much energy is wasted. Nothing is gained of endless talks. Everybody wants to show his scholarly learning and intelligence. In the end both the parties fight. A wise man will never enter into discussion. He will take every opportunity to dwell in meditation and will not entertain any thought of participating in debated and discussionsand will avoid them. It is very important to note that much study of Veda and the shastras is also not necessary and much intelligence and retentive memory is also not needed for self -realization. Only meditation is enough. One should have a calm and tranquil mind. No meditation is possible without serenity of mind. Serenity is a rare virtue. It is acquired by eradication of vasanas. With serenity, one can enjoy unruffled abiding peace of mind. When all vasanas are eradicated, mind becomes calm and serene, just as the lake becomes calm and serene as the waves subside. Hence, the Mind Management Rule here is: "Meditate as much as possible and wherever it is possible".

***Great Combinations of Meditation***

One should meditate on the Universe bearing in mind the interior relations of the earth, the air and the atmosphere. The air is the means of joining the posterior form the earth with the atmosphere, the junction. By meditating on this Infinite Universe, the mind goes beyond the trifling pre-occupations andattunes itself to the Infinite,

One should meditate upon the Light. Fire is the prior form, the Sun is the posterior form, water is the junction, and lightning is the means of joining.

One should meditate upon Learning. The Teacher is the prior form, the pupil (student) is the posterior form and the Learning is the junction. Imparting of instruction is the means of joining.

One should meditate upon the Progeny. Mother is the prior form, father is the posterior form, progeny is the junction and procreation is the means f joining.

One should meditate upon the Self. The lower Jaw is the prior form, the upper jaw is the posterior, Speech, or the vocal organ is the junction. Tongue is the means of the union.

These are called the 'Great Combinations'. He who meditates upon these conjunctions, as expounded above, will attain progeny, wealth, and the abode of heaven. There is no hard and fast rule regarding the time, place and postures, but based on the facility available and agreeableness one can meditate. All meditations except that on Paramatman are symbolic.

"Om", the symbol and designation of Brahman- the Object of profound meditation and the highest spiritual efficiency is attributed to it is the quintessence of Veda. Veda is derived from 'Vid' meaning Knowledge [*Chhandogya Upanishad II 23*].

*"Oh! The Supreme Lord, cheer me with the intellectual vigour. Oh!*

*Lord, may I be the possessor of the immortal Revelation. May I be able and active in my body; may my speech be sweet and agreeable to the highest degree; and, may I, with my ears, listen abundantly clear (so that I may learn). Thou art the sheath of the Supreme Being, the "Om", I pray to thee, to preserve my learning".*

This is a prayer addressed to the Supreme Being, the Grantor of all wishes asking for mental power and physical fitness without which Knowledge of Brahman is not possible. *[Kathopanishad I 15-17; Prashnopanishad V 2-7; Brihadaranyaka Upanishad V 1.1; Mundakopanishad II 2.6; Mandukyopanishad V. 11; Bhagavad-Gita Ch. IX. 17; and Manu XI].*

*Maditation is contemplation on one of the Mahat Tattvas, or may have for its object any of the three anthahkaranas- the Mind, the Self, and the Consciousness, or may have the Supreme Brahman.*

*"Let him meditate on the Self which consists of Min", [Shatpatha Brahmana-Madhyandina 10-6.3.2], This Vidya or Mantra is found in Agnirahasya in the Vajasaneyi Shakha.*

*Again, there is another Mantra:*

*"This being identified with the Mind" {Brihadaranyaka Upanishad, 5.6.1] which states' the object of Meditation is the 'Self' consisting Mind'.*

*In Shandilya Vidya, the above two mantra refer to meditation on the Self, consisting of mind, not exclusive of mind!*

*There is the Satya Brahman, a Vidya, or technique where meditation is on Satya Brahman. That which is Satya is the pratyaksha (that can be seen) Sun, the being who is in that orb and the being who is in the right eye.[Brihadaranyaka Upanishad 5.5.12].The two abodes of Satya Brahman are 'Ahar' (the Sun) and the 'Aham' (body).*

*Then there is meditation on the 'Saguna Brahman' (the qualified One or the One with Gunas) and the 'Nirguna Brahman' (the non-qualified One i.e., the One with out Gunas). Shrutis say, 'the one who meditates on the Saguna Brahman will attain the Brahman through the path of God, the 'Devayaana'. The one who meditates on Nirguna Brahman will attain Brahman directly He needs no path since the Knowledge paves the way.*

Meditation and Self-culture are age-old practices in vogue since the Vedic times. The preliminary process of attaining purity of mind by a life of self-control (Righteousness) is given in the following:

*"Yunjjana prathamam Manasthatvaya savithadhiya;*
*Agnerjyotirnichayya Prithvya Adhyabhavat ".*

First, harnessing the Mind and the senses with a view to realize the Truth, and then having found out the Light, of the fire, the evolving soul brought itself out of the earth. The Sun is used as a synonym for 'Antaryamin' (the Ultimate Principle) as the source of all creation, working constantly and eternally in the hearts of all beings to raise them to higher and higher levels of life (thus evolution is caused behind the scene). All evolution is to be traced ultimately to the working of divinity 'within'. Only those rare few who know the glory of the Immanent Soul (All-pervading, all-knowing, Infinite, and the Self- Luminous) undergo the necessary discipline and spiritual practices. The wise do, indeed, control the activities of the intellect, and practise meditation and Dharana, Concentration.

Sit down for a few minutes and pray:

*"Tejosi tejo mayi dehi, veeryamasi veerya mayi dehi;*
*Balamasi balam mayi dehi, ojosi ojo mayi dehi!*

This is a very simple prayer mantra to ask for purity, energy, strength and peace of mind. This is a very effective mantra from *Shukla Yajur Veda Samhita 19.9.*

It gives enormous strength of mind and self-confidence. Meditation gives good relaxation to tired mind and body. Close your eyes and take the name of the Lord and chant. If you get sleep, it is good. Continue meditation when you get up. But this going to sleep in meditation should not be developed into a habit. It will not help spiritual attainments. Meditation should be done with total awareness, not in sleep. A man getting up from sleep may be fresh and look refreshed; but a man coming out of mediation looks bright, radiant, and more energetic. Meditation helps to calm nerves and reduce tension. Very nervous people cannot meditate. So, first the tense nerves should be calmed down. We should control all our sentiments and feelings, good or bad. And make the mind passive. We should concentrate on the Infinite and tune our mind towards the Supreme Lord. Fill the mind with the holy image and the harmonizing vibrations of the holy sound, 'Om'.

Before we go to bed, we should concentrate on some holy idea, or think of some divine form; ths will help to get a sound sleep. Chanting Lord's name, or 'Om'will keep the mind engaged in the Divine. It is not good to combine Japa with sleep. Japa before and after sleep is good. Normally, japa of the required number of chantings should be completed for good results. We should find the center of consciousness at the heart level, or the 'Ajnya' level and concentrate on this at the time of japam and meditation for excellent results.

Sattvic food, rhythmic breathing, constant awareness of mind or alertness and feeling one with the environment are the important requirements for success of meditation. Patience, good disposition, kind and benevolent attitude towards others are virtues. Establishing in oneself is important for a harmonious and peaceful life. Impatience, anger, dissatisfaction and digruntled behaviour will spoil the mood and bring unhappiness to self as well asothers. Pleasant mood should be practiced despite any odds and, it is very difficult. But, it comes easy with meditataton. Our own mental impurities, desires and passions, tendencies and impressions, attachments are major obstacles to meditation. Meditation requires a pure mind and meditation creates a pure mind!

### *Japam*

Japa means chanting of a mantra. The word comprises of '*Ja*' meaning, 'destroys birth and death cycle' and the syllable '*Pa*' meaning, 'destroys all the sins' [*Agni Purana*]. Thus, Japa has the potential to unite the soul with the Supreme Being. It has miraculous powers that infuse us with courage and confidence. Vedic mantra are very sacred. Hymns of the Veda are known as *mantra*. Some of the mantra are the prayer mantra. One such hymn in the Yajur Veda is the Gayatri mantra. It is a beeja mantra or seed syllable, derived from ancient primeval sounds. Lord Shree Krishna says in the Bhagavad Gita, amongst the mantra ***I am Gayatri***. *Gayatri mantra* has the latent spiritual power by which regular japa and meditation can transform the mind into prajnya or wisdom. Chanting of this mantra, the 'Gayatri', with concentration and understanding, brings inexplicable peace, calm and solace to the disturbed mind.

Just repetition of the sacred word and hearing the same is the technique of meditation that is practiced by Christians in the Church. Here the stress is laid on the repetition of the sacred word or the verses of Bilble without involving the 'Self' as its object. The concentration on the sounds of the mantra is supposed to erase the ego. Hence, the objective of Christian meditation is the removal of 'ego' for ego is the obstruction in the path of visualization of God. However, deeper concentration (dharana) on the 'Self' will pave the way to 'Self-realization'. 'Rosary' is used in Japam, or chanting as the means of holding on to the sacred mantra both in the East and the West. The Rudraksha seeds (beads) are sacred for the Hindu spiritual seekers.

***The Gayatri Mantra***

Manu Smriti has elaborately dealt with the Gayatri mantra. It is culled out of the three Veda- the Rig Veda, Yajur Veda and Sama Veda, by none else than Brahman, Himself. It starts with the 'OM' that emanated with the sphota or Big Bang at the time of the origin of the Universe and the sound still persists in the cosmic space. The Gayatri mantra has been constructed by letters "A', 'U', and 'M' extracted out of the three Veda and by their coalition with the three mysterious words- 'Bhur', Bhuvah, and Svah, meaning earth, sky and heaven, respectively. Thus the text of the Gayatri mantra was composed as:

*"Om! Bhur bhuva svah, tatsaviturvareneeyam,*
*Bhargodevasya dheemahi, dheeyo yonah prachodayat".*

This mantra is conceived as the worship of Shree Hari, of Aditya (the Sun), and also as pure Nirguna worship of Brahman. Bhisma Pitamaha advises Yudhistir to recite this spiritually powerful mantra in the battle-field of Kurukshetra. The Goddess Gayatri Devi is the incarnation and manifestation of Brahman who resides in all human beings, rather in all living beings. *Gayatri mantra* is also known as '***Savitri***' mantra or '***Surya***' mantra and is addressed to the divine power of the Star of our Solar System the Sun.

The *Shvetasvatara Upanisad* proclaims that, "the one affluent divinity is hidden in all beings. He is All-pervading and is the inner-self of all creatures. He presides over all actions and all beings reside in Him. He is the inner-witness. He endows all with the consciousness and is Nirguna, or free from all three gunas- the tamas, Rajas and the Sattvic". *Isavasya Upanisad* also gives a similar exposition of the Gayatri mantra. However, the *Rig Veda* has defined this Gayatri mantra differently. Accordingly, "the illumined sages like Surayah constantly see that infinite all-pervading supreme reality Vishnu without any obstruction as though their vast intuitive eye or vision was spread over the spiritual sky". ***Before Gayatri japa is chanted, it is beneficial to practice Pranayama***. This helps in concentration. Of the three methods of chanting the mantra, the Vachik (chanting loudly), Upansu (in low voice) and Manasic (mental chanting), the last one is more effective. Gayatri is a spiritual weapon that protects one who chants it, and blesses him with brilliant light of the highest spiritual illumination. It should forma nitya karma for one and all, a means of realization of the self; it leads to realization of the divinity of the self and it is salvation.

Pranayama practised with Gayatri Japa is a very powerful technique (Tantra) that brings both materialistic prosperity and spiritual attainments. The method is elaborately described in many ancient scriptures. Briefly, it is as follows:

Pranayama started with Sukha Pranayama should be gradually regulated along with the Gayatri Japam.

The Pranava '***Om***' is followed by the Seven Vyahruti (Lokas) ***'Bhu', 'bhuvah', 'svarh', 'maha', 'janah', 'tapah' and the 'satyam*** (the seven worlds- earth, sky, heavens, mahat, janahlok, tapolok and the satyalok; or, the Mrutyulok (the earth), Pitrulok, Devalok, Gandharvalok, Yakshalok, Kinnaralok, Satyalok or the Brahmalok).

This is followed by ***the Gayatri mantra***:

*"Om Tatsaviturvarenyam Bhargodevasya dheemahih dheeyo yo nah prachodayat".*

This is concluded *with the 'Shiras': "Om, Apojyoti rasomrutam Bhramhah bhurbhuvasvar Om".*

These three parts of the Gayatri, i.e., ***the Vyahruti, Gayatri and the Shiras*** should be synchronized with the breathing in (Pooraka), Holding the breath within (Kumbhaka) and breathing out (Rechaka), respectively. This is called '***Gayatri viniyogah***' or technique of dispensing with the Gayatri Japa and Pranayama'. The Pooraka, Kumbhaka and the Rechaka techniques have been described under Pranayama.

*Pranayama* with Gayatri is the mantra-tantra of mano-niyantran, eternal happiness and success ***par excellence***. There is no doubt about this!

The effect of Japa and Meditation are direct. Japa and meditation keep the mind engaged. The mind dwells at least for a little while on the supreme spirit, dwells on divine blissful form, on the noble attributes. Then comes the time, when one feels the divine Presence. Many blessed souls get the spiritual vision of the divine Form. Such persons then become the Guru. *Spiritual life is like mountain climbing. One has to go slowly higher and higher, carefully*. No one can become a realized soul overnight. One has to begin with a simple thing like repetition of the name of the *Ishtadevatha*. This is called *Japa*. Repetition of the name should not be mechanical. It should be done with total devotion and bhaavartha. The significance of the name uttered should be contemplated upon. Think of the Lord as pure, blissful, luminous, all-pervading spirit. Gradually the inner meaning will unfold by itself. It will be a very enlightening experience. It brings with it cheerfulness and peace.

*Meditation is contemplation on the Divine. It is a continuous flow of thoughts towards a higher spiritual ideal in a higher spiritual 'centre of Consciousness'. One must be absorbed in the thought of the divine, but it does not come easily in the beginning. Japa is the first step in this direction. Repetition of the name of Ishtadevatha, thinking of Him, deeply absorbed in Him, will gradually lead to supreme Spirit 'Sat- Chit-Ananda'. God will appear to his devotee in the form of his Ishtadevatha.*

*Yama, Niyama, and Prathyahara should be practiced before attempting serious meditation. If one attempts meditation without having attained purity of mind, it is likely that he will concentrate more on impurities of the mind than God. The higher centers of consciousness must open in order to enable one to dwell on higher thoughts for long. Prayer and doing good work helps here.*

*Meditation is a fully conscious process, an exercise of the will. Meditation means concentration on a spiritual idea that presupposes that the aspirant is capable of rising above worldly ideas. Meditation is done usually at a particular center of consciousness, preferably the heart. It is a long drawn process and the results come automatically in due course and one should not be too eager to experience the results. Real dhyan or meditation is possible only when the out-going tendencies are controlled and the mind flows continuously as a current in the contemplation of God. Atleast, chanting of name of any personal god twenty thousand times a day is necessary.*

*In the beginning, we may need some support like the picture of our Ishtadevatha (personal god). We have to remember in our mind this picture as we repeat the name and gradually install this piecture in our heart. Then, it becomes easy to look inward and pray; we can take His form, then His attributes, and then His infinite Svaroopa or nature. Thus, progress in meditation will be made step by step. The inner shrine will be gradually revealed to us as we make progress in meditation. The seat of consciousness is the space, contentless. It is called 'chidakasha' in the heart as compared to the 'mahakasha', the external space ('Mahat' or vast outer space).*

*So long as one is not able to control his thoughts, one should not take to meditation. In early stages forbidden impure thoughts rise in the mind and overpower the aspirant leading to confusion. One should go very slowly about meditation and gain control over wandering mind. The concentrated mind, if it is not pointed, becomes a veritable demon and creates lot of trouble. Once again, it is reiterated here, that 'purity of mind and purity of heart with a disciplined austere sattvic life', are essential for a purposeful and fruitful meditation.*

*We have to meditate within the shrine of our heart, the 'chidakasha', or heart, or the seat of pure consciousness. If we perform Japa and dhyana, obstacles will be removed and a new spiritual consciousness awaken'. Our tendency to worry will disappear. The evil thoughts and anxiety that sicken our mind and body will be removed and holy thoughts take their place. Harmony is established. With the improvement in mental health, physical health will also improve. With the awakening of the spiritual consciousness we will discover that we are not mere physical body but the spirit, a part of the universal spirit, and the 'Ishtadevatha' is no other than the 'Paramatman', the source of supreme bliss, supreme peace, and supreme love.*

*Often we hear the complaint that, 'in spite of all my sincere efforts, there is no progress; nothing happens, and the like'. It should be made very clear that nothing happens in the beginning. But one should not feel disappointed. The path to spiritual progress is very slow and difficult. There shall be the effect of meditation if one does his meditation or japa with devotion, sincerely. First the physical health will improve and the mental peace prevails. In the early stages of meditation it is like waging a war with the mind. The restless mind has to be brought under control. Any attempt to resist thoughts is of no use. Thoughts should be allowed to come and go on their own; simply watch the thoughts. That will do.*

*Unless we meditate, we cannot control the mind and unless we control mind, it is difficult to meditate. So, we must start meditation with firm determination and should not leave it even for a day. It is enough if we meditate for 15 minutes every day in the beginning. At best, one should meditate 2 hours in the morning and 2 hours in the evening, in a selected secluded place without any disturbance. But, it must be remembered that we should not grumble about the environment and complain about it. We should accept whatever comes our way. That is the 'law of least effort'.*

*One should not exert too much and strain the brain in early stages. One has to go slowly and then gradually intensify the effort. Once it becomes a regular habit, it becomes easy to sit for long hours in meditation. Happiness and a feeling of freshness are the results of deep meditation.*

*Meditation is not easy to those who indulge in worldly affairs too much. Too much of anything is bad- whether eating, sleeping, talking, indulgence in sex, or pursuit of sensual happiness. In Bhagavad- Gita, Sri Krishna says, "Yoga destroys sorrow for a man who is regulated in his food, recreation, work, sleep and wakefulness". [Bhagavad-Gita VI, 17]. There should be a golden mean; 'this far and no further'. One should create hunger for God; meditate on Him, Ishtadevatha'. One can visualize his God with perseverance and patience. There is nothing superior to the happiness one derives from 'God -visualization' through meditation with a pure heart, pure mind, and pure body. Purity is the mainstay of spirituality. By thoughts, words and deeds (Kaya, vacha, manasa) one should perform his action in total submission to the Lord. Then only, the effect of japa and meditation will yield good results.*

*Slightest ego will spoil the whole effort. Veda and Upanishads make it clear that one should build up his 'ego' only to be offered at the Lotus Feet of the Lord. One must work hard to earn material wealth, earn name and fame. With all humility, he should spend his wealth to the welfare of the other less fortunate. Otherwise, what can you offer Him? Love and sacrifice are the hallmarks of a spiritual aspirant.*

### *Prathyahara and Dharana*

*'Prathyahara' means 'gathering towards'. 'When the senses giving up their own objects take the form of the mind, as it were, it is 'Prathyahara', according to Patanjali [Yoga Sutra II. 54].*

*It is detachment from all sensuous objects, thoughts, fantasies, indulgences in things that bind the mind and concentration on the Almighty. With-holding the mind from its going along the channels of perception and in gathering it is called 'Prathyahara'.*

*Moral instruction consisting in forbidding the doing of certain things is ineffective, because the power to detach the mind from the object of the senses is not present in the person. Establishing control over the mind is not easy. Mind is active like a monkey drunk and bitten by a scorpion. So it is suggested here that one should allow the mind to wander and simply watch it. After a strenuous senseless pursuit it will come to rest on its own. Thus, one can get control over the mind gradually by constant observation. This is Prathyahara in practice. This can also be done by creating an aversion to the sense objects just like one is fed up when constantly fed by same food, may be one's most favourite dish. For a spiritual spirant too much indulgence in sex should bring about aversion to sex. Similarly, too much of loose talks, drinks, entertainment, television viewing, and other habits should be nauseating. By autosuggestion, one can develop aversion to all these and turn the mind to God.*

*By 'Dharana', we mean concentration on a particular object, i.e., holding the mind on a single point. May be it is one's own heart or picture of Ishtadevatha, or a Lotus flower. Even a lit-candle will serve the purpose. Long and arduous practice is required for success in Dharana. Spiritual aspitants practising dharana should be strict in their food habits, talk less, and live alone, if possible. The results of dharana can be seen very early. They become calm, develop clear voice and good temperament. With increase in practice, they can hear anahata dhwani, sounds from distance. One can hear mantra in the right ear. The senses become very sharp and pointed and even a pin drop will be a thunderbolt! Some aspirants select one idea and concentrate wholly on it and achieve extra-ordinary success. The results of Dharana are unbelievable!*

*It is difficult to say when concentration ends and meditation begins. Meditation follows concentration. Ethical practices like Yama and Niyama are important before Dharana is practised. Concentration without purity of mind is of no use. Taking to Dharana without preliminary ethical training is like taking to long jump without practice that will end in disasters.*

*Dharana, i.e., concentration is steadfastness of mind. Continence, Brahmacharya (preserving virya), is necessary for Dharana (concentration) for it will give strength of mind. Those who practise Dharana, i.e., concentration evolve quickly and can do any work efficiently, with scientific accuracy and much quicker than others. They will gain clarity and extra in-depth perception of jobs on hand. Concentration helps in attaining material prosperity. Nothing is impossible to a person who practises Dharana regularly. But setting a goal is very important in Dharana and the process of concentration should be continuous and without break like the flow of oil.*

*Dhyana and Samadhi*

*'Dhyaana' is the continuous flow of divine thought in an unbroken chain. [PatanajliYoga Sutra III.2]. This is achieved by concentration on a particular location, may be the tip of the nose, or preferably between the eyebrows. It leads to Samadhi. Patanjali, the yoga teacher, says 'By 'Ishvarapranidhana', sacrificing all to Ishvara comes samadhi'. Learn to surrender all of your labour of your spiritual practice to the Supreme Being. Surrender yourself completely; offer all fruits of your action, connect your little will to the divine will, and then a miracle takes place. That Truth, that Reality which shines within, which also shines outside in all beings, reveals itself in all its glory, and then comes communion between the soul and the Oversoul.*

Dharana, Dhyana and Samadhi, the three together is called 'samyama'. Meditation should begin with gross objects and slowly rise to finer and finer ones until it becomes objectless. It should lead to a state of 'choiceless awareness'. The meditative state is the highest state of existence. It brings total happiness and real enjoyment incomparable to any the senses could bring.

*Samadhi (Realization)*

As already stated, there are different layers of consciousness. Normally, we work within a circle of what appears to be rational and this comes within the conscious sphere. Here, self-consciousness accompanied by an individualized will is functioning. There are the sub-conscious and super-conscious levels besides the unconscious and we are rarely aware of these in our normal work. Yogis claim that even the internal organs of our body that are normally independent of our control like breathing, pumping blood, pulses can be brought under conscious control of man. This is the ego-prompted rational level and self-conscious. This is in contrast to the ego-less and uncontrolled instinctive level commonly found in animals.

*"The Yogis hold that the mind can go beyond the self-conscious level of the mind". Just as unconscious work is beneath consciousness, so there is another kind of work which is above consciousness and which also is not accompanied with the feeling of egoism. The feeling of egoism is only in the middle plane. When the mind is above or below this line, there is no feeling of ego and yet the mind works. When the mind goes beyond this line of self-consciousness it is called 'Samadhi' or Super-consciousness. When a fool goes into Samadhi he wakes up an enlightened person. This will be the effect of Samadhi on persons who practises all the eight steps of yoga to the point of culmination in Samadhi.*

*'Samadhi' is the culmination of the steps to 'Self Realization'. It leads to Brahmananda; but it is very difficult to reach this stage in the ordinary way of life. It is said, that the culmination of spiritual exercises in 'samadhi' will bring immense happiness and bliss that is un-surpassed by any other effort. This bliss is not comparable to any other joy. Those few who have experienced this bliss will be ever ready to share their happiness and bliss with their devotees. They see divinity in all souls*

*and make no distinction of caste, creed, birth, or worldly accomplishments in their devotees. In the Hindu way of life, this is the ultimate one can achieve and it is the aspiration of all spiritual seekers to reach this stage, called 'turiya', and experience the Bliss of 'Sat-Chit-Ananda', i.e., Brahmananda.*

*The meditative state is the highest state of existence. It is only the contemplative, 'witness-like' study of objects that bring us real enjoyment and happiness. Samadhi is also known as 'Jnyana' (Knowledge) or Realization. It is not a state of un-consciousness. It is a state of 'choiceless awareness'. Samadhi is the complete forgetfulness of all thought by first making it changeless and then identifying it with Brahman* ***[Patanjali Yoga Sutra].*** *It is 'Pure Consciousness'.*

*The state of Samadhi is the final stage of spiritual attainment. But, it is very difficult to reach this stage without much effort. Many obstacles such as idleness, desire for sensual pleasure, sleep, dullness, distraction, lack of inquiry, sudden disinterestedness or loss of enthusiasm to puruse it further and eagerness to taste joy and a sense of blank-mindedness appear while practicing Samadhi. So, one has to guard against all these obstacles and get rid of them; one has to pursue the effort to reach the state of Samadhi with steadfastness and with firm determination.*

*The next highest state after 'Turiya' (Samadhi) is 'Sushupti'. One attains the Brahman in this state. There will be no body-consciousness or mind-consciousness in this state. It is Absolute Brahman! It is not possible to stay in this state for long. One has to come back to 'Turiya' and constantly strive for the 'Eternal Bliss"*

*It is not the intention here to go into the details of 'Samadhi', or 'Turiya' state, and its benefits since the main objective of this book is to live and work in this sensate world happily, peacefully and successfully. It is with this intention that the householders' approach to Self Realization is stressed. Without taking recourse to going to forest ('vanaprasthashrama'), staying in the family and achieving the fulfillment is the goal of Grihasta. The 'sat' (True) 'nyasa' (maarg) i.e., 'sanyas' through mind control or mind management is the real pathway to "Atma Sakshaatkaara", i.e., Self Realization. It is not ascetcism, Sanyas with ochre robe and total abandonment of family responsibilities that is advocated or sought for here. Life is to enjoy and everyone should enjoy it fully; the Veda and Upansihads fully support and encourage this fulfillment and offer a number of mantra or techniques for this purpose. A few such mantra are given in the opening pages of this book.*

*Transcendental Meditation (TM)*

*This is a much more simple but very effective method of controlling the mind. Maha Rishi Mahesh Yogi developed this technique based on the Vedic Science of Consciousness during the later part of the last Century and, this technique caught the whole world like wild fire. In Maha Rishi's own words, "Transcendental Meditation [TM] is a simple, natural programme for the mind; a spontaneous, effortless march of the mind unfolds its potential for unlimited awareness, transcendental awareness, Unity Consciousness- a lively field of all potential, where every possibility is naturally available to the conscious mind. The conscious mind becomes aware of its own un-bounded dignity, its unbounded essence, its infinite potential".*

*"Transcendental Meditation provides a way for the conscious mind to fathom the whole range of its existence- active and silent, point and infinity. It is not a philosophy or a religion; it is an experience, a mental technique one practices everyday for fifteen or twenty minutes".*

*In Maha Rishis's own words, "the technique of Transcendental Meditation, when practiced regularly, tends to produce normalization in all areas of life. It reduces stress, improves health, enriches mental functioning, enhances personal relationships, and increases job productivity and gives job satisfaction; besides, it is extremely simple for everyone to practice.*

*It is well known that creative intelligence is the cause of this universe and the manifestation of this intelligence is the physical and psychological features of everyday world. Transcendental Meditation approaches directly this creative intelligence aspect of creation rather than the creatures, the manifestation of intelligence. It induces the much-needed harmony and well being at the very basic level of existence. Hence, it deals with the humans rather than their problems; hence, it is very wholesome, covering the psychological, intellectual and spiritual. Thus, it is very effective.*

*Transcendental Meditation direotly deals with the mind only. It does not involve any additional aspects with which the mind is associated, such as breathing, yoga or physical exercises. Transcendental Meditation helps to fathom the whole range of its existence unhindered by any extraneous factors. There is no interference of any sort in this process of TM. The technique of TM ranges from active mind or the performing mind to- quiet mind or resting mind. In resting mind, there is purity and simplicity, and no other involvement. All expressions of intelligence are nourished since only the mind is involved. The mind meditates, gains Transcendental Consciousness and brings about transformation in different fields of manifestation. All fields of life, which are the expression of intelligence, are nourished or transformed and made better through experiencing Transcendental Meditation [TM].*

*In Maha Rishi's own words, "the nature of transcendental consciousness is unity of consciousness, an encounter with the field of unified consciousness. In transcendental consciousness, the mind experiences itself; intelligence experiences itself. The mind is the observer of its own reality. In that state, the mind is transcendental consciousness. Transcendental consciousness is the self-fulfilled state of mind; it is the source of all activity, just as the surface of the quiet ocean is the source from which all waves rise. It is called the unified field of natural law, from which all the different laws of nature emerge and conduct their specific activities in the relative world".*

*Through regular practice of TM, 'that unbounded awareness, that pure consciousness, the field of all the laws of nature, becomes ingrained in all activities of the mind'. 'Then the mind begins to live in Unity Consciousness; it becomes a living reality'.*

*The best thing is to take a course in Transcendental Meditation in any of the TM Schools run by the Maha Rishi Mahesh Yogi. This will help the aspirant to experience himself whatever happens; what happens is that the mind, in its active state, learns to experience its own less active states, experience its progressively minimized active states, until eventually it cognizes the transcendental state of consciousness. In order to realize what is the natural state, the aspirant has to be first liberated from unnatural programs, performances, and experiences. Most people have no experience with Transcendental Consciousness, pure consciousness, which is the nature of pure mind. They are aware of active mind, which is the waking state of consciousness. They are also aware of forgetful state of mind, the sleep state of mind. They are aware of the dream state of mind. But they are not aware of pure state or Transcendental Consciousness. This is taught in Transcendental Meditation courses; it is a course in natural state of mind, rather, a nature of mind.*

*Transcendental Meditation [TM] does not involve intellect. It is an experience of the mind from the active levels to the unified level. It is just an innocent experience of active mind and an innocent experience of settled mind, silent mind. Try it under some trained persons and experience it.*

*Neuro-Linguistic Programming (NLP)*

*Neuro-Linguistic Programming (NLP) is a technique of 'Mind Management'. It is an age-old practice among the Hindus to gather in small groups on auspicious days like Monday, Friday, Saturday and/or Thursday at regular intervals and sing bhajans and clap for an hour with total devotion. The modern terms 'Neuro' stands for nerves (that represents behaviour), 'linguistic' is for language that means structure; and, 'Programming' as derived from computer science stands for creating 'change'. Thus, the NLP creates 'structural behavioral changes' in our attitudes using techniques like Meditation, creative Visualisation, and 'auto-suggestion' depending on the person's mental map. Here, the five senses can be controlled by the technique of Neuro-Linguistic Programming (NLP) according to Dr. Bandier and Dr. Grinder. All the successful persons use certain common traits with the help of the five senses. These traits can be studied, decoded and programmed to produce success.*

*According to Neuro-Linguistic Programming (NLP), if you have a negative memory you have to programme it out of your system. This can be done by sitting in a comfortable position, closing the eyes and listening to special mind power music and visualizing the event that the person wants to forget, like watching a movie. This helps one to forget all unwanted memories or sad events. Like re-winding a film, by this revisualization process, the negative energy associated with a particular memory goes into trash. This technique is very helpful in eliminating fear, emerging out of trauma, sad events, or tragic events like accidents and death.*

*The visual, the auditory, and the kinesthetic are involved in the Neuro-linguistic Programming (NLP). A simple bhajan or a 'saastang namaskar' (prostrating, all parts of the body touching the ground) is the simplest method of NLP. If the whole family does this regularly it would give wonderful results. Meditation for a few minutes chanting "Om" and singing together clapping hands for a few minutes everyday is fine. It brings cohesion, understanding, mutual respect and affection and will greatly promote peace and happiness in the family. Spirituality rules and spirituality binds the family.*

*Neuro-linguistic Programming (NLP) helps to keep the mind cool and fresh. It helps concentration and increases efficiency in all daily activities. In fact, this is a regular practice in any Hindu family.*

*The origin of the Neuro-linguistic Programming is found in Rig Veda. Meditation and exercise, that is regularly practiced, enables one to vibrate with the energy of the universe. Diet is a very important factor in NLP. It has been observed that a certain kind of food interferes with the brain's function and hence avoided. Extreme Rajasic and Tamasic foods, i.e., too hot or too cold a food are avoided; Sattvic food creates ideal conditions for noble thoughts and noble deeds.*

*It is possible to attain materialistic prosperity through Vedanta. Once we understand the meaning and purpose of 'life', it is not very difficult to enjoy it peacefully, joyfully, and happily. But, we do not know the meaning and purpose of this life. We want success in our endeavour; but we do not know what this success is; we do not know whether this success brings us happiness or more problems. We have seen many successful men have commited suicide and a closer study of such cases reveal what lies under the guise of this 'success'. Worldly success is again 'Maya', Illusion and it is 'make-believe'! That is why we utter the words, 'I cannot believe it", this is how the truth comes out with out our awareness. In the heart of hearts (the soul) we know this world is unreal! It (the world or the worldly succss) is not real, is not the truth. A few people garlanding and praising you may boost your ego and you feel happy for the moment. When the same people boo-boo and pelt stones at you for no fault of yours, you feel miserable. This worldly success is the devil that haunts us throughout our life. It should always be rememebered that there is nothing wrong in working hard to gain success, but it should not be an obsession that comes in the way of real happiness. lso, the worldly success should not get into our head (boostd 'ego') and spoil our normal life.*

*We want honour, fame, wealth and all these are the qualities of the Brahman who shines in us. There is nothing wrong in aspiring for these. Even the Veda and Upanishads advise us to gain worldly success and promote your ego; promote ego only to surrender it at the feet of the Lord! Worldly success is important. But, every success in life, every accomplishment in life is to be treated as the means to an end; the end or goal of life is Self Realization, 'Atma Saakshaatkara'. This does not come easily to mortals in one or two lives; it takes hundreds of lives to purify the blemished souls, get rid of all desires, surrender the bloated ego to the Lord and live a life of pure heart and realize the Self.*

*The golden rule is: 'keep yourself happy; keep your family happy; keep your relatives happy; keep your friends and social circle happy; keep your world happy by understanding the intricacies of the functioning of the mind'. Achieve the full potential of the brain by integration of body, mind, and soul through the application of principles of Yoga. Gain self- control and get mastery over the skills that will help to excel in all fields. This will give the joy, the happiness, peace that cannot be achieved by any other means.*

*Mauna (Silence), Its Significance*

*Silence (Mauna) is deep, vast, expanse of supreme Consciousness- 'Brihat', called 'Brahman'; and Brahman is Silence. Silence is the unified state-' Samhita'. It is eternally awake in its potential dynamism 'Anyonya –Abhava' in the state of silence (Mauna) 'Atyanta-Abhava'. The entire multiverse has emerged from this Mauna, the Silence, the Hiranyagarbha. Silence is the creative process of Natural Law. To dwell in deep silence is to dwell in supreme Brahman. One must be able to reach the depth of this supreme Consciousness – Mauna (Silence) by dhyaan, japam, and meditation. One must be able to stretch this timeless silence and dwell deep in it; stretch as much as possible a second of the minute of mauna- ' Atyanta-Abhava' and reach the center of creative intelligence in 'Anyonya-Abhava' as much as possible and seek the supreme Knowledge and Bliss hidden in it and extrct the supreme intellignce and creative ability through Pradhwamsha –Abhava and Prag-Abhava. The GAPS (Sandhi) between words, or GAPS between letters in Vedic Mantra are Silence (Mauna). The Atharva Veda, the reverberating WHOLENESS (Completeness) quality of Atharva, is available in "dynamic silence" (Rk Veda), flowing wake*fulness *of Sama Veda, offering and creating Yajur Veda; and, as all the three Veda are the dynamics of the GAP (Silence), all the four Veda function together as the self-interacting dynamics of the Mauna (GAP) expressed through Pradhwamsha- Abhava, Atyanta- Abhava, Anyonya- Abhava (potential dynamism) and Prag-Abhava. These four stages are the stages of Silence- ech evolving into the other and the unified state of Silence is 'Samhita'. Thistotality or WHOLENESS of Mauna (Silence) can be experienced in the state of self-referral Transcendental Conciousness through deep Meditation. Atma or Soul is 'self-referral' for there is nothing else to refer to. Hence, Meditation on the Self will reveal the supreme Intelligence, the Brahman, the Absolute Silence-'Mauna'.*

*Sound is heard only in silence and sound is a disturbance. The Buddha would not answer any questions and would simply ask the questioner to sit near him for two or three years in silence till it was total. And then ask any question. Those who dared to do so found that when total silence engulfed them, all the questions they had vanished too. Verily, ultimate reality is beyond words. It is our very existence.*

*The significance of 'Mauna' is that words have their origin in the mind and the mind has no relationship with the unknown. Hence what all mind thinks is only repetition of the memory. It cannot think of the unknown. It stands still in the wake of anything that is wonderful, magnanimous, huge, and astounding. Only silence is aware of all great things. Kathoupanishad puts it thus: 'The Ultimate Reality cannot be known through speech or through eyes. Who but the one who says 'It Is', can know it? And that 'It Is', cannot be known by logic or words; it can only be known through silence. The silence does not reside in the mind, that is ever shifting process, but it resides in the heart. Discussion involves using words and these words collide with the mind or head and rebound to the seeker or the questioner".*

*Maharishi Bhagavan Mahesh Yogi has beautifully explained the significance of Mauna. In his "Apaurusheya Bhashya", a commentary on Rk Veda, Maharishi says:*

*"Looking deeper into the structure of the Veda, into the sequential flow of Vedic Sound, we find that the self-referral dynamics of consciousness expresses itself in the sequence of sound and silence- the creative process is in Mauna ('SILENCE'), and the creation is expressed through sound. This alternation of silence sound, and how much silence and how much sound- i.e., the quantified values of silence and sound quantify the unbounded infinity of the self-referral consciousness, creating, giving expression to, the specific Laws of Nature- the fundamental building blocks of creation."*

*Maharishi says, "It is very interesting to examine the sequence of sound and silence in the flow of consciousness- in the evolution of consciousness- in the volution of Law- in the sequential flow of the structure of the Ved, as traditionally available in the Mauna- GAPS- between sounds of the syllables, and between the verses (the Richa); between the paragraphs, the Suktas; and between the chapters, the Mandalas; of the Vedic Structure. The insight into the Mauna –GAPS- between the sounds of theVedic Literature is Maharishis's special contribution to the knowledge of the evolution of the Laws of Nature from the holistic structure of Law- th self-referral Unifid Field, or Samhita –of Rishi, Devta, Chhandas.*

*Words can perform only one function; they can make the seeker aware of the need to be silent or wordless. After this the words are useless as far as the seeker is concerned. As silence lies beyond the parameters in which words operate, the latter cannot express that which is known in silence. For words can only describe the known. The ultimate reality is unknowable to words. One should practice 'mouna vrata' one day a month, at least; and, gradually make it at least a day once a week. This will keep the mind cool and steady. This is the method of cleansing the mind. Purity of mind is very important,*

*Silence is Brahman. Silence Is existence. Everything exists in silence. The Pranava, "Om" emanates from silence. "Om" begins and ends with silence.*

*"Yasmad vaacho nivartante apraaptamanasaa saha*
*yan maunam yogibhihgamyam sarvadaa budhaa"*

*[Taittiriya Upanishad, II.9]*

*One should be established in one's Self, where the words and thoughts do not reach. Where the words and thoughts return without reaching is 'That'; and, 'That' (the silence) is existence, truth and Bliss. Consciousness, space and time exist in silence. Both Knowledge and Nescience exist in silence. Silence is there where there is no 'other' and it is Brahman, 'ekamevaadviteeyam'. In this silence lies the 'Will', the creative energy (sankalp). It is the Lord's will to create the world of 'others'- the names, forms and functions that has produced this material objective world. Hence, everything in this world is subjected to His Will, 'Daiva Saṅkalpa'.*

*Mantra, Its Significance*

*Mantra is a divine name. Mantra literally means that which frees the soul through reflection: 'Mananat thraayate iti mantra'. Utterance of a mantra is the simple and easiest way of self-realization. Maharshi Patanjali, speaking about the effect of repeating 'Om' and other holy names says that, "It ('Om') removes the various obstacles (like doubt, illness, mental disturbances) on the path and leads to the awareness of the individual Spirit" [Yoga Sutra 1.29]. Repetition of the mantra calms the nerves and unifies the powers of the mind and finally awakens the Spirit within. Each mantra contains a special syllable called the bija (seed). The bija is believed to arouse special power of our deity in us. Every individual has a bija mantra or a personal divine name which is very potent and effective; but this has to be revealed by an accomplished Guru or, should be initiated to by a person of spiritual attainment. Even parents can initiate as is usually done during the upanayanam. Sometimes, mantra is heard as 'anahata dhvani' in the right ear, or in adream, and it tallies with the one given by the Guru. In tantric tradition the mantra is a secret and never to be revealed to others for it loses its power and sanctity. It becomes a common- place utterance when revealed to everyone.*

*'Shanti Mantra' is the invocation to peace. Peace is where there is harmony, when there is acceptance, when there is Truth. The body is made up of five elements viz the air, water, fire, earth and prana (the vital force). There is harmony among these five great elements. A slight impairment in any one of these five great elements will cause sickness and death. The supreme Being, the Self unites and joins and keeps them in harmony in the body and the person is healthy and happy. These elements that are inside the body are also outside the body. There is harmony and balance between the outside and the inside. This Shanti Mantra is for the continuance of that balance and harmony.*

*The Mantra states:*

*"May Mitra, Varuna, Aryaman, Indra, Brihaspati, All-pervading Vishnu be propitious to us and grant us welfare and Bliss. I bow down to Brahman in reverence; Oh, Vayu, I bow down to thee in adoration. Thou art verily perceptible Brahman. I shall declare thou art Right. Thou art the True and the Good. May That, the Supreme Being, adored as Vayu preserve me. May He preserve the Teacher. May He protect 'Om'. May He protect both of us. May He nourish us both, together. May we work*

*conjointly with great energy. May our study be vigorous and be effective. May we not mutually dispute or we not hate any. Om! Let there be Peace and peace and Peace in me, in my environment and the forces that act on me.*

*Contemplation on any of the mantra, or Japa (chanting) or meditation on the selected mantra will help relax the mind and recharge our energy- both physocal and psychic. Some of the most potent mantra are:*

*" Sri Harih! Om!"*
*"Om Bhurbhuvahsvah, Tatsaviturvareneeyam,*
*Bhargo devasya dheemahi, dheeyo yo nah prachodayat!"*
*"Om! Namah Shivaaya'!*
*Om! Om Namo Narayanaya",*
*"Om! Namo Bhagavathe Vaasudevaya",*
*"Shree Ram Jaya Ram, Jaya jaya Ram",*
*"Hare Rama, Hare Rama, Rama Rama, Hare Hare,*
*Hare Krishna, Hare Krishna, Krishna Krishna Hare Hare"*

*Some times, these mantra are counted by their syllables (Bija mantra) that have numerological significance. The mantra arouse the latent spiritual tendencies in every man. Thus, one can contemplate or meditate on his 'Bija mantra' and this will give very good results. Continuous repetition of mantra with concentration produces what may be called 'molecular vibration', that which will persist even when there is no external repetition with effort.*

*Repetition and contemplation of the meaning can go on simultaneously. Vishnu Purana says, 'after the repetition of Om, one should have recourse to meditation, and after meditation, one should again take to chanting of Om! Through perfection of repetition and meditation, the Supreme Spirit becomes manifest'.*

*This sort of using 'bija mantra' or 'Ishta devatha namasmarane', reciting the name of God in japa or meditation is not restricted to Hindusim. In Islam, the Sufi mystics have for centuries employed the repetition of 'Allah' meaning God, or 'Ali' as a means of getting spiritual illumination. In Buddhist sect Shin, the spiritual aspirants recite the mantra, Namo Amitabha Buddhaya (Namu-amida-butsu). One can repeat the name of Amida in any posture. The Catholics use the rosary in repeating ' Ave Maria, Hail Mary'. The Greek saints of the Middle Ages perfected the system of prayer, Jesus Prayer [The Way of a Piligrim] is similar to the Hindu japa. The name of the Lord should be repeated constantly without break, with full heart, and contemplation. Meditation with bhavartha, imploring the Lords 8Grace keeping His picture in mind is very effective. The Holy Mother used to practice japa, over a lakh a day, during the sadhana period and had demonstrated the power of the divine Name. Through japa and dhyana one can rise from body consciousness to super consciousness.*

*The technique of meditation should be perfected in order to realize its full powers. That is, 'if the mind can first concentrate on an object, and then is able to continue in that concentration for some length of time, and then, by continued concentration, to dwell only on the internal part of the perception of which the object was the effect, everything comes under the control of such a mind'. 'At first meditation must begin with some gross objects and slowly rise to finer or subtler ones until finally it becomes object-less. The mind must be employed to perceive the external causes of sensations, and then move on to internal motions and then to its own reactions. When it has succeeded in perceiving the motions inside by themselves, it will gain the control of all the mental waves in itself or others, even before they have translated themselves into physical energy; and, when he will be able to perceive the mental reactions by itself, the Yogi will acquire the knowledge of everything, as every sensible object and even thought is the result of this reaction. Then he will have seen the very foundation of his mind and it will be under his control. This is the perfect method of mind control.*

*So, meditate; practise dharana, dhyana. and meditation. The golden rule is Japam-japam-japam; practice japam all the time and experience the result. This will give immense happiness.*

*Mantra and Meditation used in Buddhist Monasteries and Churches are very interesting. Buddhist Monks spend almost the whole of their life in chanting Mantra and Meditation. Christians use very simple technique of meditation. Usually, they say their prayers in Church on Sundays and Christian festival days, and solemn occasions. A short devotional passage, or a Chapter of the Bible is recited. The word "Ma-ra-na-tha", meaning, "the Lord Comes", is used for chanting and meditation. The other mantra are: "Hail Mary", and "Lord Jesus Christ, Have mercy on me" as in "The way of the Piligrim". In chanting the Mantra, thee stress is laid on the word rather than on the Self. Listening to the word, the 'mantra', is more important. It is a reasonably good technique since the only way to transcend the ego is to ignore it. The mantra enables the person to achieve this goal of transcending the 'Self'. But, Dwelling on the 'Self' is the technique adopted in the Oriental exercise. It is also important to note that, "Silence (Mauna) is a presence and at the heart of it is God" and this aspect has been recognised in the Christian Meditation; "for a Christian the practice of meditation is the practice of an awareness of God in Christ". Conversion and inner silence are the essential ingrediens of Christian meditation.*

*Peace and Happiness*

*Peace is the state of a tranquil mind. A person's Mind is at rest while he is enjoying peace. Peace is an undisturbed state of mind. Ordinarily, the mind is always agitated and there will be no peace. Peace or 'Shanti' comes with enlightenment. Peace is a calm state of Mind that comes with Jnyan, Knowledge. It can be achieved by ethical principles, Sama and Dama. It is an experience that comes with Self Realisation. Such a 'peace' of mind cannot be disturbed by any worldly disturbances caused by desire or the ari-shadvargas.*

*Ashtavakra Samhita [XI. 2] says,*

*"He who has known for certain that Ishvara is the Creator of all and*

*that there is none-else, becomes peaceful with all his inner desires set at rest, and is not attached to anything whatsoever".*

*Desires arise from thinking that there are desirable things and attractive existences outside of one self. Mind rests on them and feels restless untill it covets them and enjoys them. But, when one knows that the universe is pervaded by the Self- that there is only 'the Self' and nothing else- the feeling of 'otherness' goes and there is no desire, and hence there is peace. A person, who is perfectly happy with him self, contented, and calm and peaceful even under dire provocations, is not at all perturbed even when ridiculed and despised by his servants, sons, wife, daughters and their children and other relations. He is a Yogi, a man of knowledge.*

*Although outwardly appearing to feel pleasure and pain, a yogi is not at all affected by anything. It is only a person of dull intellect, even without doing anything, is ever agitated by distraction; but, the knowledgeable one, even doing his duties, is verily unperturbed, peaceful. His Mind is always calm and peaceful. The pure one knows for cetain that this universe is theproduct of illusion and that nothing exists. Self is revealed to him, and he naturally enjoys peace. Bliss and peace are are the very essence of the Self, the Atman. Hence, one has to realize that peace is already there within oneself. Self-knowledge is not a thing to be obtained by practice of control. The wise one neither longs for gain nor grieves at non-attainment. His cool mind is verily filled with nectar. [Ashtavakra Samhita XVIII 75, 82].*

*One has to realize the totality of existence. The unity of existence is the key to a happy and successful life on this planet. Those who do not realize this will have repeated births and deaths; no doubt they will have some glimpse of happiness and success here and there; but the higher they go deeper they fall. Every feeling of happiness is followed by misery, unhappiness. The Buddha is an example; he says that he has taken atleast a- 500 rebirths as narrated in the jataka stories. Gautama was distressed at old age and death and wanted to get himself redeemed from it; he dis not aspire for wealth for he was a prince by birth. He was not aspiring for any worldly happiness for he had everything! Although this world offers everything to everybody, the unhappiness and misery is sure to haunt some time or the other and we have to find a permanent solution to the problems of life.*

*The Magic Formula*

*The magic formula for a happy and successful life is given here. One has to carefully read this, chant this mantra three times a day- early morning at sunrise, at noon, and in the evening at sunset. It is better if one studies this mantraraja always. One has to contemplate on the meaning of the words. This is a wish-fulfilling mantra. It is Prajapati, Lord Brahman who thus spoke to the gods. One who studies this mantra will be purified, absolved from all sins, wins the seven worlds, and even elements come under his spell. This mahamantra is the panacea for all worldly ills- physical, psychological, social, and economic and is assured of the heavenly abode.*

*The Mahamantra, or the mantra-raja is:*

*Om! (The whole World including Brahman); "OMmmmmmmmmmm...."*

*Om! Namschakraya!*

*To contemplate on: the World surrounded by Vishve Devah, Vasus,*

*Rudras, Adityas, Sun, Moon and Maya; Chakra is Sudarshana - Radiating Brilliance of the self-effulegence- Narayana, the Source of energy, strength, the dynamics (Thermo) ever present behind the Sun*

*Om! namo Narayanaya! (Omniscient and Omnipotent supreme Lord; cosmic flow)*

*Om! namo bhagavathe Vasudevaya! (all-pervading cosmic energy)*

*Om! a, aa, I, ee, u, oo, ru, roo, lu, loo, ye, eye, ou, auo, am, aah!*

*(The Letters of alphabets contains beejaksharas that give basis or support to words and supports the world). Sound followed by silence-self interacting dynamics of unified nature, the unmanifest, unbounded ocean of consciousness expresses the mechanics of manifesting; each sound followed by GAP or silence is the cause of emergence of supreme intelligence since all Knowledge resides in this supreme Silence called 'Atyanta-Abhava' (PURUSHA) evolving and emanating as 'Anyonya-Abhava' (PRAKRITI).*

*Meditate on this Tantra and experience the Bliss of Jnyaan - WHOLENESS and Enjoy it- the 'BLISS'. One must reach this highest state in Dhyan chanting (Japa) of the above Mantra.*

*Yet another Mantra that gives you supreme strength is the Mantra Raja from Nrsimha Tapaniya Upanishad:*

*Om! Ugram, Viram, Mahavishnum, Om hridayaya namah!*
*Jvalantam sarvatomukham, Om! shirase svaha!*
*Narsimham* Bheeshanam bhadram, Om! shikhayai vasat!*
*Mrutyormrutyum namaamyaham, Om! kavachaya hum!*
*Om! Ugram veeram mahavishnum jvalantam sarvatomukham,*
*Nrsimham bheeshanam bhadram mrutyormrutyum namamyaham*
*Om! Asthraya phat!*
*[Nrsimha Poorva-Tapaniya Upanishad and*
*Nrsimha Uttara-Tapaniya Upanishad]*

* *Prajapati created the world by means of the Narasimha Formula. This is the magic formula of happiness and success in life! [used in the Title of this Book- See Cover Page]*

* *The mantra is in Anushtub Chandas, 'highest of all the metres' [Taittiriya Samhita 5,4,12,1].*

*This mantra includes all the Veda and Upanishads. This matra helped the gods to defeat and destroy the Asuras as directed by Lord Indra*

*This mantra is graphically inscribed on a copper plate and worshipped. It is called Shree Sudarshan Chakra (the discus of Vishnu). This Great Circle is the wish-fulfilling gate of liberation, fulfilling all desires. At its center (nave) is the delivering sign (tarakam); the syllable, which denotes Narasimha (Om). This is a very powerful tantra of wish fulfillment. Worn on the body (neck, arm or hair-tuft), this yantra (diagram put in a copper cylinder closed at the two ends) slays evil spirits and protect from death. Absolute faith is required in using this mantra, yantra, and tantra for fulfillment. Of course, all ethical and moral conditions hold good.*

*Along with this mantra, another mantra may be chanted to worship the Mother of all riches, Mahalakshmi. This is the Lakshmi-yajus or the Yajur-Lakshmi. Materialistic as well as spiritual attainments are possible with the chanting of this mantra. The mantra reads:*

*"Om! Bhur Lakshmir, bhuvar Lakshmih,*
*Svarh kaalakarni, tan no Mahalakshmih prachodayat!*

*Meaning, "Om! Earth luck, and atmosphere luck, and heaven luck, black-eared, so may the great luck promote us!*

*He who knows this Mahalakshmi contained in a sacrificial formula obtains great bliss. [Taittiriya Aranyaka, 10,11,12; 3,10,1; 2.8; 1,31;2,10; Mahanarayana Upanishad 11th Anuvaka, Verse 12; Rk Veda 2,33,11; 3,4,9; 1,154,2; 1,89,8; 10,121, 2; 1.40,5].*

**However, it is mentioned that this 'Yajur Lakshmi Mantra' should not be uttered by women since the mantra is addressed to the Goddess, and women are said to be Goddess Lakshmi incarnate.*

*Another important mantra from Ishavasya Upanishad is of great importance since the entire Universe should be seen in its entirety - a holistic view:*

*"Om! Poornamadah Poornamidham Poornaath*
*Poornamudhachyate*
*Poornasya Poornamadhaaya Poornamevaavashishyate"*
*Om! Shantih, Shantih, Shantih!*

*"Om! That is the complete; this too is complete. From the complete has come out the complete. The complete remains complete even though the complete has come out of the complete". It may be surprising that, some times, what we think as the part of the complete is more than the complete. This is the greatest mystery of this Universe! Every thing we perceive is complete in itself, may it be a unicellular amoeba or the millions of cells in Man". We have to realize this completeness of this great opportunity of being born in human life form and should strive for attainment of Supreme Bliss.*

*"Engrossment with the many without knowing the One behind it is the bane of ignorant life. The secret of the many (avidya) is that the One (vidya) can appear to be many without losing its unity [Isavasya Upanisad 10]. One who understands this attains the spiritual felicity of transcendence by absorption in the One (avidya), having overcome the weakness and delusions of mortal life by knowing how 'the many are the becomings of the One'. [Isavasya Upanisad 11]. This sense of oneness, unity, homogeneity, all-comprehensiveness, totality, fullness, completeness, should be realized. This mantra is for contemplation.*

*Select a serene, secluded place and contemplate on this idea with bhavartha in order to get an inner vision of the Self.*

*Meditation should be practised regularly in a selected serene place and at regular times. One should meditate atleast four times a day- in the early morning around 5 a.m., around 12 in the noon, around 6 in the evening, and 10 p.m. or before going to bed. Each mediatation should last for about 45 minutes at a stretch. There should be complete concentration on the Lord and nothing should disturb the mind. No effort shall be made to ward off the unwanted thoughts that occur in the mind spontaneously; just watching them is sufficient to drive them off. Mind shall be calm and serene in a few days after regular practice. It will give supreme strength and self-confidence in all other activities. It will increase efficiency and creative intelligence will take over inertia and indolence. It will give a new turn to life. It gives new energy and makes life more enjoyable.*

*A very important aspect of meditation is the 'dwelling' in Absolute Silence called 'Atyanta- Abhava' where the supreme Knowledge resides. Once you dwell in it, you evolve into 'Anyonya-Abhava' where all possibilities exist and creative abilities emanate. This is the secret! Remember, you are dwelling in suprme Consciousness in Absolute Silence!*

### *" Om", Its Significance*

*'Om' is Brahman. 'Om' is a primeaval sound. 'Om' is the imperishable Brahman, and it constitutes the universe. All Vedic prayers emerged from Om! Om is is used as prefix to all mantra as it is synonymous with Brahman. Whatsoever existed, whatsoever that exists now, and whatsoever shall exist hereafter is Om. [Mandukya Upanisad, 1]. 'Om' represents all the physical and astral bodies, both manifested and unmanifested, from the external-most physical to the internal-most spiritual on four cosmic planes. 'He who knows it attains the highest fulfillment of life' [Katha Upanisad, 1. 2. 15-16]. 'Om' is the symbol of Ishvara or God according to the Yoga Sutra of Patanjali. Patanjali says that constant repetition of this mantra leads to awakening of the soul removing all obstacles.*

'*Om*' is the most sacred mantra ever known and the origin of the word is closely linked to the origin of the universe. It is the first word that came out of Brahman. It came out with 'the Big Bang', or 'the Sphota'. 'Om' is the symbol of this sphota and the Om and the sphota cannot be separated. It is the mother of all names and forms and the whole universe may be supposed to have been created out of this holiest of the holy word Om. The divine spirit expresses itself through the divine Idea, and the Divine Idea through divine sound or word 'Om'. During his meditation, Sri Ramakrishna got the revelation of the ***Nada Brahman*** or the manifestation of Brahman as sound.

*The Katha Upanishad [1.2.15-16] says 'Om is the supreme, immutable Brahman Itself'. He who knows it attains the highest fulfillment in life. The Mundaka Upanishad [2. 2. 4] compares Om to a bow, and the purified and concentrated mind to an arrow, and exhorts us to shoot the arrow with intense alertness so that it may hit the target which is Brahman and become one with it. Om here stands for the entire meaning of the*

*Upanishads. The Mandukya Upanishad declares that, "the syllable 'Om' is the Universe. Whatsoever that existed, whatsoever now exists, whatsoever shall exist hereafter is 'Om'. The syllables A, U, and M that constitutes 'Om' stands for the vast physical universe, the vast mental universe and the causal substratum of both these universes, respectively. The soundless or the unmanifested 'Om', the amatra, however, transcends them".*

*'Om', represents the whole phenomenon of sound production and no other word can do this. This is the fittest symbol of the sphota. Sphota and Om are the same according to Swami Vivekananda. Om is truly symbolic of God. Therefore one should contemplate and meditate on Om!*

*'Om' is the only word that reached where nothing else could reach, and it is the word that originated where everything else is consequential. The mantra shastra or the science of mantra, which is a division of the Tantras, is based on the theory that the whole universe is created out of vibrations. What we call sound is only physical vibrations. Subtler than audible sound are the electromagnetic waves like the instruments within the radio-receiving sets. Subtler still are the thought waves. Thought itself is a manifestation of the eternal supersensuous cosmic pulsations of the Nada Brahman or Shabda Brahman, or the cosmic mind. Nada Brahman can be heard through the subtle mind. It only needs a highly purified mind.*

*"Om is Pranava, the Prana or the cosmic energy that flows throughout the microcosmiv jeeva and the macrocosm Brahmaanda or Hiranyagarbha. Om is prefixed and affixed to all other Mantra by virtue of its great significance. The efficacy of the Mantra depends on the Om.*

## *"ENLIGHTENMENT" AND THE "LIGHT WITHIN"*

*"The Self indeed serves as his Light".*

*[Brihadaranyaka Upanishad.4.3. 2-6]*

*All the external lights can help man only in his waking state. But, during the dream state and deep sleep, it is the Self by which man knows and enjoys himself. There is a very interesting account in Brihadaranyaka Upanishad regarding the 'light within us'. Janaka, the emperor of Videha asked Yajnavalkya, the great Upanishadic Sage about the 'Light that serves man in darkness'. Janaka, a great Jnyani, wanted this answer to enlighten the common man, the man who identifies himself with his body and mind. Yajnavalkya answered this question in a very simple way. 'It is the Sun who gives light to the world and when the Sun has set, it is the moon who reflects the sunshine and sheds the moonlight that gives light in the dark. When the moonlight is not there, it is the fire that gives the light and the heat. When the Sun, the moon and the fire are not there to give light, man uses his speech and finds his way in darkness. One can shout and make his presence known when there is no light. Likewise, man can use his ears, nose and touch to make his way in darkness. The fragrance of a flower or the smell of a plant, the touch on a wall or the sound coming from some direction will serve as light in the absence of the sun, the moon and the fire.*

*The most significant answer came when the Sage said that the inner light shines spreading light on our thoughts, intuition, dreams, and bright ideas. Srinivasa Ramanujam, the great mathematician found answer to most of his problems in his dreams! No external light helps a man in sleep; but it is his inner light, the Consciousness, the Self, the Atman that guides him, that enlightens him.*

*So far, no one has gone to the depth of the mysterious mind to unearth the precious store of wealth hidden in the layers and layers of the sub conscious. Super Consciousness will shed light on all the mysteries of man and his universe. This can be achieved by constant meditation. It is the 'choiceless awareness', the supreme consciousness an atom of which is in our Self that shines on its own and sheds light on everything within us. It is this that keeps us alive and kicking! "The Self indeed is the light of man", says Yajnvalkya.*

*There is darkness where there is no light. There is darkness in some place or the other despite the sun, fire and other sources of light available. There is only one light that can dispel darkness everywhere and that is Atman. The light of the Atman pervades everywhere. There is no darkenss where the Atman shines and the Atman shines in its own glory. It needs no other source; it is self-effulgent and self- luminiscent It is withn us, and not elsewhere outside. As long as the person is ignorant, and avidya covers him, he cannot see this light. This light is covered by the nescience and hence blurred as for as the ignorant person is concerned. It is different with the Yogin, the jnyaani whose senses are withdrawn, mind is stilled and the heart is pure. He shines in his Self.*

*The source of all light is Brahman, the Supreme Spirit and Pure Consciousness. Atman, the knowing self of the human being is identical with the Brahman, Pure Consciousness. It is the radiance of the Pure Consciousness which manifests all things at all times. Pure mind is anthahkarana, the inner instrument of this knowing self. It is not the source oflight. There is no consciousness inherent in the mind. The mind only receives the radiance of consciousness from the knowing self whose inner instrument it is, andilluminate all things including physical light.*

*Though having no light of its own the mind appears to be luminous. Though it seems to cognise, the mind is not the cognizer, but only an instrument of cognition. Shining as it does with the borrowed light of consciousness, the mind is an effective instrument of knowledge.*

*The Self is not illumined by anything but it illumines everything else. This light shines in the state of spiritual attainment, all by itself. It is for this illumination that the spiritual aspirants crave and adopt all sorts of spiritual exercises like dhyana, japa, tapa, vrata, meditation, and goes into the state of Samadhi. No one can stay in that state for long, and no one can leave that effort either. Hence, it is the desire of every aspirant to gain that state of supreme bliss and remain there forever.*

### *The Cosmic Energy*

*'Cosmic energy' is flowing through us all. We are all instruments, more or less. But, when we consciously stop the expression of this energy*

*through the lower centers (of consciousness) and let it find expression through the higher ones, we always feel fresh, then there is no old age for us so far as thought life is concerned. Sometimes we are not able to maintain the activity at higher centers (of Consciousness) because of our old impressions (samskaras or memories) and tendencies, and then there is a strong downward pull, a real tug-of-war that cannot be avoided if we are to grow at all. We can never stop the energy, but we can give it a higher direction, consciously, intelligently, with an effort of the will.*

*Conscious intelligent thinking is necessary. Conscious intelligent thinking removes the barrier, and in the process, the obstruction is removed and more psychic energy flows in us.*

*The Surya Yoga*

*This is yet another important yoga that would greatly enable us to harness the solar power. Many Sadhus and Sants have taken to this Yoga system wherein they are capable of storing the solar energy in their brain cells. These Siddhi purushas can live without solid food for several years. The Yoga is very simple. What all one has to do is to gaze at the Sun for a few seconds, not more than ten at a time every day and go on increasing this period up to 45 seconds in 45 days. This should be done fifteen minutes or half an hour after sunrise and before sunset. Over a period of a month and a half, enormous energy will be stored up in brain cells and this will give good health and longevity. Such persons who have attained siddhi in this Yoga can live on liquid diet and forego solid food for years and years!*

*Importance of 'Being'*

*"Be-ing" is existence, the Truth. The 'Supreme Being' is the Lord Himself. He is the 'Purushottama', the Mahapurusha. It is also true that the species Homo sapiens sapiens is human beings. 'Being' means 'Purusha', a divine personality, a spiritual personality. But, it is very clear from this study that we are neither 'human' nor 'being's; we have to evolve from the animal to man, and man to human first. And, then we have to learn how to 'be' (svastha- at rest), because we are always struggling without 'be'-ing (calm and peaceful). We are a confused lot and we donot know what we are doing and what we want. We madly run after things and get disillusioned when we do not get what we want. Unfortunately, it is also the experienceof most of us that we are not happy even when we get what we want! It is all a mad mad world. We have not understood the meanng of this 'Being".*

*Ashtavakra Samhita is a very beautiful treatise on philosophy of life. Having born one has to simply live; Living is an ordained duty or obligation to God, the Creator. There is nothing that one can do on the face of 'prarabhdha karma' and forces of 'samskara'. But this does not mean total abandonment of one's duty. One should live a contented life (nirlipta jeevana) of minimum needs. Remember, all knowledge leads to this!*

*This is the 'Keep Quiet Rule' of Mind Management Technique (MMT).*

*Keep quiet, or talk less if there is need to talk. Silence speaks much better than sound. There is a very interesting account of a rich and powerful person. He was going in the vicinity of an ashram and felt like meeting the saint. He went to him and asked him to tell him some secret mantra. The saint looked at him and smiled. Again this gentleman asked him to tell him quickly for he had no time to spare. Again, he smiled at him. When he persisted further, the saint said only one word "meditate'. The saint said, even uttering one word is half-truth and you have made me utter it. The more words you use, the more untruth will fall out. A meaningful glance or an all-knowing smile is enough. Never enter into discussion or argument. Take to meditation at the earliest opportunity and contemplate on Him. A wise man will never indulge in worldy affairs for he knows the futility of it all.*

*There is a big difference between a fool keeping quiet and a wise man keeping quiet; there is a big difference between the Buddha smiling and an idiot smiling. It is 'jnyaan' that makes all the difference! Jnyaan is everything! To repeat, we all know that Man is a human being; but, as men, neither we are 'Human' nor we know how to be a 'Being'. Too much of ego, too much of senseless talks, arguments, take away our energy. These have no place in this philosophy of Self Realisation. We are always restless. We keep on dabbling in things consciously or without it. Keeping a calm and cool disposition with total awareness is the Mind Management Technique. Here, it is reiterated that 'happiness is not rejoicing and unhappiness is being dull and morose. It is a state unperturbed by happenings- success or failure.*

*Equanimity is 'Sukha dukhe samekrutva, laabhaalaabhau jayaajayau' [Bhagavad-Gita II.38]. It is maintaining equanimity, balanced mind, unexcited state of mind ('anudvigna manah'), under all circumstances. It is treating happiness and sorrow, gain and loss, and conquest and defeat with equanimity; One has to engage in battle (of life), thus he will not incur sin (sorrow). This is the way to be happy and successful. Happiness is normally believed to be a state of joyfulness with elated ego; extroverts expressing it in jumping, singing and dancing and introverts enjoying it within unmindful of the goings on in the outside world. Both the expressions are not. Happiness is a cool and contemplated, meditative mind, an undisturbed state of mind, a state of equilibrium. Neither jumping with joy, nor being morose and dull with sadness are stated to be real 'happiness'. It may be called a 'nirliptata', happy and contented state of mind.*

*There are two types of 'nirliptata' or 'simply being'; one, just like a fool who keeps quite for he knows not what to do and, the other, a Jnyani who knows that he is at the mercy of the Lord. A jnyani will neither brood about the past nor get anxious about the future. He just lives now and here, at the present. Past is dead and future is unborn. Arjuna was advised even to forget the episode of 'Visvaroopa Darshan' and get down to the practical duty. Even 'vision' of the God will not bring one's duty to an end, and one has to constantly remember Him and do his duty. Here, there is no choice; there is no role to the play of the quixotic and 0fickle mind. There is absolute resolute mind, concentrating on the crdained duty. This is the sure way of achieving success and happiness in life. 'Duty first' is the Rule. One cannot abandon one's duty under any circumstance.*

# 10
# The Art of Creative Living

*To make the best use of life is wisdom. Wisdom comes from knowledge. Knowledge or 'Vid' (to know) is the essence, the goal of life. Knowledge comes from Buddhi, the disciminating power of the mind. Buddhi is the reflection of the inner light shining in the Atman. Intellect or Buddhi is thus, the most important thing that governs our life and activity. It derives all its strength and discriminative power from 'Prajnya' or Consciousness, the light called the 'Jnyaan Deep', the source of which lies in the Atman. It is the Spiritiual Light that has its source in Parabrahman, the self-effulgent source that provides the strength and power to the Sun. It is called 'Sri Hari Narayana', i.e., the ever-flowing Cosmic Energy in the Vedas.*

*Need For Spiritual Life*

Where is the need for spiritual life if one is happy and contented? Yes, this is the most perplexing question. Most of the mortals are happy and contented; even if they are not happy, they are resigned to fate and live as their fate decides. Even in day- to- day struggle, it never occurs to them that there is a simple and beautiful way to get out of all this rut. It is sheer ignorance that they enjoy. Some spiritual leaders like Sri Madhwacharya and Sri Shankara are of the opinion that, 'Divine Grace' is required to turn to Him. Without His grace, nothing can move. May be it is true that is the way many people think.

In *Vivekachudamani*, Shri Shankara says, "a human birth, desire for emancipation, and contact with holy men- these three are very rare and are attained only through the Grace of the Lord".

'Divine Grace' is something very powerful that steers your life out of all pitfalls and gives you 'awareness'. Hence, it is not something that comes from outside but that is already within you. It is the light that shines when your spark kindles it. It is the result of a pure mind and a pure heart that comes with love and sacrifice. It is self- luminous; it is always present behind Self-reliance and Self –surrender; it comes in the form of divine pulsations from within and only a strong mind can receive it. It can be felt only in the absence of ego. This requires total surrender to Him, 'sharanagati'.

Sri Krishna says in Bhagavad Gita, "abandoning all dharmas, take refuge in Me alone; I will liberate you from all sins; grieve not". 'Not even a blade of grass waves without My will'. Lord's Grace is also not that easy to get. It is like the saying, 'only the crying child gets the milk'. Only those who cry for Him will get His grace. Sant Tukaram did it; Gouranga or Chaitanya Maha Prabhu did it. Tears should flow down in utter submission and total desperation; only then will He turn towards you. Where is the need for all this? For those who do not believe in God and those who are already happy and peaceful by their poorva punya, and the Lord's Grace, there is no need for crying. But, *Narada Bhakti Sutra* clearly states that, 'happiness and peace of mind are not sufficient; one should constantly think of the Lord both in happiness and distress'. It is the ultimate goal of every human being. It is easy to live happily like any other animal; but, if one has to cross the ocean of sansar, one has to look to Him. Shri Adi Shankara has put it in a very beautiful form:

*"Punarapi jananam, punarapi maranam*
*Punrapi janani jatare shayanam...*
.........................................
*Iha Samsaare bahu dustaare,*
*Kripaya saare, Pahi Muraare,*
*Bhaja Govindam, Bhaja Govindam,*
*Govindam Bhaja, Moodha mate ".*

There are situations when your ego stands in your way to see Him, the Lord. You desperately need Him; but your ego will not allow you to think of Him. It is here we all come to what is called 'living on the periphery'. There is no sense of purpose of life. There is no set goal. There is absolute complacency and a false sense of satisfaction. There is no internal urge to develop spiritual life since the mundane world has a firm grip and does not allow to get rid of it. That is the beauty of the 'Mother Earth'!

Mother earth is the Goddess Shri Lakshmi, the bestower of everything in this sensate world. She is beautiful and bountiful. She is the supporter, the inspiration to Shriman Narayana. She is the eternal source of wealth; and, any one who prays her, praises her, will get whatever one wants. The hold of the mother over the child is astounding! Once born on this earth, even to think of the other world is very difficult. The earth is gross and finite. It is this finite world that dictates all life and activities. But no one will believe that this world is unreal!

Always remember the upanishadic doctrines. Remember, this world is bound by space and time. Anything bound by space and time is finite and limited, subject to change and cause disappointment; it is a phenomenon of 'make-believe' material world. Even the solid surface features of the earth that appear firm are not stable and give way with the earthquakes; lofty features such as the mountains, plateaus and plains have changed over the geological time of thousands and thousands of Millenia.The rivers change their course and lakes dry up. There have been major convulsions and revolutions in the earth's cycle and the finest example is that of the Himalaya Mountains. These mountains stand where once the Sea of Tethys stood. May be, one day our Great Ganga Plains will be raised up to lofty mountains higher than the Himalayas and the present Himalayas are weathered, eroded and denuded and reduced to an erosional plateau like Tibet. When such lofty mountains are reduced by denudation, what about the fragile life of the humans on this earth?

The tragedy of human life is that man believes that everything is eternal and permanent. For even a second, man cannot believe that he is mortal and would die anytime, any day. This idea of permanency of status is derived from the same divine source, the eternal 'Atman', the Brahman, who dwells in him. This taste of 'Infinite' nature is the taste that lingers in man and it is for this infinite status his subconscious lingers on. But to fathom it out is very difficult under the earthly conditions. Swamy Vivekananada used to repeat, 'each soul is potentially divine, and the goal is to manifest the divinity within'.

Both the body and mind are subject to constant change and cannot reach a state beyond change. But beyond the momentary sheath of gross matter, beyond the finer covering of the mind lies the 'Atman', the true Self of man, permanent and ever free. It is His freedom that is percolating through layers of thought and Matter; and in spite of this, the colourings of name and form is ever asserting its unshackled existence. This Atman is to be realised through faith, devotion and meditation. There is no doubt, it is the same Atman that shines in our souls and also shines in all souls. We all reflect the same Light. It is the one 'Infinite' spirit that manifests itself through all individual souls. Self-knowledge is the realisation that the individual self is part of the all- pervading spirit Sri Hari Narayana. Attaining it, all desires, even in the subtlest form, disappear. Once successful in this attempt, having attained this with the help of the enlightened ones, it is the duty to return to world to spread this divine knowledge, realization of God in man. It is this realization of the divinity that manifests in man is what is called true 'Religion'.

*The Source of Ignorance, Avidya or Nescience*

*Avidya or nescience is the mother. It is the mother who has given birth to the child and nourished it. It is the Prakriti, the uncaused cause and as such, it has no beginning. Avidya is thus self- existent.*

Ever since the child has tasted its mother's milk, the sensate world has taken a firm hold over the life of the child. As the child grows older, the hold becomes tighter and tighter fed by the food derived as it is from tamasic or rajasic sources like the minerals, water, vegetation, animal products like milk and meat and other earthly sources. All the 'ari-shad-vargas'- raga or moha, dvesha, krodha (anger), lobha, mada, matsarya that obstruct, or hinder, the realization of the Self take firm root in the body. The different juices of fruits and vegetables, or anything derived from the vegetative sources take control of the senses and dictate the moods. The 'tamasic' and the 'rajasic' juices (food) make the grip much firmer and it is very difficult to get rid of this sensate world. It leads to a state where the sense of discrmination is lost and we reach a state as one can put it, 'the pigs are happy in mire'; happy and contented as they are, persons do not have the thirst or hunger for the Lord. Is it the result of 'His Grace' that you forget Him? May be! But the sweet memories of Him is lingering somewhere in the subconscious. Immersed in the worldly affairs, forgetting Him for a while, a rude shock or a jolt shakes persons out of complacency now and then to remind this. Once in a while, this changes the direction of life of some people, but may not alter the lives of many others! This is the way the Lord cleanses our mind and makes our hearts pure; this is the way our ego is curbed and realize our Self and thus He makes us see Him in all, not merely in a few kith and kins or loved ones.

The grip of 'Vasudha',. 'Raga' or attachment of the mother earth is so great on the mortals that it is difficult to get out of it. Even Sriman Narayana was not spared; He got into the grip of ' Shree Vasudha' when He came to rescue her in 'Varaha Avatar'. It is believed that Goddess Lakshmi, the earth, was hidden in ocean and the Lord came to rescue her in 'Varaha avatar'. Since he resided in water for some time with Laksmi, he is known as Narayana, [naara meaning water, and ayana meaning abode]. On insistence from all other Divine Souls in the Heaven, Sri Narada had to come down to earth and remind Sriman Narayana of His purpose of the visit to earth and prod Him to return to Vaikunta. The Lord had forgotten his abode "Vaikunta' for a while! If this is the state of the Lord under the grip of the sensate world, how strange it is to expect the mortals to get out of the grip of this sensuous world?

We all live on the periphery of Consciousness. We are governed by the sensuous life directed by the mind. The mind controls the senses and sets them on their errands of search for happiness in small things. The supreme goal of life is happiness. This happiness has to be gained by the senses and the senses get satisfied as per the dictates of the mind. It is an outward errand and the senses go out to reach for the source of happiness. Now and then, the stint of happiness enjoyed, a 'make-believe state', is attained and the ignorant mind takes it for real happiness until it gets bored of it and strives for a different source of happiness.

Thus, the mad pursuit for the 'make-believe happy state' continues and this state of illusion is '*maya*'. All of us are carried away in this flood of illusion; once we are knocked down by the 'prajnya' or realisation, we come to our real senses. The mind takes the guidance from the 'buddhi' or intellect' and looks inward for its guidance. The senses are asked to keep quite and allow the mind to take to the inward journey. The same sensuous mind turns to the intellect and the consciousness guides it to better understanding of the real happiness through 'self- realization'.

Here, it is very interesting to note an episode that took place during the churning of the ocean for the sacred elixir 'amrut'. When the demons realised that they were cheated in the distribution of the divine elixir, the amrut, they tried to control the five senses of the mortals and prevent them from turning to God. Whenever man turned towards the spirituial sources for his happiness, the sensuous mind was diverted to the opposite of all that is good. Thus came the habbit of seeing and hearing sensuous sights and sounds, taste rajasic (hot) and tamasic (cold) foods and drinks, and dwelling in sex, in mad pursuit of sensuous life. This plan of the "Asuras' is to keep off the mortals from the attractions of the 'divine' and denying them a chance of enjoying the 'Supreme Bliss'. Thus, it appears as though 'evil prevails over good'. This is again 'maya'. This is just an illusion for it is 'Sat' only that prevails.

'*Maya*' is beautifully described in '*Brahma Rahasya Upanishad*'. [*Mantra* 13]. Maya is called 'Avyaktam' (undifferentiated or unmanifested), or Prakriti. This can be inferred from the effects it produces. It is this Maya that brings forth this whole universe. Maya playing upon Brahman causes the first manifestation of Hiranyagarbha (Cosmic Space) in the beginning of the cycle. He, in turn, creates the whole universe. [*Isavasya Upa.* 12].

Maya is Shuddha Sattva (pure, devoid of passion and inertia). Brahman is beginning-less and end-less (Anadi-Anantam). But, Maya is Anadi-Santam (beginning-less but has the end) only for the Jnyani who has the knowledge of the Self.

Matter and energy and sound exist in Maya in an undifferentiated state. The whole world exists in Maya in a seed-state during the cosmic Pralaya (dissolution). Maya is the Upadhi or causal body of the Ishvara. It is under the control of the Lord. Shri Ramakrishna Paramahansa puts it in a very interesting way. Accordingly, "the truth is that God alone is real and all else unreal. Men, universe, house, wife, children- are all unreal; all these are like the magic of the magician. The magician strikes his wand and says, 'come delusion, come confusion'! Then he says to the audience,'open the lid of the pot; see the birds fly into the sky'. But the magician alone is real and his magic unreal. The unreal exists for a second and then vanishes". Swami Shivananda puts it in a different way. He says, "All visible things are Maya. Maya will vanish through the effect of knowledge (Jnyana). One must strive to get rid of Maya that devastates the mind; the destruction of the mind". Some believe that destruction of mind, manonasha is not possible. 'Manonasha' means the annihilation of Maya, ignorance that covers Reality. "Meditation is the only way in which to dominate maya". It is possible to get out of this 'make-believe' world by meditation, contemplation, dhyan and sadhana.

***Brahma Rahasya of Happiness***

The secrets of knowing the Self, the '*Brahman*' are beautifully explained in the '*Brahma Rahasya Upanishad*'. This Upanishad contains mantras that help in understanding the attributes or the svabhava of the jeevas, and the methods of overcoming the obstacles that prevent realization of the Brahman. This whole world is a make-believe theatre of action. All are actors who come and go and the stage remains. This make-believe world, rather this unreal world or '*maya prapancha*' is the product of the mind. If the mind vanishes, the world vanishes. There is a beautiful mantra in Brahma Rahasya Upanisad where in *Manonasha* is described. [Mantra 12]

***"Jeevanmuktesu manasah saroopanashah***
***videhamukteshu svaroopanashah"***

It means, "*There is a Saroopanasha of mind in jeevanmuktas. In Videhamuktas*, i.e., *who have attained disembodied liberation, there is aroopanasha of mind*". *Thus, there are two kinds of manonasha, or destruction of mind: 1.Saroopanasha (mind with form) and 2. Aroopoanasha, (mind without form)*.

If one is free from desires from sensual objects, raga (attachment), dvesha (hatred), ahamkara (egotism), anger, lust, mama-ta (mine-ness), pride, jealousy, greed and attachment, such a person has achieved 'manonasha' (mumukshutva) or liberation. It is the Vasanas that cause bondage and attachment to sensual objects. Vasana- kshaya is extinction of Vasanas. Manonasha is destruction of mind. Tatva-Jnyana is knowledge of truth. As long as these are not equally practiced regularly and continuously the knowledge of the Self cannot be achieved. Extinction of Vasanas that causes annihilation of mind cannot be achieved easily. It requires discrimination (Viveka), meditation on the Self (Atma-Chintana), Vichara (enquiry of Atman), Sama (control of mind), control of senses (dama), Vairagya (dispassiona), Tyaga (renunciation) – all these, to destroy Vasanas.

Brahman i.e., Self- realisation can be achieved through the mind alone after abandoning its Sankalpas, or Vrittis (thoughts) and Vikalpas (imaginations). When the five organs of knowledge are subdued, when the mind is controlled and when incessant meditation is practiced, Brahman is revealed. Then alone one becomes immortal. Brahma Jnyana is the release from the trammels of one's own mind. Such a release alone leads to the attainment of Moksha.

The purpose of Brahman-realization is self-perfection and the attainment is illumination and liberation from the meshes of ignorance, desire and rebirth. Mukti is attaining perfection."***He who realizes Brahman becomes Brahman***" [***Mundaka Upanishad III-2-9***]. He realizes the final goal of evolution. This realization of Brahman is not limited to mere intellectual apprehension. It is really a profound working experience in which ordinary Consciousness working in the realm of time and space through subject-object relation is transcended, indeed, deepened into its essence, i.e., Brahman. Such a state is realized in the highest mode of in-drawn concentration known as 'Nirvikalpa Samadhi' or 'Asamprajnyata'.

One who has attained this realization has a true and immediate vision of the divine unity, and is the possessor of supreme felicity, free as he becomes, from all cravings and evanescent interests. Only when the Mind ceases from its preoccupations with the sense objects and turns to Brahman, it can enjoy the Bliss; for, Brahman is the source of the reflected happiness, which the mind experiences even in the sense contact.

One has to realize the 'Brahman' as one's own very Self. Then and then alone one can attain perfect independence. Real swarajya, or independence of the soul, can be achieved by manonasha (destruction of the mind), and burning of the Vasanas. Meditation alone can help in the control of the mind. This gives eternal happiness. This is the Brahmarahasya of happiness and supreme bliss.

***Desire***

*Desire is the seed; it is the cause of all causes and leads to eternal bondage. It is at the root of all our problems. Unless desire is completely rooted out there is no mukti or liberation. What makes desire so strong is that' desire is Brahman'. Desire is the main object of this objective world and its fulfillment is the goal of life. Desire comes in the form of dreams and the dreams become the basis of life; and, dream fulfillment becomes the goal of life.*

*The Lord has created this world of material objects for sheer enjoyment and happiness of all the creatures. He has thrown a lavish party in his garden that covers the entire universe and invites all organic beings to enjoy the everlasting feast. It is an everlasting and an inexhustible one. One can go on enjoying this Lord's Party, a Banquet at that, birth after birth until one is completely fed-up! Not only the Lord has hosted this lavish party, but also has given an unending hunger and recurring desire. It is this hunger and desire that make us run after material objects. Our hunger and thirst are never quenched. We have thirty-three parts of the body each having its desire; the eyes have the desire to look at beautiful objects and ears have the desire to hear melodious songs. The skin is ever hungry of fleeting happiness of touch! The List goes on and on. Further, the benevolent and the All-merciful Lord has created a million objects and a thousand Deities to each of the hungry part to quench the thirst and feed the hungry millions of these hungry, greedy bodies. Together, the thirty-three thousand million hungry parts of the body and an equal number of material objects to feed them fills this material world. The thirty-three thousand Vasus, Abhimaani Devatas are empowered by the Lord to look after these hungry creatures. How kind and Gracious of the Lord!*

*But, remember! Conditions apply. Note the letters in small print. There is a clause to this. The Rider says, 'no over indulgences'! Remember, it is an illusion, 'maya'; and, soon you will be disillusioned. Just watch and enjoy the drama; do not involve yourself in it. A Jnyaani will not be attracted to this attractive "just because party" of the Lord; because the party is the magic wand of bondage and once you get into its trap you are doomed to flashes of joy and ocean of misery. It is very difficult to get out of the Grand Party. It is similar to the morning sickness after the Grand Party of the previous night; the sickness sticks! Jnyaanis cleverly avoid this party and fools easily fall prey to this.*

This world is for enjoyment. Every part of our body has desire. Buddha called it the' desires of the flesh'. There are 33 parts of our body craving for fulfillment. So also, these thirty-three parts have thirty-three thousand deities who are benevolent and grant our wishes to be fulfilled. These Deities are called the Vasus,' Abhimaani Devatas'. They are empowered to grant our wishes fulfilled. With every fulfillment of our wish, the impressions we get are impreganated as 'karmic particles' into the Soul and become the cause of our next birth. Our soul is so impreganated with the memories and desires that would cause repeated births to get over. Thus we are in eternal bondage due to our 'desire'.

Desire and activity cease only when all wants are fulfilled. Ignorance begets desire and desire generates activity directed towards ephemeral ends, which in course of fulfillment produce good and bad tendencies, pulling up the individual self to higher births or dragging it down to lower life.

The person is the desire. It is the desire that makes the soul take birth repeatedly. It is the desire that is the driving force behind the formation of the body that is the means for the soul. The great elements guided by the supreme intelligence forms the body to perform this function. This is the supreme order the power of creation is the power of the Self.

The soul has the outer coverings and shines through these coverings. These coverings are the five sheaths of desire- annamaya kosha, pranamaya kosha, manomaya kosha, vignyanamaya kosha, and the anandamaya kosha. What the soul wants, it gets it. For it is the giver, that is the taker, that is the creator, and that is the 'enjoyer'. That is also the enjoyed and the 'enjoyment'. The body and mind are medium for its activities.

Till the soul is free from all types of desires, including desire for 'liberation', it goes on taking any number of bodies, transmigrating through bodies till it experiences all desires. The soul goes through different bodies evolving at every stage depending upon the nature of its desires till it attains supreme knowledge.

*'Whatever may be the nature of desire it shall be fulfilled, since the desire itself is the Brahman in its true nature i.e., 'Bliss', or 'Anand'. This is the Supreme Order.*

***"Kaamagney Namah" [Vishnu Sahasra Naamam]***

***'The Supreme Self purifies the person from all desires'.***

The 'ari-shadvargas', kama, krodha, moha, lobha, mada, matsarya can be destroyed by prayer, worship, and meditation and firm resolve. Mind is so attached to these raga, moha, mada that it is very difficult to get out of the clutch. The desire is the fire that destroys reason. It burns out the body and the brain cells. It makes man an animal. Yoga helps to get out of the grip of desire, but there should be a firm mind, a strong will power.

The Supreme Self is the creator of the desires. All desires are the reflection of creativity of the Supreme Self. These desires for the objects are the conscious desires of the ignorant soul to reach its destination. It aspires for the perishable objects due to ignorance; and when it attains knowledge it attains desire and its own true nature, the Bliss. The desire, the desirer, and the desired are one only, but in different names, forms and functions.

The Supreme Creator is the creator of desire. The desire is the illusion or 'maya', ignorance. Only by the 'Lord's Grace', a person is freed from this desire, this illusion, this ignorance.

The seat of desire is the mind. Mind is the desire. Senses are a medium for the experience of this desire. The senses coming in contact with the objects experience the quality of the sense objects that are termed as pleasure or pain. The intellect is the sharp edge of the mind. It is the guiding arm of the mind as per the dictates of the mind. '*The senses, the mind and the intellect are said to be its seat through which these delude the embodied by veiling his wisdom'. [Gita* III-40]. So, kill the mind, the destroyer of knowledge. It is not possible to kill the Mind; here, it is meant only to still the mind, i.e., to stop the vibration and establish equilibrium. The Supreme Self goes on creating the universe in newer and bewitching forms so that the persons are always enamoured to live in this world. The Lord Almighty has made breathing a pleasure, all sense objects pleasurable so that nobody wants to leave this world. Persons are so much attached to this world of bodies, the perishable bodies at that, they forget about their own true Self. They are attached to the body that is the means of bondage that eventually leads to disenchantment and disillusion. Attaining Self is the means of breaking this cycle of life and be liberated into freedom.

The Anthahkarana, internal organ (sensitivity?) that include mind (manas), intellect (Buddhi), (internal organ) will not assume the form of objects. It will be free from vrittis. 'Vrittis' are virtual 'whirlpool' in the mind-lake, thought waves in manas, or mental modifications. It will be in a state of resistence, or Nirodha, or control. In saroopanasha, the Rajas and Tamas gunas are eradicated. Sattva Guna remains. On account of this sattva Guna, a jeevanmukta possesses Sattvic virtues such as Maitri (Friendship), Karuna (Mercy), and other good qualities. In a Videhamukta, even Sattva Guna is annihilated. Therefore Aroopanasha of mind comes in.

The attributes of the three Gunas are to be clearly understood in order to achieve 'Manonasha'. Mind is formed out of the sum total of Sattva portion of Tanmatras, the subtle elements. It is not self-luminous. Because, it is very near Brahman on account of its subtlety, the light of Brahman is reflected on it. So it thinks, it doubts, plans and speculates. Just as there is death for this physical body, there is death for this mind also, 'manonasha'. When one gets knowledge of the Self, mind gets absorbed in Brahman, just as the drops of water get absorbed in a hot pan. Mind gropes in dark; it is unable to explain the Whys and Hows of the riddle of the universe. Mind is a finite and a frail instrument that is conditioned in time, space and causation.

'Manonasha' or destruction of mind is possible by 'Meditation' and Tapas. 'Manolaya' which is only temporary absorption for a short time in the object of meditation cannot give freedom. 'Vasanas' are destroyed in 'manonasha'. Pranayama can check the velocity of mind. It can calm and steady the mind. It cannot annihilate the mind. The enquiry of 'Who am I'? or Brahma Vichara will bring Manonasha. Atman and Mind are two different entities. Mind can be annihilated but not the Atman.

The characteristics of pure '*Sattva*', unmixed with Rajas and Tamas, are harmony, knowledge, bliss, supreme peace, cheerfulness, balance of mind, purity of nature (Shuddha Bhava), contentment, constant devotion unto Atman, absence of pride, hatred, hypocrisy, lust and anger, desire for liberation, divine tendencies, faith, turning away from the unreal, discrimination, enquiry, meditative mood, etc. Pure Sattva is like transparent crystal. Reflection of Atman can take place in Sattva only, like reflection of objects that can take place only in a clear mirror. When Sattva is mixed with Rajas and Tamas, it becomes impure Sattva. It is Avidya or ignorance. This becomes Upadhi or the limiting factor, the limiting adjunct of Jeevas. Transmigration takes place in this condition. Self-Realization comes when the Sattva Guna is raised to one hundred percent, reducing the proportion of Tamas and Rajas and the transmigration also ends with it. Eradicating the Sattva Guna takes one to Kaivalya- a state of mind in turiya, and makes Jeeva, a Jeevanmukta.

'*Rajo Guna*' has got the projecting capacity or Vikshepa Shakti. The phenomenal world manifests through this Vikshepa Shakti. Rajas cause attachment to objects and various sorts of activities. This brings grief or sorrow and misery. Preponderance of Rajo Guna is the cause of bondage and induces worldly tendencies. Lust, anger, greed, arrogance, hatred, pride, hypocrisy, jealosy are the attributes of Rajas.

'*Tamo Guna*' is at the root of all the problems of the Jeevas of this world. It is a veiling power. Ignorance or moudhya, carelessness, sleep, laziness, lassitude, and dullness are the attributes of Tamas. Tamas causes perverted intellect. Intellect is rendered blind. Preponderance of Tamas causes repeated transmigration. It makes things appear differently from what they are. It projects things that are non-existing. Even the learned persons are under the clutches of Tamas and lose their sense of right judgment. They lose their understanding and become seekers of pleasure. They suffer under sense of deeper attachment to worldly things and perishable objects. They mistake unreal things as real. They get swayed under the power of money, power, and authority and regard them as eternal. They regard body, wife, children, brothers and sisters as self and mistake them for Atman. These learned persons suffer grief and misery when these pleasure centers are withdrawn. Tamas is very powerful as a veiling shakti, that makes even the learned persons lose their sense of discretion and treat this 'make-believe' world as more real.

The *Brahmarahasya Upanishad* describes the method of attaining Self- Realization. By constantly thinking of Him one can attain Him. One can attain the Brahma Jnyana by eradicating or annihilating the Tamasic and Rajasic Gunas. All vrittis, such as the Ghora vrittis (impure thoughts of mind), Mudha vrittis (stupefied) and the pleasure creating vrittis, Ajnyana Vrittis (ignorance), egoism – all should be annihilated. The source of all these vrittis is the samskaras or impressions of various vasanas in a seed state. If the seed-body or mula ajnyana is removed all vrittis perish by themselves.

Practising Pranayama will help in the annihilation of all vrittis. Constant inquiry as to '*Who am I*?' will help understanding oneself and annihilation of vrittis. Whenever a vritti rises up, put this question; the vritti disappears. Do not try to fulfill the desires; the vrittis disappear. Because, fulfillment of the desire leaves a deeper impression that the mind lingers upon again and again leading to frustration and delusion. Fulfillment of desires is not the answer; repeat the question whether this will give an everlasting happiness. If it is not giving permanent happiness, discard it by 'prathyahara' technique, i.e., withdrawing the mind from the object.

*'Meditation' is the technique of rooting out 'Ajnyana'. Meditate on the Srutis: "AHAM BRAHMAASMI", ["I AM THE SELF"]" and SARVAM KHALVIDAM BRAHMA NEHA NANASTI KINCHANA", meaning, "ALL INDEED IS BRAHMAN, THERE IS NO SUCH THING AS DIVERSITY (OBJECTIVE WORLD)".*

Well, Is there anything wrong in the statement of the Lord, 'I am Brahman'? The Lord who sits in the cavity of the heart, the 'Atman', or the embodied soul proclaims "*Aham Brahmasmi*". Hear this 'anahata dhvani', (sound emanating from within). Try to experience this supreme Bliss within you meditating on your Self, say the Upanishads But, this is not so very easy to those who are not initiated into spiritual life.

"When meditation is practiced, obstacles such as absence of right enquiry, impatience, laziness, inclination to enjoyment, absorption in sensual and impure thoughts arise. Remove them through right enquiry and discrimination" [Mantra 18]. Use sense of discrimination, viveka, vichara and vairagya by asking the question 'who am I'? Sama (serenity or calmness), dama (control of senses), and uparati (abstraction) should be practiced constantly; thoughts of Atman will remove impure thoughts. *Asana*, *Prnayama*, and right sattvic diet will help reducing tamas and rajas. 'Brahma Jnyan' is the release from the trammels from one's own mind. Such a release alone leads to the attainment of moksha or liberation. One who practises contemplation or meditation on the above mantras will surely conquer his mind and attain 'Brahma Jnyan'.

*" If one regards the world as unreal, all vasanas will vanish by themselves. Ignorance, 'Ajnyana' will perish slowly. One has to realise 'the Brahman' as one's own very Self. This is the Brahma Rahasya". [Mantras 15-20].*

The individual mind is in touch with the cosmic mind and our mental energy comes from a cosmic source. We should know how to control and direct this psychic energy. Control is necessary to prevent the energy from flowing into lower centers, from flowing out through our sense organs and getting wasted through futile thinking and worrying and useless talk. This cosmic energy should be made to find expression at higher centers, the heart, the throat, the ajnya (between the eye brows).

Unconscious control is called repression, and some forms of repression are harmful to certain people. But, conscious, intelligent control is beneficial and essential for all people, not necessarily for the spiritual aspirants.

*The Power of Love*

There is a desire in all of us that others should always love us. We do not want that others should show scant respect or hate us. But, the opposite is not always true. We do not want to love others unless there is a special relation with us. We do not hesitate to show disrespect to others, especially when they are less fortunate and deprived persons. Our ego does not permit us to show respect to such persons. We love only our superiors for fear of repression, or for favours. This is normal human behaviour that we observe in our day-to-day life. Hence, the question of unqualified universal love does not arise. Honestly speaking, love in its true sense, does not exist. Otherwise we would not see so much of strife, jealousy, hatred, intolerance, wars and unrest everywhere. No two countries can co-exist peacefully with all their no-war pacts, for fear of the unknown! This is the situation in the world today. This applies to relationships between States, between cities and towns, between communities, and even families within towns and villages. Some attribute this to Kali since this is Kali Yug. But the reality is that our heart is not pure; our mind is not pure. We are possessive in nature. We are selfish and we want everything exclusively for ourselves whether we need them or not. We are jealous of others. The arishadvargas have their play for there is no control over them. Man is not bothered to control his mind; that is the problem.

Love is a very precious thing that we do not want to shower on everyone recklessly. We reserve it to a chosen few and that also for a limited time; may be till our desires are fulfilled with that person. It requires

Jesus Christ to shower love and compassion recklessly. We look at Shree Krishna's love for the Gopikas also with suspicion, lust in our mind! This is the situation today. When they say, Lord Krishna had 16,008 damsels we literally believe it and envy Him! It is a great tragedy that our mind will not rise above a certain level of consciousness. If God cannot redeem the troubled souls who else can? We do not realize that Lord Krishna redeemed all those damsels who earnestly worshiped Him with Love; you also worship Him with Love He will shower His Grace on you!

Love is defined as 'Yuj' meaning union. It is the union of souls. Any person, who loves the 'other', sees himself in that other- person, place, animal, or thing. When we love our pet birds or animals, we identify ourselves with them. We do not see any difference between our selves and our pets. We become one. That is the reason why we see some fortunate pets get luxurious treatment from their adopters and inherit huge property bequeathed to them by their rich owners. The opposite of love is hatred. This should not mean that if we cannot love we should hate. Many parents hate their children and children hate their parents for various reasons. Here, absence of love is the basic thing. Selfishness is the other important reason for this. Many a parents dis-own their children and deprive them of ancestral property; they give it away in charities and public trusts.

Mother's love for children is true love. It is true love without blemish, without selfishness, without any desire for returns and it is not even reciprocal. However, some human minds are so wretched that we find some exceptions to this, too. Paternal love is filial and, very rarely we find some fine sentiments and deep love between parents and grown up children. Some parents love their children so much that they close their eyes to all their follies and weakness. More often, children are in the grip of their own desires, likes and dislikes, and love has no place in such afflicted minds. *Pure love exists where spirituality reigns supreme*!

We often see some doctors and nurses showering love and affection on patients in hospitals and it works wonders. Love has great power of curing sickness of body and mind. Love is God for God comes in the form of love comparison of doctors and nurses and ward boys to the sick. It is extremely difficult to say that love is a constant factor in our day-to-day life. Our love is at best conditional reflex and we hesitate to love even those who love us; hence, it is not even reciprocal. It is this kind of development of man that makes the future of this world bleak. The concept of universal love is too much to ask for in this materialistic world. With so much of jealousy, intolerance, greed and avarice, cruel and merciless attitude of people, it is frightening! It is this fear that prompted Jesus Christ to preach universal love and sacrifice. Unfortunately, even today, his preachings are not taken seriously; we are eager to accept his 'love thy neighbour' concept, that too in a very narrow and limited or restricted sense of the terms. Hence the question, 'where is pure Love'?

*You can love only the Lord Almighty with pure heart and none else! Love Him whole-heartedly*. This is an important Mind Management Technique. Do It. Experience the joy of Love of God. Enjoy the Supreme Bliss. There is no other happiness that is superior to this!

Nature teaches the lessons of love and compassion and, man learns discrimination. The dualities inherent in this illusory world are responsible for the nature of man and his behavioural tendencies. Memory on the one hand and arishadvargas on the other create such a complexity in man that his actions are highly influenced by his likes and dislikes. If he likes some persons or things, his love, sympathy, benevolence, compassion, anthahkarana, overflow; if he dislikes someone, he starts hating not only him, but, everyone and everything associated with his enemy. Such is the nature of afflicted mind. This is due to ignorance that shrouds the Reality.

Love dissipates when Man loses his sense of God. Extreme ego, identification with oneself in his body and mind and the earthly possessions makes him blind. It is this blindness that is the cause of all problems of life. Pure, unconditional love is associated with spirituality. Science and rationality know no love; and, love is a divine quality, the attribute of the Brahman. Love brings bliss, total bliss at that! Home is the place of love and temple is the place of peace; we should make our homes a temple of love and peace so that our children develop integrated personality and never suffer from want; our daughters should shower love, peace and grace of the Lord wherever they go and our sons should be personification of the Lord Himself. This is the aspiration of all spiritual parents.

Love and Peace go together; where there is love, there is peace. If the nations are to prosper, there should be peace; peace is the prerequisite of progress. If the society is to prosper, it should develop mutual trust and love; only mutual trust can give the strong foundation of love. And, all these progress and development depend on the prevalence of peace that comes out of love and love comes out of spirituality. Prosperity cannot be achieved with what is called secularism; secularism is devoid of spirituality. Spirituality establishes the concept of 'unity', the 'One'; spirituality stands for the Lord who is 'One without a second'. National leaders without spirituality cannot establish peace and progress in any country. They cannot make the country great, unless they become great by spiritual attainments, love and sacrifice. The present day maladies are due to the absence of spirituality in our leaders. The first priority in India is to establish Dharma, the foundation of our Maha Bharat. Truly, it will make our country great and our people great. A strong spiritual base is the only solution to our problems; it delivers peace and progress.

Hence, our constant prayer should be "Sarve Jano Sukhino bhavantu". Om! Shantih, Shantih, Shantih".

Thus, "*We all live on the periphery and should try to reach the Centre of Consciousness*". There are many obstacles that prevent us from attaining the Brahman in one life. Even Gautama Buddha remembers his five hundred past lives and says that he had to take another twenty-one lives in different forms before attaining 'enlightenment'. So to make an earnest beginning is the first step in this direction.

***Love and Friendship***

*The relationship between Sri Hari, Lord Krishna and Sudhama is well known. It is worth remembering here the episode of Sri Krishna visiting His child-hood friend Sudhama, a poor Brahmin. Sudhama, with no source of worldy income and wealth, had nothing to offer the Lord except a handful of parched rice; this, the Lord accepted with love and affection!* This episode reminds us of our child-hood friends and our feelings that are beyond any reasoning. We love our friends so deeply that there is no scent of selfishness or desire. It is all so spontaneous that our heart is thrilled at the sight of our old friends. There is no 'give and take' here. It is this love, spontaneity of its expression, that cannot be explained but only to be realised. The basis of friendship is pure love. This is expressed at its best in situations like distress in times of war, or on board a ship in mid sea that has turned turbulent. Comrades as they are, each is ready to sacrifice himself for the other! Friendship knows no barriers. True friendship is true love and true love that blossoms in the lotus of our heart is the true God within us.

***Hatred and Jealousy***

Hatred, extreme dislike or active ill-will, or 'Dvesha' is one of the worst enemies of man. It creates ill- will and rage at the very mention of the person, place, animal or things we do not like. The reason for hatred is self-interest. *Ishavasya Upanishad* [Verse 6] clearly explains the cause and remedy of hatred. "*The wise man who perceives all beings as not distinct from his own Self at all, and his own Self as the Self of all – he does not, by virtue of that perception, hate anyone*".

When the unconditioned state of consciousness is realized, the wise man recognizes that the one Conscious Principle, Self or Atman, which witnesses the modifications of the body- mind combination, that is specially called his own, is the same as the Conscious Principle witnessing all other entities from the higher to the lowest. The feeling of separateness and the self-interest cause hatred when the 'other' is not agreeable to the self and goes against the self-interest, greed, possessive, craving for self-gratification, and may be, the self-interest. When there is a fear that things are going against one's interest, it gives rise to anger, jealousy and the mind loses its balance and sense of discrimination. Hence, it is very dangerous to entertain the very idea of jealousy and hatred, even with the enemies, for ultimately it hurts us, destroys our balance of mind and peace. "***A person who sees unity of existence and perceives all beings as his own Self will not have any sorrow***". [*Isavasya Upanishad*: Verse 7]. Before harming others, hatred and jealousy harms us first. Love is the panacea for all these ari-shadvargas, six categories of personal enemies.

***Greed and Avarice***

Greed and avarice are the worst enemies of man. It is the mean-mindedness of the person that drives him to not only covet some others property but, hides them without sharing them with others. This attitude develops very early in the child-hood and continues till death unless spirituality is developed. Whem greed takes over, people behave like animals; and, cruelty, cunningness, falsity, cheating and other bad qualities take preponderance over sacrifice, compassion, love, piety and kindness. Lobha (greed) is one of the arishadvargas that should be guarded in spiritual practices.

***Anger***

Anger (Krodha) is the worst enemy of man. It is fire and it burns. When a man is angry he has lost his balance of mind. He is not in his senses; he is prepared to go to any extent. He may even kill others in fitness of anger. The cause of anger is selfishness. When a person does not get what he wants, his reasoning fails and anger takes over. To control anger is very difficult and even the great sage like Doorvasa could not control his anger in front of the Lord of the Lords! Anger is associated with Rajas and unless Sattvic guna is cultivated, it becomes very difficult to control anger. Meditation is the only answer. It is indeed, very difficult to control the arishasvargas- kama, krodha, lobha, moha, mada and matsaruya. However, effort can be made to control all them by Meditation. Control the Mind and conquer the enemies within like anger, lust, greed, avarice, selfishness, jealousy and such other qualities that destroy peace and happiness.

Conquering the arishadvargas is the essence of life and it is the clue to happy and successful life.

***Attachment, Raaga or Moha***

***The entire Mahabharat is a story of blind attachment or moha. Dhrutarashtra's blind attachment to Duryodhana ended in the catastrophic epic war. This attachment is common to all mortals. There is an interesting story to show how this attachment prevents liberation or mukti even when it is certain, almost attainable with divine grace.***

There was a merchant with a small family of wife and two children. He was happy with his earnings from his small business and loved his children so much that he always wanted to protect them from all hardships. One day a sadhu passing by his shop asked for some water and the merchant gladly offered him some sweets and water. In return for this treat, the grateful sadhu wanted to grant him liberation and passage to Golok or Svarga. But, the merchant wanted some time and the sadhu agreed to come back again. After several years, the Sadhu came and searchd for the merchant, but found two adults quarrelling over some petty thing in a small grocery shop. This came as a surprise to the Sadhu. The flourishing business had gone and a small shop in its place! The merchant came out and told the sad story of his arrogant spoiled brats and again, requested for some more time when the Sadhu offered him liberation from all this sansar. '*Time and tide waits for none*', they say. The arrogant quarrelsome sons took to tilling a piece of land when their father died and the business flopped. Again, the Sadhu appeared and asked for the merchant. He was surprised to see the merchant born and grown up as a bullock in order to help his sons! Again the same story repeated. The bull asked some time and the Sadhu returned. After many years, the Sadhu came back only to see an old dog guarding a small hut and came out barking at him. Again, the merchant in the form of dog requested for some time. When the sadhu came back again, he found the two sons of the merchant quarrelling and rushed to beat this sadhu shouting that it is this sadhu who has brought all this misery. One of the sons said, 'You cheat in the garb of the Sadhu, you have destroyed our family. My father died and we are orphaned. You have brought misery to us. Get lost, or....". The Sadhu smiled at the irate fellow and said, "Your father is not that merciless. He has left some pot of gold coins. Dig it out and share it equally. You all will be haapy." Finally, when the fellows dug at the place pointed out by the Sdhu they found a snake guarding the pot came out hissing. Finally, they killed the snake and took out the pot of gold, and shared it. The Sadhu granted the merchant in the form of snaree mukti, or release from this bondage brought about by attachment, moha. Such is the force of attraction of attachment. Thus, the story goes to show how the mortals are in the grip of attachment.

***The Art of Living***

Life is an art and one must know how to live an artistic, attractive, happy and peaceful life. It is again all a divine grace and one's purva punya. However, it is never too late to learn. The secret of life has already been explained. If you want happiness, you must keep others happy by your thoughts and deeds, by self-less service, and love. Love is the most significant single factor that governs life and one must shower love towards all and this is the most difficult problem in life. Ego, selfishness and attachment always dominate our lives. Hence, it is very essential to live an austere and selfless life.

Many learned and wise persons take to Yoga and are partly successful in attaining peace and happiness. But, the best way to attain peace and happiness in life as also attain liberation from bondage or mukti is to take to Vedantic way of life. This has already been explained here. It is the wisdom of our ancient Rishis and Sages that made them take to deep meditation and attain to the inner secrets of life and happiness; they have conveyed the same in a very simple way. These are nothing but the Upanishadic doctrines put into actual practice. Some have lived the householders' way and some have taken to Sanyas; both ways, it is difficult. The best way is to live a happy and contented life by understanding the dualities inherent in this objective sensate world. It is essential to give up 'desire' that leads to eternal bondage and take to meditation and control the Mind.

All these are clearly explained here and one must carefully understand and practise the doctrines.

# 11

# Sansar- Ripples and Waves

*"Asato ma sadgamaya; Tamaso ma Jyotirgamaya; Mrutyor ma amrutam gamaya!"*

*Meaning, "Lead me from' asat' to 'sat', i.e., the 'Unreal' to the 'Real'; Darkness to Light, i.e., Ignorance to Knowledge; and, from Death to Immortality."*

Life on this Planet seems like a long drawn drama that has neither a beginning nor an end. Each person gets an idea as to what is life accord to his experience and ability to understand the same. But there is no one who can definitely define the meaning and scope of life on this planet. The ancient sages contemplated over this problem for quite a long time and have come to certain conclusions that are worthy of consideration. These are clearly described in our ancient scriptures. The Veda, the Upanishads, the Bhagavata and other Puranas, the Bhagavad Gita, and other scriptures hold the key to life. Any body in doubt can always go to these scriptures and get solutions to their problems. These are the 'mantra' that are like formulae of life.

What is life? Why life is a problem? Why is it for some life is a bed of roses and some always made to suffer for no fault of theirs? Why is it some people are born to poverty, misery and sickness while some are born to affluence? First of all these are not at all questions that are difficult to answer. These are the questions that may be easily answered by any knowledgeable person. While it is true that taking birth in a rich family or a poor family is not in one's hands, at least it is true that one can live properly, judiciously and it is in one's own hands and there is no doubt about it. Let us analyze this aspect clearly.

It will be surprising to know that we are born here on this earth due to our desire, own sweet will and pleasure, and Karma. It is due to our intent desire that we are born here again and again. We take birth repeatedly due to our inherent desire and it is the unfulfilled desires that make us take repeated births. The day one says to himself that he is satisfied and contented, it is the end of his cycle of rebirths. To reach this stage it is essential to attain a stage of purity of the mind and purity of the soul of the highest degree and burn all karmic particles, the seeds of birth.

*METEMPSYCHOSIS*

*The Cycle of birth and death is the nature and quality of jeevas, mortals who are ignorant of the nature of their Self. The soul embedded in the body is released when the body dies only to find another suitable body in order to fulfil its desire and run the full course of karma. Souls transmigrate here. This transmigration of souls is called 'metempsychosis'. The earth is called the 'mrutyu lok' a land of death. There seems to be no end to this repeated birth and death!*

Every organism that takes birth on the earth has to die one day; it has a cycle of birth and death and the cycle repeats till the jeeva is liberated from the shakles of desire, 'Moha Bandhan'; only a blemish-less soul has no rebirth. Desire is the blemish of the soul. Only a hundred percent sattvic soul is liberated from the cycle of rebirths, that too when it transcends time and sapce. This state of liberation could be achieved by spiritual practices that are very hard in the present day life of all sorts of distractions. When one can reach the state of 'turiya' in 'samadhi' he can visualize the world of 'Sat-Chit-Ananda' - a state of Supreme Bliss. This brings about liberation.

Jeevas are the cause of their own birth, and their 'prarabhdha karma' is the cause of their suffering. A neem seed gives rise to a neem tree and a tamarind seed gives rise to a tamarind tree. Sattvic life, purified mind and soul render jeevas to become spiritually strong and tapas can burn all the 'sanchita prarabdha karma' seeds (fruits of accumulated past actions) that are the source of re-births. A life of love and sacrifice is all that is called for here. So, cursing anybody for one's own folly is of no use. The more one does good actions in this life and the more sattvic life one lives, one will find it easy to achieve this goal of liberation.

It is in fact by one's own sweet will and sweet pleasure that one is taking birth on this earth, that too, to fulfill his desires. May be, some body wants to become a prime minister and some body wants to become a university vice chancellor and yet another wants to become a supreme court justice and yet another wants to become a pilot or army major and General. They all achieve their ambitions by taking birth in appropriate environment, get appropriate education and training, and achieve their goal. But, it is also true that they find ultimately that it is not that what they wanted. They are disillusioned and driven to search for meaning of life and ways of self-realization. Some wise persons learn by others' mistakes.

***Why Sansar is Bhandhan, Bondage?***

There are two types of people- First, People who think this world is for enjoyment and go all out seeking joy and fun wherever possible; and, the second type who are not very enthusisastic about life. The first type of people, are nescient, ignorant of the nature of their Self; they identify themselves with their body and mind. They do not know that there exists a spiritual body, Self or Atman that is self-existent, free, and Blissful. They enjoy the material objects of the world and, accept happiness and misery, joy and sorrow as their karma. They do not try to cross the boundary of nescience, avidya. They are not mature enough, spiritually ripe enough to realize the meaning and purpose of life. On the other hand, the second type, are mature, contemplative, and prone to think of the meaning and purpose of life. They are not easily carried away by the attractions of the material world. They have had a glimpse of the fleeting nature of this glittering material world. They know the 'Reality' of 'existence'.

Great Acharyas like Shankara and Madhwa have studied deeply our ancient scriptures, have performed meditation and sadhana, and have realized the secret of life. They traversed the whole country by foot and have spread their teachings through out the country. Hence, it is now possible for anybody to choose a path of his liking. One can live a reckless life of sensual enjoyment and suffer endlessly cursing every one, or one can choose a life of love and sacrifice and attain what he wants. The choice is in one's own hands.

Here it is very intereting to quote Acharya Rajaneesh, popularly known as 'Osho'. He narrates a very imteresting episode. Once a rich and famous person went to the famous Sufi Mystic Junnaid and asked him, "What do you say about, fate, luck, freedom of man?'

Junnaid asked him to stand up on one leg and, the fellow promptly did it. When he was asked to lift up the other leg also, he became angry and shouted back, "How is it possible?"

Junnaid said, "Remember, man is half free and half in bondage; but, he is free first".

Acharya Rajaneesh says, "It is this freedom, how man uses that determine his bondage. No body is responsible and there is no God. You choose a certain act and that is your freedom; that freedom brings bondage and that is your responsibility." Further, "Science says cause and effect are together. As far as the cause is concerned you are free; the effect, the consequences of action, is decided by you, by your cause. In fact, you are free in that too; it is an outcome of your freedom."

According to Rajaneesh, "There are no problems in life if one takes life in a non-theological way, a very simple way. A problem is that which can be solved; a mystery is that which can be lived, but can never be solved." Here meditation comes to help.

"Meditation is nothing but an exploration of the mystery- not an explanation, not a search to find the solution to it, but an exploration.........to dissolve into it slowly, just as a ripple disappears into the ocean; this disappearance is the only religiousness that I know of. All else is non-sense."

What is that "all else (that is non-sense)?" he refers to? Is he referring to Karma, fate, luck, etc.?

Obviously. Rajaneesh does not believe in God or luck; so also, the doctrines of Raja Yoga do not believe in some external force dictating our lives. There is nothing like God. Even if there is God, He will not interfere in the affairs of man. It is at his own sweet will and pleasure that man has come here and he wants to live, as he likes. Why should God bother?

Acharya Rajaneesh, popularly known as Osho, is very clear about the responsibility for one's action. He says, no one can avoid his responsibility for his action. It reminds us of the famous Drama 'Shaakuntala' by the most famous Poet Laureate of India, Kaalidaasa. The story goes that the King Dushyanta was on his tour of his State when he met a beautiful girl named Shakuntala. He fell in love with this beautiful girl and, he instantly married her in the style of 'Gandharva vivah' giving her a wedding ring, and quietly left the place. On reaching the palace, he forgot all about this marriage. Poor Shakuntala became pregnant, got his child in due course and went to the palace to meet the King Dushyanta. The King refused to accept the child for he had completely forgotten the whole episode! It is this son of Dushyanta-Shaakuntala, called '*Bharata*' who later became the King who ruled India i.e.,'***Bhaarat***'. It is the avoidance of responsibility for our action that binds us and life becomes bondage. We are like King Dushyanta; we want enjoyment and accept no responsibility for our action. You are free only when your responsibilities are discharged.

Osho does not believe in the doctrine of 'Karma' and the oft-repeated mantra of Bhagavda-Gita: "*Karmanyevaadhikaaraste ma phaleshu kadaachana*". He asks why should we not desire for the fruits of our action? "Why should somebody withhold our fruits? Why should somebody else decide the fruits of our action? Yes, Acharya Rajaneesh does not like that the fruits of our action be in somebody else's hands, than too, when freedom of action is in your hands. He says, "To lift one leg, the right or the left, is in your hands; but once you lift one leg, you are not free to lift the other leg. There is no freedom to lift both the legs; you are in bondage. There is no alternate but to take the responsibility for your action, just not enjoy the freedom of action." It is like the bullock tied to a long rope; It has all the freedom to move around within the spehere restricted by the rope. So also, a person who climbs a coconut tree has all the freedom to operate on the tree. Our life is just similar to that. We have all the freedom to operate within the grand design made for us by the Lord. You may call it destiny, fate, Karma or, just Luck (Adrishta),

Acharya Rajaneesh is just right when he says that our action brings responsibility on us and the fruits of action are decided by our own action and not by somebody else. We should desire the fruits of our action; we should strive for it. There is nothing wrong in looking for the fruits. But, reality of life is not that simple. In life, the simple equation of two plus two will not work out to four so easily. There are lots and lots of uncertainties. If life were to be so simple and easy, there would have been no need for a Rajaneesh to guide us. All would be Rajaneeshs!

It is sheer avidya, ignorance, nescience that binds us. We are not certain of anything in this world. While we wish one thing we get another; even when we take a well-chosen path, a pre-determined route, the destiny takes us in its own way. It is when you are ignorant, uncertain, act foolish, when you do not know whether to lift the right leg or the left leg that you get into problems; it is then that you feel the need for an Acharya like Rajaneesh. It is here, that the Lord's beckoning "Come to me, I will take care of you", *the assurance of Lord Shree Krishna in Bhagavad-Gita: "Yogakshemam vahaamyaham" becomes more valid, more meaningful.*

Meditation is good. Meditation is the panacea for all ills of this world. Do it. Meditate on the Lord; meditate on your inner Self. Act immediately when intuition drives you. Have full knowledge of the consequences of your action. Enjoy the fruits of action. Enjoy your 'being' every second; be alive to your 'existence'. Be a witness, a 'sakshin', to all your actions. Merge yourself totally in your action and the rest all is 'Bliss'! Complete your action. Fulfill your desire for action. Rather, live fully. "When there is completion what are you going to desire? Desire is always out of incompletion. Your whole energy is so fulfilled and so contented that it needs nothing. Ultimately, there are only two types of people in the world;

the beggars and the emperors. Those who live in desires are beggars; those who live in completion of silence, peace, and love- are the emperors. In order to love others, you have to love yourself first. If you can love yourself first, you can love others. If you are always unhappy, discontented, what happiness you can give others? Jesus Chrsit said, "Love thy neighbor". How can you love your neighbour if you are unhappy and do not know what is love? First, learn to love yourself, your 'Self'. Love your body, first; do not starve it with all vengeance! Eat well, be happy; let your own happiness and joy overflow spontaneously as pure love and make all others near you happy. Happiness and joy overflows when you are 'full'.

***Happiness, joy and love come out of peace; and, peace comes out of meditation. So meditate and be happy and peaceful.***

The question arises as to why is it 'this sort of a well-laid path to salvation is never followed by people and, they land them selves into trouble'. It is due to ignorance and egotism. Both egotism and ignorance are born with the person at birth; preponderance of tamasic and rajasic gunas rule the nature, or svabhava of the person and land these persons into trouble. Realised souls are those who develop sattvic guna and reduce the preponderance of tamasic and rajasic gunas in a slow and phased manner by spiritual exercises. This is one simple but very difficult method of getting rid of this 'make-believe' objective or illusory world.

This objective world is the cause of misery for we desire it; we desire it for we think it is real and it gives us happiness. In our innermost core, our heart, we know it is not real. We touch again and again to reassure ourselves the objects are real, for there is a lurking fear in us that we will be disappointed when we come to know the objects are unreal. Despite our inner voice warning us, we crave for it. We see things made of parts degenerate, fall apart and decay. We still love these objects of desire. We cannot see things as they are'. We find our faith is misplaced (not in God); our love is selfish and goes unrewarded. We fail our trusted friends and cheat ourselves. We do not have guts to take responsibility for our actions; we run away from the battlefield like Arjuna and do not have a Krishna to hold us back! It is this cowardliness that is the problem; it is lack of trust, faith in one's own Self that is the problem! It is lack of trust, faith in the Lord; that is the problem.

We have no inner peace, happiness, and joy and that is the problem. We cannot expand our mind. Our mind should be like 'aakash', the sky- all encompassing! We are selfish, narrow-minded. We have no capacity to love; that is the problem. We cannot understand the principle of 'unity of existence'; we do not merge, we stand separate and that is the problem. We cannot treat others as our own selves; that is the main problem. It is in meditation that 'I' and the 'other' disappears and we have heard of that. Even when we know that we have no mind to sit, close our eyes and meditate; that is our biggest problem.

So, try to sit down for a few minutes, close your eyes, take to deep breathing, and meditate on some simple aspect of life. Just observe your breathing. Lo! All problems disappear like the clouds dissipating revealing the clear blue sky!

Another important question is whether one can wish away this troublesome world in one birth. The answer is an emphatic 'No'. It is not possible to get rid of the clutches of 'Maya', this gross sensate world in one birth. If one starts getting tuned to sattvic and spiritual life starting with 'svaadhyaya' and satsang in this life, it may take several hundred births to get 'enlightenment' like the Buddha. Gautama Buddha, Mahaveera and many other Jnyaanis have taken several births before 'enlightenment'. It is important to note here that there is no doubt about 're-birth' in this concept of life on this planet.

In fact, the cycle of re-birth is the process of refinement of the souls. And it is the goal of life to attain fulfillment through the realization of the Self, 'atmasakhatkar' and not through fulfillment of desires. The more the desires are fulfilled, the more amd more the new ones arise out of the impressions or memories or sanskar. Hence, the salvation lies in the abnegation of the self as identified by the body and mind, and its desires, cravings for the mundane and realization of the true Self. It is a long drawn process, and evolutionary theory confirms this.

### *Hunger and Food*

*Chhandogya Upanishad gives an elaborate description of food. It is very important that one should take care of what he is eating, because "Mind consists of food" [Chhaandogya Upanishad VI 5.4]. The grossest part of food goes waste while the middle part is transformed into flesh and the subtlest part goes to form the mind. It is like the butter, the subtlest part of the curds that comes up due to churning. Pure food gives pure mind and good memory; it helps to realize the true nature of this world.*

Food is elusive. Search for food is the most important driving force in man and it is hunger that keeps him on the move. Why is food evasive? Although food is available in plenty, it is not easily obtained by man to quench his hunger; even water is available, but not food! Why is it? Remember, the birds fly long distances in search of food. One should strive for everything. Nothing comes easy. The answer lies in the mystery of the origin of the universe. It is again 'Maya'. It is the divine 'Leela'. It is God's 'will'.

When the Lord created life he also created food. First manifestation of Brahman is the Sun (Energy) and the second manifestation is the Moon (food); Moon is the food to the Sun. Sun and the moon also stand for time, the solar year, the lunar month, the Shukla Paksha and the Krishna Paksha and the days and nights, etc. The waxing and waning of moon is the consumption pattern of the Sun. In other words, the energy, space and time are the earliest manifestations of the Brahman, the Supreme Conciousness, the eternal 'cosmic flow'. Flow, as it clearly shows, is movement; the food, i.e., the Brahman ("*Annam Brahma*") in his manifest form, is evasive! When food was created in water it started moving. The Lord tried to catch it by his mind, but could not reach it; He tried by the eyes, the ears, the nose, the skin and the tongue but failed to catch it. Then He Himself entered into it through the mouth with Vayu and reached the stomach (navel). Hence, food remained elusive and it is not within the reach of the mind or the five sense organs. If it were so, by mere thinking or thought of food, one would be satisfied! One would be happy and contented with mere sight of food, sound of food, smell of food and touch of food. Even the generative organs cannot reach for food unless Brahman enters through the mouth as Prana in the form of air. It is only when food along with vital breath, Prana Vayu reaches the naval center of consciousness, Vaishvanara Deva, the 'Jataragni' consumes it, the man is satisfied; remember, the hunger continues day after day and year after year till death consumes the body!

The whole pattern of food chain is a very tricky business, like each bigger fish swallowing the smaller fish. When the tiger falls on a deer and kills it, the Jnyani knows that it is the nature of the tiger to kill and tries to help the deer with compassion; however, he also knows that all this game is the Lord's leela! There is neither the tiger, nor the deer and its death. The deer and the tiger are merely different names and forms and killing an action identified by our ignorant mind and the senses. The underlying spiritual principle is that the Soul is one and eternal; it is self-existent and, neither it is created nor can it be destroyed. The names and forms are due to our ignorance.

*The Veda proclaims: "Annam Brahma", and the Jnyani knows that neither there is an eater, nor the edible, nor the eating. It is all one 'That Inseparable Brahman'! It is the ignorance that makes us believe all that appears in this sensate world as real. Name, form and function mislead us. Meditate on Him and the screen dissolves, illusion dissolves.*

It is again the Self, the enjoyer of the food; for namesake, it appears like the one eaten by man; but actually it is a yajnya. The food offered to Vaisvanara Deva, the Jataragni (the fire in the stomach). Since the mantra says "Annam Brahma", the food is the visible God. It is not the food that is going to be rotten or decayed that is Brahman; but it is the vitality, Sattva, life force that is in it is the Brahman. Brahman is manifest in different forms and rules the life on this planet earth. Hence, it is the Vedic dictum that one should never disrespect food! Any person with spiritual attainment will not find it very difficult to get food. For him, food is available in plenty, enough and to spare! Veda proclaim that one should work hard, earn by self-effort enormous food, only to give it away to the hungry and needy.

Food sustains Prana with air (Vayu) and water (Jal). When a man is dying due to hunger, the first thing that he requires is food. Five morsels (handful) of food is just sufficient to regain the life of a man dying of hunger. With the first morsel, his dull brain will become more active (helps to regain memory); with the second morsel his closing eyes will open slowly. With the third morsel, his dying sound comes back. With the fourth his body will regain strength to sit up and the fifth morsel will make him stand on his own and he will exclaim that his life has come back! ***Offering a hungry man food is the most sacred duty of every human being.***

Here, again, there is an interesting story about Uddhalaka teaching his son Svetaketu by experiment how food is converted into mind. As we all know Milk contains butter; butter comes out of churning of milk or curds (made out of milk). Butter is thus the subtlest part that rises out of the churning of curds. Similarly, Uddalaka told Svetaketu, "That which is the subtlest part of the food that is eaten rises and becomes mind. The subtlest part of water that is drunk rises and becomes prana. Thus, my dear, the mind consists of food, prana consists of water, and speech consists of fire".

It is through sattvic food that one can develop a calm and serene mind that can perceive the Atman. A volatile mind is the cause of all the unrest, unhappiness and misery. One should avoid Rajasic food- excessively hot, sour, bitter, sweet and saline food. Similarly, Tamasic food- cold, stale, leftovers of food stacked in cold storage should be avoided. Only fresh, balanced and agreeable food should be consumed in limited quantity, enough and to sustain the body. A Jnyani or a wise man will take food in limited quantity like medicine.

Essentially man is not the mind but the Self or Atman. The Atman is ever free, infinite and eternal. It is pure consciousness. Mind is an instrument in the hands of the Self through which man apprehends and responds to the external world. Since the mind is always vascillating, changing constantly, it makes the world appear changing; if the mind is made to be calm and serene it can reflect the Atman and reveal the true nature of the world. When one knows oneself as the Atman, there is no longer a mind needing control. Hence, *sattvic food is one of the essential requirements for a happy and successful life*.

Another important question that haunts us is that of 'luck' or destiny. It is true that God's Grace protects us by giving us strength- moral and spiritual. It is also true that one who performs his functions in the name of God achieves enormous success. But, luck alone is not in any way helpful in 'self- realization'. Absence of ego is the first pre-requisite of success and happiness in life. Pride nullifies all good actions while humility and trust in God brings success.

*Absolute Faith in the 'Almighty' is a sure path to success. Devotion, total dedication, concentration and total submission are essential requirements of a successful life.*

Ultimately, it is God's Will. Since man has no knowledge of the future, it is He who will guide all persons in times of need or distress. Only those who submit totally to Lord Almighty will get His attention; in a sense He gives strength and courage to face life and provides clues to pass the test of life. Without His grace, nothing is possible in this worldly life. Even to tune oneself towards Him needs His Grace. *'Trust in God' is essential to success and happiness in life.*

Many people have asked the question, "If God's Will be done, where is the need for human effort'? This is true. If God or Lord Almighty rules our destiny, a doubt arises as to what is our role in life. The answer is simple. ***'He helps those who help themselves'***. One has to perform his duty without anticipation of anything in return. Every action is performed as if by divine inspiration and offered to the Lord. *This is the secret of success and happiness*. Giver is one who has plenty and he has got everything to give; but the actions of our past decide the results of our action. Each one gets according to his Karma. If one has done good deeds in the past, the fruits of the good actions come sooner or later in this life or in the next.

Those who do not believe in the Karma theory depend on their rational mind that does not help in understanding the sublime and infinite truth. Ego speaks in such cases. It is their 'I'-ness, their ego, 'ahamkaara' that makes them forget the Creator. *One has to do his duty and leave the rest in the hands of the Lord. Bhagavad-Gita holds the key to success and happiness in life.*

Now, as to the living and enjoyment of life on this earth, there is a very simple formula. Find out the level of consciousness at which you operate. We are living on the periphery and it is difficult to go to the center of Consciousness. Most of us are living and operating at lower levels of Consciousness that does not require much energy. The centers of Consciousness decide about the nature of one's status in life. Those who live and operate at lower levels, i.e., the level of navel are engaged in fulfilling their basic instincts of life like any other animals. Probably, they are at lower scales of evolution. They are consciously aware of their 'annamaya kosha' and 'pranamaya kosha'. Some of them excel in one of these 'koshas' and achieve great success, too. A few of them rise above the level of awareness of these two layers and reach the 'Manomaya Kosha' and try to understand the mysteries of life. But those who realize higher levels of Consciousness reach 'Vijnyanamaya Kosha', and very few reach the innermost core of 'Anandamaya Kosha' and enjoy the Supreme Bliss. It is sheer ecstasy at that!

Hence, the level of Consciousness at which one operates is very important. One can excel at any of these levels by pure will power, personal efforts and Lord's Grace. It is only the enlightened persons who realize the need to rise to higher levels of Consciousness; it takes several births to reach the higher stages of evolution. Buddha says, it took five hundred years for him to reach the highest state of Pure Consciousness,

One must consciously be aware of one's spiritual status and position in life in order to move forward; but this awareness is rarely possible. Normally, everybody has not got the capacity to understand these secrets. Hence, it is advisable to take the guidance of an enlightened person or a spiritual leader. But, it is hard to find a true guru. So one has to look inward to one's own soul for guidance and thus become one's own Guru. This is possible only by concerted sincere efforts. Develop purity of mind and heart.

Lord Jesus has stressed a good deal on this aspect of love and sacrifice, and the Bhakti cult of the Hindus stress the devotional aspect. The Buddhists try to practice a life of restraint and become monks in order to desist desire. Jainism preaches to practice compassion. So, in one way or the other, all the religions of the world preach only one thing and that is to live a simple life of love and self-sacrifice. There is happiness in giving and there is no doubt about it. Bookish knowledge is absolutely of no use, unless one practices the teachings of the enlightened souls. Not all the pages of the calendar or panchanga showing the rain-bearing stars will ever give a drop of water and no Veda or Upanishad and Puranas will show any God.

A very important secret of success of life is to shift from body-consciousness to soul-consciousness. No body asks you to resist temptations of life and feel frustrated or disappointed. Only be aware of the temptations and the way it leads you to. Live a life of full awareness and become a 'Sakshi' to yourself. Watch your thoughts and action. When you enjoy life, enjoy so well that you do not hanker after it any more. Be satisfied with what you get. Do not allow discontent and greed to take over. Once you fully enjoy what you get and do not live on its memory, you are liberated. Live a happy and contented life. Do not fall prey to greed and avarice. Contentment is very important. There is no end to greed and sensuous pleasures that only lead to sickness of body and mind. Restrain from excessive sexual indulgence, or for that matter, remember, any excessive indulgences are forbidden. That does not mean denial of the essential requirements of life. The golden rule is "*this far and no further*".

### *Marriage*

*'Maya' is the basic principle that governs this objective world. The' leela of the lord', divine play is evident in every walk of our life. Marriage is one such event when this leela of the Lord can be experienced. It is the Divine Will that binds two persons in marital ties and it is His Plan that one suffers or enjoys the bliss and blisters of marital life so that they come to know of the realities of life.*

*It is the Lord Shiva, embodiment of love that became Ardhanarishwar and led to the status of man and wife that led to procreation and Sansar. Every man has the woman in him and vice versa (X and Y chromosomes). It is the craving for fulfillment, union of 'the other' that leads to union of two individuals- a male and female. It is 'the other' and constant identification of 'the other' that leads to problems of life. The moment one recognizes that the 'the other' exists in oneself, the duality ends. The moment the person recognizes the man and wife are one in body, mind and soul the problems of life cease to exist as problems. This spiritual unification is the real marriage that never breaks. In a sense, it is the spiritual experience that 'the other' does not exist, rather reverting to the state of Ardha-Narishwar that brings fulfillment.*

Eversince the appearence of Adam and eve, this concept of sex has come under heated discussion and ended in battle of the sexes. It is the natural order that opposite poles attract each other and the entire behavior of the atom is the divine will. The most outstanding duality of this world is evident in the attracting forces of opposite qualities. Extreme opposite gunas are 'catchy' and boys and girls of teens become more charming and attractive. It is the vibrations, the gunas, that rule the life.

*The word' marriage' comes from 'marry' means 'to agree to' and this agreement without a strong basic understanding of meaning of life creates all the problems of life.*

*Marriage* is an important institution created for purposes of social, moral, ethical and spiritual progress, It is an event in life of a person that shapes or ruins the future. All of us, or most of us, enter into marriage without any preparation to embark the life journey. There is a saying that, 'marriages are made in heaven and it is only celebrated here'. How true it is! We have seen instances where the divine only will operate. Girls get their boys as if pre-determined under strange circumstances and, families distant and unknown are united. It is a upanishadic truth that the same relations of the previous births continue in permutation and combination, in different forms and functions birth after birth, death after death!

Honestly, every body marries for sex. It is natural that the institution of marriage guarantees sex within bounds. It is here the problems start. Marriages that guarantee sex at body level and mind level do not succeed for the simple reason that the boy and the girl will soon find out each other's defects for, nobody is perfect. Each one has got his or her strong points and weak points. It is but natural, that strangers as they are at first in arranged marriages, both soon form an adamantine wall on some sensitive issues and marriages collapse due to ego factor and disillusionment at the earliest opportunity.

Many marriages have hit the rock for the simple reason that the marriage partners cannot adjust, do not accept their deficiencies, and do not develop sense of trust, faith, and mutual respect, let alone love. False prestige and sense of bloated self-respect and ego rule their mind and no other consideration counts in fits of anger. It is all pure selfishness!. If any one of the marriage partners is mature enough to adjust, submit, cooperate and be considerate and sacrifice the self, the marriage will succeed. Both the boy and the girl have formed unrealistic ideas and they are in a very impressionable state of mind. Fantasy and images rule the mind and this take them away from reality. Soon both are disappointed. Fantasies melt at the first hand knowledge of reality. No body wants their dream to be disturbed!

*Love and Marriage*

Falling in love is the most common thing that we hear these days. But, rarely have we heard of 'rising in love' and enjoying the bliss of long married life. The two most contradictory and conflicting basic concepts are love and marriage. Love is a state of inebriated or intoxicated mind based on fantasy or imagination. Love is a magical transformation. It is a chemical flow, a flow of colour from the heart, that is initiated by the imageries and memories and fantasies of the mind. That is why they say love is blind. When the figure or face of a person matches its image in the memory of the sub-conscious of another person, it clicks! It may be 'love at first sight' or at 'repeated sights'. There is no rational or scientific explanation for this; but love is a basic quality of the divine inherent in all creatures. But, still, some scientists claim that the smell of a mother or father is the internal guiding factor in 'falling in love'. It may be match of gunas, likes and dislikes, mutual interests, and what not? One should study the Upanishads to know the realities of this madness of love. Love, in its true form, is the quality of a pure heart devoid of all tinge of selfishness and it is total surrender of the self, at that!

If love is blind, marriage is an eye-opener. It may appear true that marriage is a practical solution to the man or woman's natural physical urge of sex and social security. Where the love factor takes an upper hand, the person is not in the normal state of mind to understand anything, let alone the pros and cons of their action based on it. Most of the children in their teens get disappointed very early in life as the reality of life strikes and they get a jolt; some even succumb to it! It requires two strong minds to get into permanent union in love, and this is again a fantasy! No marriage is an utter success unless proved to be so to end, i.e., ripe old age and death. One may feel disappointed and dejected at the end of his life and this is the case with most of the people. It is an illusion and blind faith that one thinks that marriage would help solve all problems and jumps into it. But, soon it would br realized that marriage creates more problems. This is because of the fact that marriage is not a solution; it is only a means to salvation. The institution of marriage is a social constraint and one is not bound by it, if attainment of Supreme Bliss is the goal.

*Bliss and Blisters of Love Marriage*

Before we get into this subject, it is very interesting to know why we love. In marriages, whether arranged one or love marriage, marriage is the main concern. In Love, it is the underlying psychological disposition that is important. One is attracted to things due to two reasons. One reason, although we cannot say it is' reasoning' in the strict sense of the term for there is no reasoning in love, it is the attraction of the object that draws our mind and makes it dwell on it. This attraction may be due to the beauty of the object or the external qualities that are impressive to our mind. Some times, the object may not be really beautiful or attractive; but still we love it because our mind dwells on it of its own accord! It is this mind dwelling on a certain person, animal, place or thing and becoming one with that is what we call 'love'. There is no reasoning here. Just the mind dwells on it due to its previous impressions, memories or samskars. We cannot reason it out. Suddenly a flash of memory (may be of the previous birth?) drives the mind to such an act of 'falling in love'.

When we get good friends, lovers, or pets and intensely love them, it is this 'sanskars' that are responsible for such 'love'. That is one of the reasons why all our relationships are believed to be the result of the memories, impressions and sanskars, philosophically speaking. If a persons falls in love and gets married, may be it is the' divine will', fulfillment of a desire of the previous birth, and thus, an old relationship is re-established (in this life). In a sense, it appears as though all the multitude of creatures on this earth, including human beings and their activities are the results of a magic wand waved by the Lord. That is why this 'prapancha' is called 'maya'.

When it comes to marriage, in the beginning everything appears happy and blissful. In the heat of passion, in the dream of fulfillment, married life appears to be blissful. It appears as if a heaven on earth! It is sheer ecstasy and joy, but short-lived. The bliss turns to blisters as the reality dawns!

Married life is not a bed of roses. No marriage, whether arranged or love marriage, will ever guarantee instantaneous success unless sincere efforts are made to sustain the marriage by both the marriage partners. Dualities rule the game of marriages. It is especially so in the case of intercaste or cross-culture or internationational love marriages. When the charm fades, the reality of life stares at the face and every thing that appeared beautiful, attractive earlier begins to look ugly, repulsive and intolerable. It is always the opposites and the opposites remain the same until joined by Yoga (Yuj), by the will and grace of the Lord.

Both types of marriages, love marriage and the arranged marriage do not assure any success. Success is not assured unless and until all efforts are made by the life partners (or, at least one of them) and, both sincerely strive to make it a success. Both love and marriage lose luster and glamour soon as reality dawns to day-to-day life problems. Threat of 'break-down' stares at every corner of life and it takes time to understand and adjust in marriage. First year, the third year, the seventh year of marriages are crucial in a person's life; they are the turning points. Birth of children may bring some relief. Joint family may or may not help in this respect. Ultimately, marriage is still treated a gamble in life.

*Success in marriage*

Only spiritual union, 'union of souls', guarantee success in marriages. Both the life partners should be soul mates to succeed in married life; both must mutually strengthen the spiritual bondage and God is the only One with whom one can be reliable and happy. With every feeling of bliss of marital happiness, a blister arises and it is only a spiritual or divine blessing that can ward of this duality. This is the meaning of life; this is the reality of the world, how it exists and how it works. Meditate on Him and praise the "leela of the Lord'!

One secret of success of marriage is given here. It is the recognition of the prepondering gunas and the vibrations. A proper attention to these factors will help reduce the heat and irritations in a marriage and bring some happiness to the couple. If both the marriage partners are of the same prepondering gunas, preferably sattvic guna, their marriage will succeed. If one of the couple is of sattvic guna and the other tamasic, it may be dull but gives no serious problem. But, if both the couple are of prepondering rajasic guna and vie with each other for selfish ends and, ego rules their mind, such marriages create hell of a problem in their lives. They never compromise. It will be an indifferent marriage if the wife is of sattvic guna and the husband is of rajsic guna or vice versa.

Ultimately, it is spirituality rather than sexuality that governs a successful marriage. This is one of the reasons why the children should be given a spiritual training and should be guarded against the corrupting tendencies, Good company, family background, good moral and ethical education are the essential requirements. Western way of life, valueless moral and social behaviour of the elders are corruptive. Many evil forces are at work in our so-called modern society and children should be well guarded. They should not get any opportunity to imbibe the character and even a flavour of the soul-less materialistic society that has already pervaded life of people in the East.

Conservation of sex energy is very important for raising the level of Consciousness. Western Psychologists such as Sigmund Freud and Alfred Jung go to the extent of identifying sex as the whole life and treat all problems of life as problems of sex only. The profession of psychoanalysts and psychiatrists is thriving on this concept of sex as the root of all mental illness. While it may be partly true that sex governs life and mental sicknesses are connected with sexual fulfillment, it is not wholly incorrect to say that all problems are connected to sex. Sex plays a significant role in early adolescent life and early maturity stage of life and loses its importance as and when man becomes spiritually mature and realizes the futility of indulgence in sex in the pursuit of greater satisfaction in life.

Love and affection should govern all transactions of life at all stages of life. This is the true meaning of marriage. It is not just the physical union of a male and female body. It is the spiritual unification of the entire family that brings meaning to life. Love should flow out spontaneously from the bottom of the heart. Mind has no business there. Where mind comes, jealousy, pride, selfishness and gratification take the place of love. There are married girls who postpone bearing children for fear of losing their physical form. They are afraid of losing the physical charm and go to the extent of denying breast-feeding of babies. The question of spirituality does not arise in such a situation. The concept of spiritual union is missing in the western philosophy of life and the modern Indian families are also blindly following the West due to lack of understanding and proper guidance. One comes to know the value of things only when one loses what he has and does not get what he wants. The Western society is materialistic and technologically superior sending wrong signals. That is why there are more mentally sick people in the western countries.

What is the true path (sat-nays) to a happy and successful life? The true path is a simple life of dedication. Here, the Mind Management Technique dictate: 'dedicate your life to love and sacrifice, at the service of the Lord'. Never indulge in excess of anything, be it food, sex or sport. Svaadhyaya and meditation are important. Know what you want and why you want it before craving for it. Remember that there is always a time gap between the time of desire and time of fulfillment. This gap of time erodes the glamour and even necessity of the thing craved for and brings in discontent and disappointment. It may be in marriage, children, job, or any walk of life, there is a big gap of time between desire and fulfillment. The key to successful life lies in identification of the problem in desires and root-out them as futile.

The advice is simple and direct. Do not live like a fool and a coward; live like a hero and develop the higher levels of Consciousness. Always beware the pitfalls of life that come in the form of a golden deer that put Lakshmana into trouble. To aim high is not a crime; to feel disappointed not reaching the height is. Always be grateful to the Lord for giving this life and an opportunity to know Him. Use this opportunity to know Him. He comes to you in the form of your 'Ishta Devatha' if you earnestly long for Him. Keep a certain time of the day for dhyana and meditation; chant the name of your Ishta Devatha keeping in mind the bhavaartha (significance of the meaning of the words).

In times of distress, sadness due to bereavement of the loved ones, '*be brave*'. Take to meditation and prayer. Pray for the loved ones; pray for all. It is always better to rely on Him than those who are created by Him. Take refuge in Him; He will take care of you. Remember He will not come to your rescue as long as you depend on others. Total submission alone will rescue you and your loved ones in times of distress. So, have full faith in Him. He is the creator. He is the sustainer, and He is always aware of all his creations. He exists in the past, present and the future. The Lord knows what is the best for you and whatever happens happens for the best. Remember that 'every failure is a stepping stone of success'. Every testing time is an opportunity to remember the Lord, and re-assure oneself of His presence. Hard times are times of tuning oneself to the divine path and every blow is a warning to those who forget Him.

Here, the Rule of Mind Management Technique (MMT) is: 'Live a simple life, an austere life of constant dhyan and minimum requirements'. Do not get perturbed at the obstacles that pave the path of Realization of the Supreme Self in one's own self. Go slow; there is no hurry to reach Him for He resides very close to you. He resides nearer to you, nearer than your hands and limbs! Silence is the medium to hear His voice, and try to hear His voice in utter silence, meditation and dhyan. Always repeat the name of your Ishta Devatha whether you are working or sleeping. There are three ways to chant the name of the Ishta Devatha: One, chanting of 'Om', or any other mantra, loudly in a secluded place where nobody is disturbed by loud chantings; second, chanting without sound but only by lip movement; three, chanting in mind without either of the first two methods. The third method is supposed to be more effective. *This will keep the mind under control.*

***The Sensible way of Living***

There are two ways of living: One is living with 'choiceless awareness' living as a 'Sakshi', i.e., witness to all your thoughts and actions. This is a very sensible, a sane way of living. The other is just living unconsciously, 'without awareness' whatsoever; it is this way of life that our one hundred and odd crores of people of India have chosen to and the result is obvious. This life of utter callousness as regards consciousness and the senseless pursuit of sensuous living have led us and our country to downfall, from the status of a very great spiritual leader (upto 5th Century) to a Third World country, of virtually a dark age, today. When it comes to the general psyche of the people of India, this is evident in every walk of their life. Accumulation of garbage and mindless spitting in public places, pushing and goading through crowd are very common observations. The physical and social environment that has been created by the people in Indian villages, and towns and cities could have been easily avoided with a little conscious living. One can see how people are not conscious of their spiritual, historical and cultural past, and have forgotten the spiritual height their ancestors had reached, and the glory that was Maha Bharat and behave like an unconscious, 'Prajnya-heena' lot today.

In every walk of our lives, we exhibit our foolish, unconscious, indiscreet, senseless behaviour. Every action of ours is shortsighted and selfish. There is no national fervour or social commitment in our thoughts and action. We are neither religious nor philosophical, nor rational and scientific. We have scant respect for 'Ritam' and 'Satyam', i.e., Truth and Order, the very foundation of this universe. We are unmindful of the consequences of our action. Accumulation of wealth by a few, regardless of the oppressive poverty of their brothren, is commonly seen everywhere, particularly among the rich and the famous; we have become blind to realities of life and our ego will not permit us to think of the reality. We are purely selfish to the core.

Thus, there is need for revival of our ancient culture and spiritual way of life. Unless one willfully wants to follow the western culture and enjoy that soul-less life, people should follow the path of 'dharma' laid down here. Modern life is full of stress and strain causing numerous problems of sickness of body and mind. Western life as compared with the Eastern life is now in a disadvantageous position due to this very simple reason that it lacks harmony. But, unfortunately, mimicking the west, the present-day Eastern way of life has also become a life devoid of soul, devoid of both rationale and conscious-ness. In contrast, the Western way of life seems to be much better; it has has imbibed a system of strict discipline in social life. It has developed technological means of comfortable living. But, this has helped people only to build up physical conveniences only, and the people lack harmony within, mental peace and contentment. Hence, it is time to think about the path we have chosen. This work is relevant to all the people of the world, East or West, North or South.

Although abnegation of self is not possible at one stroke, one should learn to live with a sense of pure love and detachment; it is like a nurse looking after a baby with love, affection and tenderness and handing it over to its mother. It is like the drops of water on a lotus leaf. The discontent within oneself is at the root of the problems. One who is at peace with oneself will be happy and contented with all his relations. High expectations in relationships cause great disappointments. Even in love, one who expects reciprocal emotional response will be disappointed and later on get into trouble. Self-less love is the answer here.

Love and sacrifice are the key words to remember. Here the technique to be adopted is very simple. Find out at what level you are operating; is it at the body level, or mind level, or spiritual (soul) level? Any 'body-level' relationship is going to collapse when bodily attractions cease. 'Mind-level' attachments also collapse when mind gets bored of repitition and looks elsewhere for more thrilling or interesting attachments. But the spiritual or 'soul-level' attachments are very permanent and no one will have regrets at that level. Hence, one has to cultivate spiritual relationships with relatives and friends and these would last longer.

Living is an art. The art of living has to be cultivated. One should be consciously aware of one-self and develop the Sattvic guna. Both the Tamasic and Rajasic gunas are binding to the worldly way of life while sattvic guna leads to liberation, emancipation or mukti. The science of living is to develop a rational and experimental approach to life. Whenever doubts occur, one has to test and confirm oneself in order to accept it as truth; but actually, the majority of the people go by blind faith and irrelevant practices.

*Modern life has become more mechanical and leaves no time to enjoy life despite the numerous time- saving gadgets and mechanisms. In fact, modern technology has given an advantage to people to save time and use the same to meditation and spiritual practices. More leisure is not for more pleasure. Sensuous pleasure leaves void and brings frustration. This has to be realized. The fire of desire for sensual pleasures should be extinguished not by fulfillment but by repulsion, vivek and vairagya. The more one tries to fulfil the desires for sensual pleasures, the more one is disappointed. Ultimately, it is a peaceful and contented life that is more important. All possible means should be adopted to live a happy and successful life in this modern hectic world.*

Many persons have attained material prosperity but have failed to get peace and contentment. Here, the ignorance that material prosperity will bring happiness is responsible for the disappointment. Material prosperity comes from outside world and, peace and contentment comes from within. Hence, it is necessary to understand the source of peace and contentment. An act of selfless service gives immense satisfaction and contentment. An act of contemplation on the source of all wealth, the Lord Almighty, gives immense happiness. So constant 'dhyan' or meditation on Him will bring immense happiness and peace. But, greed for amassing wealth and constant struggle and endless effort to earn more and more without having any time to enjoy that wealth will bring misery.

Sometimes, we feel that our material prosperity comes from our hard work. But, this is an illusion. Material prosperity and efforts to attain it have no relationship! Material prosperity is the Divine Grace and it is showered according to one's past deeds, the 'poorva punya'. It is the past deeds that decide the state of material prosperity. It is also evident that material prosperity will not guarantee any spiritual progress and eternal bliss. It is also true that one has to put in effort to attain material progress, purely as a necessity, as ordained by the Lord in the Karma marga. One has to perform one's duty without aspiring for the fruits of action.

There is also an important dictum, the basic rule, of 'Ritam' and 'Satyam'. Every body should invariably strictly follow this rule in life. A table that does not have the four supporting straight legs cannot stand; or for that matter, no building where the walls are not straight can survive. How can a man or his society survive on dishonesty, lies, untruth, immoral, and unethical behaviour? Anything earned without morals and ethics, may it be in business or in any other profession, is certain to bring misery.

'Ritam' is the right path and 'Satyam' is the truthful path, sanmarg or 'sat-marg'. If the wealth earned belongs to someone else and it is coveted by wrong means, it will bring untold miseries to family members, loved-ones and kith and kin and all those who enjoy that ill-gotten wealth. Beware! Never aspire for somebody's wealth. *The first mantra of Isavasya Upanishad makes this point amply clear.* There are numerous instances of persons suffering in unimaginable ways- mental and physical, due to ill-gotten wealth. The worst affected here are the ones whom you love most. Still, many people enjoy ill-gotten wealth unmindful of the consequences. Those giving away a part of the ill-gotten wealth in charity with the hope of getting punya or Lord's Grace will be disappointed for, the Lord will accept only the hard-earned money or part of the wealth earned in *sanmarg only*.

One need not offer huge amounts of money to propitiate the God; even a handful of grains, a flower or a blade of grass, or the Tulsi -leaf and a few spoonful of milk will do to appease the God if the same has been earned in a right path, and offered with total devotion. Hence, *righteousness* in all walks of life is the first principle of *Mind Management techniques (MMT)*. All those who follow the path of Dharma (Righteousness) will come under the Lord's protection. *This is what is 'Dharmo rakshati rakshitah'. Here, one should not think that dharma is so weak that it needs someone to protect it or save it.*

Professional success is another source of happiness. Many persons are denied of this simple source of happiness. Persons occupying very high positions have cut short their life committing suicide due to stress, tension, fear and disappointments. Many young and prosperous industrialists have done this. Many scientists of repute have done this. Even the film stars of fame and wealth have taken to this unwise path due to tension, depression and lack of inner strength. Here, Mind Management Technique lays down clearly that one must be a 'dheera', and only a 'dheera' can live successfully. Cowards have no place in this world. Read Bhagavad Gita every day and realize the truth. In times of distress call for the Lord Almighty's help in total submission to Him. Do not loose your heart. Help will come in one form or the other. One who trusts God will never be letdown. Absolute faith in the Lord is the most important principle to be adhered to in life for a successful and happy life.

There is another secret of success in professional life. This should be clearly understood. Any work that comes your way is due to the Lord's Divine Grace. Invoke the Lord's blessings before taking up the job and perform it with sincere devotion, and finally offer it to Him as your service – all in His name. Perform all duties with total devotion and without any desire of its fruits. Success is yours and happiness follows. An iota of ego will spoil what would have been a success story. Always remember that 'I', or 'me' and 'mine' are ego factors that are stumbling blocks in the path of success. All the creatures on this earth are mere toys in the hands of the Lord and only His 'Will' be done. There is nothing that one can do in the odds of life except to submit to Him. Even Sri Krishna was not exempt from his past karma during his avatar in Dvapara Yuga and the same is true with Sri Rama in 'Treta Yuga'. One has to suffer, pay for the misdeeds of the past.

The Lord Almighty, '*He*' gives everyone whatever one asks for with total devotion; but what one gets depends on one's accumulated sins or good work of the past. Poorva arjitha punya is important. God's Grace will only mitigate the effect of the ghastly sins committed in the past; not even the God can escape the 'prarabhda' aspect of life. God's Grace will give strength of mind and self-confidence to face any situation in life. It will instill courage and strength of conviction and helps to pass all tests of life.

*Why Marital Discord and Divorces?*

Marital discord and, sometimes, the extreme step like divorce is a common thing in open societies. The underlying causes are not hard to find. First of all, it is the Desire. Secondly, modern life is full of stress, tension and competition. It is simply not in one's hands to get whatever one wishes for.. Third, normally, it is the lack of respect for each other and highly bloated ego of the marriage partners in addition to lack of understanding and faith in each other contribute to the collapse of marriages.

It is two opposites that attract each other and the natural law is to repel whatever comes very close to each other. In marriage, it is two persons of opposite sex having different natural, cultural, social and psychological background that come together; and it is obvious that the natural forces begin to operate sooner or later. Attraction and repulsion are the order of nature, law of nature. This duality is built-in to the mechanism since this sensate world is un-real (Maya). It is a 'make-believe' or magical world and there is no meaning taking it very seriously and worrying about the changing whims and fancies of persons and their behaviour. This is the truth!

Two persons cannot agree always on everything. A boy and a girl with extreme difference in nature (svabhava), are attracted at first sight. But this attraction wanes when reality dawns on the persons. No two persons are of same nature and each person has a capacity to bear with the nature of another person when their relationships are at body level or mind level. Body chemistry or physical attractions are temporary. When the two persons are bound by spiritual attraction, their relationship lasts longer and becomes more fruitful. Thus, marital discord appears when body or sensual attractions and mental attractions wane out. Infatuation based on fascinations or fantasies and imaginary desires brings dislIusionment sooner or later. When the real nature of a person is intolerable to the other person, either they quarrel and separate, or decide to end the marriage with mutual consent. Rarely a marriage succeeds when it is based on wealth, social status, power or other worldly achievements.

The function of billiard balls is to collide. A strong personality is like a billiard ball. Any two strong personalities always collide, and their ego forms an adamantine wall preventing proper understanding, mutual admiration, respect and love. Ego rules the roost. On the other hand, any integrated personality is a harmonious being and he operates spiritually rather than mentally. He is full of love and understanding. He knows only love and consideration for others feelings. Here, 'love' means 'to unite'. It is Yoga. Life is a yajnya and, for a successful marriage the couple should offer themselves as the fuel and burn their ego in this yajnya. Only spiritual attainment will provide an enduring relationship and happiness. There are some strange marriages that fall outside reasoning or rationale; probably this helps us to understand the spiritual relationships better.

Eternal companionship and mutual dependence is possible only with the Lord. This is the reason why many ardent devotees like Shri Ramana Maharshi, Sant Tukaram, Gouranga, Swamy Ramakrishna Pramahamsa, Andal, Akkamahadevi, and Radha have all taken refuge in their Ishta Devatha to attain liberation and enjoy Supreme Bliss.

The marriage that is bound by spiritual attraction is mostly successful. Both the man and his wife must be aware of the Lord Almighty's divine plan and submit to His will. He will grant all success and happiness in such persons' lives. But who can know His Plans? Here, total submission will help. There is no place for the self here; there is no place for worldly desires here; there is no place for excesses or over-indulgences here. One has to be careful even in basic requirements like food, clothing and shelter and should not hanker after them. Hence, this is a very difficult proposition. But there is no way out at all.

All persons bound by mutual attraction at body level or mind level will have to face unimaginable miseries in their lives; thisis true especially of those who are attracted by bodily attractions and they will suffer more. Here, the reason is very simple; physical body is subject to change and deterioration over time; and, thus the very basis of marriage disappears leading to disappointment and distress. 'Rajasic' and 'Tamasic' Gunas take an upper hand, or preponderance over 'Sattvic Guna', in such lives. Due to too much of attachment (raga), mind looses sight of realities. For example, in a state of infatuation the realities of nature are forgotten. The most beautiful face that the mind madly sought after looses its glamour for it is not spiritually enlightened. The skin looses its elasticity for it is its sharira dharma. One should always remember that all finite things, however beautiful, deteriorate and disappear.

In the West, divorces are common after the mutual attraction fades away. A day comes when the person realizes that the other person is not the person he or she sought for so ardently or for that matter, so madly fell in love with. Hence is the disappointment and the misery. But here again, the marriage built on spiritual basis is stronger and there is no place for disappointment if both the husband and wife look to the Lord Almighty for guidance in life and take whatever comes as the God's Grace. 'Sattva Guna' takes preponderance in such lives. There is no place for 'Tamasic' indulgences in 'sattvic' lives. Even if one of the marriage partners is spiritual and the other not, problems remain. Rajasic or tamasic nature of a person makes him blind to realities of life since the mind under these prepondering gunas will cloud the sense of judgment with false notions of life.

The second category persons who operate at the mind level also face the same problem. Mind is always fleeting. Mind is always changing and looking for interesting or thrilling objects. Mind operates on the basis of imagination or memories. In both these cases, the persons lose sight of the realities of the present and feel disappointed when they do not get what they imagined or what they wished for. Further, if the marriage is not based on mutual understanding, mutual respect, trust, faith, love and sacrifice, such marriages are rocked at the earliest realization of the reality. If one of the partners is spiritually oriented and knows the reality of life, the marriage is sustained for a longer period. In all these cases, spiritual bent of mind will greatly help. Ego has no place in marriage. But in almost all cases of unstable marriages ego is the destabilizing factor. Wealth and fame are not the guarantors of a successful marriage.

This is how duality exists in everyday life. Mind dwelling on fascination and imagination is very dangerous. Mind has the ability to create things that are not real and thus dupes the persons offering him or her unlimited sexual happiness that is only imaginary; such an unlimited happiness is never possible in real life for the simple reason that the human body is limited and finite. Infinite happiness can be achieved only by spiritual practices. The role of sex is well defined in the Veda and Upanisads. Although sex is important in life, it should be understood within the definition and scope of life as defined in the ancient scriptures.

Vatsayana's Kama Sutra has been completely distorted by modern interpreters with the sole aim of 'en-cashing' it. It is impossible to strictly follow all the conditions that are laid down in Kama Sutra in modern day busy life. Moreover, it was laid down for a people of acertain time and certain place and it is not for all. Purity of thoughts and purity of heart underlie the relationship of sex-partners that is hardly found in present day life. It requires a very different way of life than that exists to day to live by 'Kama Sutra' way.

The spiritual path to life is the surest path that makes life more complete and satisfying. As already stated, reducing the rajasic tendencies and attaining Sattvic guna will reduce the heat of passion and sex. Here gain, sad-vichaara, viveka and vairagya will help to gain control over the sex-obsessed mind.

Of all the obsessions, sex-obsession is the strongest. Unless the person has a spiritual samskara and practices yama, niyama, and prathyahara, it is difficult to overcome the power of mind full of sexual thoughts and infatuation. This is one of the major aspects of youthful stage of life in every person that needs physical and psychological discipline and spiritual guidance. Prathyahara, or obstruction, or restraining obsessive thoughts of sex will help to control the body and mind. All the Jnyanendriyas and Karmendriyas should be constantly kept under vigil (Sakshi) and perfect control. Brahmacharya or continence should be practiced before entertaining the idea of marriage for happiness and success in life. This aspect is mostly ignored as at present.

It is repeatedly warned here that over-indulgence in any thing is bad; this is true particularly in sex. Normally, persons who are in the grip of sensuous life think life is for enjoyment at any cost! It istrue that, life is for enjoyment; but, it is definitely not at *any cost*. Life is sheer pleasure when it is sensible, when it is full of love, a Conscious enjoyment.

One who enjoys life fully will have no regret to these small things, including sex. So one should enjoy sex to the satisfaction of both the partners and the success of marriage lies in its consummation. Acharya Rajneesh says that 'a sexual union with the beloved in a total abandonment of the self will give immense satisfaction. The sexual union with the beloved that lasts for three hours at a stretch in a night will be totally and permanently satisfying and such persons will not hanker after sex anymore'. But, it is a rare possibility. Some people who have had this experience (may be in their previous birth!) do not hanker after sex any more. Thus, it is believed that sexual satisfaction that is quite lasting is important and it can be attained! It is sheer ecstasy and contemplation in the act that releases the bondage. That is how sex is a path of salvation. Sex should not be an obsession. It hinders all other creative thoughts originating from an intuitive frame of mind.

The heat of sex or passion is reduced with avoidance of lust. Ultimately, a sense of complete satisfaction or fulfillment, although not possible ordinarily, leads to vairagya and aversion to sex. Hardly three percent of our life- time is given to sex. But fools want to revel in thoughts of sex throughout life. Continence is important if one has to gain spiritual strength. It is said that 'ojas brings tejas'. Continence or avoidance of sex in married life is also very important in order to conserve the 'dhatu' (semen) and use this conserved energy for spiritual attainments. A strong heart, lungs, and nerves derive their strength from the conservation of energy from this source. A man with a strict disciplined sexual life is more attractive, strong and self-controlled. He gets a special shine, radiance on his face.

Inadequacy of partners in marriage is an important destabilizing factor. Due to lack of proper guidance at the right time many youngsters go astray and later on suffer inadequacy in married life. An unhappy wife will become quarrelsome and revolt causing marital discord. Many marriages have ended in divorces due to this factor of inadequacy. Lack of preparation and training such as brahmacharya is primarily responsible for failure or inadequacies in marriage. Carefree life in youthful stage brings in unimaginable problems later in life. The true meaning and purpose of life has to be clearly understood in order to live a happy and successful life. Hence, the golden rule is '*practise restraint*'.

An important technique of attaining sexual satisfaction is through raising the level of consciousness. Much less energy is required for sexual arousal and indulgences, whereas, more energy is required to attain spiritual experiences. With the advance in spiritual practice, the aspirant will come to experience happiness that is superior to the happiness derived from sexual indulgences. As the level of consciousness is raised to the heart level, the aspirant experiences true love. As and when this level of Consciousness is further raised to the throat level and the ajnya (eyebrow) level, and the 'Shiras' (head), the experience will be one of supreme bliss, much superior to anything experienced so far. Hence, one should rise to higher and higher levels of Consciousness through spiritual practices. Thus, life becomes more interesting and fulfilling.

### *Parents and Children*

It is the ardent desire of parents to get children. The parents aspire for progeny to continue their family heritage and lineage and, it is one of the basic instincts. But happiness in life, particularly from children is again a matter of divine grace. Not all parents are happy with their children. In the first place, it should be understood by all parents that the secret of happiness derived from children is due to love and selflessness.It is never a give and take proposition. When love dominates all weaknesses are merged in it; when love declines judgement takes its place and all human weaknesses become significant and spoils the relations. Commanding respect and imposition of one's own likes and dislikes are the worst enemies. Total freedom is the best remedy for all problems of parent- children relationshp. Respecting children and their wishes would bring in more love and happiness in the family. Always remember, that some children want to learn their lessons by hard way, their own way. Moreover, it is the impressions of their past life, sanskar that drives them that way. It is said, '***Karmaanusaarena buddhih***'; it appears that every jeeva is designed and planned in a particular way to suit its needs, to fulfil its goal. Jnyana Yoga gives an insight to human relationships. Even the animals are included in this. All individuals, Jeevas are unique and possess gunas, independent traits governed by its 'desire' that has caused its birth. It is like the body aspires for a soul and the soul is in search of suitable body and when the two match, the jeev is formed. The same principle holds good for 'parakaya pravesh' also. But, it must be remembered that a body and its souls, or for that matter, two individuals, cannot be bound for all times. Infact, release from bondage is what every jeeva seeks!

***Pure Love***

*What is Love? Pure love transcends body and mind; it rests with the heart and soul. The impulses of Love generates as the elixir of life, 'som', or 'amrut'. It is the immensity of joy felt by' antahkarana'. Here, the senses and the mind ar silent! Pure Mind is pure Consciousness that rests with the heart and that brings out the joy, the spirit of this elixir of life and spreads this joy through Prana to all parts of body. It is then, that the subtle body stirs, and mind enjoys this inexplicable joy- 'anirvachaneya santosha'. Pure Love is Anand, 'Bliss', one of the three qualities of the Lord. When that sort of love binds persons, there is 'unity' and no diversity; there is one and no 'other'. This Love is possible only with God. All other sorts of love are self-satisfying!*

***Pure Love is a one-way traffic and knows only giving***. This simple Rule of Love is not properly understood by many people and they expect love to be reciprocal. This leads to terrible disappointment. Another Rule of Love is that it ceases when judgment takes its place. Love (spirit) and judgment (mind) are inversely proportional. As love increases sense of judgment decreases. This is evident from Mahabharata. Excessive love blinds parents as to children's follies. Similarly, when wife starts to judge the husband, her sense of pure unconditional love gives place to criticism and quarrelsome behavior and life becomes miserable. A devoted wife never finds fault with her husband and has all admiration since her love is unconditional, absolute and pure. And, unconditional love is a myth!

Thus, love (spirit of devotion and dedication emanating from heart) decreases as sense of judgment (operating mind controlled by the senses) pervades relationships. Children, as they grow into mature life, start judging parents when their love for parents is replaced by sense of selfishness, rather their mind prevails over their heart; this does not mean their concern for parents also decreases. Love and mutual concern are two different things. One can have concern without love or attachment. Concern for the others is human value. In fact, the true meaning of love is also 'Yoga', ('yuj' meaning, to unite or become one). When you become one in love, *the other* does not exist. Very rarely such relationships are seen in modern families. A person conscious of his body and who operates at the mind level cannot totally subordinate himself to his loved ones. His ego comes in the way and he remains separate and does not become one with others. This is the tragedy of life!

Mind and moods rule over the heart. Mother and daughters, father and sons get into problems for want of total submission to love factor. In this material world, when children start judging parents, they start evaluation that leads to mis-understandings, clash of ideas, frequent quarrels, and more often, difference of opinion leading to separation. Similarly, where parents or the individual family members are selfish and seek their own happiness disregarding othes (especially children), the family atmosphere is vitiated. This is especially true with the joint families where the parents-in-law or the brothers and sisters-in-law live together. Where spirituality and love rule the relationships, there is mutual love and respect and the relationships grow stronger and stronger. Love and love alone thrives. Austerity helps to bind the relationships faster and it brings peace and happiness.

***Suicide***

Suicide is forbidden in all religions. It is sin to commit suicide. Indian holy scriptures condemn suicide and warn that any person who commits suicide will repeatedly take birth and repeatedly end life abruptly without fulfilling the desires. The dissatisfied soul wanders in search of a host and it is not easy to get one. It is the desire of all parents to beget children who are happy and successful in life. There is also the belief that the soul of a person commiting suicide will never rest in peace. These souls with unfulfilled desiresare always in transit. Normally, persons who are afraid of facing life will take to suicide. They forget that success or failure is not important in life; it is living that is important. The very meaning of life is struggling for survival. One has to live and struggle in life, realize the meaning of life and attain the goal. Evolutionary process must go on. It is the soul with blemishes (desires) that seek rebirth. Persons who commit suicide in one life develop a tendency to commit the same mistake of ending life without completing the cycle due to the strong impression (sanskar) created in the departed soul and the memory recurs life after life. It is this interruption, in the middle of life, that leaves a strong impression on the blemished soul; since the impression left is so strong that it (suicidal tendency) prevails birth after birth. The seed of rebirth is desire. To break the cycle of rebirth, the 'seed of desire' should be burnt with 'tapas' (heat), meditation, that brings about Realization of the Self. One has to live a full life in order to attain this 'Self Realisation'. Hence suicide is not the answer for the life's problems. Self- Realisation is the answer. According to

Bhagavad Gita, one must live like a 'dheera' and only a 'dheera' can live in this mundane sensate competitive objectve world of 'desires' ('kaamana' or 'vasana').

*Suicide should not be mistaken with the yogic 'deha parityaga' (discarding one's body at will) through Samaadhi in Transcendental Meditation. There are the Yogis who discard their body at will when they find that the body is not suitable for further spiritual pursuits. But, they can enter another body, if a suitable similar body is found in what is called 'parakaya pravesha yoga'. The Enlightened Yogis, ie Siddhi Purushas can live as long as they like. The methos of discarding their physical body is learnt from spiritual scriptures under the instructions of a Guru, and these are closely- guarded secret even today. It is a religious function watched by hundreds as seen from the accounts of Shree Raghavendra Swamy at Mantralaya, in Andhra Pradesh, India. It is a conscious effort, one of profound peace and tranquility; and, the spirit of the Yogi remains.*

The golden Rule here is, that with maturity and experience in life, one must develop 'vairagya', the sense of detachment. The coconut is a good example. As the tender coconut ripens, the inner copra (pulp) becomes hard and separates from the outer shell. *Vichara, viveka, and vairagya* are the three 'V's of Victory in this war against ignorance of life. All relationships are governed by the principles of 'Maya' (Ma= not and ya= that, i.e., 'not that') and 'Lord's Grace'. Deriving happiness from wife or husband, brothers and sisters, children, and other relations and friends, depends on 'His Grace'. Love knows only sacrifice.

Another important thing is that many parents do not realize that their children are not their children and they are only jeevas passing through their lives as a medium, and nothing more than that! Parents are selected by the jeeva to promote its desire according to its karma. As father, he only accommodates the seeds of desire and as mother, she only provides a home for the jeevas in seed form. Moreover, the parents have their past and the children have their future and the two will not stay together forever. This aspect needs a proper understanding and, that should lead to the sense of un-attachment (not total detachment like dis-ownment); it is like the water drops on the leaves of the Lotus. There should be neither raga nor dvesha and one must be '*Raagadvesha vimukta*'. This is the secret of happiness in life.

### *Death and Immortality*

*The Upanishadic doctrine is: "There is neither death nor birth, neither a bound nor a struggling soul, neither a seeker after liberation nor a liberated one- this is the ultimate Truth" [Amritabindu Upanishad, Sloka 10; Viveka Chudamani 574].*

It is in *Katha and Kena Upanishads* that we come across Death and Immortality, respectively. Nachiketas was watching the Visvajit sacrifice performed by his father Vajasrava for heavenly rewards. At the end of the sacrifice, Vajasrava offered cows and other gifts to Brahmins. As a boy of tender age, Nachiketas was sceptic about these offerings, of these Cows that ceased to yield milk. He thought that the Visvajit Sacrifice (Yajnya) would not be complete without offering *everything* in his father's possession and this includes son, me Nachiketas. He asked his father,'to whom wilt thou give me?' Vajasrava did not pay heed to his son. When Nachiketas went on repeatedly asking him to whom would he give, he angrily said that he would give him to (Yama) Death. Nachiketas took permission from his father and went to Yama, the God of Death to know what is Death. Yama refused to divulge the secret in the beginning; finally Yama conceded to reveal the truth due to Nachiketas's shruddha, bhakti, jnyaan, and other noble qualities.

*Yama said, "The wise, who by means of the highest meditation on the Self knows the Ancient One, difficult to perceive, seated in the innermost recess, hidden in the cave of the heart, dwelling in the depth of inner being, (he who knows that One) as God, is liberated from the fetters of joy and sorrow". [Kathopanishad, Verse XII].*

*Yama went on to say that whoever knows the word 'Aum' (Om) as 'Akshara Brahman' and meditates on 'Aum', would obtain whatever he desires, because God is the fulfillment of all desires. This sacred word is the highest symbol of the Absolute. Further, 'Aum' is indeed the Supreme, the Self. This Self is never born, nor does it die. It did not spring from anything, nor did anything spring from it. This Ancient One is unknown, unborn, eternal and everlasting. It is not slain even though the body is slain. Although this Atman dwells in the heart of every living being, ordinary mortals cannot perceive it because of its subtlety".*

*"He who is free from desire and free from grief, with mind and senses tranquil, beholds the glory of the Atman. Though sitting,it travels far; though lying, it goes everywhere. The wise who know the Self, bodiless, seated within perishable bodies, great and all-pervading, grieve not" [Kathopanishad II-20-2].*

*"A wise man should control speech by mind, mind by intellect, intellect by the great Atman, and that by the Peaceful One, the Paramatman, the Supreme Self". " Knowing that which is soundless, touchless, formless, undecaying; also, odourless, tasteless, and eternal; beginningless, endless and immutable; beyond the unmanifested; knowing 'That' man escapes from the mouth of death" [Katha Upanishad, III. 13 & 15].*

*"He is the sun dwelling in the bright heaven; He is the air dwelling in space; He is the fire burning on the altar; He is the guest dwelling in the house; He dwells in man. He dwells in those greater than man. He dwells in sacrifice. He dwells in the ether. He is all that is born in water, mountains, earth and sacrifice. He is True and the Great. He it is who sends the incoming life-breath Prana upward and throws the out-going breath downward. Him all the senses worship, the adorable Atman, seated in the center, the heart. When this Atman, which is seated in the heart, goes out from the body what remains then? This verily is 'That'. No mortal lives by the in-coming breath, Prana or by the out-going breath Apana, but he lives by another on which these two depend. As the intelligent man realizes the splendour of this Supreme Spirit, he becomes*

*free from that part of his nature that grieves and suffers, and thus he attains liberation"[Katha Upanishad, V 1-5].*

*Yama relates another important secret about' what happens to Self after death', to Nachiketas. He says:*

*"Some Jeevas enter wombs to be embodied; others go into immovable forms, according to their deeds and knowledge. The Being who remains awake while all sleep, who grants all desires, That is pure, That is Brahman. That alone is said to be immortal. On That all the world rests. None goes beyond That. This verily is That" [Katha Upanishad V 7-8]. " Immortality is attained when man transcends his apparent nature and finds that subtle, eternal and inexhaustible essence which is within him" [Kena Upanishad I-2].*

Thus, at great length, Katha and Kena Upanishads describe the essentials of existence and show the path to immortality. In the real sense, there is nothing that is perishable or imperishable for everything is illusion. That unicellular amoeba which made its first appearance has multiplied itslef into innumerable self and the result is the vast multitude of living creatures of different names, forms and functions. If that is not immortal, what else is immortal? Our parents live in us and we live in our children; then where is the question of death? It is the illusory body that perished under His will. Ultimately everything is gobbled up by Him.Everything is wasting and waning over time and we do not realise this Truth due to our ignorance.

*Death* is an illusion; so also is birth. Since the whole life is a drama, leela of the Lord, where is birth and death? It is He who enters in and out of bodies at His will. This transmigration of souls is the eternal game played by Him, the Supreme Spirit, Brahman. It has already been pointed out that it is He, the Brahman, who willed it. He created the cow and He himself became the bull; for all practical purposes, there is neither the cow nor the bull. It is a make-believe, magic of the Lord. He pervades the whole macrocosm and every atom of the microcosm; He is the One and only; He is the both. So death is a matter of transition from one state to the other. It is transmigration, transformation. The physical law is 'nothing is lost when a candle is burnt'. So, also nothing is lost or gained when a soul discards the unwanted body and enters another. It is His will!

Often we hear that such and such a person is no more. Sometimes we hear people saying, 'in fact, that person was with me till late in the night yesterday, and he is no more in the morning'. Such news come as rude shock, a surprise. It never occurs to us that it (birth or death) is all His Divine Plan, leela. Still, we laugh and enjoy over birth and suffer and cry over death! Even after people die, their memories live. Even after people physically die, their genes are already transmitted and thus they live in some other name and form! So, virtually none dies and nothing lies after death since death is 'illusion' for a Jnyani and, an apparent reality for an ignorant person. Hence, "*Fear not Death! Face it Boldly. You have conquered the world".In fact, modern science has got all the knowledge and tools to make death peaceful and enjoyable. However, religious leaders, ajnyanis, do not favour such a step! Willing persons must be allowed to die.*

Death is for celebration. It is an auspicious thing to celebrate death. That is the reason why 'Vaikunt' is celebrated as a grand feast in the memory of the departed soul on the thirteenth day of death. What happens after death is another interesting story. The physical body, made of the elements disintegrate and merge into their original state. The hair becomes the root of plants; the flesh and bones merge into water and earth. Thus, unto dust goes the body that was shaped out of the elements!

The departed soul finds its own level of existence in the macrocosm according to its carat, purity (atomic weight?) since the blemishes of the soul determine its future. Purer the soul, devoid of desires, tamasic, and rajasic gunas and, full of sattvic guna, the soul rises higher and higher into the sky called the 'svar lok'. Depending on its purity, the departed soul may cross the lower levels of Pitru Lok, and reach Deva Lok, Svarga Lok or even reach the Nakshatra Lok or Brahma Lok. The different spheres of the cosmic world may be taken as the lunar sphere, the inter-planetary space of all the known and unknown planets of the solar system, the solar sphere, the stellar and inter-stellar space, the galactio and inter-galactic space and finally the endless farther beyond! Whatever might be! But, it is a fact that all departed souls from this earth, called 'Mrutyu Lok', will find their own levels in the sky, the cosmic world. Some souls take immediate re-birth and some dissatisfied souls or unfulfilled souls remain nearer their homes or even within their homes till their desires are fulfilled. Some souls might be revengeful and some benevolent friendly casper and that depends on the 'fear complex' or 'guilt complex' of the living, more than the dead. Some souls wander in search of a suitable body to fulfil their unfulfilled desires. Ultimately, it is the unfulfilled desires that make the soul go round and round. A fully satisfied soul takes refuge in the Lord, the Supreme Consciousness (Brahman) and remains there forever. Ultimately, at the end of each evolutionary cycle culminating in Pralaya, i.e., when involution takes place, the souls merge in Him (may be the Black Hole!). This is the 'Involution' that precedes 'Evolution'.

There are souls in distress; the souls which terminated their lives abruptly under strange circumstances. There are Souls that could not fulfill their desires within the allotted time of its life and, these keep looking for an opportunity to take a body again and fulfill its desire. Lucky are the souls that can catch a body immediately after leaving one 'like a grasshopper that catches another blade of grass before leaving the one on which it dwells'. Desire is Brahman and desire is the cause of birth. It is the sweet will and wish of the Soul, 'Will of the Lord to manifest, take birth after birth, unless it finally decides to call it off. This is liberation of the soul; this is 'mukti' to the departed soul. Some departed souls may be hankering for love and respect from their children; others may be waiting for the fulfillment of some of the unfulfilled desires like earning name, fame, position, status, money. May be some souls have committed such sins that they are unable to find suitable station and move about as pisachas, goblins or ghouls or ghosts. Pindopanishad and Garuda Purana give details of these souls in transit or transmigration of souls.

Hence, it is the duty of every human being to satisfy the departed souls atleast by remembrance with Shruddha and Bhakti, whoever it might be! The modern day busy life may not permit elaborate 'shraaddha' functions to celebrate death anniversaries (sarcastically, they have all the time and resources to celebrate the birth anniversaries!); atleast, a well-disposed mind and an act of self-less service will do to propitiate the departed souls. A glass of milk and a fruit will be enough to satisfy the departed souls. These departed souls always shower their blessings on all those who remember them. It is also said the the departed spiritually attained souls can protect their loved ones in times of distress! This knowledge is beyond all reason and science; it belongs to the field of Spiritual Sciences. Rituals or no rituals, the souls sustain on their own, i.e., desire. It is the Divine Will!

*Some people are always obsessed with perfection, excellence, and achievement. There is nothing wrong in it. But, the obsession is the biggest hurdle in its achievement. Here, one should understand the 'akarma' theory. Nothing should be 'obsession'. Total involvement is what is required for achieving excellence in anything. Undivided attention is the pre-requisite of perfection. A calm, cool, and well-composed Mind is essential for excellence, and thereby success and happiness.*

*Professional excellence is an obsession. As soon as one forgets about it, he achieves it*! One thinks that 'I should do this', 'I should do that', and such thinking will not help in doing it for the simple reason that thought and action are two different things. If you think too much, you will not act. If you act, you are not thinking about that. This is the nature of mind; one thing at a time, either it thinks or it acts. In examination, if you are thinking about the answer, you are not writing it. Action, as if in a trance, is what we observe in some hardworking, sincere and devoted people. These are successful people; people at the top. This is, again, the "***I am not the doer***" Principle, or the 'akarma theory'. As long you are obsessed with it, you have no free will and will not be able to tap the hidden talent in you. You have to allow the mind to be calm and serene, so that ' intuition' takes over to provide you the much needed creativity, originality, perfection and excellence. The Brain works better when its temperature is near 0 Deg. Hence, the best one can do in the circumstances is to have an overall comprehensive view of things he is doing and put whole energy and soul into it with devotion, and surrender *the outcome* to the Lord Almighty. The Lord will take care of the rest. Slightest ego will spoil the whole exercise. *When Lord takes over, the outcome of action done in His name will be the best.*

Some people have the knack of buldozing everything that comes in their way. They assert with pride and ego and seem to succeed. But, ultimately, it is the humble and the submissive ones that succeed. The weak, the timid and the shy submit to Lord's will. The Lord will take care of everything; there is nothing that the Lord does not know. Persons who submit to Divine Will will have full faith in Him. They are not perturbed by small disappointments. Even small failures lead to successes in the long run. But, the strong egoists do not bend; their ego forms an adamantine wall and does not permit the vision of the Lord's hidden hand. Total involvement is what is needed here.

Professional excellence can be achieved by a simple technique of mind control. *Just study your mind and its movement dispassionately while doing work.* Watch and see how it is engaged in all sorts of trash and even harmful thoughts. Watching your mind can help gaining control over the mind to a great extent. The brain fibers become lighter and lose much of inertia when the mind is under watch by oneself. This is the 'sakshi bhava', 'self-witnessing' technique. '*Choiceless Awareness*' is very important. One should be consciously be wakefull, be aware of what he is thinking or doing. This helps to use discretionary power in a proper way. Most of the time we are indulging in mindless activities and lose sense of discretion. We have to watch ourselves, watch our thoughts, and watch our mind.

Normally, one does not bother to know how the mind works. Actually, it is important to know how the Sub-conscious, Super-conscious, and the Conscious work. The Un-conscious activity is going on without any aim; the Conscious activity is with an aim or purpose; the Higher Conscious works with normal consciousness. Always Higher Conscious should be involved in all Conscious activity in order to get the best result. A sense of inner awareness develops with the involvement of the Higher Conscious in normal Conscious activities. This comes by practice. There is a great difference between the work done by a spiritual person and an ordinary person. This is the 'Poorna Prajnya' (total awareness) technique of mind management. This is very important for success in all activities; and, ultimately it is this approach that brings success, immense satisfaction and happiness in life.

Remember the Mantra: "*I am not the doer. I am not the enjoyer. I am not the cause of the success or failure. There is a 'Guiding Force', a cosmic force that pervades everybody and guides towards destiny*". One is mistaken if he thinks that he is the cause of success or failure in life.

"*One who thinks he knows, knows not; and one who thinks he knows not, knows. He understands It, who conceives It not; and he understands It not, who conceives It. It is the unknown to the man of knowledge, but to the ignorant It is the known*" [*Kenopanishad* 3]. If a person thinks he knows everything, he is stupid; he is living in the past. Even if he says that he knows God, he is living in the past. Even those who say that they had had 'God-Vision', are living in the past with their memory. They are not living in the present. Having known God, one has already transcended God and, remember, it is not possible to transcend Him. So what is it he is speaking?

The more one knows of religious knowledge more it becomes unknown. The more one feels it is very difficult to know, more one feels he is too ignorant and helpless, the more God moves nearer to him. When someone really enters the divine, he comes to know that He is unknowable. He comes to know that there is no possibility of knowing Him. He always remains unknown, unknowable. He, the Lord Almighty, comes very near and still stays far, far beyond reach. He is within a wink of your eye and you can perceive Him in every lightning and thunder! He is like the fire in the molten lava, the magma. He is in the sun and beyond the sun. He is knowable and the unknown, as well as the unknowable and the known! One has to constantly strive for understanding Him, knowing Him, reaching Him, experiencing Him, realizing Him!

The moment I realize or know Him I am not there; I become 'That'. Similarly, the world is the other and the moment we know it, it becomes our Self and the 'other' ceases to exist. The World of illusion ceases to exist! This is the secret! He sits in us as 'Antaryamin' and directs all our actions according to our destiny.

Ashtavakra says, *"When there is no 'I', there is liberation; when there is 'I', there is bondage". Egoism is bondage and egolessness is liberation.* When there is no ego, there is no identification of the Self with body and mind, and the Self is realized as 'One without a second', pervading the whole universe. Having this knowledge, one becomes perfectly tranquil in mind and free from desires or aversions.

The liberation process begins with the process of Self-realization and 'mukti' is attained with the spiritual attainment in 'Samadhi'. If you are prepared for this in thoughts, words and action, i.e., kaya, vacha and manasa, you will get it. No doubt about this! Always remember that,'this world is not yours'. It is not for you in the sense, you are for the world and the world does not exist for you. You may live today and die tomorrow; the world exists forever. When the world is not yours, why do you cry for it? Why do you think this is mine and that is mine when nothing is yours! You have to realize that you are a guest for a limted period of stay, may be a hundred years, and you have to live within limits ('maryada') as a guest and get out as early as possible, the earliest the better! That is the way to live happily and successfully. Here, the Rule of Mind Management Technique MMT is: '*Live with Love and make sacrifice your goal. Thus, you will enjoy supreme happiness*'.

*Further, 'Atma Jnyana' alone can give Mukti or salvation. Atma Jnyana, the knowledge of the Self is the only direct means to freedom. Shrutis, Upanishads emphatically declare:*

*"Rite Jnyananna muktih", meaning, 'there is no liberation without wisdom'.*

*Nishkama karma can at best help Chitta Shuddhi very much required for mukti; it cannot give Mukti. Karma or action cannot remove ignorance. In fact, in the long run, Karma itself becomes a bandhan, bondage. Only 'Brahma Jnyaan' can remove ignorance. Hence, a drastic sadhana, 'Hatha Yoga' is needed for eradication of 'avidya', ignorance of 'Deha-adhyasa', meaning 'I am the body'. This one idea 'I am the body' has created so much havoc that we go on taking birth after birth to erase this ignorance. It is a mysterious Nescience, Avidya, or sheer ignorance.*

*Illusion, Maya*

*How often we are disillusioned about our own success? Why is it we are not contented and happy despite our so- called success? Why is it we feel unhappy and disappointed even when we achieve what we want? Why is that, sometimes, the persons whom we love most, and/or the things we like most become a source of great unhappiness, misery, and sorrow? Do we see things as they are? What is the cause of our unhappiness? Many great leaders have died utterly disillusioned even after ruling their country for several decades. Why? Why? The answer to all these questions lie in one inexplicable, powerful, dynamic, metamorphic force,' Maaya'. As already stated, it is' avidya' or ignorance, that we cannot 'Reality' i.e., 'see things as they are'. It is due to the 'avrutti', or covering of nescience or the blemishes of our soul such as desire, fear, attachment, and other vibrations of Mind, the 'Chitta Vrittis'.*

This Mind is '*Maya*', the illusion that brings about further creation of perishable and futile objects that further covers our pure Consciousness. This Mind cannot overcome 'Maya', the illusion since the mind itself is maya, the illusion. It cannot eliminate itself. Hence, one should have a clear sense of the world he lives in and strive for understanding the 'Sat' or the truth. This is the path of redemption from cycle of births and deaths. All the worldly achievements are of no significance for a Jnyani. Hence, every person should know what he wants and why he wants that. Otherwise, it will be a mad pursuit in this illusory world. It is so sad that many people die with all honours and worldly recognition but not knowing their Self!

There is a beautiful story of evolution in our Puranas. This should be taken in its proper perspective. Brahma created Saraswati and fell in love with her, his own creation and married her! Purana says so. Who is not enomoured with one's own creative force? A painter loves his own painting. An artist loves the object of his own creative skill. So also Brahma; but what is this marriage, union with Saraswati? It is the marriage, the union of the Consciousness (of the individual self) with the Supreme Consciousness, the 'Cosmic Self'. Further, Brahma created the cow and he himself became the Bull; the bull ran after the cow and the cow ran to hide and invited the bull. Finally, the cow and the bull became the cause of further creation. The story goes on and on like this to create this world of 'make-believe', 'Maya'! One should not get into the details of this story of creation. It is figuratively clear that we are bound by attachment, mamata, raga, moha, and forget the real Self in us. The whole life on this earth is a drama like the bull running after the cow and the cow hiding to invite the bull!

'*Maya*' literally means 'not that', '*Ma*' meaning 'not' and '*ya*' meaning 'that'.

Mundane knowledge is elusiveness. Ignorance binds, rather it blinds. In youth, we are so enomoured, get so infatuated (become amorous) looking at a beautiful girl, that we fantasise her. We long for possessing her. We forget for a moment that the girl is also a human, of flesh and blood with likes and dislikes, whims and fancies. We love ourselves in her and we are ever eager to enter her. When we get possessed of her, the reality dawns on us. We realize that she is not what we longed for; she is not the person we so earnestly desired for. She is just like any one of us and disillusionment starts; her shortcomings appear glaring. At times, her presence becomes so intolerable due to her attitude and behaviour that we start finding out ways and means of getting rid of her. She is 'Illusion'; she is 'Maya'. She is delusion that sweeps away our existence. There is also another way of thinking; she is the source of our joy and happiness. But, sooner or later, when we feel we are satisfied and we lose interest in her and look elsewhere for thrill and joy; this goes on until the discriminative power in us drives us to seek an eternal source of happiness. In order to realize the true nature of our Self, we try to get rid of this source that is outside of our Self and start looking within our Self for the source of eternal joy. When the 'Purusha' within us realizes His true nature 'that he is independent, eternal and Himself all-Bliss', Prakriti, Maaya, illusion, ignorance, avidya, 'Nature' releases Him from her clutches or bondage. This is libeartion, 'mukti'.

***Moksha! What is it?***

Sarvopanishad, the quintessence of the Upanishads, gives answer to some of the most important questions !ike: What is Moksha? What is bondage of the Soul? What is Vidya? What is 'Saakshin'? What is Kutastha? What is Paramatman or Supreme Self orParabrahman? What is Atman? What is Maya?

Shri Shaṇkaracharya's 'Viveka Chudamani' gives the selected gems of aphorisms or Sutras (Formulae) that show the way out of the 'Samsara tapatrayas'. It is a handbook of sane and sensible living.

"*All this universe which through ignorance appears as of diverse forms is nothing but Brahman that is free from all limitations of human thought". [Atharva Veda]. If this universe is to be true, let it then be perceived in the state of deep sleep also. As it is not at all perceived, it must be unreal and false, like dreams. Therefore, the universe does not exist apart from the Supreme Self; and the perception of its separateness is false like the blue colour of the sky. Hence, whatever is manifested, viz. this universe, is the Supreme Brahman Itself, the Real, the One without a second, pure, taintless, calm, serene, adimadhyantarahita, the Essence of Knowledge, 'Sat-Chit-Ananada'. 'Sages realize the Supreme Truth, Brahman, in which there is no differentiation of knower, knowledge, and known, which is Infinite, transcendent, and the Essence of Knowledge Absolute". [Viveka Chudamani].*

Moksha, or liberation is not what is available some where and that can be easily achieved by some technique. Moksha is a dynamic process to attain perfection. The moment one becomes perfect, blemishless, pure in heart, mind and soul, he/she is liberated. Perfection or mukti brings peace and happiness. It is an attitude like happiness; it is a way of looking at things. Once you attain this stage or gain this attitude in life, you will enjoy every minute of life, only if you are alive to it and are aware of what is happening. Normally, one gets bored sooner or later in this mundane worldly life. You do not know what to do. Nothing is interesting. Nothing is thrilling. Time moves very slowly and you are aware of that every minute; it seems endless and it is killing. You are asking when this boring state is going to end. You want to know when there is liberation or mukti from this life. But, if you are enjoying life, you will not ask when it is going to end.

You do not want that blissful state to end. You are enjoying every minute and you do not ask when it is going end. You are already free. In the very enjoyment of life has come your freedom. You feel it is good when it ends. It is also fine if it does not end. You are enjoying it; you are living it. You accept it totally. This is moksha, the state.

Here, the Mind Control technique, the '*Manoniyantran Tantra*' is:

*"One has to develop this attitude of happiness from 'living' every moment of life. Always remember that yesterday is dead and tomorrow is not born as yet. As long as one dwells on memories of the past or the dreams, aspirations and anxieties of future, there is no space for experiencing the present. The Mind can do one thing at a time. So, do not dwell on the past memories, fantasies and sanskaras; so also, do not live on hopes, dreams and aspirations. Live now and here and enjoy every moment of this life without attaching your mind and senses to life. Attachment brings misery. Live every moment of your life; observe it as a witness or 'Sakshin'. Become a witness. Watch it like a drama unfolding in front of you. Do not add colour to it, do not attach meaning to it. Observe it in a trance as a mesmerizing act of the Lord! It is the cosmic drama of life on earth. You will enjoy the 'Sat', ' Chit' and 'Anand'. This is the supreme bliss that never ends. But you have to live it. Past second is dead and the next second has not arrived as yet. What if, even if you have had the God-vision, it is only a memory, i.e., past; what about the present? Do not dwell on the past memory. What about your existence at the present? Are you 'Being', living fully, established in your Self? Erase all your memories (of the past) and be prepared to experience the present. This very second of time you are watching has all the essence of life; it is watching the mysteries hidden in the 'Hiranyagarbha', the Golden Egg that holds immense possibilities of creations. It is the 'Self', same 'Atma', the Brahman. Try to enter into it and experience yourself".* And, this is the secret. This is *'Moksha'* here and now! What more do you want?

*Ashtavakra Samhita* is a very beautiful treatise on philosophy of practical life. It is the equivalent of the Bhagavad Gita; but very little of this is known due to inaccessibility of the original scirpture. It first came in an Indian Vernacular, Kannada and later in English versions, and till today, no satisfactory true version has come out! It is a very very practical way of living peacefully, happily, and successfully in the modern day huzzle buzzle of life. In a nutshell, *Ashtavakra says*:

*"Be calm and serene; don't be agitated. Do not go after anything. If anything comes your way accept it gracefully, gratefully, happily, and be contented. Be humble and hear your inner voice. Problems crop up when you run after something and you do not get it".*

This holds good even to the aspects of liberation and salvation. If you just 'keep quiet' you will get everything, including mukti (liberation) and moksha or salvation. If you run after it, even if you take to Yoga and Meditation, with desire you will not get it!

The essence of this philosophy is very simple but very difficult to understand and practise. It is so simple that '*anything you strive for eludes you due to the fact that your desire, conscious mental effort, itself becomes a hurdle; if you approach the same without the involvement of the Mind (concentrated) and the senses (not focussed), then the Self (the Pure Consciousness) takes over and achieves the objective very easily'*. There is nothing that is impossible for the Self (Pure Consciousness) to achieve, for the simple reason that 'the Self is Brahman'! But, it is also made clear here, that 'there is nothing to go after, *there is nothing to achieve, and, there is nothing to strive for, in this 'make believe', illusory world (Maya Prapancha)'. Whom do you want to please! Once you have realized the 'Truth' there is nothing to know.*

What is the good even if a Nobel Prize is awarded and National Honours are showered on you and all the media show you to the world when you feel hollow within, internally, and do not enjoy the internal peace and happiness? These honours may bring a few US $s and scrolls of paper inscribing your name boosting your ego. Unless you surrender all 'ego' to Him, the Lord, it is all a waste! All external aggrandizement will only enhance the ego, blur 'Reality' and create more problems. It is very essential to realize this 'Sat', the Truth! Ultimately, you may die 'a person widely known all over the world but not knowing your own Self'! That will be a great tragedy!

The Reality is this. It is so very simple. Once you realize that supreme doctrine '*Thou art That*', *there is nothing more to achieve! You are already 'That*', -"*Tat Tvam Asi*". Just realize the Self in you. It is your total awareness that "the Lord dwells in you; He is the guiding force. He is the Effulgent Self that sheds light and erases your ignorance. He is Omniscient".

*Yasmin sarvaani bhutaani hyatmatvena shijaanatah*
*Na vai tasya bhavenmoho na cha shokoadviteeyatah [Shankara's 'Aparokshaanubhuti', P. 54]*

Meaning, 'In that state of experiencing unity (with the Atman), there is neither delusion nor sorrow that arise due to duality'.

It is sheer ignorance that prevents you from realizing Him, the Lord in your self, rather visualizing Him! Look inward. Watch your 'Self; Watch your mind; observe closely the behaviour of your mind. Watch your thoughts. Be a witness, '*Sakshin*' to all your thoughts and actions. You will realize Him. It is your inferiority complex; it is your lack of confidence, the lurking fear within you that hinders your vision of Him. Be courageous; be a 'dhira' and live your life, every moment of it, neither thinking of the past nor looking anxiously at the future. It is He who has created this illusory world and it is He who will take care of it. Remember He has got a Department of Proetection; have faith in Him. He is omniscient, omnipresent and sees everything and will protect you always and under all circumstances. *Trust Him. Surrender totally to Him and Him alone.*

You can invent the whole set of gadgets to investigate this outer world, this physical universe; but you cannot invent yourself! Invent your Self! Discover your Self! It is now more important than ever to discover your Self and invent your Self because you do not know yourself; you are lost in delusion, in the floods of ignorance and every ecientific advancement and technological progress is posing new cxhallenges and a threat to your own existence, survival. You are deluded by this superficial knowledge 'avidya'.

Somebody has well said, "*How wretched is the man, with honours crowned, who having not the one thing needful found, dies known to all but himself unknown*". *[Anonymous]*

Total annihilation glares at the face of our modern scientific civilization. We have no other alternative but to look to salvation in spiritual attainments! Noble Prize Laureate Alexis Carrel, the author of "Man, the Unknown", states, "The aim of civilization is the progress not of science and machinery, but of mankind". He further said, "if men like Galileo, Newton, Lavosier, had devoted their intellect to the study of human body, mind and consciousness the world would have been entirely different". He emphasized the need for the study of man in depth. Even Einstein is of the same opinion. He says "Objective knowledge provides us with powerful instruments for the achievements of certain ends in life. But the ultimate goal of life and longing to reach it, must come from another source".

Ultimately, the aim of life, according to the Veda and Upanishads, is to "*Know thyself*". Reknown Poet D.R. Bendre has explained what is meant by 'Get into thy-self'; it is 'Be thyself' or 'know thy-self'. He says, "When we try to understand our true nature by means of proper thought, technique, inquiry, and experience we get immersed in the depths of our beings. Then we have a glimpse of the profound light latent within ourselves. We realize that this light is not a figment of our imagination but a matter of profound truth".

There are thousands of Sadhus, Saints and spiritual seekers in the Himalayas, through out the stretch of 1500 kilometres of the lofty Himalaya Mountains that reach more than 8000 Metres, here and there. From Badrinath, Kedarnath, Rishikesh, Hardwar in Himachal Pradesh to Gangtok and Lhasa in Sikkim, Tibet and Khatmandu in Nepal; and Darjeeling to the end of Arunaachal and other beautiful places in the Eastern Himalayas, thousands of spiritual seekers are found living in caves and caverns, and some in the hollow of the trees, and some in remote areas inaccessible to common people. Some don the scantiest possible rags and many do even without that in such freezing cold mountainous regions! These spiritual seekers are not the ordinary persons; many of them are profound scholars in Veda and Upanishads and some are doctors, scientists, engineers, and professsors by profession. They have deserted their worldly life to experience the secrets revealed in the Veda and practise the doctrines of Brahma Sutra and the Upanishads. They do not like any intrusion. Most of them act like mad persons and throw stones at you if you try to reach them for fear of being disturbed and diverted from their Meditation. Since almost all these spiritual men have attained mystic powers common people go to them for redressal of their problems. Some of these Sadhus dispense with Ayurvedic medicine and spiritual healing by touch therapy to the sick people living in the remote villages.

As already stated, it is not very strange to meet many a famous scientists and doctorates from reputed Universities, scantily clad, living in holes and caves like animals! Their main goal is to Meditate alone in a serene atmosphere, a peaceful environment and search for the 'Truth', or 'Reality'; and, experience the innate peace and supreme Bliss. Many of these spiritually enlightened persons are very rich and famous and often attract devoted spiritual seekers from all over the world. Many have widely traveled and delivered lectures in reputed Universities. And lo! They now live here in caves along with animals, eat scarcely, and sleep very little; simply one cannot believe these things! Why do they discard clothes and live scantily dressed. The first principle of delusion is name and form that comes with dress. These sadhus discard their family names and assume some initiated name and discard robes and dresses for that is an ID mark. Some are so famous that they are known far and wide for their spiritual powers. The very spiritual success they have attained make them wary of the dangers of losing their main goal-Self-Realiszation, 'Aatmasaakshaatakaar'. Hence, they shun worldly social and economic status. Most of them carry a simple woolen rag or Kambli (woolen shawl) and a tumbler to carry water; that is all they possess as their worldly belongings! They give away everything they get from their devotees.

Some of the famous spiritual teachers, who have made the Himalayas as their abode, teach Yoga and Upanishads, render financial assistance to poor students, run (in absentia) schools and colleges, and provide funds to research institutions and support libraries with manuscripts of ancient scriptures. Amongst themselves, they talk in Deva Bhasha almost like Vedic Samskrut. It is a much-guarded secret and we cannot understand what they communicate among themselves for they communicate in silence; even when they talk it is very difficult to understand. Most of the time they are in silent communion enjoying the supreme Bliss! Silence is the means of realizing the 'Self'. Their experiment, as far as we know, deals with clairvoyance, omnipresence, omnisience, spiritual healing, touch therapy, parakaya pravesh, and reach the state of absolute Bliss in Samadhi for hours and hours, and even several weeks at a stretch! Some Sadhus and Swamis save people in distress even in far off places, without moving an inch, by mere contemplation; and, in some cases have actually brought the dead person back to life. The mystic experiences of these spiritually enlightened persons knows no bounds and some are deeply involved in experiencing the process of energy becoming matter and matter turning into energy; they disappear like mist and reappear and this has led to many stories like the abominable snowman and the 'Yeti'. Actually, it is the 'Yati' (the Spiritually enlightened) that is mistaken for Yeti, the abominable snowman. Most of these sadhus have experienced the supreme Consciousness in deep nirvikalpa samadhi, transcendental meditation.

It is Moksha or mukti that these Sadhus and Sants have already become perfect; the have attained spiritual height by rigid yogic exercises. They have many mystic experiences and have performed miracles only when absolutely essential (not for show or money). They also accept a few disciples and teach them Yoga. Some Seekers who are going to be Swamis learn at the feet of these Yogins. Upanishadic doctrines and Yoga lessons are taught in their ashrams. If anyone is really interested in spiritual attainment, it is possible to take the help and guidance of these real spiritual teachers. Some Sadhus never stir out of their huts or caves and occasionally come down to the Plains from their Himalayan abode and preach the Upanishadic doctrines; and, their gatherings are very large, often exceeding five figures and their disciples include very well known personalities in public life. Not all can get their individual attention for, they also select their students according to 'divine will'; just as we want to select the best teacher, they want the best students- humble, obedient, sincere, devoted and those who have already shown some progress in spiritual practices. They encourage scientific research into Vedic and Upanishadic Doctrines. There are scientists who are stalwarts, well trained in modern scientific research, and have taken to spiritual pursuits in the Himalayan caves under famous Yogins. Some have succeeded in reaching great spiritual heights, and have come almost close to creating life and can easily transform matter, and turn matter into energy and vice versa. There is no wonder if something more startling and mysterious are unravelled in future. But, one must remember that the spiritual path is much more difficult than the field of research in physical or biological sciences.

There is an increasing interest in Indian Vedantic Studies among the Western Spiritual Seekers. More and more successful, rich, and famous persons are seeking spiritual guidance since modern day life has become simply unbearable. There is no such thing as stress and hypertension and sickness among these Sadhus. They hardly sleep and eat very little and their worldly possessions include a tumbler and a gunny rag. Although they are spiritually rich and famous since their disciples offer them anything and everything – cars, houses, jewellery, money, they never touch them.

It is only in the mundane world the ignorant persons are struggling hard to earn more and more and suffer sickness due to this madness to earn more; and, there are the factors of ego, disappointments, frustration, challenges and competition, standing on nerves, jealousy, cutthroat competition, greed, avarice and what not! Finally, even when one gets what he wants, he is disillusioned! About the increasing mental ailments and the present day modern man's predicaments, C.G.Jung has warned Thus:

"Psychoneurosis must be understood as the suffering of a human being who has not discovered what life means to him" In the same context, T.M.Thomas, in his 'Images of Man', has opined thus:

*"The Twentieth century neurosis is the neurosis of purposelessness, meaninglessness, valuelessness, hollowness, and emptiness". What a great fall from 'Grace of the Lord"! Thus, it is high time that we take note of this trend of development and take all precautions to avoid the unavoidable, self-annihilation. We have to remember: "Utthishtato (Arise), Jagrata (Awake)! 'A clarion call of the Veda.'*

*ATMAN–BRAHMAN UNIFIED FIELD*

*Since Vedic times, in India, it has been the main objective of all Rishis, Seers, to unravel the mysteries of this universe, the creation, and the source of all KNOWLEDGE. Ultimately, they discovered the source in Brahman, the Absolute!*

*Atman-Brahman unification is the goal of life. It is this Unity, or 'Samsathi' or fulfillment of life that is the supreme goal of all living beings on this earth. This concept of Samasthi is also called "KNOWLEDGE" and it is 'Supreme Knowledge' that answer all questions.*

*When Aruni returned proud and arrogant after his twelve-year stay with his teacher and said that he has completed a course of education, his father asked him, "Do you know "That' from the Knowledge of which everything else becomes known"? Aruni replied in the negative and was sent back to his teacher to learn that and it took him another twelve years! Even Gods had to waitupon the Great Sages for decades and decades to learn these secrets!*

*In other words, "What is that "Supreme Knowledge", the 'Knowledge of One' that will reveal the Knowledge (cause and effect) of everything else"? What is 'That' from which emanates everything else? What is the source of the diverse objective world?*

*The answer given by the Shruti Texts is very simple. The knowledge of "Brahm", or the 'Brahman' reveals the mystery of this 'Uni'-verse, the diversity unmanifest in the manifest 'Unis', or the 'One' supreme 'Brahman', the supreme Consciousness. It is sheer nescience, 'avidya' or ignorance that the universe appears diverse."**It is the non-abandonment of the distinction of the entire world from Brahman that causes the impression that this illusory world as real**". Once the 'Unity concept or Samasthi is realizd, all distinctions vanish. Brahman is the only 'Sat', the "Truth" It is the 'Brihat', Greater than the Greatest, the 'Mahat', the Unmanifest from which all manifestations of this universe are caused. Just as the differentiated butter or ghee is unmanifest in milk, the entire objective world exists in the unmanifest 'Brahman'.*

*Thus, from knowledge of one, the Brahman, everything else is known. For the Shruti says that ' the effects are not different from the cause, and consequently the cause being known, the effects will also be known'. Only Brahman, the Truth, the Existence, the Sat, the Bliss, is real; all other things of this objective world, viz the ether (the Sky or Akash), the air (Vayu), the fire (Agni), are manifestations of Brahman. In all these subsequent creations there is separateness. But it should be remembered that the Atman is not the manifestation of Brahman since it is not the creation of Brahman, but it is Brahman itself. Atman is not the effect; it is the cause of all the manifest forms of this universe. All things are created from the Atman, ie Brahman. Brahman which is existence itself, cannot be an effect of any other cause; Brahman is Self-effulgent and the source of all creations. From the general, the Brahman, all the particulars, the objective world, are created. "That great birthlss Self is undecaying" [Brihadaranyaka Upanishad 4-4-25]. Brahman is eternal- beginningless, and endless, "Aadi-madhya-anta-rahita". Ultimately everything is united in Brahman. Everything evolves from Brahman and involves in Brahman. Always remember, what is called 'Atman' in the particular, is also 'Brahman'.*

### The Unified Field

*In the field of physical sciences, too, the scientists engaged in search of the'Reality' behind all this material creation, and at last found a satisfactory explanation to the problem of Unity of existence in the 'Super-String Theory' of Physics. So far, the Lagrangian Superstring theory is the most satisfactory Unified Field Theory. [See Maharishi Mahesh Yogi:'Wholeness on the Move' and the 'Heaven on Earth', Mahesh Yogi Veda VigyanPrakaashan, Jabbalpore, India]. The Unified Field Theory explains the 'Unity of all diversities' and states that the Unified Field, the 'Samhita', as the 'Self-referral Field', the 'Atma'. The Atma is 'Self- referral' because 'it knows all' and there is nothing else to refer to; it knows everything. It is "Total Knowledge". It has got the means to know. It is the end by itself, like the ocean where all the rivers end. Thus, it (Atma) is the 'Knower' as well as the 'Knowledge'. Hence, it is three-in-one, the Knower (Rishi), the 'illumining principle' (means of knowing- Devatha), and the Knowledge (the object of search -Chhandas). Rather, it is the "Brahm", the eternal,"Self-Referral' Supreme Consciousness", i.e.,"POORNAM" (WHOLENESS), "Samhita"- union ('yuj') of the Rishi, the Devata, and the Chhandas of the Rk Vedic Mantra:*

*"Agnimeele puruhitam yajnyasy devam ritvijam hotaaram ratnadhaataram;*

*[Rk Veda 1.1.1]*

*Richo ak-kshar parame vyoman yasmin devaa adhi vishve nishedhuh*
*Yastanna veda kim rucha karishyati ya it tad vidus ta ime samasate.*

*In Bhagavad- Gita, Shri Krishna says, "I am the Kshetra (Field) the Devata; I am the Kshetrajnya (Knower of the Field), the Rishi; I am the means of Knowing, the Illumining Principle, the Chhandas."In the Samhita, the three-in-one, the wholeness, the 'yuj' or union the unmanifest United Field of Consciousness (Purusha exists through its Self-interacting Dynamics (Prakriti) expresses itself in specific quantities and in a perfect sequence (Vibrations/Waves) assuming the qualities (Gunas) and structure of the Laws of Nature (Prakruti Dharma). This is the Vision of the Origin and Evolution of Law (Dharma) or supreme Consciousness or 'Poorna Prajnya' that regulates the creation (srushti), and maintains order, (Ritam and Satyam) in the Universe.*

*Rather, all these are simply, the supreme Consciousness 'Brahman' Himself, the Unified Field (Abstract Silence) acts as Brahma the Creator, Vishnu, the Sustainer, and Maheshwara, the Terminator. The Vision of the origin of quantified values of Law in the ocean of Unifid Field of Law- the Unified Field of Consciousness -the waves, the ripples, and bubbles- this Visva- the Material Obejective World.*

*Atman-Brahman Unified Field*

*Atman is Brahman indeed! In other words, Unity of Existence (E) is A = B, where, A is Atman and B is Brahman.This is the same equation E = MxC square. Where E is the Energy derived from 'Brahm', and M is represented by 'K' of "Ak" and C is represents Vibrations created by impulses generated from Absolute Silence, 'Atyanta-Abhaava' as explained in the first Mantra of Rk Veda 1.1.1. Shrutis say, 'inasmuch as all beings are born of Brahman, the supreme Atman is verily the Brahman. [Taittiriya Upanishad III.1]. This is a very beautiful concept that lies outside the purview of modern physical and material sciences. Actually, the modern scientists have been struggling hard to discover this unifying force in all matter and have now succeeded in discovering it in the*

*Lagrangian Super String. The 'Samsthi' concept is the final product of spiritual experience and as such it lies outside ordinary knowledge (apara vidya) and common understanding. It is the supreme goal of all spiritual seekers and it is deliverance, moksha or mukti. It is 'yuj', the union of 'Atman' and 'Paramatman' through the power of supreme knowledge, Consciousness. It exists in Abstract Silence, 'Atyanta-Abhava'. It is attainable but so far no one has attained it. It is Knowable but not yet 'Known'. It can be experienced – 'Aparokshaanubhuti' as Self- Realization, "Atmasakshaatkaar". In other words, it is just 'Sri Hari Narayana', the eternal Flow of cosmic energy inherent in all living and non-living Beings.*

*What is 'Atman' and what is 'Brahman'?*

*The Atma Vaisvaanara is the 'Agni' (fire) commonly existing in all persons (body tempearature). This omnipresent Self is the 'Atman' and that is the Brahman. Agni Vaisvanara is, as a rule, named only Vaisvanara, the omnipresent world-principle that is united or reconciled with that in the head of man, as a microcosm, of the size of a mustard seed, the size of the tip of the hair split a hundred times, the size of thumb or the size of a span. When the question is asked what is this 'Vaisvanara', six Brahmanas stated that, the earth, water, space, wind, sun, and heavens constitute the Vaisvanara.*

*But, Sage Asvapati clarifies that, "The earth, water, the wind, the sun, and the heavens are mere foot, bladder, breath, eyes and head, respectively, of Vaisvanara; these are only the substructure of Vaisvanara but not the full, complete Vaisvanara. He continues, the stars are Vaisvanaras, eyes shining full of splendour are Vaisvanara, the nostrils as separate paths, the space in mouth as a manifold one, the water in the mouth as riches, and the chins are the basis of Vaisvanara. The man is, thus, the Vaisvanara, Agni Vaisvanara, as grounded in man, he averts recurring death, lives in full duration of life; not once will Vaisvanara injure him who utters his name".*

*The idea of unity of the universe and realization of this unity with man is contained in the above narration. Chandogya Upanishad proclaims the unity of the Atman.*

*"What delusion, what sorrow is there for the wise man who sees the unity of existence and perceives all beings as his own?" [Isavasya Upanishad. 7]*

*"All gods, worlds, and beings depend upon a unity- one ultimate principle" [Rk Veda 1.164; 10.129].*

*This is the Principle of Samhita, Wholeness or 'Poornam', or Unified Field of Self-Referral Consciousness- 'Poorna Prajnya' (Always Awake). It is self-existent, eternal, reverberating self-effulgent "Chaitanya" and "FULL" FOREVER..*

*The Atman is the Brahman, the Self in every person. It is the size of the thumb, "Angushtamatra Purusha" [Kathopanishad II .4. 13]; some say, 'it is of the size of the point of a needle' [Kathopanishad 4.12], size of a Barley corn [Chandogya Upanishad 3.4.2], tinier than the split hair [Svetasvatara Upa. 5.8.9]. It is located near the heart, in a cavity that is known as the sky (space) of the microcosm. It is 'Atma Vaisvanara'.*

*In Brihadaranyaka Upanishad [2.1] and Kaushitaki Upanishad, [Verse 4] Gargya Baalaaki volunteers to explain the Brahman, the Atman to King Ajatashatru. When the King tells Baalaaki that these explanations are inadequate, the latter submits himself as a student and requests the King to teach. Similarly. In Brihadaranyaka Upanishad [Verses: 3,9, 10-18, 26 and 4.1] Vidaghda, when asked by Yagnavalkya with regard to Purusha, the spirit that is the highest summit of personality, gives a number of explanations, but fails to define the spirit. Again, in Chandogya Upanishad [Verses: 5.11-24], it is mentioned that six Brahmanas (knowledgeable persons) seek explanation about the Atman Vaisvanara. After they heard that the heavens, the sun, the wind, the ether, the water, and the earth are the nature of the Atman, the King Asvapati teaches them the true nature of the Atman.*

*In Chandogya Upanishad [8 7-12], Prajapati Brahma teaching Indra says, "The Atman or the Self is in the physical body as the individual soul, and as the highest soul, which represents the three steps of knowledge deepening step by step". Again, Sanatkumara son of Brahma, or Skand, the War-Lord teaches Narada and sets forth sixteenways to adore Brahman as: Naman (name), Vac (speech), manas (Mind), samkalpa (resolution), chitta (thought), dhyana (Meditation), vijnana, balam (strength), annam (food), apah (water), Tejas (fire), Akaash (Space), Smarana (Memory), Asha (desire), Prana (vital breath) and the highest of all, the 'Bhuman' (the Infinitude). According to Paingya, Prana is verily the Brahman; just as the hub of a wheel holds all the spokes, Prana holds all the constituents of the body together.*

Again, there is the instance where the King Ajathashatru tells Balaaki that, "*When a man wakes up from deep sleep (near to Brahman) it happens that just* ***'as the sparks fly out of one another from the blazing fire'*** *towards all sides, so also out of the Atman all life forces, each according to its location- come forth, out of the life forces – speech, eyes, ears, Manas come forth the divinities Agni, Surya, Disha, Chandrama (Moon) and out of the divinities the worlds –names, forms, sounds and thoughts. It is the Prana, 'Pajnyatman' ('Consciousness' of the Self), which has entered the body as self, down to hair, down to the nails. Just as the razor is concealed in a sheath, fire in its fireplace, the 'Prajnyatman' is concealed in the body.*" So long as Indra had not known this truth, the Atman as the Self, the demons were superior to him. When Indra realized this truth, he defeated the Asuras and gained supremacy over all Gods, and all creatures.

*Ajatashatru asked Balaaki " Would you like to know where does one go to in deep sleep and whence he comes forth on awakening?"*

*'In man are the arteries which are called 'Hita' which, arising out of the heart surround the pouch of the heart (pericardium). These arteries, as fine as a hair split thousand-fold, find themselves filled by the fineness of a brown, white, dark, yellow and red sap. In these one stays in deep sleep, so that he sees no dreams'. Then he becomes one with Prana and the mind and the senses enter into him.*

*Let us see what Maharishi Mahesh Yogi sayas about the Atma. "Atma is the source of Veda- fully awake in its potentiality as totality- Brahman.*

*Atma is lively in its full potential when its Self-interacting Dynamics, the thirty-seven values of Vedic Literature, together give rise to the structure of Veda, Pure Knbowledge- the Laws of Nature- the Constitution of the Universe- which in turn evolve into th physiology and the materil creation, the Vishwa (Universe).*

*But, then, what is Brahman?*

*Here is an instance. Nachiketas asks Yama, the God of Death, "Tell me of that which you see as neither good nor bad action, as neither effect nor cause, as neither past nor future" to which Yama answers, "I will tell you in brief- it is "Om". Further it is said that, "The Self is neiher born nor does it die" [Katha Upanishad 1.2.14-15 & 18].*

*Brahman is the inexplicable. None can explain what is Brahman for none has seen Him. It is beyond words to describe Him; It is 'One' from which the thoughts and words come back without reaching ("Yatra waacho nivartante"). Yet, Brahman is described as "Anoraneeyan mahatomaheeyaan", meaning, smaller than the smallest and bigger than the biggest. Brahman is supposed to be 'nirguna' (without any Gunas or qualities), niraakaara (without form), and nirmama (without Self). Brahman is also described as the One who has three worlds for his body (with His feet resting on earth). Chhandogya Upanishad describes Brahman as One with "One foot (quarter) of Him is all beings, and three feet are what is immortal in heaven" [Verse 3-12-6]. Brahman is endowed with Maaya Shakti, the power of nescience. Brahman possesses all powers. Brahman is the 'Great Maayin'- the Ruler of Maaya Brahman is the subtlest of the subtler spirit and it is stated that that "He is myself within the heart, smaller than a grain of rice, smaller than the grain of barley". [Svetasvatara Upanishad 4-10; as also, Chhandogya Upanishad, 3.14.4; 8.7.1 & 3-14-3]."The great Lord is the Maayin, the ruler of Maayaa"; and," through His infinite power of Maayaa is able to create this world of diversity" [Shvetasvatara Upanishad 4.10; Brahma Sutra 2.1.26]*

*"Praana is Brahman" [Brahma Sutra 1-1-28]; "And that Praana is indeed the intelligent self, blessed, undecaying, immortal" [Kaushitaki Upanishad 3. 1-8]. "All this indeed is Brahman" [Chhandogya Upanishad 3-14-1].*

*Brahman is described as the "Lord who is the efficient as well as the material cause of this world". The Bhagavata doctrine declares, Brahman is Vasudeva, the Supreme Lord, the material and efficient cause of the world. By worshiping Him, meditating on Him, and knowing Him one attains liberation. From Vasudeva is born Samkarshana (the Jeeva), Pradyumna (the Mind), Anirudhdha (the Ahamkaara or ego ie 'I'-ness) the four-fold vyuha (Forms) of Vasudeva.*

*Brahman is both Saguna (qualified) and nirgunaa (non-qualified). Saguna Brahman, ie Brahman with attributes is to give some support to mind to concentrate in meditation. Nirguna Brahman is the Reality.*

***The Concept of Samashti***

The concept of '*Samashti*', which states that '***there is but one soul***

***throughout the universe, all is but one existence***' is a great Vedantic view of existence. This concept is a leveler of all inequalities, rich and poor, strong and weak, advanced and backward; and, even the ugly and the beautiful, man and animal are included in this! This is a noble idea that heralds the real and basic solidarity of the whole universe, the ideal of ' the oneness of things'. It is this basic concept that India offered to the whole world, the concept of 'universal brotherhood' and 'world peace and happiness', the concepts of "vasudaiva Kutumbakam" and Sarve Jano sukhino bhavantu", respectively. Here there is no distinction between man and beast or even the plants! This is the key to ecological balance. See the Rig Vedic Mantra given in the first page.

Adopting this basic concept 'Samashti', one can solve the present day maladies of development that have resulted in eco-degradation, environmental hazards, social inequities, and cruelty to animals. In order to understand this basic concept, one has to go to the depth of the Self, the immutable *Brahman.*

In *Brihadaranyaka Upanishad* 2.1, 4.1.as well as, *Kaushitaki Upanishad* 4, Gargya Balaaki volunteers to explain to the King Ajatasatru to explain the Brahman. In turn, Ajatasatru replies that all these definitions put forth by Balaaki are insufficient and finally reveals the Brahman. Similarly, In *Brihadaranyaka Upanishad*, 3,9, 10-18, 26 Vidaghda answers Yagnyavalkya regarding the spirit (Purusha) i.e., the highest summit. He puts forth eight definitions of Purusha and falils to mention 'the spirit' that is the essence of the Upanishadic teachings. The six definitions of Brahman offered in *Brihadaranyaka. Upanishad.* 4.1.are corrected by Yajnavalkya.

In *Chandogya Upanishad*, it is mentioned that six Brahmanas seek explanation about the Atman Vaisvaanara. King Asvapati clarifies that the heavens, the sun, the wind, the ether, the water, the earth are not suffiecient explanations. Bhrugu Maharishi himself comprehended the Brahman as food, Prana (vital breath), Manas (Mind), Consciousness (intelligence) and Bliss. [*Taittiriya Upanishad* 3]. In *Chandogya Upanishad*, 8.7-12, Prajapati teaches Indra that '*Atman is the Self*', is the *physical body*, the *individual soul and the highest soul*, which represent the three steps of knowledge deepening itself step by step.

Narada (a Kshatriya) teaches a Brahmana, Skanda (Sanatkumara) that namam (Name), Vac (words), manas (Mind), sankalpa, chittam, dhyanam, vijnyanam, balam, apah (water), tejas (fire), akasha (sky), smaranam (memory), asha (desire), Prana (vital breath), and the highest of all bhuman (infinitude) are all adored as Brahman.

*Atman* (Being) is the embodied Self. This Atman is hidden in all beings and it is not manifest to all so easily. But it can be realized by means of the sharp and subtle reason of those who have been trained to enquire into and realize subtle truths. *Isavasya Upanisad* states that, "*He, the self-existent, is everywhere, without a body, without muscles, and without the taint of sin, radiant, whole, and pure, seeing all, knowing all, and encompassing all, He duly assigned their respective duties to the eternal Prajapatis*". "*The Self is one, unmoving; it is faster than mind. Having preceded the mind, it is beyond the reach of the senses. Ever steady, it outstrips all that run. By Its mere presence, it enables the cosmic energy to sustain the activities of living beings". "It moves, and It moves not". "It is far, and it is near". "It is within all this and it is also outside all this". [Isavasya Upanisad. 4- 5, 8]. Engrossment with the many without knowing the One behind it is the bane of ignorant life. 'The secret of the many is that the One can appear to be many without losing its identity. On knowing the One, the many lose their binding influence on the seer'. "All gods, worlds and beings depend on a unity- the one ultimate principle"* ['*Rk Veda*', 1.164; 10.129]. Atman is Brahman and there are no two separate entities. There is nothing to differentiate between the two. An enquiry into the nature of the external world leads to the Brahman. Similarly, an enquiry into the nature of the Self leads to Atman. But, the entire Brahman is in the Atman. *The so-called external world has emanated from the Atman, the Self. What is realized as 'That', called the Brahman, the sub-stratum of the universe, is but his own Self; it is he himself. All that is verily Brahman; this Atman is Brahman. [Mandukya Upanishad 2].*

How to realize the Atman? Atman or the Self is so subtle, subtler than the subtlest, that it cannot be perceived as an object. Also, it is so big, bigger than the biggest, that it is beyong our ability to comprehend it. Atman cannot be realized either by mere reading of the scriptures or, simply performing the rituals as described in the Veda. Those persons who remain satisfied with the performance of the rituals only, and never strive to know the real significance of the works as explained in the scriptures, are rajasic and cannot attain to that sattvic state of life that rests upon the glorious union of the ritualistic actions with the knowledge of their full significance. But still worse are the persons who remain contented with the mere theoretical knowledge about the gods and sacrifices gathered from the scriptural study, and never stir them selves up for any action. They are tamsic, and as such, are necessarily relegated by their own inactivity to the inert state, which, of all levels of existence, is the one farthest away from the Truth. 'Mere conceptual knowledge of Brahman is not enough. It must be combined with the practice of spiritual disciplines'.

Not to speak of ordinary people, even great scholars fail to comprehend 'Atman'. Atman can be realized through pure buddhi, since it is an ever-present datum of experience.

*"Let the wisdom, 'prajnya' merge the speech in manas and the manas in buddhi; Let him merge the buddhi in the cosmic mind and merge cosmic mind again in the Self of peace, the Atman, or the Purusha".*

*Katha Upanishad* (V.12.13) presents the 'Atman', the 'Unlimited Reality' as also the 'Intimate Reality'. "*The one Supreme Controller of all the inner Self of all beings, who makes His one form manifold- those 'dhiras' (wise men) who realize Him as existing in their own self, to them belongs eternal happiness and to none else*".

"*The Eternal among the non-eternals, the intelligence in those that are intelligent, who though one, fulfills the desires of the many, - those dhiras who perceive Him as existing in their own Self, to them belongs eternal peace and to none else*".

" ... *Glory of the Self that appears as man, the most glorious God that ever existed, or ever will exist, can never be imagined in books, scriptures, or sciences*".

Another important thing is that neither the knowledge of the supreme Brahman nor the Self alone will be of any help. The knowledge of the Self is useless unless Brahman is perceived in it; so also the knowledge of Brahman is useless unless the Atman is realized in it. This perceiving the Brahman in the Atman is the 'Reality'. It is rather, perceiving spirit in matter that is very important. It is this unity of the Atman in Brahman that is known as '*aparokshanubhuti*' or Self Realisation.

The physical body, the operative mind, and the supreme Self are so integrated that an ordinary person fails to understand the real significance of each one of these major components. The difficulty is further compounded by the inexplicability of the Atman that remains un-affected by the goings on in the other two, i.e., the Mind and the body. In day-to-day life, the Self is greedily possessed of this world. Without this Self, there is no world at all. And, yet, this conscious Self dies nightly when we sleep, and we cannot trace the stages by which in its stages it crept to an awareness of its own existence. Normally, what we call personality may be only one of Nature's methods, a convenient provisional delusion of considerable strategic value. The more intelligent and comprehensive a man's picture of the Universe has become, the more intolerable has become his concentration upon the individual life with its inevitable final rejection. One escapes from his ego by this merger, i.e., identification with and participation in a greater being, and acquires an impersonal immortality in the association, his identity dissolving into the greater identity. Abnegation of the self is thus very important to know the 'Reality' or'see things as they are'.

According to the religious mysticism, the individual saves oneself by losing himself. In mystical teaching, the individual loses himself in the Deity; in the scientific interpretation, he identifies himself as 'Man'. The Buddhists teach that '*the individual life is a painful delusion from which men escape by conquest of individual desire*'.

Self must be subordinated; it s a means to an end, but not an end by itself. Ego is a part of the ceaseless flow of Nature. The reality behind this ego is the ultimate observer or '*Sakshin*'. The Sakshi is that timeless being which witnesses all flow and change in the world of thoughts and things.

'*Sakshin*' is the Supreme entity existing in a person. That is the eye of the eye, ear of the ear, taster, experiencer, thinker and all. Self is limited Man; Saakshi is the Universal (any other Man who is in similar moral and intelligent state of mind, absolute mind and unconditioned mind). The two important characteristics of the Saakshi are detachment and universality. It marks the highest point of perfection- the power of de-personalisation. In *Bhagavad Gita*, Sri Krishna tells Arjuna that,'*the true self of man is unborn, immortal, and eternal. (Gita Ch.II 16). It is also said, 'that the Sakshi being the Ultimate Subject, there is considerable difficulty in comprehending it truly'. (Gita, II. 29).* Further, '*when one attains the 'Sakshi'- consciousness, he finds life in an entirely new perspective. All the false values, which the ego attached to life and its functions, get destroyed. Thus life becomes beautiful and harmonious- in tune with everything else and with himself. Welfare of mankind and Universal Love becomes hallmark of such persons*'. (*Bhagavad-Gita*, II 71, III 17, IV 18, XII 13-14 &18-19).

There is a beautiful imagery of two birds of golden plumage sitting on the branch of a tree, ["*Dvaa Suparna*...."] one eating the fruits, sweet and bitter, and the other witnessing this, sits immersed in its own glory [*Mundaka Upanishad* 3.1.1-2]. The bird enjoying the fruit is the man enjoying the fruits of action (Karma), the man deluded and feeling helpless. The bird witnessing it is the Self, Adorable and the Sovereign, ever free, realizing himself as but His glory. As the first bird finishes eating the fruits (of its action), it comes nearer and nearer the other bird (witnessing Self) and merges itself with the other (Realises the Self).

This is the reality that reveals itself to the discerning mind as the unchanging 'saakshi' or witness of all the changing subjects and objects of the various states. Since it is not limited by any one particular state as the ego is, it is infinite. After realization of this truth, one does not desire to protect or defend oneself, because of the realization of non-duality and the attainment of the state of fearlessness. All ideas of hatred, offense, self-protection, self-defense, and assertiveness proceed from fear, from a feeling of inadequacy with respect to the environment. That is why, it is said 'fear is the key'.

Realization of the Atman means realization of one's infinite dimensions and of one's spiritual unity with all; its fruit is infinite love and infinite strength. The Vedanta presents the Atman-Brahman as the 'Unified Experience Field' and, as such,"*inside all beings and outside all beings, He there-fore is the all*".

In *Srimad Bhagavatam* VIII.3.3, it is clearly stated that:

"I take refuge in that self-existent Being, in whom is this Universe, from Whom is this Universe, by Whom is this Universe; Who Himself is this Universe and Who is beyond this (differentiated Nature) as also beyond that (Undifferentiated Nature)".

Paramatman is Immanence and Parabrahman is Transcendence. Parabrahman when described as the cause of the universe is called "Parameswara" or "Prajapati". Parabrahman conditioned by the adjuncts of the universe is 'Prajapati' (Brahman), so is the 'Parabrahman'. Conditioned by the adjuncts of the body is termed a human being- 'Praja'. The same Prajapati who sustains vast oceans, planets, eart, and heaven enters as a seed or as a 'spark' and becomes the 'Jeeva' or the acting and enjoying agent on the earth. The Paramatman enters the seed and becomes the innermost Self of all beings. Paramatman is the Supreme Self, "Virat" ensouling the universe. He that is dwelling in the body of all jeevas is the Self, the 'Atma'.

Jeeva, the individual soul is the principle intelligence that co-exists with the Supreme Being; but it is thoroughly and absolutely dependent on Him.

If the whole Universe is the product of a self-evolving cause, which

Vedanta and modern physical science uphold, then that cause must be present in all its evolutionary products, which then can have no reality apart from it. This corollary follows, whether that cause is viewed as an intelligent principle- Brahman or Atman as in Vedanta, or as a non-intelligent background material, as in modern science. That one cause must account not only for all the objects of experience, but also for all the subjects of experience, and for all experience itself. The solar system being a product of the Sun, the food that we eat, as much as the human metabolic energy which digests it, the coal we burn, and the clothes we wear are all but solar energy in different manifestations. Einstein remarked that, “there is no place in this new kind of physics both for the field and matter, for the field is the only reality.

### *Atma-sakshaatkaara [Self- Realization], the Goal of Life*

In conclusion, with all the volumes of literature laid before us, the questions still remain:Why are we here? What is our goal? Are we happy in this world? How to get the most out of this human existence? What is Self Realization? How to attain it? Is it ever possible for us, the mortals, to attain the supreme Bliss, attain the Supreme Self? The answers are very simple and direct: Life on this earth is wonderful. This material objective world is for enjoyment. The Lord enjoys creation. One must know how to live and enjoy this beautiful world. Whether it is a householders' life or an ascetic life, both are riddled with pain until you succeed. If the present day social life, materialistic life is disgusting, the alternate path is spiritual life. But, the spiritual path is very hard and extremely difficult to tread and at the end one may or may not succeed! It would require several hundred births to attain spiritual heights and fulfillment, liberation, or emancipation. But the beginning has to be made here and now. There is no second path and the only path to salvation is the spiritual path. Of course, this world is for enjoyment and one can go on living with all the little happiness, joys accompanied by sorrow and misery. But, one should not grumble about these things for they are inevitable. It is a package scheme offered to you. Select whichever you like. Joy is there; happiness is there. Joy is within you and happiness depends on others. Everlasting bliss is possible only through Realization of the Self, attained by constant meditation and there is no other path. In his mundane, sensate, objective world, we the people are all 'illusory-product' (ever-changing and perishable) of the make-believe world, Maya.

***"Anubhutoapyayam lokovyavaharakshamaopi san,***
***asadroopo yatha svapna uttara kshanabaadhatah "*** [*Shankara's Aparokshanubhuti* 56].

Meaning, "*This world is like a dream world, of the nature of non-existence. It appears as an object of reality, as a material world of our daily experience and, also, it serves our daily requirements and practical purposes; but at the very next moment it is contradicted. It is so dynamic, ever changing, and 'asat'. Such is its nature and it is called Maya*". It has come about as a result of the ‘Divine Will’. It is the cause of the uncaused, manifestation of the unmanifest and the real cause is beyond all reasoning and comprehension; the source is the Absolute that is beyond all and it is Infinite. We, as humans, have a single goal i.e., to revert to this Infinite state from the finite and limited, with the body, mind, consciousness bestowed on us by the divine will. We have to understand this, first. The goal is to reach to the Infinite and the Unlimited through transcendence of space and time overcoming the limited adjuncts of the body and mind. This is "Self- Realization". In other words, we have become what we are, spirit embodied in matter as we are derived from energy (the supreme Consciousness) and our goal is to revert to this state of energy, rather attain supreme Consciousness and that is Liberation, emancipation, mukti, or moksha, immortality and spiritual attainement. Simply, we, in the state of matter, have to revert to the state of energy. As particles of energy, you, 'the Self' exist in different speheres of the universe, called the *sapta vyahruti*. There ends the game!

First of all, the concept of *Self-Realization* has to be clearly understood. 'Self Realization' (*Aparokshanubhuti*) is spiritual attainment, the goal of life. Not all can attain this goal, end or destination in one life or two and the journey of life should go on. It is a matter of evolution from lower forms to higher forms of life; and one has to rise to levels of higher levels of Consciousness and finally reach the state of "Supreme Consciousness". This is a spiritual aspect that each one has to understand only by personal effort. *In fact, it is a personal experience only. No amount of reading of the scriptures, or guidance from the revered Guru, or teachers, will help in this matter since the effort should come from within us. We must be prepared to undergo all the rigid spiritual practices with single-minded devotion. The driving force is within us and it should push us to take the practical steps with shruddha.* One has to develop an interest, an attitude, rather should have a feverish desire to attain it, and move steadfast in that direction. The means of attaining this is through a process of 'manoniyantran' (mind control) and 'manonaasha' or stilling the Mind; and, the technique is 'dhyan', Meditation. It all starts with a few simple exercises:

***Number One***: *Practice to sit in a comfortable posture, in a calm and serene atmosphere, close your eyes and keep the mind calm and undisturbed or still atleast for a few minutes in the beginning. This seems to be very difficult in the beginning; gradually, with practise, it becomes easy. One has to sit at least 45 minutes- three to four times a day. The ideal timings are: 4 a.m. to 6 a.m.; around mid-day; in the evening; and before mid-night. Gradually the duration should be increased. Sitting posture in Padmasana, preferably in front of a candle light or Ishta Devatha is advantageous. No effort should be made to stop the thoughts passing in the mind; only, these thoughts should be observed as a 'witness'. Rest will automatically follow.*

***Number two***: *Raise the level of Consciousness. We all live and work at very low level of consciousness and this has to be raised from the navel level to heart level, then on to throat, ajnya, and sirsa levels. We must try to live at a higher level of Consciousness as much as possible; remember, it is difficult unless concerted effort is made in this direction.*

***Number Three***: *One has to cultivate the moral and ethical values of* *life, keep the body and mind clean by sattvic food and divine thoughts. There should be a 'choiceles awareness' of all our thoughts and actions. Mind should give place to intellect and intellect should take the guidance of the inner Spirit, Atman.*

***Number Four***: *Desire is the cause of misery. The destruction of desires is liberation, and this is considered to be the first priority in attaining liberation. Keep away from sense objects and keep your sense organs rivetted to divine and divine activity only. Be selfless in all your thoughts and actions. Entertain no desire for self-enjoyment or self-aggrandisement. "Owing to the desire to run after society, the passion for too much study of scriptures, and the desire to keep the body trim, people cannot attain to proper realization. Until the identification with the body is completely rooted out, do away with thy superimposition with watchfulness and concentrated mind". [Viveka Chudamani].*

***Number Five***: *Always think that- " I am not the body"; "I am not the Mind"; "I am not the Prana"; "I am not the individual soul, but the Supreme Brahman"; "I am verily Brahman, the Eternal Spirit". Meditate on the Mahat Tattvas. Always chant the name of your Ishta Devatha, day-in and day-out, 24 hours of the day and 365 days of the year and see the results!*

***Number Six***: *Practise Mauna or silence.'Keep Quiet', absolutely quiet. Do not talk unless it is essential. Practise 'Mauna' atleast once a fortnight and fasting is also helpful, once in a way. As the mind becomes gradually established in the Inner Self, it proportionately gives up the desires for external objects. And when all such desires have been eliminated there takes place the unobstructed realization of the Atman. 'Merging the finite soul in the Supreme Self by means of meditation on their identity, always keep quiet'.*

*Do not care for the universe, which is the 'other' than the Self, before whose majesty it pales into insignificance. "The three bodies- the gross (sthoola), the subtle (sookshma), and the causal (kaarana) are also false. This objective universe is absolutely unreal; neither is egoism a reality, for it is observed to be momentary. Therefore, give up the identification with this physical body ('asat') that is a lump of flesh, as well as, with the ego or the subtle body that are imagined by buddhi. Realizing thy own self, which is 'Knowledge Absolute' and not to be denied in the past, present or future, attain to peace". [Viveka Chudamani].*

*Tamas is destroyed by Sattva and Rajas Gunas; Rajas is destroyed by Sattva and the Sattva is destroyed by Pure Consciousness, Brahman. Try to transcend all the three Gunas that are the cause of desire that causes repeated births and deaths in this world. Knowing for certain that the Prarabhda karma (work) will maintain the body, remain quiet and do away with thy superimposition carefully and with patience.*

*Shri Shankara says, "Even after the Truth has been realized, there remains that strong, beginningless, obstinate impression that one is the agent and experiencer, which is the cause of one's transmigration. It has to be carefully removed by living in a state of constant identification with the Supreme Self. Sages call that 'Liberation' which is attenuation of sanskaras here and now." This will burn all 'Prarabhda Karmas' and kill desires that cause repeated births and deaths. A man who has no selfish desires will easily attain mukti.*

*There are as many ways of attaining mukti, or moksha, liberation or release from bondage as many jeevas are there. So do not be perturbed. Follow any means of Self Realization! All paths lead to salvation and much depends on the sincereity and devotion of the aspirant.*

The basic message of the Veda is "*Be Open*". Do not cling to the past. Do not close the door. Keep it open and wait for the unknown to happen. And, whenever it happens, do not try to make it known. Whatsoever happens throw it away and be ready again. Something new will happen again. The Brahman remains unknown eternally. "Indeed, he attains immortality who realizes it in and through pulsation of knowledge and awareness. No Knowledge is ultimate. It is just a vibration, a pulsation".

Do not make any vibration the ultimate. In deep meditation you will come to feel a great silence. This is just a pulsation. Whatever happens, Brahman is always more. Do not identify any happening with Brahman; otherwise you will stop. Let every wave be wave; wait for the ocean.

Many people have reached deep ecstasy and they stop because then they say, "This is the Brahman. The ultimate has been reached". Remember, it is never achieved. It is simply achievable; never achieved; approachable but never approached. The beautiful journey remains.

Be Aware! *Utthishtato Jagrata*! This is the clarion call of the Veda and the Upanishads often repeated by Swamy Vivekananada. It is now more relevant than ever before! *Shree Harih Om*! *Om Tat Sat*!

# Conclusion

In a subject that deals with the purpose of life, the Goal of life, or the ways and means of attaining to the Brahman, the supreme Bliss, unbounded happiness, there can be no conclusion of any sort. The conclusion is left to the reader and he can arrive at his own on the basis of his understanding and the ability to practise the supreme Upanishadic doctrines enunciated here. However, a brief resume or summary that serves as conclusion is given here.

*Vedanta* is the end of Knowledge and anybody who knows the Subject, the Knower, ***the Brahm***, there is nothing more to attain to for he is liberated; he is a '*Jeevanmukta*'. *But, that is a long long way to go! It is a never ending process and even after you feel you have reached the end of the journey, the journey, i.e., Sri Hari Narayana, remains. It reminds us of Osho's words:" Rememeber, the ocean never comes; "it is always the waves which are coming. The ocean comes through the waves. Do not say the waves are the ocean." The drops of water, the bubbles, and the waves cannot become the ocean. They can merge with the ocean and become one with it; but, remember the part can never become the whole. Reaching ecstasy is not reaching the ocean; it s coming near the ocean.* This is an endless quest. The physical or biological sciences, or even metaphysics for that matter, cannot answer all the questions that concern our lives. Only spiritual science has all the answers but it comes with a practical approach, and not just the theoretical knowledge. Many learned scholars have failed to grasp the subject matter of our discussion. Only the ancient Sages and Seers had a high state of purity of mind and heart that enabled them to perceive the 'Truth'.

First of all, let us recount; what is the subject matter of our discussion? It is the search for 'Truth'. It is the search for 'Reality' of our existence. It is the meaning and purpose of life on earth. It is establishing our selves in our own 'Self'. It means a state of equillibrium, a state of complete rest of body, mind, and soul in the Absolute Self. It starts with a search 'within'. It does not come within the purview of knowledge of outside world that is sensate and objective; it concerns the subject itself, the Atman, the Self. The sense objects and the sense organs are under the control of the Mind and, they always look outward; it is, now, our problem how to withdraw them and quieten them in order to open and turn our inner eye towards the inner self. It is essential to look inward to search what is within. Unfortunately, we tend to search elsewhere what is within and very near to our Self. There is a story that illustrates this point very well. An old lady who had lost her sewing needle in her house was searching for the same outside her house under the street-light. When somebody asked her why she is searching for the needle in the street and not inside the house where she had lost it, the answer she gave was that she is searching for the needle where there is light and cannot search it in darkness of her house.

It is true that it is dark inside her house and she needs light to search. There is light outside and she is right in her search outside. But, it is her sheer ignorance that she is searching in a wrong place. The scientists are doing the same. They are searching for 'Truth' in a wrong place, in their laboratories. The 'Truth', or 'Reality', is invisible in the matter, the cell, or the atom like the oil in til seeds. Breaking the matter, or dividing the cell, will not reveal the 'spirit within'. At best, it will reveal sub-atomic particles; it can never reveal the vital energy, or the life force, 'within' the cell for it is always invisible. We have lost sight of the Lord in our previous births and we still do not have an inclination to know the 'Truth'. Like the old lady searching the needle in the street, we have lost sight of God in our childhood and we are searching for the same in oldage when we are weak and infirm.

Katha Upansihad makes it very clear. "Those who are devoid of discrimination and cannot distinguish betweem the real and the unreal, the ever-changing and the permanent, aspire for the fleeting material and sensual objects of this mundane world; they entangle themselves in the net of insatiable desires and suffer disappointments and misery. They identify themselves with things that decay, and all that take birth and that dies. But, the wise who 'see things as they are', are no longer deluded by the glttering objects and the charms of the phenomenal world and do not seek permanent happiness in fleeting objects. They desist from sensual desires and keep away the desires of the flesh as if it is the nauseating thing! They always seek the Truth, real and the more satisfying permanent Bliss."

A human being is part matter and part spirit; Man is matter in his mind and body, and is spirit in the soul. It is the divine will and Grace of the Lord that human Mind is bestowed with the power of understanding and discrimination so that it can perceive the 'Truth' in its own stillness. *Yoga Sutras of Patanjali* explain in detail how to go about this search of 'Truth'. *Brahma Sutra* gives the nature of the Truth. Vedas tell everything about these things. Man is in no way different from the 'Truth' and, only he should make an effort 'to know' that! *Katha and Kena Upanishads* remove all the doubts about this. They say, "*You are verily That*".

After a detailed study of the subject, we come to the conclusion that 'Truth' is one; that is the 'Infinite' and 'the Absolute'. This Infinite or the Absolute is the supreme Self, also the supreme Consciousness, called "That", or 'the Brahman'. This 'Brahman' is the "Knowledge", 'Sat', and one who knows this is a 'Jnyaani' and he knows all; he who says, 'he knows', knows not; and he who says he 'knows not', really knows. The "Truth" is knowable but not 'known'. Almost all the religions of the world strive at this and make all effort to know this. The 'Truth' is so simple and is easy to understand that no body wants it! Almost all human beings, though in their heart of hearts are eager to know God, for it is their nature to know God, do not want God, for fear of losing the pleasures caused by ignorance. Knowledge is fire and no body wants this fire that sheds light on darkness, shed light on ignorance, and this fire that burns kaamna, Karma and sanskar, of all our previous births and release us from bondage. This is the whole truth. Pigs are happy in the mire and all are happy in ignorance. Only a Mahaveera or a Budhdha contemplated on the nature of this illusory world and wanted to save the mankind. How far they are successful, everybody knows. Ultimately, no one can help another in this matter of 'realization of the self'. Only those who suffer from stomach pain should take the medicine to get relief from pain. The doctor cannot take the medicines to cure the patients' illness. This is the spiritual world. Every one born as a human being, with an ability to think, to contemplate upon, and meditate can easily attain the spiritual goal, i.e., attaining the supreme Brahman, the "Truth". Many Saints and Seers have shown the way. In fact, God Himself has taken birth on this earth, as incarnation, 'avatar', to show the path of peace and salvation.

Now, what is this 'Truth'? This 'Truth' is our existence. Are we real? 'Are we'? Or, 'Are we not'? Are we the part of Him, or are we not a part of His Self? The answer is an emphatic "Yes". We are all part of His divine Self and that is the 'Truth'. Divinity exists in all creatures; it is inherent in all. Our ignorance covers this part of the supreme Consciousness that exists in all as "Prajnya" (Consciousness). The most significant thing is that we are not conscious of the 'Consciousness' in our self and do not make any effort to know it. We live and work with out the 'Knowledge' of it! And, in our old age, when it is too late, that is when we are physically weak and menatally unstable, we try to make an effort towards the understanding of this 'knowledge'. When we are young and energetic, our efforts are directed towards fulfilling our desires and enjoying the pleasures of the flesh; and, we live unconsciously. We are all dead in the real sense of the term, identified with the body and full of ego. We are not truthful, austere, and devoted to Him, the Lord and we are not conscious of the Lord's presence within us as the 'inner driving force'. It reminds us of the statement of Shree Krishna in *Bhagavad Gita*. "***Oh, Arjuna! Whence comes this ignorance to you?***"

Thus, the "Truth" is simple. Our existence is illusory. Our body is not real; it is subject to change, death and decay with time. It is not the 'Sat' or 'Truth'. The real 'Truth' is that 'we are all finite and subject to change. We are all merely names and forms that are subject to change. Anything that is subject to change is not real, not the 'Sat', 'Truth'. Anything bound by space and time is not real; and, only that which is not affected by time and space is real and that is the 'Truth'. Human beings, the plants, and animals, or even the inorganic substances for that matter, are all bound by space and time and hence not real. That is why this objective sensate world (world perceived by mind and the senses) is called '*Maya*' or '*illusion*'.

Now, as regards the happiness and success in life as the goal in life, the Vedanta makes things very clear. It asks you whether you want a happiness that is short-lived due to the constraints of space and time, or you want a permanent happiness that is the supreme 'Bliss', that surpasses anything and everything on this sensate, objectve, ever-changing world. Ancient Sages have experienced this supreme 'Bliss' and estimated its value; they say it gives several millions of times much more happiness than that any young, rich, powerful and famous person can enjoy from the material and physical sources on this earth. Once you taste the supreme

'Bliss' in the state of supreme Consciousness, you will never aspire for the material and physical happiness, also called desires of the flesh. It is the 'Infinitude'. The choice is yours. The path of attaining the supreme Bliss is arduous and it requires immense courage, will- power, and determination. It requires perseverence to attain the goal at any cost. It involves abnegation of the self to attain the Self, the' Atman', the 'Brahman'. It involves time, may be a few hundred years!

*Chhandogya Upanishad states that, 'elevation of Prana containing the divine to the state of the Infinitude (Bhuman) brings supreme Bliss. It becomes the highest soul encompassing all, when one strips off this empirical form of phenomenon in which one abrogating the distinction between the subject and object, elevates himself to full Infinitude, the 'Bhuman'.*

Now, how is the Infinitude attained? It is by strict adherence to the principles of '*Ritam*' and '*Satyam*' and living an austere life. A 'Yogin' who excels in all controversies through 'Ritam' and 'Satyam', the Right and the Truth, is a real speaker excelling all. The truth depends on knowledge and knowledge depends on thought and thought on 'faith'. Faith depends on that which lies at the root of all that feeling about what lies at the root depends on creation. Creation depends on desire or joy that lasts depends on the Infinitude. The joy that comes from ***Infinitude*** is supreme joy because it is identical with itself, "***Ya vai bhuma tat sukham***". 'Correspondingly, the creation (kriti) is not that of the individual; but the divine creative activity flowing out of the joy of being or becoming. With it is united one who elevates his self on the way of knowledge, thought, and faith (shruddha); 'shruddha' with bhakti, knowledge and conviction, must be rooted in the divine'.

*The Infinitude is called 'Bhuman'; Bhuman,* the Infinitude is magnificent! The Infinitude does not see, hear or know anything outside itself. Being immortal, it rests on itself, its own supra-mundane majesty, present everywhere. He who leads his life with this view-point has his joy only in the Atman and knows everything is conditional on the Atman. The 'Atman', is free, is immortal, is above pain, sorrow and death, and finds his 'I' everywhere. All distnction or duality vanishes here. When we go beyond our thoughts (chitta) we come to the realm of the Infinite. There we come into touch with the Absolute and become one with it (or merge with the Infinite). It is only when we transcend the three states of consciousness- the jagrat, svapna, sushupti and exist in the turiya, that we enter the realm of the Infinitude. The fourth state is just not a relative one that is beyond the Sushupti- the deep sleep state of Consciousness, but it is sheer ecstasy of existence, truth Bliss, and the 'Sat'. Here, the state of mind ceases to consider the three other states as real and comes to know as 'illusion'; in fact, tutriya state has crossed the limit of the adjuncts of time and space, and is thus, one with pure Consciousness, the Subject, the Brahman.

A Spiritual Seeker transcends all the four stages of the waking, dreaming, dream-less, and the deep sleep state of Consciousness and arrives at the state of '*nirvikalpa samadhi*' close to the Brahman. When he realizes the Absolute, the ' Truth', or gets off his 'delusion', he says:

***"Saasasteham dehadrushtyaasmi shambho, jaatastemsho***

***jeevadrushtya tridrushtyaah tridrushte:***
*Sarvasyatmannaatmadrishtya tvamevetyevaam me dheera nischitaa sarvashaastraih."*

*Meaning, "O Lord (Shree Hanuman addresses Shree Ram), when I think of myself as related to the physical body (as an animal with the body of a monkey), I am thy servant; Thou art my Lord. When I think of my soul that is an'ego', I am Thy part and Thou art the one stupendous Whole (you and I are equal). But, when I think of my true self, that is the Atman, that is a part of the Absolute, then I am one with thee, I am one with the Infinite (ocean of existence, intelligence, bliss, -"Sat-chit-anand" and love.)"*

It is very interesting to note here that Shree Hanuman goes one step further and tells Shree Ram that, "O Lord, at least you are in bondage as an incarnaticn of Vishnu with a vow to protect all the jeevas; and, as the King (Raja) of Ayodhya, you have the duties to perform to protect the people of Ayodhya, whereas, I am free, a 'jeevan mukta' at that, released from all bondage, and hence superior to you!

Thus, one has to get rid of all bondage. Vedanta says: "*Bhidyate hrudayagranthi-schchidyante sarva-samshayah. Ksheeyante chaasya karmaani tasmin drushte paraavare." Unless one gets rid of all bondage of "anthahkarana", rather, the raagadveshaadi ashtavargas that prevent us from attaining mukti, there is no liberation. Cut that chord of the heart that binds you to this sensate objective world and get released from eternal bondage. Only a few like the Great Raikva, the cartman, Kapila, Vemana and Bhrugu were capable of this!*

Inspite of all these detailed explanation, if anybody still asks the question why should we bother about all these, the answer is another question: Why should we bother about the "Truth", the very basis of our very existence? Should we bother about this short life on this earth and all its trivialities; should we worry about all this suffering and unhappiness and misery of life? Should we hanker after the desires of the flesh and suffer the consequences? Should we remain in our stae of ignorance thinking that ignorance is bliss? Should we go on living to suffer the heat in summer and the cold in the winter and expect that the day would go on without ever bringing the night or the night would go on without bringing the day in? Our life is not a bed of roses and no one can enjoy only happiness, eternal happiness here, on this mortal plane of existence. Here, happiness comes with misery and joy, with grief and sorrow, like the day followed by night and, winter and summer. Without going to the detailed specifics, we have the problems of poverty, affluence, diseases, incompatibility in family and marital relationships, and the problems of property, likes and dislikes, the problems of old age, sickness, death, etc. We weep and cry, as also, laugh and be merry; we have no knowledge of what is in store for us the next moment. Well, we are all happy at that! But this state of mind, too, changes and we soon brood over things past and we are anxious of our future, future of our children and their children, and suffer from stress, tension and agony. We turn to astrologers, or we take to black magic, and try all sorts of tantrics to console ourselves in distress.

the mysterious ways of this world. Aghories have attained siddhi and can transform matter ; they can easily change sand into sugar and pebbles to almond. The days of creating new life is not far off. This is the evolutionary history of man, and evolution itself, in short!

Now, it is discernible that the return journey is also by the same path-from the finite and the limited, i.e., the human soul embodied, return towards the Infinite and the Unlimited, from bondage to liberation, from evolution to involution. First, it is this embodied ignorant person, the 'Jeeva' with Mind and Spirit that seeks liberation (that seeks to attain the supreme Consciousness). 'Realisation of the Self' through abnegation of the self (that is the release from 'body-consciousness' and 'mind-consciousness'), and attaining the state of superconsciousness through Meditation, 'nirvikalpa samadhi'; it is a well-defined path. Transcending time and space in superconscious state and uniting the Self with the 'Brahman' ('Yuj' or Yoga) is 'Immortality'. It is important to remember here that, in the process of evolution we acquired the Mind (Manas), the ego (ahaṃkara), the anthahkarana, and attachment of the heart; and, on our return journey, i.e., towards involution, we have to drop all these one by one and be completely liberated from the shackles of Maya, the illusory, objective, sensate, world of names and forms. This takes a longer time than one can imagine. One has to start this return journey now only. One should realize the nature of one's Self and adopt necessary methods to attain purity of the mind and purity of the heart.

There are fifteen steps to fulfillment i.e., Self Realization ('Atmaanubhuti'). These are yama, niyama, tyaga, mauna, desha, kaala, asana, muabandha, dehasamyam dhruksthiti, pranasmayama, pratyahara, dharana, and atmadhyaana leading to samadhi. It starts with simple austere life of morals and ethics like shama, dama. One should develop 'sad-vichara' (good thoughts), 'viveka' (wisdom), and have 'vivechane' (discrimination), and 'vairagya' (renunciation). One should start a celibate life (desire-less) and practise restraint in everything, and should not lose the goal or purpose of life. While going on a long journey of pilgrimage, one should not get attracted to the fascinating and tantalizing attractions of the wayside stations and get down or interrupt the jouiney. One should live a very strict disciplined austere life without depending on any body for anything. One should remember that even the grains of salt consumed from others, will take us to eternal bondage! Hence, one must learn to live a completely independent life without asking anybody for anything! Depending on one's 'Self' is very important! This is possible by total surrender ('sharanagatim') to the Lord. One is permitted to beg food, just for survival, from one's own son; food should be taken, as medicine, only to sustain the body. One should become 'Eka-dandi' (ascetic holding a staff, the symbol of self-realisation, depending on the Atman, 'Self') first, and then become a 'Parama Hamsa', a 'jeevan mukta' (completely Free and Liberated). This is the way to get out of the shackles of bondage, indebtedness. Total surrender to the Lord is the only way. Ultimately, it brings complete independence and eternal happiness. One can certainly merge in the Brahman for, it is from there he has come. This is the 'Sat' (Truth'), it is the

'Chit' (Knowledge) and, it is 'Anand' (Eternal Bliss), or "Sachchidanand" That is Salvation, Liberation or 'mukti' or 'moksha', in this very life, not after death, now and here. That is it. "Om! Tat Sat!"

# Think It Over

*Contemplate on the following. Meditate on any one of these whichever you like most:*
*Space manifests first, then comes time. When there is time,*
*events come in succession. Our mind thinks in terms of space,*
*time, and events. Space and Time are the creation of mind and,*
*as such, these are 'unreal'. Both are beginningless and endless,*
*and, as products of 'Maya', they cause delusion of mind.*
*Silence is Brahman. Brahman is ekamevadviteeyam, one only;*
*Silence pervades Brahman and Brahman exists in Silence.*
*Silence is existence, truth and Bliss.*
*'Om' is' Pranava', 'Ekakshara Brahma'.*
*'Om' emanates from Silence and ends in silence. 'Om' is everything.*
*Everything emanates from 'Om', the sound that came out of Sphota, the Big Bang!*
*The all-pervading Prana,'Prajnya', or Consciousness acts upon the ether,*
*Then the five elements come into being,*
*The elements combine and various objects are formed.*
*Even if you imagine that nothing exists, there will be space.*
*You will have to transcend space to realize the 'Self'.*
*Transcending time and space is Realising the Self.*
*Try to experience this!*

***GOD IS EVERYWHERE!***
*Time and space are eternal.*
*The Supreme spirit covering all time and space is Shree Hari Narayana.*
*All matter- fire, water, air, earth and mind and their respective*
*Qualities emanate from the Supreme Spirit.*
*Soul, the Jeeva is the infinitesimal part and parcel of Shree Hari,*
*The Supreme Spirit pervading the Universe.*
*Realization of the fact that the whole world including the Creator*
*Is a play of matter and spirit, and is a cosmic joke is the key to*
*Freedom and escape from Sansara or cycle of life and death.*
*Any devotee who wants to see God in the name and form he wants*
*to See, can see and experience Him in that name and form.*
*In reality, the devotee and his mind itself is also a part and parcel of*
*The Supreme Spirit encompassing the whole Universe.*
*Realization of this Truth is "Aham Brahmaasmi". Or "Tat tvam asi".*
*God has no particular name or form and is not attached to any*
*Since He pervades everything.*
*"Choiceless Total Awareness is True Living".*
*Observe this phenomenon within yourself and practice it.*

*"The Atman is hidden in the hearts of all.*
*It is seen only by the Seers through their pure subtle intuition"*
*[Katha Upanishad 1.3.12]*
*Each one of us is a part of the infinite Spirit.*
*As our mind and heart becomes pure, we come to get hold of*
*Our individual inner- self. As we move further and further,*
*We find that we are all really parts of a greater Whole*
*And this is the greatest truth we need.*
*We, as souls, are inseparable parts of the Over-soul,*
*The Supreme Spirit.*
*Let us try to awaken in us the consciousness that we are the Spirit.*
*Let us try to find that we are all parts of the one Over-soul.*

***GOD KNOWS EVERYTHING!***

*"A playwright knows the plot and the sequences well before drafting his play. It is only the spectator who has to wait for sequences to be unraveled on the stage.*
*So also, a Yogi can perceive by his contemplation, meditation, And, yogic powers foresee the things to come.*
*The Lord knows the past, present and the future. He has simultaneous knowledge of all events at all times at all places.*
*Self- realization means the union of the individual spirit with The supreme Spirit.*
*Spiritual initiation brings the individual Self into harmony with the supreme Self.*
***Mind purified of thought is 'Self'.***
***'Self' filled with thoughts and desires, is the mind.*** [*Gita VI-35*]
*Mind is the enemy of one who cannot control the mind.*
*Mind is the friend who has won the mind.*
*Brihadaaranyaka Upanishad [1-5-9]*
*Mind is made up of food. [Chhaandogya Upanishad]*
***Pure food helps to keep purity of mind.***
***Pure mind is energy. Pure mind shines as consciousness.***
***Indians beware, stale and contaminated non-vegetarian food***
***Lead to impure mind leading to impure thoughts and inhuman actions.***
*All dead animals are contaminated with germs and microbes.*
*And, human digestive system is not meant for hard food from non-vegetarian sources. One should avoid non-vegetarian food.*
***He who covets the desirable things, while brooding on their virtues, is born amidst these very surroundings along with the desires.***
***But for one who has got his wishes fulfilled and is self-poised, all Longings vanish even here.*** [*Mundaka Upanishad III- ii- 2*]
*Mind is the world and world is our Mind.*
*If we want to win the world, we have to win our Mind.*
*For a person who has overcome the mind, he rests peacefully within Himself; he has no preference for time and place.*
*He has no choice since the time and space have become one.*
*He is one with Pure Consciousness.*

*When Mind is merged with consciousness, there is no 'becoming' or 'attaining'. There is nothing to be achieved. All this is in the Mind and that Mind is no more. This consciousness is the background and support of mind and all thoughts that exist*
*Mind is to be treated very kindly, tenderly and should be tutored.*
*It is the knowledge that frees the mind and dissolves the Mind.*
*"The 'fear' is the resistance to movement.*
*Fear is the feeling, for loss of attachment, for loss of what we have, and loss of whom we have.*
*We are afraid to lose something and someone since we ourselves do not matter.*
*Since we ourselves do not have self-esteem, we do not value Our selves and want someone whom we value higher and by whom our value increases.*
*We by ourselves are worthless.*
*We have to be identified with wealth, power, position, or by recognition of some higher achievement for us to have value and faith in ourselves or by others.*
*This self-abnegation, this ignorance that something, or somebody is higher, and something makes us higher, and the fear of losing that, that makes us feel higher and better, is the achievement, an illusion of our Mind.*
*Otherwise, we have no where to go, and there is nothing to attain, to attain and to become.Then there is no fear, since there is no 'becoming' and 'attaining'.*
*Conquer fear by knowing fear*
*There is only one being which is fearless.*
*This fearless and deathless entity is our 'Self', whose nature is Consciousness and Bliss. Its nature is also intelligence".*
*"Antar Pragnyam Bahor Pragnyam, Pragnyam pragnyam eva cha"*
*"The inner consciousness and the outer consciousness is one and the same Consciousness".*
*If the individual consciousness is different from outer consciousness , then each individual would have seen different sizes of objects, depending upon the size of the image etched in their memory".*
*"Since all persons and beings see the same objects, hear the same sound, taste the same taste, and experience the same touch of an object, the seer, the hearer, the taster and smeller,and experiencer is one and the same in all the bodies. But, the interpretation of the quality of objects being different from person to person depending upon one's moods, likes and dislikes, the play of the mind".*
*"It is the Universal Consciousness that is reflected in the Creative intelligence or consciousness of innumerable beings".*
*Just as the reflection changes according to the quality of the Reflecting surface, even though the object is the same, each Individual soul seated in all the different beings being one and the same, sees the same life-size objects".*

*"Going beyond Mind is going beyond space and time;
Going beyond space and time is going beyond Light".
"Brahmam Satyam, Jagat Mithyam".[ Shri Shankara].
"Brahma is Real and the world is unreal".
"Everything exists within Him; we are in this world and
the entire world is within us, in the microcosm". "Anoranecyaan Mahato Maheeyaan"
"Mind is made up of time and space, the environment in which
the person lives. Mind is a product of his past experiences,
living conditions, desires and urges and future ambitions.
A Hindu has a Hindu mind steeped in rituals,
beliefs and superstition.
A Muslim has a Muslim mind indoctrinated, fanatic,
and blindly following system irrespective of time and place.
A Christian Mind has Christian Mind trying to measure the
immeasurable and judge the infinite with the finite.
Mind does not change the path and goes on in a trodden path
by its past memories and experiences".
" Mind is the servant of the ego. The ego is the feeling of
supremacy identified with the limited adjuncts of the body.
'Ego' is truly the master of the Mind. The Mind has found its
true master in the ego and serves the ego day in day out.
Ego is based on ignorance and exists only in isolation.
This ego is not accepted by any one, since it promotes only
isolation and exclusiveness".
"Sangaat samjaayate kaamah, kaamaat khrodhobhijaayate,
Khrodaatbhavati sammoha, sammohat smrityvibhramah;
Smritibhramshat buddhinaasha, buddhinaashat pranashyati!
[Bhagavad Gita, Ch.II –62-63]
"By dwelling in objects therewith, man develops attachment,
From attachment is born desire, from thwarted desires comes
Anger; from anger ariseth delusion, there from confusion of
memory, loss of reason; when reason is gone, the man is lost"*
***"Veeta raagabhayakrodha sthithahdhir muniruchyate"***
*"That sage who is free from attachment, fear and anger,
Is a 'Muni', of stable mind, or poised understanding ".
Man of self-control and real peace is described as
"One whose thoughts shine like the cool moon-beams,
whose mind remains unruffled when confronted with fighting
in death, even as at the prospect of festivity- he indeed is
called a self-controlled man of peace".
[Yoga Vasishta Mumukshu Khanda 14. 75]
"Blessed are the pure in heart, for they shall see God".
[Bible, St,Mathews 5:8]
"Nistraigunyo bhava, Arjuna", Shree Krishna in Bhagavad Gita.
Jnyaanani Brahma bhavati saarathi Rk Veda.*

# Acknowledgments

My salutations to Sri Ramakrishna Paramahansa and Swami Vivekananda, Shri Swami Shivananda, Swami Ranganathananda, and Swami Yatishwarananda, Swami Yogananada and Swami Raama who have been the guiding spirit and light showing us the path of sensible life. Day in day out, we have to remember them and pray. Their contributions to mankind are of immense value and cannot be assessed by any means.

Bhagavad-Gita is the eternal source of knowledge. Many great thinkers and spiritual leaders have interpreted the Gita in different ways. It is an important source of inspiration to all who seek solace in times of distress. It lightens the path when left in darkness, and gives enormous moral and spiritual strength. This source is quoted at length in my Text.

Rig Veda and the Sama Veda, the Upanishads, the Vishnu Purana, Bhagavad-Gita, are all parts of the cultural and spiritual heritage of India. They are the rich source of knowledge. Sudhakara Chaturvedi has given a beautiful translation and commentaryIN Kannada language on the Sanskrit verses to Rig Veda Samhita and Sama Veda, published by Arya Samaj, Bangalore. I am indebted to Sri Sudhakar Chaturvedi. Raghavendra, T.N. has given a more modern and scientific commentary to Rig Veda and Sama Veda, and the Upanishads, the Bhagavad Gita, Vishnu Sahasra Nama, all of which I have quoted at length in my text. I am indebted to him. Raghavendra's web site Gyaanadeep.com gives a complete list of his works, with a few excerpts. Also there is a Weekly Newsletter cast on the website. His book (un- published) "The Creative Power Within Us" is the most comprehensive book on Mind and his 'Vidyas in Bhagavad-Gita' is quite refreshing.

Besides, a number of authors like Swami Vivekananda, Swami Shivananda, Swami Abhedananda, Swami Ranganathananda, Swami Yatiswarananda, Swami Yogananda, Swami Rama, Swami Paramananda, Pritjof Capra, Aldous Huxley, Thomas Huxley, Julius Huxley, Sigmund Freud, Schroedinger, Carl Jung Narayanasvami Aiyar, Raghavendra, and a host of others have been copiously quoted at length in the text. I owe my debt of gratitude to these authors, editors and their publishers.

The Author may be contacted at:
e-mail:
achyutaraotippur@hotmail.com
anugraha2k1@yahoo.com

# Further Reading


| | | |
|---|---|---|
| Arthur J. Thomson | : | Introduction to Science |
| Bertrand Russel | : | The Impact of Science on Society |
| | : | The Scientific Outlook |
| Capra, Fritjof, | : | Uncommon Wisdom, |
| | : | The Turning Point |
| | : | The Tao of Physics |
| Charles Darwin | : | Origin of the Species |
| Chardin, Teilhard de | : | The Phenomenon of Man |
| Chaturvedi, Sudhakar | : | Yoga Pradeepa, Udupi. Rig Veda Samhita, Sama Veda, Arya Samaja, Bangalore, 2001 Daniel Goleman |
| R.J. davidson | : | Consciosness: The Brain. States of Awareness, and Alternate Realities |
| Gaudapada | : | Mandukya-Karika, |
| John Welwood | : | Meeting of the Ways: Explorations in East/West Psychology |
| Jennings, J.G., | : | The Vedantic Buddhism of the Buddha, Oxford University Press |
| Julian Huxley | : | The Uniqueness of Man, Evolution after Darwin, (Vols. I -III) |
| Maharishi Mahesh Yogi | : | The Science of Being and Art of Living. Settled Mind and Silent Mind, [An interview with Maha Rishi Mahesh Yogi by Kathy Juline in Science of Mind, Nov. 1993, pp. 1-7] Wholeness on the move, MMVeda Vigyan Vidyapeetha, Jabbalpore Heaven on Earth, MM Veda Vigyan Prakashan, Jabbalpore |
| Max Muller | : | Three Lectures on Vedanta Philosophy |
| Padmanabhachar, C.M. | : | Life and Teachings of Shri Madhvacharya, Bombay 1909. |
| Penfield, Wilder. | : | The Cerebral Cortex and the Mind of Man, |
| Peter Laslet (Ed.) | : | The Physical Basis of Mind |
| Raghavendra, T.N. | : | The Power of Creation Within Us.(Un-published) Rig Veda Samhita* (Un-published) Samaveda Ishavaasya Upanishad, Gayatri Publica |

tion, Bangalore
Atmavan, Gayatri Publication, Bangalore, 2001
Chandogya Upanishad *
Mandukya Upanishad *
Vidyas in Bhagavad Gita *
Vishnu Sahasranama *
Brihadaranyaka Upanishad *
Vishnua Purana, SRGS, Bangalore
Mahanarayana Upanishad *
Ashtavakra Samhita*
Lalita Sahasranaamam*
Atmajnyaan *
Gods In Rk Veda * [*Un-published]

Radhakrishnan, S. : The Bhagavad- Gita

Richard Devenport : An Outline of Animal Development,

Schrodinger, Erwin. What is Life? Mind and Matter

Siu, R.G.H. Tao of Science, M.I.T., Mass., USA

Swami Abhedananada : True Psychology, Calcutta 2000.

Swami Gambhirananda : Prasna Upanishad, Pub.: Advaita Ashrama, 1995
Bhgavad Gita (Commentaries of Shri Shankaracharya), Tr., Advaita Ashrama, Calcutta, 1991.

Swami Madhavananda : Minor Upanishads, Advaita Ashrama,

Swami Nityasvaroopananada: Ashtavakra Samhita, Advaita Ashrama, Calcutta 1998.

Swami Rama : Living with the Himalayan Masters, Adhyatma Sanshodhan, Pennsylvania, USA

Swami Shivananda : Ten Upanishads, The Divine Life So ciety,
Bhagavad Gita
Shivanandnagar, U.P. 1973.

Swami Sarvananda : Isavasya Upanishad, Shri Ramakrishna Math, Mylapore, Chennai - 600 004
Taittiryopanishad, Madras

Swami Vimuktananada : Aparokshanubhuti, Adavaita Ashrama,

Swami Vireshwarananda : Brahma Sutras, Advaita Ashrama,Calcutta 1996

Swami Vivekananda : The Complete Works of Swami Vivekananda,
Advaita Ashrama, Calcutta 1973.

Upanishads : Advaitamruta Upanishad
Aithareya Upanishad . [1.1.4] 24; [2] 80; [IV-1] 82.

Amrutabindu Upa. [2] 80.
Ananadabindu Upanishad
Aparokashanubhuti
Aruneyi Upanisdhad
Ashtavakra Samhita [1.2] 88, 157-8, 193.
Atmopanishad
Badarayana Brahmasutra [4-1-7] 133.
Bhagavad Gita [II-29] [II 7-8] [III-17] [IV-18]
[XII-13,4,18-19] [XVII-40] 26, 31.
Brahmanubhava Upanishad
Brahma Sutra [4-1-7] 133.
Brahmopanishad [III-13] 77.
Brahmendra Upanishad
Brihadaranyaka Upanishad [4-4-9] 24
Chhaandogya Upanishad. 24, 38, 77
Isavasya Upanishad. [4-5-8] 72, 77-8, [10-11] 160.
Jyotirbindu Upanishad
Kaivalyopanishad Manthra
Katha Upanishad. [V-12-13][III-3-9] 65, [V-12-13] 24,27,
[V-15] 79, [1-2-4] 132, [1-2-15-16] 153, [III-3-9].
Kenopanishad 186,
Mahanarayana Upa. 53,
Mandukyakarika –Gaudapada 81, 86-88, [1] 153.
Muktikopanishad
Mundaka Upa. [1-2-12] 29, [1-1-35] [2-2-4] 153.
Paramahamsopanishad
Prasna Upanishad
Sarvopanishad 1 [3] 32
Shivajnyanamruta Upa. Manthra 3
Shrimad Bhagavatam, 13, 28, VIII 33, VIII 3
Shvetasvatara Upa. [1-1-2] 39, [1-3] 39, 144, [VI-20] 100.
Upanishads (Contd.) Taittiriya Up. [III-IV-1] 24, [II-1] 38.
Tejabindu Upanishad
Vedantasara Upanishad
Vicharabindu Upanishad
Vishnu Purana [II-29] 83
Vishnu Sahasranamam [5-2] 24.
Yogasara Upanishad

# Glossory of Samskrut Terms

'A': Brahmaanda, Universe (Rk Veda 1.1)
Aahara: Food
Aakasha: Sky, space.
Abhinivesha: Clinging to life
Abhokta: Non-enjoyer
Achyuta: That' which does not wear out; death-less; endless. That which has no 'Chyuti' or end; The Omniscient and the Omnipotent.
Adhyatma: The reality underlying the inner-most individual self.
Advaita: Monism
Ahara: Food, Food for body, Food for thought.
Aithareya Upanishad: deals with the spiritual character of the Absolute
Aja: Unborn
'Ak': Universe, Brahmaanda, (Rk Veda, 1.1.)
Akarta; Non-doer
Akshara: Imperishable
Alambana: Support for the mind to lean upon
Ananth: Endless; refers to time and space and the power behind the unifying force.
Actually time and space are borne out of the same Eternal called Ananth or 'Infinity'.
Antaryami: Yama inside the body
Anusandhana: Enquiry
Anthahkarana: Internal organ that includes mind and intellect, i.e., manas and buddhi
Aptakama: One in whom all desires are gratified
Asambhuti: Maya, Prakruti
Asamsakthi: Non-attachment for objects
Asmita: Egoism, with sense of Responsibility
Ashtanga Yoga: Yoga with eight limbs
Asura: Demon
Atman: Soul, the divine energy with Creative intelligence and bliss that pervades through nature having different qualities, create bodies having qualities of nature through which it (creative energy) pervades; the Soul, the Self; the Supreme Spirit.
Avidya: Nescience, Ignorance, Perverted Intelligence.
Avyakta: Unmanifest
Bhaya: Fear
Bhakta: Devotee, Disciple.
Brahm: Supreme Consciousness, KNOWLEDGE, the Brahman derived from 'Brihat'.
Brahma: the Creator, the first manifestation of Brahman.

Brahaman: Light. The Supreme Self, Supreme Being; the cosmic Intelligence; Supreme Consciousness; Supreme Knowledge; the Self-luminous power, the cosmic flow, i.e., Sri Hari Narayana. Saguna Brahman having symbols of Brahman such as Aakasha, Praana, and Manas (Mind,) are for meditation. Vaisvanara is also Brahman.

Brahmacharya: Continence, Abstinence from sex; Silence

Brahma Srotri: Person having Knowledge of Brahman bystudying books.

Brahma Nishta: One who has direct Perception of Brahman through Self-Realisation.

Brahmanda: Hiranyagarbha, Cosmic Space; The first manifestation of Brahman, Sambhuti.

Bruhadaranyaka Upanishad: deals with the Unity of Being; inherent purity and diversity of soul; Absolute is fearless.

Cha: And (Conjunction that joins two letters or words); It is the letter that joins 'Ra' meaning joy Bliss, 'Brahman', the Supreme Soul, and 'ka' that is the Jeeva, individual soul, in 'Charaka' of Vedic Literature- 'Charaka Samhita'.

Charaka Samhita: Vedic Literature that deals with the functioning of the human physiology.

Chhandogya Upanishad: deals with True Nature of Self; It is in the form of a dialogue between Satyakama and Svetaketu; 'The knower of the Self crosses all sorrow' [VII 1.8].

Chitta: Thought, the Mind-set; 'manas'.

Chitta Vritti: Thought waves

Dama: Self Restraint; Self- control; control of senses. Turning Jnanendriyas and Karmendriyas away from sense objects and placing them in their respective centers is called Dama or self control.

Dhaatu: Retas, Semen; this energy should be diverted to activating Kundalini by contenence.

Ego: 'I'-ness; Ahamkara in ordinary sense; but, means more than that. It is the ajnyana (ignorance) that makes one identify him self with Body and mind and, not the spirit or self within.

Egotism: Prepondering 'I'-ness. All defects that arise from Ahamkara.

Ekadandi: One who carries staff, -Sage or Saint. Danda is staff of authority

God; The Supreme Power behind the Universe; The all-pervading 'Vishnu'- the all-pervading, cosmic flow; the energy that sustains this universe.

Guna: Attributes such as: Saguna and Nirguna- with or without attributes.

Hatha Yoga: 'Hatha' in popular parlance, firm minded, determination;

'Ha' means Sun, and 'Tha' means moon, energu and food, respectively. Union of Prana Vayu and Apana vayu; Yoga of physical- vital culture.

Heredity: The theory of heredity is that the impressions registered in the 'Germ cell' are transferred from generation to generation, as there is continuity in the germ cell. In the bioplasmic cell, the limitless impressions of all time are compressed and transmitted to the offspring.

Hiranyagarbha: The Cosmic Sace; the Supreme Lord of the Universe.

Ishavasya Upanishad: The First Upanishad of great spiritual significance; deals with the Divinity of Man,Nature,and the inherent Spiritual nature of life. Also known asSamhitopanishad, or Manthropanishad par excellence.

Ishvara: Tat Pada, literally meaning Brahman (indicative)

Jada: Inert; inertia; laziness.

Japa: Higher formof worship

Jeevatma: Individual soul

Jnyana: Knowledge, Wisdom, Knowledge of the Self

Jnyani: the Knower of the Self, the wise man

Kama: Desire, lust, sensuousness.

Karma: Impressions of actions.

Karma Kanda: Karrma Kanda of the Vedas comprise of Samhitas and Brahmanas; Forms the source of Inspiration for one sect. As compared to Jnyana Kanda of the Vedas comprising of Aranyakas and Upanishads.

Karma Yoni: Birth for action.

Karta: Doer ('Akarta'- Non-doer).

Katha Upanishad: deals with Fear, 'Death and After' in the form of a dialogue between Yama and Nachikethas.

Kenopanishad: deals with Ultimate Reality- the Inner Self.

Knowledge: The union of subject and object; Supreme Knowledge is the Unity of subject and object in the Absilute; here neither the Subject nor the object exist. It is Relaisation of the Pure Consciousness, or the Supreme self.

Kshama: Forgiveness, ethical conduct

Laya Yoga: Yoga of absorption of mind.

Mahavakyas: Great sayings of Shritis.'the Supreme Doctrine"- "Thou art that"("Tat tvam asi"), "Aham Brahmasmi" (I am Brahm), etc.

Mandukya Upanishad: Deals with Divinity of Man; self same reality.

Manonasha: Destruction of Mind; Stilling of Mind

Manolaya: Temporary absorption of mind in the object of mediattaion, Vasanas are still present; only in manonasha, vasanas are destroyed.

Mantra Yoga: Yoga of recitation of sacred syllable OM.

Mauna: Silence; method of cleansing impure mind.

Moksha: Deliverance from cycle of birth and death.

Mundaka Upanishad: deals with Para and Apara Vidya; Sage Angirasa teaches Saunaka (Atharva Veda); Freedom and Delight; Summons to battle of life equipped properly with Upanishadic thoughts, and Meditation.

Nada Anusandhana: Concentration of Anahata or mystic sounds of heart and channelising energy.

Nature: Unmanifested Ether; Prakruti, Maya. Shakti, Ajnyana.

Nidra: Ignorance, Sleep.

Nishkama Karma: Yoga of selfless service

Om: The sound that emanated with the Sphota at the time of Origin of the Universe, the Brahman - the Nada Brahman. [See Rk Veda Samhita , IV.5.4].

Paramatman: The Supreme Soul, the Lord. The Supreme Consciousness. Pure Consciousness.

Paramahansa: Yogi who neither carries Danda (the Staff) nor the hair stuff, nor the holy thread; who has attained nirliptata.

Patanajali : Maharishi who compiled Yogic Principles and tenets taught by Hiranyagarbha according to Yagnyavalkya Smriti. Patanjali Yoga Sutra is the treatise on Yoga.

Prakruti: Nature, the universe, a manifest form of the Lord.

Prana: First Principle of life, then as Principle of Consciousness, then equated with Ultimate Reality, namely Atman.

Prashnopanishad: deals with Philosophical problems in diaogue form.

Prathyahara: Yogic practice of drawing mind to self; drawing in of sense organs into the Chitta or mindstuff, by detaching from their objects

Purusha: Dweller in the body (referred to as Brahmapura), refers to the Supreme Being, Purushottama

Purushottama : The Lord, Supreme Being

Raja yoga: Dhyana Yoga, Yoga of meditation and Samadhi.

Rebirth: There is heredity transmission so far as furnishing the materials to the soul for embodiment is concerned. But, the soul migrates and manufactures body after body, and each thought we think and each deed of ours, is stored as moral efficiency in the soul. Ready to spring again and take shape at proper time. The sum total of these impressions give the soul the direction for the next birth. If these impressions are such that they have to manufacture a new body for further experience, the soul will go to those parents who are ready to supply it with material for that body. Thus, from body to body it will go, sometimes to heaven and back again to earth; this way it will go on till it has finished its experience and completed the circle.

Revelation: It is a divine afflatus springing from within, the result of inspiration through God -intoxication. It is not a message received from outside. [Ranade]. Only he whose heart is purified and made ready so that it can receive the revelation. [Katha Upanishad, II. 5. 3,].

Rishi: Wise Seer.

Salvation: The search for a new body and fulfillment of desires come to an end when the Soul comes to know of its true nature, its ignorance vanishes, its power becomes manifest; it becomes perfect and there is no need to work through physical bodies or through finer mental bodies. It shines in its own light, and is free, no more to be born or to die. It is the desire, the ignorance that causes rebirth. Salvation lies in cleansing the soul of its blemishes of desires and samskaras (impressions).

Sama: The resting of the mind steadfastly on its goal, viz. Brahman after it has detached itself from manifold sense-objects by continuously observing the defects, is called Sama or calmness.

Samadhi: Highest State of Consciousness; Height of spiritual attainment; Yogic achievement. Nirvikalapa Samaadhi- without triputi (causalty, time and space constraints) and alambana; Thought-less Super-Conscious (Choiceless Awareness) state.

Samprajnayata Samadhi Sabija or savikalpa S: Samadhi with triputi and alambana.

Samhita: Collection. Totality, WHOLENESS of 'VID', i.e., Veda - KNOWLEDGE

Sama: Tranquility of Mind.

Samadhana: One-pointed Mind.

Samadhi: Super conscious State wherein super sensual experiences occur. Ultimate in Yoga.

Samsara: Realm of births and deaths.

Samskaras: Latent Impressions, experiences, memories stored in subconscious.

Santosha: Happiness.

Sanyasins: Spiritually consecrated seekers.

Sat: Truth, Real, the real foundation of the universe.

Satsang: Company of spiritual thinkers, seers, sages, sants, spiritual aspirants

Shikha: Tuft of hair on the crown of head (Govinda?)

Shriddha: Faith.

Siddhi: Perfection in Raja Yoga entering Asamprajnya Samadhi

Soul: The self-luminous entity that forms the core of man's personality. It can reveal itself and reveal others simultaneously and give the awareness that 'one is experiencing'. This is the spiritual Essence, the Atman in man. It is beyond causation; it is not the product of anything (not a compound of anything) and it is indestructible.

Suras: Gods; stands for noble, divine and other higher qualities.

Svastha: One who is established in oneself, 'Sthithaprajnya'.

Taijas: Luminous

Taittiriya Upanishad: deals with Nature of man- the Five Koshas.

Tanmatras: Subtle elements. "That thou art": "That" is "Brahm" or "Brahman" -Knowledge, Light, Intelligence; "thou" is Self, Atman. 'That' is Paramatman and 'thou' is Jeevaatman.

Time: Time has been calculated in terms of the rotation and revolution movements of the earth Sun in our Solar System. Once we get out of this earth and enter space, the basis of our calcultion is lost. In Vedanta, time is calculated according to the wheel of time wielded by Sriman Narayana. It consists of Brahma's 100 years of life; each year consists of 360 days and each day consists of Krita, Treta, Dvapara and Kali ages; added together and multiplied 994 times. In terms of human years it works out to: Krita Yuga 1.728 million years; Treta Yuga 1.080; Dvapara Yuga 0.72 million years and Kali Yuga 0.36 million years Together it works out to 3 million 888 thousand years- a single age of the Gods Divine Age). 71 Divine ages make up one Manvantara- i.e., one day of Brahma, the four-faced Creator, the manifestation of the Brahman, the Supreme Spirit. 100 years of Brahma (36000 Kalpas) end up in a Mahapralaya (deluge) lasting equal duration. Indras, Manus, and Rishis change at the end of every Manvantara. It seems that 21 Krita, Treta, and Dvapara Yugas have already passed in revolution since the origin of this Universe. That is why Shri Krishna refers to the cycle and says, 'that He will take birth at every dawn of a Dvapara Yuga' to restore Dharma (Dharma samsthapanarthaya Sambhavami Yuge Yuge).

The great wheel of Mahapralaya and Maha Kalpa has millions of smaller ones, wheel within wheel, rotating at the propulsion of the Supreme Spirit in the center of all, the processes of nature taking place right through in rotations. This is the Celestial Time as distinct from the time calculated in our Solar and Lunar calendars, based on rotation and revolution of earth and its satellite, the Moon, respectively.

Titiksha : Endurance.Trataka: Steady Gazing, Dharana, Concentration, Chitta ekagrata, steadiness of mind.

Trikuti: Concentrating between eye brows

| | |
|---|---|
| Triputi; | Triad, The knower, the knowledge and the knowable (in Savikalpa Samadhi); Time. Space And Causation are the Triputi of Vedanta. |
| Turiya: | Super-conscious State. |
| Upanishads: | Constitute the end and aim of Vedas (Vedanta); the sum and substance of all true wisdom; These are 1180 in number- one for each Shakha of the Vedas, but only 200 rought to light. Upanishads in Verses or Mantras are called 'Manthropanishad'. See list at end. |
| Uparati: | Renunciation. |
| Upasana: | Bhakti, Devotion, comprehension. |
| Vairagya: | Renunciation; Dispassion, Non- attachment as opposed to Raga (Attachment). It is the desire to give up all transitory enjoyments. It includes the desire to attain Saayujya of Brahman or Supreme Bliss- 'Brahmanhhod'. |
| Vaisvaanara: | Fire God that reside in human body, Cosmic form of Brahman. |
| Veda: | 'Ved" means Knowledge, Divine knowledge. The four Veda are: Rig Veda, Saama Veda, Yajur Veda, Atharva Veda, Dhanur Veda, Ayur-Veda; All Veda, ('Vid' ) are 'one' only i.e., Vidya, or Knowledge, or Upasana. Vedic Literature that sheds light on the transcendental means of achieving what is wished for and avoiding what is disliked according to Sayanacharya, Veda are transmitted by word of mouth since time immemorial, beginning-less antiquity, believed to be the first received from Brahma, the creator. |
| Vichara Shakti: | Power of enquiry |
| Vikshepa Shakti: | Projecting capacity of Mind. |
| Vikruti: | Indriyas; Pancha bhutas. |
| Vimochana: | Release from Bondage, Mukti. |
| Viveka: | Discrimination |
| Vrittis: | Thought waves; mental modifications. |
| Wisdom: | The discriminatory power. According to Vedas, Brahma, the Cretor is the first Manifestation, born of fire of Wisdom; wisdom thus existed before the other five elements were formed. |
| Yoga: | Restraint of thought waves, union with God, Union of (Jeeva) 'Atma' and 'Paramatma', Union of the individual soul (Jeevaatma) and Supreme Consciousness. |
| Yoga Nadis: | Astral nerves |
| Yogi: | One who practices yoga; a wise man. |
| 'Yuj': | to join, Knowledge. Yoga-Unity. |

# Index


A

Abnegation of self, 298
Absolute and Relative, 224
Acharyas (Hindu), 193
Adhvaryus (Yajna
performers), 35
Ahamkara, 68
Ahimsa Doctrine, 187
Aitareyopanishad, 95
Akarma (Non-action)
theory, 182-84
Amritabindu Upanishad, 121
Amritananda Upanishad, 106
Ancient
• scriptures, 21-22, 208
- publishing, 21
• civilization
(cradle of), 24
• site Indian
civilization, 44
• sages, 64
Anger, 281
Apaurusheya Bhasyah, 40
Aranyakas, 29
Arjuna to Krishna, 177-78
Arya Samaj Volume
on Vedas, 40
Asana, 229
Ashram ritulas (students/guru),
19-20
Ashtavakra Samhita, 316
Astrology, 46
Atharva Veda, 28, 30, 32, 36, 41
Atharvan (Brahma's son), 29
Atharva Veda Samhita
hymns, 34
Atma 41, 81, 93, 115, 326-27
• Brahman unity, 55, 322
• Brahman Reality, 45, 102
• way to, 147
Atma Jnana, 313
Atmabudha Upanishad, 100
Atomic energy source,
23, 49
Attachment (Moha), 281
Avidya or Nescience (source), 269

B

'Being' importance of, 264
Bereavement of
loved one, 297
Bhagavad Gita, 178
Bhakta Prahlada episode, 169
Bhakti Yoga, 220
Bhedaabheda
doctrine, 202
Bhel Samhita, 42
Big Bang Theory of
origin of universe,
38, 48, 50, 224
Black Hole Theory, 36
Bondage
• of man, 18-19
• /emancipation causes,
126-272
• sansar as, 284
Brahma Sutras, 28
Brahman, 137, 156

• Principles, 38-39
• Absolute (meaning) 52, 60, 325
• and Maya, 156
• achievement, 272
• Shankracharya on, 196
Brahma Rahasya Upanishad, 271
Brahmavidya, 126
• Upanishad, 104
Brahmabindu Uppanishad, 106
Brahmalok, 128
Brahmacharyam, 147
Brahma Sutra, 155
theme of, 152
Brahma Purana, 166
Brahma-nirvana, 179
Breathing, 135
Brihad Jataka, 21
Brihadaranayaka Upanishad, 149
Brugu Samhita, 21
Buddhi, 67
Buddhism, 190
Buddha
• life, 190
• teachings, 190

C

Charak Samhita, 42
Chhaandogya Upanishad, 134-35, 156
Chaitanya Mahaprabhu, 205-206
Children (desire for), 304-305
Chulika Upanishad, 105
Concentration, 247
Concept of Samashti, 325
Consciousness (Supreme), 270
• qualities, 28
• states, 102
• self, 185
• levels, 291
- developing, 296
Contentment and happiness, 134
Cosmic Origin Theories, 23
Cosmic/Psychic principle, 136
Cosmogony, 48
Cycle of birth and death, 283-84
• coming out of, 288

D

Death, 143
• and immortality, 307
• celebrating, 310
• and after, 160
Deities recognized by Veda, 40, 63
Departed souls (Satisfying), 311
Destruction of Manas, 61
Desire, 272-74, 310
Descartes, Reni, 19
Devotional aspect, 291
Dhanur Veda, 42
Dharma (principles), 69
Dharma
• fundamentals, 209
• Yuddha, 173
Dharana, 239, 247
benefits, 239
Dhyana
• and Samadhi, 248
• Yoga, 226-27
Dhyanabindu Upanishad, 108
Discoveries (role of), 183
Diseases
cause, cure (mantra), 33, 37
Dispersal of energy from Sun, 55
Distressed souls, 310
Divinity
path to, 218
Divisions (caste/sex) in spirituality, 214
Divorce/marital discord-reasons, 301

Doctrine of point (bindu), 106
Doctrine of Raikua, 140
Doctrine of 'neti, neti', 157
Doctrine of Maya, 162
Duty
performance, 178, 266
Dwapara Yuga, 72
Dynamics of silence, 28

**E**

Earth, 23, 50
• origin, 23
• as planet, 57
Ego-less state, 179
Epics, 165
Evolution of life, 24
• events since, 50
• and vibrations, 51

**F**

Family System
Vedic, 211
Food, 288
• chain, 289
• sattvic type, 290
Friendship, 280
Fulfillment/
Self Realization
• Steps to, 341

**G**

Gandharva Veda, 42
Gaps in sounds of
Rk Veda, 28, 51
Gaudapada Acharya, 193
Gayatri
formula, 107
Mantra, 243
God (concept), 46, 63
Good Health
formula, 138-39
Greed and Avarice,
280
Gunas, 66, 275, 298
Guru Ashram, rituals, 20
Gurukul System, 21

**H**

Hamsa Upanishad, 111
Happiness/Bliss,
47, 271, 336
and Vedanta, 47
Harita Samhita, 42
Hatred and Jealousy, 280
Hata Yoga, 230
He (God), 63
Health Care, 218
• modern/vedic, 218
Higher Knowledge
(Para Vidya), 19
Hindu
• religion, 46
• way of life, 68
• philosophy, 68
- Vedanta in, 64
- systems, 65
Hinduism
• and Buddhism
differences, 190
• changes, 70
*Hiranyagarbha*
principle (Brahman), 38
Homa Karma (Mantra for
medicine), 33
Honours/recognition, 317
Human Being, 335
Human Development history, 71
Human body constituents, 143
Hunger and food, 288

**I**

Ignorance
(source), 57
Illusion (Maya), 58, 270, 313-14
Imagination, 185
India spiritual heritage, 21, 28
Infinititude
attainment, 337

Infinite Brahman, 138
Institutions propagating
Vedic Culture, 45
Ishavasya
Upanishad, 77
• mantra, 77-78
Interpretation of Vedas, 35
Intelligence (qualities of), 42
Isvara pranidhanam, 229

J

Jainism, 188
theory, 188
Japa/Japam, 238, 242
Jnyana/Dhyana
• Yoga, 52, 220, 222
• Path, 61, 170, 176
• Bhakti relation, 224
Jyotish (Astrology), 45

K

Kaivalya Upanishad, 105
Kala Principle
Brahmah, 38
Kali Yuga, 73
Kalp, 42
Kapila Sage, 65
• on events since evolution, 50
• presentation by, 56
Karma Yoga, 220
Karma
• record of, 160
• theory, 291
• and Jainism, 188
• and Ramanujacharya, 200
• Mimamsa, 42
Katha Upanishad, 80
Kaushitaki Upanishad, 127
Keep quiet rule, 265
Kena Upanishad, 79
Knowledge, 162, 185
• Upanishad on, 19
• Types of, 19
• of Brahmah, 164
• Ramanujacharya on, 201
• path of, 178
• of one Brahman, 321
• source of, 88
Koshas types, 124
Kriti Yuga, 73
Krishna Lord
advice, 74
Krishna Yajurveda, 112
Kshurika Upanishad, 105
Kundalini, 236
adverse effects, 237
Kurukshetra war, 180

L

Life
• Vedanta on, 25
• goal, 69
• meaning, 283
Living
• art of, 282, 298
• ways of, 297
Lotus posture, 110
Love (power of), 277
• definition, 278
• and friendship, 279
• and sacrifice, 298
• and marriage, 293
• and affection, 296
• purity in, 305
Love marriage, 294
Lower Knowledge
(*Apara* Vidya), 19

M

Maaya, 156, 270-71, 292, 313
• as Shakti
(Ramanujacharya), 201
• doctrine of, 162
Madhavacharya, 202-205
Madhuparkam
doctrine, 153
Maharishi Mahesh Yogi, 44
• on Knowledge, 22

• on Veda aspects, 30
• on Yajur Veda, 31
Mahabharat, 173
central idea, 174
Maha Upanishad, 99
Mahaveer Vardhaman
• life, 187
• Buddha differences, 192
Mahavakyas, 125
Mahanarayanopanishad, 100
Mahat (cosmic intelligence), 50, 67
Mahashanti Performance, 33
Maitreya Upanishad, 119
Man
• why special, 19, 238, 275-76, 286, 331
• history of, 19, 24, 71
• fossil records, 24
Mandukya Upanishad, 91
Mantra, 36-37, 54
• significance, 255-57
• Atharva Veda, 32
• efficacy, 45
• vedic, 24
Mauna, 48, 148
significance, 253
Manusmriti, 69, 243
Marriage
• sex and, 293
• love and, 293
• success in, 295, 302
Material Creation (Reality about), 321
Material prosperity, 299
Meditation, 108,
• combination, 240
• with Om, 103
• Steps, 331-32
• themes, 240
• on Atma, 113
• processes, 241
Milky Way (Vedas), 50
Mind, 39, 303
• control, 312, 316
• and consciousness, 25
• truth about, 26
Mind Management Techniques (MMT) 264, 297
Modern/Traditional ways, 215, 299
Modern Science in Vedic scriptures, 22
*Moha*, 281
Moksha (methods), 189, 315, 318
Morning ablutions, 214
Mukti
paths to, 218
Muktikopanishad, 61
Mundakopanishad, 87
Mulabandha & Uddayana bandha, 111

**N**

Nachiketas (story), 80, 325
Nadabindu Upanishad, 105
Narayana Lord, 99
• Purushas from, 99
• as creator, 133
Nature, 39
Nature of Self, 89,
Narasimha — Uttara – Tapaniya Upanishad, 102
Narayanopanishad, 100
Nimbaaraka Philosophy, 202
Nirvana in Buddhism, 91
Niyama Principle, 228, 245-46
Non-action (Akarma) Philosophy, 182-83
Nrsimha - purva Tapaniya Upanishad, 101
Nyaya and Vaisheshika, 65

**O**

Obsession to perfection, 311
Om (Big Bang Theory), 36,

49, 50, 88, 91, 103-104, 106, 135
• contemplation, 109
• significance, 261-64
Organs (Repository), 39
• sense, 334
Origin of Man
• fossil records, 24
Origin of Vedas, 28
Origin of Universe, 36, 52
Osho (Rajaneesh), 285-86

**P**

Paingala Upanishad, 122
Panini's grammar, 45
Papanivaraka Mantra, 33
Parmatamah, 329
Patanjali's
Ashtanga, 45
Peace
and happiness,
257, 287
• formula, 258
• mantra, 259-61
Pradhaana Principle
(Brahman), 38
Prakriti, 163
Pranayama,
231-32, 276
• with Gayatri Mantra, 249
• pre-requisites, 233
• and Kundalini, 236
Prana, 96, 124, 130
• and Mind, 235
• Vidya, 129-30
Prathyahara, 247
Prashna Upanishad,
83-87
Primeaval being, 142
Professional excellence, 312
Progress
type, 215
Progeny (desire for), 304
Propitiating God, 300
Psychoneurosis, 320
Purusha Principle
Brahman, 35
Purusha/Prakriti, 67-68
Union, 50-51, 56, 60
Puranas, 165
Purusharthas, 211
Pure love, 305

**Q**

Qualities of man, 25

**R**

Radiation of energy, 55
Rajaneesh Acharya
on meditation, 285
Raj/Dhyana Yoga, 226
Rajo Guna, 275
Ramayan, 171
• authors, 172
Ramanujacharya, 199
• philosophy, 200
Realities of existence, 94
Realization of the self, 161
Reasoning, 186
Rebirth, 145
Reincarnation
and Jainism, 182
Renunciation Principles, 185
Rituals
in Vedas, 89
Ritualistic Practices
• Rk Veda, 209
• Vedic way, 212
Rk Veda, 24, 40, 62
• meaning, 25
• importance, 29
• hymns/verses, 29
• sounds, 30

**S**

Sacrificial fires, 142
Sadhus, 318-19
Sakshin, 328
Salvation, 313

• means to reach, 121
• prayer, 144
Samadhi (Realization), 235, 248
Sama Veda, 24, 34, 36, 41
Samkhya, 43
• Philosophy (Kapilas), 58, 66
• school, 66
Samhitas, 29
Santhosha, 228
Scripture, 28
Scriptures of Vedic science, 47
Secret of life, 284-84
Self-Realization, 27, 81, 330-31
• explanation, 97
• steps, 330-31
Self (nature), 148
• Knowledge of
-spiritual requirements, 159
• realization of, 161
Sense Organs
• superiority, 146
Sexual
• Practices Principles (Kamasutra), 341
• Instinct, 234-35
• Satisfaction attaining, 304
• energies diversion in Yoga, 227
Sex
• over indulgence, 303-304
• and Marriage, 293
• energy conservation, 296
Shiksha, 42
Shakhas (Schools of thought) Vedas, 29
Shakti, 171
Shankracharya
Guru, 29, 194
• Philosophy, 195
• attainment of Brahman, 198
Shanti Mantra, 255
*Shoucha*, 228
Shrutis (Vedas), 29
Shree Krishna Story, 175-76
Skanda Upanishad, 122
Sleeping, 143
Social Contract Theory, 19
Solar System, 23, 55, 58
Soma
• Ras, 34
• Sacrifice, 35
– festival, 35
– rituals, 35
Soul, 39, 67, 157-58
Soul in dreamless sleep, 162
Sounds in Rk Veda, 30, 36
Speech (Origin), 25, 97
Spiritual leaders, 63
Spiritual heritage, 44
Spiritual science, 59
Sphota (explosion), 49
Spiritual path to life, 303
Spiritual seekers, 318-19
Sreemad Bhagavatham, 175
Sphota (explosion), 49
Spiritual life need, 267
Spiritual heritage, 44
Studying of Vedàs
• methods, 45
• theme, 58
• system, 64
Subala Upanishad, 137
Subject of Knowledge, 131
Sun, 55, 137
• Veda on, 58
Success, 311
• in professional life (secret of), 300
• secret of, 290, 292
Suicide, 306
Supreme consciousness, 322
Superstring Theory, 321
Surya Yoga, 264
Sutras, 64
Svaadhyaya, 228

Sveatasuatra Upanishad, 162, 243

T

Tantra-mantras of life, 39, 93
Taittiriyopanishad, 91-92
Taittiriya Aranyaka, 107
Tamo Guna, 276
Tantras, 170
Philosophy, 170-71
Tapas, 228
Tat (Principle of), 180
Tejobindu Upanishad, 110
Thirst, 143
Traditional habits (Indian), 216
Tragedy of human life, 268
Treta Yuga, 72
Transcendental Meditation (TM), 249-51
Transmigration of soul, 160
Truth, 334-36
and Vedas, 59
TTD (Tirupati Tirumalai Devasthanam), 45
• Samskrut Vidyapeeth ancient scriptures publishing, 21

U

Uddiyana bandha postures, 117
Udgitha, 135
Ultimate goal of life, 23
Unity principle of Brahman/Atman, 144
Unified Field, 231
Union of Spirit, 49-50
Universe
• mystery, 24
• in Upanishads, 38
• origin, 36, 48
– themes, 48
Upanishads, 75
• types, 19, 22-24, 26, 29
• aspects, 23
• significance, 25
• numbers, 75
• important one, 76
• theme of, 152
• 108 in order of imp, 76-77
Upanishadic doctrine, 208

V

Vak (Speech), 97
Vairagya attainment, 115
Variety of life (Rk Veda), 37
Varnashrama Dharma, 70
Varaha Upanishad, 114-17
Vardhamana Mahaveera, 187
Vatsayana's Kama Sutra, 234
Vedas, 165
• types, origin, 28
• interpretation, 34
Vedanta, 19-20, 28
44, 46-47, 61, 165, 207, 334
• in Hindu Philosophy, 64
• on life, 25
Vedanga, 45
Vedantic way of life, 207-209
Vedic
• way of life, 37
• literature, 40, 47
• scholars of our times, 46
• cosmology, 54, 93, 122
• agriculture, 209
• health care, 210
• economy, 210
• family, 211
• education (importance), 213
Veda Vyasa, 29
Vibrations (*Kampan*) and evolution, 51
Vivêkananda, 44
Vishnu/Shiva eulogising, 122
Vishnu, 167
Vishnu Purana, 167
Vyakran, 42

W

Water as purifier, 146
Way to Atman, 147

What was at first, 133
Will (concept of), 225

**Y**

Yajnya, 145
Yajnavalkya, 124-26
Yagnya approach to study Vedanta, 22
Yajur Veda, 24, 31, 34, 36, 41
Yajnas
- rituals, 35
- performing, 35

Yamalok, 145
Yama, 80-82, 308
Yantra, Tantra, Mantra, 37
Yogasana, 230
Yoga, 26, 71-72, 107, 112
- preliminary practices, 117
- types 219
- meaning, 218
- sexual energies, 227

Yogatattva Upanishad, 112
Yoga Upanishad, 108
Yogis, 44
Yogashidhs Upanishad, 110
Yogic postures, 109, 118, 229
Yogasutra, 226